SIE Exam
Reference Guide

Coventry House Publishing

ISBN: 1734820314
ISBN-13: 978-1734820317

Table of Contents

The following Table of Contents is from the "Rules" section of the SIE Content Outline provided by FINRA. A full copy of the Outline can be found at www.finra.org.

Section 3: Understanding Trading, Customer Accounts and Prohibited Activities **197**

Section 1
Knowledge of
Capital Markets

1. FINRA Rules: 2266 – SIPC Information

All members, except those members: (a) that pursuant to Section 3(a)(2)(A)(i) through (iii) of the Securities Investor Protection Act of 1970 (SIPA) are excluded from membership in the Securities Investor Protection Corporation (SIPC) and that are not SIPC members; or (b) whose business consists exclusively of the sale of investments that are ineligible for SIPC protection, shall advise all new customers, in writing, at the opening of an account, that they may obtain information about SIPC, including the SIPC brochure, by contacting SIPC, and also shall provide the Web site address and telephone number of SIPC. In addition, such members shall provide all customers with the same information, in writing, at least once each year. In cases where both an introducing firm and clearing firm service an account, the firms may assign these requirements to one of the firms.

---

2. FINRA Rules: 2269 – Disclosure of Participation or Interest in Primary or Secondary Distribution

A member who is acting as a broker for a customer or for both such customer and some other person, or a member who is acting as a dealer and who receives or has promise of receiving a fee from a customer for advising such customer with respect to securities, shall, at or before the completion of any transaction for or with such customer in any security in the primary or secondary distribution of which such member is participating or is otherwise financially interested, give such customer written notification of the existence of such participation or interest.

---

3. MSRB Rules: G-11 – Primary Offering Practices

Summary: Establishes terms and conditions for sales by dealers of new issues of municipal securities in primary offerings, including provisions on priority of customer orders.

(a) Definitions. For purposes of this rule, the following terms have the following meanings:
   (i) The term "accumulation account" means an account established in connection with a municipal securities investment trust to hold securities pending their deposit in such trust.
   (ii) The term "date of sale" means, in the case of competitive sales, the date on which all bids for the purchase of securities must be submitted to an issuer, and, in the case of negotiated sales, the date on which the contract to purchase securities from an issuer is executed.
   (iii) The term "group order" means an order for securities held in syndicate, which order is for the account of all members of the syndicate on a pro rata basis in proportion to their respective participations in the syndicate. Any such order submitted directly to the senior syndicate manager will, for purposes of this rule, be deemed to be the submission of such order by such manager to the syndicate.

(iv) The term "municipal securities investment trust" means a unit investment trust, as defined in the Investment Company Act of 1940, the portfolio of which consists in whole or in part of municipal securities.

(v) The term "order period" means the period of time, if any, announced by a syndicate or, when no syndicate has been formed, a sole underwriter, during which orders will be solicited for the purchase of securities in a primary offering.

(vi) The term "priority provisions" means the provisions adopted by a syndicate governing the allocation of securities to different categories of orders.

(vii) The term "retail order period" means an order period during which orders that meet the issuer's designated eligibility criteria for retail orders and for which the customer is already conditionally committed will be either (i) the only orders solicited or (ii) given priority over other orders.

(viii) The term "syndicate" means an account formed by two or more persons for the purpose of purchasing, directly or indirectly, all or any part of a new issue of municipal securities from the issuer, and making a distribution thereof.

(ix) The term "qualified note syndicate" means any syndicate formed for the purpose of purchasing and distributing a new issue of municipal securities that matures in less than two years where:
    (A) the new issue is to be purchased by the syndicate on other than an "all or none" basis; or
    (B) the syndicate has provided that:
        (1) there is to be no order period;
        (2) only group orders will be accepted; and,
        (3) the syndicate may purchase and sell the municipal securities for its own account.

(x) The term "affiliate" means a person controlling, controlled by, or under common control with a syndicate member or, when no syndicate has been formed, a sole underwriter.

(xi) In the case of a primary offering for which a syndicate is formed for the purchase of municipal securities, the term "related account" includes a municipal securities investment portfolio of a syndicate member or an affiliate, an arbitrage account of a syndicate member or an affiliate, a municipal securities investment trust sponsored by a syndicate member or an affiliate, or an accumulation account established in connection with such a municipal securities investment trust. In the case of a primary offering for which a syndicate has not been formed, the term "related account" includes a municipal securities investment portfolio of the sole underwriter or an affiliate, an arbitrage account of the sole underwriter or an affiliate, a municipal securities investment trust sponsored by the sole underwriter or an affiliate, or an accumulation account established in connection with such a municipal securities investment trust.

(xii) The term "selling group" means a group of brokers, dealers, or municipal securities dealers formed for the purpose of assisting in the distribution of a new issue of municipal securities for the issuer other than members of the syndicate.

(b) Disclosure of Capacity. Every broker, dealer or municipal securities dealer that submits an order to a sole underwriter or syndicate or to a member of a syndicate for the purchase of municipal securities held by the syndicate shall disclose at the time of submission of such order if the securities are being purchased for its dealer account or for a related account of such broker, dealer or municipal securities dealer.

(c) Confirmations of Sale. Sales of securities held by a syndicate to a related account shall be confirmed by the syndicate manager directly to such related account or for the account of such related account submitting the order. Nothing herein contained shall be construed to require that sales of municipal securities to a related account be made for the benefit of the syndicate.

(d) Disclosure of Group Orders. Every broker, dealer or municipal securities dealer that submits a group order to a syndicate or to a member of a syndicate shall disclose at the time of submission of such order the identity of the person for whom the order is submitted. This section shall not apply to a qualified note syndicate as defined in subsection (a)(ix) above.

(e) Priority Provisions.
    (i) In the case of a primary offering for which a syndicate has been formed, the syndicate shall establish priority provisions and, if such priority provisions may be changed, the procedure for making changes. For

purposes of this rule, the requirement to establish priority provisions shall not be satisfied if a syndicate provides only that the syndicate manager or managers may determine in the manager's or managers' discretion the priority to be accorded different types of orders. Unless otherwise agreed to with the issuer, such priority provisions shall give priority to customer orders over orders by members of the syndicate for their own accounts or orders for their respective related accounts, to the extent feasible and consistent with the orderly distribution of securities in the offering. Notwithstanding the preceding sentence, a syndicate may include a provision permitting the syndicate manager or managers on a case-by-case basis to allocate securities in a manner other than in accordance with the priority provisions, if the syndicate manager or managers determine in its or their discretion that it is in the best interests of the syndicate. In the event any such allocation is made, the syndicate manager or managers shall have the burden of justifying that such allocation was in the best interests of the syndicate.

(ii) In the case of a primary offering for which a syndicate has not been formed, unless otherwise agreed to with the issuer, the sole underwriter shall give priority to customer orders over orders for its own account or orders for its related accounts, to the extent feasible and consistent with the orderly distribution of securities in the offering.

(f) Communications Relating to Issuer Requirements, Priority Provisions and Order Period. Prior to the first offer of any securities by a syndicate, the senior syndicate manager shall furnish in writing to the other members of the syndicate and to members of the selling group, if any, (i) a written statement of all terms and conditions required by the issuer, (ii) a written statement of all of the issuer's retail order period requirements, if any, (iii) the priority provisions, (iv) the procedure, if any, by which such priority provisions may be changed, (v) if the senior syndicate manager or managers are to be permitted on a case-by-case basis to allocate securities in a manner other than in accordance with the priority provisions, the fact that they are to be permitted to do so, (vi) if there is to be an order period, whether orders may be confirmed prior to the end of the order period, and (vii) all pricing information. Any change in the priority provisions or pricing information shall be promptly furnished in writing by the senior syndicate manager to the other members of the syndicate and the selling group, if any. Syndicate and selling group members shall promptly furnish in writing the information described in this section to others, upon request. If the senior syndicate manager, rather than the issuer, prepares the written statement of all terms and conditions required by the issuer, such statement shall be provided to the issuer for its approval. An underwriter shall promptly furnish in writing to any other broker, dealer, or municipal securities dealer with which such underwriter has an arrangement to market municipal securities that includes the issuer's new issue, all of the information provided to it from the senior syndicate manager as required by this section.

(g) Designations and Allocations of Securities. The senior syndicate manager shall:

(i) within 24 hours of the sending of the commitment wire, complete the allocation of securities; provided however, that, if at the time allocations are made the purchase contract in a negotiated sale is not yet signed or the award in a competitive sale is not yet made, such allocations shall be made subject to the signing of the purchase contract or the awarding of the securities, as appropriate, and the purchaser must be informed of this fact;

(ii) within two business days following the date of sale, disclose to the other members of the syndicate, in writing, a summary, by priority category, of all allocations of securities which are accorded priority over members' take-down orders, indicating the aggregate par value, maturity date and price of each maturity so allocated, including any allocation to an order confirmed at a price other than the original list price. The summary shall include allocations of securities to orders submitted through the end of the order period or, if the syndicate does not have an order period, through the first business day following the date of sale;

(iii) disclose, in writing, to each member of the syndicate all available information on designations paid to syndicate and non-syndicate members expressed in total dollar amounts within 10 business days following the date of sale and all information about designations paid to syndicate and non-syndicate members expressed in total dollar amounts with the sending of the designation checks pursuant to section (j) below; and

(iv) disclose to the members of the syndicate, in writing, the amount of any portion of the take-down directed to each member by the issuer. Such disclosure is to be made by the later of 15 business days following the date of sale or three business days following receipt by the senior syndicate manager of notification of such set asides of the take-down.

(h) Disclosure of Syndicate Expenses and Other Information. At or before the final settlement of a syndicate account, the senior syndicate manager shall furnish to the other members of the syndicate:

(i) an itemized statement setting forth the nature and amounts of all actual expenses incurred on behalf of the syndicate. Notwithstanding the foregoing, any such statement may include an item for miscellaneous expenses, provided that the amount shown under such item is not disproportionately large in relation to other items of expense shown on the statement and includes only minor items of expense which cannot be easily categorized elsewhere in the statement. The amount of discretionary fees for clearance costs, if any, to be imposed by a syndicate manager and the amount of management fees, if any, shall be disclosed to syndicate members prior to the submission of a bid, in the case of a competitive sale, or prior to the execution of a purchase contract with the issuer, in the case of a negotiated sale. For purposes of this section, the term "management fees" shall include, in addition to amounts categorized as management fees by the syndicate manager, any amount to be realized by a syndicate manager, and not shared with the other members of the syndicate, which is attributable to the difference in price to be paid to an issuer for the purchase of a new issue of municipal securities and the price at which such securities are to be delivered by the syndicate manager to the members of the syndicate; and

(ii) a summary statement showing:

(A) the identity of each related account submitting an order to which securities have been allocated as well as the aggregate par value and maturity date of each maturity so allocated;

(B) the identity of each person submitting a group order to which securities have been allocated as well as the aggregate par value and maturity date of each maturity so allocated except that this subparagraph shall not apply to the senior syndicate manager of a qualified note syndicate as defined in subsection (a)(ix) above; and

(C) the aggregate par values and prices (expressed in terms of dollar prices or yields) of all securities sold from the syndicate account. This subparagraph shall not apply to a qualified note syndicate as defined in subsection (a)(ix) above.

(i) Settlement of Syndicate or Similar Account. Final settlement of a syndicate or similar account formed for the purchase of securities shall be made within 30 calendar days following the date the issuer delivers the securities to the syndicate.

(j) Payments of Designations. All syndicate or similar account members shall submit the allocations of their designations according to the rules of the syndicate or similar account to the syndicate or account manager within two business days following the date the issuer delivers the securities to the syndicate. Any credit designated by a customer in connection with the purchase of securities as due to a member of a syndicate or similar account shall be distributed to such member by the broker, dealer or municipal securities dealer handling such order within 10 calendar days following the date the issuer delivers the securities to the syndicate.

(k) Retail Order Period Representations and Required Disclosures. From the end of the retail order period but no later than the Time of Formal Award (as defined in Rule G-34(a)(ii)(C)(1)(a)), each broker, dealer, or municipal securities dealer that submits an order during a retail order period to the senior syndicate manager or sole underwriter, as applicable, shall provide, in writing, which may be electronic (including, but not limited to, an electronic order entry system), the following information relating to each order designated as retail submitted during a retail order period:

(i) whether the order is from a customer that meets the issuer's eligibility criteria for participation in the retail order period;

(ii) whether the order is one for which a customer is already conditionally committed;

(iii) whether the broker, dealer, or municipal securities dealer has received more than one order from such retail customer for a security for which the same CUSIP number has been assigned;

(iv) any identifying information required by the issuer, or the senior syndicate manager on the issuer's behalf, in connection with such retail order (but not including customer names or social security numbers); and

(v) the par amount of the order.

The senior syndicate manager may rely on the information furnished by each broker, dealer, or municipal securities dealer that provided the information required by (i)-(v) unless the senior syndicate manager knows, or has reason to know, that the information is not true, accurate or complete.

(l)(i) Prohibitions on Consents by Brokers, Dealers, and Municipal Securities Dealers. No broker, dealer, or municipal securities dealer shall provide bond owner consent to amendments to authorizing documents for municipal securities, either in its capacity as an underwriter or remarketing agent, or as agent for or in lieu of bond owners, provided that this prohibition shall not apply in the following circumstances:

(A) the authorizing document expressly allows an underwriter to provide bond owner consent and the offering documents for the existing securities expressly disclosed that bond owner consents could be provided by underwriters of other securities issued under the authorizing document;

(B) such securities are owned by such broker, dealer, or municipal securities dealer other than in its capacity as underwriter or remarketing agent;

(C) all securities affected by such amendments (other than securities retained by an owner in lieu of a tender and for which such bond owner had delivered consent to such amendment), are held by the broker, dealer, or municipal securities dealer acting as remarketing agent, as a result of a mandatory tender of such securities;

(D) the broker, dealer or municipal securities dealer provides consent solely as agent for and on behalf of bond owners delivering written consent to such amendments; or

(E) such consent provided by a broker, dealer or municipal securities dealer, in its capacity as an underwriter on behalf of prospective purchasers, would not become effective until all bond owners of securities affected by the proposed amendments (other than the prospective purchasers for whom the underwriter had provided consent) had also consented to such amendments.

(ii) For purposes of this section, the term "authorizing document" shall mean the trust indenture, resolution, ordinance, or other document under which the securities are issued. The term "bond owner" shall mean the owner of municipal securities issued under the applicable authorizing document. The term "bond owner consent" shall mean any consent specified in an authorizing document that may be or is required to be given by a bond owner pursuant to such authorizing document.

---

4. MSRB Rules: G-32 – Disclosures in Connection with Primary Offerings

Summary: Requires underwriters to submit certain information to the Electronic Municipal Market Access (EMMA®) system and dealers to provide certain information to customers in connection with primary offerings.

(a) Customer Disclosure Requirements.

(i) No broker, dealer or municipal securities dealer shall sell, whether as an underwriter or otherwise, any offered municipal securities to a customer unless such broker, dealer or municipal securities dealer delivers to the customer by no later than the settlement of the transaction a copy of the official statement or, if an official statement is not being prepared, a written notice to that effect together with a copy of a preliminary official statement, if any.

(ii) Notwithstanding the provisions of subsection (a)(i) of this rule, the delivery obligation thereunder shall be deemed satisfied if the following conditions are met:

(A) the offered municipal securities being sold are not municipal fund securities; and

(B) the underwriter has made the submissions to EMMA required under paragraph (b)(i)(A) or (b)(i)(B)(1) of this rule; provided that the condition in this paragraph (B) shall apply solely to sales to customers by brokers, dealers and municipal securities dealers acting as underwriters in respect of the offered municipal securities being sold.

(iii) Any broker, dealer or municipal securities dealer that sells any offered municipal securities to a customer with respect to which the delivery obligation under subsection (a)(i) of this rule is deemed satisfied pursuant to subsection (a)(ii) of this rule shall provide or send to the customer, by no later than the settlement of such transaction, either:

(A) a copy of the official statement (or, if an official statement is not being prepared, a written notice to that effect together with a copy of a preliminary official statement, if any), and, in connection with offered municipal securities sold by the issuer on a negotiated basis to the extent not included in the official statement, (1) the underwriting spread, if any, (2) the amount of any fee received by the broker, dealer or municipal securities dealer as agent for the issuer in the distribution of the securities; and (3) the initial offering price for each maturity in the offering, including maturities that are not reoffered; or

(B) a notice advising the customer:

(1) how to obtain the official statement from EMMA, which notice may be combined, at the election of the broker, dealer or municipal securities dealer, with notice of the availability of the official statement from a qualified portal; and

(2) that a copy of the official statement will be provided by the broker, dealer or municipal securities dealer upon request.

If a broker, dealer or municipal securities dealer provides notice to a customer pursuant to paragraph (a)(iii)(B), such broker, dealer or municipal securities dealer shall, upon request from the customer, send a copy of the official statement to the customer, together with the information required pursuant to paragraph (a)(iii)(A) in connection with a negotiated offering to the extent not included in the official statement, within one business day of request by first class mail or other equally prompt means.

(iv) In the case of a sale by a broker, dealer or municipal securities dealer of municipal fund securities to a customer, the following additional provisions shall apply:

(A) notwithstanding the provisions of subsection (a)(i) of this rule, if a customer who participates in a periodic municipal fund security plan or a non-periodic municipal fund security program has previously received a copy of the official statement in connection with the purchase of municipal fund securities under such plan or program, a broker, dealer or municipal securities dealer that sells additional shares or units of the municipal fund securities under such plan or program to the customer will be deemed to have satisfied the delivery obligation under subsection (a)(i) of this rule if such broker, dealer or municipal securities dealer sends to the customer a copy of any new, supplemented, amended or "stickered" official statement, by first class mail or other equally prompt means, promptly upon receipt thereof; provided that, if the broker, dealer or municipal securities dealer sends a supplement, amendment or sticker without including the remaining portions of the official statement, such broker, dealer or municipal securities dealer includes a written statement describing which documents constitute the complete official statement and stating that the complete official statement is available upon request; and

(B) the broker, dealer or municipal securities dealer shall provide to the customer, by no later than the settlement of the transaction, written disclosure of the amount of any fee received by the broker, dealer or municipal securities dealer as agent for the issuer in the distribution of the municipal fund securities; provided, however, that if a broker, dealer or municipal securities dealer selling municipal fund securities provides periodic statements to the customer pursuant to Rule G-15(a)(viii) in lieu of individual transaction confirmations, this paragraph (iv)(B) shall be deemed to be satisfied if the broker, dealer or municipal securities dealer provides this information to the customer at least annually and provides information regarding any change in such fee on or prior to the sending of the next succeeding periodic statement to the customer.

(v) If two or more customers share the same address, a broker, dealer or municipal securities dealer may satisfy the delivery obligations set forth in this section (a) by complying with the requirements set forth in Rule 154 of the Securities Act of 1933, on delivery of prospectuses to investors at the same address. In addition, any such broker, dealer or municipal securities dealer shall comply with section (c) of Rule 154, on revocation of consent, to the extent that the provisions of paragraph (a)(iv)(A) relating to a customer who participates in a periodic municipal fund security plan or a non-periodic municipal fund security program apply.

(b) Underwriter Submissions to EMMA.

(i) Official Statements, Preliminary Official Statements, and Information Concerning Exempt Offerings.

(A) Form G-32 Information Submission. Except as otherwise provided in paragraph (F) of this subsection (i), the underwriter of a primary offering of municipal securities shall submit, in addition to any applicable documents and information required to be submitted pursuant to paragraphs (B) through (E) of this subsection (i), Form G-32 information relating to the offering in a timely and accurate manner as follows:

(1) NIIDS-Eligible Primary Offerings. For any primary offering of municipal securities that is a new issue eligible for submission of information to NIIDS under Rule G-34(a)(ii)(C), the underwriter of such offering shall submit all information required to be submitted under this paragraph (A) on Form G-32 relating to such offering at such times and in such manner as required under Rule G-34(a)(ii)(C), and the submission of such information under Rule G-34(a)(ii)(C) in a full and timely manner shall be deemed to be in compliance with the submission requirement of this subparagraph (b)(i)(A)(1); provided, however, that:

(a) Any items of information required to be included on Form G-32 but for which no corresponding data element then is available through NIIDS shall be submitted through EMMA on Form G-32 at such times and in such manner as required under subsection (b)(vi) of this rule and as set forth in the EMMA Dataport Manual; and

(b) Any corrections to data submitted pursuant to Rule G-34(a)(ii)(C) shall be made promptly and, to the extent feasible, in the manner originally submitted.

(2) Primary Offerings Ineligible for NIIDS. For any primary offering of municipal securities that is not a new issue eligible for submission of information to NIIDS under Rule G-34(a)(ii)(C) or is exempt from such submission requirement under Rule G-34(d), the underwriter of such offering shall initiate the submission of Form G-32 information relating to the offering on or prior to the date of first execution, and shall complete the submission of all information required to be submitted by Form G-32 relating to such offering at such times and in such manner as required under subsection (b)(vi) of this rule and as set forth in the EMMA Dataport Manual.

(B) Official Statement Submission.

(1) Except as otherwise provided in paragraph (C), (E) or (F) of this subsection (i), the underwriter of a primary offering of municipal securities shall submit the official statement for such offering to EMMA within one business day after receipt of the official statement from the issuer or its designee, but by no later than the closing date.

(2) If for any reason the official statement for a primary offering of municipal securities subject to this paragraph (B) is not submitted by the underwriter to EMMA by the closing date, the underwriter shall submit to EMMA:

(a) by no later than the closing date, notice to the effect that the official statement has not been submitted by the underwriter to EMMA by the closing date and that the official statement will be submitted to EMMA when it becomes available;

(b) within one business day after receipt from the issuer or its designee, the official statement; and

(c) the preliminary official statement or notice required pursuant to paragraph (D) of this subsection (i);

provided, however, that compliance with the requirements of this subparagraph (2) will not cure the failure to comply with subparagraph (1) of this paragraph (B).

(C) No Official Statement Prepared for Offering Exempt from Exchange Act Rule 15c2-12. If an official statement will not be prepared for a primary offering of municipal securities exempt from Securities Exchange Act Rule 15c2-12, the underwriter shall submit to EMMA, by no later than the closing date:

(1) notice to the effect that no official statement will be prepared; and

(2) the preliminary official statement or notice required pursuant to paragraph (D) of this subsection (i).

(D) Preliminary Official Statement Submission. The underwriter of a primary offering of municipal securities to which subparagraph (B)(2) or paragraph (C) of this subsection (i) applies shall submit to EMMA, by no later than the closing date, either:

(1) the preliminary official statement for such offering; or

(2) if no preliminary official statement has been prepared for such offering, notice that no preliminary official statement has been prepared.

(E) Exemption for Certain Limited Offerings. The underwriter of a primary offering of municipal securities not subject to Securities Exchange Act Rule 15c2-12 by virtue of paragraph (d)(1)(i) thereof for which an official statement has been prepared shall not be required to submit the official statement or any preliminary official statement to EMMA if the underwriter:

(1) complies with the requirements of paragraph (A) of this subsection (i);

(2) submits to EMMA, by no later than the closing date:

(a) notice that such primary offering is not subject to Securities Exchange Act Rule 15c2-12 by virtue of paragraph (d)(1)(i) thereof and that an official statement has been prepared but is not being submitted to EMMA; and

(b) contact information, including mailing address, telephone number, e-mail address and name of an associated person of the underwriter from whom customers may request the official statement; and

(3) delivers the official statement to each customer purchasing the offered municipal securities from the underwriter or from any other broker, dealer or municipal securities dealer, upon request, by the later of one business day after request or the settlement of the customer's transaction.

(F) Exemption for Certain Commercial Paper Offerings or Remarketings. The underwriter of a primary offering of municipal securities that consists of commercial paper not subject to Securities Exchange Act Rule 15c2-12 by virtue of paragraph (d)(1)(ii) thereof or of a remarketing of municipal securities not subject to paragraphs (b)(1) through (b)(4) of Securities Exchange Act Rule 15c2-12 by virtue of paragraph (d)(5) thereof shall not be required to comply with the requirements of paragraph (A) of this subsection (i) or to submit the official statement or any preliminary official statement to EMMA if:

(1) no official statement is prepared for the offering; or

(2) the official statement used in connection with such offering:

(a) has previously been properly submitted to EMMA in connection with a prior primary offering; and

(b) has not been supplemented or amended subsequent to such prior submission.

(ii) Advance Refunding Documents. If a primary offering advance refunds outstanding municipal securities and an advance refunding document is prepared, each underwriter in such offering shall, by no later than five business days after the closing date, submit:

    (A) the advance refunding document to EMMA; and

    (B) all information required to be submitted by Form G-32 relating to the advance refunding document as required under subsection (b)(vi) of this rule and as set forth in the EMMA Dataport Manual.

(iii) Amendments to Official Statements, Préliminary Official Statements and Advance Refunding Documents. In the event the underwriter for a primary offering has previously submitted to EMMA an official statement, preliminary official statement or advance refunding document and such document is amended by the issuer during the primary offering disclosure period, the underwriter for such primary offering must, within one business day after receipt of the amendment from the issuer or an agent of the issuer, submit:

    (A) the amendment to EMMA; and

    (B) all information required to be submitted by Form G-32 relating to the amendment as required under subsection (b)(vi) of this rule and as set forth in the EMMA Dataport Manual.

(iv) Cancellation of All or Part of Primary Offering. In the event an underwriter provides to EMMA the documents and information referred to in subsection (i), (ii) or (iii) above, but the primary offering is later cancelled, the underwriter shall notify EMMA of this fact promptly through Form G-32. If only a portion of a primary offering is cancelled, the underwriter shall amend or supplement information submitted to EMMA to reflect such partial cancellation by no later than the closing date.

(v) Underwriting Syndicate. In the event a syndicate or similar account has been formed for the underwriting of a primary offering, the managing underwriter shall take the actions required under the provisions of this rule.

(vi) Procedures for Submitting Documents and Form G-32 Information.

    (A) All official statements, preliminary official statements, advance refunding documents and amendments thereto submitted to EMMA under this rule shall be in a designated electronic format.

    (B) All submissions of information required under this rule shall be made by means of Form G-32 submitted electronically to EMMA in such format and manner, and including such items of information provided at such times, as specified herein, in Form G-32 and in the EMMA Dataport Manual.

    (C) The underwriter in any primary offering of municipal securities for which a document or information is required to be submitted to EMMA under this section (b) shall submit such information in a timely and accurate manner as follows:

        (1) Form G-32 information submissions pursuant to paragraph (b)(i)(A) hereof with respect to a primary offering shall be:

            (a) initiated on or prior to the date of first execution with the submission of CUSIP numbers (except if such CUSIP numbers are not required under Rule G-34 and have not been assigned), initial offering prices or yields (including prices or yields for maturities designated as not reoffered), if applicable, the expected closing date, whether the issuer or other obligated persons have agreed to undertake to provide continuing disclosure information as contemplated by Securities Exchange Act Rule 15c2-12, and if there was a retail order period (as defined in Rule G-11(a)(vii)) as part of a primary offering, information indicating whether a retail order period was conducted, each date and each time (beginning and end) it was conducted, together with such other items of information as set forth in Form G-32 and the EMMA Dataport Manual; and

            (b) completed by no later than the closing date, except to the extent that the provisions of subsection (b)(i) otherwise require a submission after the closing date.

        Specific items of information required by Form G-32 shall be submitted at such times and in such manners as set forth in the EMMA Dataport Manual.

        (2) Form G-32 information submissions pursuant to paragraph (b)(ii)(B) hereof with respect to an advance refunding shall be completed by no later than five business days after the closing date with the submission of CUSIP numbers, if any, of the advance refunded municipal securities (in-

cluding any CUSIP numbers newly assigned to some or all of the advance refunded municipal securities), together with such other items of information as set forth in Form G-32 and the EMMA Dataport Manual.

(3) Form G-32 information submissions pursuant to paragraph (b)(iii)(B) hereof with respect to an amendment to a previously submitted document shall be completed by no later than one business day after receipt of such amendment from the issuer or an agent of the issuer with the submission of such items of information as set forth in Form G-32 and the EMMA Dataport Manual.

(4) Form G-32 information submissions pursuant to subsection (b)(iv) hereof with respect to a cancellation of a primary offering shall be completed:

(a) in the case of a partial cancellation, by no later than the closing date for the remaining portion of such primary offering; and

(b) in the case of a cancellation of the entire primary offering, promptly after a final determination by the issuer that such offering is cancelled, provided that such information shall be deemed to have been submitted on a timely basis if submitted within five business days after cancellation by the underwriter of its transactions with customers or other brokers, dealers and municipal securities dealers in connection with such cancelled offering.

(D) Form G-32 and any related documents shall be submitted by the underwriter or by any submission agent designated by the underwriter pursuant to procedures set forth in the EMMA Dataport Manual. The failure of a submission agent designated by an underwriter to comply with any requirement of this rule shall be considered a failure by such underwriter to so comply.

(c) Preparation of Official Statements By Financial Advisors. A broker, dealer or municipal securities dealer that, acting as financial advisor, prepares an official statement on behalf of an issuer with respect to a primary offering of municipal securities shall make the official statement available to the managing underwriter or sole underwriter in a designated electronic format promptly after the issuer approves its distribution.

(d) Definitions. For purposes of this rule, the following terms have the following meanings:

(i) The term "advance refunding document" shall mean the refunding escrow trust agreement or its equivalent prepared by or on behalf of the issuer.

(ii) The term "closing date" shall mean the date of first delivery by the issuer to or through the underwriter of municipal securities sold in a primary offering.

(iii) The term "designated electronic format" shall mean portable document format, with files configured to permit documents to be saved, viewed, printed and retransmitted by electronic means. For files submitted to EMMA on or after January 1, 2010, documents in designated electronic format must be word-searchable (without regard to diagrams, images and other non-textual elements).

(iv) The term "EMMA" shall mean the Board's Electronic Municipal Market Access system, or any other electronic municipal securities information access system designated by the Board for collecting and disseminating primary offering documents and information.

(v) The term "EMMA Dataport Manual" shall mean the document(s) designated as such published by the Board from time to time setting forth the processes and procedures with respect to submissions to be made to the primary market disclosure service of EMMA by underwriters under Rule G-32(b).

(vi) The term "offered municipal securities" shall mean municipal securities that are sold by a broker, dealer or municipal securities dealer during the securities' primary offering disclosure period, including but not limited to municipal securities reoffered in a remarketing that constitutes a primary offering and municipal securities sold in a primary offering but designated as not reoffered.

(vii) The term "official statement" shall mean (A) for an offering subject to Securities Exchange Act Rule 15c2-12, a document or documents defined in Securities Exchange Act Rule 15c2-12(f)(3), or (B) for an offering not subject to Securities Exchange Act Rule 15c2-12, a document or documents prepared by or on behalf of the issuer that is complete as of the date delivered to the underwriter and that sets forth information concerning the terms of the proposed offering of securities. A notice of sale shall not be deemed to be an "official statement" for purposes of this rule.

(viii) The term "primary offering" shall mean an offering defined in Securities Exchange Act Rule 15c2-12(f)(7), including but not limited to any remarketing of municipal securities that constitutes a primary offering as such subsection (f)(7) may be interpreted from time to time by the Commission.

(ix) The term "primary offering disclosure period" shall mean, with respect to any primary offering, the period commencing with the first submission to an underwriter of an order for the purchase of offered municipal securities or the purchase of such securities from the issuer, whichever first occurs, and ending 25 days after the final delivery by the issuer or its agent of all securities of the issue to or through the underwriting syndicate or sole underwriter.

(x) The term "qualified portal" shall mean an Internet-based utility providing access by any purchaser or potential purchaser of offered municipal securities to the official statement for such offered municipal securities in a designated electronic format, and allowing such purchaser or potential purchaser to search for (using the nine-digit CUSIP number and other appropriate search parameters), view, print and save the official statement, at no charge, for a period beginning on the first business day after such official statement becomes available from EMMA and ending no earlier than 30 calendar days after the end of the primary offering disclosure period for such offered municipal securities; provided that any such utility shall not be a qualified portal unless notice to users that official statements are also available from EMMA and a hyperlink to EMMA are posted on the page on which searches on such utility for official statements may be conducted.

(xi) The term "date of first execution" shall mean the date on which the underwriter executes its first transactions with a customer or another broker, dealer or municipal securities dealer in any security offered in a primary offering; provided that, for offerings subject to Rule G-34(a)(ii)(C), "date of first execution" shall mean the date corresponding to the Time of First Execution as defined in Rule G-34(a)(ii)(C)(1)(b); further provided that, solely for purposes of this rule, the date of first execution shall be deemed to occur by no later than the closing date.

(xii) The term "underwriter" shall mean a broker, dealer or municipal securities dealer that is an underwriter as defined in Securities Exchange Act Rule 15c2-12(f)(8), including but not limited to a broker, dealer or municipal securities dealer that acts as remarketing agent for a remarketing of municipal securities that constitutes a primary offering.

(xiii) The term "commercial paper" shall mean municipal securities having a maturity of nine months or less issued pursuant to a commercial paper program permitting such municipal securities to be rolled over upon maturity into new commercial paper.

(xiv) The term "obligated person" shall mean an obligated person defined in Securities Exchange Act Rule 15c2-12(f)(10).

(xv) The term "NIIDS" shall have the meaning set forth in Rule G-34(a)(ii)(C)(3)(b).

---

5. MSRB Rules: G-34 – CUSIP Numbers, New Issue and Market Information Requirements

Summary: Establishes requirements relating to CUSIP numbers for dealers and, in competitive offerings, municipal advisors; requires underwriter participation in the New Issue Information Dissemination Service (NIIDS); and requires submission of certain information and documents related to auction rate securities and variable rate demand obligations to the SHORT system.

(a) New Issue Securities.

  (i) Assignment and Affixture of CUSIP Numbers.

    (A) Except as otherwise provided in this section (a) and section (d), a broker, dealer or municipal securities dealer acting as an underwriter in a new issue of municipal securities, and a municipal advisor advising the issuer with respect to a competitive sale of a new issue of municipal securities, shall apply in writing to the Board or its designee for assignment of a CUSIP number or numbers to such new issue, as follows:

      (1) The underwriter in a negotiated sale shall make an application by no later than the time that pricing information for the issue is finalized. Such application for CUSIP number assignment shall be made at a time sufficient to ensure final CUSIP number assignment occurs prior to the formal award of the issue.

      (2) The underwriter in a competitive sale for which no CUSIP numbers have been pre-assigned shall make an application immediately after receiving notification of the award from the issuer. The underwriter in a competitive sale shall ensure that CUSIP numbers are assigned prior to disseminating the Time of First Execution required under paragraph (a)(ii)(C) of this Rule G-34.

      (3) A municipal advisor advising the issuer with respect to a competitive sale of a new issue of municipal securities shall make an application by no later than one business day after dissemination of a notice of sale or other such request for bids. Such application for CUSIP number assignment shall be made at a time sufficient to ensure final CUSIP number assignment occurs prior to the award of the issue.

      (4) In making applications for CUSIP number assignment, the following information shall be provided:

        (a) complete name of issue and series designation, if any;

        (b) interest rate(s) and maturity date(s) (provided, however, that, if the interest rate is not established at the time of application, it may be provided at such time as it becomes available);

        (c) dated date;

        (d) type of issue (e.g., general obligation, limited tax or revenue);

        (e) type of revenue, if the issue is a revenue issue;

        (f) details of all redemption provisions;

        (g) the name of any company or other person in addition to the issuer obligated, directly or indirectly, with respect to the debt service on all or part of the issue (and, if part of the issue, an indication of which part); and

        (h) any distinction(s) in the security or source of payment of the debt service on the issue, and an indication of the part(s) of the issue to which such distinction(s) relate.

      (5) Any changes to information identified in subparagraph (a)(i)(A)(4) and included in an application for CUSIP number assignment shall be provided to the Board or its designee as soon as they are known but no later than a time sufficient to ensure final CUSIP number assignment occurs prior to disseminating the time of first execution required under subparagraph (a)(ii)(C)(1)(b) of this Rule G-34.

    (B) The information required by subparagraph (i)(A)(4) of this section (a) shall be provided in accordance with the provisions of this paragraph. The application shall include a copy of a notice of sale, official statement, legal opinion, or other similar documentation prepared by or on behalf of the issuer, or portions of such documentation, reflecting the information required by subparagraph (i)(A)(4) of this section (a). Such documentation may be submitted in preliminary form if no final documentation is available at the time of application. In such event the final documentation, or the relevant portions of such documentation, reflecting any changes in the information required by subparagraph (i)(A)(4) of this section (a) shall be submitted when such documentation becomes available. If no such documentation, whether in preliminary or final form, is available at the time application for CUSIP number assignment is made, such copy shall be provided promptly after the documentation becomes available.

(C) The provisions of subsection (i) of this section (a) shall not apply with respect to any new issue of municipal securities on which the issuer or a person acting on behalf of the issuer has submitted an application for assignment of a CUSIP number or numbers.

(D) In the event that the proceeds of the new issue will be used, in whole or in part, to refund an outstanding issue or issues of municipal securities in such a way that part but not all of the outstanding issue or issues previously assigned a single CUSIP number is to be refunded to one or more redemption date(s) and price(s) (or all of an outstanding issue is to be refunded to more than one redemption date and price), the broker, dealer or municipal securities dealer shall apply in writing to the Board or its designee for a reassignment of a CUSIP number to each part of the outstanding issue refunded to a particular redemption date and price and shall provide to the Board or its designee the following information on the issue or issues to be refunded:

(1) the previously assigned CUSIP number of each such part or issue;

(2) for each such CUSIP number, the redemption dates and prices, to be established by the refunding;

(3) for each such redemption date and price, a designation of the portion of such part or issue (e.g., the designation of use of proceeds, series, or certificate numbers) to which such redemption date and price applies.

The underwriter also shall provide documentation supporting the information provided pursuant to the requirements of this subparagraph (D).

(E) The underwriter, prior to the delivery of a new issue of municipal securities to any other person, shall affix to, or arrange to have affixed to, the securities certificates of such new issue the CUSIP number assigned to such new issue. If more than one CUSIP number is assigned to the new issue, each such number shall be affixed to the securities certificates of that part of the issue to which such number relates.

(F) A broker, dealer or municipal securities dealer acting as an underwriter of a new issue of municipal securities, or a municipal advisor advising the issuer with respect to a competitive sale of a new issue, which is being purchased directly by a bank, any entity directly or indirectly controlled by the bank or under common control with the bank, other than a broker, dealer or municipal securities dealer registered under the Securities Exchange Act of 1934, or a consortium of such entities; or by a municipal entity with funds that are, at least in part, proceeds of, or fully or partially secure or pay, the purchasing entity's issue of municipal obligations (e.g., state revolving fund or bond bank), may elect not to apply for assignment of a CUSIP number or numbers if the underwriter or municipal advisor reasonably believes (e.g., by obtaining a written representation) that the present intent of the purchasing entity or entities is to hold the municipal securities to maturity or earlier redemption or mandatory tender.

(ii) Application for Depository Eligibility and Dissemination of New Issue Information. Each underwriter shall carry out the following functions:

(A) Except as otherwise provided in this paragraph (ii)(A) and section (d), the underwriter shall apply to a securities depository registered with the Securities and Exchange Commission, in accordance with the rules and procedures of such depository, to make such new issue depository-eligible. The application required by this paragraph (ii)(A) shall be made as promptly as possible, but in no event later than one business day after award from the issuer (in the case of a competitive sale) or one business day after the execution of the contract to purchase the securities from the issuer (in the case of a negotiated sale). In the event that the full documentation and information required to establish depository eligibility is not available at the time the initial application is submitted to the depository, the underwriter shall forward such documentation as soon as it is available; provided, however, this paragraph (ii)(A) of this rule shall not apply to:

(1) an issue of municipal securities that fails to meet the criteria for depository eligibility at all depositories that accept municipal securities for deposit; or

(2) any new issue maturing in 60 days or less; or

(3) a new issue of municipal securities purchased directly by a bank, any entity directly or indirectly controlled by the bank or under common control with the bank, other than a broker, dealer or municipal securities dealer registered under the Securities Exchange Act of 1934, or a consortium of such entities; or by a municipal entity with funds that are, at least in part, proceeds of, or fully or partially secure or pay, the purchasing entity's issue of municipal obligations (e.g., state revolving fund or bond bank), from an issuer in which an underwriter reasonably believes (e.g., by obtaining a written representation) that the present intent of the purchasing entity or entities is to hold the municipal securities to maturity or earlier redemption or mandatory tender.

(B) Prior to acting as underwriter for a new issue of municipal securities eligible for submission to NIIDS:

(1) each broker, dealer or municipal securities dealer must register to use NIIDS with DTCC and shall test its capability to use NIIDS by successfully submitting two test new issues using the NIIDS Web Interface; and

(2) each broker, dealer or municipal securities dealer that plans to establish computer-to-computer connections with NIIDS (either directly or through a vendor) shall test its capability to use NIIDS by successfully submitting two test new issues using computer-to-computer connections.

(C) The underwriter of a new issue of municipal securities, which has been made depository eligible pursuant to paragraph (ii)(A) above, shall communicate information about the new issue in accordance with the requirements of this paragraph (a)(ii)(C) to ensure that other brokers, dealers and municipal securities dealers have timely access to information necessary to report, compare, confirm, and settle transactions in the new issue and to ensure that registered securities clearing agencies receive information necessary to provide comparison, clearance and depository services for the new issue; provided, however, that this paragraph (a)(ii)(C) shall not apply to commercial paper.

(1) The underwriter shall ensure that the following information is submitted to NIIDS in the manner described in the written procedures for system users and that changes or corrections to submitted information are made as soon as possible:

(a) the time of formal award.

(i) For purposes of this paragraph (a)(ii)(C), the "time of formal award" means:

(A) for competitive issues, the later of the time the issuer announces the award or the time the issuer notifies the underwriter of the award, and

(B) for negotiated issues, the later of the time the contract to purchase the securities from the issuer is executed or the time the issuer notifies the underwriter of its execution.

(ii) If the underwriter and issuer have agreed in advance on a time of formal award, that time may be submitted to NIIDS in advance of the actual time of formal award.

(b) the time of first execution.

(i) For purposes of this paragraph (a)(ii)(C), the "time of first execution" means the time the underwriter plans to execute its first transactions in the new issue.

(ii) The underwriter shall designate a time of first execution that is:

(A) for new issues consisting of variable rate instruments for which transactions occurring on the first day of trading are expected to settle on a same-day or next-day basis, any time after all information required by paragraph (a)(ii)(C) has been transmitted to NIIDS; or

(B) for all other new issues, no less than two business hours after all information required by paragraph (a)(ii)(C) has been transmitted to NIIDS; provided that the time of first execution may be designated as 9:00 A.M. Eastern Time or later on the RTRS business day following the day on which all information required by paragraph (a)(ii)(C) has been transmitted to NIIDS without regard to whether two business hours have elapsed.

(c) All other information identified as required for "Trade Eligibility" in NIIDS.

(2) The underwriter shall ensure that all information identified in this paragraph (a)(ii)(C) is transmitted to NIIDS no later than two business hours after the time of formal award. For purposes of this paragraph (a)(ii)(C):

   (a) "business hours" shall include only the hours from 9:00 A.M. to 5:00 P.M. Eastern Time on an RTRS business day.

   (b) "RTRS business day" shall have the meaning set forth in Rule G-14 RTRS Procedures subsection (d)(ii).

(3) For purposes of paragraphs (B) and (C) of this subsection (a)(ii):

   (a) "DTCC" means The Depository Trust and Clearing Corporation, a securities clearing agency registered with the Commission providing depository services for municipal securities.

   (b) "NIIDS" means the New Issue Information Dissemination Service, an automated, electronic system operated by DTCC as part of its underwriting eligibility request platform, UW Source, that receives comprehensive new issue information for municipal securities on a market-wide basis for the purposes of establishing depository eligibility and immediately re-disseminating such information to information vendors supplying formatted municipal securities information for use in automated trade processing systems.

(D) The underwriter of any new issue of municipal securities consisting of commercial paper shall, as promptly as possible, announce each item of information listed below in a manner reasonably designed to reach market participants that may trade the new issue. All information shall be announced no later than the time of the first execution of a transaction in the new issue by the underwriter.

   (1) the CUSIP number or numbers assigned to the issue and descriptive information sufficient to identify the CUSIP number corresponding to each part of the issue assigned a specific CUSIP number; and

   (2) the time of formal award as defined in subparagraph (a)(ii)(C)(1)(a).

(E) For any new issue of municipal securities eligible for comparison through the automated comparison facilities of a registered clearing agency under section (f) of rule G-12, the underwriter shall provide the registered securities clearing agency responsible for comparing when, as and if issued transactions with:

   (1) final interest rate maturity information about the new issue as soon as it is available; and

   (2) the settlement date of the new issue as soon as it is known and shall immediately inform the registered clearing agency of any changes in such settlement date.

(iii) Underwriting Syndicate. In the event a syndicate or similar account has been formed for the purchase of a new issue of municipal securities, the managing underwriter shall take the actions required of the underwriter under the provisions of this section (a).

(iv) Limited Use of NRO Designation. From and after the time of initial award of a new issue of municipal securities, a broker, dealer or municipal securities dealer may not use the term "not reoffered" or other comparable term or designation without also including the applicable price or yield information about the securities in any of its written communications, electronic or otherwise, sent by it or on its behalf. For purposes of this subsection (iv), the "time of initial award" means the earlier of (A) the time of formal award as defined in subparagraph (a)(ii)(C)(1)(a), or (B) if applicable, the time at which the issuer initially accepts the terms of a new issue of municipal securities subject to subsequent formal award.

(b) Secondary Market Securities.

(i) Each broker, dealer, or municipal securities dealer that, in connection with a sale or an offering for sale of part of a maturity of an issue of municipal securities, acquires or arranges for the acquisition of a transferable instrument applicable to such part which alters the security or source of payment of such part shall apply in writing to the Board or its designee for the assignment of a CUSIP number to designate the part of the maturity of the issue which is the subject of the instrument when traded with the instrument attached. Such instruments shall include (A) insurance with respect to the payment of debt service on such portion, (B) a put option or tender option, (C) a letter of credit or guarantee, or (D) any other similar device. This paragraph (i) shall not apply with respect to any part of an outstanding maturity of an issue of municipal securities with respect to which a CUSIP number that is applicable to such part when traded with an instrument which alters the security or source of payment of such part has already been assigned.

(ii) Each broker, dealer or municipal securities dealer, in connection with a sale or an offering for sale of part of a maturity of an issue of municipal securities which is assigned a CUSIP number that no longer designates securities identical with respect to all features of the issue listed in items (a) through (h) of subparagraph (a)(i)(A)(4) of this rule, shall apply in writing to the Board or its designee for a new CUSIP number or numbers to designate the part or parts of the maturity which are identical with respect to items (a) through (h) of subparagraph (a)(i)(A)(4).

(iii) The broker, dealer or municipal securities dealer shall make the application required under this section (b) as promptly as possible, and shall provide to the Board or its designee:

(A) the previously assigned CUSIP number;

(B) all information on the features of the maturity of the issue listed in items (a) through (h) of subparagraph (a)(i)(A)(4) of this rule and documentation of the features of such maturity sufficient to evidence the basis for CUSIP number assignment; and,

(C) if the application is based on an instrument affecting the source of payment or security for a part of a maturity of an issue, information on the nature of the instrument, including the name of any party obligated with respect to debt service under the terms of such instrument and documentation sufficient to evidence the nature of the instrument.

(c) Variable Rate Security Market Information.

(i) Auction Rate Securities.

(A) Auction Rate Securities Data.

(1) Each broker, dealer or municipal securities dealer that submits an order directly to an Auction Agent for its own account or on behalf of another account to buy, hold or sell an Auction Rate Security through the auction process program dealer shall report, or ensure the reporting of, the following information about the auction rate security and concerning the results of the auction to the Board:

(a) CUSIP number;

(b) Interest rate produced by the auction process and designation of whether the interest rate is a maximum rate, all hold rate, or rate set by auction;

(c) Identity of all program dealers that submitted orders, including but not limited to hold orders;

(d) Date and time of the auction;

(e) Length of time, in days, that the interest rate produced by the auction process is applicable;

(f) Minimum denomination;

(g) Minimum and maximum rates, if any, applicable at the time of the auction or, if not calculable as of the time of auction, indication that such rate or rates are not calculable.

(h) Date and time the interest rate determined as a result of the auction process was communicated to program dealers;

(i) Aggregate par amount of orders to sell at any interest rate and aggregate par amount of such orders that were executed;

(j) Interest rate(s) and aggregate par amount(s) of orders to hold at a specific interest rate and aggregate par amount of such orders that were successfully held;

(k) Interest rate(s) and aggregate par amount(s) of orders to buy and aggregate par amount of such orders that were executed;

(l) Interest rate(s), aggregate par amount(s), and type of order – either buy, sell or hold – for a program dealer for its own account and aggregate par amounts of such orders, by type, that were executed; and

(m) Interest rate(s), aggregate par amount(s), and type of order – either buy, sell or hold – for an issuer or conduit borrower for such auction rate security.

(2) Information identified in paragraph (c)(i)(A) shall be provided to the Board by no later than 6:30 P.M. Eastern Time on the date on which an auction occurs if such date is an RTRS business day as defined in Rule G-14 RTRS Procedures subsection (d)(ii). In the event that any item of information identified in subparagraph (c)(i)(A)(1) is not available by the deadline in this subparagraph (c)(i)(A)(2), such item shall be provided to the Board as soon as it is available. In the event that an auction occurs on a non-RTRS business day, the information identified in subparagraph (c)(i)(A)(1) shall be reported by no later than 6:30 P.M. Eastern Time on the next RTRS business day.

(3) A program dealer may designate an agent to report the information identified in subparagraph (c)(i)(A)(1) to the Board, provided that an auction agent may submit information on behalf of a program dealer absent such designation by the program dealer. The failure of a designated agent to comply with any requirement of this subsection (c)(i) shall be considered a failure by such program dealer to so comply; provided that if an auction agent has, within the time periods required under subparagraph (c)(i)(A)(2), reported the information required under subparagraph (c)(i)(A)(1), the program dealer may rely on the accuracy of such information if the program dealer makes a good faith and reasonable effort to cause the auction agent to correct any inaccuracies known to the program dealer.

(4) For Auction Rate Securities in which there are multiple program dealers, each program dealer must only report for items (i) through (m) of the items of information identified in subparagraph (c)(i)(A)(1) information reflective of the program dealer's involvement in the auction. A designated agent as described in subparagraph (c)(i)(A)(3) reporting results of an auction on behalf of multiple program dealers must report for items (i) through (m) of the items information identified in subparagraph (c)(i)(A)(1) information reflective of the aggregate of all such program dealers' involvement in the auction for which the designated agent is making a report. A program dealer may rely on the reporting of information by an auction agent as provided in subparagraph (c)(i)(A)(3) if the auction agent has undertaken to report, and the program dealer does not have reason to believe that the auction agent is not accurately reporting, all items of information identified in subparagraph (c)(i)(A)(1), to the extent applicable, for an auction that is reflective of all program dealers that were involved in the auction.

(5) Information reported to the Board pursuant to this subsection (c)(i) shall be submitted in the manner described in the written procedures for SHORT system users and changes to submitted information must be made as soon as possible.

(6) Every broker, dealer or municipal securities dealer that submits an order to a program dealer on behalf of an issuer or conduit borrower for such auction rate securities shall disclose at the time of the submission of such order that the order is on behalf of an issuer or conduit borrower for such auction rate securities.

(B) Auction Rate Securities Documents.

(1) Each program dealer shall submit to the Board current documents setting forth auction procedures and interest rate setting mechanisms associated with an outstanding auction rate security for which it acts as a program dealer by no later than September 22, 2011 and shall submit to the Board any future, subsequently amended or new versions of such documents no later than five business days after they are made available to the program dealer.

(2) All submissions of documents required under subparagraph (c)(i)(B)(1) shall be made by electronic submissions to the SHORT system in a designated electronic format (as defined in Rule G-32) at such time and in such manner as specified herein and in the SHORT System Users Manual.

(ii) Variable Rate Demand Obligations.

    (A) Variable Rate Demand Obligations Data.

        (1) Each remarketing agent for a variable rate demand obligation shall report the following information to the Board about the variable rate demand obligation applicable at the time of and concerning the results of an interest rate reset:

            (a) CUSIP number;

            (b) Interest rate and designation of whether the interest rate is a maximum rate, set by formula or set by the remarketing agent;

            (c) Identity of the remarketing agent;

            (d) Date and time of the interest rate reset;

            (e) Effective date and length of time, in days, that the interest rate is applicable;

            (f) Minimum denomination;

            (g) Length of Notification Period;

            (h) Minimum and maximum rates, if any, applicable at time of the interest rate reset or, if not calculable as of the time of interest rate reset, indication that such rate or rates are not calculable;

            (i) Identity of liquidity provider, type and expiration date of each liquidity facility applicable to the variable rate demand obligation;

            (j) Identity of the agent of the issuer to which bondholders may tender their security ("tender agent"); and

            (k) Aggregate par amount, if any, of the variable rate demand obligation held by a liquidity provider(s) (par amount held as "bank bonds"), and aggregate par amount, if any, of the variable rate demand obligation held by parties other than a liquidity provider(s), including the par amounts held by the remarketing agent and by investors.

        (2) Information identified in subparagraph (c)(ii)(A)(1) shall be provided to the Board by no later than 6:30 P.M. Eastern Time on the date on which an interest rate reset occurs if such date is an RTRS business day as defined in Rule G-14 RTRS Procedures subsection (d)(ii). In the event that any item of information identified in subparagraph (c)(ii)(A)(1) is not available by the deadline in this subparagraph (c)(ii)(A)(2), such item shall be provided to the Board as soon as it is available provided that items (i) through (k) of the information identified in subparagraph (c)(ii)(A)(1) shall reflect the information available to the remarketing agent as of the date and time of the interest rate reset. In the event that an interest rate reset occurs on a non-RTRS business day, the information identified in subparagraph (c)(ii)(A)(1) shall be reported by no later than 6:30 P.M. Eastern Time on the next RTRS business day.

        (3) A remarketing agent may designate an agent to report the information identified in subparagraph (c)(ii)(A)(1) to the Board. The failure of a designated agent to comply with any requirement of this paragraph (c)(ii) shall be considered a failure by such remarketing agent to so comply.

        (4) Information reported to the Board pursuant to this subsection (c)(ii) shall be submitted in the manner described in the written procedures for SHORT system users and changes to submitted information must be made as soon as possible.

    (B) Variable Rate Demand Obligations Documents.

        (1) Each remarketing agent shall use best efforts to obtain and shall submit to the SHORT system the current versions of the following documents detailing provisions of liquidity facilities associated with the variable rate demand obligation for which it acts as a remarketing agent by no later than September 22, 2011 and shall submit to the SHORT system any future, subsequently amended or new versions of such documents no later than five business days after they are made available to the remarketing agent:

            (a) Stand-by bond purchase agreement;

            (b) Letter of credit agreement; and

(c) any other document that establishes an obligation to provide liquidity.

(2) All submissions of documents required under this rule shall be made by electronic submissions to the SHORT system in a designated electronic format (as defined in Rule G-32) at such time and in such manner as specified herein and in the SHORT System Users Manual.

(3) In the event that a document described in subparagraph (c)(ii)(B)(1) is not able to be obtained through the best efforts of the remarketing agent, the remarketing agent shall submit notice to the SHORT system that such document will not be provided at such times as specified herein and in the SHORT System Users Manual.

(d) Exemptions. The provisions of this rule shall not apply to an issue of municipal securities (or for the purpose of section (b) any part of an outstanding maturity of an issue) which (i) does not meet the eligibility criteria for CUSIP number assignment or (ii) consists entirely of municipal fund securities.

(e) Definitions. For purposes of this rule, the following terms have the following meanings:

(i) The term "auction agent" shall mean the agent responsible for conducting the auction process for auction rate securities on behalf of the issuer or other obligated person with respect to such securities and that receives orders from brokers, dealers and municipal securities dealers.

(ii) The term "auction rate security" shall mean municipal securities in which the interest rate resets on a periodic basis under an auction process conducted by an auction agent.

(iii) The term "notification period" shall mean the specified advance notice period during which an investor in a variable rate demand obligation has the option to put the issue back to the trustee, tender agent or other agent of the issuer or obligated person.

(iv) The term "program dealer" shall mean each broker, dealer or municipal securities dealer that submits an order directly to an auction agent for its own account or on behalf of another account to buy, hold or sell an auction rate security through the auction process.

(v) The term "remarketing agent" shall mean, with respect to variable rate demand obligations, the broker, dealer or municipal securities dealer responsible for reselling to new investors securities that have been tendered for purchase by a holder.

(vi) The term "SHORT system" shall mean the Short-term Obligation Rate Transparency System, a facility operated by the Board for the collection and public dissemination of information and documents about securities bearing interest at short-term rates.

(vii) The term "underwriter" shall mean an underwriter as defined in Securities Exchange Act Rule 15c2-12(f)(8) and includes a dealer acting as a placement agent.

(viii) The term "variable rate demand obligation" shall mean securities in which the interest rate resets on a periodic basis with a frequency of up to and including every nine months, where an investor has the option to put the issue back to the trustee, tender agent or other agent of the issuer or obligated person at any time, typically within a notification period, and a broker, dealer or municipal securities dealer acts as a remarketing agent responsible for reselling to new investors securities that have been tendered for purchase by a holder.

6. SEC Rules and Regulations, Securities Act of 1933:
Section 7 – Information Required in a Registration Statement

(a) Information required in registration statement

    (1) In general

        The registration statement, when relating to a security other than a security issued by a foreign government, or political subdivision thereof, shall contain the information, and be accompanied by the documents, specified in Schedule A of section 77aa of this title, and when relating to a security issued by a foreign government, or political subdivision thereof, shall contain the information, and be accompanied by the documents, specified in Schedule B of section 77aa of this title; except that the Commission may by rules or regulations provide that any such information or document need not be included in respect of any class of issuers or securities if it finds that the requirement of such information or document is inapplicable to such class and that disclosure fully adequate for the protection of investors is otherwise required to be included within the registration statement. If any accountant, engineer, or appraiser, or any person whose profession gives authority to a statement made by him, is named as having prepared or certified any part of the registration statement, or is named as having prepared or certified a report or valuation for use in connection with the registration statement, the written consent of such person shall be filed with the registration statement. If any such person is named as having prepared or certified a report or valuation (other than a public official document or statement) which is used in connection with the registration statement, but is not named as having prepared or certified such report or valuation for use in connection with the registration statement, the written consent of such person shall be filed with the registration statement unless the Commission dispenses with such filing as impracticable or as involving undue hardship on the person filing the registration statement. Any such registration statement shall contain such other information, and be accompanied by such other documents, as the Commission may by rules or regulations require as being necessary or appropriate in the public interest or for the protection of investors.

    (2) Treatment of emerging growth companies

        An emerging growth company—

        (A) need not present more than 2 years of audited financial statements in order for the registration statement of such emerging growth company with respect to an initial public offering of its common equity securities to be effective, and in any other registration statement to be filed with the Commission, an emerging growth company need not present selected financial data in accordance with section 229.301 of title 17, Code of Federal Regulations, for any period prior to the earliest audited period presented in connection with its initial public offering; and

        (B) may not be required to comply with any new or revised financial accounting standard until such date that a company that is not an issuer (as defined under section 7201 of this title) is required to comply with such new or revised accounting standard, if such standard applies to companies that are not issuers.

(b) Registration statement for blank check companies

    (1) The Commission shall prescribe special rules with respect to registration statements filed by any issuer that is a blank check company. Such rules may, as the Commission determines necessary or appropriate in the public interest or for the protection of investors—

        (A) require such issuers to provide timely disclosure, prior to or after such statement becomes effective under section 77h of this title, of (i) information regarding the company to be acquired and the specific application of the proceeds of the offering, or (ii) additional information necessary to prevent such statement from being misleading;

        (B) place limitations on the use of such proceeds and the distribution of securities by such issuer until the disclosures required under subparagraph (A) have been made; and

        (C) provide a right of rescission to shareholders of such securities.

(2) The Commission may, as it determines consistent with the public interest and the protection of investors, by rule or order exempt any issuer or class of issuers from the rules prescribed under paragraph (1).

(3) For purposes of paragraph (1) of this subsection, the term "blank check company" means any development stage company that is issuing a penny stock (within the meaning of section 78c(a)(51) of this title) and that—

(A) has no specific business plan or purpose; or

(B) has indicated that its business plan is to merge with an unidentified company or companies.

(c) Disclosure requirements

(1) In general

The Commission shall adopt regulations under this subsection requiring each issuer of an asset-backed security to disclose, for each tranche or class of security, information regarding the assets backing that security.

(2) Content of regulations

In adopting regulations under this subsection, the Commission shall—

(A) set standards for the format of the data provided by issuers of an asset-backed security, which shall, to the extent feasible, facilitate comparison of such data across securities in similar types of asset classes; and

(B) require issuers of asset-backed securities, at a minimum, to disclose asset-level or loan-level data, if such data are necessary for investors to independently perform due diligence, including—

(i) data having unique identifiers relating to loan brokers or originators;

(ii) the nature and extent of the compensation of the broker or originator of the assets backing the security; and

(iii) the amount of risk retention by the originator and the securitizer of such assets.

(d) Registration statement for asset-backed securities. Not later than 180 days after July 21, 2010, the Commission shall issue rules relating to the registration statement required to be filed by any issuer of an asset-backed security (as that term is defined in section 78c(a)(77) [1] of this title) that require any issuer of an asset-backed security—

(1) to perform a review of the assets underlying the asset-backed security; and

(2) to disclose the nature of the review under paragraph (1).

---

7. SEC Rules and Regulations, Securities Act of 1933: Section 8 – Taking Effect of Registration Statements and Amendments Thereto

(a) Effective date of registration statement

Except as hereinafter provided, the effective date of a registration statement shall be the twentieth day after the filing thereof or such earlier date as the Commission may determine, having due regard to the adequacy of the information respecting the issuer theretofore available to the public, to the facility with which the nature of the securities to be registered, their relationship to the capital structure of the issuer and the rights of holders thereof can be understood, and to the public interest and the protection of investors. If any amendment to any such statement is filed prior to the effective date of such statement, the registration statement shall be deemed to have been filed when such amendment was filed; except that an amendment filed with the consent of the Commission, prior to the effective date of the registration statement, or filed pursuant to an order of the Commission, shall be treated as a part of the registration statement.

(b) Incomplete or inaccurate registration statement

If it appears to the Commission that a registration statement is on its face incomplete or inaccurate in any material respect, the Commission may, after notice by personal service or the sending of confirmed telegraphic notice not later than ten days after the filing of the registration statement, and opportunity for hearing (at a time fixed by the Commission) within ten days after such notice by personal service or the sending of such telegraphic notice, issue an order prior to the effective date of registration refusing to permit such statement to become effective until it has been amended in accordance with such order. When such statement has been amended in accordance with such order the Commission shall so declare and the registration shall become effective at the time provided in subsection (a) or upon the date of such declaration, whichever date is the later.

(c) Effective date of amendment to registration statement

An amendment filed after the effective date of the registration statement, if such amendment, upon its face, appears to the Commission not to be incomplete or inaccurate in any material respect, shall become effective on such date as the Commission may determine, having due regard to the public interest and the protection of investors.

(d) Untrue statements or omissions in registration statement

If it appears to the Commission at any time that the registration statement includes any untrue statement of a material fact or omits to state any material fact required to be stated therein or necessary to make the statements therein not misleading, the Commission may, after notice by personal service or the sending of confirmed telegraphic notice, and after opportunity for hearing (at a time fixed by the Commission) within fifteen days after such notice by personal service or the sending of such telegraphic notice, issue a stop order suspending the effectiveness of the registration statement. When such statement has been amended in accordance with such stop order, the Commission shall so declare and thereupon the stop order shall cease to be effective.

(e) Examination for issuance of stop order

The Commission is empowered to make an examination in any case in order to determine whether a stop order should issue under subsection (d). In making such examination the Commission or any officer or officers designated by it shall have access to and may demand the production of any books and papers of, and may administer oaths and affirmations to and examine, the issuer, underwriter, or any other person, in respect of any matter relevant to the examination, and may, in its discretion, require the production of a balance sheet exhibiting the assets and liabilities of the issuer, or its income statement, or both, to be certified to by a public or certified accountant approved by the Commission. If the issuer or underwriter shall fail to cooperate, or shall obstruct or refuse to permit the making of an examination, such conduct shall be proper ground for the issuance of a stop order.

(f) Notice requirements

Any notice required under this section shall be sent to or served on the issuer, or, in case of a foreign government or political subdivision thereof, to or on the underwriter, or, in the case of a foreign or Territorial person, to or on its duly authorized representative in the United States named in the registration statement, properly directed in each case of telegraphic notice to the address given in such statement.

---

8. SEC Rules and Regulations, Securities Act of 1933:
Section 10 – Information Required in Prospectus

(a) Information in registration statement; documents not required except to the extent otherwise permitted or required pursuant to this subsection or subsections (c), (d), or (e)—

    (1) a prospectus relating to a security other than a security issued by a foreign government or political subdivision thereof, shall contain the information contained in the registration statement, but it need not include the documents referred to in paragraphs (28) to (32), inclusive, of schedule A of section 77aa of this title;

    (2) a prospectus relating to a security issued by a foreign government or political subdivision thereof shall contain the information contained in the registration statement, but it need not include the documents referred to in paragraphs (13) and (14) of schedule B of section 77aa of this title;

    (3) notwithstanding the provisions of paragraphs (1) and (2) of this subsection when a prospectus is used more than nine months after the effective date of the registration statement, the information contained therein shall be as of a date not more than sixteen months prior to such use, so far as such information is known to the user of such prospectus or can be furnished by such user without unreasonable effort or expense;

    (4) there may be omitted from any prospectus any of the information required under this subsection which the Commission may by rules or regulations designate as not being necessary or appropriate in the public interest or for the protection of investors.

(b) Summarizations and omissions allowed by rules and regulations

In addition to the prospectus permitted or required in subsection (a), the Commission shall by rules or regulations deemed necessary or appropriate in the public interest or for the protection of investors permit the use of a prospectus for the purposes of subsection (b)(1) of section 77e of this title which omits in part or summarizes information in the prospectus specified in subsection (a). A prospectus permitted under this subsection shall, except to the extent the Commission by rules or regulations deemed necessary or appropriate in the public interest or for the protection of investors otherwise provides, be filed as part of the registration statement but shall not be deemed a part of such registration statement for the purposes of section 77k of this title. The Commission may at any time issue an order preventing or suspending the use of a prospectus permitted under this subsection, if it has reason to believe that such prospectus has not been filed (if required to be filed as part of the registration statement) or includes any untrue statement of a material fact or omits to state any material fact required to be stated therein or necessary to make the statements therein, in the light of the circumstances under which such prospectus is or is to be used, not misleading. Upon issuance of an order under this subsection, the Commission shall give notice of the issuance of such order and opportunity for hearing by personal service or the sending of confirmed telegraphic notice. The Commission shall vacate or modify the order at any time for good cause or if such prospectus has been filed or amended in accordance with such order.

(c) Additional information required by rules and regulations

Any prospectus shall contain such other information as the Commission may by rules or regulations require as being necessary or appropriate in the public interest or for the protection of investors.

(d) Classification of prospectuses

In the exercise of its powers under subsections (a), (b), or (c), the Commission shall have authority to classify prospectuses according to the nature and circumstances of their use or the nature of the security, issue, issuer, or otherwise, and, by rules and regulations and subject to such terms and conditions as it shall specify therein, to prescribe as to each class the form and contents which it may find appropriate and consistent with the public interest and the protection of investors.

(e) Information in conspicuous part of prospectus

The statements or information required to be included in a prospectus by or under authority of subsections (a), (b), (c), or (d), when written, shall be placed in a conspicuous part of the prospectus and, except as otherwise permitted by rules or regulations, in type as large as that used generally in the body of the prospectus.

(f) Prospectus consisting of radio or television broadcast

In any case where a prospectus consists of a radio or television broadcast, copies thereof shall be filed with the Commission under such rules and regulations as it shall prescribe. The Commission may by rules and regulations require the filing with it of forms and prospectuses used in connection with the offer or sale of securities registered under this subchapter.

---

9. SEC Rules and Regulations, Securities Act of 1933:
Section 23 – Unlawful Representations

Neither the fact that the registration statement for a security has been filed or is in effect nor the fact that a stop order is not in effect with respect thereto shall be deemed a finding by the Commission that the registration statement is true and accurate on its face or that it does not contain an untrue statement of fact or omit to state a material fact, or be held to mean that the Commission has in any way passed upon the merits of, or given approval to, such security. It shall be unlawful to make, or cause to be made to any prospective purchaser any representation contrary to the foregoing provisions of this section.

---

10. SEC Rules and Regulations, Securities Act of 1933:
215 – Accredited Investor

The term accredited investor as used in section 2(15)(ii) of the Securities Act of 1933 (15 U.S.C. 77b(15)(ii)) shall include the following persons:

(a) Any savings and loan association or other institution specified in section 3(a)(5)(A) of the Act whether acting in its individual or fiduciary capacity; any broker or dealer registered pursuant to section 15 of the Securities Exchange Act of 1934; any plan established and maintained by a state, its political subdivisions, or any agency or instrumentality of a state or its political subdivisions, for the benefit of its employees, if such plan has total assets in excess of $5,000,000; any employee benefit plan within the meaning of Table I of the Employee Retirement Income Security Act of 1974, if the investment decision is made by a plan fiduciary, as defined in section 3(21) of such Act, which is a savings and loan association, or if the employee benefit plan has total assets in excess of $5,000,000 or, if a self-directed plan, with investment decisions made solely by persons that are accredited investors;

(b) Any private business development company as defined in section 202(a)(22) of the Investment Advisers Act of 1940;

(c) Any organization described in section 501(c)(3) of the Internal Revenue Code, corporation, Massachusetts or similar business trust, or partnership, not formed for the specific purpose of acquiring the securities offered, with total assets in excess of $5,000,000;

(d) Any director, executive officer, or general partner of the issuer of the securities being offered or sold, or any director, executive officer, or general partner of a general partner of that issuer;

(e) Any natural person whose individual net worth, or joint net worth with that person's spouse, exceeds $1,000,000.

    (1) Except as provided in paragraph (e)(2) of this section, for purposes of calculating net worth under this paragraph (e):

        (i) The person's primary residence shall not be included as an asset;

        (ii) Indebtedness that is secured by the person's primary residence, up to the estimated fair market value of the primary residence at the time of the sale of securities, shall not be included as a liability (except that if the amount of such indebtedness outstanding at the time of the sale of securities exceeds the amount outstanding 60 days before such time, other than as a result of the acquisition of the primary residence, the amount of such excess shall be included as a liability); and

        (iii) Indebtedness that is secured by the person's primary residence in excess of the estimated fair market value of the primary residence shall be included as a liability.

    (2) Paragraph (e)(1) of this section will not apply to any calculation of a person's net worth made in connection with a purchase of securities in accordance with a right to purchase such securities, provided that:

        (i) Such right was held by the person on July 20, 2010;

        (ii) The person qualified as an accredited investor on the basis of net worth at the time the person acquired such right; and

        (iii) The person held securities of the same issuer, other than such right, on July 20, 2010.

(f) Any natural person who had an individual income in excess of $200,000 in each of the two most recent years or joint income with that person's spouse in excess of $300,000 in each of those years and has a reasonable expectation of reaching the same income level in the current year;

(g) Any trust, with total assets in excess of $5,000,000, not formed for the specific purpose of acquiring the securities offered, whose purchase is directed by a sophisticated person as described in § 230.506(b)(2)(ii); and

(h) Any entity in which all of the equity owners are accredited investors.

---

11. SEC Rules and Regulations, Securities Act of 1933:
431 – Summary Prospectuses

(a) A summary prospectus prepared and filed (except a summary prospectus filed by an open-end management investment company registered under the Investment Company Act of 1940) as part of a registration statement in accordance with this section shall be deemed to be a prospectus permitted under section 10(b) of the Act (15 U.S.C. 77j(b)) for the purposes of section 5(b)(1) of the Act (15 U.S.C. 77e(b)(1)) if the form used for registration of the securities to be offered provides for the use of a summary prospectus and the following conditions are met:

    (1)

        (i) The registrant is organized under the laws of the United States or any State or Territory or the District of Columbia and has its principal business operations in the United States or its territories; or

        (ii) The registrant is a foreign private issuer eligible to use Form F-2 (§ 239.32 of this chapter);

    (2) The registrant has a class of securities registered pursuant to section 12(b) of the Securities Exchange Act of 1934 or has a class of equity securities registered pursuant to section 12(g) of that Act or is required to file reports pursuant to section 15(d) of that Act;

(3) The registrant: (i) Has been subject to the requirements of section 12 or 15(d) of the Securities Exchange Act of 1934 and has filed all the material required to be filed pursuant to sections 13, 14 or 15(d) of that Act for a period of at least thirty-six calendar months immediately preceding the filing of the registration statement; and (ii) has filed in a timely manner all reports required to be filed during the twelve calendar months and any portion of a month immediately preceding the filing of the registration statement and, if the registrant has used (during the twelve calendar months and any portion of a month immediately preceding the filing of the registration statement) Rule 12b-25(b) under the Securities Exchange Act of 1934 (§ 240.12b-25 of this chapter) with respect to a report or portion of a report, that report or portion thereof has actually been filed within the time period prescribed by that Rule; and

(4) Neither the registrant nor any of its consolidated or unconsolidated subsidiaries has, since the end of its last fiscal year for which certified financial statements of the registrant and its consolidated subsidiaries were included in a report filed pursuant to section 13(a) or 15(d) of the Securities Exchange Act of 1934: (i) failed to pay any dividend or sinking fund installment on preferred stock; or (ii) defaulted on any installment or installments on indebtedness for borrowed money, or on any rental on one or more long term leases, which defaults in the aggregate are material to the financial position of the registrant and its consolidated and unconsolidated subsidiaries, taken as a whole.

(b) A summary prospectus shall contain the information specified in the instructions as to summary prospectuses in the form used for registration of the securities to be offered. Such prospectus may include any other information the substance of which is contained in the registration statement except as otherwise specifically provided in the instructions as to summary prospectuses in the form used for registration. It shall not include any information the substance of which is not contained in the registration statement except that a summary prospectus may contain any information specified in Rule 134(a) (§ 230.134(a)). No reference need be made to inapplicable terms and negative answers to any item of the form may be omitted.

(c) All information included in a summary prospectus, other than the statement required by paragraph (e) of this section, may be expressed in such condensed or summarized form as may be appropriate in the light of the circumstances under which the prospectus is to be used. The information need not follow the numerical sequence of the items of the form used for registration. Every summary prospectus shall be dated approximately as of the date of its first use.

(d) When used prior to the effective date of the registration statement, a summary prospectus shall be captioned a "Preliminary Summary Prospectus" and shall comply with the applicable requirements relating to a preliminary prospectus.

(e) A statement to the following effect shall be prominently set forth in conspicuous print at the beginning or at the end of every summary prospectus: *"Copies of a more complete prospectus may be obtained from" (Insert name(s), address(es) and telephone number(s))."*
Copies of a summary prospectus filed with the Commission pursuant to paragraph (g) of this section may omit the names of persons from whom the complete prospectus may be obtained.

(f) Any summary prospectus published in a newspaper, magazine or other periodical need only be set in type at least as large as 7 point modern type. Nothing in this rule shall prevent the use of reprints of a summary prospectus published in a newspaper, magazine, or other periodical, if such reprints are clearly legible.

(g) Eight copies of every proposed summary prospectus shall be filed as a part of the registration statement, or as an amendment thereto, at least 5 days (exclusive of Saturdays, Sundays and holidays) prior to the use thereof, or prior to the release for publication by any newspaper, magazine or other person, whichever is earlier. The Commission may, however, in its discretion, authorize such use or publication prior to the expiration of the 5-day period upon a written request for such authorization. Within 7 days after the first use or publication thereof, 5 additional copies shall be filed in the exact form in which it was used or published.

---

12. SEC Rules and Regulations, Securities Act of 1933:
Schedule A – Schedule of Information Required in Registration Statement

(1) The name under which the issuer is doing or intends to do business;

(2) the name of the State or other sovereign power under which the issuer is organized;

(3) the location of the issuer's principal business office, and if the issuer is a foreign or territorial person, the name and address of its agent in the United States authorized to receive notice;

(4) the names and addresses of the directors or persons performing similar functions, and the chief executive, financial and accounting officers, chosen or to be chosen if the issuer be a corporation, association, trust, or other entity; of all partners, if the issuer be a partnership; and of the issuer, if the issuer be an individual; and of the promoters in the case of a business to be formed, or formed within two years prior to the filing of the registration statement;

(5) the names and addresses of the underwriters;

(6) the names and addresses of all persons, if any, owning of record or beneficially, if known, more than 10 per centum of any class of stock of the issuer, or more than 10 per centum in the aggregate of the outstanding stock of the issuer as of a date within twenty days prior to the filing of the registration statement;

(7) the amount of securities of the issuer held by any person specified in paragraphs (4), (5), and (6) of this schedule, as of a date within twenty days prior to the filing of the registration statement, and, if possible, as of one year prior thereto, and the amount of the securities, for which the registration statement is filed, to which such persons have indicated their intention to subscribe;

(8) the general character of the business actually transacted or to be transacted by the issuer;

(9) a statement of the capitalization of the issuer, including the authorized and outstanding amounts of its capital stock and the proportion thereof paid up, the number and classes of shares in which such capital stock is divided, par value thereof, or if it has no par value, the stated or assigned value thereof, a description of the respective voting rights, preferences, conversion and exchange rights, rights to dividends, profits, or capital of each class, with respect to each other class, including the retirement and liquidation rights or values thereof;

(10) a statement of the securities, if any, covered by options outstanding or to be created in connection with the security to be offered, together with the names and addresses of all persons, if any, to be allotted more than 10 per centum in the aggregate of such options;

(11) the amount of capital stock of each class issued or included in the shares of stock to be offered;

(12) the amount of the funded debt outstanding and to be created by the security to be offered, with a brief description of the date, maturity, and character of such debt, rate of interest, character of amortization provisions, and the security, if any, therefor. If substitution of any security is permissible, a summarized statement of the conditions under which such substitution is permitted. If substitution is permissible without notice, a specific statement to that effect;

(13) the specific purposes in detail and the approximate amounts to be devoted to such purposes, so far as determinable, for which the security to be offered is to supply funds, and if the funds are to be raised in part from other sources, the amounts thereof and the sources thereof, shall be stated;

(14) the remuneration, paid or estimated to be paid, by the issuer or its predecessor, directly or indirectly, during the past year and ensuing year to (a) the directors or persons performing similar functions, and (b) its officers and other persons, naming them wherever such remuneration exceeded $25,000 during any such year;

(15) the estimated net proceeds to be derived from the security to be offered;

(16) the price at which it is proposed that the security shall be offered to the public or the method by which such price is computed and any variation therefrom at which any portion of such security is proposed to be offered to any persons or classes of persons, other than the underwriters, naming them or specifying the class. A variation in price may be proposed prior to the date of the public offering of the security, but the Commission shall immediately be notified of such variation;

(17) all commissions or discounts paid or to be paid, directly or indirectly, by the issuer to the underwriters in

respect of the sale of the security to be offered. Commissions shall include all cash, securities, contracts, or anything else of value, paid, to be set aside, disposed of, or understandings with or for the benefit of any other persons in which any underwriter is interested, made, in connection with the sale of such security. A commission paid or to be paid in connection with the sale of such security by a person in which the issuer has an interest or which is controlled or directed by, or under common control with, the issuer shall be deemed to have been paid by the issuer. Where any such commission is paid the amount of such commission paid to each underwriter shall be stated;

(18) the amount or estimated amounts, itemized in reasonable detail, of expenses, other than commissions specified in paragraph (17) of this schedule, incurred or borne by or for the account of the issuer in connection with the sale of the security to be offered or properly chargeable thereto, including legal, engineering, certification, authentication, and other charges;

(19) the net proceeds derived from any security sold by the issuer during the two years preceding the filing of the registration statement, the price at which such security was offered to the public, and the names of the principal underwriters of such security;

(20) any amount paid within two years preceding the filing of the registration statement or intended to be paid to any promoter and the consideration for any such payment;

(21) the names and addresses of the vendors and the purchase price of any property, or good will, acquired or to be acquired, not in the ordinary course of business, which is to be defrayed in whole or in part from the proceeds of the security to be offered, the amount of any commission payable to any person in connection with such acquisition, and the name or names of such person or persons, together with any expense incurred or to be incurred in connection with such acquisition, including the cost of borrowing money to finance such acquisition;

(22) full particulars of the nature and extent of the interest, if any, of every director, principal executive officer, and of every stockholder holding more than 10 per centum of any class of stock or more than 10 per centum in the aggregate of the stock of the issuer, in any property acquired, not in the ordinary course of business of the issuer, within two years preceding the filing of the registration statement or proposed to be acquired at such date;

(23) the names and addresses of counsel who have passed on the legality of the issue;

(24) dates of and parties to, and the general effect concisely stated of every material contract made, not in the ordinary course of business, which contract is to be executed in whole or in part at or after the filing of the registration statement or which contract has been made not more than two years before such filing. Any management contract or contract providing for special bonuses or profit-sharing arrangements, and every material patent or contract for a material patent right, and every contract by or with a public utility company or an affiliate thereof, providing for the giving or receiving of technical or financial advice or service (if such contract may involve a charge to any party thereto at a rate in excess of $2,500 per year in cash or securities or anything else of value), shall be deemed a material contract;

(25) a balance sheet as of a date not more than ninety days prior to the date of the filing of the registration statement showing all of the assets of the issuer, the nature and cost thereof, whenever determinable, in such detail and in such form as the Commission shall prescribe (with intangible items segregated), including any loan in excess of $20,000 to any officer, director, stockholder or person directly or indirectly controlling or controlled by the issuer, or person under direct or indirect common control with the issuer. All the liabilities of the issuer in such detail and such form as the Commission shall prescribe, including surplus of the issuer showing how and from what sources such surplus was created, all as of a date not more than ninety days prior to the filing of the registration statement. If such statement be not certified by an independent public or certified accountant, in addition to the balance sheet required to be submitted under this schedule, a similar detailed balance sheet of the assets and liabilities of the issuer, certified by an independent public or certified accountant, of a date not more than one year prior to the filing of the registration statement, shall be submitted;

(26) a profit and loss statement of the issuer showing earnings and income, the nature and source thereof, and the expenses and fixed charges in such detail and such form as the Commission shall prescribe for the latest fiscal year for which such statement is available and for the two preceding fiscal years, year by year, or, if such issuer has been in actual business for less than three years, then for such time as the issuer has been in actual business, year by year. If the date of the filing of the registration statement is more than six months after the close of the last fiscal year, a statement from such closing date to the latest practicable date. Such statement shall show what the practice of the issuer has been during the three years or lesser period as to the character of the charges, dividends or other distributions made against its various surplus accounts, and as to depreciation, depletion, and maintenance charges, in such detail and form as the Commission shall prescribe, and if stock dividends or avails from the sale of rights have been credited to income, they shall be shown separately with a statement of the basis upon which the credit is computed. Such statement shall also differentiate between any recurring and nonrecurring income and between any investment and operating income. Such statement shall be certified by an independent public or certified accountant;

(27) if the proceeds, or any part of the proceeds, of the security to be issued is to be applied directly or indirectly to the purchase of any business, a profit and loss statement of such business certified by an independent public or certified accountant, meeting the requirements of paragraph (26) of this schedule, for the three preceding fiscal years, together with a balance sheet, similarly certified, of such business, meeting the requirements of paragraph (25) of this schedule of a date not more than ninety days prior to the filing of the registration statement or at the date such business was acquired by the issuer if the business was acquired by the issuer more than ninety days prior to the filing of the registration statement;

(28) a copy of any agreement or agreements (or, if identical agreements are used, the forms thereof) made with any underwriter, including all contracts and agreements referred to in paragraph (17) of this schedule;

(29) a copy of the opinion or opinions of counsel in respect to the legality of the issue, with a translation of such opinion, when necessary, into the English language;

(30) a copy of all material contracts referred to in paragraph (24) of this schedule, but no disclosure shall be required of any portion of any such contract if the Commission determines that disclosure of such portion would impair the value of the contract and would not be necessary for the protection of the investors;

(31) unless previously filed and registered under the provisions of this subchapter, and brought up to date, (a) a copy of its articles of incorporation, with all amendments thereof and of its existing bylaws or instruments corresponding thereto, whatever the name, if the issuer be a corporation; (b) copy of all instruments by which the trust is created or declared, if the issuer is a trust; (c) a copy of its articles of partnership or association and all other papers pertaining to its organization, if the issuer is a partnership, unincorporated association, joint-stock company, or any other form of organization; and

(32) a copy of the underlying agreements or indentures affecting any stock, bonds, or debentures offered or to be offered.

In case of certificates of deposit, voting trust certificates, collateral trust certificates, certificates of interest or shares in unincorporated investment trusts, equipment trust certificates, interim or other receipts for certificates, and like securities, the Commission shall establish rules and regulations requiring the submission of information of a like character applicable to such cases, together with such other information as it may deem appropriate and necessary regarding the character, financial or otherwise, of the actual issuer of the securities and/or the person performing the acts and assuming the duties of depositor or manager.

---

13. SEC Rules and Regulations, Securities Act of 1933:
Schedule B – Schedule of Information Required in Registration Statement

(1) Name of borrowing government or subdivision thereof;

(2) specific purposes in detail and the approximate amounts to be devoted to such purposes, so far as determinable, for which the security to be offered is to supply funds, and if the funds are to be raised in part from other sources, the amounts thereof and the sources thereof, shall be stated;

(3) the amount of the funded debt and the estimated amount of the floating debt outstanding and to be created by the security to be offered, excluding intergovernmental debt, and a brief description of the date, maturity, character of such debt, rate of interest, character of amortization provisions, and the security, if any, therefor. If substitution of any security is permissible, a statement of the conditions under which such substitution is permitted. If substitution is permissible without notice, a specific statement to that effect;

(4) whether or not the issuer or its predecessor has, within a period of twenty years prior to the filing of the registration statement, defaulted on the principal or interest of any external security, excluding intergovernmental debt, and, if so, the date, amount, and circumstances of such default, and the terms of the succeeding arrangement, if any;

(5) the receipts, classified by source, and the expenditures, classified by purpose, in such detail and form as the Commission shall prescribe for the latest fiscal year for which such information is available and the two preceding fiscal years, year by year;

(6) the names and addresses of the underwriters;

(7) the name and address of its authorized agent, if any, in the United States;

(8) the estimated net proceeds to be derived from the sale in the United States of the security to be offered;

(9) the price at which it is proposed that the security shall be offered in the United States to the public or the method by which such price is computed. A variation in price may be proposed prior to the date of the public offering of the security, but the Commission shall immediately be notified of such variation;

(10) all commissions paid or to be paid, directly or indirectly, by the issuer to the underwriters in respect of the sale of the security to be offered. Commissions shall include all cash, securities, contracts, or anything else of value, paid, to be set aside, disposed of, or understandings with or for the benefit of any other persons in which the underwriter is interested, made, in connection with the sale of such security. Where any such commission is paid, the amount of such commission paid to each underwriter shall be stated;

(11) the amount or estimated amounts, itemized in reasonable detail, of expenses, other than the commissions specified in paragraph (10) of this schedule, incurred or borne by or for the account of the issuer in connection with the sale of the security to be offered or properly chargeable thereto, including legal, engineering, certification, and other charges;

(12) the names and addresses of counsel who have passed upon the legality of the issue;

(13) a copy of any agreement or agreements made with any underwriter governing the sale of the security within the United States; and

(14) an agreement of the issuer to furnish a copy of the opinion or opinions of counsel in respect to the legality of the issue, with a translation, where necessary, into the English language. Such opinion shall set out in full all laws, decrees, ordinances, or other acts of Government under which the issue of such security has been authorized.

14. SEC Rules and Regulations, Securities Exchange Act of 1934:
Section 3(a) – Definitions and Application of Title

(a) Definitions. When used in this chapter, unless the context otherwise requires—

(1) The term "exchange" means any organization, association, or group of persons, whether incorporated or unincorporated, which constitutes, maintains, or provides a market place or facilities for bringing together purchasers and sellers of securities or for otherwise performing with respect to securities the functions commonly performed by a stock exchange as that term is generally understood, and includes the market place and the market facilities maintained by such exchange.

(2) The term "facility" when used with respect to an exchange includes its premises, tangible or intangible property whether on the premises or not, any right to the use of such premises or property or any service thereof for the purpose of effecting or reporting a transaction on an exchange (including, among other things, any system of communication to or from the exchange, by ticker or otherwise, maintained by or with the consent of the exchange), and any right of the exchange to the use of any property or service.

(3)

(A) The term "member" when used with respect to a national securities exchange means (i) any natural person permitted to effect transactions on the floor of the exchange without the services of another person acting as broker, (ii) any registered broker or dealer with which such a natural person is associated, (iii) any registered broker or dealer permitted to designate as a representative such a natural person, and (iv) any other registered broker or dealer which agrees to be regulated by such exchange and with respect to which the exchange undertakes to enforce compliance with the provisions of this chapter, the rules and regulations thereunder, and its own rules. For purposes of sections 78f(b)(1), 78f(b)(4), 78f(b)(6), 78f(b)(7), 78f(d), 78q(d), 78s(d), 78s(e), 78s(g), 78s(h), and 78u of this title, the term "member" when used with respect to a national securities exchange also means, to the extent of the rules of the exchange specified by the Commission, any person required by the Commission to comply with such rules pursuant to section 78f(f) of this title.

(B) The term "member" when used with respect to a registered securities association means any broker or dealer who agrees to be regulated by such association and with respect to whom the association undertakes to enforce compliance with the provisions of this chapter, the rules and regulations thereunder, and its own rules.

(4) Broker.—

(A) In general.—
The term "broker" means any person engaged in the business of effecting transactions in securities for the account of others.

(B) Exception for certain activities.—A bank shall not be considered to be a broker because the bank engages in any one or more of the following activities under the conditions described:

(i) Third party brokerage arrangements.—The bank enters into a contractual or other written arrangement with a broker or dealer registered under this chapter under which the broker or dealer offers brokerage services on or off the premises of the bank if—

(I) such broker or dealer is clearly identified as the person performing the brokerage services;

(II) the broker or dealer performs brokerage services in an area that is clearly marked and, to the extent practicable, physically separate from the routine deposit-taking activities of the bank;

(III) any materials used by the bank to advertise or promote generally the availability of brokerage services under the arrangement clearly indicate that the brokerage services are being provided by the broker or dealer and not by the bank;

(IV) any materials used by the bank to advertise or promote generally the availability of brokerage services under the arrangement are in compliance with the Federal securities laws before distribution;

      (V) bank employees (other than associated persons of a broker or dealer who are qualified pursuant to the rules of a self-regulatory organization) perform only clerical or ministerial functions in connection with brokerage transactions including scheduling appointments with the associated persons of a broker or dealer, except that bank employees may forward customer funds or securities and may describe in general terms the types of investment vehicles available from the bank and the broker or dealer under the arrangement;

      (VI) bank employees do not receive incentive compensation for any brokerage transaction unless such employees are associated persons of a broker or dealer and are qualified pursuant to the rules of a self-regulatory organization, except that the bank employees may receive compensation for the referral of any customer if the compensation is a nominal one-time cash fee of a fixed dollar amount and the payment of the fee is not contingent on whether the referral results in a transaction;

      (VII) such services are provided by the broker or dealer on a basis in which all customers that receive any services are fully disclosed to the broker or dealer;

      (VIII) the bank does not carry a securities account of the customer except as permitted under clause (ii) or (viii) of this subparagraph; and

      (IX) the bank, broker, or dealer informs each customer that the brokerage services are provided by the broker or dealer and not by the bank and that the securities are not deposits or other obligations of the bank, are not guaranteed by the bank, and are not insured by the Federal Deposit Insurance Corporation.

   (ii) Trust activities.—The bank effects transactions in a trustee capacity, or effects transactions in a fiduciary capacity in its trust department or other department that is regularly examined by bank examiners for compliance with fiduciary principles and standards, and—

      (I) is chiefly compensated for such transactions, consistent with fiduciary principles and standards, on the basis of an administration or annual fee (payable on a monthly, quarterly, or other basis), a percentage of assets under management, or a flat or capped per order processing fee equal to not more than the cost incurred by the bank in connection with executing securities transactions for trustee and fiduciary customers, or any combination of such fees; and

      (II) does not publicly solicit brokerage business, other than by advertising that it effects transactions in securities in conjunction with advertising its other trust activities.

   (iii) Permissible transactions.—The bank effects transactions in—

      (I) commercial paper, bankers acceptances, or commercial bills;

      (II) exempted securities;

      (III) qualified Canadian government obligations as defined in section 24 of title 12, in conformity with section 78o–5 of this title and the rules and regulations thereunder, or obligations of the North American Development Bank; or

      (IV) any standardized, credit enhanced debt security issued by a foreign government pursuant to the March 1989 plan of then Secretary of the Treasury Brady, used by such foreign government to retire outstanding commercial bank loans.

   (iv) Certain stock purchase plans.—

      (I) Employee benefit plans.—

      The bank effects transactions, as part of its transfer agency activities, in the securities of an issuer as part of any pension, retirement, profit-sharing, bonus, thrift, savings, incentive, or other similar benefit plan for the employees of that issuer or its affiliates (as defined in section 1841 of title 12), if the bank does not solicit transactions or provide investment advice with respect to the purchase or sale of securities in connection with the plan.

      (II) Dividend reinvestment plans.—The bank effects transactions, as part of its transfer agency activities, in the securities of an issuer as part of that issuer's dividend reinvestment plan, if—

(aa) the bank does not solicit transactions or provide investment advice with respect to the purchase or sale of securities in connection with the plan; and

(bb) the bank does not net shareholders' buy and sell orders, other than for programs for odd-lot holders or plans registered with the Commission.

(III) Issuer plans.—The bank effects transactions, as part of its transfer agency activities, in the securities of an issuer as part of a plan or program for the purchase or sale of that issuer's shares, if—

(aa) the bank does not solicit transactions or provide investment advice with respect to the purchase or sale of securities in connection with the plan or program; and

(bb) the bank does not net shareholders' buy and sell orders, other than for programs for odd-lot holders or plans registered with the Commission.

(IV) Permissible delivery of materials.—The exception to being considered a broker for a bank engaged in activities described in subclauses (I), (II), and (III) will not be affected by delivery of written or electronic plan materials by a bank to employees of the issuer, shareholders of the issuer, or members of affinity groups of the issuer, so long as such materials are—

(aa) comparable in scope or nature to that permitted by the Commission as of November 12, 1999; or

(bb) otherwise permitted by the Commission.

(v) Sweep accounts.—

The bank effects transactions as part of a program for the investment or reinvestment of deposit funds into any no-load, open-end management investment company registered under the Investment Company Act of 1940 [15 U.S.C. 80a–1 et seq.] that holds itself out as a money market fund.

(vi) Affiliate transactions.—The bank effects transactions for the account of any affiliate of the bank (as defined in section 1841 of title 12) other than—

(I) a registered broker or dealer; or

(II) an affiliate that is engaged in merchant banking, as described in section 1843(k)(4)(H) of title 12.

(vii) Private offerings.—The bank—

(I) effects sales as part of a primary offering of securities not involving a public offering, pursuant to section 3(b), 4(2),[1] or 4(5) of the Securities Act of 1933 [15 U.S.C. 77c(b), 77d(a)(2), 77d(a)(5)] or the rules and regulations issued thereunder;

(II) at any time after the date that is 1 year after November 12, 1999, is not affiliated with a broker or dealer that has been registered for more than 1 year in accordance with this chapter, and engages in dealing, market making, or underwriting activities, other than with respect to exempted securities; and

(III) if the bank is not affiliated with a broker or dealer, does not effect any primary offering described in subclause (I) the aggregate amount of which exceeds 25 percent of the capital of the bank, except that the limitation of this subclause shall not apply with respect to any sale of government securities or municipal securities.

(viii) Safekeeping and custody activities.—

(I) In general.—The bank, as part of customary banking activities—

(aa) provides safekeeping or custody services with respect to securities, including the exercise of warrants and other rights on behalf of customers;

(bb) facilitates the transfer of funds or securities, as a custodian or a clearing agency, in connection with the clearance and settlement of its customers' transactions in securities;

(cc) effects securities lending or borrowing transactions with or on behalf of customers as part of services provided to customers pursuant to division (aa) or (bb) or invests cash collateral pledged in connection with such transactions;

(dd) holds securities pledged by a customer to another person or securities subject to purchase or resale agreements involving a customer, or facilitates the pledging or transfer of such securities by book entry or as otherwise provided under applicable law, if the bank maintains records separately identifying the securities and the customer; or

(ee) serves as a custodian or provider of other related administrative services to any individual retirement account, pension, retirement, profit sharing, bonus, thrift savings, incentive, or other similar benefit plan.

(II) Exception for carrying broker activities.—

The exception to being considered a broker for a bank engaged in activities described in subclause (I) shall not apply if the bank, in connection with such activities, acts in the United States as a carrying broker (as such term, and different formulations thereof, are used in section 78o(c)(3) of this title and the rules and regulations thereunder) for any broker or dealer, unless such carrying broker activities are engaged in with respect to government securities (as defined in paragraph (42) of this subsection).

(ix) Identified banking products.—

The bank effects transactions in identified banking products as defined in section 206 of the Gramm-Leach-Bliley Act.

(x) Municipal securities.—

The bank effects transactions in municipal securities.

(xi) De minimis exception.—

The bank effects, other than in transactions referred to in clauses (i) through (x), not more than 500 transactions in securities in any calendar year, and such transactions are not effected by an employee of the bank who is also an employee of a broker or dealer.

(C) Execution by broker or dealer.—The exception to being considered a broker for a bank engaged in activities described in clauses (ii), (iv), and (viii) of subparagraph (B) shall not apply if the activities described in such provisions result in the trade in the United States of any security that is a publicly traded security in the United States, unless—

(i) the bank directs such trade to a registered broker or dealer for execution

(ii) the trade is a cross trade or other substantially similar trade of a security that—

(I) is made by the bank or between the bank and an affiliated fiduciary; and

(II) is not in contravention of fiduciary principles established under applicable Federal or State law; or

(iii) the trade is conducted in some other manner permitted under rules, regulations, or orders as the Commission may prescribe or issue.

(D) Fiduciary capacity.—For purposes of subparagraph (B)(ii), the term "fiduciary capacity" means—

(i) in the capacity as trustee, executor, administrator, registrar of stocks and bonds, transfer agent, guardian, assignee, receiver, or custodian under a uniform gift to minor act, or as an investment adviser if the bank receives a fee for its investment advice;

(ii) in any capacity in which the bank possesses investment discretion on behalf of another; or

(iii) in any other similar capacity.

(E) Exception for entities subject to section 78o(e).1 —The term "broker" does not include a bank that—

(i) was, on the day before November 12, 1999, subject to section 78o(e) 1 of this title; and

(ii) is subject to such restrictions and requirements as the Commission considers appropriate.

(F) Joint rulemaking required.—

The Commission and the Board of Governors of the Federal Reserve System shall jointly adopt a single set of rules or regulations to implement the exceptions in subparagraph (B).

(5) Dealer.—

    (A) In general.—

    The term "dealer" means any person engaged in the business of buying and selling securities (not including security-based swaps, other than security-based swaps with or for persons that are not eligible contract participants) for such person's own account through a broker or otherwise.

    (B) Exception for not engaged in the business of dealing.—

    The term "dealer" does not include a person that buys or sells securities (not including security-based swaps, other than security-based swaps with or for persons that are not eligible contract participants) for such person's own account, either individually or in a fiduciary capacity, but not as a part of a regular business.

    (C) Exception for certain activities.—A bank shall not be considered to be a dealer because the bank engages in any of the following activities under the conditions described:

        (i) Permissible transactions.—The bank buys or sells—

            (I) commercial paper, bankers acceptances, or commercial bills;

            (II) exempted securities;

            (III) qualified Canadian government obligations as defined in section 24 of title 12, in conformity with section 78o–5 of this title and the rules and regulations thereunder, or obligations of the North American Development Bank; or

            (IV) any standardized, credit enhanced debt security issued by a foreign government pursuant to the March 1989 plan of then Secretary of the Treasury Brady, used by such foreign government to retire outstanding commercial bank loans.

        (ii) Investment, trustee, and fiduciary transactions.—The bank buys or sells securities for investment purposes—

            (I) for the bank; or

            (II) for accounts for which the bank acts as a trustee or fiduciary.

        (iii) Asset-backed transactions.—The bank engages in the issuance or sale to qualified investors, through a grantor trust or other separate entity, of securities backed by or representing an interest in notes, drafts, acceptances, loans, leases, receivables, other obligations (other than securities of which the bank is not the issuer), or pools of any such obligations predominantly originated by—

            (I) the bank;

            (II) an affiliate of any such bank other than a broker or dealer; or

            (III) a syndicate of banks of which the bank is a member, if the obligations or pool of obligations consists of mortgage obligations or consumer-related receivables.

        (iv) Identified banking products.—

        The bank buys or sells identified banking products, as defined in section 206 of the Gramm-Leach-Bliley Act.

(6) The term "bank" means (A) a banking institution organized under the laws of the United States or a Federal savings association, as defined in section 1462(5) 1 of title 12, (B) a member bank of the Federal Reserve System, (C) any other banking institution or savings association, as defined in section 1462(4) 1 of title 12, whether incorporated or not, doing business under the laws of any State or of the United States, a substantial portion of the business of which consists of receiving deposits or exercising fiduciary powers similar to those permitted to national banks under the authority of the Comptroller of the Currency pursuant to section 92a of title 12, and which is supervised and examined by State or Federal authority having supervision over banks or savings associations, and which is not operated for the purpose of evading the provisions of this chapter, and (D) a receiver, conservator, or other liquidating agent of any institution or firm included in clauses (A), (B), or (C) of this paragraph.

(7) The term "director" means any director of a corporation or any person performing similar functions with respect to any organization, whether incorporated or unincorporated.

(8) The term "issuer" means any person who issues or proposes to issue any security; except that with respect to certificates of deposit for securities, voting-trust certificates, or collateral-trust certificates, or with respect to certificates of interest or shares in an unincorporated investment trust not having a board of directors or of the fixed, restricted management, or unit type, the term "issuer" means the person or persons performing the acts and assuming the duties of depositor or manager pursuant to the provisions of the trust or other agreement or instrument under which such securities are issued; and except that with respect to equipment-trust certificates or like securities, the term "issuer" means the person by whom the equipment or property is, or is to be, used.

(9) The term "person" means a natural person, company, government, or political subdivision, agency, or instrumentality of a government.

(10) The term "security" means any note, stock, treasury stock, security future, security-based swap, bond, debenture, certificate of interest or participation in any profit-sharing agreement or in any oil, gas, or other mineral royalty or lease, any collateral-trust certificate, preorganization certificate or subscription, transferable share, investment contract, voting-trust certificate, certificate of deposit for a security, any put, call, straddle, option, or privilege on any security, certificate of deposit, or group or index of securities (including any interest therein or based on the value thereof), or any put, call, straddle, option, or privilege entered into on a national securities exchange relating to foreign currency, or in general, any instrument commonly known as a "security"; or any certificate of interest or participation in, temporary or interim certificate for, receipt for, or warrant or right to subscribe to or purchase, any of the foregoing; but shall not include currency or any note, draft, bill of exchange, or banker's acceptance which has a maturity at the time of issuance of not exceeding nine months, exclusive of days of grace, or any renewal thereof the maturity of which is likewise limited.

(11) The term "equity security" means any stock or similar security; or any security future on any such security; or any security convertible, with or without consideration, into such a security, or carrying any warrant or right to subscribe to or purchase such a security; or any such warrant or right; or any other security which the Commission shall deem to be of similar nature and consider necessary or appropriate, by such rules and regulations as it may prescribe in the public interest or for the protection of investors, to treat as an equity security.

(12)

    (A) The term "exempted security" or "exempted securities" includes—

        (i) government securities, as defined in paragraph (42) of this subsection;

        (ii) municipal securities, as defined in paragraph (29) of this subsection;

        (iii) any interest or participation in any common trust fund or similar fund that is excluded from the definition of the term "investment company" under section 3(c)(3) of the Investment Company Act of 1940 [15 U.S.C. 80a–3(c)(3)];

        (iv) any interest or participation in a single trust fund, or a collective trust fund maintained by a bank, or any security arising out of a contract issued by an insurance company, which interest, participation, or security is issued in connection with a qualified plan as defined in subparagraph (C) of this paragraph;

        (v) any security issued by or any interest or participation in any pooled income fund, collective trust fund, collective investment fund, or similar fund that is excluded from the definition of an investment company under section 3(c)(10)(B) of the Investment Company Act of 1940 [15 U.S.C. 80a–3(c)(10)(B)];

        (vi) solely for purposes of sections 78l, 78m, 78n, and 78p of this title, any security issued by or any interest or participation in any church plan, company, or account that is excluded from the definition of an investment company under section 3(c)(14) of the Investment Company Act of 1940 [15 U.S.C. 80a–3(c)(14)]; and

        (vii) such other securities (which may include, among others, unregistered securities, the market in which is predominantly intrastate) as the Commission may, by such rules and regulations as it deems consistent with the public interest and the protection of investors, either unconditionally or upon specified terms and conditions or for stated periods, exempt from the operation of any one or more provisions of this chapter which by their terms do not apply to an "exempted security" or to "exempted securities".

(B)

(i) Notwithstanding subparagraph (A)(i) of this paragraph, government securities shall not be deemed to be "exempted securities" for the purposes of section 78q–1 of this title.

(ii) Notwithstanding subparagraph (A)(ii) of this paragraph, municipal securities shall not be deemed to be "exempted securities" for the purposes of sections 78o and 78q–1 of this title.

(C) For purposes of subparagraph (A)(iv) of this paragraph, the term "qualified plan" means (i) a stock bonus, pension, or profit-sharing plan which meets the requirements for qualification under section 401 of title 26, (ii) an annuity plan which meets the requirements for the deduction of the employer's contribution under section 404(a)(2) of title 26, (iii) a governmental plan as defined in section 414(d) of title 26 which has been established by an employer for the exclusive benefit of its employees or their beneficiaries for the purpose of distributing to such employees or their beneficiaries the corpus and income of the funds accumulated under such plan, if under such plan it is impossible, prior to the satisfaction of all liabilities with respect to such employees and their beneficiaries, for any part of the corpus or income to be used for, or diverted to, purposes other than the exclusive benefit of such employees or their beneficiaries, or (iv) a church plan, company, or account that is excluded from the definition of an investment company under section 3(c)(14) of the Investment Company Act of 1940 [15 U.S.C. 80a–3(c)(14)], other than any plan described in clause (i), (ii), or (iii) of this subparagraph which (I) covers employees some or all of whom are employees within the meaning of section 401(c) of title 26, or (II) is a plan funded by an annuity contract described in section 403(b) of title 26.

(13) The terms "buy" and "purchase" each include any contract to buy, purchase, or otherwise acquire. For security futures products, such term includes any contract, agreement, or transaction for future delivery. For security-based swaps, such terms include the execution, termination (prior to its scheduled maturity date), assignment, exchange, or similar transfer or conveyance of, or extinguishing of rights or obligations under, a security-based swap, as the context may require.

(14) The terms "sale" and "sell" each include any contract to sell or otherwise dispose of. For security futures products, such term includes any contract, agreement, or transaction for future delivery. For security-based swaps, such terms include the execution, termination (prior to its scheduled maturity date), assignment, exchange, or similar transfer or conveyance of, or extinguishing of rights or obligations under, a security-based swap, as the context may require.

(15) The term "Commission" means the Securities and Exchange Commission established by section 78d of this title.

(16) The term "State" means any State of the United States, the District of Columbia, Puerto Rico, the Virgin Islands, or any other possession of the United States.

(17) The term "interstate commerce" means trade, commerce, transportation, or communication among the several States, or between any foreign country and any State, or between any State and any place or ship outside thereof. The term also includes intrastate use of (A) any facility of a national securities exchange or of a telephone or other interstate means of communication, or (B) any other interstate instrumentality.

(18) The term "person associated with a broker or dealer" or "associated person of a broker or dealer" means any partner, officer, director, or branch manager of such broker or dealer (or any person occupying a similar status or performing similar functions), any person directly or indirectly controlling, controlled by, or under common control with such broker or dealer, or any employee of such broker or dealer, except that any person associated with a broker or dealer whose functions are solely clerical or ministerial shall not be included in the meaning of such term for purposes of section 78o(b) of this title (other than paragraph (6) thereof).

(19) The terms "investment company", "affiliated person", "insurance company", "separate account", and "company" have the same meanings as in the Investment Company Act of 1940 [15 U.S.C. 80a–1 et seq.].

(20) The terms "investment adviser" and "underwriter" have the same meanings as in the Investment Advisers Act of 1940 [15 U.S.C. 80b–1 et seq.].

(21) The term "person associated with a member" or "associated person of a member" when used with respect to a member of a national securities exchange or registered securities association means any partner, officer, director, or branch manager of such member (or any person occupying a similar status or performing similar functions), any person directly or indirectly controlling, controlled by, or under common control with such member, or any employee of such member.

(22)

(A) The term "securities information processor" means any person engaged in the business of (i) collecting, processing, or preparing for distribution or publication, or assisting, participating in, or coordinating the distribution or publication of, information with respect to transactions in or quotations for any security (other than an exempted security) or (ii) distributing or publishing (whether by means of a ticker tape, a communications network, a terminal display device, or otherwise) on a current and continuing basis, information with respect to such transactions or quotations. The term "securities information processor" does not include any bona fide newspaper, news magazine, or business or financial publication of general and regular circulation, any self-regulatory organizations, any bank, broker, dealer, building and loan, savings and loan, or homestead association, or cooperative bank, if such bank, broker, dealer, association, or cooperative bank would be deemed to be a securities information processor solely by reason of functions performed by such institutions as part of customary banking, brokerage, dealing, association, or cooperative bank activities, or any common carrier, as defined in section 153 of title 47, subject to the jurisdiction of the Federal Communications Commission or a State commission, as defined in section 153 of title 47, unless the Commission determines that such carrier is engaged in the business of collecting, processing, or preparing for distribution or publication, information with respect to transactions in or quotations for any security.

(B) The term "exclusive processor" means any securities information processor or self-regulatory organization which, directly or indirectly, engages on an exclusive basis on behalf of any national securities exchange or registered securities association, or any national securities exchange or registered securities association which engages on an exclusive basis on its own behalf, in collecting, processing, or preparing for distribution or publication any information with respect to (i) transactions or quotations on or effected or made by means of any facility of such exchange or (ii) quotations distributed or published by means of any electronic system operated or controlled by such association.

(23)

(A) The term "clearing agency" means any person who acts as an intermediary in making payments or deliveries or both in connection with transactions in securities or who provides facilities for comparison of data respecting the terms of settlement of securities transactions, to reduce the number of settlements of securities transactions, or for the allocation of securities settlement responsibilities. Such term also means any person, such as a securities depository, who (i) acts as a custodian of securities in connection with a system for the central handling of securities whereby all securities of a particular class or series of any issuer deposited within the system are treated as fungible and may be transferred, loaned, or pledged by bookkeeping entry without physical delivery of securities certificates, or (ii) otherwise permits or facilitates the settlement of securities transactions or the hypothecation or lending of securities without physical delivery of securities certificates.

(B) The term "clearing agency" does not include (i) any Federal Reserve bank, Federal home loan bank, or Federal land bank; (ii) any national securities exchange or registered securities association solely by reason of its providing facilities for comparison of data respecting the terms of settlement of securities transactions effected on such exchange or by means of any electronic system operated or controlled by such association; (iii) any bank, broker, dealer, building and loan, savings and loan, or homestead association, or cooperative bank if such bank, broker, dealer, association, or cooperative bank would be deemed to be a clearing agency solely by reason of functions performed by such institution as part of customary banking, brokerage, dealing, association, or cooperative banking activities, or solely by reason of acting on behalf of a clearing agency or a participant therein in connection with the furnishing by the clearing agency of services to its participants or the use of services of the clearing agency by its participants, unless the Commission, by rule, otherwise provides as necessary or appropriate to assure the prompt and accurate clearance and settlement of securities transactions or to prevent evasion of this chapter; (iv) any life insurance company, its registered separate accounts, or a subsidiary of such insurance company solely by reason of functions commonly performed by such entities in connection with variable annuity contracts or variable life policies issued by such insurance company or its separate accounts; (v) any registered open-end investment company or unit investment trust solely by reason of functions commonly performed by it in connection with shares in such registered open-end investment company or unit investment trust, or (vi) any person solely by reason of its performing functions described in paragraph (25)(E) of this subsection.

(24) The term "participant" when used with respect to a clearing agency means any person who uses a clearing agency to clear or settle securities transactions or to transfer, pledge, lend, or hypothecate securities. Such term does not include a person whose only use of a clearing agency is (A) through another person who is a participant or (B) as a pledgee of securities.

(25) The term "transfer agent" means any person who engages on behalf of an issuer of securities or on behalf of itself as an issuer of securities in (A) countersigning such securities upon issuance; (B) monitoring the issuance of such securities with a view to preventing unauthorized issuance, a function commonly performed by a person called a registrar; (C) registering the transfer of such securities; (D) exchanging or converting such securities; or (E) transferring record ownership of securities by bookkeeping entry without physical issuance of securities certificates. The term "transfer agent" does not include any insurance company or separate account which performs such functions solely with respect to variable annuity contracts or variable life policies which it issues or any registered clearing agency which performs such functions solely with respect to options contracts which it issues.

(26) The term "self-regulatory organization" means any national securities exchange, registered securities association, or registered clearing agency, or (solely for purposes of sections 78s(b), 78s(c), and 78w(b) 1 of this title) the Municipal Securities Rulemaking Board established by section 78o–4 of this title.

(27) The term "rules of an exchange", "rules of an association", or "rules of a clearing agency" means the constitution, articles of incorporation, bylaws, and rules, or instruments corresponding to the foregoing, of an exchange, association of brokers and dealers, or clearing agency, respectively, and such of the stated policies, practices, and interpretations of such exchange, association, or clearing agency as the Commission, by rule, may determine to be necessary or appropriate in the public interest or for the protection of investors to be deemed to be rules of such exchange, association, or clearing agency.

(28) The term "rules of a self-regulatory organization" means the rules of an exchange which is a national securities exchange, the rules of an association of brokers and dealers which is a registered securities association, the rules of a clearing agency which is a registered clearing agency, or the rules of the Municipal Securities Rulemaking Board.

(29) The term "municipal securities" means securities which are direct obligations of, or obligations guaranteed as to principal or interest by, a State or any political subdivision thereof, or any agency or instrumentality of a State or any political subdivision thereof, or any municipal corporate instrumentality of one or more States, or any security which is an industrial development bond (as defined in section 103(c)(2) 1 of title 26) the interest on which is excludable from gross income under section 103(a)(1) 1 of title 26 if, by reason of the application of paragraph (4) or (6) of section 103(c) 1 of title 26 (determined

as if paragraphs (4)(A), (5), and (7) were not included in such section 103(c)),1 paragraph (1) of such section 103(c) 1 does not apply to such security.

(30) The term "municipal securities dealer" means any person (including a separately identifiable department or division of a bank) engaged in the business of buying and selling municipal securities for his own account, through a broker or otherwise, but does not include—

(A) any person insofar as he buys or sells such securities for his own account, either individually or in some fiduciary capacity, but not as a part of a regular business; or

(B) a bank, unless the bank is engaged in the business of buying and selling municipal securities for its own account other than in a fiduciary capacity, through a broker or otherwise: Provided, however, That if the bank is engaged in such business through a separately identifiable department or division (as defined by the Municipal Securities Rulemaking Board in accordance with section 78o–4(b)(2)(H) of this title), the department or division and not the bank itself shall be deemed to be the municipal securities dealer.

(31) The term "municipal securities broker" means a broker engaged in the business of effecting transactions in municipal securities for the account of others.

(32) The term "person associated with a municipal securities dealer" when used with respect to a municipal securities dealer which is a bank or a division or department of a bank means any person directly engaged in the management, direction, supervision, or performance of any of the municipal securities dealer's activities with respect to municipal securities, and any person directly or indirectly controlling such activities or controlled by the municipal securities dealer in connection with such activities.

(33) The term "municipal securities investment portfolio" means all municipal securities held for investment and not for sale as part of a regular business by a municipal securities dealer or by a person, directly or indirectly, controlling, controlled by, or under common control with a municipal securities dealer.

(34) The term "appropriate regulatory agency" means—

(A) When used with respect to a municipal securities dealer:

(i) the Comptroller of the Currency, in the case of a national bank, a subsidiary or a department or division of any such bank, a Federal savings association (as defined in section 3(b)(2) of the Federal Deposit Insurance Act (12 U.S.C. 1813(b)(2))), the deposits of which are insured by the Federal Deposit Insurance Corporation, or a subsidiary or department or division of any such Federal savings association;

(ii) the Board of Governors of the Federal Reserve System, in the case of a State member bank of the Federal Reserve System, a subsidiary or a department or division thereof, a bank holding company, a subsidiary of a bank holding company which is a bank other than a bank specified in clause (i), (iii), or (iv) of this subparagraph, a subsidiary or a department or division of such subsidiary, or a savings and loan holding company;

(iii) the Federal Deposit Insurance Corporation, in the case of a bank insured by the Federal Deposit Insurance Corporation (other than a member of the Federal Reserve System), a subsidiary or department or division of any such bank, a State savings association (as defined in section 3(b)(3) of the Federal Deposit Insurance Act (12 U.S.C. 1813(b)(3))), the deposits of which are insured by the Federal Deposit Insurance Corporation, or a subsidiary or a department or division of any such State savings association; and

(iv) the Commission in the case of all other municipal securities dealers.

(B) When used with respect to a clearing agency or transfer agent:

(i) the Comptroller of the Currency, in the case of a national bank, a subsidiary of any such bank, a Federal savings association (as defined in section 3(b)(2) of the Federal Deposit Insurance Act (12 U.S.C. 1813(b)(2))), the deposits of which are insured by the Federal Deposit Insurance Corporation, or a subsidiary of any such Federal savings association;

(ii) the Board of Governors of the Federal Reserve System, in the case of a State member bank of the Federal Reserve System, a subsidiary thereof, a bank holding company, a subsidiary of a bank holding company that is a bank other than a bank specified in clause (i) or (iii) of this subparagraph, or a savings and loan holding company;

(iii) the Federal Deposit Insurance Corporation, in the case of a bank insured by the Federal Deposit Insurance Corporation (other than a member of the Federal Reserve System), a subsidiary of any such bank, a State savings association (as defined in section 3(b)(3) of the Federal Deposit Insurance Act (12 U.S.C. 1813(b)(3))), the deposits of which are insured by the Federal Deposit Insurance Corporation, or a subsidiary of any such State savings association; and

(iv) the Commission in the case of all other clearing agencies and transfer agents.

(C) When used with respect to a participant or applicant to become a participant in a clearing agency or a person requesting or having access to services offered by a clearing agency:

(i) The Comptroller of the Currency, in the case of a national bank or a Federal savings association (as defined in section 3(b)(2) of the Federal Deposit Insurance Act (12 U.S.C. 1813(b)(2))), the deposits of which are insured by the Federal Deposit Insurance Corporation [2] when the appropriate regulatory agency for such clearing agency is not the Commission;

(ii) the Board of Governors of the Federal Reserve System in the case of a State member bank of the Federal Reserve System, a bank holding company, or a subsidiary of a bank holding company, a subsidiary of a bank holding company that is a bank other than a bank specified in clause (i) or (iii) of this subparagraph, or a savings and loan holding company when the appropriate regulatory agency for such clearing agency is not the Commission;

(iii) the Federal Deposit Insurance Corporation, in the case of a bank insured by the Federal Deposit Insurance Corporation (other than a member of the Federal Reserve System) or a State savings association (as defined in section 3(b)(3) of the Federal Deposit Insurance Act (12 U.S.C. 1813(b)(3))), the deposits of which are insured by the Federal Deposit Insurance Corporation; and [3] when the appropriate regulatory agency for such clearing agency is not the Commission; [4]

(iv) the Commission in all other cases.

(D) When used with respect to an institutional investment manager which is a bank the deposits of which are insured in accordance with the Federal Deposit Insurance Act [12 U.S.C. 1811 et seq.]:

(i) the Comptroller of the Currency, in the case of a national bank or a Federal savings association (as defined in section 3(b)(2) of the Federal Deposit Insurance Act (12 U.S.C. 1813(b)(2))), the deposits of which are insured by the Federal Deposit Insurance Corporation;

(ii) the Board of Governors of the Federal Reserve System, in the case of any other member bank of the Federal Reserve System; and

(iii) the Federal Deposit Insurance Corporation, in the case of any other insured bank or a State savings association (as defined in section 3(b)(3) of the Federal Deposit Insurance Act (12 U.S.C. 1813(b)(3))), the deposits of which are insured by the Federal Deposit Insurance Corporation.

(E) When used with respect to a national securities exchange or registered securities association, member thereof, person associated with a member thereof, applicant to become a member thereof or to become associated with a member thereof, or person requesting or having access to services offered by such exchange or association or member thereof, or the Municipal Securities Rulemaking Board, the Commission.

(F) When used with respect to a person exercising investment discretion with respect to an account; [5]

(i) the Comptroller of the Currency, in the case of a national bank or a Federal savings association (as defined in section 3(b)(2) of the Federal Deposit Insurance Act (12 U.S.C. 1813(b)(2))), the deposits of which are insured by the Federal Deposit Insurance Corporation;

(ii) the Board of Governors of the Federal Reserve System in the case of any other member bank of the Federal Reserve System;

(iii) the Federal Deposit Insurance Corporation, in the case of any other bank the deposits of which are insured in accordance with the Federal Deposit Insurance Act [12 U.S.C. 1811 et seq.] or a

State savings association (as defined in section 3(b)(3) of the Federal Deposit Insurance Act (12 U.S.C. 1813(b)(3))), the deposits of which are insured by the Federal Deposit Insurance Corporation; and

(iv) the Commission in the case of all other such persons.

(G) When used with respect to a government securities broker or government securities dealer, or person associated with a government securities broker or government securities dealer:

(i) the Comptroller of the Currency, in the case of a national bank, a Federal savings association (as defined in section 3(b)(2) of the Federal Deposit Insurance Act [12 U.S.C. 1813(b)(2)]), the deposits of which are insured by the Federal Deposit Insurance Corporation, or a Federal branch or Federal agency of a foreign bank (as such terms are used in the International Banking Act of 1978 [12 U.S.C. 3101 et seq.]);

(ii) the Board of Governors of the Federal Reserve System, in the case of a State member bank of the Federal Reserve System, a foreign bank, an uninsured State branch or State agency of a foreign bank, a commercial lending company owned or controlled by a foreign bank (as such terms are used in the International Banking Act of 1978), or a corporation organized or having an agreement with the Board of Governors of the Federal Reserve System pursuant to section 25 or section 25A of the Federal Reserve Act [12 U.S.C. 601 et seq., 611 et seq.];

(iii) the Federal Deposit Insurance Corporation, in the case of a bank insured by the Federal Deposit Insurance Corporation (other than a member of the Federal Reserve System or a Federal savings bank), a State savings association (as defined in section 3(b)(3) of the Federal Deposit Insurance Act [12 U.S.C. 1813(b)(3)]), the deposits of which are insured by the Federal Deposit Insurance Corporation, or an insured State branch of a foreign bank (as such terms are used in the International Banking Act of 1978); and

(iv) the Commission, in the case of all other government securities brokers and government securities dealers.

(H) When used with respect to an institution described in subparagraph (D), (F), or (G) of section 1841(c)(2), or held under section 1843(f) of title 12—

(i) the Comptroller of the Currency, in the case of a national bank;

(ii) the Board of Governors of the Federal Reserve System, in the case of a State member bank of the Federal Reserve System or any corporation chartered under section 25A of the Federal Reserve Act [12 U.S.C. 611 et seq.];

(iii) the Federal Deposit Insurance Corporation, in the case of any other bank the deposits of which are insured in accordance with the Federal Deposit Insurance Act [12 U.S.C. 1811 et seq.]; or

(iv) the Commission in the case of all other such institutions.

As used in this paragraph, the terms "bank holding company" and "subsidiary of a bank holding company" have the meanings given them in section 1841 of title 12. As used in this paragraph, the term "savings and loan holding company" has the same meaning as in section 1467a(a) of title 12.

(35) A person exercises "investment discretion" with respect to an account if, directly or indirectly, such person (A) is authorized to determine what securities or other property shall be purchased or sold by or for the account, (B) makes decisions as to what securities or other property shall be purchased or sold by or for the account even though some other person may have responsibility for such investment decisions, or (C) otherwise exercises such influence with respect to the purchase and sale of securities or other property by or for the account as the Commission, by rule, determines, in the public interest or for the protection of investors, should be subject to the operation of the provisions of this chapter and the rules and regulations thereunder.

(36) A class of persons or markets is subject to "equal regulation" if no member of the class has a competitive advantage over any other member thereof resulting from a disparity in their regulation under this chapter which the Commission determines is unfair and not necessary or appropriate in furtherance of the purposes of this chapter.

(37) The term "records" means accounts, correspondence, memorandums, tapes, discs, papers, books, and other documents or transcribed information of any type, whether expressed in ordinary or machine language.

(38) The term "market maker" means any specialist permitted to act as a dealer, any dealer acting in the capacity of block positioner, and any dealer who, with respect to a security, holds himself out (by entering quotations in an inter-dealer communications system or otherwise) as being willing to buy and sell such security for his own account on a regular or continuous basis.

(39) A person is subject to a "statutory disqualification" with respect to membership or participation in, or association with a member of, a self-regulatory organization, if such person—

(A) has been and is expelled or suspended from membership or participation in, or barred or suspended from being associated with a member of, any self-regulatory organization, foreign equivalent of a self-regulatory organization, foreign or international securities exchange, contract market designated pursuant to section 5 of the Commodity Exchange Act (7 U.S.C. 7), or any substantially equivalent foreign statute or regulation, or futures association registered under section 17 of such Act (7 U.S.C. 21), or any substantially equivalent foreign statute or regulation, or has been and is denied trading privileges on any such contract market or foreign equivalent;

(B) is subject to—

(i) an order of the Commission, other appropriate regulatory agency, or foreign financial regulatory authority—

(I) denying, suspending for a period not exceeding 12 months, or revoking his registration as a broker, dealer, municipal securities dealer, government securities broker, government securities dealer, security-based swap dealer, or major security-based swap participant or limiting his activities as a foreign person performing a function substantially equivalent to any of the above; or

(II) barring or suspending for a period not exceeding 12 months his being associated with a broker, dealer, municipal securities dealer, government securities broker, government securities dealer, security-based swap dealer, major security-based swap participant, or foreign person performing a function substantially equivalent to any of the above;

(ii) an order of the Commodity Futures Trading Commission denying, suspending, or revoking his registration under the Commodity Exchange Act (7 U.S.C. 1 et seq.); or

(iii) an order by a foreign financial regulatory authority denying, suspending, or revoking the person's authority to engage in transactions in contracts of sale of a commodity for future delivery or other instruments traded on or subject to the rules of a contract market, board of trade, or foreign equivalent thereof;

(C) by his conduct while associated with a broker, dealer, municipal securities dealer, government securities broker, government securities dealer, security-based swap dealer, or major security-based swap participant, or while associated with an entity or person required to be registered under the Commodity Exchange Act, has been found to be a cause of any effective suspension, expulsion, or order of the character described in subparagraph (A) or (B) of this paragraph, and in entering such a suspension, expulsion, or order, the Commission, an appropriate regulatory agency, or any such self-regulatory organization shall have jurisdiction to find whether or not any person was a cause thereof;

(D) by his conduct while associated with any broker, dealer, municipal securities dealer, government securities broker, government securities dealer, security-based swap dealer, major security-based swap participant, or any other entity engaged in transactions in securities, or while associated with an entity engaged in transactions in contracts of sale of a commodity for future delivery or other instruments traded on or subject to the rules of a contract market, board of trade, or foreign equivalent thereof, has been found to be a cause of any effective suspension, expulsion, or order by a foreign or international securities exchange or foreign financial regulatory authority empowered by a foreign government to administer or enforce its laws relating to financial transactions as described in subparagraph (A) or (B) of this paragraph;

(E) has associated with him any person who is known, or in the exercise of reasonable care should be known, to him to be a person described by subparagraph (A), (B), (C), or (D) of this paragraph; or

(F) has committed or omitted any act, or is subject to an order or finding, enumerated in subparagraph (D), (E), (H), or (G) of paragraph (4) of section 78o(b) of this title, has been convicted of any offense specified in subparagraph (B) of such paragraph (4) or any other felony within ten years of the date of the filing of an application for membership or participation in, or to become associated with a member of, such self-regulatory organization, is enjoined from any action, conduct, or practice specified in subparagraph (C) of such paragraph (4), has willfully made or caused to be made in any application for membership or participation in, or to become associated with a member of, a self-regulatory organization, report required to be filed with a self-regulatory organization, or proceeding before a self-regulatory organization, any statement which was at the time, and in the light of the circumstances under which it was made, false or misleading with respect to any material fact, or has omitted to state in any such application, report, or proceeding any material fact which is required to be stated therein.

(40) The term "financial responsibility rules" means the rules and regulations of the Commission or the rules and regulations prescribed by any self-regulatory organization relating to financial responsibility and related practices which are designated by the Commission, by rule or regulation, to be financial responsibility rules.

(41) The term "mortgage related security" means a security that meets standards of credit-worthiness as established by the Commission, and either:

(A) represents ownership of one or more promissory notes or certificates of interest or participation in such notes (including any rights designed to assure servicing of, or the receipt or timeliness of receipt by the holders of such notes, certificates, or participations of amounts payable under, such notes, certificates, or participations), which notes:

(i) are directly secured by a first lien on a single parcel of real estate, including stock allocated to a dwelling unit in a residential cooperative housing corporation, upon which is located a dwelling or mixed residential and commercial structure, on a residential manufactured home as defined in section 5402(6) of title 42, whether such manufactured home is considered real or personal property under the laws of the State in which it is to be located, or on one or more parcels of real estate upon which is located one or more commercial structures; and

(ii) were originated by a savings and loan association, savings bank, commercial bank, credit union, insurance company, or similar institution which is supervised and examined by a Federal or State authority, or by a mortgagee approved by the Secretary of Housing and Urban Development pursuant to sections 1709 and 1715b of title 12, or, where such notes involve a lien on the manufactured home, by any such institution or by any financial institution approved for insurance by the Secretary of Housing and Urban Development pursuant to section 1703 of title 12; or

(B) is secured by one or more promissory notes or certificates of interest or participations in such notes (with or without recourse to the issuer thereof) and, by its terms, provides for payments of principal in relation to payments, or reasonable projections of payments, on notes meeting the requirements of subparagraphs (A)(i) and (ii) or certificates of interest or participations in promissory notes meeting such requirements.

For the purpose of this paragraph, the term "promissory note", when used in connection with a manufactured home, shall also include a loan, advance, or credit sale as evidence [6] by a retail installment sales contract or other instrument.

(42) The term "government securities" means—

(A) securities which are direct obligations of, or obligations guaranteed as to principal or interest by, the United States;

(B) securities which are issued or guaranteed by the Tennessee Valley Authority or by corporations in which the United States has a direct or indirect interest and which are designated by the Secretary of the Treasury for exemption as necessary or appropriate in the public interest or for the protection of investors;

(C) securities issued or guaranteed as to principal or interest by any corporation the securities of which are designated, by statute specifically naming such corporation, to constitute exempt securities within the meaning of the laws administered by the Commission;

(D) for purposes of sections 78o–5 and 78q–1 of this title, any put, call, straddle, option, or privilege on a security described in subparagraph (A), (B), or (C) other than a put, call, straddle, option, or privilege—

(i) that is traded on one or more national securities exchanges; or

(ii) for which quotations are disseminated through an automated quotation system operated by a registered securities association; or

(E) for purposes of sections 78o, 78o–5, and 78q–1 of this title as applied to a bank, a qualified Canadian government obligation as defined in section 24 of title 12.

(43) The term "government securities broker" means any person regularly engaged in the business of effecting transactions in government securities for the account of others, but does not include—

(A) any corporation the securities of which are government securities under subparagraph (B) or (C) of paragraph (42) of this subsection; or

(B) any person registered with the Commodity Futures Trading Commission, any contract market designated by the Commodity Futures Trading Commission, such contract market's affiliated clearing organization, or any floor trader on such contract market, solely because such person effects transactions in government securities that the Commission, after consultation with the Commodity Futures Trading Commission, has determined by rule or order to be incidental to such person's futures-related business.

(44) The term "government securities dealer" means any person engaged in the business of buying and selling government securities for his own account, through a broker or otherwise, but does not include—

(A) any person insofar as he buys or sells such securities for his own account, either individually or in some fiduciary capacity, but not as a part of a regular business;

(B) any corporation the securities of which are government securities under subparagraph (B) or (C) of paragraph (42) of this subsection;

(C) any bank, unless the bank is engaged in the business of buying and selling government securities for its own account other than in a fiduciary capacity, through a broker or otherwise; or

(D) any person registered with the Commodity Futures Trading Commission, any contract market designated by the Commodity Futures Trading Commission, such contract market's affiliated clearing organization, or any floor trader on such contract market, solely because such person effects transactions in government securities that the Commission, after consultation with the Commodity Futures Trading Commission, has determined by rule or order to be incidental to such person's futures-related business.

(45) The term "person associated with a government securities broker or government securities dealer" means any partner, officer, director, or branch manager of such government securities broker or government securities dealer (or any person occupying a similar status or performing similar functions), and any other employee of such government securities broker or government securities dealer who is engaged in the management, direction, supervision, or performance of any activities relating to government securities, and any person directly or indirectly controlling, controlled by, or under common control with such government securities broker or government securities dealer.

(46) The term "financial institution" means—

(A) a bank (as defined in paragraph (6) of this subsection);

(B) a foreign bank (as such term is used in the International Banking Act of 1978); and

(C) a savings association (as defined in section 3(b) of the Federal Deposit Insurance Act [12 U.S.C. 1813(b)]) the deposits of which are insured by the Federal Deposit Insurance Corporation.

(47) The term "securities laws" means the Securities Act of 1933 (15 U.S.C. 77a et seq.), the Securities Exchange Act of 1934 (15 U.S.C. 78a et seq.), the Sarbanes-Oxley Act of 2002 [15 U.S.C. 7201 et seq.], the Trust Indenture Act of 1939 (15 U.S.C. 77aaa et seq.), the Investment Company Act of 1940 (15 U.S.C. 80a–1 et seq.), the Investment Advisers Act of 1940 (15 U.S.C. 80b et seq.) [15 U.S.C. 80b–1 et seq.], and the Securities Investor Protection Act of 1970 (15 U.S.C. 78aaa et seq.).

(48) The term "registered broker or dealer" means a broker or dealer registered or required to register pursuant to section 78o or 78o–4 of this title, except that in paragraph (3) of this subsection and sections 78f and 78o–3 of this title the term means such a broker or dealer and a government securities broker or government securities dealer registered or required to register pursuant to section 78o–5(a)(1)(A) of this title.

(49) The term "person associated with a transfer agent" and "associated person of a transfer agent" mean any person (except an employee whose functions are solely clerical or ministerial) directly engaged in the management, direction, supervision, or performance of any of the transfer agent's activities with respect to transfer agent functions, and any person directly or indirectly controlling such activities or controlled by the transfer agent in connection with such activities.

(50) The term "foreign securities authority" means any foreign government, or any governmental body or regulatory organization empowered by a foreign government to administer or enforce its laws as they relate to securities matters.

(51)

(A) The term "penny stock" means any equity security other than a security that is—
  (i) registered or approved for registration and traded on a national securities exchange that meets such criteria as the Commission shall prescribe by rule or regulation for purposes of this paragraph;
  (ii) authorized for quotation on an automated quotation system sponsored by a registered securities association, if system was established and in operation before January 1, 1990, and meets such criteria as the Commission shall prescribe by rule or regulation for purposes of this paragraph;
  (iii) issued by an investment company registered under the Investment Company Act of 1940 [15 U.S.C. 80a–1 et seq.];
  (iv) excluded, on the basis of exceeding a minimum price, net tangible assets of the issuer, or other relevant criteria, from the definition of such term by rule or regulation which the Commission shall prescribe for purposes of this paragraph; or
  (v) exempted, in whole or in part, conditionally or unconditionally, from the definition of such term by rule, regulation, or order prescribed by the Commission.

(B) The Commission may, by rule, regulation, or order, designate any equity security or class of equity securities described in clause (i) or (ii) of subparagraph (A) as within the meaning of the term "penny stock" if such security or class of securities is traded other than on a national securities exchange or through an automated quotation system described in clause (ii) of subparagraph (A).

(C) In exercising its authority under this paragraph to prescribe rules, regulations, and orders, the Commission shall determine that such rule, regulation, or order is consistent with the public interest and the protection of investors.

(52) The term "foreign financial regulatory authority" means any (A) foreign securities authority, (B) other governmental body or foreign equivalent of a self-regulatory organization empowered by a foreign government to administer or enforce its laws relating to the regulation of fiduciaries, trusts, commercial lending, insurance, trading in contracts of sale of a commodity for future delivery, or other instruments traded on or subject to the rules of a contract market, board of trade, or foreign equivalent, or other financial activities, or (C) membership organization a function of which is to regulate participation of its members in activities listed above.

(53)
    (A) The term "small business related security" means a security that meets standards of credit-worthiness as established by the Commission, and either—
        (i) represents an interest in 1 or more promissory notes or leases of personal property evidencing the obligation of a small business concern and originated by an insured depository institution, insured credit union, insurance company, or similar institution which is supervised and examined by a Federal or State authority, or a finance company or leasing company; or
        (ii) is secured by an interest in 1 or more promissory notes or leases of personal property (with or without recourse to the issuer or lessee) and provides for payments of principal in relation to payments, or reasonable projections of payments, on notes or leases described in clause (i).
    (B) For purposes of this paragraph—
        (i) an "interest in a promissory note or a lease of personal property" includes ownership rights, certificates of interest or participation in such notes or leases, and rights designed to assure servicing of such notes or leases, or the receipt or timely receipt of amounts payable under such notes or leases;
        (ii) the term "small business concern" means a business that meets the criteria for a small business concern established by the Small Business Administration under section 632(a) of this title;
        (iii) the term "insured depository institution" has the same meaning as in section 3 of the Federal Deposit Insurance Act [12 U.S.C. 1813]; and
        (iv) the term "insured credit union" has the same meaning as in section 1752 of title 12.
(54) Qualified investor.—
    (A) Definition.—Except as provided in subparagraph (B), for purposes of this chapter, the term "qualified investor" means—
        (i) any investment company registered with the Commission under section 8 of the Investment Company Act of 1940 [15 U.S.C. 80a–8];
        (ii) any issuer eligible for an exclusion from the definition of investment company pursuant to section 3(c)(7) of the Investment Company Act of 1940 [15 U.S.C. 80a–3(c)(7)];
        (iii) any bank (as defined in paragraph (6) of this subsection), savings association (as defined in section 3(b) of the Federal Deposit Insurance Act [12 U.S.C. 1813(b)]), broker, dealer, insurance company (as defined in section 2(a)(13) of the Securities Act of 1933 [15 U.S.C. 77b(a)(13)]), or business development company (as defined in section 2(a)(48) of the Investment Company Act of 1940 [15 U.S.C. 80a–2(a)(48)]);
        (iv) any small business investment company licensed by the United States Small Business Administration under section 301(c) [15 U.S.C. 681(c)] or (d) 1 of the Small Business Investment Act of 1958;
        (v) any State sponsored employee benefit plan, or any other employee benefit plan, within the meaning of the Employee Retirement Income Security Act of 1974 [29 U.S.C. 1001 et seq.], other than an individual retirement account, if the investment decisions are made by a plan fiduciary, as defined in section 3(21) of that Act [29 U.S.C. 1002(21)], which is either a bank, savings and loan association, insurance company, or registered investment adviser;
        (vi) any trust whose purchases of securities are directed by a person described in clauses (i) through (v) of this subparagraph;
        (vii) any market intermediary exempt under section 3(c)(2) of the Investment Company Act of 1940 [15 U.S.C. 80a–3(c)(2)];
        (viii) any associated person of a broker or dealer other than a natural person;
        (ix) any foreign bank (as defined in section 1(b)(7) of the International Banking Act of 1978 [12 U.S.C. 3101(7)]);
        (x) the government of any foreign country;
        (xi) any corporation, company, or partnership that owns and invests on a discretionary basis, not

less than $25,000,000 in investments;

(xii) any natural person who owns and invests on a discretionary basis, not less than $25,000,000 in investments;

(xiii) any government or political subdivision, agency, or instrumentality of a government who owns and invests on a discretionary basis not less than $50,000,000 in investments; or

(xiv) any multinational or supranational entity or any agency or instrumentality thereof.

(B) Altered thresholds for asset-backed and loan participations.—

For purposes of subsection (a)(5)(C)(iii) of this section and section 206(a)(5) of the Gramm-Leach-Bliley Act, the term "qualified investor" has the meaning given such term by subparagraph (A) of this paragraph except that clauses (xi) and (xii) shall be applied by substituting "$10,000,000" for "$25,000,000".

(C) Additional authority.—

The Commission may, by rule or order, define a "qualified investor" as any other person, taking into consideration such factors as the financial sophistication of the person, net worth, and knowledge and experience in financial matters.

(55)

(A) The term "security future" means a contract of sale for future delivery of a single security or of a narrow-based security index, including any interest therein or based on the value thereof, except an exempted security under paragraph (12) of this subsection as in effect on January 11, 1983 (other than any municipal security as defined in paragraph (29) of this subsection as in effect on January 11, 1983). The term "security future" does not include any agreement, contract, or transaction excluded from the Commodity Exchange Act [7 U.S.C. 1 et seq.] under section 2(c), 2(d), 2(f), or 2(g) of the Commodity Exchange Act [7 U.S.C. 2(c), (d), (f), (g)] (as in effect on December 21, 2000) or sections 27 to 27f of title 7.

(B) The term "narrow-based security index" means an index—

(i) that has 9 or fewer component securities;

(ii) in which a component security comprises more than 30 percent of the index's weighting;

(iii) in which the five highest weighted component securities in the aggregate comprise more than 60 percent of the index's weighting; or

(iv) in which the lowest weighted component securities comprising, in the aggregate, 25 percent of the index's weighting have an aggregate dollar value of average daily trading volume of less than $50,000,000 (or in the case of an index with 15 or more component securities, $30,000,000), except that if there are two or more securities with equal weighting that could be included in the calculation of the lowest weighted component securities comprising, in the aggregate, 25 percent of the index's weighting, such securities shall be ranked from lowest to highest dollar value of average daily trading volume and shall be included in the calculation based on their ranking starting with the lowest ranked security.

(C) Notwithstanding subparagraph (B), an index is not a narrow-based security index if—

(i)

(I) it has at least nine component securities;

(II) no component security comprises more than 30 percent of the index's weighting; and

(III) each component security is—

(aa) registered pursuant to section 78l of this title;

(bb) one of 750 securities with the largest market capitalization; and

(cc) one of 675 securities with the largest dollar value of average daily trading volume;

(ii) a board of trade was designated as a contract market by the Commodity Futures Trading Commission with respect to a contract of sale for future delivery on the index, before December 21, 2000;

(iii)

    (I) a contract of sale for future delivery on the index traded on a designated contract market or registered derivatives transaction execution facility for at least 30 days as a contract of sale for future delivery on an index that was not a narrow-based security index; and

    (II) it has been a narrow-based security index for no more than 45 business days over 3 consecutive calendar months;

(iv) a contract of sale for future delivery on the index is traded on or subject to the rules of a foreign board of trade and meets such requirements as are jointly established by rule or regulation by the Commission and the Commodity Futures Trading Commission;

(v) no more than 18 months have passed since December 21, 2000, and—

    (I) it is traded on or subject to the rules of a foreign board of trade;

    (II) the offer and sale in the United States of a contract of sale for future delivery on the index was authorized before December 21, 2000; and

    (III) the conditions of such authorization continue to be met; or

(vi) a contract of sale for future delivery on the index is traded on or subject to the rules of a board of trade and meets such requirements as are jointly established by rule, regulation, or order by the Commission and the Commodity Futures Trading Commission.

(D) Within 1 year after December 21, 2000, the Commission and the Commodity Futures Trading Commission jointly shall adopt rules or regulations that set forth the requirements under clause (iv) of subparagraph (C).

(E) An index that is a narrow-based security index solely because it was a narrow-based security index for more than 45 business days over 3 consecutive calendar months pursuant to clause (iii) of subparagraph (C) shall not be a narrow-based security index for the 3 following calendar months.

(F) For purposes of subparagraphs (B) and (C) of this paragraph—

(i) the dollar value of average daily trading volume and the market capitalization shall be calculated as of the preceding 6 full calendar months; and

(ii) the Commission and the Commodity Futures Trading Commission shall, by rule or regulation, jointly specify the method to be used to determine market capitalization and dollar value of average daily trading volume.

(56) The term "security futures product" means a security future or any put, call, straddle, option, or privilege on any security future.

(57)

(A) The term "margin", when used with respect to a security futures product, means the amount, type, and form of collateral required to secure any extension or maintenance of credit, or the amount, type, and form of collateral required as a performance bond related to the purchase, sale, or carrying of a security futures product.

(B) The terms "margin level" and "level of margin", when used with respect to a security futures product, mean the amount of margin required to secure any extension or maintenance of credit, or the amount of margin required as a performance bond related to the purchase, sale, or carrying of a security futures product.

(C) The terms "higher margin level" and "higher level of margin", when used with respect to a security futures product, mean a margin level established by a national securities exchange registered pursuant to section 78f(g) of this title that is higher than the minimum amount established and in effect pursuant to section 78g(c)(2)(B) of this title.

(58) Audit committee.—The term "audit committee" means—

(A) a committee (or equivalent body) established by and amongst the board of directors of an issuer for the purpose of overseeing the accounting and financial reporting processes of the issuer and audits of the financial statements of the issuer; and

(B) if no such committee exists with respect to an issuer, the entire board of directors of the issuer.

(59) Registered public accounting firm.—
The term "registered public accounting firm" has the same meaning as in section 2 of the Sarbanes-Oxley Act of 2002 [15 U.S.C. 7201].

(60) Credit rating.—
The term "credit rating" means an assessment of the creditworthiness of an obligor as an entity or with respect to specific securities or money market instruments.

(61) Credit rating agency.—The term "credit rating agency" means any person—
(A) engaged in the business of issuing credit ratings on the Internet or through another readily accessible means, for free or for a reasonable fee, but does not include a commercial credit reporting company;
(B) employing either a quantitative or qualitative model, or both, to determine credit ratings; and
(C) receiving fees from either issuers, investors, or other market participants, or a combination thereof.

(62) Nationally recognized statistical rating organization.—The term "nationally recognized statistical rating organization" means a credit rating agency that—
(A) issues credit ratings certified by qualified institutional buyers, in accordance with section 78o–7(a)(1)(B)(ix) of this title, with respect to—
(i) financial institutions, brokers, or dealers;
(ii) insurance companies;
(iii) corporate issuers;
(iv) issuers of asset-backed securities (as that term is defined in section 1101(c) of part 229 of title 17, Code of Federal Regulations, as in effect on September 29, 2006);
(v) issuers of government securities, municipal securities, or securities issued by a foreign government; or
(vi) a combination of one or more categories of obligors described in any of clauses (i) through (v); and
(B) is registered under section 78o–7 of this title.

(63) Person associated with a nationally recognized statistical rating organization.—
The term "person associated with" a nationally recognized statistical rating organization means any partner, officer, director, or branch manager of a nationally recognized statistical rating organization (or any person occupying a similar status or performing similar functions), any person directly or indirectly controlling, controlled by, or under common control with a nationally recognized statistical rating organization, or any employee of a nationally recognized statistical rating organization.

(64) Qualified institutional buyer.—
The term "qualified institutional buyer" has the meaning given such term in section 230.144A(a) of title 17, Code of Federal Regulations, or any successor thereto.

(65) Eligible contract participant.—
The term "eligible contract participant" has the same meaning as in section 1a of the Commodity Exchange Act (7 U.S.C. 1a).

(66) Major participant.—
The term "major swap participant" has the same meaning as in section 1a of the Commodity Exchange Act (7 U.S.C. 1a).

(67) Major -based.—
(A) In general.—The term "major security-based swap participant" means any person—
(i) who is not a security-based swap dealer; and
(ii)
(I) who maintains a substantial position in security-based swaps for any of the major security-based swap categories, as such categories are determined by the Commission, excluding both positions held for hedging or mitigating commercial risk and positions maintained by any employee benefit plan (or any contract held by such a plan) as defined in paragraphs (3) and (32) of section 3 of the Employee Retirement Income Security Act of 1974 (29 U.S.C. 1002) for the

primary purpose of hedging or mitigating any risk directly associated with the operation of the plan;

(II) whose outstanding security-based swaps create substantial counterparty exposure that could have serious adverse effects on the financial stability of the United States banking system or financial markets; or

(III) that is a financial entity that—

(aa) is highly leveraged relative to the amount of capital such entity holds and that is not subject to capital requirements established by an appropriate Federal banking agency; and

(bb) maintains a substantial position in outstanding security-based swaps in any major security-based swap category, as such categories are determined by the Commission.

(B) Definition of substantial position.—

For purposes of subparagraph (A), the Commission shall define, by rule or regulation, the term "substantial position" at the threshold that the Commission determines to be prudent for the effective monitoring, management, and oversight of entities that are systemically important or can significantly impact the financial system of the United States. In setting the definition under this subparagraph, the Commission shall consider the person's relative position in uncleared as opposed to cleared security-based swaps and may take into consideration the value and quality of collateral held against counterparty exposures.

(C) Scope of designation.—

For purposes of subparagraph (A), a person may be designated as a major security-based swap participant for 1 or more categories of security-based swaps without being classified as a major security-based swap participant for all classes of security-based swaps.

(68) Security-based.—

(A) In general.—Except as provided in subparagraph (B), the term "security-based swap" means any agreement, contract, or transaction that—

(i) is a swap, as that term is defined under section 1a of the Commodity Exchange Act [7 U.S.C. 1a] (without regard to paragraph (47)(B)(x) of such section); and

(ii) is based on—

(I) an index that is a narrow-based security index, including any interest therein or on the value thereof;

(II) a single security or loan, including any interest therein or on the value thereof; or

(III) the occurrence, nonoccurrence, or extent of the occurrence of an event relating to a single issuer of a security or the issuers of securities in a narrow-based security index, provided that such event directly affects the financial statements, financial condition, or financial obligations of the issuer.

(B) Rule of construction regarding master agreements.—

The term "security-based swap" shall be construed to include a master agreement that provides for an agreement, contract, or transaction that is a security-based swap pursuant to subparagraph (A), together with all supplements to any such master agreement, without regard to whether the master agreement contains an agreement, contract, or transaction that is not a security-based swap pursuant to subparagraph (A), except that the master agreement shall be considered to be a security-based swap only with respect to each agreement, contract, or transaction under the master agreement that is a security-based swap pursuant to subparagraph (A).

(C) Exclusions.—

The term "security-based swap" does not include any agreement, contract, or transaction that meets the definition of a security-based swap only because such agreement, contract, or transaction references, is based upon, or settles through the transfer, delivery, or receipt of an exempted security under paragraph (12), as in effect on January 11, 1983 (other than any municipal security as defined in paragraph (29) as in effect on January 11, 1983), unless such agreement, contract, or transaction is of the character of, or is commonly known in the trade as, a put, call, or other option.

(D) Mixed swap.—

The term "security-based swap" includes any agreement, contract, or transaction that is as described in subparagraph (A) and also is based on the value of 1 or more interest or other rates, currencies, commodities, instruments of indebtedness, indices, quantitative measures, other financial or economic interest or property of any kind (other than a single security or a narrow-based security index), or the occurrence, non-occurrence, or the extent of the occurrence of an event or contingency associated with a potential financial, economic, or commercial consequence (other than an event described in subparagraph (A)(ii)(III)).

(E) Rule of construction regarding use of the term index.—

The term "index" means an index or group of securities, including any interest therein or based on the value thereof.

(69) Swap.—

The term "swap" has the same meaning as in section 1a of the Commodity Exchange Act (7 U.S.C. 1a).

(70) Person associated with a -based or major based.—

(A) In general.—The term "person associated with a security-based swap dealer or major security-based swap participant" or "associated person of a security-based swap dealer or major security-based swap participant" means—

(i) any partner, officer, director, or branch manager of such security-based swap dealer or major security-based swap participant (or any person occupying a similar status or performing similar functions);

(ii) any person directly or indirectly controlling, controlled by, or under common control with such security-based swap dealer or major security-based swap participant; or

(iii) any employee of such security-based swap dealer or major security-based swap participant.

(B) Exclusion.—

Other than for purposes of section 78o–10(l)(2) of this title, the term "person associated with a security-based swap dealer or major security-based swap participant" or "associated person of a security-based swap dealer or major security-based swap participant" does not include any person associated with a security-based swap dealer or major security-based swap participant whose functions are solely clerical or ministerial.

(71) Security-based.—

(A) In general.—The term "security-based swap dealer" means any person who—

(i) holds themself out as a dealer in security-based swaps;

(ii) makes a market in security-based swaps;

(iii) regularly enters into security-based swaps with counterparties as an ordinary course of business for its own account; or

(iv) engages in any activity causing it to be commonly known in the trade as a dealer or market maker in security-based swaps.

(B) Designation by type or class.—

A person may be designated as a security-based swap dealer for a single type or single class or category of security-based swap or activities and considered not to be a security-based swap dealer for other types, classes, or categories of security-based swaps or activities.

(C) Exception.—

The term "security-based swap dealer" does not include a person that enters into security-based swaps for such person's own account, either individually or in a fiduciary capacity, but not as a part of regular business.

(D) De minimis exception.—

The Commission shall exempt from designation as a security-based swap dealer an entity that engages in a de minimis quantity of security-based swap dealing in connection with transactions with or on behalf of its customers. The Commission shall promulgate regulations to establish factors with respect to the making of any determination to exempt.

(72) Appropriate federal banking agency.—

The term "appropriate Federal banking agency" has the same meaning as in section 3(q) of the Federal Deposit Insurance Act (12 U.S.C. 1813(q)).

(73) Board.—

The term "Board" means the Board of Governors of the Federal Reserve System.

(74) Prudential regulator.—

The term "prudential regulator" has the same meaning as in section 1a of the Commodity Exchange Act (7 U.S.C. 1a).

(75) Security-based data repository.—

The term "security-based swap data repository" means any person that collects and maintains information or records with respect to transactions or positions in, or the terms and conditions of, security-based swaps entered into by third parties for the purpose of providing a centralized recordkeeping facility for security-based swaps.

(76) Swap dealer.—

The term "swap dealer" has the same meaning as in section 1a of the Commodity Exchange Act (7 U.S.C. 1a).

(77) Security-based execution facility.—The term "security-based swap execution facility" means a trading system or platform in which multiple participants have the ability to execute or trade security-based swaps by accepting bids and offers made by multiple participants in the facility or system, through any means of interstate commerce, including any trading facility, that—

(A) facilitates the execution of security-based swaps between persons; and

(B) is not a national securities exchange.

(78) Security-based agreement.—

(A) In general.—

For purposes of sections 78i, 78j, 78p, 78t, and 78u–1 of this title, and section 17 of the Securities Act of 1933 (15 U.S.C. 77q), the term "security-based swap agreement" means a swap agreement as defined in section 206A of the Gramm-Leach-Bliley Act (15 U.S.C. 78c note) of which a material term is based on the price, yield, value, or volatility of any security or any group or index of securities, or any interest therein.

(B) Exclusions.—

The term "security-based swap agreement" does not include any security-based swap.

(79) Asset-backed security.—The term "asset-backed security"—

(A) means a fixed-income or other security collateralized by any type of self-liquidating financial asset (including a loan, a lease, a mortgage, or a secured or unsecured receivable) that allows the holder of the security to receive payments that depend primarily on cash flow from the asset, including—

(i) a collateralized mortgage obligation;

(ii) a collateralized debt obligation;

(iii) a collateralized bond obligation;

(iv) a collateralized debt obligation of asset-backed securities;

(v) a collateralized debt obligation of collateralized debt obligations; and

(vi) a security that the Commission, by rule, determines to be an asset-backed security for purposes of this section; and

(B) does not include a security issued by a finance subsidiary held by the parent company or a company controlled by the parent company, if none of the securities issued by the finance subsidiary are held by an entity that is not controlled by the parent company.

(80) Emerging growth company.—The term "emerging growth company" means an issuer that had total annual gross revenues of less than $1,000,000,000 (as such amount is indexed for inflation every 5 years by the Commission to reflect the change in the Consumer Price Index for All Urban Consumers published by the Bureau of Labor Statistics, setting the threshold to the nearest 1,000,000) during its most recently completed fiscal year. An issuer that is an emerging growth company as of the first day of that fiscal year shall continue to be deemed an emerging growth company until the earliest of—

(A) the last day of the fiscal year of the issuer during which it had total annual gross revenues of $1,000,000,000 (as such amount is indexed for inflation every 5 years by the Commission to reflect the change in the Consumer Price Index for All Urban Consumers published by the Bureau of Labor Statistics, setting the threshold to the nearest 1,000,000) or more;

(B) the last day of the fiscal year of the issuer following the fifth anniversary of the date of the first sale of common equity securities of the issuer pursuant to an effective registration statement under the Securities Act of 1933;

(C) the date on which such issuer has, during the previous 3-year period, issued more than $1,000,000,000 in non-convertible debt; or

(D) the date on which such issuer is deemed to be a "large accelerated filer", as defined in section 240.12b–2 of title 17, Code of Federal Regulations, or any successor thereto.

---

15. SEC Rules and Regulations, Securities Exchange Act of 1934: Section 12 — Registration Requirements for Securities

(a) General requirement of registration

It shall be unlawful for any member, broker, or dealer to effect any transaction in any security (other than an exempted security) on a national securities exchange unless a registration is effective as to such security for such exchange in accordance with the provisions of this chapter and the rules and regulations thereunder. The provisions of this subsection shall not apply in respect of a security futures product traded on a national securities exchange.

(b) Procedure for registration; information

A security may be registered on a national securities exchange by the issuer filing an application with the exchange (and filing with the Commission such duplicate originals thereof as the Commission may require), which application shall contain—

(1) Such information, in such detail, as to the issuer and any person directly or indirectly controlling or controlled by, or under direct or indirect common control with, the issuer, and any guarantor of the security as to principal or interest or both, as the Commission may by rules and regulations require, as necessary or appropriate in the public interest or for the protection of investors, in respect of the following:

(A) the organization, financial structure, and nature of the business;

(B) the terms, position, rights, and privileges of the different classes of securities outstanding;

(C) the terms on which their securities are to be, and during the preceding three years have been, offered to the public or otherwise;

(D) the directors, officers, and underwriters, and each security holder of record holding more than 10 per centum of any class of any equity security of the issuer (other than an exempted security), their remuneration and their interests in the securities of, and their material contracts with, the issuer and any person directly or indirectly controlling or controlled by, or under direct or indirect common control with, the issuer;

(E) remuneration to others than directors and officers exceeding $20,000 per annum;

(F) bonus and profit-sharing arrangements;

(G) management and service contracts;

(H) options existing or to be created in respect of their securities;

(I) material contracts, not made in the ordinary course of business, which are to be executed in whole or in part at or after the filing of the application or which were made not more than two years before such filing, and every material patent or contract for a material patent right shall be deemed a material contract;

(J) balance sheets for not more than the three preceding fiscal years, certified if required by the rules and regulations of the Commission by a registered public accounting firm;

(K) profit and loss statements for not more than the three preceding fiscal years, certified if required by the rules and regulations of the Commission by a registered public accounting firm; and

(L) any further financial statements which the Commission may deem necessary or appropriate for the protection of investors.

(2) Such copies of articles of incorporation, bylaws, trust indentures, or corresponding documents by whatever name known, underwriting arrangements, and other similar documents of, and voting trust agreements with respect to, the issuer and any person directly or indirectly controlling or controlled by, or under direct or indirect common control with, the issuer as the Commission may require as necessary or appropriate for the proper protection of investors and to insure fair dealing in the security.

(3) Such copies of material contracts, referred to in paragraph (1)(I), as the Commission may require as necessary or appropriate for the proper protection of investors and to insure fair dealing in the security.

(c) Additional or alternative information

If in the judgment of the Commission any information required under subsection (b) is inapplicable to any specified class or classes of issuers, the Commission shall require in lieu thereof the submission of such other information of comparable character as it may deem applicable to such class of issuers.

(d) Effective date of registration; withdrawal of registration

If the exchange authorities certify to the Commission that the security has been approved by the exchange for listing and registration, the registration shall become effective thirty days after the receipt of such certification by the Commission or within such shorter period of time as the Commission may determine. A security registered with a national securities exchange may be withdrawn or stricken from listing and registration in accordance with the rules of the exchange and, upon such terms as the Commission may deem necessary to impose for the protection of investors, upon application by the issuer or the exchange to the Commission; whereupon the issuer shall be relieved from further compliance with the provisions of this section and section 78m and any rules or regulations under such sections as to the securities so withdrawn or stricken. An unissued security may be registered only in accordance with such rules and regulations as the Commission may prescribe as necessary or appropriate in the public interest or for the protection of investors.

(e) Exemption from provisions of section for period ending not later than July 1, 1935

Notwithstanding the foregoing provisions of this section, the Commission may by such rules and regulations as it deems necessary or appropriate in the public interest or for the protection of investors, permit securities listed on any exchange at the time the registration of such exchange as a national securities exchange becomes effective, to be registered for a period ending not later than July 1, 1935, without complying with the provisions of this section.

(f) Unlisted trading privileges for security originally listed on another national exchange

(1)

(A) Notwithstanding the preceding subsections of this section, any national securities exchange, in accordance with the requirements of this subsection and the rules hereunder, may extend unlisted trading privileges to—

(i) any security that is listed and registered on a national securities exchange, subject to subparagraph (B); and

(ii) any security that is otherwise registered pursuant to this section, or that would be required to be so registered except for the exemption from registration provided in subparagraph (B) or (G) of subsection (g)(2), subject to subparagraph (E) of this paragraph.

(B) A national securities exchange may not extend unlisted trading privileges to a security described in subparagraph (A)(i) during such interval, if any, after the commencement of an initial public offering of such security, as is or may be required pursuant to subparagraph (C).

(C) Not later than 180 days after October 22, 1994, the Commission shall prescribe, by rule or regulation, the duration of the interval referred to in subparagraph (B), if any, as the Commission determines to be necessary or appropriate for the maintenance of fair and orderly markets, the protection of investors and the public interest, or otherwise in furtherance of the purposes of this chapter. Until the earlier of the effective date of such rule or regulation or 240 days after October 22, 1994, such interval shall begin at the opening of trading on the day on which such security commences trading on the national securities exchange with which such security is registered and end at the conclusion of the next day of trading.

(D) The Commission may prescribe, by rule or regulation such additional procedures or requirements for extending unlisted trading privileges to any security as the Commission deems necessary or appropriate for the maintenance of fair and orderly markets, the protection of investors and the public interest, or otherwise in furtherance of the purposes of this chapter.

(E) No extension of unlisted trading privileges to securities described in subparagraph (A)(ii) may occur except pursuant to a rule, regulation, or order of the Commission approving such extension or extensions. In promulgating such rule or regulation or in issuing such order, the Commission—

(i) shall find that such extension or extensions of unlisted trading privileges is consistent with the maintenance of fair and orderly markets, the protection of investors and the public interest, and otherwise in furtherance of the purposes of this chapter;

(ii) shall take account of the public trading activity in such securities, the character of such trading, the impact of such extension on the existing markets for such securities, and the desirability of removing impediments to and the progress that has been made toward the development of a national market system; and

(iii) shall not permit a national securities exchange to extend unlisted trading privileges to such securities if any rule of such national securities exchange would unreasonably impair the ability of a dealer to solicit or effect transactions in such securities for its own account, or would unreasonably restrict competition among dealers in such securities or between such dealers acting in the capacity of market makers who are specialists and such dealers who are not specialists.

(F) An exchange may continue to extend unlisted trading privileges in accordance with this paragraph only if the exchange and the subject security continue to satisfy the requirements for eligibility under this paragraph, including any rules and regulations issued by the Commission pursuant to this paragraph, except that unlisted trading privileges may continue with regard to securities which had been admitted on such exchange prior to July 1, 1964, notwithstanding the failure to satisfy such requirements. If unlisted trading privileges in a security are discontinued pursuant to this subparagraph, the exchange shall cease trading in that security, unless the exchange and the subject security thereafter satisfy the requirements of this paragraph and the rules issued hereunder.

(G) For purposes of this paragraph—

(i) a security is the subject of an initial public offering if—

(I) the offering of the subject security is registered under the Securities Act of 1933 [15 U.S.C. 77a et seq.]; and

(II) the issuer of the security, prior to filing the registration statement with respect to the offering, was not subject to the reporting requirements of section 78m or 78o(d) of this title; and

(ii) an initial public offering of such security commences at the opening of trading on the day on which such security commences trading on the national securities exchange with which such security is registered.

(2)

(A) At any time within 60 days of commencement of trading on an exchange of a security pursuant to unlisted trading privileges, the Commission may summarily suspend such unlisted trading privileges on the exchange. Such suspension shall not be reviewable under section 78y of this title and shall not be deemed to be a final agency action for purposes of section 704 of title 5. Upon such suspension—

(i) the exchange shall cease trading in the security by the close of business on the date of such suspension, or at such time as the Commission may prescribe by rule or order for the maintenance of fair and orderly markets, the protection of investors and the public interest, or otherwise in furtherance of the purposes of this chapter; and

(ii) if the exchange seeks to extend unlisted trading privileges to the security, the exchange shall file an application to reinstate its ability to do so with the Commission pursuant to such procedures as the Commission may prescribe by rule or order for the maintenance of fair and orderly markets, the protection of investors and the public interest, or otherwise in furtherance of the purposes of this chapter.

(B) A suspension under subparagraph (A) shall remain in effect until the Commission, by order, grants approval of an application to reinstate, as described in subparagraph (A)(ii).

(C) A suspension under subparagraph (A) shall not affect the validity or force of an extension of unlisted trading privileges in effect prior to such suspension.

(D) The Commission shall not approve an application by a national securities exchange to reinstate its ability to extend unlisted trading privileges to a security unless the Commission finds, after notice and opportunity for hearing, that the extension of unlisted trading privileges pursuant to such application is consistent with the maintenance of fair and orderly markets, the protection of investors and the public interest, and otherwise in furtherance of the purposes of this chapter. If the application is made to reinstate unlisted trading privileges to a security described in paragraph (1)(A)(ii), the Commission—

(i) shall take account of the public trading activity in such security, the character of such trading, the impact of such extension on the existing markets for such a security, and the desirability of removing impediments to and the progress that has been made toward the development of a national market system; and

(ii) shall not grant any such application if any rule of the national securities exchange making application under this subsection would unreasonably impair the ability of a dealer to solicit or effect transactions in such security for its own account, or would unreasonably restrict competition among dealers in such security or between such dealers acting in the capacity of marketmakers who are specialists and such dealers who are not specialists.

(3) Notwithstanding paragraph (2), the Commission shall by rules and regulations suspend unlisted trading privileges in whole or in part for any or all classes of securities for a period not exceeding twelve months, if it deems such suspension necessary or appropriate in the public interest or for the protection of investors or to prevent evasion of the purposes of this chapter.

(4) On the application of the issuer of any security for which unlisted trading privileges on any exchange have been continued or extended pursuant to this subsection, or of any broker or dealer who makes or creates a market for such security, or of any other person having a bona fide interest in the question of termination or suspension of such unlisted trading privileges, or on its own motion, the Commission shall by order terminate, or suspend for a period not exceeding twelve months, such unlisted trading privileges for such security if the Commission finds, after appropriate notice and opportunity for hearing, that such termination or suspension is necessary or appropriate in the public interest or for the protection of investors.

(5) In any proceeding under this subsection in which appropriate notice and opportunity for hearing are required, notice of not less than ten days to the applicant in such proceeding, to the issuer of the security involved, to the exchange which is seeking to continue or extend or has continued or extended unlisted trading privileges for such security, and to the exchange, if any, on which such security is listed and registered, shall be deemed adequate notice, and any broker or dealer who makes or creates a market for such security, and any other person having a bona fide interest in such proceeding, shall upon application be entitled to be heard.

(6) Any security for which unlisted trading privileges are continued or extended pursuant to this subsection shall be deemed to be registered on a national securities exchange within the meaning of this chapter. The powers and duties of the Commission under this chapter shall be applicable to the rules of an exchange in respect of any such security. The Commission may, by such rules and regulations as it deems necessary or appropriate in the public interest or for the protection of investors, either unconditionally or upon specified terms and conditions, or for stated periods, exempt such securities from the operation of any provision of section 78m, 78n, or 78p of this title.

(g) Registration of securities by issuer; exemptions

(1) Every issuer engaged in interstate commerce, or in a business affecting interstate commerce, or whose securities are traded by use of the mails or any means or instrumentality of interstate commerce shall—

(A) within 120 days after the last day of its first fiscal year ended on which the issuer has total assets exceeding $10,000,000 and a class of equity security (other than an exempted security) held of record by either—

(i) 2,000 persons, or

(ii) 500 persons who are not accredited investors (as such term is defined by the Commission), and

(B) in the case of an issuer that is a bank, a savings and loan holding company (as defined in section 1467a of title 12), or a bank holding company, as such term is defined in section 1841 of title 12, not later than 120 days after the last day of its first fiscal year ended after the effective date of this subsection, on which the issuer has total assets exceeding $10,000,000 and a class of equity security (other than an exempted security) held of record by 2,000 or more persons, register such security by filing with the Commission a registration statement (and such copies thereof as the Commission may require) with respect to such security containing such information and documents as the Commission may specify comparable to that which is required in an application to register a security pursuant to subsection (b) of this section. Each such registration statement shall become effective sixty days after filing with the Commission or within such shorter period as the Commission may direct. Until such registration statement becomes effective it shall not be deemed filed for the purposes of section 78r of this title. Any issuer may register any class of equity security not required to be registered by filing a registration statement pursuant to the provisions of this paragraph. The Commission is authorized to extend the date upon which any issuer or class of issuers is required to register a security pursuant to the provisions of this paragraph.

(2) The provisions of this subsection shall not apply in respect of—

(A) any security listed and registered on a national securities exchange.

(B) any security issued by an investment company registered pursuant to section 80a–8 of this title.

(C) any security, other than permanent stock, guaranty stock, permanent reserve stock, or any similar certificate evidencing nonwithdrawable capital, issued by a savings and loan association, building and loan association, cooperative bank, homestead association, or similar institution, which is supervised and examined by State or Federal authority having supervision over any such institution.

(D) any security of an issuer organized and operated exclusively for religious, educational, benevolent, fraternal, charitable, or reformatory purposes and not for pecuniary profit, and no part of the net earnings of which inures to the benefit of any private shareholder or individual; or any security of a fund that is excluded from the definition of an investment company under section 80a–3(c)(10)(B) of this title.

(E) any security of an issuer which is a "cooperative association" as defined in the Agricultural Marketing Act, approved June 15, 1929, as amended [12 U.S.C. 1141 et seq.], or a federation of such cooperative associations, if such federation possesses no greater powers or purposes than cooperative associations so defined.

(F) any security issued by a mutual or cooperative organization which supplies a commodity or service primarily for the benefit of its members and operates not for pecuniary profit, but only if the security is part of a class issuable only to persons who purchase commodities or services from the issuer, the security is transferable only to a successor in interest or occupancy of premises serviced or to be served by the issuer, and no dividends are payable to the holder of the security.

(G) any security issued by an insurance company if all of the following conditions are met:

    (i) Such insurance company is required to and does file an annual statement with the Commissioner of Insurance (or other officer or agency performing a similar function) of its domiciliary State, and such annual statement conforms to that prescribed by the National Association of Insurance Commissioners or in the determination of such State commissioner, officer or agency substantially conforms to that so prescribed.

    (ii) Such insurance company is subject to regulation by its domiciliary State of proxies, consents, or authorizations in respect of securities issued by such company and such regulation conforms to that prescribed by the National Association of Insurance Commissioners.

    (iii) After July 1, 1966, the purchase and sales of securities issued by such insurance company by beneficial owners, directors, or officers of such company are subject to regulation (including reporting) by its domiciliary State substantially in the manner provided in section 78p of this title.

(H) any interest or participation in any collective trust funds maintained by a bank or in a separate account maintained by an insurance company which interest or participation is issued in connection with (i) a stock-bonus, pension, or profit-sharing plan which meets the requirements for qualification under section 401 of title 26, (ii) an annuity plan which meets the requirements for deduction of the employer's contribution under section 404(a)(2) of title 26, or (iii) a church plan, company, or account that is excluded from the definition of an investment company under section 80a–3(c)(14) of this title.

(3) The Commission may by rules or regulations or, on its own motion, after notice and opportunity for hearing, by order, exempt from this subsection any security of a foreign issuer, including any certificate of deposit for such a security, if the Commission finds that such exemption is in the public interest and is consistent with the protection of investors.

(4) Registration of any class of security pursuant to this subsection shall be terminated ninety days, or such shorter period as the Commission may determine, after the issuer files a certification with the Commission that the number of holders of record of such class of security is reduced to less than 300 persons, or, in the case of a bank, a savings and loan holding company (as defined in section 1467a of title 12), or a bank holding company, as such term is defined in section 1841 of title 12, 1,200 persons persons.[1] The Commission shall after notice and opportunity for hearing deny termination of registration if it finds that the certification is untrue. Termination of registration shall be deferred pending final determination on the question of denial.

(5) For the purposes of this subsection the term "class" shall include all securities of an issuer which are of substantially similar character and the holders of which enjoy substantially similar rights and privileges. The Commission may for the purpose of this subsection define by rules and regulations the terms "total assets" and "held of record" as it deems necessary or appropriate in the public interest or for the protection of investors in order to prevent circumvention of the provisions of this subsection. For purposes of this subsection, a security futures product shall not be considered a class of equity security of the issuer of the securities underlying the security futures product. For purposes of determining whether an issuer is required to register a security with the Commission pursuant to paragraph (1), the definition of "held of record" shall not include securities held by persons who received the securities pursuant to an employee

compensation plan in transactions exempted from the registration requirements of section 5 of the Securities Act of 1933 [15 U.S.C. 77e].

(6) Exclusion for holding certain securities.—

The Commission shall, by rule, exempt, conditionally or unconditionally, securities acquired pursuant to an offering made under section 4(6) [2] of the Securities Act of 1933 [15 U.S.C. 77d(a)(6)] from the provisions of this subsection.

(h) Exemption by rules and regulations from certain provisions of section

The Commission may by rules and regulations, or upon application of an interested person, by order, after notice and opportunity for hearing, exempt in whole or in part any issuer or class of issuers from the provisions of subsection (g) of this section or from section 78m, 78n, or 78o(d) of this title or may exempt from section 78p of this title any officer, director, or beneficial owner of securities of any issuer, any security of which is required to be registered pursuant to subsection (g) hereof, upon such terms and conditions and for such period as it deems necessary or appropriate, if the Commission finds, by reason of the number of public investors, amount of trading interest in the securities, the nature and extent of the activities of the issuer, income or assets of the issuer, or otherwise, that such action is not inconsistent with the public interest or the protection of investors. The Commission may, for the purposes of any of the above-mentioned sections or subsections of this chapter, classify issuers and prescribe requirements appropriate for each such class.

(i) Securities issued by banks

In respect of any securities issued by banks and savings associations the deposits of which are insured in accordance with the Federal Deposit Insurance Act [12 U.S.C. 1811 et seq.], the powers, functions, and duties vested in the Commission to administer and enforce this section and sections 78j–1(m), 78m, 78n(a), 78n(c), 78n(d), 78n(f), and 78p of this title, and sections 7241, 7242, 7243, 7244, 7261(b), 7262, 7264, and 7265 of this title, (1) with respect to national banks and Federal savings associations, the accounts of which are insured by the Federal Deposit Insurance Corporation [3] are vested in the Comptroller of the Currency, (2) with respect to all other member banks of the Federal Reserve System are vested in the Board of Governors of the Federal Reserve System, and (3) with respect to all other insured banks and State savings associations, the accounts of which are insured by the Federal Deposit Insurance Corporation, are vested in the Federal Deposit Insurance Corporation. The Comptroller of the Currency, the Board of Governors of the Federal Reserve System, and the Federal Deposit Insurance Corporation shall have the power to make such rules and regulations as may be necessary for the execution of the functions vested in them as provided in this subsection. In carrying out their responsibilities under this subsection, the agencies named in the first sentence of this subsection shall issue substantially similar regulations to regulations and rules issued by the Commission under this section and sections 78j–1(m), 78m, 78n(a), 78n(c), 78n(d), 78n(f), and 78p of this title, and sections 7241, 7242, 7243, 7244, 7261(b), 7262, 7264, and 7265 of this title, unless they find that implementation of substantially similar regulations with respect to insured banks and insured institutions are not necessary or appropriate in the public interest or for protection of investors, and publish such findings, and the detailed reasons therefor, in the Federal Register. Such regulations of the above-named agencies, or the reasons for failure to publish such substantially similar regulations to those of the Commission, shall be published in the Federal Register within 120 days of October 28, 1974, and, thereafter, within 60 days of any changes made by the Commission in its relevant regulations and rules.

(j) Denial, suspension, or revocation of registration; notice and hearing

The Commission is authorized, by order, as it deems necessary or appropriate for the protection of investors to deny, to suspend the effective date of, to suspend for a period not exceeding twelve months, or to revoke the registration of a security, if the Commission finds, on the record after notice and opportunity for hearing, that the issuer, of such security has failed to comply with any provision of this chapter or the rules and regulations thereunder. No member of a national securities exchange, broker, or dealer shall make use of the mails or any means or instrumentality of interstate commerce to effect any transaction in, or to induce the purchase or sale of, any security the registration of which has been and is suspended or revoked pursuant to the preceding sentence.

(k) Trading suspensions; emergency authority
  (1) Trading suspensions. If in its opinion the public interest and the protection of investors so require, the Commission is authorized by order—
    (A) summarily to suspend trading in any security (other than an exempted security) for a period not exceeding 10 business days, and
    (B) summarily to suspend all trading on any national securities exchange or otherwise, in securities other than exempted securities, for a period not exceeding 90 calendar days.
    The action described in subparagraph (B) shall not take effect unless the Commission notifies the President of its decision and the President notifies the Commission that the President does not disapprove of such decision. If the actions described in subparagraph (A) or (B) involve a security futures product, the Commission shall consult with and consider the views of the Commodity Futures Trading Commission.
  (2) Emergency orders
    (A) In general the Commission, in an emergency, may by order summarily take such action to alter, supplement, suspend, or impose requirements or restrictions with respect to any matter or action subject to regulation by the Commission or a self-regulatory organization under the securities laws, as the Commission determines is necessary in the public interest and for the protection of investors—
      (i) to maintain or restore fair and orderly securities markets (other than markets in exempted securities);
      (ii) to ensure prompt, accurate, and safe clearance and settlement of transactions in securities (other than exempted securities); or
      (iii) to reduce, eliminate, or prevent the substantial disruption by the emergency of—
        (I) securities markets (other than markets in exempted securities), investment companies, or any other significant portion or segment of such markets; or
        (II) the transmission or processing of securities transactions (other than transactions in exempted securities).
    (B) Effective period
    An order of the Commission under this paragraph shall continue in effect for the period specified by the Commission, and may be extended. Except as provided in subparagraph (C), an order of the Commission under this paragraph may not continue in effect for more than 10 business days, including extensions.
    (C) Extension
    An order of the Commission under this paragraph may be extended to continue in effect for more than 10 business days if, at the time of the extension, the Commission finds that the emergency still exists and determines that the continuation of the order beyond 10 business days is necessary in the public interest and for the protection of investors to attain an objective described in clause (i), (ii), or (iii) of subparagraph (A). In no event shall an order of the Commission under this paragraph continue in effect for more than 30 calendar days.
    (D) Security futures
    If the actions described in subparagraph (A) involve a security futures product, the Commission shall consult with and consider the views of the Commodity Futures Trading Commission.
    (E) Exemption. In exercising its authority under this paragraph, the Commission shall not be required to comply with the provisions of—
      (I) section 78s(c) of this title; or
      (ii) section 553 of title 5.
  (3) Termination of emergency actions by President
  The President may direct that action taken by the Commission under paragraph (1)(B) or paragraph (2) of this subsection shall not continue in effect.
  (4) Compliance with orders
  No member of a national securities exchange, broker, or dealer shall make use of the mails or any means

or instrumentality of interstate commerce to effect any transaction in, or to induce the purchase or sale of, any security in contravention of an order of the Commission under this subsection unless such order has been stayed, modified, or set aside as provided in paragraph (5) of this subsection or has ceased to be effective upon direction of the President as provided in paragraph (3).

(5) Limitations on review of orders

An order of the Commission pursuant to this subsection shall be subject to review only as provided in section 78y(a) of this title. Review shall be based on an examination of all the information before the Commission at the time such order was issued. The reviewing court shall not enter a stay, writ of mandamus, or similar relief unless the court finds, after notice and hearing before a panel of the court, that the Commission's action is arbitrary, capricious, an abuse of discretion, or otherwise not in accordance with law.

(6) Consultation

Prior to taking any action described in paragraph (1)(B), the Commission shall consult with and consider the views of the Secretary of the Treasury, the Board of Governors of the Federal Reserve System, and the Commodity Futures Trading Commission, unless such consultation is impracticable in light of the emergency.

(7) Definition. For purposes of this subsection, the term "emergency" means—

(A) a major market disturbance characterized by or constituting—

(i) sudden and excessive fluctuations of securities prices generally, or a substantial threat thereof, that threaten fair and orderly markets; or

(ii) a substantial disruption of the safe or efficient operation of the national system for clearance and settlement of transactions in securities, or a substantial threat thereof; or

(B) a major disturbance that substantially disrupts, or threatens to substantially disrupt—

(i) the functioning of securities markets, investment companies, or any other significant portion or segment of the securities markets; or

(ii) the transmission or processing of securities transactions.

(l) Issuance of any security in contravention of rules and regulations; application to annuity contracts and variable life policies

It shall be unlawful for an issuer, any class of whose securities is registered pursuant to this section or would be required to be so registered except for the exemption from registration provided by subsection (g)(2)(B) or (g)(2)(G) of this section, by the use of any means or instrumentality of interstate commerce, or of the mails, to issue, either originally or upon transfer, any of such securities in a form or with a format which contravenes such rules and regulations as the Commission may prescribe as necessary or appropriate for the prompt and accurate clearance and settlement of transactions in securities. The provisions of this subsection shall not apply to variable annuity contracts or variable life policies issued by an insurance company or its separate accounts.

---

16. SEC Rules and Regulations, Securities Exchange Act of 1934: Section 15 – Registration and Regulation of Brokers and Dealers

(a) Registration of all persons utilizing exchange facilities to effect transactions; exemptions

(1) It shall be unlawful for any broker or dealer which is either a person other than a natural person or a natural person not associated with a broker or dealer which is a person other than a natural person (other

than such a broker or dealer whose business is exclusively intrastate and who does not make use of any facility of a national securities exchange) to make use of the mails or any means or instrumentality of interstate commerce to effect any transactions in, or to induce or attempt to induce the purchase or sale of, any security (other than an exempted security or commercial paper, bankers' acceptances, or commercial bills) unless such broker or dealer is registered in accordance with subsection (b) of this section.

(2) The Commission, by rule or order, as it deems consistent with the public interest and the protection of investors, may conditionally or unconditionally exempt from paragraph (1) of this subsection any broker or dealer or class of brokers or dealers specified in such rule or order.

(b) Manner of registration of brokers and dealers

(1) A broker or dealer may be registered by filing with the Commission an application for registration in such form and containing such information and documents concerning such broker or dealer and any persons associated with such broker or dealer as the Commission, by rule, may prescribe as necessary or appropriate in the public interest or for the protection of investors. Within forty-five days of the date of the filing of such application (or within such longer period as to which the applicant consents), the Commission shall—

(A) by order grant registration, or

(B) institute proceedings to determine whether registration should be denied. Such proceedings shall include notice of the grounds for denial under consideration and opportunity for hearing and shall be concluded within one hundred twenty days of the date of the filing of the application for registration. At the conclusion of such proceedings, the Commission, by order, shall grant or deny such registration. The Commission may extend the time for conclusion of such proceedings for up to ninety days if it finds good cause for such extension and publishes its reasons for so finding or for such longer period as to which the applicant consents.

The Commission shall grant such registration if the Commission finds that the requirements of this section are satisfied. The order granting registration shall not be effective until such broker or dealer has become a member of a registered securities association, or until such broker or dealer has become a member of a national securities exchange, if such broker or dealer effects transactions solely on that exchange, unless the Commission has exempted such broker or dealer, by rule or order, from such membership. The Commission shall deny such registration if it does not make such a finding or if it finds that if the applicant were so registered, its registration would be subject to suspension or revocation under paragraph (4) of this subsection.

(2)

(A) An application for registration of a broker or dealer to be formed or organized may be made by a broker or dealer to which the broker or dealer to be formed or organized is to be the successor. Such application, in such form as the Commission, by rule, may prescribe, shall contain such information and documents concerning the applicant, the successor, and any persons associated with the applicant or the successor, as the Commission, by rule, may prescribe as necessary or appropriate in the public interest or for the protection of investors. The grant or denial of registration to such an applicant shall be in accordance with the procedures set forth in paragraph (1) of this subsection. If the Commission grants such registration, the registration shall terminate on the forty-fifth day after the effective date thereof, unless prior thereto the successor shall, in accordance with such rules and regulations as the Commission may prescribe, adopt the application for registration as its own.

(B) Any person who is a broker or dealer solely by reason of acting as a municipal securities dealer or municipal securities broker, who so acts through a separately identifiable department or division, and who so acted in such a manner on June 4, 1975, may, in accordance with such terms and conditions as the Commission, by rule, prescribes as necessary and appropriate in the public interest and for the protection of investors, register such separately identifiable department or division in accordance with this subsection. If any such department or division is so registered, the department or division and not such person himself shall be the broker or dealer for purposes of this chapter.

(C) Within six months of the date of the granting of registration to a broker or dealer, the Commission, or upon the authorization and direction of the Commission, a registered securities association or national securities exchange of which such broker or dealer is a member, shall conduct an inspection of the broker or dealer to determine whether it is operating in conformity with the provisions of this chapter and the rules and regulations thereunder: Provided, however, That the Commission may delay such inspection of any class of brokers or dealers for a period not to exceed six months.

(3) Any provision of this chapter (other than section 78e of this title and subsection (a) of this section) which prohibits any act, practice, or course of business if the mails or any means or instrumentality of interstate commerce is used in connection therewith shall also prohibit any such act, practice, or course of business by any registered broker or dealer or any person acting on behalf of such a broker or dealer, irrespective of any use of the mails or any means or instrumentality of interstate commerce in connection therewith.

(4) The Commission, by order, shall censure, place limitations on the activities, functions, or operations of, suspend for a period not exceeding twelve months, or revoke the registration of any broker or dealer if it finds, on the record after notice and opportunity for hearing, that such censure, placing of limitations, suspension, or revocation is in the public interest and that such broker or dealer, whether prior or subsequent to becoming such, or any person associated with such broker or dealer, whether prior or subsequent to becoming so associated—

(A) has willfully made or caused to be made in any application for registration or report required to be filed with the Commission or with any other appropriate regulatory agency under this chapter, or in any proceeding before the Commission with respect to registration, any statement which was at the time and in the light of the circumstances under which it was made false or misleading with respect to any material fact, or has omitted to state in any such application or report any material fact which is required to be stated therein.

(B) has been convicted within ten years preceding the filing of any application for registration or at any time thereafter of any felony or misdemeanor or of a substantially equivalent crime by a foreign court of competent jurisdiction which the Commission finds—

(i) involves the purchase or sale of any security, the taking of a false oath, the making of a false report, bribery, perjury, burglary, any substantially equivalent activity however denominated by the laws of the relevant foreign government, or conspiracy to commit any such offense;

(ii) arises out of the conduct of the business of a broker, dealer, municipal securities dealer municipal advisor,,[1] government securities broker, government securities dealer, investment adviser, bank, insurance company, fiduciary, transfer agent, nationally recognized statistical rating organization, foreign person performing a function substantially equivalent to any of the above, or entity or person required to be registered under the Commodity Exchange Act (7 U.S.C. 1 et seq.) or any substantially equivalent foreign statute or regulation;

(iii) involves the larceny, theft, robbery, extortion, forgery, counterfeiting, fraudulent concealment, embezzlement, fraudulent conversion, or misappropriation of funds, or securities, or substantially equivalent activity however denominated by the laws of the relevant foreign government; or

(iv) involves the violation of section 152, 1341, 1342, or 1343 or chapter 25 or 47 of title 18 or a violation of a substantially equivalent foreign statute.

(C) is permanently or temporarily enjoined by order, judgment, or decree of any court of competent jurisdiction from acting as an investment adviser, underwriter, broker, dealer, municipal securities dealer municipal advisor, government securities broker, government securities dealer, security-based swap dealer, major security-based swap participant, transfer agent, nationally recognized statistical rating organization, foreign person performing a function substantially equivalent to any of the above, or entity or person required to be registered under the Commodity Exchange Act or any substantially equivalent foreign statute or regulation, or as an affiliated person or employee of any investment company, bank, insurance company, foreign entity substantially equivalent to any of the above, or entity or person required to be registered under the Commodity Exchange Act or any substantially equivalent foreign statute or regulation, or from engaging in or continuing any conduct or practice in connection with any such activity, or in connection with the purchase or sale of any security.

(D) has willfully violated any provision of the Securities Act of 1933 [15 U.S.C. 77a et seq.], the Investment Advisers Act of 1940 [15 U.S.C. 80b–1 et seq.], the Investment Company Act of 1940 [15 U.S.C. 80a–1 et seq.], the Commodity Exchange Act, this chapter, the rules or regulations under any of such statutes, or the rules of the Municipal Securities Rulemaking Board, or is unable to comply with any such provision.

(E) has willfully aided, abetted, counseled, commanded, induced, or procured the violation by any other person of any provision of the Securities Act of 1933, the Investment Advisers Act of 1940, the Investment Company Act of 1940, the Commodity Exchange Act, this chapter, the rules or regulations under any of such statutes, or the rules of the Municipal Securities Rulemaking Board, or has failed reasonably to supervise, with a view to preventing violations of the provisions of such statutes, rules, and regulations, another person who commits such a violation, if such other person is subject to his supervision. For the purposes of this subparagraph (E) no person shall be deemed to have failed reasonably to supervise any other person, if—

  (i) there have been established procedures, and a system for applying such procedures, which would reasonably be expected to prevent and detect, insofar as practicable, any such violation by such other person, and

  (ii) such person has reasonably discharged the duties and obligations incumbent upon him by reason of such procedures and system without reasonable cause to believe that such procedures and system were not being complied with.

(F) is subject to any order of the Commission barring or suspending the right of the person to be associated with a broker, dealer, security-based swap dealer, or a major security-based swap participant;

(G) has been found by a foreign financial regulatory authority to have—

  (i) made or caused to be made in any application for registration or report required to be filed with a foreign financial regulatory authority, or in any proceeding before a foreign financial regulatory authority with respect to registration, any statement that was at the time and in the light of the circumstances under which it was made false or misleading with respect to any material fact, or has omitted to state in any application or report to the foreign financial regulatory authority any material fact that is required to be stated therein;

  (ii) violated any foreign statute or regulation regarding transactions in securities, or contracts of sale of a commodity for future delivery, traded on or subject to the rules of a contract market or any board of trade;

  (iii) aided, abetted, counseled, commanded, induced, or procured the violation by any person of any provision of any statutory provisions enacted by a foreign government, or rules or regulations thereunder, empowering a foreign financial regulatory authority regarding transactions in securities, or contracts of sale of a commodity for future delivery, traded on or subject to the rules of a contract market or any board of trade, or has been found, by a foreign financial regulatory authority, to have failed reasonably to supervise, with a view to preventing violations of such statutory provisions, rules, and regulations, another person who commits such a violation, if such other person is subject to his supervision; or

(H) is subject to any final order of a State securities commission (or any agency or officer performing like functions), State authority that supervises or examines banks, savings associations, or credit unions, State insurance commission (or any agency or office performing like functions), an appropriate Federal banking agency (as defined in section 3 of the Federal Deposit Insurance Act (12 U.S.C. 1813(q))), or the National Credit Union Administration, that—

  (i) bars such person from association with an entity regulated by such commission, authority, agency, or officer, or from engaging in the business of securities, insurance, banking, savings association activities, or credit union activities; or

    (ii) constitutes a final order based on violations of any laws or regulations that prohibit fraudulent, manipulative, or deceptive conduct.

(5) Pending final determination whether any registration under this subsection shall be revoked, the Commission, by order, may suspend such registration, if such suspension appears to the Commission, after notice and opportunity for hearing, to be necessary or appropriate in the public interest or for the protection of investors. Any registered broker or dealer may, upon such terms and conditions as the Commission deems necessary or appropriate in the public interest or for the protection of investors, withdraw from registration by filing a written notice of withdrawal with the Commission. If the Commission finds that any registered broker or dealer is no longer in existence or has ceased to do business as a broker or dealer, the Commission, by order, shall cancel the registration of such broker or dealer.

(6)

  (A) With respect to any person who is associated, who is seeking to become associated, or, at the time of the alleged misconduct, who was associated or was seeking to become associated with a broker or dealer, or any person participating, or, at the time of the alleged misconduct, who was participating, in an offering of any penny stock, the Commission, by order, shall censure, place limitations on the activities or functions of such person, or suspend for a period not exceeding 12 months, or bar any such person from being associated with a broker, dealer, investment adviser, municipal securities dealer, municipal advisor, transfer agent, or nationally recognized statistical rating organization, or from participating in an offering of penny stock, if the Commission finds, on the record after notice and opportunity for a hearing, that such censure, placing of limitations, suspension, or bar is in the public interest and that such person—

    (i) has committed or omitted any act, or is subject to an order or finding, enumerated in subparagraph (A), (D), (E), (H), or (G) of paragraph (4) of this subsection;

    (ii) has been convicted of any offense specified in subparagraph (B) of such paragraph (4) within 10 years of the commencement of the proceedings under this paragraph; or

    (iii) is enjoined from any action, conduct, or practice specified in subparagraph (C) of such paragraph (4).

  (B) It shall be unlawful—

    (i) for any person as to whom an order under subparagraph (A) is in effect, without the consent of the Commission, willfully to become, or to be, associated with a broker or dealer in contravention of such order, or to participate in an offering of penny stock in contravention of such order;

    (ii) for any broker or dealer to permit such a person, without the consent of the Commission, to become or remain, a person associated with the broker or dealer in contravention of such order, if such broker or dealer knew, or in the exercise of reasonable care should have known, of such order; or

    (iii) for any broker or dealer to permit such a person, without the consent of the Commission, to participate in an offering of penny stock in contravention of such order, if such broker or dealer knew, or in the exercise of reasonable care should have known, of such order and of such participation.

  (C) For purposes of this paragraph, the term "person participating in an offering of penny stock" includes any person acting as any promoter, finder, consultant, agent, or other person who engages in activities with a broker, dealer, or issuer for purposes of the issuance or trading in any penny stock, or inducing or attempting to induce the purchase or sale of any penny stock. The Commission may, by rule or regulation, define such term to include other activities, and may, by rule, regulation, or order, exempt any person or class of persons, in whole or in part, conditionally or unconditionally, from such term.

(7) No registered broker or dealer or government securities broker or government securities dealer registered (or required to register) under section 78o–5(a)(1)(A) of this title shall effect any transaction in, or induce the purchase or sale of, any security unless such broker or dealer meets such standards of operational capability and such broker or dealer and all natural persons associated with such broker or dealer meet such standards of training, experience, competence, and such other qualifications as the Commission finds necessary or appropriate in the public interest or for the protection of investors. The Commission shall establish such standards by rules and regulations, which may—

    (A) specify that all or any portion of such standards shall be applicable to any class of brokers and dealers and persons associated with brokers and dealers;

    (B) require persons in any such class to pass tests prescribed in accordance with such rules and regulations, which tests shall, with respect to any class of partners, officers, or supervisory employees (which latter term may be defined by the Commission's rules and regulations and as so defined shall include branch managers of brokers or dealers) engaged in the management of the broker or dealer, include questions relating to bookkeeping, accounting, internal control over cash and securities, supervision of employees, maintenance of records, and other appropriate matters; and

    (C) provide that persons in any such class other than brokers and dealers and partners, officers, and supervisory employees of brokers or dealers, may be qualified solely on the basis of compliance with such standards of training and such other qualifications as the Commission finds appropriate.

    The Commission, by rule, may prescribe reasonable fees and charges to defray its costs in carrying out this paragraph, including, but not limited to, fees for any test administered by it or under its direction. The Commission may cooperate with registered securities associations and national securities exchanges in devising and administering tests and may require registered brokers and dealers and persons associated with such brokers and dealers to pass tests administered by or on behalf of any such association or exchange and to pay such association or exchange reasonable fees or charges to defray the costs incurred by such association or exchange in administering such tests.

(8) It shall be unlawful for any registered broker or dealer to effect any transaction in, or induce or attempt to induce the purchase or sale of, any security (other than or [2] commercial paper, bankers' acceptances, or commercial bills), unless such broker or dealer is a member of a securities association registered pursuant to section 78o–3 of this title or effects transactions in securities solely on a national securities exchange of which it is a member.

(9) The Commission by rule or order, as it deems consistent with the public interest and the protection of investors, may conditionally or unconditionally exempt from paragraph (8) of this subsection any broker or dealer or class of brokers or dealers specified in such rule or order.

(10) For the purposes of determining whether a person is subject to a statutory disqualification under section 78f(c)(2), 78o–3(g)(2), or 78q–1(b)(4)(A) of this title, the term "Commission" in paragraph (4)(B) of this subsection shall mean "exchange", "association", or "clearing agency", respectively.

(11) Broker/dealer registration with respect to transactions in.—

    (A) Notice registration.—

        (i) Contents of notice.—

        Notwithstanding paragraphs (1) and (2), a broker or dealer required to register only because it effects transactions in security futures products on an exchange registered pursuant to section 78f(g) of this title may register for purposes of this section by filing with the Commission a written notice in such form and containing such information concerning such broker or dealer and any persons associated with such broker or dealer as the Commission, by rule, may prescribe as necessary or appropriate in the public interest or for the protection of investors. A broker or dealer may not register under this paragraph unless that broker or dealer is a member of a national securities association registered under section 78o–3(k) of this title.

        (ii) Immediate effectiveness.—

        Such registration shall be effective contemporaneously with the submission of notice, in written or electronic form, to the Commission, except that such registration shall not be effective if the registration would be subject to suspension or revocation under paragraph (4).

(iii) Suspension.—

Such registration shall be suspended immediately if a national securities association registered pursuant to section 78o–3(k) of this title suspends the membership of that broker or dealer.

(iv) Termination.—

Such registration shall be terminated immediately if any of the above stated conditions for registration set forth in this paragraph are no longer satisfied.

(B) Exemptions for registered brokers and dealers.—A broker or dealer registered pursuant to the requirements of subparagraph (A) shall be exempt from the following provisions of this chapter and the rules thereunder with respect to transactions in security futures products:

(i) Section 78h of this title.

(ii) Section 78k of this title.

(iii) Subsections (c)(3) and (c)(5) of this section.

(iv) Section 78o–4 of this title.

(v) Section 78o–5 of this title.

(vi) Subsections (d), (e), (f), (g), (h), and (i) [3] of section 78q of this title.

(12) Exemption for members.—

(A) Registration exemption.—A natural person shall be exempt from the registration requirements of this section if such person—

(i) is a member of a designated contract market registered with the Commission as an exchange pursuant to section 78f(g) of this title;

(ii) effects transactions only in securities on the exchange of which such person is a member; and

(iii) does not directly accept or solicit orders from public customers or provide advice to public customers in connection with the trading of security futures products.

(B) Other exemptions.—A natural person exempt from registration pursuant to subparagraph (A) shall also be exempt from the following provisions of this chapter and the rules thereunder:

(i) Section 78h of this title.

(ii) Section 78k of this title.

(iii) Subsections (c)(3), (c)(5), and (e) of this section.

(iv) Section 78o–4 of this title.

(v) Section 78o–5 of this title.

(vi) Subsections (d), (e), (f), (g), (h), and (i) 3 of section 78q of this title.

(c) Use of manipulative or deceptive devices; contravention of rules and regulations

(1)

(A) No broker or dealer shall make use of the mails or any means or instrumentality of interstate commerce to effect any transaction in, or to induce or attempt to induce the purchase or sale of, any security (other than commercial paper, bankers' acceptances, or commercial bills), or any security-based swap agreement by means of any manipulative, deceptive, or other fraudulent device or contrivance.

(B) No broker, dealer, or municipal securities dealer shall make use of the mails or any means or instrumentality of interstate commerce to effect any transaction in, or to induce or attempt to induce the purchase or sale of, any municipal security or any security-based swap agreement involving a municipal security by means of any manipulative, deceptive, or other fraudulent device or contrivance.

(C) No government securities broker or government securities dealer shall make use of the mails or any means or instrumentality of interstate commerce to effect any transaction in, or to induce or to attempt to induce the purchase or sale of, any government security or any security-based swap agreement involving a government security by means of any manipulative, deceptive, or other fraudulent device or contrivance.

(2)

(A) No broker or dealer shall make use of the mails or any means or instrumentality of interstate commerce to effect any transaction in, or to induce or attempt to induce the purchase or sale of, any security (other than an exempted security or commercial paper, bankers' acceptances, or commercial bills) otherwise than on a national securities exchange of which it is a member, in connection with which such broker or dealer engages in any fraudulent, deceptive, or manipulative act or practice, or makes any fictitious quotation.

(B) No broker, dealer, or municipal securities dealer shall make use of the mails or any means or instrumentality of interstate commerce to effect any transaction in, or to induce or attempt to induce the purchase or sale of, any municipal security in connection with which such broker, dealer, or municipal securities dealer engages in any fraudulent, deceptive, or manipulative act or practice, or makes any fictitious quotation.

(C) No government securities broker or government securities dealer shall make use of the mails or any means or instrumentality of interstate commerce to effect any transaction in, or induce or attempt to induce the purchase or sale of, any government security in connection with which such government securities broker or government securities dealer engages in any fraudulent, deceptive, or manipulative act or practice, or makes any fictitious quotation.

(D) The Commission shall, for the purposes of this paragraph, by rules and regulations define, and prescribe means reasonably designed to prevent, such acts and practices as are fraudulent, deceptive, or manipulative and such quotations as are fictitious.

(E) The Commission shall, prior to adopting any rule or regulation under subparagraph (C), consult with and consider the views of the Secretary of the Treasury and each appropriate regulatory agency. If the Secretary of the Treasury or any appropriate regulatory agency comments in writing on a proposed rule or regulation of the Commission under such subparagraph (C) that has been published for comment, the Commission shall respond in writing to such written comment before adopting the proposed rule. If the Secretary of the Treasury determines, and notifies the Commission, that such rule or regulation, if implemented, would, or as applied does (i) adversely affect the liquidity or efficiency of the market for government securities; or (ii) impose any burden on competition not necessary or appropriate in furtherance of the purposes of this section, the Commission shall, prior to adopting the proposed rule or regulation, find that such rule or regulation is necessary and appropriate in furtherance of the purposes of this section notwithstanding the Secretary's determination.

(3)

(A) No broker or dealer (other than a government securities broker or government securities dealer, except a registered broker or dealer) shall make use of the mails or any means or instrumentality of interstate commerce to effect any transaction in, or to induce or attempt to induce the purchase or sale of, any security (other than an exempted security (except a government security) or commercial paper, bankers' acceptances, or commercial bills) in contravention of such rules and regulations as the Commission shall prescribe as necessary or appropriate in the public interest or for the protection of investors to provide safeguards with respect to the financial responsibility and related practices of brokers and dealers including, but not limited to, the acceptance of custody and use of customers' securities and the carrying and use of customers' deposits or credit balances. Such rules and regulations shall (A) require the maintenance of reserves with respect to customers' deposits or credit balances, and (B) no later than September 1, 1975, establish minimum financial responsibility requirements for all brokers and dealers.

(B) Consistent with this chapter, the Commission, in consultation with the Commodity Futures Trading Commission, shall issue such rules, regulations, or orders as are necessary to avoid duplicative or conflicting regulations applicable to any broker or dealer registered with the Commission pursuant to subsection (b) (except paragraph (11) thereof), that is also registered with the Commodity Futures Trading Commission pursuant to section 4f(a) of the Commodity Exchange Act [7 U.S.C. 6f(a)] (except paragraph (2) thereof), with respect to the application of: (i) the provisions of section 78h of this title, subsection (c)(3), and section 78q of this title and the rules and regulations thereunder related to the treatment of customer funds, securities, or property, maintenance of books and records, financial reporting, or other financial responsibility rules, involving security futures products; and (ii) similar provisions of the Commodity Exchange Act [7 U.S.C. 1 et seq.] and rules and regulations thereunder involving security futures products.

(C) Notwithstanding any provision of sections 2(a)(1)(C)(i) or 4d(a)(2) of the Commodity Exchange Act [7 U.S.C. 2(a)(1)(C)(i), 6d(a)(2)] and the rules and regulations thereunder, and pursuant to an exemption granted by the Commission under section 78mm of this title or pursuant to a rule or regulation, cash and securities may be held by a broker or dealer registered pursuant to subsection (b)(1) and also registered as a futures commission merchant pursuant to section 4f(a)(1) of the Commodity Exchange Act [7 U.S.C. 6f(a)(1)], in a portfolio margining account carried as a futures account subject to section 4d of the Commodity Exchange Act [7 U.S.C. 6d] and the rules and regulations thereunder, pursuant to a portfolio margining program approved by the Commodity Futures Trading Commission, and subject to subchapter IV of chapter 7 of title 11 and the rules and regulations thereunder. The Commission shall consult with the Commodity Futures Trading Commission to adopt rules to ensure that such transactions and accounts are subject to comparable requirements to the extent practicable for similar products.

(4) If the Commission finds, after notice and opportunity for a hearing, that any person subject to the provisions of section 78l, 78m, 78n of this title or subsection (d) or any rule or regulation thereunder has failed to comply with any such provision, rule, or regulation in any material respect, the Commission may publish its findings and issue an order requiring such person, and any person who was a cause of the failure to comply due to an act or omission the person knew or should have known would contribute to the failure to comply, to comply, or to take steps to effect compliance, with such provision or such rule or regulation thereunder upon such terms and conditions and within such time as the Commission may specify in such order.

(5) No dealer (other than a specialist registered on a national securities exchange) acting in the capacity of market maker or otherwise shall make use of the mails or any means or instrumentality of interstate commerce to effect any transaction in, or to induce or attempt to induce the purchase or sale of, any security (other than an exempted security or a municipal security) in contravention of such specified and appropriate standards with respect to dealing as the Commission, by rule, shall prescribe as necessary or appropriate in the public interest and for the protection of investors, to maintain fair and orderly markets, or to remove impediments to and perfect the mechanism of a national market system. Under the rules of the Commission a dealer in a security may be prohibited from acting as a broker in that security.

(6) No broker or dealer shall make use of the mails or any means or instrumentality of interstate commerce to effect any transaction in, or to induce or attempt to induce the purchase or sale of, any security (other than an exempted security, municipal security, commercial paper, bankers' acceptances, or commercial bills) in contravention of such rules and regulations as the Commission shall prescribe as necessary or appropriate in the public interest and for the protection of investors or to perfect or remove impediments to a national system for the prompt and accurate clearance and settlement of securities transactions, with respect to the time and method of, and the form and format of documents used in connection with, making settlements of and payments for transactions in securities, making transfers and deliveries of securities, and closing accounts. Nothing in this paragraph shall be construed (A) to affect the authority of the Board of Governors of the Federal Reserve System, pursuant to section 78g of this title, to prescribe rules and regulations for the purpose of preventing the excessive use of credit for the purchase or carrying of securities, or (B) to authorize the Commission to prescribe rules or regulations for such purpose.

(7) In connection with any bid for or purchase of a government security related to an offering of government securities by or on behalf of an issuer, no government securities broker, government securities dealer, or

bidder for or purchaser of securities in such offering shall knowingly or willfully make any false or misleading written statement or omit any fact necessary to make any written statement made not misleading.

(8) Prohibition of referral fees.—

No broker or dealer, or person associated with a broker or dealer, may solicit or accept, directly or indirectly, remuneration for assisting an attorney in obtaining the representation of any person in any private action arising under this chapter or under the Securities Act of 1933 [15 U.S.C. 77a et seq.].

(d) Supplementary and periodic information

(1) In general

Each issuer which has filed a registration statement containing an undertaking which is or becomes operative under this subsection as in effect prior to August 20, 1964, and each issuer which shall after such date file a registration statement which has become effective pursuant to the Securities Act of 1933, as amended [15 U.S.C. 77a et seq.], shall file with the Commission, in accordance with such rules and regulations as the Commission may prescribe as necessary or appropriate in the public interest or for the protection of investors, such supplementary and periodic information, documents, and reports as may be required pursuant to section 78m of this title in respect of a security registered pursuant to section 78l of this title. The duty to file under this subsection shall be automatically suspended if and so long as any issue of securities of such issuer is registered pursuant to section 78l of this title. The duty to file under this subsection shall also be automatically suspended as to any fiscal year, other than the fiscal year within which such registration statement became effective, if, at the beginning of such fiscal year, the securities of each class, other than any class of asset-backed securities, to which the registration statement relates are held of record by less than 300 persons, or, in the case of a bank, a savings and loan holding company (as defined in section 1467a of title 12), or a bank holding company, as such term is defined in section 1841 of title 12, 1,200 persons. For the purposes of this subsection, the term "class" shall be construed to include all securities of an issuer which are of substantially similar character and the holders of which enjoy substantially similar rights and privileges. The Commission may, for the purpose of this subsection, define by rules and regulations the term "held of record" as it deems necessary or appropriate in the public interest or for the protection of investors in order to prevent circumvention of the provisions of this subsection. Nothing in this subsection shall apply to securities issued by a foreign government or political subdivision thereof.

(2) Asset-backed securities

(A) Suspension of duty to file

The Commission may, by rule or regulation, provide for the suspension or termination of the duty to file under this subsection for any class of asset-backed security, on such terms and conditions and for such period or periods as the Commission deems necessary or appropriate in the public interest or for the protection of investors.

(B) Classification of issuers

The Commission may, for purposes of this subsection, classify issuers and prescribe requirements appropriate for each class of issuers of asset-backed securities.

(e) Notices to customers regarding securities lending

Every registered broker or dealer shall provide notice to its customers that they may elect not to allow their fully paid securities to be used in connection with short sales. If a broker or dealer uses a customer's securities in connection with short sales, the broker or dealer shall provide notice to its customer that the broker or dealer may receive compensation in connection with lending the customer's securities. The Commission, by rule, as it deems necessary or appropriate in the public interest and for the protection of investors, may prescribe the form, content, time, and manner of delivery of any notice required under this paragraph.

(f) Compliance with this chapter by members not required to be registered

The Commission, by rule, as it deems necessary or appropriate in the public interest and for the protection of investors or to assure equal regulation, may require any member of a national securities exchange not required to register under this section and any person associated with any such member to comply with any provision of this chapter (other than subsection (a)) or the rules or regulations thereunder which by its terms regulates or prohibits any act, practice, or course of business by a "broker or dealer" or "registered broker or dealer" or a "person associated with a broker or dealer," respectively.

(g) Prevention of misuse of material, nonpublic information

Every registered broker or dealer shall establish, maintain, and enforce written policies and procedures reasonably designed, taking into consideration the nature of such broker's or dealer's business, to prevent the misuse in violation of this chapter, or the rules or regulations thereunder, of material, nonpublic information by such broker or dealer or any person associated with such broker or dealer. The Commission, as it deems necessary or appropriate in the public interest or for the protection of investors, shall adopt rules or regulations to require specific policies or procedures reasonably designed to prevent misuse in violation of this chapter (or the rules or regulations thereunder) of material, nonpublic information.

(h) Requirements for transactions in penny stocks

(1) In general no broker or dealer shall make use of the mails or any means or instrumentality of interstate commerce to effect any transaction in, or to induce or attempt to induce the purchase or sale of, any penny stock by any customer except in accordance with the requirements of this subsection and the rules and regulations prescribed under this subsection.

(2) Risk disclosure with respect to penny stocks. Prior to effecting any transaction in any penny stock, a broker or dealer shall give the customer a risk disclosure document that—

(A) contains a description of the nature and level of risk in the market for penny stocks in both public offerings and secondary trading;

(B) contains a description of the broker's or dealer's duties to the customer and of the rights and remedies available to the customer with respect to violations of such duties or other requirements of Federal securities laws;

(C) contains a brief, clear, narrative description of a dealer market, including "bid" and "ask" prices for penny stocks and the significance of the spread between the bid and ask prices;

(D) contains the toll free telephone number for inquiries on disciplinary actions established pursuant to section 78o–3(i) of this title;

(E) defines significant terms used in the disclosure document or in the conduct of trading in penny stocks; and

(F) contains such other information, and is in such form (including language, type size, and format), as the Commission shall require by rule or regulation.

(3) Commission rules relating to disclosure. The Commission shall adopt rules setting forth additional standards for the disclosure by brokers and dealers to customers of information concerning transactions in penny stocks. Such rules—

(A) shall require brokers and dealers to disclose to each customer, prior to effecting any transaction in, and at the time of confirming any transaction with respect to any penny stock, in accordance with such procedures and methods as the Commission may require consistent with the public interest and the protection of investors—

(i) the bid and ask prices for penny stock, or such other information as the Commission may, by rule, require to provide customers with more useful and reliable information relating to the price of such stock;

(ii) the number of shares to which such bid and ask prices apply, or other comparable information relating to the depth and liquidity of the market for such stock; and

(iii) the amount and a description of any compensation that the broker or dealer and the associated person thereof will receive or has received in connection with such transaction;

(B) shall require brokers and dealers to provide, to each customer whose account with the broker or dealer contains penny stocks, a monthly statement indicating the market value of the penny stocks in that account or indicating that the market value of such stock cannot be determined because of the unavailability of firm quotes; and

(C) may, as the Commission finds necessary or appropriate in the public interest or for the protection of investors, require brokers and dealers to disclose to customers additional information concerning transactions in penny stocks.

(4) Exemptions

The Commission, as it determines consistent with the public interest and the protection of investors, may by rule, regulation, or order exempt in whole or in part, conditionally or unconditionally, any person or class of persons, or any transaction or class of transactions, from the requirements of this subsection. Such exemptions shall include an exemption for brokers and dealers based on the minimal percentage of the broker's or dealer's commissions, commission-equivalents, and markups received from transactions in penny stocks.

(5) Regulations

It shall be unlawful for any person to violate such rules and regulations as the Commission shall prescribe in the public interest or for the protection of investors or to maintain fair and orderly markets—

(A) as necessary or appropriate to carry out this subsection; or

(B) as reasonably designed to prevent fraudulent, deceptive, or manipulative acts and practices with respect to penny stocks.

(i) Limitations on State law

(1) Capital, margin, books and records, bonding, and reports

No law, rule, regulation, or order, or other administrative action of any State or political subdivision thereof shall establish capital, custody, margin, financial responsibility, making and keeping records, bonding, or financial or operational reporting requirements for brokers, dealers, municipal securities dealers, government securities brokers, or government securities dealers that differ from, or are in addition to, the requirements in those areas established under this chapter. The Commission shall consult periodically the securities commissions (or any agency or office performing like functions) of the States concerning the adequacy of such requirements as established under this chapter.

(2) Funding portals

(A) Limitation on State laws

Except as provided in subparagraph (B), no State or political subdivision thereof may enforce any law, rule, regulation, or other administrative action against a registered funding portal with respect to its business as such.

(B) Examination and enforcement authority

Subparagraph (A) does not apply with respect to the examination and enforcement of any law, rule, regulation, or administrative action of a State or political subdivision thereof in which the principal place of business of a registered funding portal is located, provided that such law, rule, regulation, or administrative action is not in addition to or different from the requirements for registered funding portals established by the Commission.

(C) Definition

For purposes of this paragraph, the term "State" includes the District of Columbia and the territories of the United States.

(3) De minimis transactions by associated persons

No law, rule, regulation, or order, or other administrative action of any State or political subdivision thereof may prohibit an associated person of a broker or dealer from effecting a transaction described in paragraph (3) for a customer in such State if—

(A) such associated person is not ineligible to register with such State for any reason other than such a transaction;

(B) such associated person is registered with a registered securities association and at least one State; and

(C) the broker or dealer with which such person is associated is registered with such State.

(4) Described transactions

    (A) In general, a transaction is described in this paragraph if—

        (i) such transaction is effected—

            (I) on behalf of a customer that, for 30 days prior to the day of the transaction, maintained an account with the broker or dealer; and

            (II) by an associated person of the broker or dealer—

                (aa) to which the customer was assigned for 14 days prior to the day of the transaction; and

                (bb) who is registered with a State in which the customer was a resident or was present for at least 30 consecutive days during the 1-year period prior to the day of the transaction; or

        (ii) the transaction is effected—

            (I) on behalf of a customer that, for 30 days prior to the day of the transaction, maintained an account with the broker or dealer; and

            (II) during the period beginning on the date on which such associated person files an application for registration with the State in which the transaction is effected and ending on the earlier of—

                (aa) 60 days after the date on which the application is filed; or

                (bb) the date on which such State notifies the associated person that it has denied the application for registration or has stayed the pendency of the application for cause.

    (B) Rules of construction. For purposes of subparagraph (A)(i)(II)—

        (i) each of up to 3 associated persons of a broker or dealer who are designated to effect transactions during the absence or unavailability of the principal associated person for a customer may be treated as an associated person to which such customer is assigned; and

        (ii) if the customer is present in another State for 30 or more consecutive days or has permanently changed his or her residence to another State, a transaction is not described in this paragraph, unless the associated person of the broker or dealer files an application for registration with such State not later than 10 business days after the later of the date of the transaction, or the date of the discovery of the presence of the customer in the other State for 30 or more consecutive days or the change in the customer's residence.

(j) Rulemaking to extend requirements to new hybrid products

    (1) Consultation

    Prior to commencing a rulemaking under this subsection, the Commission shall consult with and seek the concurrence of the Board concerning the imposition of broker or dealer registration requirements with respect to any new hybrid product. In developing and promulgating rules under this subsection, the Commission shall consider the views of the Board, including views with respect to the nature of the new hybrid product; the history, purpose, extent, and appropriateness of the regulation of the new product under the Federal banking laws; and the impact of the proposed rule on the banking industry.

    (2) Limitation

    The Commission shall not—

        (A) require a bank to register as a broker or dealer under this section because the bank engages in any transaction in, or buys or sells, a new hybrid product; or

        (B) bring an action against a bank for a failure to comply with a requirement described in subparagraph (A), unless the Commission has imposed such requirement by rule or regulation issued in accordance with this section.

    (3) Criteria for rulemaking

    The Commission shall not impose a requirement under paragraph (2) of this subsection with respect to any new hybrid product unless the Commission determines that—

        (A) the new hybrid product is a security; and

(B) imposing such requirement is necessary and appropriate in the public interest and for the protection of investors.

(4) Considerations

In making a determination under paragraph (3), the Commission shall consider—

(A) the nature of the new hybrid product; and

(B) the history, purpose, extent, and appropriateness of the regulation of the new hybrid product under the Federal securities laws and under the Federal banking laws.

(5) Objection to Commission regulation

(A) Filing of petition for review

The Board may obtain review of any final regulation described in paragraph (2) in the United States Court of Appeals for the District of Columbia Circuit by filing in such court, not later than 60 days after the date of publication of the final regulation, a written petition requesting that the regulation be set aside. Any proceeding to challenge any such rule shall be expedited by the Court of Appeals.

(B) Transmittal of petition and record

A copy of a petition described in subparagraph (A) shall be transmitted as soon as possible by the Clerk of the Court to an officer or employee of the Commission designated for that purpose. Upon receipt of the petition, the Commission shall file with the court the regulation under review and any documents referred to therein, and any other relevant materials prescribed by the court.

(C) Exclusive jurisdiction

On the date of the filing of the petition under subparagraph (A), the court has jurisdiction, which becomes exclusive on the filing of the materials set forth in subparagraph (B), to affirm and enforce or to set aside the regulation at issue.

(D) Standard of review

The court shall determine to affirm and enforce or set aside a regulation of the Commission under this subsection, based on the determination of the court as to whether—

(i) the subject product is a new hybrid product, as defined in this subsection;

(ii) the subject product is a security; and

(iii) imposing a requirement to register as a broker or dealer for banks engaging in transactions in such product is appropriate in light of the history, purpose, and extent of regulation under the Federal securities laws and under the Federal banking laws, giving deference neither to the views of the Commission nor the Board.

(E) Judicial stay

The filing of a petition by the Board pursuant to subparagraph (A) shall operate as a judicial stay, until the date on which the determination of the court is final (including any appeal of such determination).

(F) Other authority to challenge

Any aggrieved party may seek judicial review of the Commission's rulemaking under this subsection pursuant to section 78y of this title.

(6) Definitions

For purposes of this subsection:

(A) New hybrid product. The term "new hybrid product" means a product that—

(i) was not subjected to regulation by the Commission as a security prior to the date of the enactment of the Gramm-Leach-Bliley Act [Nov. 12, 1999];

(ii) is not an identified banking product as such term is defined in section 206 of such Act; and

(iii) is not an equity swap within the meaning of section 206(a)(6) of such Act.

(B) Board

The term "Board" means the Board of Governors of the Federal Reserve System.

(k) Registration or succession to a United States broker or dealer

In determining whether to permit a foreign person or an affiliate of a foreign person to register as a United

States broker or dealer, or succeed to the registration of a United States broker or dealer, the Commission may consider whether, for a foreign person, or an affiliate of a foreign person that presents a risk to the stability of the United States financial system, the home country of the foreign person has adopted, or made demonstrable progress toward adopting, an appropriate system of financial regulation to mitigate such risk.

(l) Termination of a United States broker or dealer

For a foreign person or an affiliate of a foreign person that presents such a risk to the stability of the United States financial system, the Commission may determine to terminate the registration of such foreign person or an affiliate of such foreign person as a broker or dealer in the United States, if the Commission determines that the home country of the foreign person has not adopted, or made demonstrable progress toward adopting, an appropriate system of financial regulation to mitigate such risk.

(m) Harmonization of enforcement

The enforcement authority of the Commission with respect to violations of the standard of conduct applicable to a broker or dealer providing personalized investment advice about securities to a retail customer shall include—

(1) the enforcement authority of the Commission with respect to such violations provided under this chapter; and

(2) the enforcement authority of the Commission with respect to violations of the standard of conduct applicable to an investment adviser under the Investment Advisers Act of 1940 [15 U.S.C. 80b–1 et seq.], including the authority to impose sanctions for such violations, and the Commission shall seek to prosecute and sanction violators of the standard of conduct applicable to a broker or dealer providing personalized investment advice about securities to a retail customer under this chapter to [9] same extent as the Commission prosecutes and sanctions violators of the standard of conduct applicable to an investment advisor under the Investment Advisers Act of 1940 [15 U.S.C. 80b–1 et seq.].

(n) Disclosures to retail investors

(1) In general

Notwithstanding any other provision of the securities laws, the Commission may issue rules designating documents or information that shall be provided by a broker or dealer to a retail investor before the purchase of an investment product or service by the retail investor.

(2) Considerations

In developing any rules under paragraph (1), the Commission shall consider whether the rules will promote investor protection, efficiency, competition, and capital formation.

(3) Form and contents of documents and information

Any documents or information designated under a rule promulgated under paragraph (1) shall—

(A) be in a summary format; and

(B) contain clear and concise information about—

(i) investment objectives, strategies, costs, and risks; and

(ii) any compensation or other financial incentive received by a broker, dealer, or other intermediary in connection with the purchase of retail investment products.

(o) Authority to restrict mandatory pre-dispute arbitration

The Commission, by rule, may prohibit, or impose conditions or limitations on the use of, agreements that require customers or clients of any broker, dealer, or municipal securities dealer to arbitrate any future dispute between them arising under the Federal securities laws, the rules and regulations thereunder, or the rules of a self-regulatory organization if it finds that such prohibition, imposition of conditions, or limitations are in the public interest and for the protection of investors.

17. SEC Rules and Regulations, Securities Exchange Act of 1934:
Section 15A – Registered Securities Associations

(a) Registration; application

An association of brokers and dealers may be registered as a national securities association pursuant to subsection (b), or as an affiliated securities association pursuant to subsection (d), under the terms and conditions hereinafter provided in this section and in accordance with the provisions of section 78s(a) of this title, by filing with the Commission an application for registration in such form as the Commission, by rule, may prescribe containing the rules of the association and such other information and documents as the Commission, by rule, may prescribe as necessary or appropriate in the public interest or for the protection of investors.

(b) Determinations by Commission requisite to registration of applicant as national securities association. An association of brokers and dealers shall not be registered as a national securities association unless the Commission determines that—

(1) By reason of the number and geographical distribution of its members and the scope of their transactions, such association will be able to carry out the purposes of this section.

(2) Such association is so organized and has the capacity to be able to carry out the purposes of this chapter and to comply, and (subject to any rule or order of the Commission pursuant to section 78q(d) or 78s(g)(2) of this title) to enforce compliance by its members and persons associated with its members, with the provisions of this chapter, the rules and regulations thereunder, the rules of the Municipal Securities Rulemaking Board, and the rules of the association.

(3) Subject to the provisions of subsection (g) of this section, the rules of the association provide that any registered broker or dealer may become a member of such association and any person may become associated with a member thereof.

(4) The rules of the association assure a fair representation of its members in the selection of its directors and administration of its affairs and provide that one or more directors shall be representative of issuers and investors and not be associated with a member of the association, broker, or dealer.

(5) The rules of the association provide for the equitable allocation of reasonable dues, fees, and other charges among members and issuers and other persons using any facility or system which the association operates or controls.

(6) The rules of the association are designed to prevent fraudulent and manipulative acts and practices, to promote just and equitable principles of trade, to foster cooperation and coordination with persons engaged in regulating, clearing, settling, processing information with respect to, and facilitating transactions in securities, to remove impediments to and perfect the mechanism of a free and open market and a national market system, and, in general, to protect investors and the public interest; and are not designed to permit unfair discrimination between customers, issuers, brokers, or dealers, to fix minimum profits, to impose any schedule or fix rates of commissions, allowances, discounts, or other fees to be charged by its members, or to regulate by virtue of any authority conferred by this chapter matters not related to the purposes of this chapter or the administration of the association.

(7) The rules of the association provide that (subject to any rule or order of the Commission pursuant to section 78q(d) or 78s(g)(2) of this title) its members and persons associated with its members shall be appropriately disciplined for violation of any provision of this chapter, the rules or regulations thereunder, the rules of the Municipal Securities Rulemaking Board, or the rules of the association, by expulsion, suspension, limitation of activities, functions, and operations, fine, censure, being suspended or barred from being associated with a member, or any other fitting sanction.

(8) The rules of the association are in accordance with the provisions of subsection (h) of this section, and, in general, provide a fair procedure for the disciplining of members and persons associated with members, the denial of membership to any person seeking membership therein, the barring of any person from becoming associated with a member thereof, and the prohibition or limitation by the association of any

person with respect to access to services offered by the association or a member thereof.

(9) The rules of the association do not impose any burden on competition not necessary or appropriate in furtherance of the purposes of this chapter.

(10) The requirements of subsection (c), insofar as these may be applicable, are satisfied.

(11) The rules of the association include provisions governing the form and content of quotations relating to securities sold otherwise than on a national securities exchange which may be distributed or published by any member or person associated with a member, and the persons to whom such quotations may be supplied. Such rules relating to quotations shall be designed to produce fair and informative quotations, to prevent fictitious or misleading quotations, and to promote orderly procedures for collecting, distributing, and publishing quotations.

(12) The rules of the association to promote just and equitable principles of trade, as required by paragraph (6), include rules to prevent members of the association from participating in any limited partnership rollup transaction (as such term is defined in paragraphs (4) and (5) of section 78n(h) of this title) unless such transaction was conducted in accordance with procedures designed to protect the rights of limited partners, including—

(A) the right of dissenting limited partners to one of the following:

    (i) an appraisal and compensation;

    (ii) retention of a security under substantially the same terms and conditions as the original issue;

    (iii) approval of the limited partnership rollup transaction by not less than 75 percent of the outstanding securities of each of the participating limited partnerships;

    (iv) the use of a committee that is independent, as determined in accordance with rules prescribed by the association, of the general partner or sponsor, that has been approved by a majority of the outstanding securities of each of the participating partnerships, and that has such authority as is necessary to protect the interest of limited partners, including the authority to hire independent advisors, to negotiate with the general partner or sponsor on behalf of the limited partners, and to make a recommendation to the limited partners with respect to the proposed transaction; or

    (v) other comparable rights that are prescribed by rule by the association and that are designed to protect dissenting limited partners;

(B) the right not to have their voting power unfairly reduced or abridged;

(C) the right not to bear an unfair portion of the costs of a proposed limited partnership rollup transaction that is rejected; and

(D) restrictions on the conversion of contingent interests or fees into non-contingent interests or fees and restrictions on the receipt of a non-contingent equity interest in exchange for fees for services which have not yet been provided.

As used in this paragraph, the term "dissenting limited partner" means a person who, on the date on which soliciting material is mailed to investors, is a holder of a beneficial interest in a limited partnership that is the subject of a limited partnership rollup transaction, and who casts a vote against the transaction and complies with procedures established by the association, except that for purposes of an exchange or tender offer, such person shall file an objection in writing under the rules of the association during the period in which the offer is outstanding.

(13) The rules of the association prohibit the authorization for quotation on an automated interdealer quotation system sponsored by the association of any security designated by the Commission as a national market system security resulting from a limited partnership rollup transaction (as such term is defined in paragraphs (4) and (5) of section 78n(h) of this title), unless such transaction was conducted in accordance with procedures designed to protect the rights of limited partners, including—

(A) the right of dissenting limited partners to one of the following:

    (i) an appraisal and compensation;

    (ii) retention of a security under substantially the same terms and conditions as the original issue;

(iii) approval of the limited partnership rollup transaction by not less than 75 percent of the outstanding securities of each of the participating limited partnerships;

(iv) the use of a committee that is independent, as determined in accordance with rules prescribed by the association, of the general partner or sponsor, that has been approved by a majority of the outstanding securities of each of the participating partnerships, and that has such authority as is necessary to protect the interest of limited partners, including the authority to hire independent advisors, to negotiate with the general partner or sponsor on behalf of the limited partners, and to make a recommendation to the limited partners with respect to the proposed transaction; or

(v) other comparable rights that are prescribed by rule by the association and that are designed to protect dissenting limited partners;

(B) the right not to have their voting power unfairly reduced or abridged;

(C) the right not to bear an unfair portion of the costs of a proposed limited partnership rollup transaction that is rejected; and

(D) restrictions on the conversion of contingent interests or fees into non-contingent interests or fees and restrictions on the receipt of a non-contingent equity interest in exchange for fees for services which have not yet been provided.

As used in this paragraph, the term "dissenting limited partner" means a person who, on the date on which soliciting material is mailed to investors, is a holder of a beneficial interest in a limited partnership that is the subject of a limited partnership rollup transaction, and who casts a vote against the transaction and complies with procedures established by the association, except that for purposes of an exchange or tender offer, such person shall file an objection in writing under the rules of the association during the period during which the offer is outstanding.

(14) The rules of the association include provisions governing the sales, or offers of sales, of securities on the premises of any military installation to any member of the Armed Forces or a dependent thereof, which rules require—

(A) the broker or dealer performing brokerage services to clearly and conspicuously disclose to potential investors—

(i) that the securities offered are not being offered or provided by the broker or dealer on behalf of the Federal Government, and that its offer is not sanctioned, recommended, or encouraged by the Federal Government; and

(ii) the identity of the registered broker-dealer offering the securities;

(B) such broker or dealer to perform an appropriate suitability determination, including consideration of costs and knowledge about securities, prior to making a recommendation of a security to a member of the Armed Forces or a dependent thereof; and

(C) that no person receive any referral fee or incentive compensation in connection with a sale or offer of sale of securities, unless such person is an associated person of a registered broker or dealer and is qualified pursuant to the rules of a self-regulatory organization.

(15) The rules of the association provide that the association shall—

(A) request guidance from the Municipal Securities Rulemaking Board in interpretation of the rules of the Municipal Securities Rulemaking Board; and

(B) provide information to the Municipal Securities Rulemaking Board about the enforcement actions and examinations of the association under section 78o–4(b)(2)(E) of this title, so that the Municipal Securities Rulemaking Board may—

(i) assist in such enforcement actions and examinations; and

(ii) evaluate the ongoing effectiveness of the rules of the Board.

(c) National association rules; provision for registration of affiliated securities association

The Commission may permit or require the rules of an association applying for registration pursuant to subsection (b), to provide for the admission of an association registered as an affiliated securities association pursuant to subsection (d), to participation in said applicant association as an affiliate thereof, under terms permitting such powers and responsibilities to such affiliate, and under such other appropriate terms and conditions, as may be provided by the rules of said applicant association, if such rules appear to the Commission to be necessary or appropriate in the public interest or for the protection of investors and to carry out the purposes of this section. The duties and powers of the Commission with respect to any national securities association or any affiliated securities association shall in no way be limited by reason of any such affiliation.

(d) Registration as affiliated association; prerequisites; association rules

An applicant association shall not be registered as an affiliated securities association unless it appears to the Commission that—

(1) such association, notwithstanding that it does not satisfy the requirements set forth in paragraph (1) of subsection (b), will, forthwith upon the registration thereof, be admitted to affiliation with an association registered as a national securities association pursuant to subsection (b), in the manner and under the terms and conditions provided by the rules of said national securities association in accordance with subsection (c); and

(2) such association and its rules satisfy the requirements set forth in paragraphs (2) to (10), inclusive, and paragraph (12),[1] of subsection (b); except that in the case of any such association any restrictions upon membership therein of the type authorized by paragraph (3) of subsection (b) shall not be less stringent than in the case of the national securities association with which such association is to be affiliated.

(e) Dealings with nonmember professionals

(1) The rules of a registered securities association may provide that no member thereof shall deal with any nonmember professional (as defined in paragraph (2) of this subsection) except at the same prices, for the same commissions or fees, and on the same terms and conditions as are by such member accorded to the general public.

(2) For the purposes of this subsection, the term "nonmember professional" shall include (A) with respect to transactions in securities other than municipal securities, any registered broker or dealer who is not a member of any registered securities association, except such a broker or dealer who deals exclusively in commercial paper, bankers' acceptances, and commercial bills, and (B) with respect to transactions in municipal securities, any municipal securities dealer (other than a bank or division or department of a bank) who is not a member of any registered securities association and any municipal securities broker who is not a member of any such association.

(3) Nothing in this subsection shall be so construed or applied as to prevent (A) any member of a registered securities association from granting to any other member of any registered securities association any dealer's discount, allowance, commission, or special terms, in connection with the purchase or sale of securities, or (B) any member of a registered securities association or any municipal securities dealer which is a bank or a division or department of a bank from granting to any member of any registered securities association or any such municipal securities dealer any dealer's discount, allowance, commission, or special terms in connection with the purchase or sale of municipal securities: Provided, however, That the granting of any such discount, allowance, commission, or special terms in connection with the purchase or sale of municipal securities shall be subject to rules of the Municipal Securities Rulemaking Board adopted pursuant to section 78o–4(b)(2)(K) of this title.

(f) Transactions in municipal securities

Nothing in subsection (b)(6) or (b)(11) of this section shall be construed to permit a registered securities association to make rules concerning any transaction by a registered broker or dealer in a municipal security.

(g) Denial of membership

(1) A registered securities association shall deny membership to any person who is not a registered broker or dealer.

(2) A registered securities association may, and in cases in which the Commission, by order, directs as necessary or appropriate in the public interest or for the protection of investors shall, deny membership to any registered broker or dealer, and bar from becoming associated with a member any person, who is subject to a statutory disqualification. A registered securities association shall file notice with the Commission

not less than thirty days prior to admitting any registered broker or dealer to membership or permitting any person to become associated with a member, if the association knew, or in the exercise of reasonable care should have known, that such broker or dealer or person was subject to a statutory disqualification. The notice shall be in such form and contain such information as the Commission, by rule, may prescribe as necessary or appropriate in the public interest or for the protection of investors.

(3)
    (A) A registered securities association may deny membership to, or condition the membership of, a registered broker or dealer if (i) such broker or dealer does not meet such standards of financial responsibility or operational capability or such broker or dealer or any natural person associated with such broker or dealer does not meet such standards of training, experience, and competence as are prescribed by the rules of the association or (ii) such broker or dealer or person associated with such broker or dealer has engaged and there is a reasonable likelihood he will again engage in acts or practices inconsistent with just and equitable principles of trade. A registered securities association may examine and verify the qualifications of an applicant to become a member and the natural persons associated with such an applicant in accordance with procedures established by the rules of the association.

    (B) A registered securities association may bar a natural person from becoming associated with a member or condition the association of a natural person with a member if such natural person (i) does not meet such standards of training, experience, and competence as are prescribed by the rules of the association or (ii) has engaged and there is a reasonable likelihood he will again engage in acts or practices inconsistent with just and equitable principles of trade. A registered securities association may examine and verify the qualifications of an applicant to become a person associated with a member in accordance with procedures established by the rules of the association and require a natural person associated with a member, or any class of such natural persons, to be registered with the association in accordance with procedures so established.

    (C) A registered securities association may bar any person from becoming associated with a member if such person does not agree (i) to supply the association with such information with respect to its relationship and dealings with the member as may be specified in the rules of the association and (ii) to permit examination of its books and records to verify the accuracy of any information so supplied.

    (D) Nothing in subparagraph (A), (B), or (C) of this paragraph shall be construed to permit a registered securities association to deny membership to or condition the membership of, or bar any person from becoming associated with or condition the association of any person with, a broker or dealer that engages exclusively in transactions in municipal securities.

(4) A registered securities association may deny membership to a registered broker or dealer not engaged in a type of business in which the rules of the association require members to be engaged: Provided, however, That no registered securities association may deny membership to a registered broker or dealer by reason of the amount of such type of business done by such broker or dealer or the other types of business in which he is engaged.

(h) Discipline of registered securities association members and persons associated with members; summary proceedings

(1) In any proceeding by a registered securities association to determine whether a member or person associated with a member should be disciplined (other than a summary proceeding pursuant to paragraph (3) of this subsection) the association shall bring specific charges, notify such member or person of, and give him an opportunity to defend against, such charges, and keep a record. A determination by the association to impose a disciplinary sanction shall be supported by a statement setting forth—

    (A) any act or practice in which such member or person associated with a member has been found to have engaged, or which such member or person has been found to have omitted;

    (B) the specific provision of this chapter, the rules or regulations thereunder, the rules of the Municipal

Securities Rulemaking Board, or the rules of the association which any such act or practice, or omission to act, is deemed to violate; and

(C) the sanction imposed and the reason therefor.

(2) In any proceeding by a registered securities association to determine whether a person shall be denied membership, barred from becoming associated with a member, or prohibited or limited with respect to access to services offered by the association or a member thereof (other than a summary proceeding pursuant to paragraph (3) of this subsection), the association shall notify such person of and give him an opportunity to be heard upon, the specific grounds for denial, bar, or prohibition or limitation under consideration and keep a record. A determination by the association to deny membership, bar a person from becoming associated with a member, or prohibit or limit a person with respect to access to services offered by the association or a member thereof shall be supported by a statement setting forth the specific grounds on which the denial, bar, or prohibition or limitation is based.

(3) A registered securities association may summarily (A) suspend a member or person associated with a member who has been and is expelled or suspended from any self-regulatory organization or barred or suspended from being associated with a member of any self-regulatory organization, (B) suspend a member who is in such financial or operating difficulty that the association determines and so notifies the Commission that the member cannot be permitted to continue to do business as a member with safety to investors, creditors, other members, or the association, or (C) limit or prohibit any person with respect to access to services offered by the association if subparagraph (A) or (B) of this paragraph is applicable to such person or, in the case of a person who is not a member, if the association determines that such person does not meet the qualification requirements or other prerequisites for such access and such person cannot be permitted to continue to have such access with safety to investors, creditors, members, or the association. Any person aggrieved by any such summary action shall be promptly afforded an opportunity for a hearing by the association in accordance with the provisions of paragraph (1) or (2) of this subsection. The Commission, by order, may stay any such summary action on its own motion or upon application by any person aggrieved thereby, if the Commission determines summarily or after notice and opportunity for hearing (which hearing may consist solely of the submission of affidavits or presentation of oral arguments) that such stay is consistent with the public interest and the protection of investors.

(i) Obligation to maintain registration, disciplinary, and other data

(1) Maintenance of system to respond to inquiries

A registered securities association shall—

(A) establish and maintain a system for collecting and retaining registration information;

(B) establish and maintain a toll-free telephone listing, and a readily accessible electronic or other process, to receive and promptly respond to inquiries regarding—

(i) registration information on its members and their associated persons; and

(ii) registration information on the members and their associated persons of any registered national securities exchange that uses the system described in subparagraph (A) for the registration of its members and their associated persons; and

(C) adopt rules governing the process for making inquiries and the type, scope, and presentation of information to be provided in response to such inquiries in consultation with any registered national securities exchange providing information pursuant to subparagraph (B)(ii).

(2) Recovery of costs

A registered securities association may charge persons making inquiries described in paragraph (1)(B), other than individual investors, reasonable fees for responses to such inquiries.

(3) Process for disputed information

Each registered securities association shall adopt rules establishing an administrative process for disputing the accuracy of information provided in response to inquiries under this subsection in consultation with any registered national securities exchange providing information pursuant to paragraph (1)(B)(ii).

(4) Limitation on liability

A registered securities association, or an exchange reporting information to such an association, shall not have any liability to any person for any actions taken or omitted in good faith under this subsection.

(5) Definition

For purposes of this subsection, the term "registration information" means the information reported in connection with the registration or licensing of brokers and dealers and their associated persons, including disciplinary actions, regulatory, judicial, and arbitration proceedings, and other information required by law, or exchange or association rule, and the source and status of such information.

(j) Registration for sales of private securities offerings

A registered securities association shall create a limited qualification category for any associated person of a member who effects sales as part of a primary offering of securities not involving a public offering, pursuant to section 77c(b), 77d(2),1 or 77d(6) 1 of this title and the rules and regulations thereunder, and shall deem qualified in such limited qualification category, without testing, any bank employee who, in the six month period preceding November 12, 1999, engaged in effecting such sales.

(k) Limited purpose national securities association

(1) Regulation of members with respect to security futures products

A futures association registered under section 21 of title 7 shall be a registered national securities association for the limited purpose of regulating the activities of members who are registered as brokers or dealers in security futures products pursuant to section 78o(b)(11) of this title.

(2) Requirements for registration

Such a securities association shall—

(A) be so organized and have the capacity to carry out the purposes of the securities laws applicable to security futures products and to comply, and (subject to any rule or order of the Commission pursuant to section 78s(g)(2) of this title) to enforce compliance by its members and persons associated with its members, with the provisions of the securities laws applicable to security futures products, the rules and regulations thereunder, and its rules;

(B) have rules that—

(i) are designed to prevent fraudulent and manipulative acts and practices, to promote just and equitable principles of trade, and, in general, to protect investors and the public interest, including rules governing sales practices and the advertising of security futures products reasonably comparable to those of other national securities associations registered pursuant to subsection (a) that are applicable to security futures products; and

(ii) are not designed to regulate by virtue of any authority conferred by this chapter matters not related to the purposes of this chapter or the administration of the association;

(C) have rules that provide that (subject to any rule or order of the Commission pursuant to section 78s(g)(2) of this title) its members and persons associated with its members shall be appropriately disciplined for violation of any provision of the securities laws applicable to security futures products, the rules or regulations thereunder, or the rules of the association, by expulsion, suspension, limitation of activities, functions, and operations, fine, censure, being suspended or barred from being associated with a member, or any other fitting sanction; and

(D) have rules that ensure that members and natural persons associated with members meet such standards of training, experience, and competence necessary to effect transactions in security futures products and are tested for their knowledge of securities and security futures products.

(3) Exemption from rule change submission

Such a securities association shall be exempt from submitting proposed rule changes pursuant to section 78s(b) of this title, except that—

(A) the association shall file proposed rule changes related to higher margin levels, fraud or manipulation, recordkeeping, reporting, listing standards, or decimal pricing for security futures products, sales practices for, advertising of, or standards of training, experience, competence, or other qualifications for security futures products for persons who effect transactions in security futures products, or rules effectuating the association's obligation to enforce the securities laws pursuant to section 78s(b)(7) of this title;

(B) the association shall file pursuant to sections 78s(b)(1) and 78s(b)(2) of this title proposed rule changes related to margin, except for changes resulting in higher margin levels; and

(C) the association shall file pursuant to section 78s(b)(1) of this title proposed rule changes that have been abrogated by the Commission pursuant to section 78s(b)(7)(C) of this title.

(4) Other exemptions

Such a securities association shall be exempt from and shall not be required to enforce compliance by its members, and its members shall not, solely with respect to their transactions effected in security futures products, be required to comply, with the following provisions of this chapter and the rules thereunder:

(A) Section 78h of this title.

(B) Subsections (b)(1), (b)(3), (b)(4), (b)(5), (b)(8), (b)(10), (b)(11), (b)(12), (b)(13), (c), (d), (e), (f), (g), (h), and (i) of this section.

(C) Subsections (d), (f), and (k) 1 of section 78q of this title.

(D) Subsections (a), (f), and (h) of section 78s of this title.

(l) Rules to avoid duplicative regulation of dual registrants

Consistent with this chapter, each national securities association registered pursuant to subsection (a) of this section shall issue such rules as are necessary to avoid duplicative or conflicting rules applicable to any broker or dealer registered with the Commission pursuant to section 78o(b) of this title (except paragraph (11) thereof), that is also registered with the Commodity Futures Trading Commission pursuant to section 6f(a) of title 7 (except paragraph (2) thereof), with respect to the application of—

(1) rules of such national securities association of the type specified in section 78o(c)(3)(B) of this title involving security futures products; and

(2) similar rules of national securities associations registered pursuant to subsection (k) of this section and national securities exchanges registered pursuant to section 78f(g) of this title involving security futures products.

(m) Procedures and rules for security future products

A national securities association registered pursuant to subsection (a) shall, not later than 8 months after December 21, 2000, implement the procedures specified in section 78f(h)(5)(A) of this title and adopt the rules specified in subparagraphs (B) and (C) of section 78f(h)(5) of this title.

---

18. SEC Rules and Regulations: Regulation D – Rules Governing the Limited Offer and Sale of Securities Without Registration Under the Securities Act of 1933

Preliminary Notes

1. The following rules relate to transactions exempted from the registration requirements of section 5 of the Securities Act of 1933 (the Act). Such transactions are not exempt from the anti fraud, civil liability, or other provisions of the federal securities laws. Issuers are reminded of their obligation to provide such further material information, if any, as may be necessary to make the information required under this regulation, in light of the circumstances under which it is furnished, not misleading.

2. Nothing in these rules obviates the need to comply with any applicable state law relating to the offer and sale

of securities. Regulation D is intended to be a basic element in a uniform system of Federal-State limited offering exemptions consistent with the provisions of sections 18 and 19(c) of the Act. In those states that have adopted Regulation D, or any version of Regulation D, special attention should be directed to the applicable state laws and regulations, including those relating to registration of person who receive remuneration in connection with the offer and sale of securities, to disqualification of issuers and other persons associated with offerings based on state administrative orders or judgments, and to requirements for filings of notices of sales.

3. Attempted compliance with any rule in Regulation D does not act as an exclusive election; the issuer can also claim the availability of any other applicable exemption. For instance, an issuer's failure to satisfy all the terms and conditions of Rule 506 shall not raise any presumption that the exemption provided by section 4(2) of the Act is not available.

4. These rules are available only to the issuer of the securities and not to any affiliate of that issuer or to any other person for resales of the issuer's securities. The rules provide an exemption only for the transactions in which the securities are offered or sold by the issuer, not for the securities themselves.

5. These rules may be used for business combinations that involve sales by virtue of rule 145(a) or otherwise.

6. In view of the objectives of these rules and the policies underlying the Act, regulation D is not available to any issuer for any transaction or chain of transactions that, although in technical compliance with these rules, is part of a plan or scheme to evade the registration provisions of the Act. In such cases, registration under the Act is required.

7. Securities offered and sold outside the United States in accordance with Regulation S need not be registered under the Act. See Release No. 33-6863. Regulation S may be relied upon for such offers and sales even if coincident offers and sales are made in accordance with Regulation D inside the United States. Thus, for example, persons who are offered and sold securities in accordance with Regulation S would not be counted in the calculation of the number of purchasers under Regulation D. Similarly, proceeds from such sales would not be included in the aggregate offering price. The provisions of this note, however, do not apply if the issuer elects to rely solely on Regulation D for offers or sales to persons made outside the United States.

Rule 501 - Definitions and Terms Used in Regulation D
As used in Regulation D, the following terms shall have the meaning indicated:
a. Accredited investor. Accredited investor shall mean any person who comes within any of the following categories, or who the issuer reasonably believes comes within any of the following categories, at the time of the sale of the securities to that person:
   1. Any bank as defined in section 3(a)(2) of the Act, or any savings and loan association or other institution as defined in section 3(a)(5)(A) of the Act whether acting in its individual or fiduciary capacity; any broker or dealer registered pursuant to section 15 of the Securities Exchange Act of 1934; any insurance company as defined in section 2(13) of the Act; any investment company registered under the Investment Company Act of 1940 or a business development company as defined in section 2(a)(48) of that Act; any Small Business Investment Company licensed by the U.S. Small Business Administration under section 301(c) or (d) of the Small Business Investment Act of 1958; any plan established and maintained by a state, its political subdivisions, or any agency or instrumentality of a state or its political subdivisions, for the benefit of its employees, if such plan has total assets in excess of $5,000,000; any employee benefit plan within the meaning of the Employee Retirement Income Security Act of 1974 if the investment decision is made by a plan fiduciary, as defined in section 3(21) of such act, which is either a bank, savings and loan association, insurance company, or registered investment adviser, or if the employee benefit plan has total assets in excess of $5,000,000 or, if a self-directed plan, with investment decisions made solely by persons that are accredited investors;
   2. Any private business development company as defined in section 202(a)22 of the Investment Advisers Act of 1940;
   3. Any organization described in section 501(c)3 of the Internal Revenue Code, corporation, Massachusetts

or similar business trust, or partnership, not formed for the specific purpose of acquiring the securities offered, with total assets in excess of $5,000,000;

    4. Any director, executive officer, or general partner of the issuer of the securities being offered or sold, or any director, executive officer, or general partner of a general partner of that issuer;

    5. Any natural person whose individual net worth, or joint net worth with that person's spouse, at the time of his purchase exceeds $1,000,000;

    6. Any natural person who had an individual income in excess of $200,000 in each of the two most recent years or joint income with that person's spouse in excess of $300,000 in each of those years and has a reasonable expectation of reaching the same income level in the current year;

    7. Any trust, with total assets in excess of $5,000,000, not formed for the specific purpose of acquiring the securities offered, whose purchase is directed by a sophisticated person as described in Rule 506(b)(2)(ii) and

    8. Any entity in which all of the equity owners are accredited investors.

b. Affiliate. An affiliate of, or person affiliated with, a specified person shall mean a person that directly, or indirectly through one or more intermediaries, controls or is controlled by, or is under common control with, the person specified.

c. Aggregate offering price. Aggregate offering price shall mean the sum of all cash, services, property, notes, cancellation of debt, or other consideration to be received by an issuer for issuance of its securities. Where securities are being offered for both cash and non-cash consideration, the aggregate offering price shall be based on the price at which the securities are offered for cash. Any portion of the aggregate offering price attributable to cash received in a foreign currency shall be translated into United States currency at the currency exchange rate in effect at a reasonable time prior to or on the date of the sale of the securities. If securities are not offered for cash, the aggregate offering price shall be based on the value of the consideration as established by bona fide sales of that consideration made within a reasonable time, or, in the absence of sales, on the fair value as determined by an accepted standard. Such valuations of non-cash consideration must be reasonable at the time made.

d. Business combination. Business combination shall mean any transaction of the type specified in paragraph (a) of Rule 145 under the Act and any transaction involving the acquisition by one issuer, in exchange for all or a part of its own or its parent's stock, of stock of another issuer if, immediately after the acquisition, the acquiring issuer has control of the other issuer (whether or not it had control before the acquisition).

e. Calculation of number of purchasers. For purposes of calculating the number of purchasers under Rule 505(b) and Rule 506(b) only, the following shall apply:

    1. The following purchasers shall be excluded:

        i. Any relative, spouse or relative of the spouse of a purchaser who has the same principal residence as the purchaser;

        ii. Any trust or estate in which a purchaser and any of the persons related to him as specified in paragraph (e)1(i) or (e)1(iii) of this section collectively have more than 50 percent of the beneficial interest (excluding contingent interests);

        iii. Any corporation or other organization of which a purchaser and any of the persons related to him as specified in paragraph (e)1(i) or (e)1(ii) of this section collectively are beneficial owners of more than 50 percent of the equity securities (excluding directors' qualifying shares) or equity interests; and

        iv. Any accredited investor.

    2. A corporation, partnership or other entity shall be counted as one purchaser. If, however, that entity is organized for the specific purpose of acquiring the securities offered and is not an accredited investor under paragraph (a)8 of this section, then each beneficial owner of equity securities or equity interests in the entity shall count as a separate purchaser for all provisions of Regulation D, except to the extent provided in paragraph (e)1 of this section.

    3. A non-contributory employee benefit plan within the meaning of Title I of the Employee Retirement In-

come Security Act of 1974 shall be counted as one purchaser where the trustee makes all investment decisions for the plan.

f. Executive officer. Executive officer shall mean the president, any vice president in charge of a principal business unit, division or function (such as sales, administration or finance), any other officer who performs a policy making function, or any other person who performs similar policy making functions for the issuer. Executive officers of subsidiaries may be deemed executive officers of the issuer if they perform such policy making functions for the issuer.

g. Issuer. The definition of the term issuer in section 2(4) of the Act shall apply, except that in the case of a proceeding under the Federal Bankruptcy Code (11 U.S.C. 101 et seq.), the trustee or debtor in possession shall be considered the issuer in an offering under a plan or reorganization, if the securities are to be issued under the plan.

h. Purchaser representative. Purchaser representative shall mean any person who satisfies all of the following conditions or who the issuer reasonably believes satisfies all of the following conditions:

1. Is not an affiliate, director, officer or other employee of the issuer, or beneficial owner of 10 percent or more of any class of the equity securities or 10 percent or more of the equity interest in the issuer, except where the purchaser is:

   i. A relative of the purchaser representative by blood, marriage or adoption and not more remote than a first cousin;

   ii. A trust or estate in which the purchaser representative and any persons related to him as specified in paragraph (h)1(i) or (h)1(iii) of this section collectively have more than 50 percent of the beneficial interest (excluding contingent interest) or of which the purchaser representative serves as trustee, executor, or in any similar capacity; or

   iii. A corporation or other organization of which the purchaser representative and any persons related to him as specified in paragraph (h)1(i) or (h)1(ii) of this section collectively are the beneficial owners of more than 50 percent of the equity securities (excluding directors' qualifying shares) or equity interests;

2. Has such knowledge and experience in financial and business matters that he is capable of evaluating, alone, or together with other purchaser representatives of the purchaser, or together with the purchaser, the merits and risks of the prospective investment;

3. Is acknowledged by the purchaser in writing, during the course of the transaction, to be his purchaser representative in connection with evaluating the merits and risks of the prospective investment; and

4. Discloses to the purchaser in writing a reasonable time prior to the sale of securities to that purchaser any material relationship between himself or his affiliates and the issuer or its affiliates that then exists, that is mutually understood to be contemplated, or that has existed at any time during the previous two years, and any compensation received or to be received as a result of such relationship.

Rule 502 - General Conditions to Be Met

The following conditions shall be applicable to offers and sales made under Regulation D:

a. Integration. All sales that are part of the same Regulation D offering must meet all of the terms and conditions of Regulation D. Offers and sales that are made more than six months before the start of a Regulation D offering or are made more than six months after completion of a Regulation D offering will not be considered part of that Regulation D offering, so long as during those six month periods there are no offers or sales of securities by or for the issuer that are of the same or a similar class as those offered or sold under Regulation D, other than those offers or sales of securities under an employee benefit plan as defined in rule 405 under the Act.

b. Information requirements-

1. When information must be furnished. If the issuer sells securities under Rule 505 or Rule 506 to any purchaser that is not an accredited investor, the issuer shall furnish the information specified in paragraph

(b)(2) of this section to such purchaser a reasonable time prior to sale. The issuer is not required to furnish the specified information to purchasers when it sells securities under Rule 504, or to any accredited investor.

2. Type of information to be furnished.

    i. If the issuer is not subject to the reporting requirements of section 13 or 15(d) of the Exchange Act, at a reasonable time prior to the sale of securities the issuer shall furnish to the purchaser, to the extent material to an understanding of the issuer, its business and the securities being offered:

        A. Non-financial statement information. If the issuer is eligible to use Regulation A, the same kind of information as would be required in Part II of Form 1-A. If the issuer is not eligible to use Regulation A, the same kind of information as required in Part I of a registration statement filed under the Securities Act on the form that the issuer would be entitled to use.

        B. Financial statement information.

            1. Offerings up to $2,000,000. The information required in Item 310 of Regulation S-B, except that only the issuer's balance sheet, which shall be dated within 120 days of the start of the offering, must be audited.

            2. Offerings up to $7,500,000. The financial statement information required in Form SB-2. If an issuer, other than a limited partnership, cannot obtain audited financial statements without unreasonable effort or expense, then only the issuer's balance sheet, which shall be dated within 120 days of the start of the offering, must be audited. If the issuer is a limited partnership and cannot obtain the required financial statements without unreasonable effort or expense, it may furnish financial statements that have been prepared on the basis of Federal income tax requirements and examined and reported on in accordance with generally accepted auditing standards by an independent public or certified accountant.

            3. Offerings over $7,500,000. The financial statement as would be required in a registration statement filed under the Act on the form that the issuer would be entitled to use. If an issuer, other than a limited partnership, cannot obtain audited financial statements without unreasonable effort or expense, then only the issuer's balance sheet, which shall be dated within 120 days of the start of the offering, must be audited. If the issuer is a limited partnership and cannot obtain the required financial statements without unreasonable effort or expense, it may furnish financial statements that have been prepared on the basis of Federal income tax requirements and examined and reported on in accordance with generally accepted auditing standards by an independent public or certified accountant.

        C. If the issuer is a foreign private issuer eligible to use Form 20-F, the issuer shall disclose the same kind of information required to be included in a registration statement filed under the Act on the form that the issuer would be entitled to use. The financial statements need be certified only to the extent required by paragraph (b)2(i) (B) (1), (2) or (3) of this section, as appropriate.

    ii. If the issuer is subject to the reporting requirements of section 13 or 15(d) of the Exchange Act, at a reasonable time prior to the sale of securities the issuer shall furnish to the purchaser the information specified in paragraph (b)2(ii)(A) or (B) of this section, and in either event the information specified in paragraph (b)(2)(ii)(C) of this section:

        A. The issuer's annual report to shareholders for the most recent fiscal year, if such annual report meets the requirements of Rule 14a-3 or Rule14c-3 under the Exchange Act, the definitive proxy statement filed in connection with that annual report, and, if requested by the purchaser in writing, a copy of the issuer's most recent Form 10-K and Form 10-KSB under the Exchange Act.

        B. The information contained in an annual report on Form 10-K or 10-KSB under the Exchange Act or in a registration statement on Form S-1, SB-1, SB-2 or S-11 under the Act or on Form 10 or Form 10-SB under the Exchange Act, whichever filing is the most recent required to be filed.

        C. The information contained in any reports or documents required to be filed by the issuer under sections 13(a), 14(a), 14(c), and 15(d) of the Exchange Act since the distribution or filing of the report or registration statement specified in paragraphs (b)2(ii) (A) or (B), and a brief description of the securities being offered, the use of the proceeds from the offering, and any material changes in the issuer's affairs that are not disclosed in the documents furnished.

    D. If the issuer is a foreign private issuer, the issuer may provide in lieu of the information specified in paragraph (b)2(ii) (A) or (B) of this section, the information contained in its most recent filing on Form 20-F or Form F-1.

iii. Exhibits required to be filed with the Commission as part of a registration statement or report, other than an annual report to shareholders or parts of that report incorporated by reference in a Form 10-K and Form 10-KSB report, need not be furnished to each purchaser that is not an accredited investor if the contents of material exhibits are identified and such exhibits are made available to a purchaser, upon his written request, a reasonable time prior to his purchase.

iv. At a reasonable time prior to the sale of securities to any purchaser that is not an accredited investor in a transaction under Rule 505 or Rule 506, the issuer shall furnish to the purchaser a brief description in writing of any material written information concerning the offering that has been provided by the issuer to any accredited investor but not previously delivered to such unaccredited purchaser. The issuer shall furnish any portion or all of this information to the purchaser, upon his written request a reasonable time prior to his purchase.

v. The issuer shall also make available to each purchaser at a reasonable time prior to his purchase of securities in a transaction under Rule 505 or Rule 506 the opportunity to ask questions and receive answers concerning the terms and conditions of the offering and to obtain any additional information which the issuer possesses or can acquire without unreasonable effort or expense that is necessary to verify the accuracy of information furnished under paragraph (b)2(i) or (ii) of this section.

vi. For business combinations or exchange offers, in addition to information required by Form S-4, the issuer shall provide to each purchaser at the time the plan is submitted to security holders, or, with an exchange, during the course of the transaction and prior to sale, written information about any terms or arrangements of the proposed transactions that are materially different from those for all other security holders. For purposes of this subsection, an issuer which is not subject to the reporting requirements of section 13 or 15(d) of the Exchange Act may satisfy the requirements of Part I.B.or C. of Form S-4 by compliance with paragraph (b)2(i) of this Rule 502.

vii. At a reasonable time prior to the sale of securities to any purchaser that is not an accredited investor in a transaction under Rule 505 or Rule 506, the issuer shall advise the purchaser of the limitations on resale in the manner contained in paragraph (d)2 of this section. Such disclosure may be contained in other materials required to be provided by this paragraph.

c. Limitation on manner of offering. Except as provided in Rule 504(b)(1), neither the issuer nor any person acting on its behalf shall offer or sell the securities by any form of general solicitation or general advertising, including, but not limited to, the following:

    1. Any advertisement, article, notice or other communication published in any newspaper, magazine, or similar media or broadcast over television or radio; and

    2. Any seminar or meeting whose attendees have been invited by any general solicitation or general advertising;

    Provided, however, that publication by an issuer of a notice in accordance with Rule 135c shall not be deemed to constitute general solicitation or general advertising for purposes of this section; Provided further, that, if the requirements of Rule 135e are satisfied, providing any journalist with access to press conferences held outside of the United States, to meeting with issuer or selling security holder representatives conducted outside of the United States, or to written press-related materials released outside the United States, at or in which a present or proposed offering of securities is discussed, will not be deemed to constitute general solicitation or general advertising for purposes of this section.

d. Limitations on resale. Except as provided in Rule 504(b)(1), securities acquired in a transaction under Regulation D shall have the status of securities acquired in a transaction under section 4(2) of the Act and cannot be resold without registration under the Act or an exemption therefrom. The issuer shall exercise reasonable care to assure that the purchasers of the securities are not underwriters within the meaning of section 2(11) of the Act, which reasonable care may be demonstrated by the following:

1. Reasonable inquiry to determine if the purchaser is acquiring the securities for himself or for other persons;
2. Written disclosure to each purchaser prior to sale that the securities have not been registered under the Act and, therefore, cannot be resold unless they are registered under the Act or unless an exemption from registration is available; and
3. Placement of a legend on the certificate or other document that evidences the securities stating that the securities have not been registered under the Act and setting forth or referring to the restrictions on transferability and sale of the securities.

    While taking these actions will establish the requisite reasonable care, it is not the exclusive method to demonstrate such care. Other actions by the issuer may satisfy this provision. In addition, Rule 502(b)2(vii) requires the delivery of written disclosure of the limitations on resale to investors in certain instances.

Rule 503 - Filing of Notice of Sales

a. An issuer offering or selling securities in reliance on Rule 504, Rule 505 or Rule 506 shall file with the Commission five copies of a notice on Form D no later than 15 days after the first sale of securities.
b. One copy of every notice on Form D shall be manually signed by a person duly authorized by the issuer.
c. If sales are made under Rule 505, the notice shall contain an undertaking by the issuer to furnish to the Commission, upon the written request of its staff, the information furnished by the issuer under Rule 502(b) to any purchaser that is not an accredited investor.
d. Amendments to notices filed under paragraph (a) of this Rule 503 need only report the issuer's name and the information required by Part C and any material change in the facts from those set forth in Parts A and B.
e. A notice on Form D shall be considered filed with the Commission under paragraph (a) of this Rule 503:
    1. As of the date on which it is received at the Commission's principal office in Washington, DC; or
    2. As of the date on which the notice is mailed by means of United States registered or certified mail to the Commission's principal office in Washington, DC, if the notice is delivered to such office after the date on which it is required to be filed.

Rule 504 - Exemption for Limited Offerings and Sales of Securities Not Exceeding $1,000,000

a. Exemption. Offers and sales of securities that satisfy the conditions in paragraph (b) of this Rule 504 by an issuer that is not:
    1. subject to the reporting requirements of section 13 or 15(d) of the Exchange Act:
    2. an investment company; or
    3. a development stage company that either has no specific business plan or purpose or has indicated that its business plan is to engage in a merger or acquisition with an unidentified company or companies, or other entity or person, shall be exempt from the provision of section 5 of the Act under section 3(b) of the Act.
b. Conditions to be met
    1. General conditions. To qualify for exemption under this Rule 504, offers and sales must satisfy the terms and conditions of Rule 501 and Rule 502 (a), (c) and (d), except that the provisions of Rule 502 (c) and (d) will not apply to offers and sales of securities under this Rule 504 that are made:
        i. Exclusively in one or more states that provide for the registration of the securities, and require the public filing and delivery to investors of a substantive disclosure document before sale, and are made in accordance with those state provisions;
        ii. In one or more states that have no provision for the registration of the securities or the public filing or delivery of a disclosure document before sale, if the securities have been registered in at least one

state that provides for such registration, public filing and delivery before sale, offers and sales are made in that state in accordance with such provisions, and the disclosure document is delivered before sale to all purchasers (including those in the states that have no such procedure); or

iii. Exclusively according to state law exemptions from registration that permit general solicitation and general advertising so long as sales are made only to "accredited investors" as defined in Rule 501(a).

2. The aggregate offering price for an offering of securities under this Rule 504, as defined in Rule 501(c), shall not exceed $1,000,000, less the aggregate offering price for all securities sold within the twelve months before the start of and during the offering of securities under this Rule 504, in reliance on any exemption under section 3(b), or in violation of section 5(a) of the Securities Act.

Rule 505 - Exemption for Limited Offers and Sales of Securities Not Exceeding $5,000,000

a. Exemption. Offers and sales of securities that satisfy the conditions in paragraph (b) by an issuer that is not an investment company shall be exempt from the provisions of section 5 of the Act under section 3(b) of the Act.

b. Conditions to be met

1. General conditions. To qualify for exemption under this section, offers and sales must satisfy the terms and conditions of Rule 501 and Rule 502.

2. Specific conditions

i. Limitation on aggregate offering price. The aggregate offering price for an offering of securities under this Rule 505, as defined in Rule 501(c), shall not exceed $5,000,000, less the aggregate offering price for all securities sold within the twelve months before the start of and during the offering of securities under this Rule 505 in reliance on any exemption under section 3(b) of the Act or in violation of section 5(a) of the Act.

ii. Limitation on number of purchasers. There are no more than or the issuer reasonably believes that there are no more than 35 purchasers of securities from the issuer in any offering under this section.

iii. Disqualifications. No exemption under this section shall be available for the securities of any issuer described in Rule 262 of Regulation A, except that for purposes of this section only:

A. The term "filing of the offering statement required by Rule 252" as used in Rule 262(a), (b) and (c) shall mean the first sale of securities under this section;

B. The term "underwriter" as used in Rule 262 (b) and (c) shall mean a person that has been or will be paid directly or indirectly remuneration for solicitation of purchasers in connection with sales of securities under this section; and

C. Paragraph (b) (2) (iii) of this Rule 505 shall not apply to any issuer if the Commission determines, upon a showing of good cause, that it is not necessary under the circumstances that the exemption be denied. Any such determination shall be without prejudice to any other action by the Commission in any other proceeding or matter with respect to the issuer or any other person.

Rule 506 - Exemption for Limited Offers and Sales without Regard to Dollar Amount of Offering

a. Exemption. Offers and sales of securities by an issuer that satisfy the conditions in paragraph (b) shall be deemed to be transactions not involving any public offering within the meaning of section 4 (2) of the Act.

b. Conditions to be met-

1. General conditions. To qualify for an exemption under this section, offers and sales must satisfy all the terms and conditions of Rule 501 and Rule 502.

2. Specific Conditions-

i. Limitation on number of purchasers. There are no more than or the issuer reasonably believes that there are no more than 35 purchasers of securities from the issuer in any offering under this section.

ii. Nature of purchasers. Each purchaser who is not an accredited investor either alone or with his purchaser representative(s) has such knowledge and experience in financial and business matters that he is capable of evaluating the merits and risks of the prospective investment, or the issuer reasonably believes immediately prior to making any sale that such purchaser comes within this description.

Rule 507 - Disqualifying Provision Relating to Exemptions Under Rule 504, Rule 505 and Rule 506

a. No exemption under Rule 504, Rule 505 or Rule 506 shall be available for an issuer if such issuer, any of its predecessors or affiliates have been subject to any order, judgment, or decree of any court of competent jurisdiction temporarily, preliminary or permanently enjoining such person for failure to comply with Rule 503.

b. Paragraph (a) of this section shall not apply if the Commission determines, upon a showing of good cause, that it is not necessary under the circumstances that the exemption be denied.

Rule 508 - Insignificant Deviations from a Term, Condition or Requirement of Regulation D

a. A failure to comply with a term, condition or requirement of Rule 504, Rule 505 or Rule 506 will not result in the loss of the exemption from the requirements of section 5 of the Act for any offer or sale to a particular individual or entity, if the person relying on the exemption shows:

    1. The failure to comply did not pertain to a term, condition or requirement directly intended to protect that particular individual or entity; and

    2. The failure to comply was insignificant with respect to the offering as a whole, provided that any failure to comply with paragraph (c) of Rule 502, paragraph (b)(2) of Rule 504, paragraph (b)(2)(i) and paragraph(b)(2)(ii) of Rule 505 and paragraph (b)(2)(i) of Rule 506 shall be deemed to be significant to the offering as a whole; and

    3. A good faith and reasonable attempt was made to comply with all applicable terms, conditions and requirements of Rule 504, Rule 505 or Rule 506.

b. A transaction made in reliance on Rule 504, Rule 505 or Rule 506 shall comply with all applicable terms, conditions and requirements of Regulation D. Where an exemption is established only through reliance upon paragraph (a) of this section, the failure to comply shall nonetheless be actionable by the Commission under section 20 of the Act.

---

19. SEC Rules and Regulations: 144 – Persons Deemed Not to Be Engaged in a Distribution and Therefore Not Underwriters

Preliminary Note: Certain basic principles are essential to an understanding of the registration requirements in the Securities Act of 1933 (the Act or the Securities Act) and the purposes underlying Rule 144: 1. If any person sells a non-exempt security to any other person, the sale must be registered unless an exemption can be found for the transaction. 2. Section 4(1) of the Securities Act provides one such exemption for a transaction "by a person other than an issuer, underwriter, or dealer." Therefore, an understanding of the term "underwriter" is important in determining whether or not the Section 4(1) exemption from registration is available for the sale of the securities. The term "underwriter" is broadly defined in Section 2(a)(11) of the Securities Act to mean any person who has purchased from an issuer with a view to, or offers or sells for an issuer in connection with, the distribution of any security, or participates, or has a direct or indirect participation in any such undertaking, or participates or has a participation in the direct or indirect underwriting of any such undertaking. The interpretation of this definition traditionally has focused on the words "with a view to" in the phrase "purchased from an issuer with a view to * * * distribution." An investment banking firm which arranges with an issuer for the public sale of its securities is clearly an "underwriter" under that section. However, individual investors who are not professionals in the securities business also may be "underwriters" if they act as links in a chain of transactions through which securities move from an issuer to the public. Since it is difficult to ascertain the mental state of the purchaser at the time of an acquisition of securities, prior to and since the adoption of Rule 144, subsequent acts and circumstances have been considered to determine whether the purchaser took the securities "with a view to distribution" at the time of the acquisition. Emphasis has been placed on factors such as the length of time the person held the securities and whether there has been an unforeseeable change in circumstances of the holder. Experience has shown, however, that reliance upon such factors alone has led to uncertainty in the application of the registration provisions of the Act. The Commission adopted Rule 144 to establish specific criteria for determining whether a person is not engaged in a distribution. Rule 144 creates a safe harbor from the Section 2(a)(11) definition of "underwriter." A person satisfying the applicable conditions of the Rule 144 safe harbor is deemed not to be engaged in a distribution of the securities and therefore not an underwriter of the securities for purposes of Section 2(a)(11). Therefore, such a person is deemed not to be an underwriter when determining whether a sale is eligible for the Section 4(1) exemption for "transactions by any person other than an issuer, underwriter, or dealer." If a sale of securities complies with all of the applicable conditions of Rule 144: 1. Any affiliate or other person who sells restricted securities will be deemed not to be engaged in a distribution and therefore not an underwriter for that transaction; 2. Any person who sells restricted or other securities on behalf of an affiliate of the issuer will be deemed not to be engaged in a distribution and therefore not an underwriter for that transaction; and 3. The purchaser in such transaction will receive securities that are not restricted securities. Rule 144 is not an exclusive safe harbor. A person who does not meet all of the applicable conditions of Rule 144 still may claim any other available exemption under the Act for the sale of the securities. The Rule 144 safe harbor is not available to any person with respect to any transaction or series of transactions that, although in technical compliance with Rule 144, is part of a plan or scheme to evade the registration requirements of the Act.

(a) Definitions. The following definitions shall apply for the purposes of this section.

   (1) An affiliate of an issuer is a person that directly, or indirectly through one or more intermediaries, controls, or is controlled by, or is under common control with, such issuer.

   (2) The term person when used with reference to a person for whose account securities are to be sold in reliance upon this section includes, in addition to such person, all of the following persons:

   (i) Any relative or spouse of such person, or any relative of such spouse, any one of whom has the same home as such person;

   (ii) Any trust or estate in which such person or any of the persons specified in paragraph (a)(2)(i) of this section collectively own 10 percent or more of the total beneficial interest or of which any of such persons serve as trustee, executor or in any similar capacity; and

   (iii) Any corporation or other organization (other than the issuer) in which such person or any of the persons specified in paragraph (a)(2)(i) of this section are the beneficial owners collectively of 10 percent or more of any class of equity securities or 10 percent or more of the equity interest.

   (3) The term restricted securities means:

   (i) Securities acquired directly or indirectly from the issuer, or from an affiliate of the issuer, in a transaction or chain of transactions not involving any public offering;

   (ii) Securities acquired from the issuer that are subject to the resale limitations of § 230.502(d) under Regulation D or § 230.701(c);

   (iii) Securities acquired in a transaction or chain of transactions meeting the requirements of § 230.144A;

   (iv) Securities acquired from the issuer in a transaction subject to the conditions of Regulation CE (§ 230.1001);

   (v) Equity securities of domestic issuers acquired in a transaction or chain of transactions subject to the conditions of § 230.901 or § 230.903 under Regulation S (§ 230.901 through § 230.905, and Preliminary Notes);

   (vi) Securities acquired in a transaction made under § 230.801 to the same extent and proportion that the securities held by the security holder of the class with respect to which the rights offering was made were, as of the record date for the rights offering, "restricted securities" within the meaning of this paragraph (a)(3);

(vii) Securities acquired in a transaction made under § 230.802 to the same extent and proportion that the securities that were tendered or exchanged in the exchange offer or business combination were "restricted securities" within the meaning of this paragraph (a)(3); and

(viii) Securities acquired from the issuer in a transaction subject to an exemption under section 4(5) (15 U.S.C. 77d(5)) of the Act.

(4) The term debt securities means:

(i) Any security other than an equity security as defined in § 230.405;

(ii) Non-participatory preferred stock, which is defined as non-convertible capital stock, the holders of which are entitled to a preference in payment of dividends and in distribution of assets on liquidation, dissolution, or winding up of the issuer, but are not entitled to participate in residual earnings or assets of the issuer; and

(iii) Asset-backed securities, as defined in § 229.1101 of this chapter.

(b) Conditions to be met. Subject to paragraph (i) of this section, the following conditions must be met:

(1) Non-affiliates.

(i) If the issuer of the securities is, and has been for a period of at least 90 days immediately before the sale, subject to the reporting requirements of section 13 or 15(d) of the Securities Exchange Act of 1934 (the Exchange Act), any person who is not an affiliate of the issuer at the time of the sale, and has not been an affiliate during the preceding three months, who sells restricted securities of the issuer for his or her own account shall be deemed not to be an underwriter of those securities within the meaning of section 2(a)(11) of the Act if all of the conditions of paragraphs (c)(1) and (d) of this section are met. The requirements of paragraph (c)(1) of this section shall not apply to restricted securities sold for the account of a person who is not an affiliate of the issuer at the time of the sale and has not been an affiliate during the preceding three months, provided a period of one year has elapsed since the later of the date the securities were acquired from the issuer or from an affiliate of the issuer.

(ii) If the issuer of the securities is not, or has not been for a period of at least 90 days immediately before the sale, subject to the reporting requirements of section 13 or 15(d) of the Exchange Act, any person who is not an affiliate of the issuer at the time of the sale, and has not been an affiliate during the preceding three months, who sells restricted securities of the issuer for his or her own account shall be deemed not to be an underwriter of those securities within the meaning of section 2(a)(11) of the Act if the condition of paragraph (d) of this section is met.

(2) Affiliates or persons selling on behalf of affiliates. Any affiliate of the issuer, or any person who was an affiliate at any time during the 90 days immediately before the sale, who sells restricted securities, or any person who sells restricted or any other securities for the account of an affiliate of the issuer of such securities, or any person who sells restricted or any other securities for the account of a person who was an affiliate at any time during the 90 days immediately before the sale, shall be deemed not to be an underwriter of those securities within the meaning of section 2(a)(11) of the Act if all of the conditions of this section are met.

(c) Current public information. Adequate current public information with respect to the issuer of the securities must be available. Such information will be deemed to be available only if the applicable condition set forth in this paragraph is met:

(1) Reporting issuers. The issuer is, and has been for a period of at least 90 days immediately before the sale, subject to the reporting requirements of section 13 or 15(d) of the Exchange Act and has:

(i) Filed all required reports under section 13 or 15(d) of the Exchange Act, as applicable, during the 12 months preceding such sale (or for such shorter period that the issuer was required to file such reports), other than Form 8-K reports (§ 249.308 of this chapter); and

(ii) Submitted electronically every Interactive Data File (§ 232.11 of this chapter) required to be submitted pursuant to § 232.405 of this chapter, during the 12 months preceding such sale (or for such shorter period that the issuer was required to submit such files); or

(2) Non-reporting issuers. If the issuer is not subject to the reporting requirements of section 13 or 15(d) of the Exchange Act, there is publicly available the information concerning the issuer specified in paragraphs (a)(5)(i) to (xiv), inclusive, and paragraph (a)(5)(xvi) of § 240.15c2-11 of this chapter, or, if the issuer is an insurance company, the information specified in section 12(g)(2)(G)(i) of the Exchange Act (15 U.S.C. 78l(g)(2)(G)(i)).

(d) Holding period for restricted securities. If the securities sold are restricted securities, the following provisions apply:

(1) General rule.

(i) If the issuer of the securities is, and has been for a period of at least 90 days immediately before the sale, subject to the reporting requirements of section 13 or 15(d) of the Exchange Act, a minimum of six months must elapse between the later of the date of the acquisition of the securities from the issuer, or from an affiliate of the issuer, and any resale of such securities in reliance on this section for the account of either the acquiror or any subsequent holder of those securities.

(ii) If the issuer of the securities is not, or has not been for a period of at least 90 days immediately before the sale, subject to the reporting requirements of section 13 or 15(d) of the Exchange Act, a minimum of one year must elapse between the later of the date of the acquisition of the securities from the issuer, or from an affiliate of the issuer, and any resale of such securities in reliance on this section for the account of either the acquiror or any subsequent holder of those securities.

(iii) If the acquiror takes the securities by purchase, the holding period shall not begin until the full purchase price or other consideration is paid or given by the person acquiring the securities from the issuer or from an affiliate of the issuer.

(2) Promissory notes, other obligations or installment contracts. Giving the issuer or affiliate of the issuer from whom the securities were purchased a promissory note or other obligation to pay the purchase price, or entering into an installment purchase contract with such seller, shall not be deemed full payment of the purchase price unless the promissory note, obligation or contract:

(i) Provides for full recourse against the purchaser of the securities;

(ii) Is secured by collateral, other than the securities purchased, having a fair market value at least equal to the purchase price of the securities purchased; and

(iii) Shall have been discharged by payment in full prior to the sale of the securities.

(3) Determination of holding period. The following provisions shall apply for the purpose of determining the period securities have been held:

(i) Stock dividends, splits and recapitalizations. Securities acquired from the issuer as a dividend or pursuant to a stock split, reverse split or recapitalization shall be deemed to have been acquired at the same time as the securities on which the dividend or, if more than one, the initial dividend was paid, the securities involved in the split or reverse split, or the securities surrendered in connection with the recapitalization.

(ii) Conversions and exchanges. If the securities sold were acquired from the issuer solely in exchange for other securities of the same issuer, the newly acquired securities shall be deemed to have been acquired at the same time as the securities surrendered for conversion or exchange, even if the securities surrendered were not convertible or exchangeable by their terms.

(iii) Contingent issuance of securities. Securities acquired as a contingent payment of the purchase price of an equity interest in a business, or the assets of a business, sold to the issuer or an affiliate of the issuer shall be deemed to have been acquired at the time of such sale if the issuer or affiliate was then committed to issue the securities subject only to conditions other than the payment of further consideration for such securities. An agreement entered into in connection with any such purchase to remain in the employment of, or not to compete with, the issuer or affiliate or the rendering of services pursuant to such agreement shall not be deemed to be the payment of further consideration for such securities.

(iv) Pledged securities. Securities which are bona-fide pledged by an affiliate of the issuer when sold by the pledgee, or by a purchaser, after a default in the obligation secured by the pledge, shall be deemed to have been acquired when they were acquired by the pledgor, except that if the securities were pledged without recourse they shall be deemed to have been acquired by the pledgee at the time of the pledge or by the purchaser at the time of purchase.

(v) Gifts of securities. Securities acquired from an affiliate of the issuer by gift shall be deemed to have been acquired by the donee when they were acquired by the donor.

(vi) Trusts. Where a trust settlor is an affiliate of the issuer, securities acquired from the settlor by the trust, or acquired from the trust by the beneficiaries thereof, shall be deemed to have been acquired when such securities were acquired by the settlor.

(vii) Estates. Where a deceased person was an affiliate of the issuer, securities held by the estate of such person or acquired from such estate by the estate beneficiaries shall be deemed to have been acquired when they were acquired by the deceased person, except that no holding period is required if the estate is not an affiliate of the issuer or if the securities are sold by a beneficiary of the estate who is not such an affiliate.

(viii) Rule 145(a) transactions. The holding period for securities acquired in a transaction specified in § 230.145(a) shall be deemed to commence on the date the securities were acquired by the purchaser in such transaction, except as otherwise provided in paragraphs (d)(3)(ii) and (ix) of this section.

(ix) Holding company formations. Securities acquired from the issuer in a transaction effected solely for the purpose of forming a holding company shall be deemed to have been acquired at the same time as the securities of the predecessor issuer exchanged in the holding company formation where:

(A) The newly formed holding company's securities were issued solely in exchange for the securities of the predecessor company as part of a reorganization of the predecessor company into a holding company structure;

(B) Holders received securities of the same class evidencing the same proportional interest in the holding company as they held in the predecessor, and the rights and interests of the holders of such securities are substantially the same as those they possessed as holders of the predecessor company's securities; and

(C) Immediately following the transaction, the holding company has no significant assets other than securities of the predecessor company and its existing subsidiaries and has substantially the same assets and liabilities on a consolidated basis as the predecessor company had before the transaction.

(x) Cashless exercise of options and warrants. If the securities sold were acquired from the issuer solely upon cashless exercise of options or warrants issued by the issuer, the newly acquired securities shall be deemed to have been acquired at the same time as the exercised options or warrants, even if the options or warrants exercised originally did not provide for cashless exercise by their terms.

(e) Limitation on amount of securities sold. Except as hereinafter provided, the amount of securities sold for the account of an affiliate of the issuer in reliance upon this section shall be determined as follows:

(1) If any securities are sold for the account of an affiliate of the issuer, regardless of whether those securities are restricted, the amount of securities sold, together with all sales of securities of the same class sold for the account of such person within the preceding three months, shall not exceed the greatest of:

(i) One percent of the shares or other units of the class outstanding as shown by the most recent report or statement published by the issuer, or

(ii) The average weekly reported volume of trading in such securities on all national securities exchanges and/or reported through the automated quotation system of a registered securities association during the four calendar weeks preceding the filing of notice required by paragraph (h), or if no such notice is required the date of receipt of the order to execute the transaction by the broker or the date of execution of the transaction directly with a market maker, or

(iii) The average weekly volume of trading in such securities reported pursuant to an effective transaction reporting plan or an effective national market system plan as those terms are defined in §

242.600 of this chapter during the four-week period specified in paragraph (e)(1)(ii) of this section.

(2) If the securities sold are debt securities, then the amount of debt securities sold for the account of an affiliate of the issuer, regardless of whether those securities are restricted, shall not exceed the greater of the limitation set forth in paragraph (e)(1) of this section or, together with all sales of securities of the same tranche (or class when the securities are non-participatory preferred stock) sold for the account of such person within the preceding three months, ten percent of the principal amount of the tranche (or class when the securities are non-participatory preferred stock) attributable to the securities sold.

(3) Determination of amount. For the purpose of determining the amount of securities specified in paragraph (e)(1) of this section and, as applicable, paragraph (e)(2) of this section, the following provisions shall apply:

    (i) Where both convertible securities and securities of the class into which they are convertible are sold, the amount of convertible securities sold shall be deemed to be the amount of securities of the class into which they are convertible for the purpose of determining the aggregate amount of securities of both classes sold;

    (ii) The amount of securities sold for the account of a pledgee of those securities, or for the account of a purchaser of the pledged securities, during any period of three months within six months (or within one year if the issuer of the securities is not, or has not been for a period of at least 90 days immediately before the sale, subject to the reporting requirements of section 13 or 15(d) of the Exchange Act) after a default in the obligation secured by the pledge, and the amount of securities sold during the same three-month period for the account of the pledgor shall not exceed, in the aggregate, the amount specified in paragraph (e)(1) or (2) of this section, whichever is applicable;

(f) Manner of sale.

    (1) The securities shall be sold in one of the following manners:

        (i) Brokers' transactions within the meaning of section 4(4) of the Act;

        (ii) Transactions directly with a market maker, as that term is defined in section 3(a)(38) of the Exchange Act; or

        (iii) Riskless principal transactions where:

            (A) The offsetting trades must be executed at the same price (exclusive of an explicitly disclosed markup or markdown, commission equivalent, or other fee);

            (B) The transaction is permitted to be reported as riskless under the rules of a self-regulatory organization; and

            (C) The requirements of paragraphs (g)(2)(applicable to any markup or markdown, commission equivalent, or other fee), (g)(3), and (g)(4) of this section are met.

    (2) The person selling the securities shall not:

        (i) Solicit or arrange for the solicitation of orders to buy the securities in anticipation of or in connection with such transaction, or

        (ii) Make any payment in connection with the offer or sale of the securities to any person other than the broker or dealer who executes the order to sell the securities.

    (3) Paragraph (f) of this section shall not apply to:

        (i) Securities sold for the account of the estate of a deceased person or for the account of a beneficiary of such estate provided the estate or estate beneficiary is not an affiliate of the issuer; or

        (ii) Debt securities.

(g) Brokers' transactions. The term brokers' transactions in section 4(4) of the Act shall for the purposes of this rule be deemed to include transactions by a broker in which such broker:

    (1) Does no more than execute the order or orders to sell the securities as agent for the person for whose account the securities are sold;

    (2) Receives no more than the usual and customary broker's commission;

    (3) Neither solicits nor arranges for the solicitation of customers' orders to buy the securities in anticipation of or in connection with the transaction; Provided, that the foregoing shall not preclude:

(i) Inquiries by the broker of other brokers or dealers who have indicated an interest in the securities within the preceding 60 days;

(ii) Inquiries by the broker of his customers who have indicated an unsolicited bona fide interest in the securities within the preceding 10 business days;

(iii) The publication by the broker of bid and ask quotations for the security in an inter-dealer quotation system provided that such quotations are incident to the maintenance of a bona fide inter-dealer market for the security for the broker's own account and that the broker has published bona fide bid and ask quotations for the security in an inter-dealer quotation system on each of at least twelve days within the preceding thirty calendar days with no more than four business days in succession without such two-way quotations; or

(iv) The publication by the broker of bid and ask quotations for the security in an alternative trading system, as defined in § 242.300 of this chapter, provided that the broker has published bona fide bid and ask quotations for the security in the alternative trading system on each of the last twelve business days; and

(h) Notice of proposed sale.

(1) If the amount of securities to be sold in reliance upon this rule during any period of three months exceeds 5,000 shares or other units or has an aggregate sale price in excess of $50,000, three copies of a notice on Form 144 (§ 239.144 of this chapter) shall be filed with the Commission. If such securities are admitted to trading on any national securities exchange, one copy of such notice also shall be transmitted to the principal exchange on which such securities are admitted.

(2) The Form 144 shall be signed by the person for whose account the securities are to be sold and shall be transmitted for filing concurrently with either the placing with a broker of an order to execute a sale of securities in reliance upon this rule or the execution directly with a market maker of such a sale. Neither the filing of such notice nor the failure of the Commission to comment on such notice shall be deemed to preclude the Commission from taking any action that it deems necessary or appropriate with respect to the sale of the securities referred to in such notice. The person filing the notice required by this paragraph shall have a bona fide intention to sell the securities referred to in the notice within a reasonable time after the filing of such notice.

(i) Unavailability to securities of issuers with no or nominal operations and no or nominal non-cash assets.

(1) This section is not available for the resale of securities initially issued by an issuer defined below:

(i) An issuer, other than a business combination related shell company, as defined in § 230.405, or an asset-backed issuer, as defined in Item 1101(b) of Regulation AB (§ 229.1101(b) of this chapter), that has:

(A) No or nominal operations; and

(B) Either:

(1) No or nominal assets;

(2) Assets consisting solely of cash and cash equivalents; or

(3) Assets consisting of any amount of cash and cash equivalents and nominal other assets; or

(ii) An issuer that has been at any time previously an issuer described in paragraph (i)(1)(i).

(2) Notwithstanding paragraph (i)(1), if the issuer of the securities previously had been an issuer described in paragraph (i)(1)(i) but has ceased to be an issuer described in paragraph (i)(1)(i); is subject to the reporting requirements of section 13 or 15(d) of the Exchange Act; has filed all reports and other materials required to be filed by section 13 or 15(d) of the Exchange Act, as applicable, during the preceding 12 months (or for such shorter period that the issuer was required to file such reports and materials), other than Form 8-K reports (§ 249.308 of this chapter); and has filed current "Form 10 information" with the Commission reflecting its status as an entity that is no longer an issuer described in paragraph (i)(1)(i), then those securities may be sold subject to

the requirements of this section after one year has elapsed from the date that the issuer filed "Form 10 information" with the Commission.

(3) The term "Form 10 information" means the information that is required by Form 10 or Form 20-F (§ 249.210 or § 249.220f of this chapter), as applicable to the issuer of the securities, to register under the Exchange Act each class of securities being sold under this rule. The issuer may provide the Form 10 information in any filing of the issuer with the Commission. The Form 10 information is deemed filed when the initial filing is made with the Commission.

---

20. SEC Rules and Regulations: 144A – Private Resales of Securities to Institutions

Preliminary Notes: This section relates solely to the application of section 5 of the Act and not to antifraud or other provisions of the federal securities laws. 2. Attempted compliance with this section does not act as an exclusive election; any seller hereunder may also claim the availability of any other applicable exemption from the registration requirements of the Act. 3. In view of the objective of this section and the policies underlying the Act, this section is not available with respect to any transaction or series of transactions that, although in technical compliance with this section, is part of a plan or scheme to evade the registration provisions of the Act. In such cases, registration under the Act is required. 4. Nothing in this section obviates the need for any issuer or any other person to comply with the securities registration or broker-dealer registration requirements of the Securities Exchange Act of 1934 (the Exchange Act), whenever such requirements are applicable. 5. Nothing in this section obviates the need for any person to comply with any applicable state law relating to the offer or sale of securities. 6. Securities acquired in a transaction made pursuant to the provisions of this section are deemed to be restricted securities within the meaning of § 230.144(a)(3) of this chapter. 7. The fact that purchasers of securities from the issuer thereof may purchase such securities with a view to reselling such securities pursuant to this section will not affect the availability to such issuer of an exemption under section 4(a)(2) of the Act, or Regulation D under the Act, from the registration requirements of the Act.

(a) Definitions.

(1) For purposes of this section, qualified institutional buyer shall mean:

(i) Any of the following entities, acting for its own account or the accounts of other qualified institutional buyers, that in the aggregate owns and invests on a discretionary basis at least $100 million in securities of issuers that are not affiliated with the entity:

(A) Any insurance company as defined in section 2(a)(13) of the Act;

(B) Any investment company registered under the Investment Company Act or any business development company as defined in section 2(a)(48) of that Act;

(C) Any Small Business Investment Company licensed by the U.S. Small Business Administration under section 301(c) or (d) of the Small Business Investment Act of 1958;

(D) Any plan established and maintained by a state, its political subdivisions, or any agency or instrumentality of a state or its political subdivisions, for the benefit of its employees;

(E) Any employee benefit plan within the meaning of title I of the Employee Retirement Income Security Act of 1974;

(F) Any trust fund whose trustee is a bank or trust company and whose participants are exclusively plans of the types identified in paragraph (a)(1)(i) (D) or (E) of this section, except trust funds that include as participants individual retirement accounts or H.R. 10 plans.

    (G) Any business development company as defined in section 202(a)(22) of the Investment Advisers Act of 1940;

    (H) Any organization described in section 501(c)(3) of the Internal Revenue Code, corporation (other than a bank as defined in section 3(a)(2) of the Act or a savings and loan association or other institution referenced in section 3(a)(5)(A) of the Act or a foreign bank or savings and loan association or equivalent institution), partnership, or Massachusetts or similar business trust; and

    (I) Any investment adviser registered under the Investment Advisers Act.

(ii) Any dealer registered pursuant to section 15 of the Exchange Act, acting for its own account or the accounts of other qualified institutional buyers, that in the aggregate owns and invests on a discretionary basis at least $10 million of securities of issuers that are not affiliated with the dealer, Provided, That securities constituting the whole or a part of an unsold allotment to or subscription by a dealer as a participant in a public offering shall not be deemed to be owned by such dealer;

(iii) Any dealer registered pursuant to section 15 of the Exchange Act acting in a riskless principal transaction on behalf of a qualified institutional buyer;

(iv) Any investment company registered under the Investment Company Act, acting for its own account or for the accounts of other qualified institutional buyers, that is part of a family of investment companies which own in the aggregate at least $100 million in securities of issuers, other than issuers that are affiliated with the investment company or are part of such family of investment companies. Family of investment companies means any two or more investment companies registered under the Investment Company Act, except for a unit investment trust whose assets consist solely of shares of one or more registered investment companies, that have the same investment adviser (or, in the case of unit investment trusts, the same depositor), Provided That, for purposes of this section:

    (A) Each series of a series company (as defined in Rule 18f-2 under the Investment Company Act [17 CFR 270.18f-2]) shall be deemed to be a separate investment company; and

    (B) Investment companies shall be deemed to have the same adviser (or depositor) if their advisers (or depositors) are majority-owned subsidiaries of the same parent, or if one investment company's adviser (or depositor) is a majority-owned subsidiary of the other investment company's adviser (or depositor);

(v) Any entity, all of the equity owners of which are qualified institutional buyers, acting for its own account or the accounts of other qualified institutional buyers; and

(vi) Any bank as defined in section 3(a)(2) of the Act, any savings and loan association or other institution as referenced in section 3(a)(5)(A) of the Act, or any foreign bank or savings and loan association or equivalent institution, acting for its own account or the accounts of other qualified institutional buyers, that in the aggregate owns and invests on a discretionary basis at least $100 million in securities of issuers that are not affiliated with it and that has an audited net worth of at least $25 million as demonstrated in its latest annual financial statements, as of a date not more than 16 months preceding the date of sale under the Rule in the case of a U.S. bank or savings and loan association, and not more than 18 months preceding such date of sale for a foreign bank or savings and loan association or equivalent institution.

(2) In determining the aggregate amount of securities owned and invested on a discretionary basis by an entity, the following instruments and interests shall be excluded: bank deposit notes and certificates of deposit; loan participations; repurchase agreements; securities owned but subject to a repurchase agreement; and currency, interest rate and commodity swaps.

(3) The aggregate value of securities owned and invested on a discretionary basis by an entity shall be the cost of such securities, except where the entity reports its securities holdings in its financial statements on the basis of their market value, and no current information with respect to the cost of those securities has been published. In the latter event, the securities may be valued at market for purposes of this section.

(4) In determining the aggregate amount of securities owned by an entity and invested on a discretionary basis, securities owned by subsidiaries of the entity that are consolidated with the entity in its financial statements prepared in accordance with generally accepted accounting principles may be included if the investments of such subsidiaries are managed under the direction of the entity, except that, unless the entity is a reporting company under section 13 or 15(d) of the Exchange Act, securities owned by such subsidiaries may not be included if the entity itself is a majority-owned subsidiary that would be included in the consolidated financial statements of another enterprise.

(5) For purposes of this section, riskless principal transaction means a transaction in which a dealer buys a security from any person and makes a simultaneous offsetting sale of such security to a qualified institutional buyer, including another dealer acting as riskless principal for a qualified institutional buyer.

(6) For purposes of this section, effective conversion premium means the amount, expressed as a percentage of the security's conversion value, by which the price at issuance of a convertible security exceeds its conversion value.

(7) For purposes of this section, effective exercise premium means the amount, expressed as a percentage of the warrant's exercise value, by which the sum of the price at issuance and the exercise price of a warrant exceeds its exercise value.

(b) Sales by persons other than issuers or dealers. Any person, other than the issuer or a dealer, who offers or sells securities in compliance with the conditions set forth in paragraph (d) of this section shall be deemed not to be engaged in a distribution of such securities and therefore not to be an underwriter of such securities within the meaning of sections 2(a)(11) and 4(a)(1) of the Act.

(c) Sales by dealers. Any dealer who offers or sells securities in compliance with the conditions set forth in paragraph (d) of this section shall be deemed not to be a participant in a distribution of such securities within the meaning of section 4(a)(3)(C) of the Act and not to be an underwriter of such securities within the meaning of section 2(a)(11) of the Act, and such securities shall be deemed not to have been offered to the public within the meaning of section 4(a)(3)(A) of the Act.

(d) Conditions to be met. To qualify for exemption under this section, an offer or sale must meet the following conditions:

(1) The securities are sold only to a qualified institutional buyer or to a purchaser that the seller and any person acting on behalf of the seller reasonably believe is a qualified institutional buyer. In determining whether a prospective purchaser is a qualified institutional buyer, the seller and any person acting on its behalf shall be entitled to rely upon the following non-exclusive methods of establishing the prospective purchaser's ownership and discretionary investments of securities:

(i) The prospective purchaser's most recent publicly available financial statements, Provided That such statements present the information as of a date within 16 months preceding the date of sale of securities under this section in the case of a U.S. purchaser and within 18 months preceding such date of sale for a foreign purchaser;

(ii) The most recent publicly available information appearing in documents filed by the prospective purchaser with the Commission or another United States federal, state, or local governmental agency or self-regulatory organization, or with a foreign governmental agency or self-regulatory organization, Provided That any such information is as of a date within 16 months preceding the date of sale of securities under this section in the case of a U.S. purchaser and within 18 months preceding such date of sale for a foreign purchaser;

(iii) The most recent publicly available information appearing in a recognized securities manual, Provided That such information is as of a date within 16 months preceding the date of sale of securities under this section in the case of a U.S. purchaser and within 18 months preceding such date of sale for a foreign purchaser; or

(iv) A certification by the chief financial officer, a person fulfilling an equivalent function, or other executive officer of the purchaser, specifying the amount of securities owned and invested on a discretionary basis by the purchaser as of a specific date on or since the close of the purchaser's most recent fiscal year, or, in the case of a purchaser that is a member of a family of investment companies, a certification by an executive officer of the investment adviser specifying the amount of securities owned by the family of investment companies as of a specific date on or since the close of the purchaser's most recent fiscal year;

(2) The seller and any person acting on its behalf takes reasonable steps to ensure that the purchaser is aware that the seller may rely on the exemption from the provisions of section 5 of the Act provided by this section;

(3) The securities offered or sold:

(i) Were not, when issued, of the same class as securities listed on a national securities exchange registered under section 6 of the Exchange Act or quoted in a U.S. automated inter-dealer quotation system; Provided, That securities that are convertible or exchangeable into securities so listed or quoted at the time of issuance and that had an effective conversion premium of less than 10 percent, shall be treated as securities of the class into which they are convertible or exchangeable; and that warrants that may be exercised for securities so listed or quoted at the time of issuance, for a period of less than 3 years from the date of issuance, or that had an effective exercise premium of less than 10 percent, shall be treated as securities of the class to be issued upon exercise; and Provided further, That the Commission may from time to time, taking into account then-existing market practices, designate additional securities and classes of securities that will not be deemed of the same class as securities listed on a national securities exchange or quoted in a U.S. automated inter-dealer quotation system; and

(ii) Are not securities of an open-end investment company, unit investment trust or face-amount certificate company that is or is required to be registered under section 8 of the Investment Company Act; and

(4)

(i) In the case of securities of an issuer that is neither subject to section 13 or 15(d) of the Exchange Act, nor exempt from reporting pursuant to Rule 12g3-2(b) (§ 240.12g3-2(b) of this chapter) under the Exchange Act, nor a foreign government as defined in Rule 405 (§ 230.405 of this chapter) eligible to register securities under Schedule B of the Act, the holder and a prospective purchaser designated by the holder have the right to obtain from the issuer, upon request of the holder, and the prospective purchaser has received from the issuer, the seller, or a person acting on either of their behalf, at or prior to the time of sale, upon such prospective purchaser's request to the holder or the issuer, the following information (which shall be reasonably current in relation to the date of resale under this section): a very brief statement of the nature of the business of the issuer and the products and services it offers; and the issuer's most recent balance sheet and profit and loss and retained earnings statements, and similar financial statements for such part of the two preceding fiscal years as the issuer has been in operation (the financial statements should be audited to the extent reasonably available).

(ii) The requirement that the information be reasonably current will be presumed to be satisfied if:

(A) The balance sheet is as of a date less than 16 months before the date of resale, the statements of profit and loss and retained earnings are for the 12 months preceding the date of such balance sheet, and if such balance sheet is not as of a date less than 6 months before the date of resale, it shall be accompanied by additional statements of profit and loss and retained earnings for the period from the date of such balance sheet to a date less than 6 months before the date of resale; and

(B) The statement of the nature of the issuer's business and its products and services offered is as of a date within 12 months prior to the date of resale; or

(C) With regard to foreign private issuers, the required information meets the timing requirements of the issuer's home country or principal trading markets.

(e) Offers and sales of securities pursuant to this section shall be deemed not to affect the availability of any exemption or safe harbor relating to any previous or subsequent offer or sale of such securities by the issuer or any prior or subsequent holder thereof.

---

21. SEC Rules and Regulations: 145 – Reclassification of Securities, Mergers, Consolidations and Acquisitions of Assets

Preliminary Note: Rule 145 (§ 230.145 of this chapter) is designed to make available the protection provided by registration under the Securities Act of 1933, as amended (Act), to persons who are offered securities in a business combination of the type described in paragraphs (a) (1), (2) and (3) of the rule. The thrust of the rule is that an offer, offer to sell, offer for sale, or sale occurs when there is submitted to security holders a plan or agreement pursuant to which such holders are required to elect, on the basis of what is in substance a new investment decision, whether to accept a new or different security in exchange for their existing security. Rule 145 embodies the Commission's determination that such transactions are subject to the registration requirements of the Act, and that the previously existing no-sale theory of Rule 133 is no longer consistent with the statutory purposes of the Act. See Release No. 33-5316 (October 6, 1972) [37 FR 23631]. Securities issued in transactions described in paragraph (a) of Rule 145 may be registered on Form S-4 or F-4 (§ 239.25 or § 239.34 of this chapter) or Form N-14 (§ 239.23 of this chapter) under the Act.
Transactions for which statutory exemptions under the Act, including those contained in sections 3(a)(9), (10), (11) and 4(2), are otherwise available are not affected by Rule 145. Reference is made to Rule 153a (§ 230.153a of this chapter) describing the prospectus delivery required in a transaction of the type referred to in Rule 145. A reclassification of securities covered by Rule 145 would be exempt from registration pursuant to section 3(a)(9) or (11) of the Act if the conditions of either of these sections are satisfied.

(a) Transactions within this section. An offer, offer to sell, offer for sale, or sale shall be deemed to be involved, within the meaning of section 2(3) of the Act, so far as the security holders of a corporation or other person are concerned where, pursuant to statutory provisions of the jurisdiction under which such corporation or other person is organized, or pursuant to provisions contained in its certificate of incorporation or similar controlling instruments, or otherwise, there is submitted for the vote or consent of such security holders a plan or agreement for:
  (1) Reclassifications. A reclassification of securities of such corporation or other person, other than a stock split, reverse stock split, or change in par value, which involves the substitution of a security for another security;
  (2) Mergers of consolidations. A statutory merger or consolidation or similar plan or acquisition in which securities of such corporation or other person held by such security holders will become or be exchanged for securities of any person, unless the sole purpose of the transaction is to change an issuer's domicile solely within the United States; or
  (3) Transfers of assets. A transfer of assets of such corporation or other person, to another person in consideration of the issuance of securities of such other person or any of its affiliates, if:
    (i) Such plan or agreement provides for dissolution of the corporation or other person whose security holders are voting or consenting; or
    (ii) Such plan or agreement provides for a pro rata or similar distribution of such securities to the security holders voting or consenting; or

    (iii) The board of directors or similar representatives of such corporation or other person, adopts resolutions relative to paragraph (a)(3) (i) or (ii) of this section within 1 year after the taking of such vote or consent; or

    (iv) The transfer of assets is a part of a preexisting plan for distribution of such securities, notwithstanding paragraph (a)(3) (i), (ii), or (iii) of this section.

(b) Communications before a Registration Statement is filed. Communications made in connection with or relating to a transaction described in paragraph (a) of this section that will be registered under the Act may be made under § 230.135, § 230.165 or § 230.166.

(c) Persons and parties deemed to be underwriters. For purposes of this section, if any party to a transaction specified in paragraph (a) of this section is a shell company, other than a business combination related shell company, as those terms are defined in § 230.405, any party to that transaction, other than the issuer, or any person who is an affiliate of such party at the time such transaction is submitted for vote or consent, who publicly offers or sells securities of the issuer acquired in connection with any such transaction, shall be deemed to be engaged in a distribution and therefore to be an underwriter thereof within the meaning of Section 2(a)(11) of the Act.

(d) Resale provisions for persons and parties deemed underwriters. Notwithstanding the provisions of paragraph (c), a person or party specified in that paragraph shall not be deemed to be engaged in a distribution and therefore not to be an underwriter of securities acquired in a transaction specified in paragraph (a) that was registered under the Act if:

    (1) The issuer has met the requirements applicable to an issuer of securities in paragraph (i)(2) of § 230.144; and

    (2) One of the following three conditions is met:

        (i) Such securities are sold by such person or party in accordance with the provisions of paragraphs (c), (e), (f), and (g) of § 230.144 and at least 90 days have elapsed since the date the securities were acquired from the issuer in such transaction; or

        (ii) Such person or party is not, and has not been for at least three months, an affiliate of the issuer, and at least six months, as determined in accordance with paragraph (d) of § 230.144, have elapsed since the date the securities were acquired from the issuer in such transaction, and the issuer meets the requirements of paragraph (c) of § 230.144; or

        (iii) Such person or party is not, and has not been for at least three months, an affiliate of the issuer, and at least one year, as determined in accordance with paragraph (d) of § 230.144, has elapsed since the date the securities were acquired from the issuer in such transaction.

(e) Definitions.

    (1) The term affiliate as used in paragraphs (c) and (d) of this section shall have the same meaning as the definition of that term in § 230.144.

    (2) The term party as used in paragraphs (c) and (d) of this section shall mean the corporations, business entities, or other persons, other than the issuer, whose assets or capital structure are affected by the transactions specified in paragraph (a) of this section.

    (3) The term person as used in paragraphs (c) and (d) of this section, when used in reference to a person for whose account securities are to be sold, shall have the same meaning as the definition of that term in paragraph (a)(2) of § 230.144.

---

22. SEC Rules and Regulations: 147 – "Part of an Issue," "Person Resident," and "Doing Business Within" for Purposes of Section 3(a)(11)

1. This rule shall not raise any presumption that the exemption provided by section 3(a)(11) of the Act is not available for transactions by an issuer which do not satisfy all of the provisions of the rule.
2. Nothing in this rule obviates the need for compliance with any state law relating to the offer and sale of the securities.
3. Section 5 of the Act requires that all securities offered by the use of the mails or by any means or instruments of transportation or communication in interstate commerce be registered with the Commission. Congress, however, provided certain exemptions in the Act from such registration provisions where there was no practical need for registration or where the benefits of registration were too remote. Among those exemptions is that provided by section 3(a)(11) of the Act for transactions in any security which is a part of an issue offered and sold only to persons resident within a single State or Territory, where the issuer of such security is a person resident and doing business within * * * such State or Territory. The legislative history of that Section suggests that the exemption was intended to apply only to issues genuinely local in character, which in reality represent local financing by local industries, carried out through local investment. Rule 147 is intended to provide more objective standards upon which responsible local businessmen intending to raise capital from local sources may rely in claiming the section 3(a)(11) exemption.

   All of the terms and conditions of the rule must be satisfied in order for the rule to be available. These are: (i) That the issuer be a resident of and doing business within the state or territory in which all offers and sales are made; and (ii) that no part of the issue be offered or sold to non-residents within the period of time specified in the rule. For purposes of the rule the definition of issuer in section 2(4) of the Act shall apply.

   All offers, offers to sell, offers for sale, and sales which are part of the same issue must meet all of the conditions of Rule 147 for the rule to be available. The determination whether offers, offers to sell, offers for sale and sales of securities are part of the same issue (i.e., are deemed to be integrated) will continue to be a question of fact and will depend on the particular circumstances. See Securities Act of 1933 Release No. 4434 (December 6, 1961) (26 FR 9158). Securities Act Release No. 4434 indicated that in determining whether offers and sales should be regarded as part of the same issue and thus should be integrated any one or more of the following factors may be determinative:
   (i) Are the offerings part of a single plan of financing;
   (ii) Do the offerings involve issuance of the same class of securities;
   (iii) Are the offerings made at or about the same time;
   (iv) Is the same type of consideration to be received; and
   (v) Are the offerings made for the same general purpose.
4. The rule provides an exemption for offers and sales by the issuer only. It is not available for offers or sales of securities by other persons. Section 3(a)(11) of the Act has been interpreted to permit offers and sales by persons controlling the issuer, if the exemption provided by that section would have been available to the issuer at the time of the offering. See Securities Act Release No. 4434. Controlling persons who want to offer or sell securities pursuant to section 3(a)(11) may continue to do so in accordance with applicable judicial and administrative interpretations.
   (a) Transactions covered. Offers, offers to sell, offers for sale and sales by an issuer of its securities made in accordance with all of the terms and conditions of this rule shall be deemed to be part of an issue offered and sold only to persons resident within a single state or territory where the issuer is a person resident and doing business within such state or territory, within the meaning of section 3(a)(11) of the Act.
   (b) Part of an issue. (1) For purposes of this rule, all securities of the issuer which are part of an issue shall be offered, offered for sale or sold in accordance with all of the terms and conditions of this rule. (2) For purposes of this rule only, an issue shall be deemed not to include offers, offers to sell, offers for sale or sales of securities of the issuer pursuant to the exemption provided by section 3 or section 4(a)(2) of the Act or

pursuant to a registration statement filed under the Act, that take place prior to the six month period immediately preceding or after the six month period immediately following any offers, offers for sale or sales pursuant to this rule, Provided, That, there are during either of said six month periods no offers, offers for sale or sales of securities by or for the issuer of the same or similar class as those offered, offered for sale or sold pursuant to the rule.

(c) Nature of the issuer. The issuer of the securities shall at the time of any offers and the sales be a person resident and doing business within the state or territory in which all of the offers, offers to sell, offers for sale and sales are made.

(1) The issuer shall be deemed to be a resident of the state or territory in which:

(i) It is incorporated or organized, if a corporation, limited partnership, trust or other form of business organization that is organized under state or territorial law;

(ii) Its principal office is located, if a general partnership or other form of business organization that is not organized under any state or territorial law;

(iii) His principal residence is located if an individual.

(2) The issuer shall be deemed to be doing business within a state or territory if:

(i) The issuer derived at least 80 percent of its gross revenues and those of its subsidiaries on a consolidated basis.

(A) For its most recent fiscal year, if the first offer of any part of the issue is made during the first six months of the issuer's current fiscal year; or

(B) For the first six months of its current fiscal year or during the twelve-month fiscal period ending with such six-month period, if the first offer of any part of the issue is made during the last six months of the issuer's current fiscal year from the operation of a business or of real property located in or from the rendering of services within such state or territory; provided, however, that this provision does not apply to any issuer which has not had gross revenues in excess of $5,000 from the sale of products or services or other conduct of its business for its most recent twelve-month fiscal period;

(ii) The issuer had at the end of its most recent semi-annual fiscal period prior to the first offer of any part of the issue, at least 80 percent of its assets and those of its subsidiaries on a consolidated basis located within such state or territory;

(iii) The issuer intends to use and uses at least 80 percent of the net proceeds to the issuer from sales made pursuant to this rule in connection with the operation of a business or of real property, the purchase of real property located in, or the rendering of services within such state or territory; and

(iv) The principal office of the issuer is located within such state or territory.

(d) Offerees and purchasers: Person resident. Offers, offers to sell, offers for sale and sales of securities that are part of an issue shall be made only to persons resident within the state or territory of which the issuer is a resident. For purposes of determining the residence of offerees and purchasers:

(1) A corporation, partnership, trust or other form of business organization shall be deemed to be a resident of a state or territory if, at the time of the offer and sale to it, it has its principal office within such state or territory.

(2) An individual shall be deemed to be a resident of a state or territory if such individual has, at the time of the offer and sale to him, his principal residence in the state or territory.

(3) A corporation, partnership, trust or other form of business organization which is organized for the specific purpose of acquiring part of an issue offered pursuant to this rule shall be deemed not to be a resident of a state or territory unless all of the beneficial owners of such organization are residents of such state or territory.

(e) Limitation of resales. During the period in which securities that are part of an issue are being offered and sold by the issuer, and for a period of nine months from the date of the last sale by the issuer, all resales of any part of the issue, by any person, shall be made only to persons resident within such state or territory.

(f) Precautions against interstate offers and sales.

    (1) The issuer shall, in connection with any securities sold by it pursuant to this rule:

        (i) Place a legend on the certificate or other document evidencing the security stating that the securities have not been registered under the Act and setting forth the limitations on resale contained in paragraph (e) of this section;

        (ii) Issue stop transfer instructions to the issuer's transfer agent, if any, with respect to the securities, or, if the issuer transfers its own securities make a notation in the appropriate records of the issuer; and

        (iii) Obtain a written representation from each purchaser as to his residence.

    (2) The issuer shall, in connection with the issuance of new certificates for any of the securities that are part of the same issue that are presented for transfer during the time period specified in paragraph (e), take the steps required by paragraphs (f)(1) (i) and (ii) of this section.

    (3) The issuer shall, in connection with any offers, offers to sell, offers for sale or sales by it pursuant to this rule, disclose, in writing, the limitations on resale contained in paragraph (e) and the provisions of paragraphs (f)(1) (i) and (ii) and paragraph (f)(2) of this section.

---

23. SEC Rules and Regulations: 164 – Post-filing Free Writing Prospectuses in Connection with Certain Registered Offerings

Preliminary Notes: This section is not available for any communication that, although in technical compliance with this section, is part of a plan or scheme to evade the requirements of section 5 of the Act. 2. Attempted compliance with this section does not act as an exclusive election and the person relying on this section also may claim the availability of any other applicable exemption or exclusion. Reliance on this section does not affect the availability of any other exemption or exclusion from the requirements of section 5 of the Act.

(a) In connection with a registered offering of an issuer meeting the requirements of this section, a free writing prospectus, as defined in Rule 405 (§ 230.405), of the issuer or any other offering participant, including any underwriter or dealer, after the filing of the registration statement will be a section 10(b) prospectus for purposes of section 5(b)(1) of the Act provided that the conditions set forth in Rule 433 (§ 230.433) are satisfied.

(b) An immaterial or unintentional failure to file or delay in filing a free writing prospectus as necessary to satisfy the filing conditions contained in Rule 433 will not result in a violation of section 5(b)(1) of the Act or the loss of the ability to rely on this section so long as:

  (1) A good faith and reasonable effort was made to comply with the filing condition; and

  (2) The free writing prospectus is filed as soon as practicable after discovery of the failure to file.

(c) An immaterial or unintentional failure to include the specified legend in a free writing prospectus as necessary to satisfy the legend condition contained in Rule 433 will not result in a violation of section 5(b)(1) of the Act or the loss of the ability to rely on this section so long as:

  (1) A good faith and reasonable effort was made to comply with the legend condition;

  (2) The free writing prospectus is amended to include the specified legend as soon as practicable after discovery of the omitted or incorrect legend; and

(3) If the free writing prospectus has been transmitted without the specified legend, the free writing prospectus must be retransmitted with the legend by substantially the same means as, and directed to substantially the same prospective purchasers to whom, the free writing prospectus was originally transmitted.

(d) Solely for purposes of this section, an immaterial or unintentional failure to retain a free writing prospectus as necessary to satisfy the record retention condition contained in Rule 433 will not result in a violation of section 5(b)(1) of the Act or the loss of the ability to rely on this section so long as a good faith and reasonable effort was made to comply with the record retention condition. Nothing in this paragraph will affect, however, any other record retention provisions applicable to the issuer or any offering participant.

(e) Ineligible issuers.

(1) This section and Rule 433 are available only if at the eligibility determination date for the offering in question, determined pursuant to paragraph (h) of this section, the issuer is not an ineligible issuer as defined in Rule 405 (or in the case of any offering participant, other than the issuer, the participant has a reasonable belief that the issuer is not an ineligible issuer);

(2) Notwithstanding paragraph (e)(1) of this section, this section and Rule 433 are available to an ineligible issuer with respect to a free writing prospectus that contains only descriptions of the terms of the securities in the offering or the offering (or in the case of an offering of asset-backed securities, contains only information specified in paragraphs (a)(1), (2), (3), (4), (6), (7), and (8) of the definition of ABS informational and computational materials in Item 1101 of Regulation AB (§ 229.1101 of this chapter), unless the issuer is or during the last three years the issuer or any of its predecessors was:

(i) A blank check company as defined in Rule 419(a)(2) (§ 230.419(a)(2));

(ii) A shell company, other than a business combination related shell company, as defined in Rule 405; or

(iii) An issuer for an offering of penny stock as defined in Rule 3a51-1 of the Securities Exchange Act of 1934 (§ 240.3a51-1 of this chapter).

(f) Excluded issuers. This section and Rule 433 are not available if the issuer is an investment company registered under the Investment Company Act of 1940 (15 U.S.C. 80a-1et seq.) or a business development company as defined in section 2(a)(48) of the Investment Company Act of 1940 (15 U.S.C. 80a-2(a)(48)).

(g) Excluded offerings. This section and Rule 433 are not available if the issuer is registering a business combination transaction as defined in Rule 165(f)(1) (§ 230.165(f)(1)) or the issuer, other than a well-known seasoned issuer, is registering an offering on Form S-8 (§ 239.16b of this chapter).

(h) For purposes of this section and Rule 433, the determination date as to whether an issuer is an ineligible issuer in respect of an offering shall be:

(1) Except as provided in paragraph (h)(2) of this section, the time of filing of the registration statement covering the offering; or

(2) If the offering is being registered pursuant to Rule 415 (§ 230.415), the earliest time after the filing of the registration statement covering the offering at which the issuer, or in the case of an underwritten offering the issuer or another offering participant, makes a bona fide offer, including without limitation through the use of a free writing prospectus, in the offering.

_____

24. SEC Rules and Regulations: Securities Investor Protection Act of 1970 (SIPA)

<u>§78aaa. Short title</u>
This chapter may be cited as the "Securities Investor Protection Act of 1970".

<u>§78bbb. Application of Securities Exchange Act of 1934</u>
Except as otherwise provided in this chapter, the provisions of the Securities Exchange Act of 1934 [15 U.S.C. 78a et seq.] (hereinafter referred to as the "1934 Act") apply as if this chapter constituted an amendment to, and was included as a section of, such Act.

<u>§78ccc. Securities Investor Protection Corporation</u>
(a) Creation and membership
   (1) Creation
      There is hereby established a body corporate to be known as the "Securities Investor Protection Corporation" (hereafter in this chapter referred to as "SIPC"). SIPC shall be a nonprofit corporation and shall have succession until dissolved by Act of the Congress. SIPC shall—
      (A) not be an agency or establishment of the United States Government; and
      (B) except as otherwise provided in this chapter, be subject to, and have all the powers conferred upon a nonprofit corporation by, the District of Columbia Nonprofit Corporation Act.
   (2) Membership
      (A) Members of SIPC
         SIPC shall be a membership corporation the members of which shall be all persons registered as brokers or dealers under section 78o(b) of this title, other than—
         (i) persons whose principal business, in the determination of SIPC, taking into account business of affiliated entities, is conducted outside the United States and its territories and possessions;
         (ii) persons whose business as a broker or dealer consists exclusively of (I) the distribution of shares of registered open end investment companies or unit investment trusts, (II) the sale of variable annuities, (III) the business of insurance, or (IV) the business of rendering investment advisory services to one or more registered investment companies or insurance company separate accounts; and
         (iii) persons who are registered as a broker or dealer pursuant to section 78o(b)(11)(A) of this title.
      (B) Commission review
         SIPC shall file with the Commission a copy of any determination made pursuant to subparagraph (A)(i). Within thirty days after the date of such filing, or within such longer period as the Commission may designate of not more than ninety days after such date if it finds such longer period to be appropriate and publishes its reasons for so finding, the Commission shall, consistent with the public interest and the purposes of this chapter, affirm, reverse, or amend any such determination of SIPC.
      (C) Additional members
         SIPC shall provide by rule that persons excluded from membership in SIPC under subparagraph (A)(i) may become members of SIPC under such conditions and upon such terms as SIPC shall require by rule, taking into account such matters as the availability of assets and the ability to conduct a liquidation if necessary.
      (D) Disclosure
         Any broker or dealer excluded from membership in SIPC under subparagraph (A)(i) shall, as required by the Commission by rule, make disclosures of its exclusion and other relevant information to the customers of such broker or dealer who are living in the United States or its territories and possessions.
(b) Powers
   In addition to the powers granted to SIPC elsewhere in this chapter, SIPC shall have the power—

(1) to sue and be sued, complain and defend, in its corporate name and through its own counsel, in any State, Federal, or other court;

(2) to adopt, alter, and use a corporate seal, which shall be judicially noticed;

(3) to adopt, amend, and repeal, by its Board of Directors, such bylaws as may be necessary or appropriate to carry out the purposes of this chapter, including bylaws relating to—

   (A) the conduct of its business; and

   (B) the indemnity of its directors, officers, and employees (including any such person acting as trustee or otherwise in connection with a liquidation proceeding) for liabilities and expenses actually and reasonably incurred by any such person in connection with the defense or settlement of an action or suit if such person acted in good faith and in a manner reasonably believed to be consistent with the purposes of this chapter.

(4) to adopt, amend, and repeal, by its Board of Directors, such rules as may be necessary or appropriate to carry out the purposes of this chapter, including rules relating to—

   (A) the definition of terms used in this chapter, other than those terms for which a definition is provided in section 78lll of this title;

   (B) the procedures for the liquidation of members and direct payment procedures, including the transfer of customer accounts, the distribution of customer property, and the advance and payment of SIPC funds; and

   (C) the exercise of all other rights and powers granted to it by this chapter;

(5) to conduct its business (including the carrying on of operations and the maintenance of offices) and to exercise all other rights and powers granted to it by this chapter in any State or other jurisdiction without regard to any qualification, licensing, or other statute in such State or other jurisdiction;

(6) to lease, purchase, accept gifts or donations of or otherwise acquire, to own, hold, improve, use, or otherwise deal in or with, and to sell, convey, mortgage, pledge, lease, exchange or otherwise dispose of, any property, real, personal or mixed, or any interest therein, wherever situated;

(7) subject to the provisions of subsection (c), to elect or appoint such officers, attorneys, employees, and agents as may be required, to determine their qualifications, to define their duties, to fix their salaries, require bonds for them and fix the penalty thereof;

(8) to enter into contracts, to execute instruments, to incur liabilities, and to do any and all other acts and things as may be necessary or incidental to the conduct of its business and the exercise of all other rights and powers granted to SIPC by this chapter; and

(9) by bylaw, to establish its fiscal year.

(c) Board of Directors

   (1) Functions

   SIPC shall have a Board of Directors which, subject to the provisions of this chapter, shall determine the policies which shall govern the operations of SIPC.

   (2) Number and appointment

   The Board of Directors shall consist of seven persons as follows:

   (A) One director shall be appointed by the Secretary of the Treasury from among the officers and employees of the Department of the Treasury.

   (B) One director shall be appointed by the Federal Reserve Board from among the officers and employees of the Federal Reserve Board.

   (C) Five directors shall be appointed by the President, by and with the advice and consent of the Senate, as follows—

      (i) three such directors shall be selected from among persons who are associated with, and representative of different aspects of, the securities industry, not all of whom shall be from the same geographical area of the United States, and

      (ii) two such directors shall be selected from the general public from among persons who are not associated with a broker or dealer or associated with a member of a national securities exchange, within the meaning of section 78c(a)(18) or section 78c(a)(21), respectively, of this title, or similarly associated with any self-regulatory organization or other securities industry group, and who have not had any such association during the two years preceding appointment.

(3) Chairman and Vice Chairman

The President shall designate a Chairman and Vice Chairman from among those directors appointed under paragraph (2)(C)(ii) of this subsection.

(4) Terms

(A) Except as provided in subparagraphs (B) and (C), each director shall be appointed for a term of three years.

(B) Of the directors first appointed under paragraph (2)—

(i) two shall hold office for a term expiring on December 31, 1971,

(ii) two shall hold office for a term expiring on December 31, 1972, and

(iii) three shall hold office for a term expiring on December 31, 1973,

as designated by the President at the time they take office. Such designation shall be made in a manner which will assure that no two persons appointed under the authority of the same clause of paragraph (2)(C) shall have terms which expire simultaneously.

(C) A vacancy in the Board shall be filled in the same manner as the original appointment was made. Any director appointed to fill a vacancy occurring prior to the expiration of the term for which his predecessor was appointed shall be appointed only for the remainder of such term. A director may serve after the expiration of his term until his successor has taken office.

(5) Compensation

All matters relating to compensation of directors shall be as provided in the bylaws of SIPC.

(d) Meetings of Board

The Board of Directors shall meet at the call of its Chairman, or as otherwise provided by the bylaws of SIPC.

(e) Bylaws and rules

(1) Proposed bylaw changes

The Board of Directors of SIPC shall file with the Commission a copy of any proposed bylaw or any proposed amendment to or repeal of any bylaw of SIPC (hereinafter in this paragraph collectively referred to as a "proposed bylaw change"), accompanied by a concise general statement of the basis and purpose of such proposed bylaw change. Each such proposed bylaw change shall take effect thirty days after the date of the filing of a copy thereof with the Commission, or upon such later date as SIPC may designate or such earlier date as the Commission may determine, unless—

(A) the Commission, by notice to SIPC setting forth the reasons therefor, disapproves such proposed bylaw change as being contrary to the public interest or contrary to the purposes of this chapter; or

(B) the Commission finds that such proposed bylaw change involves a matter of such significant public interest that public comment should be obtained, in which case it may, after notifying SIPC in writing of such finding, require that the procedures set forth in paragraph (2) be followed with respect to such proposed bylaw change, in the same manner as if such proposed bylaw change were a proposed rule change within the meaning of such paragraph.

(2) Proposed rule changes

(A) Filing of proposed rule changes

The Board of Directors of SIPC shall file with the Commission, in accordance with such rules as the Commission may prescribe, a copy of any proposed rule or any proposed amendment to or repeal of any rule of SIPC (hereinafter in this subsection collectively referred to as a "proposed rule change"), accompanied by a concise general statement of the basis and purpose of such proposed rule change. The Commission shall, upon the filing of any proposed rule change, publish notice thereof, together with the terms of substance of such proposed rule change or a description of the subjects and issues involved. The Commission shall give interested persons an opportunity to submit written data, views, and arguments with respect to such proposed rule change. No proposed rule change shall take effect unless approved by the Commission or otherwise permitted in accordance with the provisions of this paragraph.

(B) Action by the Commission

Within thirty-five days after the date of publication of notice of the filing of a proposed rule change, or within such longer period as the Commission may designate of not more than ninety days after such date if it finds such longer period to be appropriate and publishes its reasons for so finding, or as to which SIPC consents, the Commission shall—

   (i) by order approve such proposed rule change; or

   (ii) institute proceedings to determine whether such proposed rule change should be disapproved.

(C) Proceedings

Proceedings instituted with respect to a proposed rule change pursuant to subparagraph (B)(ii) shall include notice of the grounds for disapproval under consideration and opportunity for hearing, and shall be concluded within one hundred eighty days after the date of publication of notice of the filing of such proposed rule change. At the conclusion of such proceedings, the Commission shall, by order, approve or disapprove such proposed rule change. The Commission may extend the time for conclusion of such proceedings for not more than sixty days if it finds good cause for such extension and publishes its reasons for so finding, or for such longer period as to which SIPC consents.

(D) Grounds for approval or disapproval

The Commission shall approve a proposed rule change if it finds that such proposed rule change is in the public interest and is consistent with the purposes of this chapter, and any proposed rule change so approved shall be given force and effect as if promulgated by the Commission. The Commission shall disapprove a proposed rule change if it does not make the finding referred to in the preceding sentence. The Commission shall not approve any proposed rule change prior to thirty days after the date of publication of notice of the filing thereof, unless the Commission finds good cause for so doing and publishes its reasons for so finding.

(E) Exception

Notwithstanding any other provision of this paragraph, a proposed rule change may take effect—

   (i) upon the date of filing with the Commission, if such proposed rule change is designated by SIPC as relating solely to matters which the Commission, consistent with the public interest and the purposes of this subsection, determines by rule do not require the procedures set forth in this paragraph; or

   (ii) upon such date as the Commission shall for good cause determine. Any proposed rule change which takes effect under this clause shall be filed promptly thereafter and reviewed in accordance with the provisions of subparagraph (A).

At any time within sixty days after the date of filing of any rule change which has taken effect pursuant to this subparagraph, the Commission may summarily abrogate such rule change and require that it be refiled and reviewed in accordance with the provisions of this paragraph, if the Commission finds that such action is necessary or appropriate in the public interest, for the protection of investors, or otherwise in furtherance of the purposes of this chapter. Any action of the Commission pursuant to the preceding sentence shall not affect the validity or force of a rule change during the period it was in effect and shall not be reviewable under section 78y of this title or deemed to be final agency action for purposes of section 704 of title 5.

(3) Action required by Commission

The Commission may, by such rules as it determines to be necessary or appropriate in the public interest or to carry out the purposes of this chapter, require SIPC to adopt, amend, or repeal any SIPC bylaw or rule, whenever adopted.

§78ddd. SIPC Fund

(a) In general

  (1) Establishment of fund

    SIPC shall establish a "SIPC Fund" (hereinafter in this chapter referred to as the "fund"). All amounts received by SIPC (other than amounts paid directly to any lender pursuant to any pledge securing a borrowing by SIPC) shall be deposited in the fund, and all expenditures made by SIPC shall be made out of the fund.

  (2) Balance of the fund

    Except as otherwise provided in this section, the balance of the fund at any time shall consist of the aggregate at such time of the following items:

    (A) Cash on hand or on deposit.

    (B) Amounts invested in United States Government or agency securities.

    (C) Such confirmed lines of credit as SIPC may from time to time maintain, other than those maintained pursuant to paragraph (4).

  (3) Confirmed lines of credit

    For purposes of this section, the amount of confirmed lines of credit as of any time is the aggregate amount which SIPC at such time has the right to borrow from banks and other financial institutions under confirmed lines of credit or other written agreements which provide that moneys so borrowed are to be repayable by SIPC not less than one year from the time of such borrowings (including, for purposes of determining when such moneys are repayable, all rights of extension, refunding, or renewal at the election of SIPC).

  (4) Other lines

    SIPC may maintain such other confirmed lines of credit as it considers necessary or appropriate, and such other confirmed lines of credit shall not be included in the balance of the fund, but amounts received from such lines of credit may be disbursed by SIPC under this chapter as though such amounts were part of the fund.

(b) Initial required balance for fund

  Within one hundred and twenty days from December 30, 1970, the balance of the fund shall aggregate not less than $75,000,000, less any amounts expended from the fund within that period.

(c) Assessments

  (1) Initial assessments

    Each member of SIPC shall pay to SIPC, or the collection agent for SIPC specified in section 78iii(a) of this title, on or before the one hundred and twentieth day following December 30, 1970, an assessment equal to one-eighth of 1 per centum of the gross revenues from the securities business of such member during the calendar year 1969, or if the Commission shall determine that, for purposes of assessment pursuant to this paragraph, a lesser percentage of gross revenues from the securities business is appropriate for any class or classes of members (taking into account relevant factors, including but not limited to types of business done and nature of securities sold), such lesser percentages as the Commission, by rule or regulation, shall establish for such class or classes, but in no event less than one sixteenth of 1 per centum for any such class. In no event shall any assessment upon a member pursuant to this paragraph be less than $150.

  (2) General assessment authority

    SIPC shall, by bylaw, impose upon its members such assessments as, after consultation with self-regulatory organizations, SIPC may deem necessary and appropriate to establish and maintain the fund and to repay any borrowings by SIPC. Any assessments so made shall be in conformity with contractual obligations made by SIPC in connection with any borrowing incurred by SIPC. Subject to paragraph (3) and subsection (d)(1)(A), any such assessment upon the members, or any one or more classes thereof, may, in whole or in part, be based upon or measured by (A) the amount of their gross revenues from the securities business, or (B) all or any of the following factors: the amount or composition of their gross revenues from the securities business, the number or dollar volume of transactions effected by them, the number of customer accounts maintained by them or the amounts of cash and securities in such accounts, their net capital, the nature of their activities (whether in the securities business or otherwise) and the consequent risks, or other relevant factors.

(3) Limitations

Notwithstanding any other provision of this chapter—

(A) no assessment shall be made upon a member otherwise than pursuant to paragraph (1) or (2) of this subsection,

(B) an assessment may be made under paragraph (2) of this subsection at a rate in excess of one-half of one per centum during any twelve-month period if SIPC determines, in accordance with a bylaw, that such rate of assessment during such period will not have a material adverse effect on the financial condition of its members or their customers, except that no assessments shall be made pursuant to such paragraph upon a member which require payments during any such period which exceed in the aggregate one per centum of such member's gross revenues from the securities business for such period, and

(C) no assessment shall include any charge based upon the member's activities (i) in the distribution of shares of registered open end investment companies or unit investment trusts, (ii) in the sale of variable annuities, (iii) in the business of insurance, or (iv) in the business of rendering investment advisory services to one or more registered investment companies or insurance company separate accounts.

(d) Requirements respecting assessments and lines of credit

(1) Assessments

(A) ½ of 1 percent assessment

Subject to subsection (c)(3), SIPC shall impose upon each of its members an assessment at a rate of not less than one-half of 1 per centum per annum of the gross revenues from the securities business of such member—

(i) until the balance of the fund aggregates not less than $150,000,000 (or such other amount as the Commission may determine in the public interest),

(ii) during any period when there is outstanding borrowing by SIPC pursuant to subsection (f) or subsection (g) of this section, and

(iii) whenever the balance of the fund (exclusive of confirmed lines of credit) is below $100,000,000 (or such other amount as the Commission may determine in the public interest).

(B) ¼ of 1 percent assessment

During any period during which—

(i) the balance of the fund (exclusive of confirmed lines of credit) aggregates less than $150,000,000 (or such other amount as the Commission has determined under paragraph (2)(B)), or

(ii) SIPC is required under paragraph (2)(B) to phase out of the fund all confirmed lines of credit,

SIPC shall endeavor to make assessments in such a manner that the aggregate assessments payable by its members during such period shall not be less than one-fourth of 1 per centum per annum of the aggregate gross revenues from the securities business for such members during such period.

(C) Minimum assessment

The minimum assessment imposed upon each member of SIPC shall be $25 per annum through the year ending December 31, 1979, and thereafter shall be the amount from time to time set by SIPC bylaw, but in no event shall the minimum assessment be greater than 0.02 percent of the gross revenues from the securities business of such member of SIPC.

(2) Lines of credit

(A) $50,000,000 limit after 1973

After December 31, 1973, confirmed lines of credit shall not constitute more than $50,000,000 of the balance of the fund.

(B) Phaseout requirement

When the balance of the fund aggregates $150,000,000 (or such other amount as the Commission may determine in the public interest) SIPC shall phase out of the fund all confirmed lines of credit.

(e) Prior trusts; overpayments and underpayments

(1) Prior trusts

There may be contributed and transferred at any time to SIPC any funds held by any trust established by a self-regulatory organization prior to January 1, 1970, and the amounts so contributed and transferred shall be applied, as may be determined by SIPC with approval of the Commission, as a reduction in the amounts payable pursuant to assessments made or to be made by SIPC upon members of such self-regulatory organization pursuant to subsection (c)(2). No such reduction shall be made at any time when there is outstanding any borrowing by SIPC pursuant to subsection (g) of this section or any borrowings under confirmed lines of credit.

(2) Overpayments

To the extent that any payment by a member exceeds the maximum rate permitted by subsection (c) of this section, the excess shall be recoverable only against future payments by such member, except as otherwise provided by SIPC bylaw.

(3) Underpayments

If a member fails to pay when due all or any part of an assessment made upon such member, the unpaid portion thereof shall bear interest at such rate as may be determined by SIPC bylaw and, in addition to such interest, SIPC may impose such penalty charge as may be determined by SIPC bylaw. Any such penalty charge imposed upon a SIPC member shall not exceed 25 per centum of any unpaid portion of the assessment. SIPC may waive such penalty charge in whole or in part in circumstances where it considers such waiver appropriate.

(f) Borrowing authority

SIPC shall have the power to borrow moneys and to evidence such borrowed moneys by the issuance of bonds, notes, or other evidences of indebtedness, all upon such terms and conditions as the Board of Directors may determine in the case of a borrowing other than pursuant to subsection (g) of this section, or as may be prescribed by the Commission in the case of a borrowing pursuant to subsection (g). The interest payable on a borrowing pursuant to subsection (g) shall be equal to the interest payable on the related notes or other obligations issued by the Commission to the Secretary of the Treasury. To secure the payment of the principal of, and interest and premium, if any, on, all bonds, notes, or other evidences of indebtedness so issued, SIPC may make agreements with respect to the amount of future assessments to be made upon members and may pledge all or any part of the assets of SIPC and of the assessments made or to be made upon members. Any such pledge of future assessments shall (subject to any prior pledge) be valid and binding from the time that it is made, and the assessments so pledged and thereafter received by SIPC, or any collection agent for SIPC, shall immediately be subject to the lien of such pledge without any physical delivery thereof or further act, and the lien of such pledge shall be valid and binding against all parties having claims of any kind against SIPC or such collection agent whether pursuant to this chapter, in tort, contract or otherwise, irrespective of whether such parties have notice thereof. During any period when a borrowing by SIPC pursuant to subsection (g) of this section is outstanding, no pledge of any assessment upon a member to secure any bonds, notes, or other evidences of indebtedness issued other than pursuant to subsection (g) of this section shall be effective as to the excess of the payments under the assessment on such member during any twelve-month period over one-fourth of 1 per centum of such member's gross revenues from the securities business for such period. Neither the instrument by which a pledge is authorized or created, nor any statement or other document relative thereto, need be filed or recorded in any State or other jurisdiction. The Commission may by rule or regulation provide for the filing of any instrument by which a pledge or borrowing is authorized or created, but the failure to make or any defect in any such filing shall not affect the validity of such pledge or borrowing.

(g) SEC loans to SIPC

In the event that the fund is or may reasonably appear to be insufficient for the purposes of this chapter, the Commission is authorized to make loans to SIPC. At the time of application for, and as a condition to, any such loan, SIPC shall file with the Commission a statement with respect to the anticipated use of the proceeds of the loan. If the Commission determines that such loan is necessary for the protection of customers of brokers or dealers and the maintenance of confidence in the United States securities markets and the SIPC has submitted a plan which provides as reasonable an assurance of prompt repayment as may be feasible under the circumstances, then the Commission shall so certify to the Secretary of the Treasury, and issue notes or other obligations to the Secretary of the Treasury pursuant to subsection (h). If the Commission determines that the amount or time for payment of the assessments pursuant to such plan would not satisfactorily provide for the repayment of such loan, it may, by rules and regulations, impose upon the purchasers of equity securities in transactions on national securities exchanges and in the over-the-counter markets a transaction fee in such amount as at any time or from time to time it may determine to be appropriate, but not exceeding one-fiftieth of 1 per centum of the purchase price of the securities. No such fee shall be imposed on a transaction (as defined by rules or regulations of the Commission) of less than $5,000. For the purposes of the next preceding sentence, (1) the fee shall be based upon the total dollar amount of each purchase; (2) the fee shall not apply to any purchase on a national securities exchange or in an over-the-counter market by or for the account of a broker or dealer registered under section 78o(b) of this title unless such purchase is for an investment account of such broker or dealer (and for this purpose any transfer from a trading account to an investment account shall be deemed a purchase at fair market value); and (3) the Commission may, by rule, exempt any transaction in the over-the-counter markets or on any national securities exchange where necessary to provide for the assessment of fees on purchasers in transactions in such markets and exchanges on a comparable basis. Such fee shall be collected by the broker or dealer effecting the transaction for or with the purchaser, or by such other person as provided by the Commission by rule, and shall be paid to SIPC in the same manner as assessments imposed pursuant to subsection (c) but without regard to the limits on such assessments, or in such other manner as the Commission may by rule provide.

(h) SEC notes issued to Treasury

To enable the Commission to make loans under subsection (g), the Commission is authorized to issue to the Secretary of the Treasury notes or other obligations in an aggregate amount of not to exceed $2,500,000,000, in such forms and denominations, bearing such maturities, and subject to such terms and conditions, as may be prescribed by the Secretary of the Treasury. Such notes or other obligations shall bear interest at a rate determined by the Secretary of the Treasury, taking into consideration the current average market yield on outstanding marketable obligations of the United States of comparable maturities during the month preceding the issuance of the notes or other obligations. The Secretary of the Treasury may reduce the interest rate if he determines such reduction to be in the national interest. The Secretary of the Treasury is authorized and directed to purchase any notes and other obligations issued hereunder and for that purpose he is authorized to use as a public debt transaction the proceeds from the sale of any securities issued under chapter 31 of title 31, and the purposes for which securities may be issued under that chapter are extended to include any purchase of such notes and obligations. The Secretary of the Treasury may at any time sell any of the notes or other obligations acquired by him under this subsection. All redemptions, purchases, and sales by the Secretary of the Treasury of such notes or other obligations shall be treated as public debt transactions of the United States.

(i) Consolidated group

Except as otherwise provided by SIPC bylaw, gross revenues from the securities business of a member of SIPC shall be computed on a consolidated basis for such member and all its subsidiaries (other than the foreign subsidiaries of such member), and the operations of a member of SIPC shall include those of any business to which such member has succeeded.

§78eee. Protection of customers

(a) Determination of need of protection

(1) Notice to SIPC

If the Commission or any self-regulatory organization is aware of facts which lead it to believe that any broker or dealer subject to its regulation is in or is approaching financial difficulty, it shall immediately notify SIPC, and, if such notification is by a self-regulatory organization, the Commission.

(2) Action by self-regulatory organization

If a self-regulatory organization has given notice to SIPC pursuant to subsection (a)(1) with respect to a broker or dealer, and such broker or dealer undertakes to liquidate or reduce its business either pursuant to the direction of a self-regulatory organization or voluntarily, such self-regulatory organization may render such assistance or oversight to such broker or dealer as it considers appropriate to protect the interests of customers of such broker or dealer. The assistance or oversight by a self-regulatory organization shall not be deemed the assumption or adoption by such self-regulatory organization of any obligation or liability to customers, other creditors, shareholders, or partners of the broker or dealer, and shall not prevent or act as a bar to any action by SIPC.

(3) Action by SIPC

(A) In general

SIPC may, upon notice to a member of SIPC, file an application for a protective decree with any court of competent jurisdiction specified in section 78u(e) or 78aa of this title, except that no such application shall be filed with respect to a member, the only customers of which are persons whose claims could not be satisfied by SIPC advances pursuant to section 78fff–3 of this title, if SIPC determines that—

(i) the member (including any person who was a member within one hundred eighty days prior to such determination) has failed or is in danger of failing to meet its obligations to customers; and

(ii) one or more of the conditions specified in subsection (b)(1) exist with respect to such member.

(B) Consent required

No member of SIPC that has a customer may enter into an insolvency, receivership, or bankruptcy proceeding, under Federal or State law, without the specific consent of SIPC, except as provided in title II of the Dodd-Frank Wall Street Reform and Consumer Protection Act [12 U.S.C. 5381 et seq.].

(4) Effect of other pending actions

An application with respect to a member of SIPC filed with a court under paragraph (3)—

(A) may, with the consent of the Commission, be combined with any action brought by the Commission, including an action by the Commission for a temporary receiver pending an appointment of a trustee under subsection (b)(3); and

(B) may be filed notwithstanding the pendency in the same or any other court of any bankruptcy, mortgage foreclosure, or equity receivership proceeding or any proceeding to reorganize, conserve, or liquidate such member or its property, or any proceeding to enforce a lien against property of such member.

(b) Court action

(1) Issuance of protective decree

Upon receipt of an application by SIPC under subsection (a)(3), the court shall forthwith issue a protective decree if the debtor consents thereto, if the debtor fails to contest such application, or if the court finds that such debtor—

(A) is insolvent within the meaning of section 101 of title 11, or is unable to meet its obligations as they mature;

(B) is the subject of a proceeding pending in any court or before any agency of the United States or any State in which a receiver, trustee, or liquidator for such debtor has been appointed;

(C) is not in compliance with applicable requirements under the 1934 Act [15 U.S.C. 78a et seq.] or rules of the Commission or any self-regulatory organization with respect to financial responsibility or hypothecation of customers' securities; or

(D) is unable to make such computations as may be necessary to establish compliance with such financial responsibility or hypothecation rules.

Unless the debtor consents to the issuance of a protective decree, the application shall be heard three business days after the date on which it is filed, or at such other time as the court shall determine, taking into consideration the urgency which the circumstances require.

(2) Jurisdiction and powers of court

(A) Exclusive jurisdiction

Upon the filing of an application with a court for a protective decree with respect to a debtor, such court—

(i) shall have exclusive jurisdiction of such debtor and its property wherever located (including property located outside the territorial limits of such court and property held by any other person as security for a debt or subject to a lien);

(ii) shall have exclusive jurisdiction of any suit against the trustee with respect to a liquidation proceeding; and

(iii) except as inconsistent with the provisions of this chapter, shall have the jurisdiction, powers, and duties conferred upon a court of the United States having jurisdiction over cases under title 11, together with such other jurisdiction, powers, and duties as are prescribed by this chapter.

(B) Stay of pending actions

Pending the issuance of a protective decree under paragraph (1), the court with which an application has been filed—

(i) shall stay any pending bankruptcy, mortgage foreclosure, equity receivership, or other proceeding to reorganize, conserve, or liquidate the debtor or its property and any other suit against any receiver, conservator, or trustee of the debtor or its property, and shall continue such stay upon appointment of a trustee pursuant to paragraph (3);

(ii) may stay any proceeding to enforce a lien against property of the debtor or any other suit against the debtor, including a suit by stockholders of the debtor which interferes with prosecution by the trustee of claims against former directors, officers, or employees of the debtor, and may continue such stay upon appointment of a trustee pursuant to paragraph (3);

(iii) may stay enforcement of, and upon appointment of a trustee pursuant to paragraph (3), may continue the stay for such period of time as may be appropriate, but shall not abrogate any right of setoff, except to the extent such right may be affected under section 553 of title 11, and shall not abrogate the right to enforce a valid, nonpreferential lien or pledge against the property of the debtor; and

(iv) may appoint a temporary receiver.

(C) Exception from stay

(i) Notwithstanding section 362 of title 11, neither the filing of an application under subsection (a)(3) nor any order or decree obtained by SIPC from the court shall operate as a stay of any contractual rights of a creditor to liquidate, terminate, or accelerate a securities contract, commodity contract, forward contract, repurchase agreement, swap agreement, or master netting agreement, as those terms are defined in sections 101, 741, and 761 of title 11, to offset or net termination values, payment amounts, or other transfer obligations arising under or in connection with one or more of such contracts or agreements, or to foreclose on any cash collateral pledged by the debtor, whether or not with respect to one or more of such contracts or agreements.

(ii) Notwithstanding clause (i), such application, order, or decree may operate as a stay of the foreclosure on, or disposition of, securities collateral pledged by the debtor, whether or not with respect to one or more of such contracts or agreements, securities sold by the debtor under a repurchase agreement, or securities lent under a securities lending agreement.

(iii) As used in this subparagraph, the term "contractual right" includes a right set forth in a rule or bylaw of a derivatives clearing organization (as defined in the Commodity Exchange Act [7 U.S.C. 1 et seq.]), a multilateral clearing organization (as defined in the Federal Deposit Insurance Corporation Improvement Act of 1991), a national securities exchange, a national securities association, a securities clearing agency, a contract market designated under the Commodity Exchange Act, a derivatives transaction execution facility registered under the Commodity Exchange Act, or a board of trade (as defined in the Commodity Exchange Act), or in a resolution of the governing board thereof, and a right, whether or not in writing, arising under common law, under law merchant, or by reason of normal business practice.

(3) Appointment of trustee and attorney

If the court issues a protective decree under paragraph (1), such court shall forthwith appoint, as trustee for the liquidation of the business of the debtor and as attorney for the trustee, such persons as SIPC, in its sole discretion, specifies. The persons appointed as trustee and as attorney for the trustee may be associated with the same firm. SIPC may, in its sole discretion, specify itself or one of its employees as trustee in any case in which SIPC has determined that the liabilities of the debtor to unsecured general creditors and to subordinated lenders appear to aggregate less than $750,000 and that there appear to be fewer than five hundred customers of such debtor. No person may be appointed to serve as trustee or attorney for the trustee if such person is not disinterested within the meaning of paragraph (6), except that for any specified purpose other than to represent a trustee in conducting a liquidation proceeding, the trustee may, with the approval of SIPC and the court, employ an attorney who is not disinterested. A trustee appointed under this paragraph shall qualify by filing a bond in the manner prescribed by section 322 of title 11, except that neither SIPC nor any employee of SIPC shall be required to file a bond when appointed as trustee.

(4) Removal to bankruptcy court

Upon the issuance of a protective decree and appointment of a trustee, or a trustee and counsel, under this section, the court shall forthwith order the removal of the entire liquidation proceeding to the court of the United States in the same judicial district having jurisdiction over cases under title 11. The latter court shall thereupon have all of the jurisdiction, powers, and duties conferred by this chapter upon the court to which application for the issuance of the protective decree was made.

(5) Compensation for services and reimbursement of expenses

(A) Allowances in general

The court shall grant reasonable compensation for services rendered and reimbursement for proper costs and expenses incurred (hereinafter in this paragraph referred to as "allowances") by a trustee, and by the attorney for such a trustee, in connection with a liquidation proceeding. No allowances (other than reimbursement for proper costs and expenses incurred) shall be granted to SIPC or any employee of SIPC for serving as trustee. Allowances may be granted on an interim basis during the course of the liquidation proceeding at such times and in such amounts as the court considers appropriate.

(B) Application for allowances

Any person seeking allowances shall file with the court an application which complies in form and content with the provisions of title 11 governing applications for allowances under such title. A copy of such application shall be served upon SIPC when filed. The court shall fix a time for a hearing on such application, and notice of such hearing shall be given to the applicant, the trustee, the debtor, the creditors, SIPC, and such other persons as the court may designate, except that notice need not be given to customers whose claims have been or will be satisfied in full or to creditors who cannot reasonably be expected to receive any distribution during the course of the liquidation proceeding.

(C) Recommendations of SIPC and awarding of allowances

Whenever an application for allowances is filed pursuant to subparagraph (B), SIPC shall file its recommendation with respect to such allowances with the court prior to the hearing on such application and shall, if it so requests, be allowed a reasonable time after such hearing within which to file a further recommendation. In any case in which such allowances are to be paid by SIPC without reasonable expectation of recoupment thereof as provided in this chapter and there is no difference between the amounts requested and the amounts recommended by SIPC, the court shall award the amounts recommended by SIPC. In determining the amount of allowances in all other cases, the court shall give due consideration to the nature, extent, and value of the services rendered, and shall place considerable reliance on the recommendation of SIPC.

    (D) Applicable restrictions

        The restrictions on sharing of compensation set forth in section 504 of title 11 shall apply to allowances.

    (E) Charge against estate

        Allowances granted by the court, including interim allowances, shall be charged against the general estate of the debtor as a cost and expense of administration. If the general estate is insufficient to pay allowances in whole or in part, SIPC shall advance such funds as are necessary for such payment.

  (6) Disinterestedness

    (A) Standards

        For purposes of paragraph (3), a person shall not be deemed disinterested if—

        (i) such person is a creditor (including a customer), stockholder, or partner of the debtor;

        (ii) such person is or was an underwriter of any of the outstanding securities of the debtor or within five years prior to the filing date was the underwriter of any securities of the debtor;

        (iii) such person is, or was within two years prior to the filing date, a director, partner, officer, or employee of the debtor or such an underwriter, or an attorney for the debtor or such an underwriter; or

        (iv) it appears that such person has, by reason of any other direct or indirect relationship to, connection with, or interest in the debtor or such an underwriter, or for any other reason, an interest materially adverse to the interests of any class of creditors (including customers) or stockholders, except that SIPC shall in all cases be deemed disinterested, and an employee of SIPC shall be deemed disinterested if such employee would, except for his association with SIPC, meet the standards set forth in this subparagraph.

    (B) Hearing

        The court shall fix a time for a hearing on disinterestedness, to be held promptly after the appointment of a trustee. Notice of such hearing shall be mailed at least ten days prior thereto to each person who, from the books and records of the debtor, appears to have been a customer of the debtor with an open account within the past twelve months, to the address of such person as it appears from the books and records of the debtor, and to the creditors and stockholders of the debtor, to SIPC, and to such other persons as the court may designate. The court may, in its discretion, also require that notice be given by publication in such newspaper or newspapers of general circulation as it may designate. At such hearing, at any adjournment thereof, or upon application, the court shall hear objections to the retention in office of a trustee or attorney for a trustee on the grounds that such person is not disinterested.

(c) SEC participation in proceedings

  The Commission may, on its own motion, file notice of its appearance in any proceeding under this chapter and may thereafter participate as a party.

(d) SIPC participation

  SIPC shall be deemed to be a party in interest as to all matters arising in a liquidation proceeding, with the right to be heard on all such matters, and shall be deemed to have intervened with respect to all such matters with the same force and effect as if a petition for such purpose had been allowed by the court.

§78fff. General provisions of a liquidation proceeding

(a) Purposes

The purposes of a liquidation proceeding under this chapter shall be—

(1) as promptly as possible after the appointment of a trustee in such liquidation proceeding, and in accordance with the provisions of this chapter—

(A) to deliver customer name securities to or on behalf of the customers of the debtor entitled thereto as provided in section 78fff–2(c)(2) of this title; and

(B) to distribute customer property and (in advance thereof or concurrently therewith) otherwise satisfy net equity claims of customers to the extent provided in this section;

(2) to sell or transfer offices and other productive units of the business of the debtor;

(3) to enforce rights of subrogation as provided in this chapter; and

(4) to liquidate the business of the debtor.

(b) Application of title 11

To the extent consistent with the provisions of this chapter, a liquidation proceeding shall be conducted in accordance with, and as though it were being conducted under chapters 1, 3, and 5 and subchapters I and II of chapter 7 of title 11. For the purposes of applying such title in carrying out this section, a reference in such title to the date of the filing of the petition shall be deemed to be a reference to the filing date under this chapter.

(c) Determination of customer status

In a liquidation proceeding under this chapter, whenever a person has acted with respect to cash or securities with the debtor after the filing date and in a manner which would have given him the status of a customer with respect to such cash or securities had the action occurred prior to the filing date, and the trustee is satisfied that such action was taken by the customer in good faith and prior to the appointment of the trustee, the date on which such action was taken shall be deemed to be the filing date for purposes of determining the net equity of such customer with respect to such cash or securities.

(d) Apportionment

In a liquidation proceeding under this chapter, any cash or securities remaining after the liquidation of a lien or pledge made by a debtor shall be apportioned between his general estate and customer property in the proportion in which the general property of the debtor and the cash and securities of the customers of such debtor contributed to such lien or pledge. Securities apportioned to the general estate under this subsection shall be subject to the provisions of section 78lll(5)(A) of this title.

(e) Costs and expenses of administration

All costs and expenses of administration of the estate of the debtor and of the liquidation proceeding shall be borne by the general estate of the debtor to the extent it is sufficient therefor, and the priorities of distribution from the general estate shall be as provided in section 726 of title 11. Costs and expenses of administration shall include payments pursuant to section 78fff–2(e) of this title and section 78fff–3(c)(1) of this title (to the extent such payments recovered securities which were apportioned to the general estate pursuant to subsection (d)) and costs and expenses of SIPC employees utilized by the trustee pursuant to section 78fff–1(a)(2) of this title. All funds advanced by SIPC to a trustee for such costs and expenses of administration shall be recouped from the general estate under section 507(a)(2) of title 11.

§78fff–1. Powers and duties of a trustee

(a) Trustee powers

A trustee shall be vested with the same powers and title with respect to the debtor and the property of the debtor, including the same rights to avoid preferences, as a trustee in a case under title 11. In addition, a trustee may, with the approval of SIPC but without any need for court approval—

(1) hire and fix the compensation of all personnel (including officers and employees of the debtor and of its examining authority) and other persons (including accountants) that are deemed by the trustee necessary for all or any purposes of the liquidation proceeding;

    (2) utilize SIPC employees for all or any purposes of a liquidation proceeding; and

    (3) margin and maintain customer accounts of the debtor for the purposes of section 78fff–2(f) of this title.

(b) Trustee duties

To the extent consistent with the provisions of this chapter or as otherwise ordered by the court, a trustee shall be subject to the same duties as a trustee in a case under chapter 7 of title 11, including, if the debtor is a commodity broker, as defined under section 101 of such title, the duties specified in subchapter IV of such chapter 7, except that a trustee may, but shall have no duty to, reduce to money any securities constituting customer property or in the general estate of the debtor. In addition, the trustee shall—

    (1) deliver securities to or on behalf of customers to the maximum extent practicable in satisfaction of customer claims for securities of the same class and series of an issuer; and

    (2) subject to the prior approval of SIPC but without any need for court approval, pay or guarantee all or any part of the indebtedness of the debtor to a bank, lender, or other person if the trustee determines that the aggregate market value of securities to be made available to the trustee upon the payment or guarantee of such indebtedness does not appear to be less than the total amount of such payment or guarantee.

(c) Reports by trustee to court

The trustee shall make to the court and to SIPC such written reports as may be required of a trustee in a case under chapter 7 of title 11, and shall include in such reports information with respect to the progress made in distributing cash and securities to customers. Such reports shall be in such form and detail as the Commission determines by rule to present fairly the results of the liquidation proceeding as of the date of or for the period covered by such reports, having due regard for the requirements of section 78q of this title and the rules prescribed under such section and the magnitude of items and transactions involved in connection with the operations of a broker or dealer.

(d) Investigations

The trustee shall—

    (1) as soon as practicable, investigate the acts, conduct, property, liabilities, and financial condition of the debtor, the operation of its business, and any other matter, to the extent relevant to the liquidation proceeding, and report thereon to the court;

    (2) examine, by deposition or otherwise, the directors and officers of the debtor and any other witnesses concerning any of the matters referred to in paragraph (1);

    (3) report to the court any facts ascertained by the trustee with respect to fraud, misconduct, mismanagement, and irregularities, and to any causes of action available to the estate; and

    (4) as soon as practicable, prepare and submit, to SIPC and such other persons as the court designates and in such form and manner as the court directs, a statement of his investigation of matters referred to in paragraph (1).

§78fff–2. Special provisions of a liquidation proceeding

(a) Notice and claims

    (1) Notice of proceedings

        Promptly after the appointment of the trustee, such trustee shall cause notice of the commencement of proceedings under this section to be published in one or more newspapers of general circulation in the form and manner determined by the court, and at the same time shall cause a copy of such notice to be mailed to each person who, from the books and records of the debtor, appears to have been a customer of the debtor with an open account within the past twelve months, to the address of such person as it appears from the books and records of the debtor. Notice to creditors other than customers shall be given in the manner prescribed by title 11, except that such notice shall be given by the trustee.

    (2) Statement of claim

        A customer shall file with the trustee a written statement of claim but need not file a formal proof of claim, except that no obligation of the debtor to any person associated with the debtor within the meaning of section 78c(a)(18) of this title or section 78c(a)(21) of this title, any beneficial owner of 5 per centum or more of the voting stock of the debtor, or any member of the immediate family of any such person or owner may be satisfied without formal proof of claim.

(3) Time limitations

No claim of a customer or other creditor of the debtor which is received by the trustee after the expiration of the six-month period beginning on the date of publication of notice under paragraph (1) shall be allowed, except that the court may, upon application within such period and for cause shown, grant a reasonable, fixed extension of time for the filing of a claim by the United States, by a State or political subdivision thereof, or by an infant or incompetent person without a guardian. Any claim of a customer for net equity which is received by the trustee after the expiration of such period of time as may be fixed by the court (not exceeding sixty days after the date of publication of notice under paragraph (1)) need not be paid or satisfied in whole or in part out of customer property, and, to the extent such claim is satisfied from moneys advanced by SIPC, it shall be satisfied in cash or securities (or both) as the trustee determines is most economical to the estate.

(4) Effect on claims

Except as otherwise provided in this section, and without limiting the powers and duties of the trustee to discharge obligations promptly as specified in this section, nothing in this section shall limit the right of any person, including any subrogee, to establish by formal proof or otherwise as the court may provide such claims as such person may have against the debtor, including claims for the payment of money and the delivery of specific securities, without resort to moneys advanced by SIPC to the trustee.

(b) Payments to customers

After receipt of a written statement of claim pursuant to subsection (a)(2), the trustee shall promptly discharge, in accordance with the provisions of this section, all obligations of the debtor to a customer relating to, or net equity claims based upon, securities or cash, by the delivery of securities or the making of payments to or for the account of such customer (subject to the provisions of subsection (d) and section 78fff–3(a) of this title) insofar as such obligations are ascertainable from the books and records of the debtor or are otherwise established to the satisfaction of the trustee. For purposes of distributing securities to customers, all securities shall be valued as of the close of business on the filing date. For purposes of this subsection, the court shall, among other things—

(1) with respect to net equity claims, authorize the trustee to satisfy claims out of moneys made available to the trustee by SIPC notwithstanding the fact that there has not been any showing or determination that there are sufficient funds of the debtor available to satisfy such claims; and

(2) with respect to claims relating to, or net equities based upon, securities of a class and series of an issuer which are ascertainable from the books and records of the debtor or are otherwise established to the satisfaction of the trustee, authorize the trustee to deliver securities of such class and series if and to the extent available to satisfy such claims in whole or in part, with partial deliveries to be made pro rata to the greatest extent considered practicable by the trustee.

Any payment or delivery of property pursuant to this subsection may be conditioned upon the trustee requiring claimants to execute, in a form to be determined by the trustee, appropriate receipts, supporting affidavits, releases, and assignments, but shall be without prejudice to any right of a claimant to file formal proof of claim within the period specified in subsection (a)(3) for any balance of securities or cash to which such claimant considers himself entitled.

(c) Customer related property

(1) Allocation of customer property

The trustee shall allocate customer property of the debtor as follows:

(A) first, to SIPC in repayment of advances made by SIPC pursuant to section 78fff–3(c)(1) of this title, to the extent such advances recovered securities which were apportioned to customer property pursuant to section 78fff(d) of this title;

(B) second, to customers of such debtor, who shall share ratably in such customer property on the basis and to the extent of their respective net equities;

(C) third, to SIPC as subrogee for the claims of customers;

(D) fourth, to SIPC in repayment of advances made by SIPC pursuant to section 78fff–3(c)(2) of this title. Any customer property remaining after allocation in accordance with this paragraph shall become part of the general estate of the debtor. To the extent customer property and SIPC advances pursuant to section 78fff–3(a) of this title are not sufficient to pay or otherwise satisfy in full the net equity claims of customers, such customers shall be entitled, to the extent only of their respective unsatisfied net equities, to participate in the general estate as unsecured creditors. For purposes of allocating customer property under this paragraph, securities to be delivered in payment of net equity claims for securities of the same class and series of an issuer shall be valued as of the close of business on the filing date.

(2) Delivery of customer name securities

The trustee shall deliver customer name securities to or on behalf of a customer of the debtor entitled thereto if the customer is not indebted to the debtor. If the customer is so indebted, such customer may, with the approval of the trustee, reclaim customer name securities upon payment to the trustee, within such period of time as the trustee determines, of all indebtedness of such customer to the debtor.

(3) Recovery of transfers

Whenever customer property is not sufficient to pay in full the claims set forth in subparagraphs (A) through (D) of paragraph (1), the trustee may recover any property transferred by the debtor which, except for such transfer, would have been customer property if and to the extent that such transfer is voidable or void under the provisions of title 11. Such recovered property shall be treated as customer property. For purposes of such recovery, the property so transferred shall be deemed to have been the property of the debtor and, if such transfer was made to a customer or for his benefit, such customer shall be deemed to have been a creditor, the laws of any State to the contrary notwithstanding.

(d) Purchase of securities

The trustee shall, to the extent that securities can be purchased in a fair and orderly market, purchase securities as necessary for the delivery of securities to customers in satisfaction of their claims for net equities based on securities under section 78fff–1(b)(1) of this title and for the transfer of customer accounts under subsection (f), in order to restore the accounts of such customers as of the filing date. To the extent consistent with subsection (c), customer property and moneys advanced by SIPC may be used by the trustee to pay for securities so purchased. Moneys advanced by SIPC for each account of a separate customer may not be used to purchase securities to the extent that the aggregate value of such securities on the filing date exceeded the amount permitted to be advanced by SIPC under the provisions of section 78fff–3(a) of this title.

(e) Closeouts

(1) In general, any contract of the debtor for the purchase or sale of securities in the ordinary course of its business with other brokers or dealers which is wholly executory on the filing date shall not be completed by the trustee, except to the extent permitted by SIPC rule. Upon the adoption by SIPC of rules with respect to the closeout of such a contract but prior to the adoption of rules with respect to the completion of such a contract, the other broker or dealer shall close out such contract, without unnecessary delay, in the best available market and pursuant to such SIPC rules. Until such time as SIPC adopts rules with respect to the completion or closeout of such a contract, such a contract shall be closed out in accordance with Commission Rule S6(d)–1 as in effect on May 21, 1978, or any comparable rule of the Commission subsequently adopted, to the extent not inconsistent with the provisions of this subsection.

(2) Net profit or loss

A broker or dealer shall net all profits and losses on all contracts closed out under this subsection and—

(A) if such broker or dealer shows a net profit on such contracts, he shall pay such net profit to the trustee; and

(B) if such broker or dealer sustains a net loss on such contracts, he shall be entitled to file a claim against the debtor with the trustee in the amount of such net loss.

To the extent that a net loss sustained by a broker or dealer arises from contracts pursuant to which such broker or dealer was acting for its own customer, such broker or dealer shall be entitled to receive funds advanced by SIPC to the trustee in the amount of such loss, except that such broker or dealer may not receive more than $40,000 for each separate customer with respect to whom it sustained a loss. With respect to a net loss which is not payable under the preceding sentence from funds advanced by SIPC, the broker or dealer shall be entitled to participate in the general estate as an unsecured creditor.

(3) Registered clearing agencies

Neither a registered clearing agency which by its rules has an established procedure for the closeout of open contracts between an insolvent broker or dealer and its participants, nor its participants to the extent such participants' claims are or may be processed within the registered clearing agency, shall be entitled to receive SIPC funds in payment of any losses on such contracts, except as SIPC may otherwise provide by rule. If such registered clearing agency or its participants sustain a net loss on the closeout of such contracts with the debtor, they shall have the right to participate in the general estate as unsecured creditors to the extent of such loss. Any funds or other property owed to the debtor, after the closeout of such contracts, shall be promptly paid to the trustee. Rules adopted by SIPC under this paragraph shall provide that in no case may a registered clearing agency or its participants, to the extent such participants' claims are or may be processed within the registered clearing agency, be entitled to receive funds advanced by SIPC in an amount greater, in the aggregate, than could be received by the participants if such participants proceeded individually under paragraph (1) and (2).

(4) "Customer" defined

For purposes of this subsection, the term "customer" does not include any person who—

(A) is a broker or dealer;

(B) had a claim for cash or securities which by contract, agreement, or understanding, or by operation of law, was part of the capital of the claiming broker or dealer or was subordinated to the claims of any or all creditors of such broker or dealer; or

(C) had a relationship of the kind specified in section 78fff–3(a)(5) of this title with the debtor.

A claiming broker or dealer shall be deemed to have been acting on behalf of its customer if it acted as agent for such customer or if it held such customer's order which was to be executed as a part of its contract with the debtor.

(f) Transfer of customer accounts

In order to facilitate the prompt satisfaction of customer claims and the orderly liquidation of the debtor, the trustee may, pursuant to terms satisfactory to him and subject to the prior approval of SIPC, sell or otherwise transfer to another member of SIPC, without consent of any customer, all or any part of the account of a customer of the debtor. In connection with any such sale or transfer to another member of SIPC and subject to the prior approval of SIPC, the trustee may—

(1) waive or modify the need to file a written statement of claim pursuant to subsection (a)(2); and

(2) enter into such agreements as the trustee considers appropriate under the circumstances to indemnify any such member of SIPC against shortages of cash or securities in the customer accounts sold or transferred.

The funds of SIPC may be made available to guarantee or secure any indemnification under paragraph (2). The prior approval of SIPC to such indemnification shall be conditioned, among such other standards as SIPC may determine, upon a determination by SIPC that the probable cost of any such indemnification can reasonably be expected not to exceed the cost to SIPC of proceeding under section 78fff–3(a) of this title and section 78fff–3(b) of this title.

§78fff–3. SIPC advances

(a) Advances for customers' claims

In order to provide for prompt payment and satisfaction of net equity claims of customers of the debtor, SIPC shall advance to the trustee such moneys, not to exceed $500,000 for each customer, as may be required to pay or otherwise satisfy claims for the amount by which the net equity of each customer exceeds his ratable share of customer property, except that—

(1) if all or any portion of the net equity claim of a customer in excess of his ratable share of customer property is a claim for cash, as distinct from a claim for securities or options on commodity futures contracts, the amount advanced to satisfy such claim for cash shall not exceed the standard maximum cash advance amount for each such customer, as determined in accordance with subsection (d);

(2) a customer who holds accounts with the debtor in separate capacities shall be deemed to be a different customer in each capacity;

(3) if all or any portion of the net equity claim of a customer in excess of his ratable share of customer property is satisfied by the delivery of securities purchased by the trustee pursuant to section 78fff–2(d) of this title, the securities so purchased shall be valued as of the filing date for purposes of applying the dollar limitations of this subsection;

(4) no advance shall be made by SIPC to the trustee to pay or otherwise satisfy, directly or indirectly, any net equity claim of a customer who is a general partner, officer, or director of the debtor, a beneficial owner of five per centum or more of any class of equity security of the debtor (other than a nonconvertible stock having fixed preferential dividend and liquidation rights), a limited partner with a participation of five per centum or more in the net assets or net profits of the debtor, or a person who, directly or indirectly and through agreement or otherwise, exercised or had the power to exercise a controlling influence over the management or policies of the debtor; and

(5) no advance shall be made by SIPC to the trustee to pay or otherwise satisfy any net equity claim of any customer who is a broker or dealer or bank, other than to the extent that it shall be established to the satisfaction of the trustee, from the books and records of the debtor or from the books and records of a broker or dealer or bank, or otherwise, that the net equity claim of such broker or dealer or bank against the debtor arose out of transactions for customers of such broker or dealer or bank (which customers are not themselves a broker or dealer or bank or a person described in paragraph (4)), in which event each such customer of such broker or dealer or bank shall be deemed a separate customer of the debtor.

To the extent moneys are advanced by SIPC to the trustee to pay or otherwise satisfy the claims of customers, in addition to all other rights it may have at law or in equity, SIPC shall be subrogated to the claims of such customers with the rights and priorities provided in this chapter, except that SIPC as subrogee may assert no claim against customer property until after the allocation thereof to customers as provided in section 78fff–2(c) of this title.

(b) Other advances

SIPC shall advance to the trustee—

(1) such moneys as may be required to carry out section 78fff–2(e) of this title; and

(2) to the extent the general estate of the debtor is not sufficient to pay any and all costs and expenses of administration of the estate of the debtor and of the liquidation proceeding, the amount of such costs and expenses.

(c) Discretionary advances

SIPC may advance to the trustee such moneys as may be required to—

(1) pay or guarantee indebtedness of the debtor to a bank, lender, or other person under section 78fff–1(b)(2) of this title;

(2) guarantee or secure any indemnity under section 78fff–2(f) of this title; and

(3) purchase securities under section 78fff–2(d) of this title.

(d) Standard maximum cash advance amount defined

For purposes of this section, the term "standard maximum cash advance amount" means $250,000, as such amount may be adjusted after December 31, 2010, as provided under subsection (e).

(e) Inflation adjustment

(1) In general

Not later than January 1, 2011, and every 5 years thereafter, and subject to the approval of the Commission as provided under section 78ccc(e)(2) of this title, the Board of Directors of SIPC shall determine whether an inflation adjustment to the standard maximum cash advance amount is appropriate. If the Board of Directors of SIPC determines such an adjustment is appropriate, then the standard maximum cash advance amount shall be an amount equal to—

(A) $250,000 multiplied by—

(B) the ratio of the annual value of the Personal Consumption Expenditures Chain-Type Price Index (or any successor index thereto), published by the Department of Commerce, for the calendar year preceding the year in which such determination is made, to the published annual value of such index for the calendar year preceding 2010.

The index values used in calculations under this paragraph shall be, as of the date of the calculation, the values most recently published by the Department of Commerce.

(2) Rounding

If the standard maximum cash advance amount determined under paragraph (1) for any period is not a multiple of $10,000, the amount so determined shall be rounded down to the nearest $10,000.

(3) Publication and report to the Congress

Not later than April 5 of any calendar year in which a determination is required to be made under paragraph (1)—

(A) the Commission shall publish in the Federal Register the standard maximum cash advance amount; and

(B) the Board of Directors of SIPC shall submit a report to the Congress stating the standard maximum cash advance amount.

(4) Implementation period

Any adjustment to the standard maximum cash advance amount shall take effect on January 1 of the year immediately succeeding the calendar year in which such adjustment is made.

(5) Inflation adjustment considerations

In making any determination under paragraph (1) to increase the standard maximum cash advance amount, the Board of Directors of SIPC shall consider—

(A) the overall state of the fund and the economic conditions affecting members of SIPC;

(B) the potential problems affecting members of SIPC; and

(C) such other factors as the Board of Directors of SIPC may determine appropriate.

§78fff–4. Direct payment procedure

(a) Determination regarding direct payments

If SIPC determines that—

(1) any member of SIPC (including a person who was a member within one hundred eighty days prior to such determination) has failed or is in danger of failing to meet its obligations to customers;

(2) one or more of the conditions specified in section 78eee(b)(1) of this title exist with respect to such member;

(3) the claim of each customer of the member is within the limits of protection provided in section 78fff–3(a) of this title;

(4) the claims of all customers of the member aggregate less than $250,000;

(5) the cost to SIPC of satisfying customer claims under this section will be less than the cost under a liquidation proceeding; and

(6) such member's registration as a broker-dealer under section 78o(b) of this title has been terminated, or such member has consented to the use of the direct payment procedure set forth in this section,

SIPC may, in its discretion, use the direct payment procedure set forth in this section in lieu of instituting a liquidation proceeding with respect to such member.

(b) Notice

Promptly after a determination under subsection (a) that the direct payment procedure is to be used with respect to a member, SIPC shall cause notice of such direct payment procedure to be published in one or more newspapers of general circulation in a form and manner determined by SIPC, and at the same time shall cause to be mailed a copy of such notice to each person who appears, from the books and records of such member, to have been a customer of the member with an open account within the past twelve months, to the address of such person as it appears from the books and records of such member. Such notice shall state that SIPC will satisfy customer claims directly, without a liquidation proceeding, and shall set forth the form and manner in which claims may be presented. A direct payment procedure shall be deemed to commence on the date of first publication under this subsection and no claim by a customer shall be paid or otherwise satisfied by SIPC unless received within the six-month period beginning on such date, except that SIPC shall, upon application within such period, and for cause shown, grant a reasonable, fixed extension of time for the filing of a claim by the United States, by a State or political subdivision thereof, or by an infant or incompetent person without a guardian.

(c) Payments to customers

SIPC shall promptly satisfy all obligations of the member to each of its customers relating to, or net equity claims based upon, securities or cash by the delivery of securities or the effecting of payments to such customer (subject to the provisions of section 78fff–2(d) of this title and section 78fff–3(a) of this title insofar as such obligations are ascertainable from the books and records of the member or are otherwise established to the satisfaction of SIPC. For purposes of distributing securities to customers, all securities shall be valued as of the close of business on the date of publication under subsection (b). Any payment or delivery of securities pursuant to this section may be conditioned upon the execution and delivery, in a form to be determined by SIPC, of appropriate receipts, supporting affidavits, releases, and assignments. To the extent moneys of SIPC are used to satisfy the claims of customers, in addition to all other rights it may have at law or in equity, SIPC shall be subrogated to the claims of such customers against the member.

(d) Effect on claims

Except as otherwise provided in this section, nothing in this section shall limit the right of any person, including any subrogee, to establish by formal proof or otherwise such claims as such person may have against the member, including claims for the payment of money and the delivery of specific securities, without resort to moneys of SIPC.

(e) Jurisdiction of Bankruptcy Courts

After SIPC has published notice of the institution of a direct payment procedure under this section, any person aggrieved by any determination of SIPC with respect to his claim under subsection (c) may, within six months following mailing by SIPC of its determination with respect to such claim, seek a final adjudication of such claim. The courts of the United States having jurisdiction over cases under title 11 shall have original and exclusive jurisdiction of any civil action for the adjudication of such claim. Any such action shall be brought in the judicial district where the head office of the debtor is located. Any determination of the rights of a customer under subsection (c) shall not prejudice any other right or remedy of the customer against the member.

(f) Discontinuance of direct payment procedures

If, at any time after the institution of a direct payment procedure with respect to a member, SIPC determines, in its discretion, that continuation of such direct payment procedure is not appropriate, SIPC may cease such direct payment procedure and, upon so doing, may seek a protective decree pursuant to section 78eee of this title. To the extent payments of cash, distributions of securities, or determinations with respect to the validity of a customer's claim are made under this section, such payments, distributions, and determinations shall be recognized and given full effect in the event of any subsequent liquidation proceeding. Any action brought under subsection (e) and pending at the time of the appointment of a trustee under section 78eee(b)(3) of this title shall be permanently stayed by the court at the time of such appointment, and the court shall enter an order directing the transfer or removal to it of such suit. Upon such removal or transfer the complaint in such action shall constitute the plaintiff's claim in the liquidation proceeding, if appropriate, and shall be deemed received by the trustee on the date of his appointment regardless of the date of actual transfer or removal of such action.

(g) References

For purposes of this section, any reference to the trustee in sections 78fff–1(b)(1), 78fff–2(d), 78fff–2(f), 78fff–3(a), 78lll(5) and 78lll(12) of this title shall be deemed a reference to SIPC, and any reference to the date of publication of notice under section 78fff–2(a) of this title shall be deemed a reference to the publication of notice under this section.

§78ggg. SEC functions

(a) Administrative procedure

Determinations of the Commission, for purposes of making rules pursuant to section 78ccc(e)(3) and section 78iii(f) of this title shall be after appropriate notice and opportunity for a hearing, and for submission of views of interested persons in accordance with the rulemaking procedures specified in section 553 of title 5, but the holding of a hearing shall not prevent adoption of any such rule or regulation upon expiration of the notice period specified in subsection (d) of such section and shall not be required to be on a record within the meaning of subchapter II of chapter 5 of such title.

(b) Enforcement of actions

In the event of the refusal of SIPC to commit its funds or otherwise to act for the protection of customers of any member of SIPC, the Commission may apply to the district court of the United States in which the principal office of SIPC is located for an order requiring SIPC to discharge its obligations under this chapter and for such other relief as the court may deem appropriate to carry out the purposes of this chapter.

(c) Examinations and reports

(1) Examination of SIPC, etc.

The Commission may make such examinations and inspections of SIPC and require SIPC to furnish it with such reports and records or copies thereof as the Commission may consider necessary or appropriate in the public interest or to effectuate the purposes of this chapter.

(2) Reports from SIPC

As soon as practicable after the close of each fiscal year, SIPC shall submit to the Commission a written report relative to the conduct of its business, and the exercise of the other rights and powers granted by this chapter, during such fiscal year. Such report shall include financial statements setting forth the financial position of SIPC at the end of such fiscal year and the results of its operations (including the source and application of its funds) for such fiscal year. The financial statements so included shall be examined by an independent public accountant or firm of independent public accountants, selected by SIPC and satisfactory to the Commission, and shall be accompanied by the report thereon of such accountant or firm. The Commission shall transmit such report to the President and the Congress with such comment thereon as the Commission may deem appropriate.

§78hhh. Examining authority functions

Each member of SIPC shall file with such member's examining authority, or collection agent if a collection agent has been designated pursuant to section 78iii(a) of this title, such information (including reports of, and information with respect to, the gross revenues from the securities business of such member, including the composition thereof, transactions in securities effected by such member, and other information with respect to such member's activities, whether in the securities business or otherwise, including customer accounts maintained, net capital employed, and activities conducted) as SIPC may determine to be necessary or appropriate for the purpose of making assessments under section 78ddd of this title. The examining authority or collection agent shall file with SIPC all or such part of such information (and such compilations and analyses thereof) as SIPC, by bylaw or rule, shall prescribe. No application, report, or document filed pursuant to this section shall be deemed to be filed pursuant to section 78r of this title.

§78iii. Functions of self-regulatory organizations

(a) Collection agent

Each self-regulatory organization shall act as collection agent for SIPC to collect the assessments payable by all members of SIPC for whom such self-regulatory organization is the examining authority, unless SIPC designates a self-regulatory organization other than the examining authority to act as collection agent for any member of SIPC who is a member of or participant in more than one self-regulatory organization. If the only self-regulatory organization of which a member of SIPC is a member or in which it is a participant is a registered clearing agency that is not the examining authority for the member, SIPC may, nevertheless, designate such registered clearing agency as collection agent for the member or may require that payments be made directly to SIPC. The collection agent shall be obligated to remit to SIPC assessments made under section 78ddd of this title only to the extent that payments of such assessment are received by such collection agent. Members of SIPC who are not members of or participants in a self-regulatory organization shall make payments directly to SIPC.

(b) Immunity

No self-regulatory organization shall have any liability to any person for any action taken or omitted in good faith pursuant to section 78eee(a)(1) and section 78eee(a)(2) of this title.

(c) Inspections

The self-regulatory organization of which a member of SIPC is a member or in which it is a participant shall inspect or examine such member for compliance with applicable financial responsibility rules, except that—

(1) if the self-regulatory organization is a registered clearing agency, the Commission may designate itself as responsible for the examination of such member for compliance with applicable financial responsibility rules; and

(2) if a member of SIPC is a member of or participant in more than one self-regulatory organization, the Commission, pursuant to section 78q(d) of this title, shall designate one of such self-regulatory organizations or itself as responsible for the examination of such member for compliance with applicable financial responsibility rules.

(d) Reports

There shall be filed with SIPC by the self-regulatory organizations such reports of inspections or examinations of the members of SIPC (or copies thereof) as may be designated by SIPC by bylaw or rule.

(e) Consultation

SIPC shall consult and cooperate with the self-regulatory organizations toward the end:

(1) that there may be developed and carried into effect procedures reasonably designed to detect approaching financial difficulty upon the part of any member of SIPC;

(2) that, as nearly as may be practicable, examinations to ascertain whether members of SIPC are in compliance with applicable financial responsibility rules will be conducted by the self-regulatory organizations under appropriate standards (both as to method and scope) and reports of such examinations will, where appropriate, be standard in form; and

(3) that, as frequently as may be practicable under the circumstances, each member of SIPC will file financial information with, and be examined by, the self-regulatory organization which is the examining authority for such member.

(f) Financial condition of members

The Commission may, by such rules as it determines necessary or appropriate in the public interest and to carry out the purposes of this chapter, require any self-regulatory organization to furnish SIPC with reports and records (or copies thereof) relating to the financial condition of members of or participants in such self-regulatory organization.

§78jjj. Prohibited acts

(a) Failure to pay assessment, etc.

If a member of SIPC shall fail to file any report or information required pursuant to this chapter, or shall fail to pay when due all or any part of an assessment made upon such member pursuant to this chapter, and such failure shall not have been cured, by the filing of such report or information or by the making of such payment, together with interest and penalty thereon, within five days after receipt by such member of written notice of such failure given by or on behalf of SIPC, it shall be unlawful for such member, unless specifically authorized by the Commission, to engage in business as a broker or dealer. If such member denies that it owes all or any part of the amount specified in such notice, it may after payment of the full amount so specified commence an action against SIPC in the appropriate United States district court to recover the amount it denies owing.

(b) Engaging in business after appointment of trustee or initiation of direct payment procedure

It shall be unlawful for any broker or dealer for whom a trustee has been appointed pursuant to this chapter or for whom a direct payment procedure has been initiated to engage thereafter in business as a broker or dealer, unless the Commission otherwise determines in the public interest. The Commission may by order bar or suspend for any period, any officer, director, general partner, owner of 10 per centum or more of the voting securities, or controlling person of any broker or dealer for whom a trustee has been appointed pursuant to this chapter or for whom a direct payment procedure has been initiated from being or becoming associated with a broker or dealer, if after appropriate notice and opportunity for hearing, the Commission shall determine such bar or suspension to be in the public interest.

(c) Concealment of assets; false statements or claims

(1) Specific prohibited acts

Any person who, directly or indirectly, in connection with or in contemplation of any liquidation proceeding or direct payment procedure—

(A) employs any device, scheme, or artifice to defraud;

(B) engages in any act, practice, or course of business which operates or would operate as a fraud or deceit upon any person; or

(C) fraudulently or with intent to defeat this chapter—

(i) conceals or transfers any property belonging to the estate of a debtor;

(ii) makes a false statement or account;

(iii) presents or uses any false claim for proof against the estate of a debtor;

(iv) receives any material amount of property from a debtor;

(v) gives, offers, receives, transfers, or obtains any money or property, remuneration, compensation, reward, advantage, other consideration, or promise thereof, for acting or forebearing to act;

(vi) conceals, destroys, mutilates, falsifies, makes a false entry in, or otherwise falsifies any document affecting or relating to the property or affairs of a debtor; or

(vii) withholds, from any person entitled to its possession, any document affecting or relating to the property or affairs of a debtor,

shall be fined not more than $250,000 or imprisoned for not more than five years, or both.

(2) Fraudulent conversion

Any person who, directly or indirectly steals, embezzles, or fraudulently, or with intent to defeat this chapter, abstracts or converts to his own use or to the use of another any of the moneys, securities, or other assets of SIPC, or otherwise defrauds or attempts to defraud SIPC or a trustee by any means, shall be fined not more than $250,000 or imprisoned not more than five years, or both.

(d) Misrepresentation of SIPC membership or protection

(1) In general

Any person who falsely represents by any means (including, without limitation, through the Internet or any other medium of mass communication), with actual knowledge of the falsity of the representation and with an intent to deceive or cause injury to another, that such person, or another person, is a member of SIPC or that any person or account is protected or is eligible for protection under this chapter or by SIPC, shall be liable for any damages caused thereby and shall be fined not more than $250,000 or imprisoned for not more than 5 years.

(2) Injunctions

Any court having jurisdiction of a civil action arising under this chapter may grant temporary injunctions and final injunctions on such terms as the court deems reasonable to prevent or restrain any violation of paragraph (1). Any such injunction may be served anywhere in the United States on the person enjoined, shall be operative throughout the United States, and shall be enforceable, by proceedings in contempt or otherwise, by any United States court having jurisdiction over that person. The clerk of the court granting the injunction shall, when requested by any other court in which enforcement of the injunction is sought, transmit promptly to the other court a certified copy of all papers in the case on file in such clerk's office.

§78kkk. Miscellaneous provisions

(a) Public inspection of reports

Any notice, report, or other document filed with SIPC pursuant to this chapter shall be available for public inspection unless SIPC or the Commission shall determine that disclosure thereof is not in the public interest. Nothing herein shall act to deny documents or information to the Congress of the United States or the committees of either House having jurisdiction over financial institutions, securities regulation, or related matters under the rules of each body. Nor shall the Commission be denied any document or information which the Commission, in its judgment, needs.

(b) Liability of members of SIPC

Except for such assessments as may be made upon such member pursuant to the provisions of section 78ddd of this title, no member of SIPC shall have any liability under this chapter as a member of SIPC for, or in connection with, any act or omission of any other broker or dealer whether in connection with the conduct of the business or affairs of such broker or dealer or otherwise and, without limiting the generality of the foregoing, no member shall have any liability for or in respect of any indebtedness or other liability of SIPC.

(c) Liability of SIPC and Directors, officers, or employees

Neither SIPC nor any of its Directors, officers, or employees shall have any liability to any person for any action taken or omitted in good faith under or in connection with any matter contemplated by this chapter.

(d) Advertising

SIPC shall by bylaw prescribe the manner in which a member of SIPC may display any sign or signs (or include in any advertisement a statement) relating to the protection to customers and their accounts, or any other protections, afforded under this chapter. No member may display any such sign, or include in an advertisement any such statement, except in accordance with such bylaws. SIPC may also by bylaw prescribe such minimal requirements as it considers necessary and appropriate to require a member of SIPC to provide public notice of its membership in SIPC.

(e) SIPC exempt from taxation

SIPC, its property, its franchise, capital, reserves, surplus, and its income, shall be exempt from all taxation now or hereafter imposed by the United States or by any State or local taxing authority, except that any real property and any tangible personal property (other than cash and securities) of SIPC shall be subject to State and local taxation to the same extent according to its value as other real and tangible personal property is taxed. Assessments made upon a member of SIPC shall constitute ordinary and necessary expenses in carrying on the business of such member for the purpose of section 162(a) of title 26. The contribution and transfer to SIPC of funds or securities held by any trust established by a national securities exchange prior to January 1, 1970, for the purpose of providing assistance to customers of members of such exchange, shall not result in any taxable gain to such trust or give rise to any taxable income to any member of SIPC under any provision of title 26, nor shall such contribution or transfer, or any reduction in assessments made pursuant to this chapter, in any way affect the status, as ordinary and necessary expenses under section 162(a) of title 26, of any contributions made to such trust by such exchange at any time prior to such transfer. Upon dissolution of SIPC, none of its net assets shall inure to the benefit of any of its members.

(f) Section 78t(a) of this title not to apply

The provisions of subsection (a) of section 78t of this title shall not apply to any liability under or in connection with this chapter.

(g) SEC study of unsafe or unsound practices

Not later than twelve months after December 30, 1970, the Commission shall compile a list of unsafe or unsound practices by members of SIPC in conducting their business and report to the Congress (1) the steps being taken under the authority of existing law to eliminate those practices and (2) recommendations concerning additional legislation which may be needed to eliminate those unsafe or unsound practices.

§78lll. Definitions

For purposes of this chapter, including the application of the Bankruptcy Act to a liquidation proceeding:

(1) Commission

The term "Commission" means the Securities and Exchange Commission.

(2) Customer

(A) In general

The term "customer" of a debtor means any person (including any person with whom the debtor deals as principal or agent) who has a claim on account of securities received, acquired, or held by the debtor in the ordinary course of its business as a broker or dealer from or for the securities accounts of such person for safekeeping, with a view to sale, to cover consummated sales, pursuant to purchases, as collateral, security, or for purposes of effecting transfer.

(B) Included persons

The term "customer" includes—

(i) any person who has deposited cash with the debtor for the purpose of purchasing securities;

(ii) any person who has a claim against the debtor for cash, securities, futures contracts, or options on futures contracts received, acquired, or held in a portfolio margining account carried as a securities account pursuant to a portfolio margining program approved by the Commission; and

(iii) any person who has a claim against the debtor arising out of sales or conversions of such securities.

(C) Excluded persons

The term "customer" does not include any person, to the extent that—

(i) the claim of such person arises out of transactions with a foreign subsidiary of a member of SIPC; or

(ii) such person has a claim for cash or securities which by contract, agreement, or understanding, or by operation of law, is part of the capital of the debtor, or is subordinated to the claims of any or all creditors of the debtor, notwithstanding that some ground exists for declaring such contract, agreement, or understanding void or voidable in a suit between the claimant and the debtor.

(3) Customer name securities

The term "customer name securities" means securities which were held for the account of a customer on the filing date by or on behalf of the debtor and which on the filing date were registered in the name of the customer, or were in the process of being so registered pursuant to instructions from the debtor, but does not include securities registered in the name of the customer which, by endorsement or otherwise, were in negotiable form.

(4) Customer property

The term "customer property" means cash and securities (except customer name securities delivered to the customer) at any time received, acquired, or held by or for the account of a debtor from or for the securities accounts of a customer, and the proceeds of any such property transferred by the debtor, including property unlawfully converted. The term "customer property" includes—

(A) securities held as property of the debtor to the extent that the inability of the debtor to meet its obligations to customers for their net equity claims based on securities of the same class and series of an issuer is attributable to the debtor's noncompliance with the requirements of section 78o(c)(3) of this title and the rules prescribed under such section;

(B) resources provided through the use or realization of customers' debit cash balances and other customer-related debit items as defined by the Commission by rule;

(C) any cash or securities apportioned to customer property pursuant to section 78fff(d) of this title;

(D) in the case of a portfolio margining account of a customer that is carried as a securities account pursuant to a portfolio margining program approved by the Commission, a futures contract or an option on a futures contract received, acquired, or held by or for the account of a debtor from or for such portfolio margining account, and the proceeds thereof; and

(E) any other property of the debtor which, upon compliance with applicable laws, rules, and regulations, would have been set aside or held for the benefit of customers, unless the trustee determines that including such property within the meaning of such term would not significantly increase customer property.

(5) Debtor

The term "debtor" means a member of SIPC with respect to whom an application for a protective decree has been filed under section 78eee(a)(3) of this title or a direct payment procedure has been instituted under section 78fff–4(b) of this title.

(6) Examining authority

The term "examining authority" means, with respect to any member of SIPC (A) the self-regulatory organization which inspects or examines such member of SIPC, or (B) the Commission if such member of SIPC is not a member of or participant in any self-regulatory organization or if the Commission has designated itself examining authority for such member pursuant to section 78iii(c) of this title.

(7) Filing date

The term "filing date" means the date on which an application for a protective decree is filed under section 78eee(a)(3) of this title, except that—

(A) if a petition under title 11 concerning the debtor was filed before such date, the term "filing date" means the date on which such petition was filed;

(B) if the debtor is the subject of a proceeding pending in any court or before any agency of the United States or any State in which a receiver, trustee, or liquidator for such debtor has been appointed and such proceeding was commenced before the date on which such application was filed, the term "filing date" means the date on which such proceeding was commenced; or

(C) if the debtor is the subject of a direct payment procedure or was the subject of a direct payment procedure discontinued by SIPC pursuant to section 78fff–4(f) of this title, the term "filing date" means the date on which notice of such direct payment procedure was published under section 78fff–4(b) of this title.

(8) Foreign subsidiary

The term "foreign subsidiary" means any subsidiary of a member of SIPC which has its principal place of business in a foreign country or which is organized under the laws of a foreign country.

(9) Gross revenues from the securities business

The term "gross revenues from the securities business" means the sum of (but without duplication)—

(A) commissions earned in connection with transactions in securities effected for customers as agent (net of commissions paid to other brokers and dealers in connection with such transactions) and markups with respect to purchases or sales of securities as principal;

(B) charges for executing or clearing transactions in securities for other brokers and dealers;

(C) the net realized gain, if any, from principal transactions in securities in trading accounts;

(D) the net profit, if any, from the management of or participation in the underwriting or distribution of securities;

(E) interest earned on customers' securities accounts;

(F) fees for investment advisory services (except when rendered to one or more registered investment companies or insurance company separate accounts) or account supervision with respect to securities;

(G) fees for the solicitation of proxies with respect to, or tenders or exchanges of, securities;

(H) income from service charges or other surcharges with respect to securities;

(I) except as otherwise provided by rule of the Commission, dividends and interest received on securities in investment accounts of the broker or dealer;

(J) fees in connection with put, call, and other option transactions in securities;

(K) commissions earned from transactions in (i) certificates of deposit, and (ii) Treasury bills, bankers acceptances, or commercial paper which have a maturity at the time of issuance of not exceeding nine months, exclusive of days of grace, or any renewal thereof, the maturity of which is likewise limited, except that SIPC shall by bylaw include in the aggregate of gross revenues only an appropriate percentage of such commissions based on SIPC's loss experience with respect to such instruments over at least the preceding five years; and

(L) fees and other income from such other categories of the securities business as SIPC shall provide by bylaw.

Such term includes revenues earned by a broker or dealer in connection with a transaction in the portfolio margining account of a customer carried as securities accounts pursuant to a portfolio margining program approved by the Commission. Such term does not include revenues received by a broker or dealer in connection with the distribution of shares of a registered open end investment company or unit investment trust or revenues derived by a broker or dealer from the sale of variable annuities or from the conduct of the business of insurance.

(10) Liquidation proceeding

The term "liquidation proceeding" means any proceeding for the liquidation of a debtor under this chapter in which a trustee has been appointed under section 78eee(b)(3) of this title.

(11) Net equity

The term "net equity" means the dollar amount of the account or accounts of a customer, to be determined by—

(A) calculating the sum which would have been owed by the debtor to such customer if the debtor had liquidated, by sale or purchase on the filing date—

(i) all securities positions of such customer (other than customer name securities reclaimed by such customer); and

(ii) all positions in futures contracts and options on futures contracts held in a portfolio margining account carried as a securities account pursuant to a portfolio margining program approved by the Commission, including all property collateralizing such positions, to the extent that such property is not otherwise included herein; minus

(B) any indebtedness of such customer to the debtor on the filing date; plus

(C) any payment by such customer of such indebtedness to the debtor which is made with the approval of the trustee and within such period as the trustee may determine (but in no event more than sixty days after the publication of notice under section 78fff–2(a) of this title).

A claim for a commodity futures contract received, acquired, or held in a portfolio margining account pursuant to a portfolio margining program approved by the Commission or a claim for a security futures contract, shall be deemed to be a claim with respect to such contract as of the filing date, and such claim shall be treated as a claim for cash. In determining net equity under this paragraph, accounts held by a customer in separate capacities shall be deemed to be accounts of separate customers.

(12) Persons registered as brokers or dealers

The term "persons registered as brokers or dealers" includes any person who is a member of a national securities exchange other than a government securities broker or government securities dealer registered under section 78o–5(a)(1)(A) of this title.

(13) Protective decree

The term "protective decree" means a decree, issued by a court upon application of SIPC under section 78eee(a)(3) of this title, that the customers of a member of SIPC are in need of the protection provided under this chapter.

(14) Security

The term "Security" means any note, stock, treasury stock, bond, debenture, evidence of indebtedness, any collateral trust certificate, preorganization certificate or subscription, transferable share, voting trust certificate, certificate of deposit, certificate of deposit for a security, or any security future as that term is defined in section 78c(a)(55)(A) of this title, any investment contract or certificate of interest or participation in any profit-sharing agreement or in any oil, gas, or mineral royalty or lease (if such investment contract or interest is the subject of a registration statement with the Commission pursuant to the provisions of the Securities Act of 1933 [15 U.S.C. 77a et seq.]), any put, call, straddle, option, or privilege on any security, or group or index of securities (including any interest therein or based on the value thereof), or any put, call, straddle, option, or privilege entered into on a national securities exchange relating to foreign currency, any certificate of interest or participation in, temporary or interim certificate for, receipt for, guarantee of, or warrant or right to subscribe to or purchase or sell any of the foregoing, and any other instrument commonly known as a security. Except as specifically provided above, the term "security" does not include any currency, or any commodity or related contract or futures contract, or any warrant or right to subscribe to or purchase or sell any of the foregoing.

Section 2

Understanding Products
and Their Risks

1. FINRA Rules: 2261 – Disclosure of Financial Condition

(a) A member shall make available to inspection by any bona fide regular customer, upon request, the information relative to such member's financial condition as disclosed in its most recent balance sheet prepared either in accordance with such member's usual practice or as required by any state or federal securities laws, or any rule or regulation thereunder. In lieu of making such balance sheet available to inspection, a member may deliver the balance sheet to the requesting bona fide regular customer in paper or electronic form; provided that, with respect to electronic delivery, the customer must consent to receive the balance sheet in electronic form.

(b) Any member who is a party to an open transaction or who has on deposit cash or securities of another member shall deliver upon written request of the other member, in paper or electronic form, a statement of its financial condition as disclosed in its most recent balance sheet prepared either in accordance with such member's usual practice or as required by any state or federal securities laws, or any rule or regulation thereunder.

(c) As used in paragraph (a) of this Rule, the term "customer" means any person who, in the regular course of such member's business, has cash or securities in the possession of such member.

---

2. FINRA Rules: 2262 – Disclosure of Financial Relationship with Issuer

A member controlled by, controlling, or under common control with, the issuer of any security, shall, before entering into any contract with or for a customer for the purchase or sale of such security, disclose to such customer the existence of such control, and if such disclosure is not made in writing, it shall be supplemented by the giving or sending of written disclosure at or before the completion of the transaction.

---

3. FINRA Rules: 2310 – Direct Participation Programs

(a) Definitions

For the purposes of this Rule, the following terms shall have the stated meanings:

(1) Affiliate — when used with respect to a member or sponsor, shall mean any person which controls, is controlled by, or is under common control with, such member or sponsor and includes:

(A) any partner, officer or director (or person performing similar functions) of (i) such member or sponsor, or (ii) a person which beneficially owns 50% or more of the equity interest in, or has the power to vote 50% or more of the voting interest in, such member or sponsor;

(B) any person which beneficially owns or has the right to acquire 10% or more of the equity interest in or has the power to vote 10% or more of the voting interest in (i) such member or sponsor, or (ii) a person which beneficially owns 50% or more of the equity interest in, or has the power to vote 50% or more of the voting interest in, such member or sponsor;

(C) any person with respect to which such member or sponsor, the persons specified in subparagraph (A) or (B), and the immediate families of partners, officers or directors (or persons performing similar functions) specified in subparagraph (A), or other person specified in subparagraph (B), in the aggregate beneficially own or have the right to acquire 10% or more of the equity interest or have the power to vote 10% or more of the voting interest;

(D) any person an officer of which is also a person specified in subparagraph (A) or (B) and any person a majority of the board of directors of which is comprised of persons specified in subparagraph (A) or (B); or

(E) any person controlled by a person or persons specified in subparagraphs (A), (B), (C) or (D).

(2) Cash available for distribution — cash flow less amount set aside for restoration or creation of reserves.

(3) Cash flow — cash funds provided from operations, including lease payments on net leases from builders and sellers, without deduction for depreciation, but after deducting cash funds used to pay all other expenses, debt payments, capital improvements and replacements.

(4) Direct participation program (program) — a program which provides for flow-through tax consequences regardless of the structure of the legal entity or vehicle for distribution including, but not limited to, oil and gas programs, real estate programs, agricultural programs, cattle programs, condominium securities, Subchapter S corporate offerings and all other programs of a similar nature, regardless of the industry represented by the program, or any combination thereof. A program may be composed of one or more legal entities or programs but when used herein and in any rules or regulations adopted pursuant hereto the term shall mean each of the separate entities or programs making up the overall program and/or the overall program itself. Excluded from this definition are real estate investment trusts, tax qualified pension and profit sharing plans pursuant to Sections 401 and 403(a) of the Internal Revenue Code and individual retirement plans under Section 408 of that Code, tax sheltered annuities pursuant to the provisions of Section 403(b) of the Internal Revenue Code, and any company including separate accounts, registered pursuant to the Investment Company Act.

(5) Dissenting limited partner — a person who, on the date on which soliciting material is mailed to investors, is a holder of a beneficial interest in a limited partnership that is the subject of a limited partnership rollup transaction, and who casts a vote against the transaction and complies with procedures established by FINRA, except that for purposes of an exchange or tender offer, such person shall file an objection in writing under FINRA rules during the period in which the offer is outstanding. Such objection in writing shall be filed with the party responsible for tabulating the votes or tenders.

(6) Equity interest — when used with respect to a corporation, means common stock and any security convertible into, exchangeable or exercisable for common stock, and, when used with respect to a partnership, means an interest in the capital or profits or losses of the partnership.

(7) Fair market net worth — total assets computed at fair market value less total liabilities.

(8) Limited partner or investor in a limited partnership — the purchaser of an interest in a direct participation program that is a limited partnership who is not involved in the day-to-day management of the limited partnership and bears limited liability.

(9) Limited partnership — an unincorporated association that is a direct participation program organized as a limited partnership whose partners are one or more general partners and one or more limited partners, which conforms to the provisions of the Revised Uniform Limited Partnership Act or the applicable statute that regulates the organization of such partnership.

(10) Limited partnership rollup transaction — a transaction involving the combination or reorganization of one or more limited partnerships, directly or indirectly, in which:

(A) some or all of the investors in any of such limited partnerships will receive new securities, or securities in another entity, that will be reported under a transaction reporting plan declared effective before January 1, 1991, by the SEC under Section 11A of the Exchange Act.

(B) any of the investors' limited partnership securities are not, as of the date of the filing, reported under a transaction reporting plan declared effective before January 1, 1991, by the SEC under Section 11A of the Exchange Act.

(C) investors in any of the limited partnerships involved in the transaction are subject to a significant adverse change with respect to voting rights, the term of existence of the entity, management compensation, or investment objectives; and

(D) any of such investors are not provided an option to receive or retain a security under substantially the same terms and conditions as the original issue. Notwithstanding the foregoing definition, a "limited partnership rollup transaction" does not include:

  (i) a transaction that involves only a limited partnership or partnerships having an operating policy or practice of retaining cash available for distribution and reinvesting proceeds from the sale, financing, or refinancing of assets in accordance with such criteria as the SEC determines appropriate;

  (ii) a transaction involving only limited partnerships wherein the interests of the limited partners are repurchased, recalled or exchanged pursuant to the terms of the pre-existing limited partnership agreements for securities in an operating company specifically identified at the time of the formation of the original limited partnership;

  (iii) a transaction in which the securities to be issued or exchanged are not required to be and are not registered under the Securities Act;

  (iv) a transaction that involves only issuers that are not required to register or report under Section 12 of the Exchange Act, both before and after the transaction;

  (v) a transaction, except as the SEC may otherwise provide for by rule for the protection of investors, involving the combination or reorganization of one or more limited partnerships in which a non-affiliated party succeeds to the interests of the general partner or sponsor, if:

    a. such action is approved by not less than 66 2/3 percent of the outstanding units of each of the participating limited partnerships; and

    b. as a result of the transaction, the existing general partners will receive only compensation to which they are entitled as expressly provided for in the pre-existing partnership agreements; or

  (vi) a transaction, except as the SEC may otherwise provide for by rule for the protection of investors, in which the securities offered to investors are securities of another entity that are reported under a transaction reporting plan declared effective before January 1, 1991, by the SEC under Section 11A of the Exchange Act; if:

    a. such other entity was formed, and such class of securities was reported and regularly traded, not less than 12 months before the date on which soliciting material is mailed to investors; and

    b. the securities of that entity issued to investors in the transaction do not exceed 20 percent of the total outstanding securities of the entity, exclusive of any securities of such class held by or for the account of the entity or a subsidiary of the entity.

  (vii) a transaction involving only entities registered under the Investment Company Act or any Business Development Company as defined in Section 2(a)(48) of that Act.

(11) Management fee — a fee paid to the sponsor, general partner(s), their affiliates, or other persons for management and administration of a direct participation program.

(12) Organization and offering expenses — expenses incurred in preparing a direct participation program for registration and subsequently offering interests in the program to the public, including all forms of compensation paid to underwriters, broker-dealers, or affiliates thereof in connection with the offering of the program.

(13) Participant — the purchaser of an interest in a direct participation program.

(14) Person — any natural person, partnership, corporation, association or other legal entity.

(15) Prospectus — a prospectus as defined by Section 2(10) of the Securities Act, as amended, an offering circular as described in Securities Act Rule 256 or, in the case of an intrastate offering, any document utilized for the purpose of announcing the offer and sale of securities to the public.

(16) Registration statement — a registration statement as defined by Section 2(8) of the Securities Act, as amended, a notification on Form 1-A filed with the SEC pursuant to the provisions of Securities Act Rule 255 and, in the case of an intrastate offering, any document initiating a registration or similar process for an issue of securities which is required to be filed by the laws or regulations of any state.

(17) Solicitation expenses — direct marketing expenses incurred by a member, in connection with a limited partnership rollup transaction such as telephone calls, broker-dealer fact sheets, members' legal and other fees related to the solicitation, as well as direct solicitation compensation to members.

(18) Sponsor — a person who directly or indirectly provides management services for a direct participation program whether as general partner, pursuant to contract or otherwise.

(19) Transaction costs — costs incurred in connection with a limited partnership rollup transaction, including printing and mailing the proxy, prospectus or other documents; legal fees not related to the solicitation of votes or tenders; financial advisory fees; investment banking fees; appraisal fees; accounting fees; independent committee expenses; travel expenses; and all other fees related to the preparatory work of the transaction, but not including costs that would have otherwise been incurred by the subject limited partnerships in the ordinary course of business or solicitation expenses.

(b) Requirements

(1) Application

No member or person associated with a member shall participate in a public offering of a direct participation program, a limited partnership rollup transaction or, where expressly provided below, a real estate investment trust as defined in Rule 2231(d)(4)("REIT"), except in accordance with this paragraph (b).

(2) Suitability

(A) A member or person associated with a member shall not underwrite or participate in a public offering of a direct participation program unless standards of suitability have been established by the program for participants therein and such standards are fully disclosed in the prospectus and are consistent with the provisions of subparagraph (B).

(B) In recommending to a participant the purchase, sale or exchange of an interest in a direct participation program, a member or person associated with a member shall:

(i) have reasonable grounds to believe, on the basis of information obtained from the participant concerning his investment objectives, other investments, financial situation and needs, and any other information known by the member or associated person, that:

a. the participant is or will be in a financial position appropriate to enable him to realize to a significant extent the benefits described in the prospectus, including the tax benefits where they are a significant aspect of the program;

b. the participant has a fair market net worth sufficient to sustain the risks inherent in the program, including loss of investment and lack of liquidity; and

c. the program is otherwise suitable for the participant; and

(ii) maintain in the files of the member documents disclosing the basis upon which the determination of suitability was reached as to each participant.

(C) Notwithstanding the provisions of subparagraphs (A) and (B) hereof, no member shall execute any transaction in direct participation program in a discretionary account without prior written approval of the transaction by the customer.

(D) Subparagraphs (A) and (B), and, only in situations where the member is not affiliated with the direct participation program, subparagraph (C) shall not apply to:

(i) a secondary public offering of or a secondary market transaction in a unit, depositary receipt, or other interest in a direct participation program that is listed on a national securities exchange; or

(ii) an initial public offering of a unit, depositary receipt or other interest in a direct participation program for which an application for listing on a national securities exchange has been approved by such exchange and the applicant makes a good faith representation that it believes such listing on an exchange will occur within a reasonable period of time following the formation of the program.

(3) Disclosure

(A) Prior to participating in a public offering of a direct participation program or REIT, a member or person associated with a member shall have reasonable grounds to believe, based on information made available to him by the sponsor through a prospectus or other materials, that all material facts are adequately and accurately disclosed and provide a basis for evaluating the program.

(B) In determining the adequacy of disclosed facts pursuant to subparagraph (A) hereof, a member or person associated with a member shall obtain information on material facts relating at a minimum to the following, if relevant in view of the nature of the program:

(i) items of compensation;

(ii) physical properties;

(iii) tax aspects;

(iv) financial stability and experience of the sponsor;

(v) the program's conflict and risk factors; and

(vi) appraisals and other pertinent reports.

(C) For purposes of subparagraphs (A) or (B) hereof, a member or person associated with a member may rely upon the results of an inquiry conducted by another member or members, provided that:

(i) the member or person associated with a member has reasonable grounds to believe that such inquiry was conducted with due care;

(ii) the results of the inquiry were provided to the member or person associated with a member with the consent of the member or members conducting or directing the inquiry; and

(iii) no member that participated in the inquiry is a sponsor of the program or an affiliate of such sponsor.

(D) Prior to executing a purchase transaction in a direct participation program or a REIT, a member or person associated with a member shall inform the prospective participant of all pertinent facts relating to the liquidity and marketability of the program or REIT during the term of the investment. Included in the pertinent facts shall be information regarding whether the sponsor has offered prior programs or REITs in which disclosed in the offering materials was a date or time period at which the program or REIT might be liquidated, and whether the prior program(s) or REIT(s) in fact liquidated on or around that date or during the time period; provided however, this subparagraph (D) shall not apply to an initial or secondary public offering of or a secondary market transaction in a unit, depositary receipt or other interest in a direct participation program that meets the criteria in paragraph (b)(2)(D)(i) or (ii).

(4) Organization and Offering Expenses

(A) No member or person associated with a member shall underwrite or participate in a public offering of a direct participation program or REIT if the organization and offering expenses are not fair and reasonable, taking into consideration all relevant factors.

(B) In determining the fairness and reasonableness of organization and offering expenses that are deemed to be in connection with or related to the distribution of the public offering for purposes of subparagraph (A) hereof, the arrangements shall be presumed to be unfair and unreasonable if:

(i) organization and offering expenses, as defined in paragraph (b)(4)(C), in which a member or an affiliate of a member is a sponsor, exceed an amount that equals fifteen percent of the gross proceeds of the offering;

(ii) the total amount of all items of compensation from whatever source, including compensation paid from offering proceeds and in the form of "trail commissions," payable to underwriters, broker-dealers, or affiliates thereof exceeds an amount that equals ten percent of the gross proceeds of the offering (excluding securities purchased through the reinvestment of dividends);

(iii) any compensation in connection with an offering is to be paid to underwriters, broker-dealers, or affiliates thereof out of the proceeds of the offering prior to the release of such proceeds from escrow, provided, however, that any such payment from sources other than proceeds of the offering shall be made only on the basis of bona fide transactions;

(iv) commissions or other compensation are to be paid or awarded either directly or indirectly, to any person engaged by a potential investor for investment advice as an inducement to such advisor to advise the purchaser of interests in a particular program or REIT, unless such person is a registered broker-dealer or a person associated with such a broker-dealer;

(v) the program or REIT provides for compensation of an indeterminate nature to be paid to members or persons associated with members for sales of the program or REIT, or for services of any kind rendered in connection with or related to the distribution thereof, including, but not necessarily limited to, the following: a percentage of the management fee, a profit sharing arrangement, brokerage commissions, an over-riding royalty interest, a net profits interest, a percentage of revenues, a reversionary interest, a working interest, a security or right to acquire a security having an indeterminate value, or other similar incentive items;

(vi) the program or REIT charges a sales load or commission on securities that are purchased through the reinvestment of dividends, unless the registration statement registering the securities under the Securities Act became effective prior to August 6, 2008; or

(vii) the member has received reimbursement for due diligence expenses that are not included in a detailed and itemized invoice, unless the amount of the reimbursement is included in the calculation of underwriting compensation as a non-accountable expense allowance, which when aggregated with all other such non-accountable expenses, does not exceed three percent of offering proceeds.

(C) The organization and offering expenses subject to the limitations in paragraph (b)(4)(B)(i) above include the following:

(i) issuer expenses that are reimbursed or paid for with offering proceeds, including overhead expenses, which issuer expenses include, but are not limited to, expenses for:

a. assembling, printing and mailing offering materials, processing subscription agreements, generating advertising and sales materials;

b. legal and accounting services provided to the sponsor or issuer;

c. salaries and non-transaction-based compensation paid to employees or agents of the sponsor or issuer for performing services for the issuer;

d. transfer agents, escrow holders depositories, engineers and other experts; and

e. registration and qualification of securities under federal and state law, including taxes and fees and FINRA fees;

(ii) underwriting compensation, which includes but is not limited to items of compensation listed in Rule 5110(c)(3) including payments:

a. to any wholesaling or retailing firm that is engaged in the solicitation, marketing, distribution or sales of the program or REIT securities;

b. to any registered representative of a member who receives transaction-based compensation in connection with the offering, except to the extent that such compensation has been included in a. above;

c. to any registered representative who is engaged in the solicitation, marketing, distribution or sales of the program or REIT securities, except:

1. to the extent that such compensation has been included in a. above;

2. for a registered representative whose functions in connection with the offering are solely and exclusively clerical or ministerial; and

3. for a registered representative whose sales activities are de minimis and incidental to his or her clerical or ministerial job functions; or

    d. for training and education meetings, legal services provided to a member in connection with the offering, advertising and sales material generated by the member and contributions to conferences and meetings held by non-affiliated members for registered representatives.

  (iii) due diligence expenses incurred when a member affirmatively discharges its responsibilities to ensure that all material facts pertaining to a program or REIT are adequately and accurately disclosed in the offering document.

(D) Notwithstanding paragraphs (b)(4)(C)(ii)b. and c. above, for every program or REIT filed with the Corporate Financing Department (the "Department") for review, the Department shall, based upon the information provided, make a determination as to whether some portion of a registered representative's non-transaction-based compensation should not be deemed to be underwriting compensation if the registered representative is either:

  (i) a dual employee of a member and the sponsor, issuer or other affiliate with respect to a program or REIT with ten or fewer registered representatives engaged in wholesaling, in which instance the Department may make such determination with respect to the ten or fewer registered representatives engaged in wholesaling; or

  (ii) a dual employee of a member and the sponsor, issuer or other affiliate who is one of the top ten highest paid executives based on non-transaction-based compensation in any program or REIT.

(E) All items of compensation paid by the program or REIT directly or indirectly from whatever source to underwriters, broker-dealers, or affiliates thereof, including, but not limited to, sales commissions, wholesaling fees, due diligence expenses, other underwriter's expenses, underwriter's counsel's fees, securities or rights to acquire securities, rights of first refusal, consulting fees, finder's fees, investor relations fees, and any other items of compensation for services of any kind or description, which are deemed to be in connection with or related to the public offering, shall be taken into consideration in computing the amount of compensation for purposes of determining compliance with the provisions of subparagraphs (A) and (B).

(F) The determination of whether compensation paid to underwriters, broker-dealers, or affiliates thereof is in connection with or related to a public offering, for purposes of this subparagraph (4), shall be made on the basis of such factors as the timing of the transaction, the consideration rendered, the investment risk, and the role of the member or affiliate in the organization, management and direction of the enterprise in which the sponsor is involved.

  (i) An affiliate of a member which acts or proposes to act as a general partner, associate general partner, or other sponsor of a program or REIT shall be presumed to be bearing investment risk for purposes of this paragraph (b) if the affiliate:

    a. is subject to potential liability as a general partner to the same extent as any other general partner;

    b. is not indemnified against potential liability as a general partner to any greater or different extent than any other general partner for its actions or those of any other general partner;

    c. has a net worth equal to at least five percent of the net proceeds of the public offering or $1.0 million, whichever is less; provided, however, that the computation of the net worth shall not include an interest in the program offered but may include net worth applied to satisfy the requirements of this paragraph (b) with respect to other programs or REITs; and

    d. agrees to maintain net worth as required by subparagraph c. above under its control until the earlier of the removal or withdrawal of the affiliate as a general partner, associate general partner, or other sponsor, or the dissolution of the program or REIT.

  (ii) For purposes of determining the factors to be utilized in computing compensation derived from securities received in connection with a public offering, the guidelines set forth in Rule 5110 shall govern to the extent applicable.

(G) Subject to the limitations on direct and indirect non-cash compensation provided under subparagraph (C), no member shall accept any cash compensation unless all of the following conditions are satisfied:

(i) all compensation is paid directly to the member in cash and the distribution, if any, of all compensation to the member's associated persons is controlled solely by the member;

(ii) the value of all compensation to be paid in connection with an offering is included as compensation to be received in connection with the offering for purposes of subparagraph (B);

(iii) arrangements relating to the proposed payment of all compensation are disclosed in the prospectus or similar offering document;

(iv) the value of all compensation paid in connection with an offering is reflected on the books and records of the recipient member as compensation received in connection with the offering; and

(v) no compensation paid in connection with an offering is directly or indirectly related to any non-cash compensation or sales incentive items provided by the member to its associated persons.

(5) Valuation for Customer Account Statements

A member shall not participate in a public offering of the securities of a direct participation program (DPP) that is not subject to the requirements of the Investment Company Act of 1940 or of a REIT unless the issuer of the DPP or REIT has agreed to disclose:

(A) a per share estimated value of the DPP or REIT security, developed in a manner reasonably designed to ensure it is reliable, in the DPP or REIT periodic reports filed pursuant to Section 13(a) or 15(d) of the Exchange Act;

(B) an explanation of the method by which the per share estimated value was developed;

(C) the date of the valuation; and

(D) in a periodic or current report filed pursuant to Section 13(a) or 15(d) of the Exchange Act within 150 days following the second anniversary of breaking escrow and in each annual report thereafter, a per share estimated value:

(i) based on valuations of the assets and liabilities of the DPP or REIT performed at least annually, by, or with the material assistance or confirmation of, a third-party valuation expert or service;

(ii) derived from a methodology that conforms to standard industry practice; and

(iii) accompanied by a written opinion or report by the issuer, delivered at least annually, that explains the scope of the review, the methodology used to develop the valuation or valuations, and the basis for the value or values reported.

(6) Participation in Rollups

(A) No member or person associated with a member shall participate in the solicitation of votes or tenders from limited partners in connection with a limited partnership rollup transaction, irrespective of the form of the resulting entity (i.e., a partnership, real estate investment trust or corporation), unless any compensation received by the member:

(i) is payable and equal in amount regardless of whether the limited partner votes affirmatively or negatively in the proposed limited partnership rollup transaction;

(ii) in the aggregate, does not exceed 2% of the exchange value of the newly created securities; and

(iii) is paid regardless of whether the limited partners reject the proposed limited partnership rollup transaction.

(B) No member or person associated with a member shall participate in the solicitation of votes or tenders from limited partners in connection with a limited partnership rollup transaction unless the general partner(s) or sponsor(s) proposing the limited partnership rollup transaction agrees to pay all solicitation expenses related to the limited partnership rollup transaction, including all preparatory work related thereto, in the event the limited partnership rollup transaction is rejected.

(C) No member or person associated with a member shall participate in any capacity in a limited partnership rollup transaction if the transaction is unfair or unreasonable.

(i) A limited partnership rollup transaction will be presumed not to be unfair or unreasonable if the limited partnership rollup transaction provides for the right of dissenting limited partners:

a. to receive compensation for their limited partnership units based on an appraisal of the limited partnership assets performed by an independent appraiser unaffiliated with the sponsor or general partner of the program that values the assets as if sold in an orderly manner in a reasonable period of time, plus or minus other balance sheet items, and less the cost of sale or refinancing and in a manner consistent with the appropriate industry practice. Compensation to dissenting limited partners of limited partnership rollup transactions may be cash, secured debt instruments, unsecured debt instruments, or freely tradeable securities; provided, however, that:

    1. limited partnership rollup transactions which utilize debt instruments as compensation must provide for a trustee and an indenture to protect the rights of the debt holders and provide a rate of interest equal to at least 120% of the applicable federal rate as determined in accordance with Section 1274 of the Internal Revenue Code of 1986;

    2. limited partnership rollup transactions which utilize unsecured debt instruments as compensation, in addition to the requirements of subparagraph 1., must limit total leverage to 70% of the appraised value of the assets;

    3. all debt securities must have a term no greater than 8 years and provide for prepayment with 80% of the net proceeds of any sale or refinancing of the assets previously owned by the partnership entitles subject to the limited partnership rollup transaction or any part thereof; and

    4. freely tradeable securities used as compensation to dissenting limited partners must be previously listed on a national securities exchange prior to the limited partnership rollup transaction, and the number of securities to be received in return for limited partnership interests must be determined in relation to the average last sale price of the freely tradeable securities in the 20-day period following the date of the meeting at which the vote on the limited partnership rollup transaction occurs. If the issuer of the freely tradeable securities is affiliated with the sponsor or general partner, newly issued securities to be used as compensation to dissenting limited partners shall not represent more than 20 percent of the issued and outstanding shares of that class of securities after giving effect to the issuance. For purposes of the preceding sentence, a sponsor or general partner is "affiliated" with the issuer of the freely tradeable securities if the sponsor or general partner receives any material compensation from the issuer or its affiliates in conjunction with the limited partnership rollup transaction or the purchase of the general partner's interest; provided, however, that nothing herein shall restrict the ability of a sponsor or general partner to receive any payment for its equity interests and compensation as otherwise provided by this subparagraph.

b. to receive or retain a security with substantially the same terms and conditions as the security originally held. Securities received or retained will be considered to have the same terms and conditions as the security originally held if:

    1. there is no material adverse change to dissenting limited partners' rights with respect to the business plan or the investment, distribution and liquidation policies of the limited partnership; and

    2. the dissenting limited partners receive substantially the same rights, preferences and priorities as they had pursuant to the security originally held; or

c. to receive other comparable rights including, but not limited to:

    1. approval of the limited partnership rollup transaction by 75% of the outstanding units of each of the individual participating limited partnerships and the exclusion of any individual limited partnership from the limited partnership rollup transaction which fails to

reach the 75% threshold. The third-party appointed to tabulate votes and dissents pursuant to subparagraph (C)(ii)b.4. hereof shall submit the results of such tabulation to FINRA;

2. review of the limited partnership rollup transaction by an independent committee of persons not affiliated with the general partner(s) or sponsor. Whenever utilized, the independent committee:

   A. shall be approved by a majority of the outstanding securities of each of the participating partnerships;

   B. shall have access to the books and records of the partnerships;

   C. shall prepare a report to the limited partners subject to the limited partnership rollup transaction that presents its findings and recommendations, including any minority views;

   D. shall have the authority to negotiate the proposed transaction with the general partner or sponsor on behalf of the limited partners, but not the authority to approve the transaction on behalf of the limited partners;

   E. shall not deliberate for a period longer than 60 days, although extensions will be permitted if unanimously agreed upon by the members of the independent committee or if approved by FINRA;

   F. may be compensated and reimbursed by the limited partnerships subject to the limited partnership rollup transaction and shall have the ability to retain independent counsel and financial advisors to represent all limited partners at the limited partnerships' expense provided the fees are reasonable; and

   G. shall be entitled to indemnification to the maximum extent permitted by law from the limited partnerships subject to the limited partnership rollup transaction from claims, causes of action or lawsuits related to any action or decision made in furtherance of their responsibilities; provided, however, that general partners or sponsors may also agree to indemnify the independent committee; or

3. any other comparable rights for dissenting limited partners proposed by general partners or sponsors, provided, however, that the general partner(s) or sponsor demonstrates to the satisfaction of FINRA or, if FINRA determines appropriate, to the satisfaction of an independent committee, that the rights proposed are comparable.

(ii) Regardless of whether a limited partnership rollup transaction is in compliance with subparagraph (C)(i), a limited partnership rollup transaction will be presumed to be unfair and unreasonable:

a. if the general partner(s):

   1. converts an equity interest in any limited partnership(s) subject to a limited partnership rollup transaction for which consideration was not paid and which was not otherwise provided for in the limited partnership agreement and disclosed to limited partners, into a voting interest in the new entity (provided, however, an interest originally obtained in order to comply with the provisions of Internal Revenue Service Revenue Proclamation 89-12 may be converted);

   2. fails to follow the valuation provisions, if any, in the limited partnership agreements of the subject limited partnerships when valuing their limited partnership interests; or

   3. utilizes a future value of their equity interest in the limited partnership rather than the current value of their equity interest, as determined by an appraisal conducted in a manner consistent with subparagraph (C)(i)a., when determining their interest in the new entity;

b. as to voting rights, if:

   1. the voting rights in the entity resulting from a limited partnership rollup transaction do not generally follow the original voting rights of the limited partnerships participating in

the limited partnership rollup transaction; provided, however, that changes to voting rights may be effected if FINRA determines that such changes are not unfair or if the changes are approved by an independent committee;

2. a majority of the interests in an entity resulting from a limited partnership rollup transaction may not, without concurrence by the sponsor, general partner(s), board of directors, trustee, or similar governing entity, depending on the form of entity and to the extent not inconsistent with applicable state law, vote to:

   A. amend the limited partnership agreement, articles of incorporation or by-laws, or indenture;

   B. dissolve the entity;

   C. remove the general partner, board of directors, trustee or similar governing entity, and elect a new general partner, board of directors, trustee or similar governing entity; or

   D. approve or disapprove the sale of substantially all of the assets of the entity;

3. the general partner(s) or sponsor(s) proposing a limited partnership rollup transaction do not provide each limited partner with a document which instructs the limited partner on the proper procedure for voting against or dissenting from the transaction; or

4. the general partner(s) or sponsor(s) does not utilize an independent third party to receive and tabulate all votes and dissents in connection with the limited partnership rollup transaction, and require that the third party make the tabulation available to the general partner and any limited partner upon request at any time during and after voting occurs;

c. as to transaction costs, if:

1. transaction costs of a rejected limited partnership rollup transaction are not apportioned between general and limited partners of the subject limited partnerships according to the final vote on the proposed transaction as follows:

   A. the general partner(s) or sponsor(s) bear all transaction costs in proportion to the total number of abstentions and votes to reject the limited partnership rollup transaction; and

   B. limited partners bear transaction costs in proportion to the number of votes to approve the limited partnership rollup transaction; or

2. individual limited partnerships that do not approve a limited partnership rollup transaction are required to pay any of the transaction costs, and the general partner or sponsor is not required to pay the transaction costs on behalf of the non-approving limited partnerships, in a limited partnership rollup transaction in which one or more limited partnerships determines not to approve the transaction, but where the transaction is consummated with respect to one or more approving limited partnerships; or

d. as to fees of general partners, if:

1. general partners are not prevented from receiving both unearned management fees discounted to a present value (if such fees were not previously provided for in the limited partnership agreement and disclosed to limited partners) and new asset-based fees;

2. property management fees and other general partner fees are inappropriate, unreasonable and more than, or not competitive with, what would be paid to third parties for performing similar services; or

3. changes in fees which are substantial and adverse to limited partners are not approved by an independent committee according to the facts and circumstances of each transaction.

(c) Non-Cash Compensation

   (1) Definitions

   The terms "compensation," "non-cash compensation" and "offeror" for the purposes of this paragraph (c) shall have the following meanings:

(A) "Compensation" shall mean cash compensation and non-cash compensation.

(B) "Non-cash compensation" shall mean any form of compensation received in connection with the sale and distribution of direct participation securities that is not cash compensation, including but not limited to merchandise, gifts and prizes, travel expenses, meals and lodging.

(C) "Offeror" shall mean an issuer, sponsor, an adviser to an issuer or sponsor, an underwriter and any affiliated person of such entities.

(2) Restriction on Non-Cash Compensation

In connection with the sale and distribution of direct participation program or REIT securities, no member or person associated with a member shall directly or indirectly accept or make payments or offers of payments of any non-cash compensation, except as provided in this provision. Non-cash compensation arrangements are limited to the following:

(A) Gifts that do not exceed an annual amount per person fixed periodically by the Board of Governors and are not conditioned on achievement of a sales target.

(B) An occasional meal, a ticket to a sporting event or the theater, or comparable entertainment which is neither so frequent nor so extensive as to raise any question of propriety and is not preconditioned on achievement of a sales target.

(C) Payment or reimbursement by offerors in connection with meetings held by an offeror or by a member for the purpose of training or education of associated persons of a member, provided that:

　(i) associated persons obtain the member's prior approval to attend the meeting and attendance by a member's associated persons is not conditioned by the member on the achievement of a sales target or any other incentives pursuant to a non-cash compensation arrangement permitted by paragraph (c)(2)(D);

　(ii) the location is appropriate to the purpose of the meeting, which shall mean a United States office of the offeror or the member holding the meeting, or a facility located in the vicinity of such office, or a United States regional location with respect to meetings of associated persons who work within that region or, with respect to meetings with direct participation programs or REITs, a United States location at which a significant or representative asset of the program or REIT is located;

　(iii) the payment or reimbursement is not applied to the expenses of guests of the associated person; and

　(iv) the payment or reimbursement by the offeror is not conditioned by the offeror on the achievement of a sales target or any other non-cash compensation arrangement permitted by paragraph (c)(2)(D).

(D) Non-cash compensation arrangements between a member and its associated persons or a company that controls a member company and the member's associated persons, provided that no unaffiliated non-member company or other unaffiliated member directly or indirectly participates in the member's or non-member's organization of a permissible non-cash compensation arrangement; and

(E) Contributions by a non-member company or other member to a non-cash compensation arrangement between a member and its associated persons, provided that the arrangement meets the criteria in paragraph (c)(2)(D).

A member shall maintain records of all non-cash compensation received by the member or its associated persons in arrangements permitted by paragraphs (c)(2)(C) through (E). The records shall include: the names of the offerors, non-members or other members making the non-cash compensation contributions; the names of the associated persons participating in the arrangements; the nature and value of non-cash compensation received; the location of training and education meetings; and any other information that proves compliance by the member and its associated persons with paragraph (c)(2)(C) through (E).

4. FINRA Rules: 2330 – Members' Responsibilities Regarding Deferred Variable Annuities

(a) General Considerations

   (1) Application

      This Rule applies to recommended purchases and exchanges of deferred variable annuities and recommended initial subaccount allocations. This Rule does not apply to reallocations among subaccounts made or to funds paid after the initial purchase or exchange of a deferred variable annuity. This Rule also does not apply to deferred variable annuity transactions made in connection with any tax-qualified, employer-sponsored retirement or benefit plan that either is defined as a "qualified plan" under Section 3(a)(12)(C) of the Exchange Act or meets the requirements of Internal Revenue Code Sections 403(b), 457(b), or 457(f), unless, in the case of any such plan, a member or person associated with a member makes recommendations to an individual plan participant regarding a deferred variable annuity, in which case the Rule would apply as to the individual plan participant to whom the member or person associated with the member makes such recommendations.

   (2) Creation, Storage, and Transmission of Documents

      For purposes of this Rule, documents may be created, stored, and transmitted in electronic or paper form, and signatures may be evidenced in electronic or other written form.

   (3) Definitions

      For purposes of this Rule, the term "registered principal" shall mean a person registered as a General Securities Sales Supervisor (Series 9/10), a General Securities Principal (Series 24) or an Investment Company Products/Variable Contracts Principal (Series 26), as applicable.

(b) Recommendation Requirements

   (1) No member or person associated with a member shall recommend to any customer the purchase or exchange of a deferred variable annuity unless such member or person associated with a member has a reasonable basis to believe

     (A) that the transaction is suitable in accordance with Rule 2111 and, in particular, that there is a reasonable basis to believe that

        (i) the customer has been informed, in general terms, of various features of deferred variable annuities, such as the potential surrender period and surrender charge; potential tax penalty if customers sell or redeem deferred variable annuities before reaching the age of 59½; mortality and expense fees; investment advisory fees; potential charges for and features of riders; the insurance and investment components of deferred variable annuities; and market risk;

        (ii) the customer would benefit from certain features of deferred variable annuities, such as tax-deferred growth, annuitization, or a death or living benefit; and

        (iii) the particular deferred variable annuity as a whole, the underlying subaccounts to which funds are allocated at the time of the purchase or exchange of the deferred variable annuity, and riders and similar product enhancements, if any, are suitable (and, in the case of an exchange, the transaction as a whole also is suitable) for the particular customer based on the information required by paragraph (b)(2) of this Rule; and

     (B) in the case of an exchange of a deferred variable annuity, the exchange also is consistent with the suitability determination required by paragraph (b)(1)(A) of this Rule, taking into consideration whether

        (i) the customer would incur a surrender charge, be subject to the commencement of a new surrender period, lose existing benefits (such as death, living, or other contractual benefits), or be subject to increased fees or charges (such as mortality and expense fees, investment advisory fees, or charges for riders and similar product enhancements);

        (ii) the customer would benefit from product enhancements and improvements; and

(iii) the customer has had another deferred variable annuity exchange within the preceding 36 months.

The determinations required by this paragraph shall be documented and signed by the associated person recommending the transaction.

(2) Prior to recommending the purchase or exchange of a deferred variable annuity, a member or person associated with a member shall make reasonable efforts to obtain, at a minimum, information concerning the customer's age, annual income, financial situation and needs, investment experience, investment objectives, intended use of the deferred variable annuity, investment time horizon, existing assets (including investment and life insurance holdings), liquidity needs, liquid net worth, risk tolerance, tax status, and such other information used or considered to be reasonable by the member or person associated with the member in making recommendations to customers.

(3) Promptly after receiving information necessary to prepare a complete and correct application package for a deferred variable annuity, a person associated with a member who recommends the deferred variable annuity shall transmit the complete and correct application package to an office of supervisory jurisdiction of the member.

(c) Principal Review and Approval

Prior to transmitting a customer's application for a deferred variable annuity to the issuing insurance company for processing, but no later than seven business days after an office of supervisory jurisdiction of the member receives a complete and correct application package, a registered principal shall review and determine whether he or she approves of the recommended purchase or exchange of the deferred variable annuity.

A registered principal shall approve the recommended transaction only if he or she has determined that there is a reasonable basis to believe that the transaction would be suitable based on the factors delineated in paragraph (b) of this Rule.

The determinations required by this paragraph shall be documented and signed by the registered principal who reviewed and then approved or rejected the transaction.

(d) Supervisory Procedures

In addition to the general supervisory and recordkeeping requirements of Rules 3110, 3120, 3130, 3150, and 4510 Series, a member must establish and maintain specific written su-pervisory procedures reasonably designed to achieve compliance with the standards set forth in this Rule. The member also must (1) implement surveillance procedures to determine if any of the member's associ-ated persons have rates of effecting deferred variable annuity exchanges that raise for review whether such rates of exchanges evidence conduct inconsistent with the applicable provisions of this Rule, other applicable FINRA rules, or the federal securities laws ("inappropriate exchanges") and (2) have policies and procedures reasonably designed to implement corrective measures to address inappropriate exchanges and the conduct of associated persons who engage in inappropriate exchanges.

(e) Training

Members shall develop and document specific training policies or programs reasonably designed to ensure that associated persons who effect and registered principals who review transactions in deferred variable annuities comply with the requirements of this Rule and that they understand the material features of deferred variable annuities, including those described in paragraph (b)(1)(A)(i) of this Rule.

---

5. FINRA Rules: 2342 – "Breakpoint" Sales

(a) No member shall sell investment company shares in dollar amounts just below the point at which the sales charge is reduced on quantity transactions so as to share in the higher sales charges applicable on sales below the breakpoint.

(b) For purposes of determining whether a sale in dollar amounts just below a breakpoint was made in order to share in a higher sales charge, FINRA will consider the facts and circumstances, including, for example, whether a member has retained records that demonstrate that the trade was executed in accordance with a bona fide asset allocation program that the member offers to its customers:

    (1) which is designed to meet their diversification needs and investment goals; and

    (2) under which the member discloses to its customers that they may not qualify for breakpoint reductions that are otherwise available.

---

6. FINRA Rules: 2360 – Options

(a) Definitions

    The following terms shall, unless the context otherwise requires, have the stated meanings:

    (1) Aggregate Exercise Price — The term "aggregate exercise price" means the exercise price of an option contract multiplied by the number of units of the underlying security covered by such option contract.

    (2) Call — The term "call" means an option contract under which the holder of the option has the right, in accordance with the terms of the option, to purchase the number of units of the underlying security or to receive a dollar equivalent of the underlying index covered by the option contract. In the case of a "call" issued by The Options Clearing Corporation on common stock, it shall mean an option contract under which the holder of the option has the right, in accordance with the terms of the option, to purchase from The Options Clearing Corporation the number of units of the underlying security or receive a dollar equivalent of the underlying index covered by the option contract.

    (3) Class of Options — The term "class of options" means all option contracts of the same type of option covering the same underlying security or index.

    (4) Clearing Member — The term "clearing member" means a FINRA member which has been admitted to membership in The Options Clearing Corporation pursuant to the provisions of the rules of The Options Clearing Corporation.

    (5) Closing Sale Transaction — The term "closing sale transaction" means an option transaction in which the seller's intention is to reduce or eliminate a long position in the series of options involved in such transaction.

    (6) Control

        (A) The term "control" means the power or ability of an individual or entity to make investment decisions for an account or accounts, or influence directly or indirectly the investment decisions of any person or entity who makes investment decisions for an account. In addition, control will be presumed in the following circumstances:

            (i) among all parties to a joint account who have authority to act on behalf of the account;

            (ii) among all general partners to a partnership account;

            (iii) when a person or entity:

    a. holds an ownership interest of 10 percent or more in an entity (ownership interest of less than 10 percent will not preclude aggregation), or

    b. shares in 10 percent or more of profits and/or losses of an account;

   (iv) when accounts have common directors or management;

   (v) where a person or entity has the authority to execute transactions in an account.

  (B) Control, presumed by one or more of the above powers, abilities or circumstances, can be rebutted by proving the factor does not exist or by showing other factors which negate the presumption of control. The rebuttal proof must be submitted by affidavit and/or such other evidence as may be appropriate in the circumstances.

  (C) FINRA will also consider the following factors in determining if aggregation of accounts is required:

   (i) similar patterns of trading activity among separate entities;

   (ii) the sharing of kindred business purposes and interests;

   (iii) whether there is common supervision of the entities which extends beyond assuring adherence to each entity's investment objectives and/or restrictions;

   (iv) the degree of contact and communication between directors and/or managers of separate accounts.

(7) Controls, Is Controlled by or Is Under Common Control With — The terms "controls," "is controlled by" and "is under common control with" shall have the meanings specified in Rule 405 of SEC Regulation C.

(8) Conventional Index Option — The term "conventional index option" means any options contract not issued, or subject to issuance, by The Options Clearing Corporation, or an OCC Cleared OTC Option, that, as of the trade date, overlies a basket or index of securities that:

 (A) Underlies a standardized index option; or

 (B) Satisfies the following criteria:

  (i) The basket or index comprises 9 or more equity securities;

  (ii) No equity security comprises more than 30% of the equity security component of the basket's or index's weighting; and

  (iii) Each equity security comprising the basket or index:

   a. is a component security in either the Russell 3000 Index or the FTSE All-World Index Series; or

   b. has

    1. market capitalization of at least $75 million or, in the case of the lowest weighted component securities in the basket or index that in the aggregate account for no more than 10% of the weight of the index, $50 million; and

    2. trading volume for each of the preceding six months of at least one million shares or, in the case of each of the lowest weighted component securities in the basket or index that in the aggregate account for no more than 10% of the weight of the index, 500,000 shares.

(9) Conventional Option — The term "conventional option" shall mean: (A) any option contract not issued, or subject to issuance, by The Options Clearing Corporation; or (B) an OCC Cleared OTC Option.

(10) Covered — The term "covered" in respect of a short position in a call option contract means that the writer's obligation is secured by a "specific deposit" or an "escrow deposit," meeting the conditions of Rules 610(e) or 610(g), respectively, of the rules of The Options Clearing Corporation, or the writer holds in the same account as the short position, on a unit-for-unit basis, a long position either in the underlying security or in an option contract of the same class of options where the exercise price of the option contract in such long position is equal to or less than the exercise price of the option contract in such short position. The term "covered" in respect of a short position in a put option contract means that the writer holds in the same account as the short position, on a unit-for-unit basis, a long position in an option contract of the same class of options having an exercise price equal to or greater than the exercise price of the option contract in such short position.

(11) Delta Neutral — The term "delta neutral" describes an equity options position that has been fully hedged, in accordance with a Permitted Pricing Model as defined in paragraph (b)(3)(A)(ii)b. with a portfolio of instruments including or relating to the same underlying security to offset the risk that the value of the equity options position will change with incremental changes in the price of the security underlying the options position.

(12) Disclosure Document(s) — The term "disclosure document" or "disclosure documents" shall mean those documents filed with the SEC, prepared by one or more options markets and meeting the requirements of SEA Rule 9b-1. They shall contain general explanatory information relating to the mechanics of buying, writing and exercising options; the risks involved, the uses of and market for the options; transaction costs and applicable margin requirements; tax consequences of trading options; identification of the options issuer and the instrument underlying the options class; and the availability of the prospectus and the information in Part II of the registration statement.

(13) Exercise Price — The term "exercise price" in respect of an option contract means the stated price per unit at which the underlying security may be purchased (in the case of a call) or sold (in the case of a put) upon the exercise of such option contract.

(14) Expiration Date — The term "expiration date" of an option contract issued by The Options Clearing Corporation means the day and time fixed in accordance with the rules of The Options Clearing Corporation for the expiration of such option contract. The term "expiration date" of all other option contracts means the date specified thereon for such.

(15) Expiration Month — The term "expiration month" in respect of an option contract means the month and year in which such option contract expires.

(16) FLEX Equity Option — The term "FLEX Equity Option" means any options contract issued, or subject to issuance by, The Options Clearing Corporation, other than an OCC Cleared OTC Option, whereby the parties to the transaction have the ability to negotiate the terms of the contract consistent with the rules of the exchange on which the options contract is traded.

(17) Long Position — The term "long position" means the number of outstanding option contracts of a given series of options held by a person (purchaser).

(18) Net Delta — The term "net delta" means the number of shares that must be maintained (either long or short) to offset the risk that the value of an equity options position will change with incremental changes in the price of the security underlying the options position.

(19) OCC Cleared OTC Option — The term "OCC Cleared OTC Option" means any put, call, straddle or other option or privilege that meets the definition of an "option" under Rule 2360(a)(21), and is cleared by The Options Clearing Corporation, is entered into other than on or through the facilities of a national securities exchange, and is entered into exclusively by persons who are "eligible contract participants" as defined in the Exchange Act.

(20) Opening Writing Transaction — The term "opening writing transaction" means an option transaction in which the seller's (writer's) intention is to create or increase a short position in the series of options involved in such transaction.

(21) Option — The term "option" shall mean any put, call, straddle or other option or privilege, which is a "security" as defined in Section 2(1) of the Securities Act, as amended, but shall not include any (A) tender offer, (B) registered warrant, (C) right, (D) convertible security or (E) any other option in respect to which the writer (seller) is the issuer of the security which may be purchased or sold upon the exercise of the option.

(22) Option Transaction — The term "option transaction" means a transaction effected by a member for the purchase or sale of an option contract, or for the closing out of a long or short position in such option.

(23) Options Contract — The term "options contract" means any option as defined in paragraph (a)(21). For purposes of paragraphs (b)(3) through (12), an option to purchase or sell common stock shall be deemed to cover 100 shares of such stock at the time the contract granting such option is written. If a stock option is granted covering some other number of shares, then for purposes of paragraphs (b)(3)

through (12), it shall be deemed to constitute as many option contracts as that other number of shares divided by 100 (e.g., an option to buy or sell five hundred shares of common stock shall be considered as five option contracts). A stock option contract that, when written, grants the right to purchase or sell 100 shares of common stock shall continue to be considered as one contract throughout its life, notwithstanding that, pursuant to its terms, the number of shares that it covers may be adjusted to reflect stock dividends, stock splits, reverse splits, or other similar actions by the issuer of such stock.

(24) Options Contract Equivalent of the Net Delta – the term "options contract equivalent of the net delta" means the net delta divided by the number of shares underlying the options contract.

(25) Options Trading — The term "options trading" means trading (A) in any option issued by The Options Clearing Corporation, and (B) in any conventional option.

(26) Outstanding — The term "outstanding" in respect of an option contract means an option contract which has neither been the subject of a closing sale transaction nor has been exercised nor reached its expiration date.

(27) Premium — The term "premium" means the aggregate price of the option contracts agreed upon between the buyer and writer/seller or their agents.

(28) Put — The term "put" means an option contract under which the holder of the option has the right, in accordance with the terms of the option, to sell the number of units of the underlying security or deliver a dollar equivalent of the underlying index covered by the option contract. In the case of a "put" issued by The Options Clearing Corporation on common stock, it shall mean an option contract under which the holder of the option has the right, in accordance with terms of the option, to sell to The Options Clearing Corporation the number of units of the underlying security covered by the option contract or to tender the dollar equivalent of the underlying index.

(29) Rules of The Options Clearing Corporation — The term "rules of The Options Clearing Corporation" means the by-laws and the rules of The Options Clearing Corporation, and all written interpretations thereof as may be in effect from time to time.

(30) Series of Options — The term "series of options" means all option contracts of the same class of options having the same exercise price and expiration date and which cover the same number of units of the underlying security or index.

(31) Short Position — The term "short position" means the number of outstanding option contracts of a given series of options with respect to which a person is obligated as a writer (seller).

(32) Standardized Equity Option — The term "standardized equity option" means any equity options contract issued, or subject to issuance by, The Options Clearing Corporation that is not a FLEX Equity Option and not an OCC Cleared OTC Option.

(33) Standardized Index Option — The term "standardized index option" means any options contract issued, or subject to issuance, by The Options Clearing Corporation that is based upon an index and is not an OCC Cleared OTC Option.

(34) The Options Clearing Corporation — The term "The Options Clearing Corporation" means The Options Clearing Corporation.

(35) Type of Option — The term "type of option" means classification of an option contract as a put or a call.

(36) Uncovered — The term "uncovered" in respect of a short position in an option contract means the short position is not covered. For purposes of paragraph (b)(16) (Opening of Accounts), paragraph (b)(20) (Supervision of Accounts) and paragraph (b)(11) (Delivery of Current Disclosure Document(s)), the term "writing uncovered short option positions" shall include combinations and any other transactions which involve uncovered writing.

(37) Underlying Index — The term "underlying index" means an index underlying a Standardized Index Option or a Conventional Index Option.

(38) Underlying Security — The term "underlying security" in respect of an option contract means the security which The Options Clearing Corporation or another person shall be obligated to sell (in the case of a call) or purchase (in the case of a put) upon the valid exercise of such option contract.

(39) Unit — The term "unit" shall mean the smallest interest in a particular security which can be purchased or sold, such as one share of stock, one warrant, one bond, and so forth.

(b) Requirements

(1) Applicability

This Rule shall be applicable to the extent appropriate unless otherwise stated herein: (A) to the conduct of accounts, the execution of transactions, and the handling of orders in exchange-listed options by members that are not members of an exchange on which the option executed is listed; (B) to the conduct of accounts, the execution of transactions, and the handling of orders in conventional options by all members; and (C) to other matters related to options trading.

Subparagraphs (3) through (12) shall apply only to standardized and conventional options on common stock. Subparagraphs (13) through (24) shall apply to transactions in all options as defined in paragraph (a)(21), including common stock unless otherwise indicated herein.

(2) FLEX Equity Options

The position and exercise limits for FLEX Equity Options for members that are not also members of the exchange on which FLEX Equity Options trade shall be the same as the position and exercise limits as applicable to members of the exchange on which such FLEX Equity Options are traded.

(3) Position Limits

(A) Stock Options —

(i) Standardized Equity Options

Except in highly unusual circumstances, and with the prior written approval of FINRA pursuant to the Rule 9600 Series for good cause shown in each instance, no member shall effect for any account in which such member has an interest, or for the account of any partner, officer, director or employee thereof, or for the account of any customer, non-member broker, or non-member dealer, an opening transaction on any exchange in a stock option contract of any class of stock options if the member has reason to believe that as a result of such transaction the member or partner, officer, director or employee thereof, or customer, non-member broker, or non-member dealer, would, acting alone or in concert with others, directly or indirectly, hold or control or be obligated in respect of an aggregate standardized equity options position in excess of the highest position limit established by an exchange on which the option trades, or such other number of stock option contracts as may be fixed from time to time by FINRA as the position limit for one or more classes or series of options provided that reasonable notice shall be given of each new position limit fixed by FINRA.

(ii) Equity Option Hedge Exemptions

a. The following qualified hedge strategies and positions described in subparagraphs 1. through 6. below shall be exempt from the established position limits under this Rule for standardized options. Hedge strategies and positions described in subparagraphs 7. and 8. below in which one of the option components consists of a conventional option, shall be subject to a position limit of five times the established position limits contained in paragraphs (b)(3)(A)(iii)a.1. through 6. below. Hedge strategies and positions in conventional options as described in subparagraphs 1. through 6. below shall be subject to a position limit of five times the established position limits contained in paragraphs (b)(3)(A)(iii)a.1. through 6. below. Options positions limits established under this subparagraph shall be separate from limits established in other provisions of this Rule.

1. Where each option contract is "hedged" or "covered" by 100 shares of the underlying security or securities convertible into the underlying security, or, in the case of an adjusted option, the same number of shares represented by the adjusted contract: (a) long call and short stock; (b) short call and long stock; (c) long put and long stock; or (d) short put and short stock.

2. Reverse Conversions — A long call position accompanied by a short put position, where the long call expires with the short put, and the strike price of the long call and short put is equal, and where each long call and short put position is hedged with 100 shares (or other adjusted number of shares) of the underlying security or securities convertible into such underlying security.

3. Conversions — A short call position accompanied by a long put position where the short call expires with the long put, and the strike price of the short call and long put is equal, and where each short call and long put position is hedged with 100 shares (or other adjusted number of shares) of the underlying security or securities convertible into such underlying security.

4. Reverse Collars — A long call position accompanied by a short put position where the long call expires with the short put and the strike price of the long call equals or exceeds the short put and where each long call and short put position is hedged with 100 shares of the underlying security (or other adjusted number of shares). Neither side of the long call, short put position can be in-the-money at the time the position is established.

5. Collars — A short call position accompanied by a long put position, where the short call expires with the long put, and the strike price of the short call equals or exceeds the strike price of the long put position and where each short call and long put position is hedged with 100 shares (or other adjusted number of shares) of the underlying security or securities convertible into such underlying security. Neither side of the short call/long put position can be in-the-money at the time the position is established.

6. Box Spreads — A long call position accompanied by a short put position with the same strike price and a short call position accompanied by a long put position with a different strike price.

7. Back-to-Back Options — A listed option position hedged on a one-for-one basis with an over-the-counter (OTC) option position on the same underlying security. The strike price of the listed option position and corresponding OTC option position must be within one strike price interval of each other and no more than one expiration month apart.

8. For reverse conversion, conversion, reverse collar and collar strategies set forth above in subparagraphs 2., 3., 4. and 5., one of the option components can be an OTC option guaranteed or endorsed by the firm maintaining the proprietary position or carrying the customer account.

b. Delta Hedging Exemption For Members and Non- Member Affiliates

An equity options position of a member or non-member affiliate in standardized and/or conventional equity options that is delta neutral under a Permitted Pricing Model shall be exempt from position limits under this Rule. Any equity options position of such member or non-member affiliate that is not delta neutral shall be subject to position limits, subject to the availability of other options position limit exemptions. The number of options contracts attributable to a position that is not delta neutral shall be the options contract equivalent of the net delta.

1. Permitted Pricing Model shall mean:

A. A pricing model maintained and operated by the Options Clearing Corporation ("OCC Model") when used by a member, or non-member affiliate permitted to rely on subparagraphs B or C;

B. A pricing model maintained and used by a member subject to consolidated supervision by the SEC pursuant to Appendix E of SEA Rule 15c3-1, or by an affiliate that is part of such member's consolidated supervised holding company group, in accordance with its internal risk management control system and consistent with the requirements of Appendices E or G, as applicable, to SEA Rule 15c3-1 and SEA Rule

15c3-4, as amended from time to time, in connection with the calculation of risk-based deductions from capital or capital allowances for market risk thereunder, provided that the member or affiliate of a member relying on this exemption in connection with the use of such model is an entity that is part of such member's consolidated supervised holding company group;

C. A pricing model maintained and used by a financial holding company ("FHC") or a company treated as an FHC under the Bank Holding Company Act, or by an affiliate that is part of either such company's consolidated supervised holding company group, in accordance with its internal risk management control system and consistent with:

i. the requirements of the Board of Governors of the Federal Reserve System, as amended from time to time, in connection with the calculation of risk-based adjustments to capital for market risk under capital requirements of the Board of Governors of the Federal Reserve System, provided that the member or affiliate of a member relying on this exemption in connection with the use of such model is an entity that is part of such company's consolidated supervised holding company group; or

ii. the standards published by the Basel Committee on Banking Supervision, as amended from time to time and as implemented by such company's principal regulator, in connection with the calculation of risk-based deductions or adjustments to or allowances for the market risk capital requirements of such principal regulator applicable to such company – where "principal regulator" means a member of the Basel Committee on Banking Supervision that is the home country consolidated supervisor of such company – provided that the member or affiliate of a member relying on this exemption in connection with the use of such model is an entity that is part of such company's consolidated supervised holding company group;

D. A pricing model maintained and used by an OTC derivatives dealer registered with the SEC pursuant to SEA Rule 15c3-1(a)(5) in accordance with its internal risk management control system and consistent with the requirements of Appendix F to SEA Rule 15c3-1 and SEA Rule 15c3-4, as amended from time to time, in connection with the calculation of risk-based deductions from capital for market risk thereunder, provided that only such OTC derivatives dealer and no other affiliated entity (including a member) may rely on this subparagraph D; or

E. A pricing model used by a national bank under the National Bank Act maintained and used in accordance with its internal risk management control system and consistent with the requirements of the Office of the Comptroller of the Currency, as amended from time to time, in connection with the calculation of risk-based adjustments to capital for market risk under capital requirements of the Office of the Comptroller of the Currency, provided that only such national bank and no other affiliated entity (including a member) may rely on this exemption.

2. Effect on Aggregation of Account Positions

A. Members and non-member affiliates who rely on this exemption must ensure that the Permitted Pricing Model is applied to all positions in or relating to the security underlying the relevant options position that are owned or controlled by such member or non-member affiliate.

B. Notwithstanding subparagraph b.2.A. of this Rule, the Net Delta of an options position held by an entity entitled to rely on this exemption, or by a separate and distinct trading unit of such entity, may be calculated without regard to positions in or relating to the security underlying the options positions held by an affiliated entity or by another trading unit within the same entity, provided that:

    i. the entity demonstrates to FINRA's satisfaction that no control relationship, as discussed in Supplementary Material .02, exists between such affiliates or trading units; and

    ii. the entity has provided FINRA written notice in advance that it intends to be considered separate and distinct from any affiliate, or — as applicable — which trading units within the entity are to be considered separate and distinct from each other for purposes of this exemption.

C. Notwithstanding subparagraph b.2.A. or b.2.B. of this Rule, a member or non-member affiliate who relies on this exemption shall designate, by prior written notice to FINRA, each trading unit or entity whose options positions are required under FINRA rules to be aggregated with the option positions of such member or non-member affiliate that is relying on this exemption for purposes of compliance with FINRA position limits or exercise limits. In any such case:

    i. the Permitted Pricing Model shall be applied, for purposes of calculating such member's or affiliate's net delta, only to the positions in or relating to the security underlying any relevant option position owned and controlled by those entities and trading units who are relying on this exemption; and

    ii. the net delta of the positions owned or controlled by the entities and trading units who are relying on this exemption shall be aggregated with the nonexempt option positions of all other entities and trading units whose options positions are required under FINRA rules to be aggregated with the option positions of such member or affiliate.

3. Obligations of Members and Affiliates

A member that relies, or whose affiliate relies, upon this exemption must provide a written certification to FINRA that it and/or its affiliates are using a Permitted Pricing Model pursuant to subparagraph 1. above and that if the affiliate ceases to hedge stock options positions in accordance with such Permitted Pricing Model, it will provide immediate written notice to the member.

The options positions of a non-member relying on this exemption must be carried by a member with which it is affiliated.

4. Reporting

A. Each member must report in accordance with paragraph (b)(5), all equity option positions (including those that are delta neutral) of 200 or more contracts (whether long or short) on the same side of the market covering the same underlying security that are effected by the member.

B. In addition, each member on its own behalf or on behalf of a designated aggregation unit pursuant to paragraph (b)(3)(A)(ii)b.2. shall report in a manner specified by FINRA the options contract equivalent of the net delta of each position that represents 200 or more contracts (whether long or short) on the same side of the market covering the same underlying security that are effected by the member.

(iii) Conventional Equity Options

a. For purposes of this paragraph (b), standardized equity option contracts of the put class and call class on the same side of the market overlying the same security shall not be aggregated with conventional equity option contracts or FLEX Equity Option contracts overlying the same security on the same side of the market. Conventional equity option contracts of the put class and call class on the same side of the market overlying the same security shall be subject to a position limit of:

1. 25,000 option contracts, combining for purposes of this position limit long positions in put options with short positions in call options, and short positions in put options with long positions in call options; or
2. 50,000 option contracts for option contracts on securities that underlie exchange-traded options qualifying under applicable rules for a position limit of 50,000 option contracts; or
3. 75,000 option contracts for option contracts on securities that underlie exchange-traded options qualifying under applicable rules for a position limit of 75,000 option contracts; or
4. 200,000 option contracts for option contracts on securities that underlie exchange-traded options qualifying under applicable rules for a position limit of 200,000 option contracts; or
5. 250,000 option contracts for option contracts on securities that underlie exchange-traded options qualifying under applicable rules for a position limit of 250,000 option contracts; or
6. for selected conventional options on exchange-traded funds ("ETF"), the position limits are listed in the chart below:

Security Underlying Option	Position Limit
The DIAMONDS Trust (DIA)	300,000 contracts
The Standard and Poor's Depositary Receipts Trust (SPY)	900,000 contracts
The iShares Russell 2000 Index Fund (IWM)	500,000 contracts
The PowerShares QQQ Trust (QQQQ)	900,000 contracts
The iShares MSCI Emerging Markets Index Fund (EEM)	500,000 contracts

b. In order for a security not subject to standardized equity options trading to qualify for an options position limit of more than 25,000 contracts, a member must first demonstrate to FINRA's Market Regulation Department that the underlying security meets the standards for such higher options position limit and the initial listing standards for standardized options trading.

Provided, however, that for certain securities in an index designated by FINRA, a member may claim such higher position limit as permitted in accordance with the volume and float criteria specified by FINRA; provided further, that a member claiming a higher position limit under this subparagraph must notify FINRA's Market Regulation Department in writing in such form as may be prescribed by FINRA and shall be filed no later than the close of business day on the next business day following the day on which the transaction or transactions requiring such limits occurred; and provided further, that the member must agree to reduce its position in the event that FINRA staff determines different position limits shall apply.

(B) Index Options

Except in highly unusual circumstances, and with the prior written approval of FINRA pursuant to the Rule 9600 Series for good cause shown in each instance, no member shall effect for any account in which such member has an interest, or for the account of any partner, officer, director or employee thereof, or for the account of any customer, an opening transaction in an option contract of any class of index options dealt in on an exchange if the member has reason to believe that as a result of such transaction the member or partner, officer, director or employee thereof, or customer, would, acting alone or in concert with others, directly or indirectly, hold or control or be obligated in respect of an aggregate position in excess of position limits established by the exchange on which the option trades.

(C) Index option contracts shall not be aggregated with option contracts on any stocks whose prices are the basis for calculation of the index.

(D) FINRA will notify the SEC at any time it approves a request to exceed the limits established pursuant to paragraph (b)(3).

(4) Exercise Limits

Except in highly unusual circumstances, and with the prior written approval of FINRA pursuant to the Rule 9600 Series for good cause shown in each instance, no member or person associated with a member shall exercise, for any account in which such member or person associated with a member has an interest, or for the account of any partner, officer, director or employee thereof or for the account of any customer, non-member broker, or non-member dealer, any option contract if as a result thereof such member or partner, officer, director or employee thereof or customer, non-member broker, or non-member dealer, acting alone or in concert with others, directly or indirectly, has or will have exercised within any five (5) consecutive business days a number of option contracts of a particular class of options in excess of the limits for options positions in paragraph (b)(3). FINRA may institute other limitations concerning the exercise of option contracts from time to time by action of FINRA. Reasonable notice shall be given of each new limitation fixed by FINRA.

(5) Reporting of Options Positions

(A)(i)a. Conventional Options

Each member shall file or cause to be filed with FINRA a report with respect to each account in which the member has an interest, each account of a partner, officer, director or employee of such member, and each customer, non-member broker, or non-member dealer account, which, acting alone or in concert, has established an aggregate position of 200 or more option contracts (whether long or short) of the put class and the call class on the same side of the market covering the same underlying security or index, combining for purposes of this subparagraph long positions in put options with short positions in call options and short positions in put options with long positions in call options, provided, however, that such reporting with respect to positions in conventional index options shall apply only to an option that is based on an index that underlies, or is substantially similar to an index that underlies, a standardized index option.

b. Standardized Options

Each member that conducts a business in standardized options but is not a member of the options exchange upon which the standardized options are listed and traded shall file or cause to be filed with FINRA a report with respect to each account in which the member has an interest, each account of a partner, officer, director or employee of such member, and each customer, non-member broker, or non-member dealer account, which, acting alone or in concert, has established an aggregate position of 200 or more option contracts (whether long or short) of the put class and the call class on the same side of the market covering the same underlying security or index, combining for purposes of this subparagraph long positions in put options with short positions in call options and short positions in put options with long positions in call options.

(ii) The reports required by this subparagraph shall identify the person or persons having an interest in such account and shall identify separately the total number of option contracts of each such class comprising the reportable position in such account. The reports shall be in such form as may be prescribed by FINRA and shall be filed no later than the close of business on the next business day following the day on which the transaction or transactions requiring the filing of such report occurred. Whenever a report shall be required to be filed with respect to an account pursuant to this subparagraph, the member filing such shall file with FINRA such additional periodic reports with respect to such account as FINRA may from time to time prescribe.

(B) In addition to the reports required by subparagraph (A) above, each member shall report promptly to FINRA any instance in which such member has a reason to believe that a person, acting alone or in concert with others, has exceeded or is attempting to exceed the position limits or the exercise limits set forth in paragraphs (b)(3) and (4).

(6) Liquidation of Positions and Restrictions on Access

(A) Whenever FINRA determines that a person or group of persons acting in concert holds or controls, or is obligated in respect of, an aggregate position in option contracts covering any underlying security or index in excess of the position limitations established by paragraph (b)(3), it may, when deemed necessary or appropriate in the public interest and for the protection of investors, direct:

(i) any member or all members carrying a position in option contracts covering such underlying security or index for such person or persons to liquidate such position or positions, or portions thereof, as expeditiously as possible and consistent with the maintenance of an orderly market, so as to bring such person or persons into compliance with the position limitations contained in paragraph (b)(3);

(ii) that such person or persons named therein not be permitted to execute an opening transaction, and that no member shall accept and/or execute for any person or persons named in such directive, any order for an opening transaction in any option contract, unless in each instance express approval therefor is given by FINRA, the directive is rescinded, or the directive specifies another restriction appropriate under the circumstances.

(B) Prior to the issuance of any directive provided for in subparagraph (A), FINRA shall notify, in the most expeditious manner possible, such person, or group of persons of such action, the specific grounds therefor and provide them an opportunity to be heard thereon. In the absence of unusual circumstances, in the case of a directive pursuant to the provisions of subparagraph (A)(i) hereof, the hearing shall be held within one business day of notice. In the case of a directive pursuant to the provisions of subparagraph (A)(ii) hereof, the hearing shall be held as promptly as possible under the circumstances. In any such proceeding a record shall be kept. A determination by FINRA after hearing or waiver of hearing, to implement such directive shall be in writing and shall be supported by a statement setting forth the specific grounds on which the determination is based. Any person aggrieved by action taken by FINRA pursuant to this subparagraph may make application for review to the SEC in accordance with Section 19 of the Exchange Act.

(7) Limit on Uncovered Short Positions

Whenever FINRA shall determine in light of current conditions in the markets for options, or in the markets for underlying securities, that there are outstanding a number of uncovered short positions in option contracts of a given class in excess of the limits established by FINRA for purposes of this subparagraph or that a percentage of outstanding short positions in option contracts of a given class are uncovered, in excess of the limits established by FINRA for purposes of this subparagraph, FINRA, upon its determination that such action is in the public interest and necessary for the protection of investors and the maintenance of a fair and orderly market in the option contracts or underlying securities, may prohibit any further opening writing transactions in option contracts of that class unless the resulting short position will be covered, and it may prohibit the uncovering of any existing covered short position in option contracts of one or more series of options of that class.

(8) Restrictions on Option Transactions and Exercises

FINRA may impose from time to time such restrictions on option transactions or the exercise of option contracts in one or more series of options of any class which it determines are necessary in the interest of maintaining a fair and orderly market in option contracts, or in the underlying securities covered by such option contracts, or otherwise necessary in the public interest or for the protection of investors. During the period of any such restriction, no member shall effect any option transaction or exercise any option contract in contravention of such restriction. Notwithstanding the foregoing, during the ten (10) business days prior to the expiration date of a given series of options, no restriction established pursuant to this subparagraph on the exercise of option contracts shall remain in effect with respect to that series of options.

(9) Rights and Obligations of Holders and Writers

Subject to the provisions of paragraphs (b)(4), (6), and (8), the rights and obligations of holders and writers of option contracts of any class of options issued by The Options Clearing Corporation shall be set forth in the rules of The Options Clearing Corporation.

(10) Open Orders on "Ex-Date"

Open orders for one or more option contracts of any class of options issued by The Options Clearing Corporation held by members prior to the effective date of an adjustment by The Options Clearing Corporation to the terms of a class of options pursuant to Article VI, Section 11A of the By-Laws of The Options Clearing Corporation shall be adjusted on the "ex-date" by such amount as The Options Clearing Corporation shall specify, unless otherwise instructed by the customer.

(11) Delivery of Current Disclosure Documents

(A)(i) Characteristics and Risks of Standardized Options (the "ODD"). Every member shall deliver the current ODD to each customer at or prior to the time such customer's account is approved for trading options issued by The Options Clearing Corporation, other than an OCC Cleared OTC Option. Thereafter, a copy of each amendment to the ODD shall be distributed to each customer to whom the member previously delivered the ODD not later than the time a confirmation of a transaction in the category of options to which the amendment pertains is delivered to such customer.

(ii) Special Statement for Uncovered Option Writers ("Special Written Statement"). In the case of customers approved for writing uncovered short options transactions, the Special Written Statement required by paragraph (b)(16) shall be in a format prescribed by FINRA and delivered to customers in accordance with paragraph (b)(16). A copy of each new or revised Special Written Statement shall be distributed to each customer having an account approved for writing uncovered short options not later than the time a confirmation of a transaction is delivered to each customer who enters into a transaction in options issued by The Options Clearing Corporation, other than an OCC Cleared OTC Option.

(iii) FINRA will advise members when a new or revised current disclosure document meeting the requirements of SEA Rule 9b-1 is available.

(B) Where a broker or dealer enters his orders with another member in a single omnibus account, the member holding the account shall take reasonable steps to assure that such broker or dealer is furnished reasonable quantities of current disclosure documents, as requested by him in order to enable him to comply with the requirements of SEA Rule 9b-1.

(C) Where an introducing broker or dealer enters orders for his customers with, or clears transactions through, a member on a fully disclosed basis and that member carries the accounts of such customers, the responsibility for delivering the current disclosure document(s) as provided in this paragraph (b)(11) shall rest with the member carrying the accounts. However, such member may rely upon the good faith representation of the introducing broker or dealer that the current disclosure document(s) has been delivered in compliance with paragraph (b)(11).

(12) Confirmations

Every member shall promptly furnish to each customer a written confirmation of each transaction in option contracts for such customer's account. Each such confirmation shall show the type of option, the underlying security or index, the expiration month, the exercise price, the number of option contracts, the premium, the commission, the trade and settlement dates, whether the transaction was a purchase or a sale (writing) transaction, whether the transaction was an opening or a closing transaction, whether the transaction was effected on a principal or agency basis and, for other than options issued by The Options Clearing Corporation, the date of expiration. The confirmation shall by appropriate symbols distinguish between exchange listed and other transactions in option contracts though such confirmation does not need to specify the exchange or exchanges on which such options contracts were executed.

(13) Transactions with Issuers

No member shall enter a transaction for the sale (writing) of a call option contract for the account of any corporation which is the issuer of the underlying security thereof.

(14) Restricted Stock

For the purposes of covering a short position in a call option contract, delivery pursuant to the exercise of a put option contract, or satisfying an exercise notice assigned in respect of a call option contract, no member shall accept shares of an underlying stock, which may not be sold by the holder thereof except upon registration pursuant to the provisions of the Securities Act or pursuant to SEC rules promulgated under the Securities Act, unless, at the time such securities are accepted and at any later time such securities are delivered, applicable provisions of the Securities Act and the rules thereunder have been complied with by the holder of such securities.

(15) Statements of Account

(A) Statements of account showing security and money positions, entries, interest charges and any special charges that have been assessed against such account during the period covered by the statement shall be sent no less frequently than once every month to each customer in whose account there has been an entry during the preceding month with respect to an option contract and quarterly to all customers having an open option position or money balance. Interest charges and any special charges assessed during the period covered by the statement need not be specifically delineated if they are otherwise accounted for on the statement and have been itemized on transaction confirmations. With respect to options customers having a general (margin) account, such statements shall also provide the mark-to-market price and market value of each option position and other security position in the general (margin) account, the total market value of all positions in the account, the outstanding debit or credit balance in the account, and the general (margin) account equity. The statements shall bear a legend stating that further information with respect to commissions and other charges related to the execution of option transactions has been included in confirmations of such transactions previously furnished to the customer, and that such information will be made available to the customer promptly upon request. The statements shall also bear a legend requesting the customer promptly to advise the member of any material change in the customer's investment objectives or financial situation.

(B) For purposes of this subparagraph (15), general (margin) account equity shall be computed by subtracting the total of the "short" security values and any debit balance from the total of the "long" security values and any credit balance.

(16) Opening of Accounts

(A) Approval Required

No member or person associated with a member shall accept an order from a customer to purchase or write an option contract relating to an options class that is the subject of an options disclosure document, or approve the customer's account for the trading of such option, unless the broker or dealer furnishes or has furnished to the customer the appropriate options disclosure document(s) and the customer's account has been approved for options trading in accordance with the provisions of subparagraphs (B) through (D) hereof.

(B) Diligence in Opening Accounts

In approving a customer's account for options trading, a member or any person associated with a member shall exercise due diligence to ascertain the essential facts relative to the customer, his financial situation and investment objectives. Based upon such information, the branch office manager, a Registered Options Principal or a Limited Principal—General Securities Sales Supervisor shall specifically approve or disapprove in writing the customer's account for options trading; provided, that if the branch office manager is not a Registered Options Principal or a Limited Principal—General Securities Sales Supervisor, account approval or disapproval shall within ten (10) business days be submitted to and approved or disapproved by a Registered Options Principal or a Limited Principal—General Securities Sales Supervisor.

(i) With respect to options customers who are natural persons, members shall seek to obtain the following information at a minimum (information shall be obtained for all participants in a joint account):

    a. Investment objectives (e.g., safety of principal, income, growth, trading profits, speculation);

    b. Employment status (name of employer, self-employed or retired);

    c. Estimated annual income from all sources;

    d. Estimated net worth (exclusive of family residence);

    e. Estimated liquid net worth (cash, securities, other);

    f. Marital status; number of dependents;

    g. Age; and

    h. Investment experience and knowledge (e.g., number of years, size, frequency and type of transactions) for options, stocks and bonds, commodities, and other financial instruments.

(ii) In addition, a customer's account records shall contain the following information, if applicable:

    a. Source or sources of background and financial information (including estimates) concerning the customer;

    b. Discretionary authorization agreement on file, name, relationship to customer and experience of person holding trading authority;

    c. Date disclosure document(s) furnished to customer;

    d. Nature and types of transactions for which account is approved (e.g., buying covered writing, uncovered writing, spreading, discretionary transactions);

    e. Name of registered representative;

    f. Name of Registered Options Principal or Limited Principal—General Securities Sales Supervisor approving account; date of approval; and

    g. Dates of verification of currency of account information.

(iii) Members shall consider utilizing a standard account approval form so as to ensure the receipt of all the required information.

(iv) Refusal of a customer to provide any of the information called for in subparagraph (i) shall be so noted on the customer's records at the time the account is opened. Information provided shall be considered together with the other information available in determining whether and to what extent to approve the account for options trading.

(v) A record of the information obtained pursuant to this subparagraph and of the approval or disapproval of each such account shall be maintained by the member as part of its permanent records in accordance with paragraph (b)(17).

(C) Verification of Customer Background and Financial Information

The background and financial information upon which the account of every new options customer that is a natural person has been approved for options trading, unless the information is included in the customer's account agreement, shall be sent to the customer for verification within fifteen (15) days after the customer's account has been approved for options trading. A copy of the background and financial information on file with a member shall also be sent to the customer for verification within fifteen (15) days after the member becomes aware of any material change in the customer's financial situation.

Members shall satisfy the initial and subsequent verification of customer background and financial information by sending to the customer the information required in subparagraphs (B)(i)a. through f. hereof, as contained in the member's records and providing the customer with an opportunity to correct or complete the information. In all cases, absent advice from the customer to the contrary, the information will be deemed to be verified.

(D) Account Agreement

Within fifteen (15) days after a customer's account has been approved for options trading, a member shall obtain from the customer a written agreement that the customer is aware of and agrees to be bound by FINRA rules applicable to the trading of option contracts and, if he desires to engage in transactions in options issued by The Options Clearing Corporation, other than solely for OCC Cleared OTC Options, that the customer has received a copy of the current disclosure document(s) required to be furnished under this subparagraph (16) and that he is aware of and agrees to be bound by the rules of The Options Clearing Corporation. In addition, the customer shall indicate on such written agreement that he is aware of and agrees not to violate the position limits established pursuant to paragraph (b)(3) and the exercise limits established pursuant to paragraph (b)(4).

(E) Uncovered Short Option Contracts

Each member transacting business with the public in writing uncovered short option contracts shall develop, implement and maintain specific written procedures governing the conduct of such business which shall include, at least, the following:

(i) Specific criteria and standards to be used in evaluating the suitability of a customer for writing uncovered short option transactions;

(ii) Specific procedures for approval of accounts engaged in writing uncovered short option contracts, including written approval of such accounts by a Registered Options Principal;

(iii) Designation of a specific Registered Options Principal(s) as responsible for approving customer accounts that do not meet the specific criteria and standards for writing uncovered short option transactions and for maintaining written records of the reasons for every account so approved;

(iv) Establishment of specific minimum net equity requirements for initial approval and maintenance of customer accounts writing uncovered short option transactions; and

(v) Requirements that customers approved for writing uncovered short options transactions be provided with a special written statement for uncovered option writers approved by FINRA that describes the risks inherent in writing uncovered short option transactions, at or prior to the initial writing of an uncovered short option transaction.

(17) Maintenance of Records

(A) In addition to the requirements of Rules 2268, 5340 and Rule 4510 Series, every member shall maintain and keep current a separate central log, index or other file for all options-related complaints, through which these complaints can easily be identified and retrieved. The central file shall be located at the principal place of business of the member or such other principal office as shall be designated by the member. At a minimum, the central file shall include:

(i) identification of complainant;

(ii) date complaint was received;

(iii) identification of registered representative servicing the account;

(iv) a general description of the matter complained of; and

(v) a record of what action, if any, has been taken by the member with respect to the complaint.

For purposes of this subparagraph, the term "options-related complaint" shall mean any written statement by a customer or person acting on behalf of a customer alleging a grievance arising out of or in connection with options. Each options-related complaint received by a branch office of a member shall be forwarded to the office in which the separate, central file is located not later than 30 days after receipt by the branch office that is the subject of the complaint. A copy of every options-related complaint shall also be maintained at the branch office that is the subject of the complaint.

(B) Background and financial information of customers who have been approved for options trading shall be maintained at both the branch office servicing the customer's account and the principal supervisory office having jurisdiction over that branch office. Copies of account statements of options customers shall also be maintained at both the branch office supervising the accounts and the principal supervisory office having jurisdiction over that branch for the most recent six-month period. With respect solely to the above-noted record retention requirements applicable to principal supervisory offices, however, the customer information and account statements may be maintained at a location other than the principal supervisory office if such documents and information are readily accessible and promptly retrievable. Other records necessary to the proper supervision of accounts shall be maintained at a place easily accessible both to the branch office servicing the customer's account and to the principal supervisory office having jurisdiction over that branch office.

(18) Discretionary Accounts

    (A) Authorization and Approval

        (i) No member and no person associated with a member shall exercise any discretionary power with respect to trading in option contracts in a customer's account, or accept orders for option contracts for an account from a person other than the customer, except in compliance with the provisions of Rule 3260 and unless:

           a. The written authorization of the customer required by Rule 3260 shall specifically authorize options trading in the account; and

           b. the account shall have been accepted in writing by a Registered Options Principal or Limited Principal—General Securities Sales Supervisor.

        (ii) Each firm shall designate specific Registered Options Principals as described below to review discretionary accounts. A Registered Options Principal other than the Registered Options Principal or Limited Principal—General Securities Sales Supervisor who accepted the account shall review the acceptance of each discretionary account to determine that the Registered Options Principal or Limited Principal—General Securities Sales Supervisor accepting the account had a reasonable basis for believing that the customer was able to understand and bear the risk of the strategies or transactions proposed, and shall maintain a record of the basis for such determination. Every discretionary order shall be identified as discretionary on the order at the time of entry. Discretionary accounts shall receive frequent appropriate supervisory review by a Registered Options Principal who is not exercising the discretionary authority. The provisions of this subparagraph (18) shall not apply to discretion as to the price at which or the time when an order given by a customer for the purchase or sale of a definite number of option contracts in a specified security shall be executed, except that the authority to exercise time and price discretion will be considered to be in effect only until the end of the business day on which the customer granted such discretion, absent specific, written contrary indication signed and dated by the customer. This limitation shall not apply to time and price discretion exercised in an institutional account, as defined in Rule 4512(c), pursuant to valid Good-Till-Cancelled instructions issued on a "not held" basis. Any exercise of time and price discretion must be reflected on the order ticket.

        (iii) Any member that does not utilize computerized surveillance tools for the frequent and appropriate review of discretionary activity must establish and implement procedures to require specific Registered Options Principals who have been designated to review discretionary accounts to approve and initial each discretionary order on the day entered.

    (B) Record of Transactions

    A record shall be made of every transaction in option contracts in respect to which a member or person associated with a member has exercised discretionary authority, clearly reflecting such fact and indicating the name of the customer, the designation and number of the option contracts, the premium and the date and time when such transaction was effected.

    (C) Option Programs

    Where the discretionary account utilizes options programs involving the systematic use of one or more options strategies, the customer shall be furnished with a written explanation of the nature and risks of such programs.

(19) Suitability

    (A) No member or person associated with a member shall recommend to any customer any transaction for the purchase or sale (writing) of an option contract unless such member or person associated therewith has reasonable grounds to believe upon the basis of information furnished by such customer after reasonable inquiry by the member or person associated therewith concerning the customer's investment objectives, financial situation and needs, and any other information known by such member or associated person, that the recommended transaction is not unsuitable for such customer.

(B) No member or person associated with a member shall recommend to a customer an opening transaction in any option contract unless the person making the recommendation has a reasonable basis for believing, at the time of making the recommendation, that the customer has such knowledge and experience in financial matters that he may reasonably be expected to be capable of evaluating the risks of the recommended transaction, and is financially able to bear the risks of the recommended position in the option contract.

(20) Supervision of Accounts

(A) Duty to Supervise

Each member that conducts a public customer options business shall ensure that its written supervisory system policies and procedures pursuant to Rules 3110, 3120, and 3130 adequately address the member's public customer options business.

(B) Branch Offices

No branch office of a member shall transact an options business unless the principal supervisor of such branch office accepting options transactions has been qualified as either a Registered Options Principal or a Limited Principal—General Securities Sales Supervisor; provided that this requirement shall not apply to branch offices in which no more than three registered representatives are located, so long as the options activities of such branch offices are appropriately supervised by either a Registered Options Principal or a Limited Principal—General Securities Sales Supervisor.

(C) Headquarters Review of Accounts

Each member shall maintain at the principal supervisory office having jurisdiction over the office servicing customer accounts, or have readily accessible and promptly retrievable, information to permit review of each customer's options account on a timely basis to determine:

(i) the compatibility of options transactions with investment objectives and with the types of transactions for which the account was approved;

(ii) the size and frequency of options transactions;

(iii) commission activity in the account;

(iv) profit or loss in the account;

(v) undue concentration in any options class or classes, and

(vi) compliance with the provisions of Regulation T of the Federal Reserve Board.

(21) Violation of By-Laws and Rules of FINRA or The Options Clearing Corporation

(A) In FINRA disciplinary proceedings, a finding of violation of any provision of the rules, regulations or by-laws of The Options Clearing Corporation by any member or person associated with a member engaged in transactions involving options issued, or subject to issuance, by The Options Clearing Corporation, may be deemed to be conduct inconsistent with just and equitable principles of trade and a violation of Rule 2010.

(B) In FINRA disciplinary proceedings, a finding of violation of any provision of the FINRA rules, regulations or By-Laws by any member engaged in option transactions may be deemed to be conduct inconsistent with just and equitable principles of trade and a violation of Rule 2010.

(22) Stock Transfer Tax

Any stock transfer or similar tax payable in accordance with applicable laws and regulations of a taxing jurisdiction upon the sale, transfer or delivery of securities pursuant to the exercise of an option contract shall be the responsibility of the seller (writer) to whom the exercise notice is assigned in the case of a call option contract or the exercising holder in the case of a put option contract except that (A) in the case of a call option contract where the incidents of the tax are attributable solely to the exercising holder, the member representing such holder or another member which acts on its behalf as a clearing member of The Options Clearing Corporation, the tax shall be the responsibility of the exercising holder, and (B) in the case of a put option contract where the incidents of the tax are attributable solely to the seller (writer) to whom the exercise notice is assigned, the member representing such seller (writer) or another member which acts on its behalf as a clearing member of The Options Clearing Corporation, the tax shall be the responsibility of such seller (writer). Each delivery of securities subject to such tax must be accompanied by a sales ticket stamped in accordance with the regulations of the State imposing such tax, or if required by applicable law, such tax shall be remitted by the clearing member having responsibility therefor to the clearing corporation through which it customarily pays stock transfer taxes, in accordance with the applicable rules of such clearing corporation.

(23) Tendering Procedures for Exercise of Options

    (A) Exercise of Options Contracts

        (i) Subject to the restrictions established pursuant to paragraphs (b)(4) and (b)(8) hereof and such other restrictions that may be imposed by FINRA, The Options Clearing Corporation or an options exchange pursuant to appropriate rules, an outstanding option contract issued by The Options Clearing Corporation may be exercised during the time period specified in the rules of The Options Clearing Corporation by the tender to The Options Clearing Corporation of an exercise notice in accordance with rules of The Options Clearing Corporation. An exercise notice may be tendered to The Options Clearing Corporation only by the clearing member in whose account the option contract is carried. Members may establish fixed procedures as to the latest time they will accept exercise instructions from customers.

        (ii) Special procedures apply to the exercise of standardized equity options on the business day of their expiration, or, in the case of standardized equity options expiring on a day that is not a business day, on the last business day before their expiration ("expiring options"). Unless waived by The Options Clearing Corporation, expiring standardized equity options are subject to the Exercise-by-Exception ("Ex-by-Ex") procedure under The Options Clearing Corporation Rule 805. This Rule provides that, unless contrary instructions are given, standardized equity option contracts that are in-the-money by specified amounts shall be automatically exercised. In addition to The Options Clearing Corporation rules, the following FINRA requirements apply with respect to expiring standardized equity options. Option holders desiring to exercise or not exercise expiring standardized equity options must either:

           a. take no action and allow exercise determinations to be made in accordance with The Options Clearing Corporation's Ex-by-Ex procedure where applicable; or

           b. submit a "Contrary Exercise Advice" by the deadline specified below.

        (iii) Exercise cut-off time. Option holders have until 5:30 p.m. Eastern Time ("ET") on the business day of expiration, or, in the case of a standardized equity option expiring on a day that is not a business day, on the business day immediately prior to the expiration date to make a final exercise decision to exercise or not exercise an expiring option. Members may not accept exercise instructions for customer or non-customer accounts after 5:30 p.m. ET.

        (iv) Submission of Contrary Exercise Advice. A Contrary Exercise Advice is a form approved by the national options exchanges, FINRA or The Options Clearing Corporation for use by a member to submit a final exercise decision committing an options holder to either: (1) not exercise an option position which would automatically be exercised pursuant to The Options Clearing Corporation's Ex-by-Ex procedure; or (2) to exercise a standardized equity option position which would not automatically be exercised pursuant to The Options Clearing Corporation's Ex-by-Ex procedure. A Contrary Exercise Advice may be canceled by filing an "Advice Cancel" or resubmitted at any time up to the submission cut-off times specified herein. For customer accounts, members have until 7:30 p.m. ET to submit a Contrary Exercise Advice. For non-customer accounts, members have until 7:30 p.m. ET to submit a Contrary Exercise Advice if such member employs an electronic submission procedure with time stamp for the submission of exercise instructions by option holders. Members are required to manually submit a Contrary Exercise Advice by 5:30 p.m. ET for non-customer accounts if such members do not employ an electronic submission procedure with time stamp for the submission of exercise instructions by option holders. Each member shall establish fixed procedures to ensure secure time stamps in connection with their electronic systems employed for the recording of submissions to exercise or not exercise expiring options. For purposes of this Rule 2360(b)(23)(A), the terms "customer account" and "non-customer account" shall have the meanings as defined in The Options Clearing Corporation By-laws. Contrary Exercise Advices and/or Advice Cancels may be submitted by any member to:

    a. a place designated for that purpose by any national options exchange of which it is a member and where the standardized equity option is listed;

    b. a place designated for that purpose by any national options exchange that lists and trades the standardized equity option via a member of such exchange if the member is not a member of such exchange;

    c. any national options exchange of which it is a member and where the standardized equity option is listed via The Options Clearing Corporation in a form prescribed by The Options Clearing Corporation; or

    d. any national options exchange where the standardized equity option is listed via The Options Clearing Corporation in a form prescribed by The Options Clearing Corporation, provided the member is a member of The Options Clearing Corporation.

(v) In those instances when The Options Clearing Corporation has waived the Ex-by-Ex procedure for an options class, members must either:

    a. submit to any of the places listed in subparagraphs (iv)a. through d. above, a Contrary Exercise Advice, within the time limits specified in subparagraph (iv) above if the holder intends to exercise the standardized equity option, or

    b. take no action and allow the standardized equity option to expire without being exercised.

The applicable underlying security price in such instances will be as described in The Options Clearing Corporation Rule 805(1), which is normally the last sale price in the primary market for the underlying security. In cases where the Ex-by-Ex procedure has been waived for an options class, The Options Clearing Corporation rules require that members wanting to exercise such options must submit an affirmative Exercise Notice to The Options Clearing Corporation, whether or not a Contrary Exercise Advice has been filed.

(vi) Members that maintain proprietary or public customer positions in expiring standardized equity options shall take necessary steps to ensure that final exercise decisions are properly indicated to the relevant national options exchange with respect to such positions. Members that have accepted the responsibility to indicate final exercise decisions on behalf of another member also shall take necessary steps to ensure that such decisions are properly indicated to the relevant national options exchange. Members may establish a processing cut-off time prior to FINRA's exercise cut-off time at which they will no longer accept final exercise decisions in expiring standardized equity options from customers.

(vii) Members may effect or amend exercise decisions for standardized equity options after the exercise cut-off time (but prior to expiration) under the following circumstances:

    a. in order to remedy mistakes or errors made in good faith;

    b. to take appropriate action as the result of a failure to reconcile unmatched option transactions; or

    c. where extraordinary circumstances restricted a customer's or member's ability to inform the respective member of such decisions (or a member's ability to receive such decisions) by the cut-off time.

The burden of establishing an exception for a proprietary or customer account of a member rests solely on the member seeking to rely on such exception.

(viii) In the event a national options exchange or The Options Clearing Corporation provides advance notice on or before 5:30 p.m. ET on the business day immediately prior to the business day of expiration, or, in the case of a standardized equity option expiring on a day that is not a business day, the business day immediately prior to the last business day before the expiration date, indicating that a modified time for the close of trading in standardized equity options on such business day of expiration, or, in the case of a standardized option expiring on a day that is not a business day, such last business day before expiration will occur, then the deadline for an option holder to make a final decision to exercise or not exercise an expiring option shall be 1 hour 30 minutes following the time announced for the close of trading on that day instead of the 5:30 p.m. ET deadline found in subparagraph (iii) above. However, members have until 7:30 p.m. ET to deliver a Contrary Exercise Advice or Advice Cancel to the places specified in subparagraphs (iv)a. through d. above for customer accounts and non-customer accounts where such member firm employs an electronic submission procedure with time stamp for the submission of exercise instructions. For non-customer accounts, members that do not employ an electronic procedure with time stamp for the submission of exercise instructions are required to manually deliver a Contrary Exercise Advice or Advice Cancel within 1 hour and 30 minutes following the time announced for the close of trading on that day instead of the 5:30 p.m. ET deadline found in subparagraph (iv) above.

(ix) The filing of a final exercise decision, exercise instruction, exercise advice, Contrary Exercise Advice or Advice Cancel required by subparagraph (A) hereof does not serve as a substitute to the effective notice required to be submitted to The Options Clearing Corporation for the exercise or non-exercise of expiring standardized equity options.

(x) Submitting or preparing an exercise instruction after the exercise cut-off time in any expiring standardized equity option on the basis of material information released after the exercise cut-off time is activity inconsistent with just and equitable principles of trade.

(xi) The exercise cut-off requirements contained in this subparagraph (A) do not apply to any currency option or standardized index option products listed on a national options exchange.

(B) In the event a member receives and acts on an exercise instruction (for its own proprietary account or on behalf of a customer's account) pursuant to an exception set forth in subparagraphs a., b., or c. of subparagraph (A)(vii) hereof, the member shall maintain a memorandum setting forth the circumstances giving rise to such exception and shall file a copy of the memorandum with the Market Regulation Department of the national options exchange trading the option, if it is a member of such exchange, or FINRA's Market Regulation Department if it is not a member of such exchange, no later than 12:00 p.m. ET, on the business day following that expiration. Such memorandum must additionally include the time when such final exercise decision was made or, in the case of a customer, received, and shall be subject to the requirements of SEA Rules 17a-3(a)(6) and 17a-4(b).

(C) Allocation of Exercise Assignment Notices.

(i) Each member shall establish fixed procedures for the allocation to customers of exercise notices assigned in respect of a short position in option contracts in such member's customer accounts. Such allocation shall be on a "first in-first out" or automated random selection basis that has been approved by FINRA or on a manual random selection basis that has been specified by FINRA. Each member shall inform its customers in writing of the method it uses to allocate exercise notices to its customer's accounts, explaining its manner of operation and the consequences of that system.

(ii) Each member shall report its proposed method of allocation to FINRA and obtain FINRA's prior approval thereof, and no member shall change its method of allocation unless the change has been reported to and been approved by FINRA. The requirements of this subparagraph (C) shall not be applicable to allocation procedures submitted to and approved by another self-regulatory organization having comparable standards pertaining to methods of allocation.

(iii) Each member shall preserve for a three-year period sufficient work papers and other documentary materials relating to the allocation of exercise assignment notices to establish the manner in which allocation of such exercise assignment notices is in fact being accomplished.

(D) Delivery and Payment

Delivery of the shares of an underlying security upon the exercise of an option contract and payment of the aggregate exercise price in respect thereto, shall be effected in accordance with the rules of The Options Clearing Corporation. As promptly as practicable after the exercise of an option contract by a customer, the member shall require the customer to make full cash payment of the aggregate exercise price in the case of a call option contract or to deposit the underlying stock in the case of a put option contract, or, in either case, to make the required margin deposit in respect thereto if such transaction is effected in a margin account, in accordance with the applicable regulations of the Federal Reserve Board and Rule 4210. As promptly as practicable after the assignment to a customer of an exercise notice, the member shall require the customer to deposit the underlying stock in the case of a call option contract if the shares of the underlying security are not carried in the customer's account, or to make full cash payment of the aggregate exercise price in the case of a put option contract, or, in either case, to make the required market deposit in respect thereof, if such transaction is effected in a margin account, in accordance with Rule 4210 and the applicable regulations of the Federal Reserve Board.

(24) Options Transactions and Reports by Market Makers in Listed Securities

Every member who is an off-board market maker in a security listed on a national securities exchange shall report to FINRA in accordance with such procedures as may be prescribed by the Board of Governors, transactions involving 50 or more option contracts on such listed securities which are either directly for the benefit of (A) the member or (B) any employee, partner, officer, or director of the member who, by virtue of his position with the member, is directly involved in the purchase or sale of the underlying security for the firm's proprietary account(s) or is directly responsible for supervision of such persons; or who by virtue of his position in the firm, is authorized to, and regularly does, obtain information on the proprietary account(s) of the member in which the underlying security is traded. This subparagraph shall apply to all options transactions including those executed on an exchange to which the member may belong.

(c) Portfolio Margining Disclosure Statement and Acknowledgement

The special written disclosure statement describing the nature and risks of portfolio margining, and acknowledgement for an eligible participant signature, required by Rule 4210(g)(5)(C) shall be in a format prescribed by FINRA or in a format developed by the member, provided it contains substantially similar information as in the prescribed FINRA format and has received the prior written approval of FINRA.

---

7. MSRB Rules: D-12 – Definition of Municipal Fund Securities

The term "municipal fund security" shall mean a municipal security issued by an issuer that, but for the application of Section 2(b) of the Investment Company Act of 1940, would constitute an investment company within the meaning of Section 3 of the Investment Company Act of 1940.

---

8. MSRB Rules: G-17 – Conduct of Municipal Securities and Municipal Advisory Activities

Summary: Requires dealers and municipal advisors to deal fairly with all persons and not to engage in any deceptive, dishonest or unfair practice.

In the conduct of its municipal securities or municipal advisory activities, each broker, dealer, municipal securities dealer, and municipal advisor shall deal fairly with all persons and shall not engage in any deceptive, dishonest, or unfair practice.

---

9. MSRB Rules: G-30 – Pricing and Commissions

Summary: Requires dealers to effect transactions in municipal securities with customers at fair and reasonable prices, if acting as principal, and to make reasonable efforts to obtain fair and reasonable prices for customers and to charge fair and reasonable commissions, if acting as agent.

(a) Principal Transactions.
   No broker, dealer or municipal securities dealer shall purchase municipal securities for its own account from a customer, or sell municipal securities for its own account to a customer, except at an aggregate price (including any mark-up or mark-down) that is fair and reasonable.
(b) Agency Transactions.
   (i) Each broker, dealer and municipal securities dealer, when executing a transaction in municipal securities for or on behalf of a customer as agent, shall make a reasonable effort to obtain a price for the customer that is fair and reasonable in relation to prevailing market conditions.
   (ii) No broker, dealer or municipal securities dealer shall purchase or sell municipal securities as agent for a customer for a commission or service charge in excess of a fair and reasonable amount.

---

10. MSRB Rules: G-45 – Reporting of Information on Municipal Fund Securities

Summary: Requires dealers, when acting in the capacity of an underwriter for a 529 savings plan or ABLE program, to submit information on a semi-annual or, in the case of performance data, annual basis, to the MSRB.

(a) Form G-45 Reporting Requirements. Each underwriter of a primary offering of municipal fund securities that are not interests in local government investment pools shall report to the Board the information relating to such offering required by Form G-45 by no later than 60 days following the end of each semi-annual reporting period ending on June 30 and December 31 and in the manner prescribed in the Form G-45 procedures below and as set forth in the Form G-45 Manual; provided, however, that performance data shall be reported annually by no later than 60 days following the end of the reporting period ending on December 31. Each submitter shall indicate on Form G-45 the identity of each underwriter that has identified itself as such and on whose behalf the information is submitted.

(b) Form G-45 Reporting Procedures.

(i) All submissions of information required under this rule shall be made by means of Form G-45 submitted in a designated electronic format to the Board in such manner, and including such items of information, as specified herein, in Form G-45 and in the Form G-45 Manual.

(ii) Form G-45 shall be submitted by the underwriter or by any submission agent designated by the underwriter pursuant to the procedures set forth in the Form G-45 Manual. The failure of a submission agent designated by the underwriter to comply with any requirement of this rule shall be considered a failure by such underwriter to so comply.

(c) Form G-45 Manual. The Form G-45 Manual is comprised of the specifications for reporting of information required under this rule, the user guide for submitting Form G-45, and other information relevant to reporting under this rule. The Form G-45 Manual is located at www.msrb.org and may be updated from time to time with additional guidance or revisions to existing documents.

(d) Definitions.

(i) The term "asset class" shall mean domestic equities, international equities, fixed income products, commodities, insurance products, bank products, cash or cash equivalents or other product types.

(ii) The term "benchmark" shall mean an established index or a blended index that combines the benchmarks for each of the underlying mutual funds or other investments held by an investment option during the relevant time period weighted according to the allocations of those underlying mutual funds or other investments and adjusted to reflect any changes in the allocations and the benchmarks during the relevant time period.

(iii) The term "contributions" shall mean all deposits into the plan or investment option but shall not include reallocations.

(iv) The term "designated electronic format" shall mean the format specified in the Form G-45 Manual.

(v) The term "distributions" shall mean the withdrawal of funds from a plan or investment option, but shall not include reallocations.

(vi) The term "investment option" shall mean an option, as described in a plan disclosure document or supplement thereto, available to account owners in a plan to which funds may be allocated.

(vii) The term "marketing channel" shall mean the manner by which municipal fund securities that are not local government investment pools are sold to the public, such as through a broker, dealer or municipal securities dealer that has a selling agreement with an underwriter (commonly known as "advisor-sold") or through a website, or toll-free telephone number or other direct means (commonly known as "direct-sold").

(viii) The term "performance" shall mean total returns of the investment option expressed as a percentage, net of all generally applicable fees and costs.

(ix) The term "plan" shall mean a college savings plan or program established by a state, or agency or instrumentality of a state, to operate as a Qualified Tuition Program in accordance with Section 529 of the Internal Revenue Code.

(x) The term "program manager" shall mean an entity that enters into a contract directly with the trustee of the plan to provide, directly or indirectly through service providers, investment advisory and management services, administration and accounting functions, and/or marketing and other services related to the day-to-day operation of the plan.

(xi) The term "primary offering" shall mean an offering defined in Securities Exchange Act Rule 15c2-12(f)(7).

(xii) The term "reallocation" shall mean the withdrawal of funds from one investment option in a plan and deposit of the same funds into one or more investment options in the same plan, such as where an account owner selects a different investment option or funds are moved from one age-band to another as beneficiaries approach college age.

(xiii) The term "underlying investment" shall mean a registered investment company, unit investment trust, or other investment product in which an investment option invests.

(xiv) The term "underwriter" shall mean a broker, dealer or municipal securities dealer that is an underwriter, as defined in Securities Exchange Act Rule 15c2-12(f)(8), of municipal fund securities that are not local government investment pools.

---

11. CBOE Rule: Chapter I – Definitions

Scope of Definitions
Unless otherwise specifically provided in the Rules of the Exchange or the context otherwise requires, the terms defined in this Chapter shall for all purposes of the Rules of the Exchange have the meanings specified below.

Administrator: The term "administrator" has the meaning set forth in Rule 513(a).

Affiliate: An "Affiliate" of, or a Person "Affiliated" with, another Person is a Person who, directly or indirectly, Controls, is Controlled by, or is under common Control with, such other Person.

AMERIBOR Futures: The term "AMERIBOR Futures" means collectively Cboe Three-Month AMERIBOR futures, Cboe One-Month AMERIBOR futures, Cboe 14-Day AMERIBOR futures, and Cboe 7-Day AMERIBOR futures.

Appeals Committee: The term "Appeals Committee" means the appeals committee constituted in accordance with, and with the authority and rights set forth or referred to, in Rule 211.

Applicable Law: The term "Applicable Law" includes, but is not limited to, the CEA, Commission Regulations, margin rules adopted by the Board of Governors of the Federal Reserve System (as amended from time to time) and, to the extent applicable, the Exchange Act and Exchange Act Regulations.

Authorized Reporter: The term "Authorized Reporter" has the meaning set forth in Rule 414(i) in relation to Exchange of Contract for Related Position transactions and has the meaning set forth in Rule 415(f) in relation to Block Trades.

Authorized Trader: The term "Authorized Trader" means any natural person who is a Trading Privilege Holder or who is authorized by a Trading Privilege Holder to access the CFE System on behalf of the Trading Privilege Holder.

Average Price System: The term "Average Price System" means any system used by a Trading Privilege Holder that is a registered futures commission merchant to calculate and confirm to its Customers an average price for any Contract when multiple execution prices are received on any Order or series of Orders for such Contract.

Bankruptcy Code: The term "Bankruptcy Code" means Title 11 of the United States Code, as amended from time to time.

BCC Panel: The term "BCC Panel" has the meaning set forth in Rule 209.

BOE: The term "BOE" means the Binary Order Entry protocol for interfacing with the CFE System.

Block Trade: The term "Block Trade" has the meaning set forth in Rule 415(a).

Board: The term "Board" means the board of directors of the Exchange constituted in accordance with the Constitutive Documents.

Business Conduct Committee: The term "Business Conduct Committee" means the business conduct committee of the Exchange constituted in accordance with, and with the authority and rights set forth or referred to in, Rule 209.

Business Day: The term "Business Day" has the meaning set forth in Rule 402(a).

Cboe Options: The term "Cboe Options" means Cboe Exchange, Inc., a Delaware corporation (including its successors).

Cboe Global Markets: The term "Cboe Global Markets" means Cboe Global Markets, Inc., a Delaware Corporation (including its successors).

CEA: The term "CEA" means the Commodity Exchange Act, as amended from time to time.

CFE System: The term "CFE System" means (i) the electronic systems administered by or on behalf of the Exchange which perform the functions set out in the Rules of the Exchange, including controlling, monitoring and recording trading on the Exchange and (ii) any connectivity to the foregoing electronic systems that is administered by or on behalf of the Exchange, such as a communications hub in a foreign jurisdiction.

CFE Workstation: The term "CFE Workstation" means any computer connected directly to the CFE System, including by means of an Exchange defined protocol, for the purpose of trading Contracts.

Chairman of the Board: The term "Chairman of the Board" means the individual designated as the chairman of the board of the Exchange in accordance with the Constitutive Documents from time to time.

Chief Executive Officer: The term "Chief Executive Officer" means the individual serving as chief executive officer of Cboe Global Markets from time to time.

Chief Regulatory Officer: The term "Chief Regulatory Officer" or "CRO" means the individual appointed by the Board from time to time to serve as Chief Regulatory Officer of the Exchange.

Class of Options: The term "Class of Options" means Options of the same category (e.g., traditional or binary) covering the same underlying Future of commodity.

Clearing Corporation: The term "Clearing Corporation" means The Options Clearing Corporation, a Delaware corporation (including its successors), or such other clearing organization as the Exchange may designate in the future to provide clearing services with respect to any or all of its Contracts.

Clearing Member: The term "Clearing Member" means a member of the Clearing Corporation that is a Trading Privilege Holder and that is authorized under the Rules of the Clearing Corporation to clear trades in any or all Contracts.

Commission: The term "Commission" means the Commodity Futures Trading Commission, and includes any successor agency or authority.

Commission Regulation: The term "Commission Regulation" means any rule, regulation, order, directive and any interpretation thereof adopted or amended from time to time by the Commission.

Commodity: The term "Commodity" has the same meaning as that term is defined under the CEA.

Complainant: The term "Complainant" has the meaning set forth in Rule 702(a).Constitutive Documents The term "Constitutive Documents" means the certificate of formation and the operating agreement of the Exchange, each as amended or otherwise modified from time to time.

Contract: The term "Contract" means any Future, Option or Security Future offered for trading on the Exchange. Each single leg expiration is a separate Contract. Each spread for a product is treated like a separate Contract from a system perspective. If TAS transactions are permitted in a product, each TAS single leg expiration and TAS spread for the product is treated like a separate Contract from a system perspective.

Control: The term "Control" means the power to exercise a controlling influence over the management or policies of a Person, unless such power is solely the result of an official position with such Person. Any Person who owns beneficially, directly or indirectly, more than 20% of the voting power in the election of directors of a corporation, or more than 25% of the voting power in the election of directors of any other corporation which directly or through one or more Affiliates owns beneficially more than 25% of the voting power in the election of directors of such corporation, shall be presumed to control such corporation. The terms "controlling" or "controlled" shall have meanings correlative to the foregoing.

Credentials: The term "Credentials" has the meaning set forth in Rule 513(b).

Customer: The term "Customer" means any Person for whom a Trading Privilege Holder or Market Participant carries an account (other than such Trading Privilege Holder or Market Participant or any Affiliates of such Trading Privilege Holder or Market Participant) or from whom a Trading Privilege Holder or Market Participant solicits or accepts an Order.

Delaware LLC Act: The term "Delaware LLC Act" means the Delaware Limited Liability Company Act, as amended from time to time.

Director of Enforcement: The term "Director of Enforcement" means the individual appointed by the Exchange from time to time to serve as its director of enforcement.

DPM: The term "DPM" means any designated primary market maker approved by the Exchange from time to time in accordance with Rule 515 and with the duties and responsibilities set forth in Rule 515 and Exchange Policy and Procedure X.

DPM Designee: The term "DPM Designee" has the meaning set forth in Rule 515(b)(iii).

EFID: The term "EFID" means an Executing Firm ID that is described in Rule 302(f).

Emergency: The term "Emergency" means any occurrence or circumstance which requires immediate action and threatens or may threaten the fair and orderly trading in, or the liquidation of or delivery pursuant to, any Contract or the integrity of the market, whether the need for intervention arises exclusively from the Exchange's market or as part of a coordinated, cross-market intervention. An Emergency may include, without limitation, any of the following: (a) Any manipulative activity or disruptive trading practices or attempted manipulative activity or disruptive trading practices; (b) Any actual, attempted or threatened corner, squeeze, congestion or undue concentration of positions; (c) Any circumstance which may materially adversely affect the performance of Contracts, including any failure of the payment system; (d) Any action taken by the federal or any foreign government, any other governmental body or any other exchange or trading facility (foreign or domestic), in each case which may have a direct adverse effect on trading on the Exchange; (e) Any circumstance which may have a severe, adverse effect upon the physical functions of the Exchange, including fire or other casualty, bomb threats, terrorist acts, substantial inclement weather, power failures, communications breakdowns, computer system breakdowns, malfunctions of plumbing, heating, ventilation and air conditioning systems and transportation breakdowns; (f) The bankruptcy or insolvency of any Trading Privilege Holder or the imposition of any injunction or other restraint by any government agency, court or arbitrator upon a Trading Privilege Holder which may affect the ability of that Trading Privilege Holder to perform on its Contracts; (g) Any circumstance in which it appears that a Trading Privilege Holder or any other Person has failed to perform its Contracts, is insolvent, or is in such financial or operational condition or is conducting business in such a manner that such Person cannot be permitted to continue in business without jeopardizing the safety of Customer funds, other Trading Privilege Holders, the Exchange or the Clearing Corporation; and (h) Any other unusual, unforeseeable and adverse circumstance with respect to which it is impracticable for the Exchange to submit in a timely fashion a reviewable rule to the Commission.

Exchange: The term "Exchange" means Cboe Futures Exchange, LLC, a Delaware limited liability company (including its successors), and when used with reference to the administration of any Rule of the Exchange means either the Board or the officer, employee, agent, committee or delegee to whom appropriate authority to administer such provision has been delegated. The Exchange may also be referred to as "CFE".

Exchange Act: The term "Exchange Act" means the Securities Exchange Act of 1934, as amended from time to time.

Exchange Act Regulation: The term "Exchange Act Regulation" means any rule, regulation, order, directive and any interpretation thereof adopted or amended from time to time by the Securities and Exchange Commission, including any successor agency or authority.

Exchange of Contract for Related Position or ECRP: The term "Exchange of Contract for Related Position" or "ECRP" means an exchange of a Contract listed on the Exchange for a Related Position, as that term is defined in Rule 414(b), that is entered into in accordance with the Rules of the Exchange.

Executive Committee: The term "Executive Committee" means the executive committee of the Board, as constituted in accordance with, and with the authority and rights set forth in, Rule 207.

Exercise Price or Strike Price: The terms "Exercise Price" and "Strike Price" shall be synonymous and mean the price at which a person may purchase or sell the underlying Future or commodity upon exercise of the Option.

Ex Parte Communication: The term "Ex Parte Communication" means any oral or written communication made without notice to all parties. A written communication is an Ex Parte Communication unless a copy thereof has been delivered to all interested parties. An oral communication is an Ex Parte Communication unless it is made in the presence of all interested parties other than those who, after receiving adequate prior notice, declined to be present.

Expiration Date: The term "Expiration Date" means, with respect to any Contract, the day and time set forth in the Rules of the Exchange governing such Contract for the termination or expiration of such Contract.

Expiration Month: The term "Expiration Month" means, with respect to any Contract, the month and year set forth in the Rules of the Exchange governing such Contract for the termination or expiration of such Contract.

FINRA: The term "FINRA" means the Financial Industry Regulatory Authority, and includes any successor organization.

FIX: The term "FIX" means the Financial Information Exchange protocol for interfacing with the CFE System.

Future: The term "Future" means any contract for the purchase or sale of any commodity for future delivery from time to time traded on or subject to the Rules of the Exchange.

Implied Spread Bid: The term "Implied Spread Bid" has the meaning set forth in Rule 404A(d)(i)(A).

Implied Spread Offer: The term "Implied Spread Offer" has the meaning set forth in Rule 404A(d)(i)(B).

Independent Software Vendor: The term "Independent Software Vendor" (also referred to as a "Service Bureau") has the meaning set forth in Rule 302(g).

Lower Price Limit: The term "Lower Price Limit" has the meanings set forth in contract specification rule chapters for products with price limits, such as in Rule 1202(i)(i).

Market Data: The term "Market Data" has the meaning set forth in Rule 408.

Market Participant: The term "Market Participant" has the meaning set forth in Rule 308(c).

Match Capacity Allocation: A "match capacity allocation" provides the ability to submit Orders to the CFE System within an Order rate limit designated by the Exchange. Match capacity allocations are made available in a form and manner prescribed the Exchange.

Maximum Price: The term "Maximum Price" has the meaning set forth in Rule 406(f).

Minimum Price: The term "Minimum Price" has the meaning set forth in Rule 406(f).

Narrow-Based Stock Index Future: The term "Narrow-Based Stock Index Future" has the meaning set forth in Rule 1901.

NFA: The term "NFA" means the National Futures Association, and includes any successor organization fulfilling similar functions under the CEA.

Option: The term "Option" means any commodity option, as that term is defined in Commission Regulation § 1.3(hh), from time to time traded subject to the Rules of the Exchange and issued or subject to issuance by the Clearing Corporation pursuant to the Rules of the Clearing Corporation.

Order: The term "Order" means any Market Order, Limit Order, Spread Order, Stop Limit Order, Cancel Order, Cancel Replace/Modify Order, Day Order, Good-'til Canceled Order, Good-'til-Date Order, Immediate or Cancel Order or Fill or Kill Order, all having the respective meanings set forth in Rule 404, as well as any other types of Orders that may be approved by the Exchange from time to time.

Order Entry Operator ID: The term "Order Entry Operator ID" has the meaning set forth in Rule 303A.

Order Rate Limit: The term "Order rate limit" has the meaning set forth in Rule 513A(h).

Person: The term "Person" means any natural person, association, partnership, limited liability company, joint venture, trust or corporation.

Pool: The term "Pool" has the meaning set forth in Rule 305A.

Pool Manager: The term "Pool Manager" has the meaning set forth in Rule 305A.

Port: The term "port" includes different types of ports. A "physical port" provides a physical connection to the CFE System. A physical port may provide access to multiple logical ports and match capacity allocations. A "logical port" provides the ability within the CFE System to accomplish a specific function, such as data receipt or access to information. A logical port may also be referred to as a logical session. A "purge port" is a type of that enables a Trading Privilege Holder through a single purge request to: (a) cancel all or a subset of pending Orders submitted through multiple match capacity allocations, and (b) at the option of the Trading Privilege Holder submitting the purge request, also cause the CFE System to reject or cancel back to the sender all or a subset of new Orders, until a reset request is received by the CFE System. Ports are made available in a form and manner prescribed the Exchange.

Portal: The term "Portal" has the meaning set forth in Rule 513(a).

Premium: The term "Premium" means the amount agreed upon between the purchaser and seller for the purchase or sale of an Option.

Pre-Opening Notice: The term "Pre-Opening Notice" has the meaning set forth in Rule 405A(a)(iii)(C)(1).

President: The term "President" means the individual serving as president of Cboe Global Markets from time to time.

Public Director: The term "Public Director" has the meaning set forth in Rule 201(b).

Regulatory Oversight Committee: The term "Regulatory Oversight Committee" means the regulatory oversight committee of the Board, as constituted in accordance with, and with the authority and rights set forth in, Rule 208.

Related Party: The term "Related Party" means, with respect to any Trading Privilege Holder: any partner, director, officer, branch manager, employee or agent of such Trading Privilege Holder (or any Person occupying a similar status or performing similar functions); any Person directly or indirectly Controlling, Controlled by, or under common Control with, such Trading Privilege Holder; or any Authorized Trader of such Trading Privilege Holder.

Respondent: The term "Respondent" has the meaning set forth in Rule 704(b).

Rule of the Clearing Corporation: The term "Rule of the Clearing Corporation" means the Certificate of Incorporation, the By-laws and any rule, interpretation, stated policy, or instrument corresponding to any of the foregoing, in each case as adopted or amended from time to time by the Clearing Corporation relating to the Exchange or any or all of the Contracts.

Rule of the Exchange: The term "Rule of the Exchange" means any rule, interpretation, stated policy, or instrument corresponding to any of the foregoing, in each case as adopted or amended from time to time by the Exchange.

Secretary: The term "Secretary" means the individual appointed by the Board from time to time to serve as secretary of the Exchange.

Security Future: The term "Security Future" has the meaning set forth in Section 1a(31) of the CEA.

Senior Person in Charge of the Trade Desk: The term "Senior Person in Charge of the Trade Desk" means the individual in charge of the Trade Desk at the applicable time.

Series of Options: The term "Series of Options" means options of the same class and the same type (e.g., put or call) with the same strike price and the same Expiration Date.

Single Stock Future: The term "Single Stock Future" has the meaning set forth in Rule 1801.

Specifications Supplement: The term "Specification Supplement" has the meaning set forth in Rule 1802.

Spread Processing Sequence: The term "Spread Processing Sequence" has the meaning set forth in Rule 405A(a)(iii)(B).

Standing Committee: The term "Standing Committee" has the meaning set forth in Rule 206(a).

Subject: The term "Subject" has the meaning set forth in Rule 702(e).

Strip: The term "strip" has the meaning set forth in Rule 404(c).

Threshold Width: The term "Threshold Width" means, with respect to a particular Contract, a range between the highest bid and lowest offer starting at the highest bid and going up to the lowest offer that is the greater of (i) a designated percentage of the mid-point between the highest bid and lowest offer in the Contract as set forth in the rules governing the Contract and (ii) the minimum increment in the Contract. If the range between the highest bid and lowest offer is less than or equal to the Threshold Width amount, a Threshold Width is deemed to exist and is not exceeded. If there is no bid or no offer, a Threshold Width is deemed not to exist and is deemed to be exceeded.

Trade at Settlement or TAS Transaction: The term "Trade at Settlement" or "TAS" transaction has the meaning set forth in Rule 404A(a).

Trade Desk: The term "Trade Desk" means the office established by the Exchange to assist Trading Privilege Holders and Authorized Traders in connection with their trading subject to the Rules of the Exchange.

Trading Hours: The term "Trading Hours" has the meaning set forth in Rule 402(a).

Trading Privilege Holder: The term "Trading Privilege Holder" means any Person holding Trading Privileges. Trading Privilege Holders shall be deemed to be members of the Exchange for purposes of the CEA and Commission Regulations thereunder.

Trading Privileges: The term "Trading Privileges" means a permit conferred by the Exchange on any Person in accordance with Rule 305 to access the CFE System to trade in Contracts and to enter into Exchange of Contract for Related Position transactions and Block Trades in Contracts in accordance with the Rules of the Exchange.

Treasurer: The term "Treasurer" means the individual appointed by the Board from time to time to serve as treasurer of the Exchange.

Upper Price Limit: The term "Upper Price Limit" has the meanings set forth in contract specification rule chapters for products with price limits, such as in Rule 1202(i)(i).

Volume-Based Tie Breaker or VBTB: The term "Volume-Based Tie Breaker" or "VBTB" has the meaning set forth in Rule 405A(d)(i).

Vice President: The term "Vice President" means any individual appointed by the Board from time to time to serve as a vice president of the Exchange.

---

12. SEC Rules and Regulations, Securities Exchange Act of 1934: 3a11-1 – Definition of the Term "Equity Security"

The term equity security is hereby defined to include any stock or similar security, certificate of interest or participation in any profit sharing agreement, preorganization certificate or subscription, transferable share, voting trust certificate or certificate of deposit for an equity security, limited partnership interest, interest in a joint venture, or certificate of interest in a business trust; any security future on any such security; or any security convertible, with or without consideration into such a security, or carrying any warrant or right to subscribe to or purchase such a security; or any such warrant or right; or any put, call, straddle, or other option or privilege of buying such a security from or selling such a security to another without being bound to do so.

---

13. SEC Rules and Regulations, Securities Exchange Act of 1934: 10b-18 – Purchases of Certain Equity Securities by the Issuer and Others

Preliminary Notes: Section 240.10b-18 provides an issuer (and its affiliated purchasers) with a "safe harbor" from liability for manipulation under sections 9(a)(2) of the Act and § 240.10b-5 under the Act solely by reason of the manner, timing, price, and volume of their repurchases when they repurchase the issuer's common stock in the market in accordance with the section's manner, timing, price, and volume conditions. As a safe harbor, compliance with § 240.10b-18 is voluntary. To come within the safe harbor, however, an issuer's repurchases must satisfy (on a daily basis) each of the section's four conditions. Failure to meet any one of the four conditions will remove all of the issuer's repurchases from the safe harbor for that day. The safe harbor, moreover, is not available for repurchases that, although made in technical compliance with the section, are part of a plan or scheme to evade the federal securities laws. 2. Regardless of whether the repurchases are effected in accordance with § 240.10b-18, reporting issuers must report their repurchasing activity as required by Item 703 of Regulations S-K and S-B (17 CFR 229.703 and 228.703) and Item 15(e) of Form 20-F (17 CFR 249.220f) (regarding foreign private issuers), and closed-end management investment companies that are registered under the Investment Company Act of 1940 must report their repurchasing activity as required by Item 8 of Form N-CSR (17 CFR 249.331; 17 CFR 274.128).

(a) Definitions. Unless otherwise provided, all terms used in this section shall have the same meaning as in the Act. In addition, the following definitions shall apply:

(1) ADTV means the average daily trading volume reported for the security during the four calendar weeks preceding the week in which the Rule 10b-18 purchase is to be effected.

(2) Affiliate means any person that directly or indirectly controls, is controlled by, or is under common control with, the issuer.

(3) Affiliated purchaser means:

(i) A person acting, directly or indirectly, in concert with the issuer for the purpose of acquiring the issuer's securities; or

(ii) An affiliate who, directly or indirectly, controls the issuer's purchases of such securities, whose purchases are controlled by the issuer, or whose purchases are under common control with those of the issuer; Provided, however, that "affiliated purchaser" shall not include a broker, dealer, or other person solely by reason of such broker, dealer, or other person effecting Rule 10b-18 purchases on behalf of the issuer or for its account, and shall not include an officer or director of the issuer solely by reason of that officer or director's participation in the decision to authorize Rule 10b-18 purchases by or on behalf of the issuer.

(4) Agent independent of the issuer has the meaning contained in § 242.100 of this chapter.

(5) Block means a quantity of stock that either:

(i) Has a purchase price of $200,000 or more; or

(ii) Is at least 5,000 shares and has a purchase price of at least $50,000; or

(iii) Is at least 20 round lots of the security and totals 150 percent or more of the trading volume for that security or, in the event that trading volume data are unavailable, is at least 20 round lots of the security and totals at least one-tenth of one percent (.001) of the outstanding shares of the security, exclusive of any shares owned by any affiliate; Provided, however, That a block under paragraph (a)(5)(i), (ii), and (iii) shall not include any amount a broker or dealer, acting as principal, has accumulated for the purpose of sale or resale to the issuer or to any affiliated purchaser of the issuer if the issuer or such affiliated purchaser knows or has reason to know that such amount was accumulated for such purpose, nor shall it include any amount that a broker or dealer has sold short to the issuer or to any affiliated purchaser of the issuer if the issuer or such affiliated purchaser knows or has reason to know that the sale was a short sale.

(6) Consolidated system means a consolidated transaction or quotation reporting system that collects and publicly disseminates on a current and continuous basis transaction or quotation information in common equity securities pursuant to an effective transaction reporting plan or an effective national market system plan (as those terms are defined in § 242.600 of this chapter).

(7) Market-wide trading suspension means a market-wide trading halt of 30 minutes or more that is:

(i) Imposed pursuant to the rules of a national securities exchange or a national securities association in response to a market-wide decline during a single trading session; or

(ii) Declared by the Commission pursuant to its authority under section 12(k) of the Act (15 U.S.C. 78l (k)).

(8) Plan has the meaning contained in § 242.100 of this chapter.

(9) Principal market for a security means the single securities market with the largest reported trading volume for the security during the six full calendar months preceding the week in which the Rule 10b-18 purchase is to be effected.

(10) Public float value has the meaning contained in § 242.100 of this chapter.

(11) Purchase price means the price paid per share as reported, exclusive of any commission paid to a broker acting as agent, or commission equivalent, mark-up, or differential paid to a dealer.

(12) Riskless principal transaction means a transaction in which a broker or dealer after having received an order from an issuer to buy its security, buys the security as principal in the market at the same price to satisfy the issuer's buy order. The issuer's buy order must be effected at the same price per-share at which the broker or dealer bought the shares to satisfy the issuer's buy order, exclusive of any explicitly disclosed markup or markdown, commission equivalent, or other fee. In addition, only the first leg of the transaction, when the broker or dealer buys the security in the market as principal, is reported under the rules of a self-regulatory organization or under the Act. For purposes of this section, the broker or dealer must have written policies and procedures in place to assure that, at a minimum, the issuer's buy order was received prior to the offsetting transaction; the offsetting transaction is allocated to a riskless principal account or the issuer's account within 60 seconds of the execution; and the broker or dealer has supervisory systems in place to produce records that enable the broker or dealer to accurately and readily reconstruct, in a time-sequenced manner, all orders effected on a riskless principal basis.

(13) Rule 10b-18 purchase means a purchase (or any bid or limit order that would effect such purchase) of an issuer's common stock (or an equivalent interest, including a unit of beneficial interest in a trust or limited partnership or a depository share) by or for the issuer or any affiliated purchaser (including riskless principal transactions). However, it does not include any purchase of such security:

(i) Effected during the applicable restricted period of a distribution that is subject to § 242.102 of this chapter;

(ii) Effected by or for an issuer plan by an agent independent of the issuer;

(iii) Effected as a fractional share purchase (a fractional interest in a security) evidenced by a script certificate, order form, or similar document;

(iv) Effected during the period from the time of public announcement (as defined in § 230.165(f)) of a merger, acquisition, or similar transaction involving a recapitalization, until the earlier of the completion of such transaction or the completion of the vote by target shareholders. This exclusion does not apply to Rule 10b-18 purchases:

(A) Effected during such transaction in which the consideration is solely cash and there is no valuation period; or

(B) Where:

(1) The total volume of Rule 10b-18 purchases effected on any single day does not exceed the lesser of 25% of the security's four-week ADTV or the issuer's average daily Rule 10b-18 purchases during the three full calendar months preceding the date of the announcement of such transaction;

(2) The issuer's block purchases effected pursuant to paragraph (b)(4) of this section do not exceed the average size and frequency of the issuer's block purchases effected pursuant to paragraph (b)(4) of this section during the three full calendar months preceding the date of the announcement of such transaction; and

(3) Such purchases are not otherwise restricted or prohibited;

(v) Effected pursuant to § 240.13e-1;

(vi) Effected pursuant to a tender offer that is subject to § 240.13e-4 or specifically excepted from § 240.13e-4; or

(vii) Effected pursuant to a tender offer that is subject to section 14(d) of the Act (15 U.S.C. 78n(d)) and the rules and regulations thereunder.

(b) Conditions to be met. Rule 10b-18 purchases shall not be deemed to have violated the anti-manipulation provisions of sections 9(a)(2) or 10(b) of the Act (15 U.S.C. 78i(a)(2) or 78j(b)), or § 240.10b-5 under the Act, solely by reason of the time, price, or amount of the Rule 10b-18 purchases, or the number of brokers or dealers used in connection with such purchases, if the issuer or affiliated purchaser of the issuer effects the Rule 10b-18 purchases according to each of the following conditions:

(1) One broker or dealer. Rule 10b-18 purchases must be effected from or through only one broker or dealer on any single day; Provided, however, that:

(i) The "one broker or dealer" condition shall not apply to Rule 10b-18 purchases that are not solicited by or on behalf of the issuer or its affiliated purchaser(s);

(ii) Where Rule 10b-18 purchases are effected by or on behalf of more than one affiliated purchaser of the issuer (or the issuer and one or more of its affiliated purchasers) on a single day, the issuer and all affiliated purchasers must use the same broker or dealer; and

(iii) Where Rule 10b-18 purchases are effected on behalf of the issuer by a broker-dealer that is not an electronic communication network (ECN) or other alternative trading system (ATS), that broker-dealer can access ECN or other ATS liquidity in order to execute repurchases on behalf of the issuer (or any affiliated purchaser of the issuer) on that day.

(2) Time of purchases. Rule 10b-18 purchases must not be:

(i) The opening (regular way) purchase reported in the consolidated system;

(ii) Effected during the 10 minutes before the scheduled close of the primary trading session in the principal market for the security, and the 10 minutes before the scheduled close of the primary trading session in the market where the purchase is effected, for a security that has an ADTV value of $1 million or more and a public float value of $150 million or more; and

(iii) Effected during the 30 minutes before the scheduled close of the primary trading session in the principal market for the security, and the 30 minutes before the scheduled close of the primary trading session in the market where the purchase is effected, for all other securities;

(iv) However, for purposes of this section, Rule 10b-18 purchases may be effected following the close of the primary trading session until the termination of the period in which last sale prices are reported in the consolidated system so long as such purchases are effected at prices that do not exceed the lower of the closing price of the primary trading session in the principal market for the security and any lower bids or sale prices subsequently reported in the consolidated system, and all of this section's conditions are met. However, for purposes of this section, the issuer may use one broker or dealer to effect Rule 10b-18 purchases during this period that may be different from the broker or dealer that it used during the primary trading session. However, the issuer's Rule 10b-18 purchase may not be the opening transaction of the session following the close of the primary trading session.

(3) Price of purchases. Rule 10b-18 purchases must be effected at a purchase price that:

(i) Does not exceed the highest independent bid or the last independent transaction price, whichever is higher, quoted or reported in the consolidated system at the time the Rule 10b-18 purchase is effected;

(ii) For securities for which bids and transaction prices are not quoted or reported in the consolidated system, Rule 10b-18 purchases must be effected at a purchase price that does not exceed the highest independent bid or the last independent transaction price, whichever is higher, displayed and disseminated on any national securities exchange or on any inter-dealer quotation system (as defined in § 240.15c2-11) that displays at least two priced quotations for the security, at the time the Rule 10b-18 purchase is effected; and

(iii) For all other securities, Rule 10b-18 purchases must be effected at a price no higher than the highest independent bid obtained from three independent dealers.

(4) Volume of purchases. The total volume of Rule 10b-18 purchases effected by or for the issuer and any affiliated purchasers effected on any single day must not exceed 25 percent of the ADTV for that security; However, once each week, in lieu of purchasing under the 25 percent of ADTV limit for that day, the issuer or an affiliated purchaser of the issuer may effect one block purchase if:

    (i) No other Rule 10b-18 purchases are effected that day, and

    (ii) The block purchase is not included when calculating a security's four week ADTV under this section.

(c) Alternative conditions. The conditions of paragraph (b) of this section shall apply in connection with Rule 10b-18 purchases effected during a trading session following the imposition of a market-wide trading suspension, except:

    (1) That the time of purchases condition in paragraph (b)(2) of this section shall not apply, either:

        (i) From the reopening of trading until the scheduled close of trading on the day that the market-wide trading suspension is imposed; or

        (ii) At the opening of trading on the next trading day until the scheduled close of trading that day, if a market-wide trading suspension was in effect at the close of trading on the preceding day; and

    (2) The volume of purchases condition in paragraph (b)(4) of this section is modified so that the amount of Rule 10b-18 purchases must not exceed 100 percent of the ADTV for that security.

(d) Other purchases. No presumption shall arise that an issuer or an affiliated purchaser has violated the anti-manipulation provisions of sections 9(a)(2) or 10(b) of the Act (15 U.S.C. 78i(a)(2) or 78j(b)), or § 240.10b-5 under the Act, if the Rule 10b-18 purchases of such issuer or affiliated purchaser do not meet the conditions specified in paragraph (b) or (c) of this section.

---

14. SEC Rules and Regulations, Investment Company Act of 1940: Section 3(a) – Definitions – "Investment Company"

(a) Definitions

    (1) When used in this subchapter, "investment company" means any issuer which—

        (A) is or holds itself out as being engaged primarily, or proposes to engage primarily, in the business of investing, reinvesting, or trading in securities;

        (B) is engaged or proposes to engage in the business of issuing face-amount certificates of the installment type, or has been engaged in such business and has any such certificate outstanding; or

        (C) is engaged or proposes to engage in the business of investing, reinvesting, owning, holding, or trading in securities, and owns or proposes to acquire investment securities having a value exceeding 40 per centum of the value of such issuer's total assets (exclusive of Government securities and cash items) on an unconsolidated basis.

    (2) As used in this section, "investment securities" includes all securities except (A) Government securities, (B) securities issued by employees' securities companies, and (C) securities issued by majority-owned subsidiaries of the owner which (i) are not investment companies, and (ii) are not relying on the exception from the definition of investment company in paragraph (1) or (7) of subsection (c).

(b) Exemption from provisions

    Notwithstanding paragraph (1)(C) of subsection (a), none of the following persons is an investment company within the meaning of this subchapter:

    (1) Any issuer primarily engaged, directly or through a wholly-owned subsidiary or subsidiaries, in a business or businesses other than that of investing, reinvesting, owning, holding, or trading in securities.

(2) Any issuer which the Commission, upon application by such issuer, finds and by order declares to be primarily engaged in a business or businesses other than that of investing, reinvesting, owning, holding, or trading in securities either directly or (A) through majority-owned subsidiaries or (B) through controlled companies conducting similar types of businesses. The filing of an application under this paragraph in good faith by an issuer other than a registered investment company shall exempt the applicant for a period of sixty days from all provisions of this subchapter applicable to investment companies as such. For cause shown, the Commission by order may extend such period of exemption for an additional period or periods. Whenever the Commission, upon its own motion or upon application, finds that the circumstances which gave rise to the issuance of an order granting an application under this paragraph no longer exist, the Commission shall by order revoke such order.

(3) Any issuer all the outstanding securities of which (other than short-term paper and directors' qualifying shares) are directly or indirectly owned by a company excepted from the definition of investment company by paragraph (1) or (2) of this subsection.

(c) Further exemptions

Notwithstanding subsection (a), none of the following persons is an investment company within the meaning of this subchapter:

(1) Any issuer whose outstanding securities (other than short-term paper) are beneficially owned by not more than one hundred persons (or, in the case of a qualifying venture capital fund, 250 persons) and which is not making and does not presently propose to make a public offering of its securities. Such issuer shall be deemed to be an investment company for purposes of the limitations set forth in subparagraphs (A)(i) and (B)(i) of section 80a–12(d)(1) of this title governing the purchase or other acquisition by such issuer of any security issued by any registered investment company and the sale of any security issued by any registered open-end investment company to any such issuer. For purposes of this paragraph:

(A) Beneficial ownership by a company shall be deemed to be beneficial ownership by one person, except that, if the company owns 10 per centum or more of the outstanding voting securities of the issuer, and is or, but for the exception provided for in this paragraph or paragraph (7), would be an investment company, the beneficial ownership shall be deemed to be that of the holders of such company's outstanding securities (other than short-term paper).

(B) Beneficial ownership by any person who acquires securities or interests in securities of an issuer described in the first sentence of this paragraph shall be deemed to be beneficial ownership by the person from whom such transfer was made, pursuant to such rules and regulations as the Commission shall prescribe as necessary or appropriate in the public interest and consistent with the protection of investors and the purposes fairly intended by the policy and provisions of this subchapter, where the transfer was caused by legal separation, divorce, death, or other involuntary event.

(C)

(i) The term "qualifying venture capital fund" means a venture capital fund that has not more than $10,000,000 in aggregate capital contributions and uncalled committed capital, with such dollar amount to be indexed for inflation once every 5 years by the Commission, beginning from a measurement made by the Commission on a date selected by the Commission, rounded to the nearest $1,000,000.

(ii) The term "venture capital fund" has the meaning given the term in section 275.203(l)–1 of title 17, Code of Federal Regulations, or any successor regulation.

(2)

(A) Any person primarily engaged in the business of underwriting and distributing securities issued by other persons, selling securities to customers, acting as broker, and acting as market intermediary, or any one or more of such activities, whose gross income normally is derived principally from such business and related activities.

(B) For purposes of this paragraph—

(i) the term "market intermediary" means any person that regularly holds itself out as being willing contemporaneously to engage in, and that is regularly engaged in, the business of entering into transactions on both sides of the market for a financial contract or one or more such financial contracts; and

    (ii) the term "financial contract" means any arrangement that—

        (I) takes the form of an individually negotiated contract, agreement, or option to buy, sell, lend, swap, or repurchase, or other similar individually negotiated transaction commonly entered into by participants in the financial markets;

        (II) is in respect of securities, commodities, currencies, interest or other rates, other measures of value, or any other financial or economic interest similar in purpose or function to any of the foregoing; and

        (III) is entered into in response to a request from a counter party for a quotation, or is otherwise entered into and structured to accommodate the objectives of the counter party to such arrangement.

(3) Any bank or insurance company; any savings and loan association, building and loan association, cooperative bank, homestead association, or similar institution, or any receiver, conservator, liquidator, liquidating agent, or similar official or person thereof or therefor; or any common trust fund or similar fund maintained by a bank exclusively for the collective investment and reinvestment of moneys contributed thereto by the bank in its capacity as a trustee, executor, administrator, or guardian, if—

    (A) such fund is employed by the bank solely as an aid to the administration of trusts, estates, or other accounts created and maintained for a fiduciary purpose;

    (B) except in connection with the ordinary advertising of the bank's fiduciary services, interests in such fund are not—

        (i) advertised; or

        (ii) offered for sale to the general public; and

    (C) fees and expenses charged by such fund are not in contravention of fiduciary principles established under applicable Federal or State law.

(4) Any person substantially all of whose business is confined to making small loans, industrial banking, or similar businesses.

(5) Any person who is not engaged in the business of issuing redeemable securities, face-amount certificates of the installment type or periodic payment plan certificates, and who is primarily engaged in one or more of the following businesses: (A) Purchasing or otherwise acquiring notes, drafts, acceptances, open accounts receivable, and other obligations representing part or all of the sales price of merchandise, insurance, and services; (B) making loans to manufacturers, wholesalers, and retailers of, and to prospective purchasers of, specified merchandise, insurance, and services; and (C) purchasing or otherwise acquiring mortgages and other liens on and interests in real estate.

(6) Any company primarily engaged, directly or through majority-owned subsidiaries, in one or more of the businesses described in paragraphs (3), (4), and (5) of this subsection, or in one or more of such businesses (from which not less than 25 per centum of such company's gross income during its last fiscal year was derived) together with an additional business or businesses other than investing, reinvesting, owning, holding, or trading in securities.

(7)

    (A) Any issuer, the outstanding securities of which are owned exclusively by persons who, at the time of acquisition of such securities, are qualified purchasers, and which is not making and does not at that time propose to make a public offering of such securities. Securities that are owned by persons who received the securities from a qualified purchaser as a gift or bequest, or in a case in which the transfer was caused by legal separation, divorce, death, or other involuntary event, shall be deemed to be owned by a qualified purchaser, subject to such rules, regulations, and orders as the Commission may prescribe as necessary or appropriate in the public interest or for the protection of investors.

    (B) Notwithstanding subparagraph (A), an issuer is within the exception provided by this paragraph if—

(i) in addition to qualified purchasers, outstanding securities of that issuer are beneficially owned by not more than 100 persons who are not qualified purchasers, if—

(I) such persons acquired any portion of the securities of such issuer on or before September 1, 1996; and

(II) at the time at which such persons initially acquired the securities of such issuer, the issuer was excepted by paragraph (1); and

(ii) prior to availing itself of the exception provided by this paragraph—

(I) such issuer has disclosed to each beneficial owner, as determined under paragraph (1), that future investors will be limited to qualified purchasers, and that ownership in such issuer is no longer limited to not more than 100 persons; and

(II) concurrently with or after such disclosure, such issuer has provided each beneficial owner, as determined under paragraph (1), with a reasonable opportunity to redeem any part or all of their interests in the issuer, notwithstanding any agreement to the contrary between the issuer and such persons, for that person's proportionate share of the issuer's net assets.

(C) Each person that elects to redeem under subparagraph (B)(ii)(II) shall receive an amount in cash equal to that person's proportionate share of the issuer's net assets, unless the issuer elects to provide such person with the option of receiving, and such person agrees to receive, all or a portion of such person's share in assets of the issuer. If the issuer elects to provide such persons with such an opportunity, disclosure concerning such opportunity shall be made in the disclosure required by subparagraph (B)(ii)(I).

(D) An issuer that is excepted under this paragraph shall nonetheless be deemed to be an investment company for purposes of the limitations set forth in subparagraphs (A)(i) and (B)(i) of section 80a–12(d)(1) of this title relating to the purchase or other acquisition by such issuer of any security issued by any registered investment company and the sale of any security issued by any registered open-end investment company to any such issuer.

(E) For purposes of determining compliance with this paragraph and paragraph (1), an issuer that is otherwise excepted under this paragraph and an issuer that is otherwise excepted under paragraph (1) shall not be treated by the Commission as being a single issuer for purposes of determining whether the outstanding securities of the issuer excepted under paragraph (1) are beneficially owned by not more than 100 persons or whether the outstanding securities of the issuer excepted under this paragraph are owned by persons that are not qualified purchasers. Nothing in this subparagraph shall be construed to establish that a person is a bona fide qualified purchaser for purposes of this paragraph or a bona fide beneficial owner for purposes of paragraph (1).

(8) [Repealed]

(9) Any person substantially all of whose business consists of owning or holding oil, gas, or other mineral royalties or leases, or fractional interests therein, or certificates of interest or participation in or investment contracts relative to such royalties, leases, or fractional interests.

(10)

(A) Any company organized and operated exclusively for religious, educational, benevolent, fraternal, charitable, or reformatory purposes—

(i) no part of the net earnings of which inures to the benefit of any private shareholder or individual; or

(ii) which is or maintains a fund described in subparagraph (B).

(B) For the purposes of subparagraph (A)(ii), a fund is described in this subparagraph if such fund is a pooled income fund, collective trust fund, collective investment fund, or similar fund maintained by a charitable organization exclusively for the collective investment and reinvestment of one or more of the following:

(i) assets of the general endowment fund or other funds of one or more charitable organizations;

(ii) assets of a pooled income fund;

(iii) assets contributed to a charitable organization in exchange for the issuance of charitable gift annuities;

(iv) assets of a charitable remainder trust or of any other trust, the remainder interests of which are irrevocably dedicated to any charitable organization;

(v) assets of a charitable lead trust;

(vi) assets of a trust, the remainder interests of which are revocably dedicated to or for the benefit of 1 or more charitable organizations, if the ability to revoke the dedication is limited to circumstances involving—

(I) an adverse change in the financial circumstances of a settlor or an income beneficiary of the trust;

(II) a change in the identity of the charitable organization or organizations having the remainder interest, provided that the new beneficiary is also a charitable organization; or

(III) both the changes described in subclauses (I) and (II);

(vii) assets of a trust not described in clauses (i) through (v), the remainder interests of which are revocably dedicated to a charitable organization, subject to subparagraph (C); or

(viii) such assets as the Commission may prescribe by rule, regulation, or order in accordance with section 80a–6(c) of this title.

(C) A fund that contains assets described in clause (vii) of subparagraph (B) shall be excluded from the definition of an investment company for a period of 3 years after December 8, 1995, but only if—

(i) such assets were contributed before the date which is 60 days after December 8, 1995; and

(ii) such assets are commingled in the fund with assets described in one or more of clauses (i) through (vi) and (viii) of subparagraph (B).

(D) For purposes of this paragraph—

(i) a trust or fund is "maintained" by a charitable organization if the organization serves as a trustee or administrator of the trust or fund or has the power to remove the trustees or administrators of the trust or fund and to designate new trustees or administrators;

(ii) the term "pooled income fund" has the same meaning as in section 642(c)(5) of title 26;

(iii) the term "charitable organization" means an organization described in paragraphs (1) through (5) of section 170(c) or section 501(c)(3) of title 26;

(iv) the term "charitable lead trust" means a trust described in section 170(f)(2)(B), 2055(e)(2)(B), or 2522(c)(2)(B) of title 26;

(v) the term "charitable remainder trust" means a charitable remainder annuity trust or a charitable remainder unitrust, as those terms are defined in section 664(d) of title 26; and

(vi) the term "charitable gift annuity" means an annuity issued by a charitable organization that is described in section 501(m)(5) of title 26.

(11) Any employee's stock bonus, pension, or profit-sharing trust which meets the requirements for qualification under section 401 of title 26; or any governmental plan described in section 77c(a)(2)(C) of this title; or any collective trust fund maintained by a bank consisting solely of assets of one or more of such trusts, government plans, or church plans, companies or accounts that are excluded from the definition of an investment company under paragraph (14) of this subsection; or any separate account the assets of which are derived solely from (A) contributions under pension or profit-sharing plans which meet the requirements of section 401 of title 26 or the requirements for deduction of the employer's contribution under section 404(a)(2) of title 26, (B) contributions under governmental plans in connection with which interests, participations, or securities are exempted from the registration provisions of section 77e of this title by section 77c(a)(2)(C) of this title, and (C) advances made by an insurance company in connection with the operation of such separate account.

(12) Any voting trust the assets of which consist exclusively of securities of a single issuer which is not an investment company.

(13) Any security holders' protective committee or similar issuer having outstanding and issuing no securities other than certificates of deposit and short-term paper.

(14) Any church plan described in section 414(e) of title 26, if, under any such plan, no part of the assets may be used for, or diverted to, purposes other than the exclusive benefit of plan participants or beneficiaries, or any company or account that is—

   (A) established by a person that is eligible to establish and maintain such a plan under section 414(e) of title 26; and

   (B) substantially all of the activities of which consist of—

   (i) managing or holding assets contributed to such church plans or other assets which are permitted to be commingled with the assets of church plans under title 26; or

   (ii) administering or providing benefits pursuant to church plans.

_____

15. SEC Rules and Regulations, Investment Company Act of 1940: Section 4 – Classification of Investment Companies

For the purposes of this subchapter, investment companies are divided into three principal classes, defined as follows:

(1) "Face-amount certificate company" means an investment company which is engaged or proposes to engage in the business of issuing face-amount certificates of the installment type, or which has been engaged in such business and has any such certificate outstanding.

(2) "Unit investment trust" means an investment company which (A) is organized under a trust indenture, contract of custodianship or agency, or similar instrument, (B) does not have a board of directors, and (C) issues only redeemable securities, each of which represents an undivided interest in a unit of specified securities; but does not include a voting trust.

(3) "Management company" means any investment company other than a face-amount certificate company or a unit investment trust.

_____

16. SEC Rules and Regulations, Investment Company Act of 1940: Section 5 – Subclassification of Management Companies

(a) Open-end and closed-end companies

For the purposes of this subchapter, management companies are divided into open-end and closed-end companies, defined as follows:

(1) "Open-end company" means a management company which is offering for sale or has outstanding any redeemable security of which it is the issuer.

(2) "Closed-end company" means any management company other than an open-end company.

(b) Diversified and non-diversified companies

Management companies are further divided into diversified companies and non-diversified companies, defined as follows:

(1) "Diversified company" means a management company which meets the following requirements: At least 75 per centum of the value of its total assets is represented by cash and cash items (including receivables), Government securities, securities of other investment companies, and other securities for the purposes of this calculation limited in respect of any one issuer to an amount not greater in value than 5 per centum of the value of the total assets of such management company and to not more than 10 per centum of the outstanding voting securities of such issuer.

(2) "Non-diversified company" means any management company other than a diversified company.

(c) Loss of status as diversified company

A registered diversified company which at the time of its qualification as such meets the requirements of paragraph (1) of subsection (b) shall not lose its status as a diversified company because of any subsequent discrepancy between the value of its various investments and the requirements of said paragraph, so long as any such discrepancy existing immediately after its acquisition of any security or other property is neither wholly nor partly the result of such acquisition.

---

17. SEC Rules and Regulations, Investment Company Act of 1940: 12b-1 – Distribution of Shares by Registered Open-end Management Investment Company

(a)

(1) Except as provided in this section, it shall be unlawful for any registered open-end management investment company (other than a company complying with the provisions of section 10(d) of the Act (15 U.S.C. 80a-10(d))) to act as a distributor of securities of which it is the issuer, except through an underwriter;

(2) For purposes of this section, such a company will be deemed to be acting as a distributor of securities of which it is the issuer, other than through an underwriter, if it engages directly or indirectly in financing any activity which is primarily intended to result in the sale of shares issued by such company, including, but not necessarily limited to, advertising, compensation of underwriters, dealers, and sales personnel, the printing and mailing of prospectuses to other than current shareholders, and the printing and mailing of sales literature;

(b) A registered, open-end management investment company ("Company") may act as a distributor of securities of which it is the issuer: Provided, That any payments made by such company in connection with such distribution are made pursuant to a written plan describing all material aspects of the proposed financing of distribution and that all agreements with any person relating to implementation of the plan are in writing: And further provided, That:

(1) Such plan has been approved by a vote of at least a majority of the outstanding voting securities of such company, if adopted after any public offering of the company's voting securities or the sale of such securities to persons who are not affiliated persons of the company, affiliated persons of such persons, promoters of the company, or affiliated persons of such promoters;

(2) Such plan, together with any related agreements, has been approved by a vote of the board of directors of such company, and of the directors who are not interested persons of the company and have no direct

or indirect financial interest in the operation of the plan or in any agreements related to the plan, cast in person at a meeting called for the purpose of voting on such plan or agreements;

(3) Such plan or agreement provides, in substance:

(i) That it shall continue in effect for a period of more than one year from the date of its execution or adoption only so long as such continuance is specifically approved at least annually in the manner described in paragraph (b)(2) of this section;

(ii) That any person authorized to direct the disposition of monies paid or payable by such company pursuant to the plan or any related agreement shall provide to the company's board of directors, and the directors shall review, at least quarterly, a written report of the amounts so expended and the purposes for which such expenditures were made; and

(iii) In the case of a plan, that it may be terminated at any time by vote of a majority of the members of the board of directors of the company who are not interested persons of the company and have no direct or indirect financial interest in the operation of the plan or in any agreements related to the plan or by vote of a majority of the outstanding voting securities of such company;

(iv) In the case of an agreement related to a plan:

(A) That it may be terminated at any time, without the payment of any penalty, by vote of a majority of the members of the board of directors of such company who are not interested persons of the company and have no direct or indirect financial interest in the operation of the plan or in any agreements related to the plan or by vote of a majority of the outstanding voting securities of such company on not more than sixty days' written notice to any other party to the agreement, and

(B) For its automatic termination in the event of its assignment;

(4) Such plan provides that it may not be amended to increase materially the amount to be spent for distribution without shareholder approval and that all material amendments of the plan must be approved in the manner described in paragraph (b)(2) of this section; and

(5) Such plan is implemented and continued in a manner consistent with the provisions of paragraphs (c), (d), and (e) of this section;

(c) A registered open-end management investment company may rely on the provisions of paragraph (b) of this section only if its board of directors satisfies the fund governance standards as defined in § 270.0-1(a)(7);

(d) In considering whether a registered open-end management investment company should implement or continue a plan in reliance on paragraph (b) of this section, the directors of such company shall have a duty to request and evaluate, and any person who is a party to any agreement with such company relating to such plan shall have a duty to furnish, such information as may reasonably be necessary to an informed determination of whether such plan should be implemented or continued; in fulfilling their duties under this paragraph the directors should consider and give appropriate weight to all pertinent factors, and minutes describing the factors considered and the basis for the decision to use company assets for distribution must be made and preserved in accordance with paragraph (f) of this section;

(e) A registered open-end management investment company may implement or continue a plan pursuant to paragraph (b) of this section only if the directors who vote to approve such implementation or continuation conclude, in the exercise of reasonable business judgment and in light of their fiduciary duties under state law and under sections 36(a) and (b) (15 U.S.C. 80a-35 (a) and (b)) of the Act, that there is a reasonable likelihood that the plan will benefit the company and its shareholders;

(f) A registered open-end management investment company must preserve copies of any plan, agreement or report made pursuant to this section for a period of not less than six years from the date of such plan, agreement or report, the first two years in an easily accessible place;

(g) If a plan covers more than one series or class of shares, the provisions of the plan must be severable for each series or class, and whenever this rule provides for any action to be taken with respect to a plan, that action must be taken separately for each series or class affected by the matter. Nothing in this paragraph (g) shall affect the rights of any purchase class under § 270.18f-3(f)(2)(iii).

(h) Notwithstanding any other provision of this section, a company may not:

(1) Compensate a broker or dealer for any promotion or sale of shares issued by that company by directing to the broker or dealer:

(i) The company's portfolio securities transactions; or

(ii) Any remuneration, including but not limited to any commission, mark-up, mark-down, or other fee (or portion thereof) received or to be received from the company's portfolio transactions effected through any other broker (including a government securities broker) or dealer (including a municipal securities dealer or a government securities dealer); and

(2) Direct its portfolio securities transactions to a broker or dealer that promotes or sells shares issued by the company, unless the company (or its investment adviser):

(i) Is in compliance with the provisions of paragraph (h)(1) of this section with respect to that broker or dealer; and

(ii) Has implemented, and the company's board of directors (including a majority of directors who are not interested persons of the company) has approved, policies and procedures reasonably designed to prevent:

(A) The persons responsible for selecting brokers and dealers to effect the company's portfolio securities transactions from taking into account the brokers' and dealers' promotion or sale of shares issued by the company or any other registered investment company; and

(B) The company, and any investment adviser and principal underwriter of the company, from entering into any agreement (whether oral or written) or other understanding under which the company directs, or is expected to direct, portfolio securities transactions, or any remuneration described in paragraph (h)(1)(ii) of this section, to a broker (including a government securities broker) or dealer (including a municipal securities dealer or a government securities dealer) in consideration for the promotion or sale of shares issued by the company or any other registered investment company.

Section 3

**Understanding Trading, Customer
Accounts and Prohibited Activities**

1. FINRA Rules: 2010 – Standards of Commercial Honor and Principles of Trade

A member, in the conduct of its business, shall observe high standards of commercial honor and just and equitable principles of trade.

---

2. FINRA Rules: 2020 – Use of Manipulative, Deceptive or Other Fraudulent Devices

No member shall effect any transaction in, or induce the purchase or sale of, any security by means of any manipulative, deceptive or other fraudulent device or contrivance.

---

3. FINRA Rules: 2040 – Payments to Unregistered Persons

(a) General

No member or associated person shall, directly or indirectly, pay any compensation, fees, concessions, discounts, commissions or other allowances to:

(1) any person that is not registered as a broker-dealer under Section 15(a) of the Exchange Act but, by reason of receipt of any such payments and the activities related thereto, is required to be so registered under applicable federal securities laws and SEA rules and regulations; or

(2) any appropriately registered associated person unless such payment complies with all applicable federal securities laws, FINRA rules and SEA rules and regulations.

(b) Retiring Representatives

(1) A member may pay continuing commissions to a retiring registered representative of the member, after he or she ceases to be associated with such member, that are derived from accounts held for continuing customers of the retiring registered representative regardless of whether customer funds or securities are added to the accounts during the period of retirement, provided that:

(A) a bona fide contract between the member and the retiring registered representative providing for the payments was entered into in good faith while the person was a registered representative of the member and such contract, among other things, prohibits the retiring registered representative from soliciting new business, opening new accounts, or servicing the accounts generating the continuing commission payments; and

(B) the arrangement complies with applicable federal securities laws, SEA rules and regulations.

(2) The term "retiring registered representative," as used in this Rule shall mean an individual who retires from a member (including as a result of a total disability) and leaves the securities industry. In the case of death of the retiring registered representative, the retiring registered representative's beneficiary designated in the written contract or the retiring registered representative's estate if no beneficiary is so designated may be the beneficiary of the respective member's agreement with the deceased representative.

(c) Nonregistered Foreign Finders

A member may pay to a nonregistered foreign person (the "finder") transaction-related compensation based upon the business of customers the finder directs to the member if the following conditions are met:

(1) the member has assured itself that the finder who will receive the compensation is not required to register in the United States as a broker-dealer nor is subject to a disqualification as defined in Article III, Section 4 of FINRA's By-Laws, and has further assured itself that the compensation arrangement does not violate applicable foreign law;

(2) the finder is a foreign national (not a U.S. citizen) or foreign entity domiciled abroad;

(3) the customers are foreign nationals (not U.S. citizens) or foreign entities domiciled abroad transacting business in either foreign or U.S. securities;

(4) customers receive a descriptive document, similar to that required by Rule 206(4)-3(b) of the Investment Advisers Act, that discloses what compensation is being paid to finders;

(5) customers provide written acknowledgment to the member of the existence of the compensation arrangement and such acknowledgment is retained and made available for inspection by FINRA;

(6) records reflecting payments to finders are maintained on the member's books, and actual agreements between the member and the finder are available for inspection by FINRA; and

(7) the confirmation of each transaction indicates that a referral or finders fee is being paid pursuant to an agreement.

---

4. FINRA Rules: 2090 – Know Your Customer

Every member shall use reasonable diligence, in regard to the opening and maintenance of every account, to know (and retain) the essential facts concerning every customer and concerning the authority of each person acting on behalf of such customer.

---

5. FINRA Rules: 2111 – Suitability

(a) A member or an associated person must have a reasonable basis to believe that a recommended transaction or investment strategy involving a security or securities is suitable for the customer, based on the information obtained through the reasonable diligence of the member or associated person to ascertain the customer's investment profile. A customer's investment profile includes, but is not limited to, the customer's age, other investments, financial situation and needs, tax status, investment objectives, investment experience, investment time horizon, liquidity needs, risk tolerance, and any other information the customer may disclose to the member or associated person in connection with such recommendation.

(b) A member or associated person fulfills the customer-specific suitability obligation for an institutional account, as defined in Rule 4512(c), if (1) the member or associated person has a reasonable basis to believe that the institutional customer is capable of evaluating investment risks independently, both in general and with regard to particular transactions and investment strategies involving a security or securities and (2) the institutional customer affirmatively indicates that it is exercising independent judgment in evaluating the member's or associated person's recommendations. Where an institutional customer has delegated decision-making authority to an agent, such as an investment adviser or a bank trust department, these factors shall be applied to the agent.

---

6. FINRA Rules: 2120 – Commissions, Mark Ups and Charges

2121. Fair Prices and Commissions
In securities transactions, whether in "listed" or "unlisted" securities, if a member buys for his own account from his customer, or sells for his own account to his customer, he shall buy or sell at a price which is fair, taking into consideration all relevant circumstances, including market conditions with respect to such security at the time of the transaction, the expense involved, and the fact that he is entitled to a profit; and if he acts as agent for his customer in any such transaction, he shall not charge his customer more than a fair commission or service charge, taking into consideration all relevant circumstances, including market conditions with respect to such security at the time of the transaction, the expense of executing the order and the value of any service he may have rendered by reason of his experience in and knowledge of such security and the market therefor.

2122. Charges for Services Performed
Charges, if any, for services performed, including, but not limited to, miscellaneous services such as collection of monies due for principal, dividends, or interest; exchange or transfer of securities; appraisals, safe-keeping or custody of securities, and other services shall be reasonable and not unfairly discriminatory among customers.

2124. Net Transactions with Customers
(a) Prior to executing a transaction for or with a customer on a "net" basis as defined in paragraph (e) below, a member must provide disclosure to and obtain consent from the customer as provided in this Rule.
(b) With respect to non-institutional customers, the member must obtain the customer's written consent on an order-by-order basis prior to executing a transaction for or with the customer on a "net" basis and such consent must evidence the customer's understanding of the terms and conditions of the order.
(c) With respect to institutional customers, a member must obtain the customer's consent prior to executing a transaction for or with the customer on a "net" basis in accordance with one of the following methods:
  (1) a negative consent letter that clearly discloses to the institutional customer in writing the terms and conditions for handling the customer order(s) and provides the institutional customer with a meaningful opportunity to object to the execution of transactions on a net basis. If the customer does not object, then the member may reasonably conclude that the institutional customer has consented to the member trading on a "net" basis with the customer and the member may rely on such letter for all or a portion of the customer's orders (as instructed by the customer) pursuant to this Rule;
  (2) oral disclosure to and consent from the customer on an order-by-order basis. Such oral disclosure and consent must clearly explain the terms and conditions for handling the customer order and provide the institutional customer with a meaningful opportunity to object to the execution of the transaction on a net basis. The member also must document, on an order-by-order basis, the customer's understanding of the terms and conditions of the order and the customer's consent; or

(3) written consent on an order-by-order basis prior to executing a transaction for or with the customer on a "net" basis and such consent must evidence the customer's understanding of the terms and conditions of the order.

(d) For those customers that have granted trading discretion to a fiduciary (e.g. an investment adviser), a member is permitted to obtain the consent required under this Rule from the fiduciary. If the fiduciary meets the definition of "institutional customer" in paragraph (e), the member may meet the disclosure and consent requirements under this Rule in the same manner permitted for institutional customers.

(e) For purposes of this Rule:

(1) "institutional customer" shall mean a customer whose account qualifies as an "institutional account" under Rule 4512(c); and

(2) "net" transaction shall mean a principal transaction in which a market maker, after having received an order to buy (sell) an equity security, purchases (sells) the equity security at one price (from (to) another broker-dealer or another customer) and then sells to (buys from) the customer at a different price.

(f) Members must retain and preserve all documentation relating to consent obtained pursuant to this Rule in accordance with Rule 4511.

------

7. FINRA Rules: 2150 – Improper Use of Customers' Securities or Funds; Prohibition Against Guarantees and Sharing in Accounts

(a) Improper Use

No member or person associated with a member shall make improper use of a customer's securities or funds.

(b) Prohibition Against Guarantees

No member or person associated with a member shall guarantee a customer against loss in connection with any securities transaction or in any securities account of such customer.

(c) Sharing in Accounts; Extent Permissible

(1)(A) Except as provided in paragraph (c)(2), no member or person associated with a member shall share directly or indirectly in the profits or losses in any account of a customer carried by the member or any other member; provided, however, that a member or person associated with a member may share in the profits or losses in such an account if:

(i) such person associated with a member obtains prior written authorization from the member employing the associated person;

(ii) such member or person associated with a member obtains prior written authorization from the customer; and

(iii) such member or person associated with a member shares in the profits or losses in any account of such customer only in direct proportion to the financial contributions made to such account by either the member or person associated with a member.

(B) Exempt from the direct proportionate share limitation of paragraph (c)(1)(A)(iii) are accounts of the immediate family of such member or person associated with a member. For purposes of this Rule, the term "immediate family" shall include parents, mother-in-law or father-in-law, husband or wife, children or any relative to whose support the member or person associated with a member otherwise contributes directly or indirectly.

(2) Notwithstanding the prohibition of paragraph (c)(1), a member or person associated with a member that is acting as an investment adviser may receive compensation based on a share in profits or gains in an account if:

    (A) such person associated with a member seeking such compensation obtains prior written authorization from the member employing the associated person

    (B) such member or person associated with a member seeking such compensation obtains prior written authorization from the customer; and

    (C) all of the conditions in Rule 205-3 of the Investment Advisers Act (as the same may be amended from time to time) are satisfied.

---

8. FINRA Rules: 2165 – Financial Exploitation of Specified Adults

(a) Definitions

    (1) For purposes of this Rule, the term "Specified Adult" shall mean: (A) a natural person age 65 and older; or (B) a natural person age 18 and older who the member reasonably believes has a mental or physical impairment that renders the individual unable to protect his or her own interests.

    (2) For purposes of this Rule, the term "Account" shall mean any account of a member for which a Specified Adult has the authority to transact business.

    (3) For purposes of this Rule, the term "Trusted Contact Person" shall mean the person who may be contacted about the Specified Adult's Account in accordance with Rule 4512.

    (4) For purposes of this Rule, the term "financial exploitation" means:

        (A) the wrongful or unauthorized taking, withholding, appropriation, or use of a Specified Adult's funds or securities; or

        (B) any act or omission by a person, including through the use of a power of attorney, guardianship, or any other authority regarding a Specified Adult, to:

            (i) obtain control, through deception, intimidation or undue influence, over the Specified Adult's money, assets or property; or

            (ii) convert the Specified Adult's money, assets or property.

(b) Temporary Hold on Disbursements

    (1) A member may place a temporary hold on a disbursement of funds or securities from the Account of a Specified Adult if:

        (A) The member reasonably believes that financial exploitation of the Specified Adult has occurred, is occurring, has been attempted, or will be attempted; and

        (B) The member, not later than two business days after the date that the member first placed the temporary hold on the disbursement of funds or securities, provides notification orally or in writing, which may be electronic, of the temporary hold and the reason for the temporary hold to:

            (i) all parties authorized to transact business on the Account, unless a party is unavailable or the member reasonably believes that the party has engaged, is engaged, or will engage in the financial exploitation of the Specified Adult; and

            (ii) the Trusted Contact Person(s), unless the Trusted Contact Person is unavailable or the member reasonably believes that the Trusted Contact Person(s) has engaged, is engaged, or will engage in the financial exploitation of the Specified Adult; and

(C) The member immediately initiates an internal review of the facts and circumstances that caused the member to reasonably believe that the financial exploitation of the Specified Adult has occurred, is occurring, has been attempted, or will be attempted.

(2) The temporary hold authorized by this Rule will expire not later than 15 business days after the date that the member first placed the temporary hold on the disbursement of funds or securities, unless otherwise terminated or extended by a state regulator or agency of competent jurisdiction or a court of competent jurisdiction, or extended pursuant to paragraph (b)(3) of this Rule.

(3) Provided that the member's internal review of the facts and circumstances under paragraph (b)(1)(C) of this Rule supports the member's reasonable belief that the financial exploitation of the Specified Adult has occurred, is occurring, has been attempted, or will be attempted, the temporary hold authorized by this Rule may be extended by the member for no longer than 10 business days following the date authorized by paragraph (b)(2) of this Rule, unless otherwise terminated or extended by a state regulator or agency of competent jurisdiction or a court of competent jurisdiction.

(c) Supervision

(1) In addition to the general supervisory and recordkeeping requirements of Rules 3110, 3120, 3130, 3150, and Rule 4510 Series, a member relying on this Rule shall establish and maintain written supervisory procedures reasonably designed to achieve compliance with this Rule, including, but not limited to, procedures related to the identification, escalation and reporting of matters related to the financial exploitation of Specified Adults.

(2) A member's written supervisory procedures also shall identify the title of each person authorized to place, terminate or extend a temporary hold on behalf of the member pursuant to this Rule. Any such person shall be an associated person of the member who serves in a supervisory, compliance or legal capacity for the member.

(d) Record Retention

Members shall retain records related to compliance with this Rule, which shall be readily available to FINRA, upon request. The retained records shall include records of: (1) request(s) for disbursement that may constitute financial exploitation of a Specified Adult and the resulting temporary hold; (2) the finding of a reasonable belief that financial exploitation has occurred, is occurring, has been attempted, or will be attempted underlying the decision to place a temporary hold on a disbursement; (3) the name and title of the associated person that authorized the temporary hold on a disbursement; (4) notification(s) to the relevant parties pursuant to paragraph (b)(1)(B) of this Rule; and (5) the internal review of the facts and circumstances pursuant to paragraph (b)(1)(C) of this Rule.

---

9. FINRA Rules: 2210 – Communications with the Public

(a) Definitions

For purposes of this Rule and any interpretation thereof:

(1) "Communications" consist of correspondence, retail communications and institutional communications.

(2) "Correspondence" means any written (including electronic) communication that is distributed or made available to 25 or fewer retail investors within any 30 calendar-day period.

(3) "Institutional communication" means any written (including electronic) communication that is distributed or made available only to institutional investors, but does not include a member's internal communications.

(4) "Institutional investor" means any:

    (A) person described in Rule 4512(c), regardless of whether the person has an account with a member;

    (B) governmental entity or subdivision thereof;

    (C) employee benefit plan, or multiple employee benefit plans offered to employees of the same employer, that meet the requirements of Section 403(b) or Section 457 of the Internal Revenue Code and in the aggregate have at least 100 participants, but does not include any participant of such plans;

    (D) qualified plan, as defined in Section 3(a)(12)(C) of the Exchange Act, or multiple qualified plans offered to employees of the same employer, that in the aggregate have at least 100 participants, but does not include any participant of such plans;

    (E) member or registered person of such a member; and

    (F) person acting solely on behalf of any such institutional investor.

No member may treat a communication as having been distributed to an institutional investor if the member has reason to believe that the communication or any excerpt thereof will be forwarded or made available to any retail investor.

(5) "Retail communication" means any written (including electronic) communication that is distributed or made available to more than 25 retail investors within any 30 calendar-day period.

(6) "Retail investor" means any person other than an institutional investor, regardless of whether the person has an account with a member.

(7) "Covered investment fund research report" has the meaning given that term in paragraph (c)(3) of Securities Act Rule 139b.

(b) Approval, Review and Recordkeeping

    (1) Retail Communications

        (A) An appropriately qualified registered principal of the member must approve each retail communication before the earlier of its use or filing with FINRA's Advertising Regulation Department ("Department").

        (B) The requirements of paragraph (b)(1)(A) may be met by a Supervisory Analyst approved pursuant to Rule 1220(a)(14) with respect to: (i) research reports on debt and equity securities as described in Rules 2241(a)(11) and 2242(a)(3); (ii) retail communications as described in Rules 2241(a)(11)(A) and 2242(a)(3)(A); and (iii) other research communications, provided that the Supervisory Analyst has technical expertise in the particular product area. A Supervisory Analyst may not approve a retail communication that requires a separate registration unless the Supervisory Analyst also has such other registration.

        (C) The requirements of paragraph (b)(1)(A) shall not apply with regard to any retail communication if, at the time that a member intends to publish or distribute it:

            (i) another member has filed it with the Department and has received a letter from the Department stating that it appears to be consistent with applicable standards; and

            (ii) the member using it in reliance upon this subparagraph has not materially altered it and will not use it in a manner that is inconsistent with the conditions of the Department's letter.

        (D) The requirements of paragraph (b)(1)(A) shall not apply with regard to the following retail communications, provided that the member supervises and reviews such communications in the same manner as required for supervising and reviewing correspondence pursuant to Rules 3110(b) and 3110.06 through .09:

            (i) any retail communication that is excepted from the definition of "research report" pursuant to Rule 2241(a)(11)(A) or "debt research report" under Rule 2242(a)(3)(A), unless the communication makes any financial or investment recommendation;

            (ii) any retail communication that is posted on an online interactive electronic forum; and

            (iii) any retail communication that does not make any financial or investment recommendation or otherwise promote a product or service of the member.

(E) Pursuant to the Rule 9600 Series, FINRA may conditionally or unconditionally grant an exemption from paragraph (b)(1)(A) for good cause shown after taking into consideration all relevant factors, to the extent such exemption is consistent with the purposes of the Rule, the protection of investors, and the public interest.

(F) Notwithstanding any other provision of this Rule, an appropriately qualified principal must approve a communication prior to a member filing the communication with the Department.

(2) Correspondence

All correspondence is subject to the supervision and review requirements of Rules 3110(b) and 3110.06 through .09.

(3) Institutional Communications

Each member shall establish written procedures that are appropriate to its business, size, structure, and customers for the review by an appropriately qualified registered principal of institutional communications used by the member and its associated persons. Such procedures must be reasonably designed to ensure that institutional communications comply with applicable standards. When such procedures do not require review of all institutional communications prior to first use or distribution, they must include provision for the education and training of associated persons as to the firm's procedures governing institutional communications, documentation of such education and training, and surveillance and follow-up to ensure that such procedures are implemented and adhered to. Evidence that these supervisory procedures have been implemented and carried out must be maintained and made available to FINRA upon request.

(4) Recordkeeping

(A) Members must maintain all retail communications and institutional communications for the retention period required by SEA Rule 17a-4(b) and in a format and media that comply with SEA Rule 17a-4. The records must include:

(i) a copy of the communication and the dates of first and (if applicable) last use of such communication;

(ii) the name of any registered principal who approved the communication and the date that approval was given;

(iii) in the case of a retail communication or an institutional communication that is not approved prior to first use by a registered principal, the name of the person who prepared or distributed the communication;

(iv) information concerning the source of any statistical table, chart, graph or other illustration used in the communication;

(v) for any retail communication for which principal approval is not required pursuant to paragraph (b)(1)(C), the name of the member that filed the retail communication with the Department, and a copy of the corresponding review letter from the Department; and

(vi) for any retail communication that includes or incorporates a performance ranking or performance comparison of a registered investment company, a copy of the ranking or performance used in the retail communication.

(B) Members must maintain all correspondence in accordance with the record-keeping requirements of Rules 3110.09 and 4511.

(c) Filing Requirements and Review Procedures

(1) Requirement for Certain Members to File Retail Communications Prior to First Use

(A) For a period of one year beginning on the date reflected in the Central Registration Depository (CRD®) system as the date that FINRA membership became effective, the member must file with the Department at least 10 business days prior to first use any retail communication that is published or used in any electronic or other public media, including any generally accessible website, newspaper, magazine or other periodical, radio, television, telephone or audio recording, video display, signs or billboards, motion pictures, or telephone directories (other than routine listings). To the extent any retail communication that is subject to this filing requirement is a free writing prospectus that has been filed with the SEC pursuant to Securities Act Rule 433(d)(1)(ii), the member may file such retail communication within 10 business days of first use rather than at least 10 business days prior to first use.

(B) Notwithstanding the foregoing provisions, if the Department determines that a member has departed from the standards of this Rule, it may require that such member file all communications, or the portion of such member's communications that is related to any specific types or classes of securities or services, with the Department at least 10 business days prior to first use. The Department will notify the member in writing of the types of communications to be filed and the length of time such requirement is to be in effect. Any filing requirement imposed under this subparagraph will take effect 21 calendar days after service of the written notice, during which time the member may request a hearing under Rules 9551 and 9559.

(2) Requirement to File Certain Retail Communications Prior to First Use

At least 10 business days prior to first use or publication (or such shorter period as the Department may allow), a member must file the following retail communications with the Department and withhold them from publication or circulation until any changes specified by the Department have been made:

(A) Retail communications concerning registered investment companies (including mutual funds, exchange-traded funds, variable insurance products, closed-end funds and unit investment trusts) that include or incorporate performance rankings or performance comparisons of the investment company with other investment companies when the ranking or comparison category is not generally published or is the creation, either directly or indirectly, of the investment company, its underwriter or an affiliate. Such filings must include a copy of the data on which the ranking or comparison is based.

(B) Retail communications concerning security futures. The requirements of this paragraph (c)(2)(B) shall not be applicable to:

(i) retail communications concerning security futures that are submitted to another self-regulatory organization having comparable standards pertaining to such retail communications; and

(ii) retail communications in which the only reference to security futures is contained in a listing of the services of a member.

(3) Requirement to File Certain Retail Communications

Within 10 business days of first use or publication, a member must file the following communications with the Department:

(A) Retail communications that promote or recommend a specific registered investment company or family of registered investment companies (including mutual funds, exchange-traded funds, variable insurance products, closed-end funds, and unit investment trusts) not included within the requirements of paragraphs(c)(1) or (c)(2).

(B) Retail communications concerning public direct participation programs (as defined in Rule 2310).

(C) Retail communications concerning collateralized mortgage obligations registered under the Securities Act.

(D) Retail communications concerning any security that is registered under the Securities Act and that is derived from or based on a single security, a basket of securities, an index, a commodity, a debt issuance or a foreign currency, not included within the requirements of paragraphs (c)(1), (c)(2) or subparagraphs (A) through (C) of paragraph (c)(3).

(4) Filing of Television or Video Retail Communications

If a member has filed a draft version or "story board" of a television or video retail communication pursuant to a filing requirement, then the member also must file the final filmed version within 10 business days of first use or broadcast.

(5) Date of First Use and Approval Information

A member must provide with each filing the actual or anticipated date of first use, the name, title and

Central Registration Depository (CRD®) number of the registered principal who approved the retail communication, and the date that the approval was given.

(6) Spot-Check Procedures

In addition to the foregoing requirements, each member's written (including electronic) communications may be subject to a spot-check procedure. Upon written request from the Department, each member must submit the material requested in a spot-check procedure within the time frame specified by the Department.

(7) Exclusions from Filing Requirements

The following communications are excluded from the filing requirements of paragraphs (c)(1) through (c)(4):

(A) Retail communications that previously have been filed with the Department and that are to be used without material change.

(B) Retail communications that are based on templates that were previously filed with the Department the changes to which are limited to:

(i) updates of more recent statistical or other non-narrative information; and

(ii) non-predictive narrative information that describes market events during the period covered by the communication or factual changes in portfolio composition or is sourced from a registered investment company's regulatory documents filed with the SEC.

(C) Retail communications that do not make any financial or investment recommendation or otherwise promote a product or service of the member.

(D) Retail communications that do no more than identify a national securities exchange symbol of the member or identify a security for which the member is a registered market maker.

(E) Retail communications that do no more than identify the member or offer a specific security at a stated price.

(F) Prospectuses, preliminary prospectuses, fund profiles, offering circulars, annual or semi-annual reports and similar documents that have been filed with the SEC or any state in compliance with applicable requirements, similar offering documents concerning securities offerings that are exempt from SEC and state registration requirements, and free writing prospectuses that are exempt from filing with the SEC, except that an investment company prospectus published pursuant to Securities Act Rule 482 and a free writing prospectus that is required to be filed with the SEC pursuant to Securities Act Rule 433(d)(1)(ii) will not be considered a prospectus for purposes of this exclusion.

(G) Retail communications prepared in accordance with Section 2(a)(10)(b) of the Securities Act, as amended, or any rule thereunder, such as Rule 134, and announcements as a matter of record that a member has participated in a private placement, unless the retail communications are related to publicly offered direct participation programs or securities issued by registered investment companies.

(H) Press releases that are made available only to members of the media.

(I) Any reprint or excerpt of any article or report issued by a publisher ("reprint"), provided that:

(i) the publisher is not an affiliate of the member using the reprint or any underwriter or issuer of a security mentioned in the reprint that the member is promoting;

(ii) neither the member using the reprint nor any underwriter or issuer of a security mentioned in the reprint has commissioned the reprinted article or report; and

(iii) the member using the reprint has not materially altered its contents except as necessary to make the reprint consistent with applicable regulatory standards or to correct factual errors.

(J) Correspondence.

(K) Institutional communications.

(L) Communications that refer to types of investments solely as part of a listing of products or services offered by the member.

(M) Retail communications that are posted on an online interactive electronic forum.

(N) Press releases issued by closed-end investment companies that are listed on the New York Stock Exchange (NYSE) pursuant to section 202.06 of the NYSE Listed Company Manual (or any successor provision).

(O) Research reports as defined in Rule 2241 that concern only securities that are listed on a national securities exchange, other than research reports required to be filed with the Commission pursuant to Section 24(b) of the Investment Company Act.

(P) Any covered investment fund research report that is deemed for the purposes of sections 2(a)(10) and 5(c) of the Securities Act not to constitute an offer for sale or offer to sell a security under Securities Act Rule 139b.

(8) Communications Deemed Filed with FINRA

Although the communications described in paragraphs (c)(7)(H) through (K) are excluded from the foregoing filing requirements, investment company communications described in those paragraphs shall be deemed filed with FINRA for purposes of Section 24(b) of the Investment Company Act and Rule 24b-3 thereunder.

(9) Filing Exemptions

(A) Pursuant to the Rule 9600 Series, FINRA may exempt a member from the pre-use filing requirements of paragraph (c)(1)(A) for good cause shown.

(B) Pursuant to the Rule 9600 Series, FINRA may conditionally or unconditionally grant an exemption from paragraph (c)(3) for good cause shown after taking into consideration all relevant factors, to the extent such exemption is consistent with the purposes of the Rule, the protection of investors, and the public interest.

(d) Content Standards

(1) General Standards

(A) All member communications must be based on principles of fair dealing and good faith, must be fair and balanced, and must provide a sound basis for evaluating the facts in regard to any particular security or type of security, industry, or service. No member may omit any material fact or qualification if the omission, in light of the context of the material presented, would cause the communications to be misleading.

(B) No member may make any false, exaggerated, unwarranted, promissory or misleading statement or claim in any communication. No member may publish, circulate or distribute any communication that the member knows or has reason to know contains any untrue statement of a material fact or is otherwise false or misleading.

(C) Information may be placed in a legend or footnote only in the event that such placement would not inhibit an investor's understanding of the communication.

(D) Members must ensure that statements are clear and not misleading within the context in which they are made, and that they provide balanced treatment of risks and potential benefits. Communications must be consistent with the risks of fluctuating prices and the uncertainty of dividends, rates of return and yield inherent to investments.

(E) Members must consider the nature of the audience to which the communication will be directed and must provide details and explanations appropriate to the audience.

(F) Communications may not predict or project performance, imply that past performance will recur or make any exaggerated or unwarranted claim, opinion or forecast; provided, however, that this paragraph (d)(1)(F) does not prohibit:

(i) A hypothetical illustration of mathematical principles, provided that it does not predict or project the performance of an investment or investment strategy;

(ii) An investment analysis tool, or a written report produced by an investment analysis tool, that meets the requirements of Rule 2214; and

(iii) A price target contained in a research report on debt or equity securities, provided that the price target has a reasonable basis, the report discloses the valuation methods used to determine the price target, and the price target is accompanied by disclosure concerning the risks that may impede achievement of the price target.

(2) Comparisons

Any comparison in retail communications between investments or services must disclose all material differences between them, including (as applicable) investment objectives, costs and expenses, liquidity, safety, guarantees or insurance, fluctuation of principal or return, and tax features.

(3) Disclosure of Member's Name

All retail communications and correspondence must:

(A) prominently disclose the name of the member, or the name under which the member's broker-dealer business primarily is conducted as disclosed on the member's Form BD, and may also include a fictional name by which the member is commonly recognized or which is required by any state or jurisdiction;

(B) reflect any relationship between the member and any non-member or individual who is also named; and

(C) if it includes other names, reflect which products or services are being offered by the member.

This paragraph (d)(3) does not apply to so-called "blind" advertisements used to recruit personnel.

(4) Tax Considerations

(A) In retail communications and correspondence, references to tax-free or tax-exempt income must indicate which income taxes apply, or which do not, unless income is free from all applicable taxes. If income from an investment company investing in municipal bonds is subject to state or local income taxes, this fact must be stated, or the illustration must otherwise make it clear that income is free only from federal income tax.

(B) Communications may not characterize income or investment returns as tax-free or exempt from income tax when tax liability is merely postponed or deferred, such as when taxes are payable upon redemption.

(C) A comparative illustration of the mathematical principles of tax-deferred versus taxable compounding must meet the following requirements:

(i) The illustration must depict both the taxable investment and the tax-deferred investment using identical investment amounts and identical assumed gross investment rates of return, which may not exceed 10 percent per annum.

(ii) The illustration must use and identify actual federal income tax rates.

(iii) The illustration may reflect an actual state income tax rate, provided that the communication prominently discloses that the illustration is applicable only to investors that reside in the identified state.

(iv) Tax rates used in an illustration that is intended for a target audience must reasonably reflect its tax bracket or brackets as well as the tax character of capital gains and ordinary income.

(v) If the illustration covers the payout period for an investment, the illustration must reflect the impact of taxes during this period.

(vi) The illustration may not assume an unreasonable period of tax deferral.

(vii) The illustration must disclose, as applicable:

a. the degree of risk in the investment's assumed rate of return, including a statement that the assumed rate of return is not guaranteed;

b. the possible effects of investment losses on the relative advantage of the taxable versus the tax-deferred investments;

c. the extent to which tax rates on capital gains and dividends would affect the taxable investment's return;

d. the fact that ordinary income tax rates will apply to withdrawals from a tax-deferred investment;

e. its underlying assumptions;

       f. the potential impact resulting from federal or state tax penalties (e.g., for early withdrawals or use on non-qualified expenses); and

       g. that an investor should consider his or her current and anticipated investment horizon and income tax bracket when making an investment decision, as the illustration may not reflect these factors.

(5) Disclosure of Fees, Expenses and Standardized Performance

    (A) Retail communications and correspondence that present non-money market fund open-end management investment company performance data as permitted by Securities Act Rule 482 and Rule 34b-1 under the Investment Company Act must disclose:

      (i) the standardized performance information mandated by Securities Act Rule 482 and Rule 34b-1 under the Investment Company Act; and

      (ii) to the extent applicable:

        a. the maximum sales charge imposed on purchases or the maximum deferred sales charge, as stated in the investment company's prospectus current as of the date of distribution or submission for publication of a communication; and

        b. the total annual fund operating expense ratio, gross of any fee waivers or expense reimbursements, as stated in the fee table of the investment company's prospectus described in paragraph (d)(5)(A)(ii)(a).

    (B) All of the information required by paragraph (d)(5)(A) must be set forth prominently, and in any print advertisement, in a prominent text box that contains only the required information and, at the member's option, comparative performance and fee data and disclosures required by Securities Act Rule 482 and Rule 34b-1 under the Investment Company Act.

(6) Testimonials

    (A) If any testimonial in a communication concerns a technical aspect of investing, the person making the testimonial must have the knowledge and experience to form a valid opinion.

    (B) Retail communications or correspondence providing any testimonial concerning the investment advice or investment performance of a member or its products must prominently disclose the following:

      (i) The fact that the testimonial may not be representative of the experience of other customers.

      (ii) The fact that the testimonial is no guarantee of future performance or success.

      (iii) If more than $100 in value is paid for the testimonial, the fact that it is a paid testimonial.

(7) Recommendations

    (A) Retail communications that include a recommendation of securities must have a reasonable basis for the recommendation and must disclose, if applicable, the following:

      (i) that at the time the communication was published or distributed, the member was making a market in the security being recommended, or in the underlying security if the recommended security is an option or security future, or that the member or associated persons will sell to or buy from customers on a principal basis;

      (ii) that the member or any associated person that is directly and materially involved in the preparation of the content of the communication has a financial interest in any of the securities of the issuer whose securities are recommended, and the nature of the financial interest (including, without limitation, whether it consists of any option, right, warrant, future, long or short position), unless the extent of the financial interest is nominal; and

      (iii) that the member was manager or co-manager of a public offering of any securities of the issuer whose securities are recommended within the past 12 months.

    (B) A member must provide, or offer to furnish upon request, available investment information supporting the recommendation. When a member recommends a corporate equity security, the member must provide the price at the time the recommendation is made.

(C) A retail communication or correspondence may not refer, directly or indirectly, to past specific recommendations of the member that were or would have been profitable to any person; provided, however, that a retail communication or correspondence may set out or offer to furnish a list of all recommendations as to the same type, kind, grade or classification of securities made by the member within the immediately preceding period of not less than one year, if the communication or list:

(i) states the name of each such security recommended, the date and nature of each such recommendation (e.g., whether to buy, sell or hold), the market price at that time, the price at which the recommendation was to be acted upon, and the market price of each such security as of the most recent practicable date; and

(ii) contains the following cautionary legend, which must appear prominently within the communication or list: "it should not be assumed that recommendations made in the future will be profitable or will equal the performance of the securities in this list."

(D)(i) This paragraph (d)(7) does not apply to any communication that meets the definition of "research report" for purposes of Rule 2241 or that meets the definition of "debt research report" for purposes of Rule 2242, and includes all of the disclosures required by Rule 2241 or 2242, as applicable.

(ii) Paragraphs (d)(7)(A) and (d)(7)(C) do not apply to any communication that recommends only registered investment companies or variable insurance products; provided, however, that such communications must have a reasonable basis for the recommendation.

(8) BrokerCheck

(A) Each of a member's websites must include a readily apparent reference and hyperlink to BrokerCheck on:

(i) the initial webpage that the member intends to be viewed by retail investors; and

(ii) any other webpage that includes a professional profile of one or more registered persons who conduct business with retail investors.

(B) The requirements of subparagraph (A) shall not apply to:

(i) a member that does not provide products or services to retail investors; and

(ii) a directory or list of registered persons limited to names and contact information.

(9) Prospectuses Filed with the SEC

Prospectuses, preliminary prospectuses, fund profiles and similar documents that have been filed with the SEC and free writing prospectuses that are exempt from filing with the SEC are not subject to the standards of this paragraph (d); provided, however, that the standards of this paragraph (d) shall apply to an investment company prospectus published pursuant to Securities Act Rule 482 and a free writing prospectus that is required to be filed with the SEC pursuant to Securities Act Rule 433(d)(1)(ii).

(e) Limitations on Use of FINRA's Name and Any Other Corporate Name Owned by FINRA

Members may indicate FINRA membership in conformity with Article XV, Section 2 of the FINRA By-Laws in one or more of the following ways:

(1) in any communication that complies with the applicable standards of this Rule and neither states nor implies that FINRA, or any other corporate name or facility owned by FINRA, or any other regulatory organization endorses, indemnifies, or guarantees the member's business practices, selling methods, the class or type of securities offered, or any specific security, and provided further that any reference to the Department's review of a communication is limited to either "Reviewed by FINRA" or "FINRA Reviewed";

(2) in a confirmation statement for an over-the-counter transaction that states: "This transaction has been executed in conformity with the FINRA Uniform Practice Code"; and

(3) on a member's website, provided that the member provides a hyperlink to FINRA's internet home page, www.finra.org, in close proximity to the member's indication of FINRA membership. A member is not required to provide more than one such hyperlink on its website. If the member's website contains more than one indication of FINRA membership, the member may elect to provide any one hyperlink in close proximity to any reference reasonably designed to draw the public's attention to FINRA membership. This

provision also shall apply to an internet website relating to the member's investment banking or securities business maintained by or on behalf of any person associated with a member.

(f) Public Appearances

(1) When sponsoring or participating in a seminar, forum, radio or television interview, or when otherwise engaged in public appearances or speaking activities that are unscripted and do not constitute retail communications, institutional communications or correspondence ("public appearance"), persons associated with members must follow the standards of paragraph (d)(1).

(2) If an associated person recommends a security in a public appearance, the associated person must have a reasonable basis for the recommendation. The associated person also must disclose, as applicable:

  (A) that the associated person has a financial interest in any of the securities of the issuer whose securities are recommended, and the nature of the financial interest (including, without limitation, whether it consists of any option, right, warrant, future, long or short position), unless the extent of the financial interest is nominal; and

  (B) any other actual, material conflict of interest of the associated person or member of which the associated person knows or has reason to know at the time of the public appearance.

(3) Each member shall establish written procedures that are appropriate to its business, size, structure, and customers to supervise its associated persons' public appearances. Such procedures must provide for the education and training of associated persons who make public appearances as to the firm's procedures, documentation of such education and training, and surveillance and follow-up to ensure that such procedures are implemented and adhered to. Evidence that these supervisory procedures have been implemented and carried out must be maintained and made available to FINRA upon request.

(4) Any scripts, slides, handouts or other written (including electronic) materials used in connection with public appearances are considered communications for purposes of this Rule, and members must comply with all applicable provisions of this Rule based on those communications' audience, content and use.

(5) Paragraph (f)(2) does not apply to any public appearance by a research analyst for purposes of Rule 2241 or by a debt research analyst for purposes of Rule 2242 that includes all of the disclosures required by Rule 2241 or 2242, as applicable. Paragraph (f)(2) also does not apply to a recommendation of investment company securities or variable insurance products; provided, however, that the associated person must have a reasonable basis for the recommendation.

(g) Violation of Other Rules

Any violation by a member of any rule of the SEC, the Securities Investor Protection Corporation or the Municipal Securities Rulemaking Board applicable to member communications will be deemed a violation of this Rule 2210.

---

10. FINRA Rules: 2231 – Customer Account Statements

(a) General

Except as otherwise provided by paragraph (b), each general securities member shall, with a frequency of not less than once every calendar quarter, send a statement of account ("account statement") containing a description of any securities positions, money balances, or account activity to each customer whose account had a security position, money balance, or account activity during the period since the last such statement was sent to the customer. In addition, each general securities member shall include in the account statement a statement that advises the customer to report promptly any inaccuracy or discrepancy in that person's account to his or her brokerage firm. (In cases where the customer's account is serviced by both an introducing and clearing firm, each general securities member must include in the advisory a reference that such reports be made to both firms.) Such statement also shall advise the customer that any oral communications should be re-confirmed in writing to further protect the customer's rights, including rights under the Securities Investor Protection Act (SIPA).

(b) Delivery Versus Payment/Receive Versus Payment (DVP/RVP) Accounts

Quarterly account statements need not be sent to a customer pursuant to paragraph (a) of this Rule if:

(1) the customer's account is carried solely for the purpose of execution on a DVP/RVP basis;

(2) all transactions effected for the account are done on a DVP/RVP basis in conformity with Rule 11860;

(3) the account does not show security or money positions at the end of the quarter (provided, however that positions of a temporary nature, such as those arising from fails to receive or deliver, errors, questioned trades, dividend or bond interest entries and other similar transactions, shall not be deemed security or money positions for the purpose of this paragraph (b));

(4) the customer consents to the suspension of such statements in writing. The member must maintain such consents in a manner consistent with Rule 4512 and SEA Rule 17a-4;

(5) the member undertakes to provide any particular statement or statements to the customer promptly upon request; and

(6) the member undertakes to promptly reinstate the delivery of such statements to the customer upon request.

Nothing in this Rule shall be seen to qualify or condition the obligations of a member under SEA Rule 15c3-3(j)(1) concerning quarterly notices of free credit balances on statements.

(c) DPP and Unlisted REIT Securities

A general securities member shall include in a customer account statement a per share estimated value of a direct participation program (DPP) or unlisted real estate investment trust (REIT) security, developed in a manner reasonably designed to ensure that the per share estimated value is reliable, and the disclosures in paragraph (c)(2) as applicable.

(1) For purposes of this paragraph (c), a per share estimated value for a DPP or REIT security will be deemed to have been developed in a manner reasonably designed to ensure that it is reliable if the member uses one of the following per share estimated value methodologies.

(A) Net Investment

At any time before 150 days following the second anniversary of breaking escrow, the member may include a per share estimated value reflecting the "net investment" disclosed in the issuer's most recent periodic or current report ("Issuer Report"). "Net investment" shall be based on the "amount available for investment" percentage in the "Estimated Use of Proceeds" section of the offering prospectus or, where "amount available for investment" is not provided, another equivalent disclosure that reflects the estimated percentage deduction from the aggregate dollar amount of securities registered for sale to the public of sales commissions, dealer manager fees, and estimated issuer offering and organization expenses. When the issuer provides a range of amounts available for investment, the member may use the maximum offering percentage unless the member has reason to believe that such percentage is unreliable, in which case the member shall use the minimum offering percentage.

(B) Appraised Value

At any time, the member may include a per share estimated value reflecting an appraised valuation disclosed in the Issuer Report, which, in the case of DPPs subject to the Investment Company Act ("1940 Act"), shall be consistent with the valuation requirements of the 1940 Act and the rules thereunder or, in the case of all other DPPs and REITs, shall be:

(i) based on valuations of the assets and liabilities of the DPP or REIT performed at least annually, by, or with the material assistance or confirmation of, a third-party valuation expert or service; and

   (ii) derived from a methodology that conforms to standard industry practice.

  (2) Disclosures

   (A) An account statement that provides a "net investment" per share estimated value for a DPP or REIT security under paragraph (c)(1)(A) shall disclose, if applicable, prominently and in proximity to disclosure of distributions and the per share estimated value the following statements: "IMPORTANT—Part of your distribution includes a return of capital. Any distribution that represents a return of capital reduces the estimated per share value shown on your account statement."

   (B) Any account statement that provides a per share estimated value for a DPP or REIT security shall disclose that the DPP or REIT securities are not listed on a national securities exchange, are generally illiquid and that, even if a customer is able to sell the securities, the price received may be less than the per share estimated value provided in the account statement.

(d) Definitions

 For purposes of this Rule, the following terms will have the stated meanings:

  (1) "account activity" includes, but is not limited to, purchases, sales, interest credits or debits, charges or credits, dividend payments, transfer activity, securities receipts or deliveries, and/or journal entries relating to securities or funds in the possession or control of the member.

  (2) a "general securities member" refers to any member that conducts a general securities business and is required to calculate its net capital pursuant to the provisions of SEA Rule 15c3-1(a). Notwithstanding the foregoing definition, a member that does not carry customer accounts and does not hold customer funds or securities is exempt from the provisions of this section.

  (3) "direct participation program" or "direct participation program security" refers to the publicly issued equity securities of a direct participation program as defined in Rule 2310 (including limited liability companies), but does not include securities listed on a national securities exchange or any program registered as a commodity pool with the Commodity Futures Trading Commission.

  (4) "real estate investment trust" or "real estate investment trust security" refers to the publicly issued equity securities of a real estate investment trust as defined in Section 856 of the Internal Revenue Code, but does not include securities listed on a national securities exchange.

  (5) "annual report" means the most recent annual report of the DPP or REIT distributed to investors pursuant Section 13(a) of the Exchange Act.

  (6) a "DVP/RVP account" is an arrangement whereby payment for securities purchased is made to the selling customer's agent and/or delivery of securities sold is made to the buying customer's agent in exchange for payment at time of settlement, usually in the form of cash.

(e) Exemptions

 Pursuant to the Rule 9600 Series, FINRA may exempt any member from the provisions of this Rule for good cause shown.

---

11. FINRA Rules: 2251 – Forwarding of Proxy and Other Issuer-related Materials

(a) A member shall process and forward promptly all information as required by this Rule and applicable SEC rules regarding a security to the beneficial owner (or the beneficial owner's designated investment adviser) if the member carries the account in which the security is held for the beneficial owner and the security is registered in a name other than the name of the beneficial owner.

  (1) Equity Securities

For an equity security, the member, subject to paragraph (e) of this Rule and applicable SEC rules, shall process and forward:

    (A) all proxy material, as provided in paragraph (c) of this Rule, that is furnished to the member by the issuer of the securities or a stockholder of such issuer; and

    (B) all annual reports, information statements and other material sent to stockholders that are furnished to the member by the issuer of the securities.

(2) Debt Securities

For a debt security other than a municipal security, the member, subject to paragraph (e) of this Rule and applicable SEC rules, shall make reasonable efforts to process and forward any communication, document, or collection of documents pertaining to the issue that:

    (A) was prepared by or on behalf of, the issuer, or was prepared by or on behalf of, the trustee of the specific issue of the security; and

    (B) contains material information about such issue including, but not limited to, notices concerning monetary or technical defaults, financial reports, information statements, and material event notices.

(b) No member shall give a proxy to vote stock that is registered in its name, except as required or permitted under the provisions of paragraphs (c) or (d), unless such member is the beneficial owner of stock.

(c)(1) Whenever an issuer or stockholder of such issuer soliciting proxies shall, subject to paragraph (e) of this Rule and applicable SEC rules, timely furnish to a member:

    (A) sufficient copies of all soliciting material that such person is sending to registered holders, and

    (B) satisfactory assurance that he or she will reimburse such member for all out-of-pocket expenses, including reasonable clerical expenses incurred by such member in connection with such solicitation, such member shall process and transmit promptly to each beneficial owner of stock of such issuer (or the beneficial owner's designated investment adviser) that is in its possession or control and registered in a name other than the name of the beneficial owner, all such material furnished. Such material shall include a signed proxy indicating the number of shares held for such beneficial owner and bearing a symbol identifying the proxy with proxy records maintained by the member, and a letter informing the beneficial owner (or the beneficial owner's designated investment adviser) of the time limit and necessity for completing the proxy form and processing and forwarding it to the person soliciting proxies prior to the expiration of the time limit in order for the shares to be represented at the meeting. A member shall furnish a copy of the symbols to the person soliciting the proxies and shall also retain a copy thereof pursuant to the provisions of SEA Rule 17a-4.

(2) Notwithstanding the provisions of paragraph (c)(1) of this Rule, a member may give a proxy to vote any stock pursuant to the rules of any national securities exchange of which it is a member provided that the records of the member clearly indicate the procedure it is following.

(3) This paragraph (c) shall not apply to beneficial owners residing outside of the United States, although members may voluntarily comply with the provisions hereof in respect to such persons if they so desire.

(d)(1) A member may give a proxy to vote any stock registered in its name if such member holds such stock as executor, administrator, guardian, trustee, or in a similar representative or fiduciary capacity with authority to vote.

(2) A member that has in its possession or within its control stock registered in the name of another member and that desires to process and transmit signed proxies pursuant to the provisions of paragraph (c) of this Rule, shall obtain the requisite number of signed proxies from such holder of record.

(3) Notwithstanding the foregoing,

    (A) any member designated by a named Employee Retirement Income Security Act of 1974 ("ERISA") Plan fiduciary as the investment manager of stock held as assets of the ERISA Plan may vote the proxies in accordance with the ERISA Plan fiduciary responsibilities if the ERISA Plan expressly grants discretion to the investment manager to manage, acquire, or dispose of any plan asset and has not expressly reserved the proxy voting right for the named ERISA Plan fiduciary; and

    (B) any designated investment adviser may vote such proxies.

(e)(1) As required in paragraph (a) of this Rule, a member must process and forward promptly the material set forth in paragraph (a)(1), in connection with an equity security, or must make reasonable efforts to process and forward promptly the material set forth in paragraph (a)(2), in connection with a debt security, provided that the member:

    (A) is furnished with sufficient copies of the material (e.g., annual reports, information statements or other material sent to security holders) by the issuer, stockholder, or trustee;

    (B) is requested by the issuer, stockholder, or trustee to process and forward the material to security holders; and,

    (C) receives satisfactory assurance that it will be reimbursed, consistent with Rule 2251.01 and applicable SEC rules, by such issuer, stockholder, or trustee for all out-of-pocket expenses, including reasonable clerical expenses.

    (2) This paragraph (e) shall not apply to beneficial owners residing outside of the United States although members may voluntarily comply with the provisions hereof in respect to such persons if they so desire.

(f) For purposes of this Rule, the term "designated investment adviser" is a person registered under the Investment Advisers Act, or registered as an investment adviser under the laws of a state, who exercises investment discretion pursuant to an advisory contract for the beneficial owner and is designated in writing by the beneficial owner to receive proxy and related materials and vote the proxy, and to receive annual reports and other material sent to security holders.

    (1) For purposes of this Rule, the term "state" shall have the meaning given to such term in Section 202(a)(19) of the Investment Advisers Act (as the same may be amended from time to time).

    (2) The written designation must be signed by the beneficial owner; be addressed to the member; and include the name of the designated investment adviser.

    (3) Members that receive such a written designation from a beneficial owner must ensure that the designated investment adviser is registered with the SEC pursuant to the Investment Advisers Act, or with a state as an investment adviser under the laws of such state, and that the investment adviser is exercising investment discretion over the customer's account pursuant to an advisory contract to vote proxies and/or to receive proxy soliciting material, annual reports and other material. Members must keep records substantiating this information.

    (4) Beneficial owners have an unqualified right at any time to rescind designation of the investment adviser to receive materials and to vote proxies. The rescission must be in writing and submitted to the member.

(g) The Board of Governors for the guidance of members is authorized to establish a suggested rate of reimbursement of members for expenses incurred in connection with processing and transmitting the proxy solicitation to the beneficial owners of the securities pursuant to paragraph (c) of this Rule or in processing and transmitting information statements or other material to the beneficial owners of securities pursuant to paragraph (e) of this Rule.

---

12. FINRA Rules: 2264 – Margin Disclosure Statement

(a) No member shall open a margin account, as specified in Regulation T of the Board of Governors of the Federal Reserve System, for or on behalf of a non-institutional customer, unless, prior to or at the time of opening the account, the member has furnished to the customer, individually, in paper or electronic form, and in a separate document (or contained by itself on a separate page as part of another document), the margin disclosure statement specified in this paragraph (a). In addition, any member that permits non-institutional customers either to open accounts online or to engage in transactions in securities online must post such margin disclosure statement on the member's Web site in a clear and conspicuous manner.

Margin Disclosure Statement

Your brokerage firm is furnishing this document to you to provide some basic facts about purchasing securities on margin, and to alert you to the risks involved with trading securities in a margin account. Before trading stocks in a margin account, you should carefully review the margin agreement provided by your firm. Consult your firm regarding any questions or concerns you may have with your margin accounts.

When you purchase securities, you may pay for the securities in full or you may borrow part of the purchase price from your brokerage firm. If you choose to borrow funds from your firm, you will open a margin account with the firm. The securities purchased are the firm's collateral for the loan to you. If the securities in your account decline in value, so does the value of the collateral supporting your loan, and, as a result, the firm can take action, such as issue a margin call and/or sell securities or other assets in any of your accounts held with the member, in order to maintain the required equity in the account.

It is important that you fully understand the risks involved in trading securities on margin. These risks include the following:

- <u>You can lose more funds than you deposit in the margin account.</u> A decline in the value of securities that are purchased on margin may require you to provide additional funds to the firm that has made the loan to avoid the forced sale of those securities or other securities or assets in your account(s).
- <u>The firm can force the sale of securities or other assets in your account(s).</u> If the equity in your account falls below the maintenance margin requirements, or the firm's higher "house" requirements, the firm can sell the securities or other assets in any of your accounts held at the firm to cover the margin deficiency. You also will be responsible for any short fall in the account after such a sale.
- <u>The firm can sell your securities or other assets without contacting you.</u> Some investors mistakenly believe that a firm must contact them for a margin call to be valid, and that the firm cannot liquidate securities or other assets in their accounts to meet the call unless the firm has contacted them first. This is not the case. Most firms will attempt to notify their customers of margin calls, but they are not required to do so. However, even if a firm has contacted a customer and provided a specific date by which the customer can meet a margin call, the firm can still take necessary steps to protect its financial interests, including immediately selling the securities without notice to the customer.
- <u>You are not entitled to choose which securities or other assets in your account(s) are liquidated or sold to meet a margin call.</u> Because the securities are collateral for the margin loan, the firm has the right to decide which security to sell in order to protect its interests.
- <u>The firm can increase its "house" maintenance margin requirements at any time and is not required to provide you advance written notice.</u> These changes in firm policy often take effect immediately and may result in the issuance of a maintenance margin call. Your failure to satisfy the call may cause the member to liquidate or sell securities in your account(s).
- <u>You are not entitled to an extension of time on a margin call.</u> While an extension of time to meet margin requirements may be available to customers under certain conditions, a customer does not have a right to the extension.

(b) Members shall, with a frequency of not less than once a calendar year, deliver individually, in paper or electronic form, the disclosure statement described in paragraph (a) or the following bolded disclosures to all non-institutional customers with margin accounts:
Securities purchased on margin are the firm's collateral for the loan to you. If the securities in your account

decline in value, so does the value of the collateral supporting your loan, and, as a result, the firm can take action, such as issue a margin call and/or sell securities or other assets in any of your accounts held with the member, in order to maintain the required equity in the account. It is important that you fully understand the risks involved in trading securities on margin. These risks include the following:

- You can lose more funds than you deposit in the margin account.
- The firm can force the sale of securities or other assets in your account(s).
- The firm can sell your securities or other assets without contacting you.
- You are not entitled to choose which securities or other assets in your account(s) are liquidated or sold to meet a margin call.
- The firm can increase its "house" maintenance margin requirements at any time and is not required to provide you advance written notice.
- You are not entitled to an extension of time on a margin call.

The annual disclosure statement required pursuant to this paragraph (b) may be delivered within or as part of other account documentation, and is not required to be provided in a separate document or on a separate page.

(c) In lieu of providing the disclosures specified in paragraphs (a) and (b), a member may provide to the customer and, to the extent required under paragraph (a) post on its Web site, an alternative disclosure statement, provided that the alternative disclosures shall be substantially similar to the disclosures specified in paragraphs (a) and (b).

(d) For purposes of this Rule, the term "non-institutional customer" means a customer that does not qualify as an "institutional account" under Rule 4512(c).

---

13. FINRA Rules: 2232 – Customer Confirmations

(a) A member shall, at or before the completion of any transaction in any security effected for or with an account of a customer, give or send to such customer written notification ("confirmation") in conformity with the requirements of SEA Rule 10b-10.

(b) A confirmation given or sent pursuant to this Rule shall further disclose:
  (1) with respect to any transaction in any NMS stock, as defined in Rule 600 of SEC Regulation NMS, or any security subject to the reporting requirements of the FINRA Rule 6600 Series, other than direct participation programs as defined in FINRA Rule 6420, the settlement date of the transaction; and
  (2) with respect to any transaction in a callable equity security, that:
    (A) the security is a callable equity security; and
    (B) a customer may contact the member for more information concerning the security.

(c) A confirmation shall include the member's mark-up or mark-down for the transaction, to be calculated in compliance with Rule 2121, expressed as a total dollar amount and as a percentage of the prevailing market price if:
  (1) the member is effecting a transaction in a principal capacity in a corporate or agency debt security with a non-institutional customer, and
  (2) the member purchased (sold) the security in one or more offsetting transactions in an aggregate trading size meeting or exceeding the size of such sale to (purchase from) the non-institutional customer on the same trading day as the non-institutional customer transaction. If any such transaction occurs with an affiliate of the member and is not an arms-length transaction, the member is required to "look through"

to the time and terms of the affiliate's transaction with a third party in the security in determining whether the conditions of this paragraph have been met.

(d) A member shall not be required to include the disclosure specified in paragraph (c) above if:

(1) the non-institutional customer transaction was executed by a principal trading desk that is functionally separate from the principal trading desk within the same member that executed the member purchase (in the case of a sale to a customer) or member sale (in the case of a purchase from a customer) of the security, and the member had in place policies and procedures reasonably designed to ensure that the functionally separate principal trading desk through which the member purchase or member sale was executed had no knowledge of the customer transaction; or

(2) the member acquired the security in a fixed-price offering and sold the security to non-institutional customers at the fixed price offering price on the day the securities were acquired.

(e) For all transactions in corporate or agency debt securities with non-institutional customers, the member shall also provide on the confirmation: (1) a reference, and hyperlink if the confirmation is electronic, to a web page hosted by FINRA that contains Trade Reporting And Compliance Engine (TRACE) publicly available trading data for the specific security that was traded, in a format specified by FINRA, along with a brief description of the type of information available on that page; and (2) the execution time of the customer transaction, expressed to the second.

(f) Definitions

For purposes of this Rule, the term:

(1) "agency debt security" shall have the same meaning as in Rule 6710(l);

(2) "corporate debt security" shall mean a debt security that is United States ("U.S.") dollar-denominated and issued by a U.S. or foreign private issuer and, if a "restricted security" as defined in Securities Act Rule 144(a)(3), sold pursuant to Securities Act Rule 144A, but does not include a Money Market Instrument as defined in Rule 6710(o) or an Asset-Backed Security as defined in Rule 6710(cc);

(3) "arms-length transaction" shall mean a transaction that was conducted through a competitive process in which non-affiliate firms could also participate, and where the affiliate relationship did not influence the price paid or proceeds received by the member; and

(4) "non-institutional customer" shall mean a customer with an account that is not an institutional account, as defined in Rule 4512(c).

----

14. FINRA Rules: 3150 – Holding of Customer Mail

(a) A member may hold mail for a customer who will not be receiving mail at his or her usual address, provided that:

(1) the member receives written instructions from the customer that include the time period during which the member is requested to hold the customer's mail. If the requested time period included in the instructions is longer than three consecutive months (including any aggregation of time periods from prior requests), the customer's instructions must include an acceptable reason for the request (e.g., safety or security concerns). Convenience is not an acceptable reason for holding mail longer than three months;

(2) the member:

(A) informs the customer in writing of any alternate methods, such as email or access through the member's website, that the customer may use to receive or monitor account activity and information; and

(B) obtains the customer's confirmation of the receipt of such information; and

(3) the member verifies at reasonable intervals that the customer's instructions still apply.

(b) During the time that a member is holding mail for a customer, the member must be able to communicate with the customer in a timely manner to provide important account information (e.g., privacy notices, the SIPC information disclosures required by Rule 2266), as necessary.

(c) A member holding a customer's mail pursuant to this Rule must take actions reasonably designed to ensure that the customer's mail is not tampered with, held without the customer's consent, or used by an associated person of the member in any manner that would violate FINRA rules or the federal securities laws.

---

15. FINRA Rules: 3210 – Accounts at Other Broker-Dealers and Financial Institutions

(a) No person associated with a member ("employer member") shall, without the prior written consent of the member, open or otherwise establish at a member other than the employer member ("executing member"), or at any other financial institution, any account in which securities transactions can be effected and in which the associated person has a beneficial interest.

(b) Any associated person, prior to opening or otherwise establishing an account subject to this Rule, shall notify in writing the executing member, or other financial institution, of his or her association with the employer member.

(c) An executing member shall, upon written request by an employer member, transmit duplicate copies of confirmations and statements, or the transactional data contained therein, with respect to an account subject to this Rule.

---

16. FINRA Rules: 3230 – Telemarketing

(a) General Telemarketing Requirements

No member or person associated with a member shall initiate any outbound telephone call to:

(1) Time of Day Restriction

Any residence of a person before the hour of 8 a.m. or after 9 p.m. (local time at the called party's location), unless

(A) the member has an established business relationship with the person pursuant to paragraph (m)(12)(A),

(B) the member has received that person's prior express invitation or permission, or

(C) the person called is a broker or dealer;

(2) Firm-Specific Do-Not-Call List

Any person that previously has stated that he or she does not wish to receive an outbound telephone call made by or on behalf of the member; or

(3) National Do-Not-Call List

Any person who has registered his or her telephone number on the Federal Trade Commission's national do-not-call registry.

(b) National Do-Not-Call List Exceptions

A member making outbound telephone calls will not be liable for violating paragraph (a)(3) if:

(1) Established Business Relationship Exception

The member has an established business relationship with the recipient of the call. A person's request to be placed on the firm-specific do-not-call list terminates the established business relationship exception to that national do-not-call list provision for that member even if the person continues to do business with the member;

(2) Prior Express Written Consent Exception

The member has obtained the person's prior express invitation or permission. Such permission must be evidenced by a signed, written agreement (which may be obtained electronically under the E-Sign Act) between the person and member which states that the person agrees to be contacted by the member and includes the telephone number to which the calls may be placed; or

(3) Personal Relationship Exception

The associated person making the call has a personal relationship with the recipient of the call.

(c) Safe Harbor Provision

A member or person associated with a member making outbound telephone calls will not be liable for violating paragraph (a)(3) if the member or person associated with a member demonstrates that the violation is the result of an error and that as part of the member's routine business practice, it meets the following standards:

(1) Written procedures. The member has established and implemented written procedures to comply with the national do-not-call rules;

(2) Training of personnel. The member has trained its personnel, and any entity assisting in its compliance, in procedures established pursuant to the national do-not-call rules;

(3) Recording. The member has maintained and recorded a list of telephone numbers that it may not contact; and

(4) Accessing the national do-not-call database. The member uses a process to prevent outbound telephone calls to any telephone number on any list established pursuant to the do-not-call rules, employing a version of the national do-not-call registry obtained from the administrator of the registry no more than 31 days prior to the date any call is made, and maintains records documenting this process.

(d) Procedures

Prior to engaging in telemarketing, a member must institute procedures to comply with paragraph (a). Such procedures must meet the following minimum standards:

(1) Written policy. Members must have a written policy for maintaining a do-not-call list.

(2) Training of personnel engaged in telemarketing. Personnel engaged in any aspect of telemarketing must be informed and trained in the existence and use of the do-not-call list.

(3) Recording, disclosure of do-not-call requests. If a member receives a request from a person not to receive calls from that member, the member must record the request and place the person's name, if provided, and telephone number on the firm's do-not-call list at the time the request is made. Members must honor a person's do-not-call request within a reasonable time from the date such request is made. This period may not exceed 30 days from the date of such request. If such requests are recorded or maintained by a party other than the member on whose behalf the outbound telephone call is made, the member on whose behalf the outbound telephone call is made will be liable for any failures to honor the do-not-call request.

(4) Identification of sellers and telemarketers. A member or person associated with a member making an outbound telephone call must provide the called party with the name of the individual caller, the name of the member, an address or telephone number at which the member may be contacted, and that the

purpose of the call is to solicit the purchase of securities or related service. The telephone number provided may not be a 900 number or any other number for which charges exceed local or long distance transmission charges.

(5) Affiliated persons or entities. In the absence of a specific request by the person to the contrary, a person's do-not-call request shall apply to the member making the call, and will not apply to affiliated entities unless the consumer reasonably would expect them to be included given the identification of the caller and the product being advertised.

(6) Maintenance of do-not-call lists. A member making outbound telephone calls must maintain a record of a person's request not to receive further calls.

(e) Wireless Communications

The provisions set forth in this Rule are applicable to members and persons associated with a member making outbound telephone calls to wireless telephone numbers.

(f) Outsourcing Telemarketing

If a member uses another appropriately registered or licensed entity or person to perform telemarketing services on its behalf, the member remains responsible for ensuring compliance with all provisions contained in this Rule.

(g) Caller Identification Information

(1) Any member that engages in telemarketing, as defined in paragraph (m)(20) of this Rule, must transmit or cause to be transmitted the telephone number, and, when made available by the member's telephone carrier, the name of the member, to any caller identification service in use by a recipient of an outbound telephone call.

(2) The telephone number so provided must permit any person to make a do-not-call request during regular business hours.

(3) Any member that engages in telemarketing, as defined in paragraph (m)(20) of this Rule, is prohibited from blocking the transmission of caller identification information.

(h) Unencrypted Consumer Account Numbers

No member or person associated with a member shall disclose or receive, for consideration, unencrypted consumer account numbers for use in telemarketing. The term "unencrypted" means not only complete, visible account numbers, whether provided in lists or singly, but also encrypted information with a key to its decryption. This paragraph shall not apply to the disclosure or receipt of a customer's billing information to process a payment pursuant to a telemarketing transaction.

(i) Submission of Billing Information

For any telemarketing transaction, a member or person associated with a member must obtain the express informed consent of the person to be charged and to be charged using the identified account.

(1) In any telemarketing transaction involving preacquired account information and a free-to-pay conversion feature, the member or person associated with a member must:

(A) obtain from the customer, at a minimum, the last four digits of the account number to be charged;

(B) obtain from the customer an express agreement to be charged and to be charged using the account number pursuant to paragraph (i)(1)(A); and

(C) make and maintain an audio recording of the entire telemarketing transaction.

(2) In any other telemarketing transaction involving preacquired account information not described in paragraph (i)(1), the member or person associated with a member must:

(A) identify the account to be charged with sufficient specificity for the customer to understand what account will be charged; and

(B) obtain from the customer an express agreement to be charged and to be charged using the account number identified pursuant to paragraph (i)(2)(A).

(j) Abandoned Calls

(1) No member or person associated with a member shall "abandon" any outbound telephone call. An out-

bound telephone call is "abandoned" if a person answers it and the call is not connected to a person associated with a member within two seconds of the person's completed greeting.

(2) A member or person associated with a member shall not be liable for violating paragraph (j)(1) if:

   (A) the member or person associated with a member employs technology that ensures abandonment of no more than three percent of all outbound telephone calls answered by a person, measured over the duration of a single calling campaign, if less than 30 days, or separately over each successive 30-day period or portion thereof that the campaign continues;

   (B) the member or person associated with a member, for each outbound telephone call placed, allows the telephone to ring for at least 15 seconds or four rings before disconnecting an unanswered call;

   (C) whenever a person associated with a member is not available to speak with the person answering the outbound telephone call within two seconds after the person's completed greeting, the member or person associated with a member promptly plays a recorded message that states the name and telephone number of the member or person associated with the member on whose behalf the call was placed; and

   (D) the member retains records establishing compliance with paragraph (j)(2).

(k) Prerecorded Messages

   (1) No member or person associated with a member shall initiate any outbound telephone call that delivers a prerecorded message other than a prerecorded message permitted for compliance with the call abandonment safe harbor in paragraph (j)(2)(C) unless:

      (A) the member has obtained from the recipient of the call an express agreement, in writing, that:

         (i) the member obtained only after a clear and conspicuous disclosure that the purpose of the agreement is to authorize the member to place prerecorded calls to such person;

         (ii) the member obtained without requiring, directly or indirectly, that the agreement be executed as a condition of opening an account or purchasing any good or service;

         (iii) evidences the willingness of the recipient of the call to receive calls that deliver prerecorded messages by or on behalf of a specific member; and

         (iv) includes such person's telephone number and signature (which may be obtained electronically under the E-Sign Act);

      (B) the member or person associated with a member allows the telephone to ring for at least 15 seconds or four rings before disconnecting an unanswered call; and within two seconds after the completed greeting of the person called, plays a prerecorded message that promptly provides the disclosures in paragraph (d)(4), followed immediately by a disclosure of one or both of the following:

         (i) for a call that could be answered by a person, that the person called can use an automated interactive voice and/or keypress-activated opt-out mechanism to assert a firm-specific do-not-call request pursuant to the member's procedures instituted under paragraph (d)(3) at any time during the message. The mechanism must:

            a. automatically add the number called to the member's firm-specific do-not-call list;

            b. once invoked, immediately disconnect the call; and

            c. be available for use at any time during the message;

         (ii) for a call that could be answered by an answering machine or voicemail service, that the person called can use a toll-free telephone number to assert a firm-specific do-not-call request pursuant to the member's procedures instituted under paragraph (d)(3). The number provided must connect directly to an automated interactive voice or keypress-activated opt-out mechanism that:

            a. automatically adds the number called to the member's firm-specific do-not-call list;

            b. immediately thereafter disconnects the call; and

            c. is accessible at any time throughout the duration of the telemarketing campaign; and

      (C) the member complies with all requirements of this Rule and other applicable federal and state laws.

   (2) Any call that complies with all applicable requirements of paragraph (k) shall not be deemed to violate paragraph (j).

(l) Credit Card Laundering.

Except as expressly permitted by the applicable credit card system, no member or person associated with a member shall:.

(1) present to or deposit into, the credit card system for payment, a credit card sales draft generated by a telemarketing transaction that is not the result of a telemarketing credit card transaction between the cardholder and the member;.

(2) employ, solicit, or otherwise cause a merchant, or an employee, representative or agent of the merchant, to present to or to deposit into the credit card system for payment, a credit card sales draft generated by a telemarketing transaction that is not the result of a telemarketing credit card transaction between the cardholder and the merchant; or.

(3) obtain access to the credit card system through the use of a business relationship or an affiliation with a merchant, when access is not authorized by the merchant agreement or applicable credit card system.

(m) Definitions

For purposes of this Rule:

(1) The term "account activity" shall include, but not be limited to, purchases, sales, interest credits or debits, charges or credits, dividend payments, transfer activity, securities receipts or deliveries, and/or journal entries relating to securities or funds in the possession or control of the member.

(2) The term "acquirer" means a business organization, financial institution, or an agent of a business organization or financial institution that has authority from an organization that operates or licenses a credit card system to authorize merchants to accept, transmit, or process payment by credit card through the credit card system for money, goods or services, or anything else of value.

(3) The term "billing information" means any data that enables any person to access a customer's or donor's account, for example a credit or debit card number, a brokerage, checking, or savings account number, or a mortgage loan account number.

(4) The term "broker-dealer of record" refers to the broker-dealer identified on a customer's account application for accounts held directly at a mutual fund or variable insurance product issuer.

(5) The term "caller identification service" means a service that allows a telephone subscriber to have the telephone number, and, where available, name of the calling party transmitted contemporaneously with the telephone call, and displayed on a device in or connected to the subscriber's telephone.

(6) The term "cardholder" means a person to whom a credit card is issued or who is authorized to use a credit card on behalf of or in addition to the person to whom the credit card is issued.

(7) The term "credit" means the right granted by a creditor to a debtor to defer payment of debt or to incur debt and defer its payment.

(8) The term "credit card" means any card, plate, coupon book, or other credit device existing for the purpose of obtaining money, property, labor, or services on credit.

(9) The term "credit card sales draft" means any record or evidence of a credit card transaction.

(10) The term "credit card system" means any method or procedure used to process credit card transactions involving credit cards issued or licensed by the operator of that system.

(11) The term "customer" means any person who is or may be required to pay for goods or services offered through telemarketing.

(12) The term "established business relationship" means a relationship between a member and a person if:

(A) the person has made a financial transaction or has a security position, a money balance, or account activity with the member or at a clearing firm that provides clearing services to such member within the previous 18 months immediately preceding the date of the telemarketing call;

(B) the member is the broker-dealer of record for an account of the person within the previous 18 months immediately preceding the date of the telemarketing call; or

(C) the person has contacted the member to inquire about a product or service offered by the member within the previous three months immediately preceding the date of the telemarketing call.

A person's established business relationship with a member does not extend to the member's affiliated entities unless the person would reasonably expect them to be included. Similarly, a person's established business relationship with a member's affiliate does not extend to the member unless the person would reasonably expect the member to be included.

(13) The term "free-to-pay conversion" means, in an offer or agreement to sell or provide any goods or services, a provision under which a customer receives a product or service for free for an initial period and will incur an obligation to pay for the product or service if he or she does not take affirmative action to cancel before the end of that period.

(14) The term "merchant" means a person who is authorized under a written contract with an acquirer to honor or accept credit cards, or to transmit or process for payment credit card payments, for the purchase of goods or services or a charitable contribution. A "charitable contribution" means any donation or gift of money or any other thing of value, for example a transfer to a pooled income fund.

(15) The term "merchant agreement" means a written contract between a merchant and an acquirer to honor or accept credit cards, or to transmit or process for payment credit card payments, for the purchase of goods or services or a charitable contribution.

(16) The term "outbound telephone call" means a telephone call initiated by a telemarketer to induce the purchase of goods or services or to solicit a charitable contribution from a donor. A "donor" means any person solicited to make a charitable contribution.

(17) The term "person" means any individual, group, unincorporated association, limited or general partnership, corporation, or other business entity.

(18) The term "personal relationship" means any family member, friend, or acquaintance of the person associated with a member making an outbound telephone call.

(19) The term "preacquired account information" means any information that enables a seller or telemarketer to cause a charge to be placed against a customer's or donor's account without obtaining the account number directly from the customer or donor during the telemarketing transaction pursuant to which the account will be charged.

(20) The term "telemarketing" means consisting of or relating to a plan, program, or campaign involving at least one outbound telephone call, for example cold-calling. The term does not include the solicitation of sales through the mailing of written marketing materials, when the person making the solicitation does not solicit customers by telephone but only receives calls initiated by customers in response to the marketing materials and during those calls takes orders only without further solicitation. For purposes of the previous sentence, the term "further solicitation" does not include providing the customer with information about, or attempting to sell, anything promoted in the same marketing materials that prompted the customer's call.

---

17. FINRA Rules: 3240 – Borrowing from or Lending to Customers

(a) Permissible Lending Arrangements; Conditions

No person associated with a member in any registered capacity may borrow money from or lend money to any customer of such person unless:

(1) the member has written procedures allowing the borrowing and lending of money between such registered persons and customers of the member;

(2) the borrowing or lending arrangement meets one of the following conditions:

(A) the customer is a member of such person's immediate family;

(B) the customer (i) is a financial institution regularly engaged in the business of providing credit, financing, or loans, or other entity or person that regularly arranges or extends credit in the ordinary course of business and (ii) is acting in the course of such business;

(C) the customer and the registered person are both registered persons of the same member;

(D) the lending arrangement is based on a personal relationship with the customer, such that the loan would not have been solicited, offered, or given had the customer and the registered person not maintained a relationship outside of the broker-customer relationship; or

(E) the lending arrangement is based on a business relationship outside of the broker-customer relationship; and

(3) the requirements of paragraph (b) of this Rule are satisfied.

(b) Notification and Approval

(1) The registered person shall notify the member of the borrowing or lending arrangements described in paragraphs (a)(2)(C), (D), and (E) above prior to entering into such arrangements and the member shall pre-approve in writing such arrangements. The registered person shall also notify the member and the member shall pre-approve in writing any modifications to such arrangements, including any extension of the duration of such arrangements.

(2) With respect to the borrowing or lending arrangements described in paragraph (a)(2)(A) above, a member's written procedures may indicate that registered persons are not required to notify the member or receive member approval either prior to or subsequent to entering into such borrowing or lending arrangements.

(3) With respect to the borrowing or lending arrangements described in paragraph (a)(2)(B) above, a member's written procedures may indicate that registered persons are not required to notify the member or receive member approval either prior to or subsequent to entering into such borrowing or lending arrangements, provided that, the loan has been made on commercial terms that the customer generally makes available to members of the general public similarly situated as to need, purpose and creditworthiness. For purposes of this subparagraph, the member may rely on the registered person's representation that the terms of the loan meet the above-described standards.

(c) Definition of Immediate Family

The term "immediate family" means parents, grandparents, mother-in-law or father-in-law, husband or wife, brother or sister, brother-in-law or sister-in-law, son-in law or daughter-in-law, children, grandchildren, cousin, aunt or uncle, or niece or nephew, and any other person whom the registered person supports, directly or indirectly, to a material extent.

---

18. FINRA Rules: 3250 – Designation of Accounts

No member shall carry an account on its books in the name of a person other than that of the customer, except that an account may be designated by a number or symbol, provided the member has on file a written statement signed by the customer attesting the ownership of such account.

---

19. FINRA Rules: 3260 – Discretionary Accounts

(a) Excessive Transactions

No member shall effect with or for any customer's account in respect to which such member or his agent or employee is vested with any discretionary power any transactions of purchase or sale which are excessive in size or frequency in view of the financial resources and character of such account.

(b) Authorization and Acceptance of Account

No member or registered representative shall exercise any discretionary power in a customer's account unless such customer has given prior written authorization to a stated individual or individuals and the account has been accepted by the member, as evidenced in writing by the member or the partner, officer or manager, duly designated by the member, in accordance with Rule 3110.

(c) Approval and Review of Transactions

The member or the person duly designated shall approve promptly in writing each discretionary order entered and shall review all discretionary accounts at frequent intervals in order to detect and prevent transactions which are excessive in size or frequency in view of the financial resources and character of the account.

(d) Exceptions

This Rule shall not apply to:

(1) discretion as to the price at which or the time when an order given by a customer for the purchase or sale of a definite amount of a specified security shall be executed, except that the authority to exercise time and price discretion will be considered to be in effect only until the end of the business day on which the customer granted such discretion, absent a specific, written contrary indication signed and dated by the customer. This limitation shall not apply to time and price discretion exercised in an institutional account, as defined in Rule 4512(c), pursuant to valid Good-Till-Cancelled instructions issued on a "not-held" basis. Any exercise of time and price discretion must be reflected on the order ticket;

(2) bulk exchanges at net asset value of money market mutual funds ("funds") utilizing negative response letters provided:

(A) The bulk exchange is limited to situations involving mergers and acquisitions of funds, changes of clearing members and exchanges of funds used in sweep accounts;

(B) The negative response letter contains a tabular comparison of the nature and amount of the fees charged by each fund;

(C) The negative response letter contains a comparative description of the investment objectives of each fund and a prospectus of the fund to be purchased; and

(D) The negative response feature will not be activated until at least 30 days after the date on which the letter was mailed.

---

20. FINRA Rules: 3310 – Anti-money Laundering Compliance Program

Each member shall develop and implement a written anti-money laundering program reasonably designed to achieve and monitor the member's compliance with the requirements of the Bank Secrecy Act (31 U.S.C. 5311, *et seq.*), and the implementing regulations promulgated thereunder by the Department of the Treasury. Each member's anti-money laundering program must be approved, in writing, by a member of senior management. The anti-money laundering programs required by this Rule shall, at a minimum,

(a) Establish and implement policies and procedures that can be reasonably expected to detect and cause the reporting of transactions required under 31 U.S.C. 5318(g) and the implementing regulations thereunder;

(b) Establish and implement policies, procedures, and internal controls reasonably designed to achieve compliance with the Bank Secrecy Act and the implementing regulations thereunder;

(c) Provide for annual (on a calendar-year basis) independent testing for compliance to be conducted by member personnel or by a qualified outside party, unless the member does not execute transactions for customers or otherwise hold customer accounts or act as an introducing broker with respect to customer accounts (e.g., engages solely in proprietary trading or conducts business only with other broker-dealers), in which case such "independent testing" is required every two years (on a calendar-year basis);

(d) Designate and identify to FINRA (by name, title, mailing address, e-mail address, telephone number, and facsimile number) an individual or individuals responsible for implementing and monitoring the day-to-day operations and internal controls of the program (such individual or individuals must be an associated person of the member) and provide prompt notification to FINRA regarding any change in such designation(s);

(e) Provide ongoing training for appropriate personnel; and

(f) Include appropriate risk-based procedures for conducting ongoing customer due diligence, to include, but not be limited to:

    (i) Understanding the nature and purpose of customer relationships for the purpose of developing a customer risk profile; and

    (ii) Conducting ongoing monitoring to identify and report suspicious transactions and, on a risk basis, to maintain and update customer information. For purposes of paragraph (f)(ii), customer information shall include information regarding the beneficial owners of legal entity customers (as defined in 31 CFR 1010.230(e)).

---

21. FINRA Rules: 4210 – Margin Requirements

(a) Definitions

    For purposes of this Rule, the following terms shall have the meanings specified below:

    (1) The term "basket" shall mean a group of stocks that FINRA or any national securities exchange designates as eligible for execution in a single trade through its trading facilities and that consists of stocks whose inclusion and relative representation in the group are determined by the inclusion and relative representation of their current market prices in a widely disseminated stock index reflecting the stock market as a whole.

    (2) The term "current market value" means the total cost or net proceeds of a security on the day it was purchased or sold or at any other time the preceding business day's closing price as shown by any regularly published reporting or quotation service except for security futures contracts (see paragraph (f)(10)(C)(ii)). If there is no closing price, a member may use a reasonable estimate of the market value of the security as of the close of business on the preceding business day.

    (3) The term "customer" means any person for whom securities are purchased or sold or to whom securities are purchased or sold whether on a regular way, when issued, delayed or future delivery basis. It will also include any person for whom securities are held or carried and to or for whom a member extends, arranges or maintains any credit. The term will not include the following: (A) a broker or dealer from whom a security has been purchased or to whom a security has been sold for the account of the member or its customers, or (B) an "exempted borrower" as defined by Regulation T of the Board of Governors of the

Federal Reserve System ("Regulation T"), except for the proprietary account of a broker-dealer carried by a member pursuant to paragraph (e)(6) of this Rule.

(4) The term "designated account" means the account of:

(A) a bank (as defined in Section 3(a)(6) of the Exchange Act),

(B) a savings association (as defined in Section 3(b) of the Federal Deposit Insurance Act), the deposits of which are insured by the Federal Deposit Insurance Corporation,

(C) an insurance company (as defined in Section 2(a)(17) of the Investment Company Act),

(D) an investment company registered with the SEC under the Investment Company Act,

(E) a state or political subdivision thereof, or

(F) a pension or profit sharing plan subject to the Employee Retirement Income Security Act (ERISA) or of an agency of the United States or of a state or a political subdivision thereof.

(5) The term "equity" means the customer's ownership interest in the account, computed by adding the current market value of all securities "long" and the amount of any credit balance and subtracting the current market value of all securities "short" and the amount of any debit balance. Any variation settlement received or paid on a security futures contract shall be considered a credit or debit to the account for purposes of equity.

(6) The term "exempted security" or "exempted securities" has the meaning as in Section 3(a)(12) of the Exchange Act.

(7) The term "margin" means the amount of equity to be maintained on a security position held or carried in an account.

(8) The term "person" has the meaning as in Section 3(a)(9) of the Exchange Act.

(9) The term "highly rated foreign sovereign debt securities" means any debt securities (including major foreign sovereign debt securities) issued or guaranteed by the government of a foreign country, its provinces, state or cities, or a supranational entity, if at the time of the extension of credit the issue, the issuer or guarantor, or any other outstanding obligation of the issuer or guarantor ranked junior to or on a parity with the issue or the guarantee is assigned a rating (implicitly or explicitly) in one of the top two rating categories by at least one nationally recognized statistical rating organization.

(10) The term "investment grade debt securities" means any debt securities (including those issued by the government of a foreign country, its provinces, states or cities, or a supranational entity), if at the time of the extension of credit the issue, the issuer or guarantor, or any other outstanding obligation of the issuer or guarantor ranked junior to or on a parity with the issue or the guarantee is assigned a rating (implicitly or explicitly) in one of the top four rating categories by at least one nationally recognized statistical rating organization.

(11) The term "major foreign sovereign debt" means any debt securities issued or guaranteed by the government of a foreign country or a supranational entity, if at the time of the extension of credit the issue, the issuer or guarantor, or any other outstanding obligation of the issuer or guarantor ranked junior to or on a parity with the issue or the guarantee is assigned a rating (implicitly or explicitly) in the top rating category by at least one nationally recognized statistical rating organization.

(12) The term "mortgage related securities" means securities falling within the definition in Section 3(a)(41) of the Exchange Act.

(13) The term "exempt account" means:

(A) a member, non-member broker-dealer registered as a broker or dealer under the Exchange Act, a "designated account," or

(B) any person that:

(i) has a net worth of at least $45 million and financial assets of at least $40 million for purposes of paragraphs (e)(2)(F) and (e)(2)(G), and

(ii) either:

a. has securities registered pursuant to Section 12 of the Exchange Act, has been subject to the reporting requirements of Section 13 of the Exchange Act for a period of at least 90 days and has filed all the reports required to be filed thereunder during the preceding 12 months (or such shorter period as it was required to file such reports), or

b. has securities registered pursuant to the Securities Act, has been subject to the reporting requirements of Section 15(d) of the Exchange Act for a period of at least 90 days and has filed all the reports required to be filed thereunder during the preceding 12 months (or such shorter period as it was required to file such reports), or

c. if such person is not subject to Section 13 or 15(d) of the Exchange Act, is a person with respect to which there is publicly available the information specified in paragraphs (a)(5)(i) through (xiv), inclusive, of SEA Rule 15c2-11, or

d. furnishes information to the SEC as required by SEA Rule 12g3-2(b), or

e. makes available to the member such current information regarding such person's ownership, business, operations and financial condition (including such person's current audited statement of financial condition, statement of income and statement of changes in stockholder's equity or comparable financial reports), as reasonably believed by the member to be accurate, sufficient for the purposes of performing a risk analysis in respect of such person.

(14) The term "non-equity securities" means any securities other than equity securities as defined in Section 3(a)(11) of the Exchange Act.

(15) The term "listed non-equity securities" means any non-equity securities that: (A) are listed on a national securities exchange; or (B) have unlisted trading privileges on a national securities exchange.

(16) The term "other marginable non-equity securities" means:

(A) Any debt securities not traded on a national securities exchange meeting all of the following requirements:

(i) At the time of the original issue, a principal amount of not less than $25 million of the issue was outstanding;

(ii) The issue was registered under Section 5 of the Securities Act and the issuer either files periodic reports pursuant to Section 13(a) or 15(d) of the Exchange Act or is an insurance company which meets all of the conditions specified in Section 12(g)(2)(G) of the Exchange Act; and

(iii) At the time of the extensions of credit, the creditor has a reasonable basis for believing that the issuer is not in default on interest or principal payments; or

(B) Any private pass-through securities (not guaranteed by any agency of the U.S. government) meeting all of the following requirements:

(i) An aggregate principal amount of not less than $25 million (which may be issued in series) was issued pursuant to a registration statement filed with the SEC under Section 5 of the Securities Act;

(ii) Current reports relating to the issue have been filed with the SEC; and

(iii) At the time of the credit extension, the creditor has a reasonable basis for believing that mortgage interest, principal payments and other distributions are being passed through as required and that the servicing agent is meeting its material obligations under the terms of the offering.

(b) Initial Margin

For the purpose of effecting new securities transactions and commitments, the customer shall be required to deposit margin in cash and/or securities in the account which shall be at least the greater of:

(1) the amount specified in Regulation T, or Rules 400 through 406 of SEC Customer Margin Requirements for Security Futures, or Rules 41.42 through 41.49 under the Commodity Exchange Act ("CEA"); or

(2) the amount specified in paragraph (c) of this Rule; or

(3) such greater amount as FINRA may from time to time require for specific securities; or

(4) equity of at least $2,000 except that cash need not be deposited in excess of the cost of any security purchased (this equity and cost of purchase provision shall not apply to "when distributed" securities in a cash account). The minimum equity requirement for a "pattern day trader" is $25,000 pursuant to paragraph (f)(8)(B)(iv)a. of this Rule.

Withdrawals of cash or securities may be made from any account which has a debit balance, "short" position or commitments, provided it is in compliance with Regulation T and Rules 400 through 406 of SEC Customer Margin Requirements for Security Futures and Rules 41.42 through 41.49 under the CEA, and after such withdrawal the equity in the account is at least the greater of $2,000 ($25,000 in the case of a "pattern day trader") or an amount sufficient to meet the maintenance margin requirements of this Rule.

(c) Maintenance Margin

The margin which must be maintained in all accounts of customers, except as set forth in paragraph (e), (f) or (g) and for cash accounts subject to other provisions of this Rule, shall be as follows:

(1) 25 percent of the current market value of all margin securities, as defined in Section 220.2 of Regulation T, except for security futures contracts, "long" in the account.

(2) $2.50 per share or 100 percent of the current market value, whichever amount is greater, of each stock "short" in the account selling at less than $5.00 per share; plus

(3) $5.00 per share or 30 percent of the current market value, whichever amount is greater, of each stock "short" in the account selling at $5.00 per share or above; plus

(4) 5 percent of the principal amount or 30 percent of the current market value, whichever amount is greater, of each bond "short" in the account.

(5) The minimum maintenance margin levels for security futures contracts, "long" and "short", shall be 20 percent of the current market value of such contract. (See paragraph (f)(10) of this Rule for other provisions pertaining to security futures contracts.)

(6) 100 percent of the current market value for each non-margin eligible equity security held "long" in the account.

(d) Additional Margin

Procedures shall be established by members to:

(1) review limits and types of credit extended to all customers;

(2) formulate their own margin requirements; and

(3) review the need for instituting higher margin requirements, mark-to-markets and collateral deposits than are required by this Rule for individual securities or customer accounts.

(e) Exceptions to Rule

The foregoing requirements of this Rule are subject to the following exceptions:

(1) Offsetting "Long" and "Short" Positions

When a security carried in a "long" position is exchangeable or convertible within a reasonable time, without restriction other than the payment of money, into a security carried in a "short" position for the same customer, the margin to be maintained on such positions shall be 10 percent of the current market value of the "long" securities. When the same security is carried "long" and "short" the margin to be maintained on such positions shall be 5 percent of the current market value of the "long" securities. In determining such margin requirements "short" positions shall be marked to the market.

(2) Exempted Securities, Non-equity Securities and Baskets

(A) Obligations of the United States and Highly Rated Foreign Sovereign Debt Securities

On net "long" or net "short" positions in obligations (including zero coupon bonds, i.e., bonds with coupons detached or non-interest bearing bonds) issued or guaranteed as to principal or interest by the United States Government or by corporations in which the United States has a direct or indirect interest as shall be designated for exemption by the Secretary of the Treasury, or in obligations that are highly rated foreign sovereign debt securities, the margin to be maintained shall be the percentage of the current market value of such obligations as specified in the applicable category that follows:

(i)	Less than one year to maturity	1 percent
(ii)	One year but less than three years to maturity	2 percent
(iii)	Three years but less than five years to maturity	3 percent
(iv)	Five years but less than ten years to maturity	4 percent
(v)	Ten years but less than twenty years to maturity	5 percent
(vi)	Twenty years or more to maturity	6 percent

Notwithstanding the above, on zero coupon bonds with five years or more to maturity the margin to be maintained shall not be less than 3 percent of the principal amount of the obligation.

When such obligations other than United States Treasury bills are due to mature in 30 calendar days or less, a member, at its discretion, may permit the customer to substitute another such obligation for the maturing obligation and use the margin held on the maturing obligation to reduce the margin required on the new obligation, provided the customer has given the member irrevocable instructions to redeem the maturing obligation.

(B) All Other Exempted Securities

On any "long" or "short" positions in exempted securities other than obligations of the United States, the margin to be maintained shall be 7 percent of the current market value.

(C) Non-Equity Securities

On any "long" or "short" positions in non-equity securities, the margin to be maintained (except where a lesser requirement is imposed by other provisions of this Rule) shall be:

(i) 10 percent of the current market value in the case of investment grade debt securities; and

(ii) 20 percent of the current market value or 7 percent of the principal amount, whichever amount is greater, in the case of all other listed non-equity securities, and all other margin eligible non-equity securities as defined in paragraph (a)(16) of this Rule.

(D) Baskets

Notwithstanding the other provisions of this Rule, a member may clear and carry basket transactions of one or more members registered as market makers (who are deemed specialists for purposes of Section 7 of the Exchange Act pursuant to the rules of a national securities exchange) upon a margin basis satisfactory to the concerned parties, provided all real and potential risks in accounts carried under such arrangements are at all times adequately covered by the margin maintained in the account or, in the absence thereof, by the carrying member when computing net capital under SEA Rule 15c3-1 and, if applicable, Rule 4110(a).

(E) Special Provisions

Notwithstanding the foregoing in this paragraph (e)(2):

(i) A member may, at its discretion, permit the use of accrued interest as an offset to the maintenance margin required to be maintained; and

(ii) FINRA, upon written application, may permit lower margin requirements on a case-by-case basis.

(F) Transactions with Exempt Accounts Involving Certain "Good Faith" Securities

On any "long" or "short" position resulting from a transaction involving exempted securities, mortgage related securities, or major foreign sovereign debt securities made for or with an "exempt account," no margin need be required and any marked to the market loss on such position need not be collected. However, the amount of any uncollected marked to the market loss shall be deducted in computing the member's net capital as provided in SEA Rule 15c3-1 and, if applicable, Rule 4110(a), subject to the limits provided in paragraph (e)(2)(I) of this Rule.

Members shall maintain a written risk analysis methodology for assessing the amount of credit extended to exempt accounts pursuant to paragraph (e)(2)(F) of this Rule which shall be made available to FINRA upon request. The risk limit determination shall be made by a designated credit risk officer or credit risk committee in accordance with the member's written risk policies and procedures.

(G) Transactions With Exempt Accounts Involving Highly Rated Foreign Sovereign Debt Securities and Investment Grade Debt Securities

On any "long" or "short" position resulting from a transaction made for or with an "exempt account" (other than a position subject to paragraph (e)(2)(F)), the margin to be maintained on highly rated foreign sovereign debt and investment grade debt securities shall be, in lieu of any greater requirements imposed under this Rule, (i) 0.5 percent of current market value in the case of highly rated foreign sovereign debt securities, and (ii) 3 percent of current market value in the case of all other investment grade debt securities. The member need not collect any such margin, provided the amount equal to the margin required shall be deducted in computing the member's net capital as provided in SEA Rule 15c3-1 and, if applicable, Rule 4110(a), subject to the limits provided in paragraph (e)(2)(I) of this Rule.

Members shall maintain a written risk analysis methodology for assessing the amount of credit extended to exempt accounts pursuant to paragraph (e)(2)(G) of this Rule which shall be made available to FINRA upon request. The risk limit determination shall be made by a designated credit risk officer or credit risk committee in accordance with the member's written risk policies and procedures.

(H) Covered Agency Transactions

(i) Definitions

For purposes of paragraph (e)(2)(H) of this Rule:

a. (To be Implemented on March 25, 2020).

b. The term "counterparty" means any person that enters into a Covered Agency Transaction with a member and includes a "customer" as defined in paragraph (a)(3) of this Rule.

c. The term "Covered Agency Transaction" means:

1. To Be Announced ("TBA") transactions, as defined in Rule 6710(u), inclusive of adjustable rate mortgage ("ARM") transactions, for which the difference between the trade date and contractual settlement date is greater than one business day;

2. Specified Pool Transactions, as defined in Rule 6710(x), for which the difference between the trade date and contractual settlement date is greater than one business day; and

3. Transactions in Collateralized Mortgage Obligations ("CMOs"), as defined in Rule 6710(dd), issued in conformity with a program of an Agency, as defined in Rule 6710(k), or a Government-Sponsored Enterprise, as defined in Rule 6710(n), for which the difference between the trade date and contractual settlement date is greater than three business days.

d. through j. (To be Implemented on March 25, 2020).

(ii) Margin Requirements for Covered Agency Transactions

a. (To be Implemented on March 25, 2020)

b. A member that engages in Covered Agency Transactions with any counterparty shall make a determination in writing of a risk limit for each such counterparty that the member shall enforce. The risk limit determination shall be made by a designated credit risk officer or credit risk committee in accordance with the member's written risk policies and procedures.

c. through g. (To be Implemented on March 25, 2020).

(I) Limits on Net Capital Deductions for Exempt Accounts

(i) Members shall maintain a written risk analysis methodology for assessing the amount of credit extended to exempt accounts pursuant to paragraphs (e)(2)(F) and (e)(2)(G) which shall be made available to FINRA upon request.

(ii) In the event that the net capital deductions taken by a member as a result of marked to the market losses incurred under paragraphs (e)(2)(F) and (e)(2)(G) (exclusive of the percentage requirements established thereunder) exceed:

a. on any one account or group of commonly controlled accounts, 5 percent of the member's tentative net capital (as such term is defined in SEA Rule 15c3-1), or

b. on all accounts combined, 25 percent of the member's tentative net capital (as such term is defined in SEA Rule 15c3-1),

and, such excess exists on the fifth business day after it was incurred, the member shall give prompt written notice to FINRA and shall not enter into any new transaction(s) subject to the provisions of paragraph (e)(2)(F) or (e)(2)(G) that would result in an increase in the amount of such excess under, as applicable, subparagraph (ii).

(3) Joint Accounts in Which the Carrying Member or a Partner or Stockholder Therein Has an Interest

In the case of a joint account carried by a member in which such member, or any partner, or stockholder (other than a holder of freely transferable stock only) of such member participates with others, each participant other than the carrying member shall maintain an equity with respect to such interest pursuant to the margin provisions of this paragraph as if such interest were in a separate account.

Pursuant to the Rule 9600 Series, FINRA may grant an exemption from the provisions of this paragraph (e)(3), if the account is confined exclusively to transactions and positions in exempted securities.

In the case of an account conforming to the conditions described in this paragraph (e)(3), the exemption application shall also include the following information as of the date of the request:

(A) complete description of the security;

(B) cost price, offering price and principal amount of obligations which have been purchased or may be required to be purchased;

(C) date on which the security is to be purchased or on which there will be a contingent commitment to purchase the security;

(D) approximate aggregate indebtedness;

(E) approximate net capital; and

(F) approximate total market value of all readily marketable securities (i) exempted and (ii) non-exempted, held in member accounts, partners' capital accounts, partners' individual accounts covered by approved agreements providing for their inclusion as partnership property, accounts covered by subordination agreements approved by FINRA and customers' accounts in deficit.

(4) International Arbitrage Accounts

International arbitrage accounts for non-member foreign brokers or dealers who are members of a foreign securities exchange shall not be subject to this Rule. The amount of any deficiency between the equity in such an account and the margin required by the other provisions of this Rule shall be charged against the member's net capital when computing net capital under SEA Rule 15c3-1 and, if applicable, Rule 4110(a).

(5) Specialists' and Market Makers' Accounts

(A) A member may carry the account of an "approved specialist" or "approved market maker," which account is limited to specialist or market making transactions, upon a margin basis which is satisfactory to both parties. The amount of any deficiency between the equity in the account and the haircut requirements pursuant to SEA Rule 15c3-1 and, if applicable, Rule 4110(a), shall be charged against the member's net capital when computing net capital under SEA Rule 15c3-1 and Rule 4110(a). However, when computing charges against net capital for transactions in securities covered by paragraphs (e)(2)(F) and (e)(2)(G) of this Rule, absent a greater haircut requirement that may have been imposed on such securities pursuant to Rule 4110(a), the respective requirements of those paragraphs may be used, rather than the haircut requirements of SEA Rule 15c3-1.

For the purpose of this paragraph (e)(5)(A), the term "approved specialist" or "approved market maker" means either:

(i) a specialist or market maker, who is deemed a specialist for all purposes under the Exchange Act and who is registered pursuant to the rules of a national securities exchange; or

(ii) an OTC market maker or third market maker, who meets the requirements of Section 220.7(g)(5) of Regulation T.

(B) In the case of a joint account carried by a member in accordance with subparagraph (i) above in which the member participates, the equity maintained in the account by the other participants may be in any amount which is mutually satisfactory. The amount of any deficiency between the equity maintained in the account by the other participants and their proportionate share of the haircut requirements pursuant to SEA Rule 15c3-1 and, if applicable, Rule 4110(a), shall be charged against the member's net capital when computing net capital under SEA Rule 15c3-1 and Rule 4110(a). However, when computing charges against net capital for transactions in securities covered by paragraphs (e)(2)(F) and (e)(2)(G) of this Rule, absent a greater haircut requirement that may have been imposed on such securities pursuant to Rule 4110(a), the respective requirements of those paragraphs may be used, rather than the haircut requirements of SEA Rule 15c3-1.

(6) Broker-Dealer Accounts

(A) A member may carry the proprietary account of another broker-dealer, which is registered with the SEC, upon a margin basis which is satisfactory to both parties, provided the requirements of Regulation T and Rules 400 through 406 of SEC Customer Margin Requirements for Security Futures and Rules 41.42 through 41.49 under the CEA are adhered to and the account is not carried in a deficit equity condition. The amount of any deficiency between the equity maintained in the account and the haircut requirements pursuant to SEA Rule 15c3-1 and, if applicable, Rule 4110(a), shall be charged against the member's net capital when computing net capital under SEA Rule 15c3-1 and Rule 4110(a). However, when computing charges against net capital for transactions in securities covered by paragraphs (e)(2)(F) and (e)(2)(G) of this Rule, absent a greater haircut requirement that may have been imposed on such securities pursuant to Rule 4110(a), the respective requirements of those paragraphs may be used, rather than the haircut requirements of SEA Rule 15c3-1.

(B) Joint Back Office Arrangements

An arrangement may be established between two or more registered broker-dealers pursuant to Regulation T Section 220.7, to form a joint back office ("JBO") arrangement for carrying and clearing or carrying accounts of participating broker-dealers. Members must provide written notification to FINRA prior to establishing a JBO arrangement.

(i) A carrying and clearing, or carrying member must:

a. maintain a minimum tentative net capital (as such term is defined in SEA Rule 15c3-1) of $25 million as computed pursuant to SEA Rule 15c3-1 and, if applicable, Rule 4110(a), except that a member whose primary business consists of the clearance of options market-maker accounts may carry JBO accounts provided that it maintains a minimum net capital of $7 million as computed pursuant to SEA Rule 15c3-1 and, if applicable, Rule 4110(a). In addition, the member must include in its ratio of gross options market maker deductions to net capital required by the provisions of SEA Rule 15c3-1 and, if applicable, Rule 4110(a), gross deductions for JBO participant accounts. Clearance of option market maker accounts shall be deemed a broker-dealer's primary business if a minimum of 60 percent of the aggregate deductions in the above ratio are options market maker deductions. In the event that a carrying and clearing, or a carrying member's tentative net capital (as such term is defined in SEA Rule 15c3-1), or net capital, respectively, has fallen below the above requirements, the firm shall: 1. promptly notify FINRA in writing of such deficiency, 2. take appropriate action to resolve such deficiency within three consecutive business days, or not permit any new transactions to be entered into pursuant to the JBO arrangement;

b. maintain a written risk analysis methodology for assessing the amount of credit extended to participating broker-dealers which shall be made available to FINRA on request; and

c. deduct from net capital haircut requirements pursuant to SEA Rule 15c3-1 and, if applicable, Rule 4110(a), amounts in excess of the equity maintained in the accounts of participating broker-dealers. However, when computing charges against net capital for transactions in securities covered by paragraphs (e)(2)(F) and (e)(2)(G) of this Rule, absent a greater haircut requirement that may have been imposed on such securities pursuant to Rule 4110(a), the respective requirements of those paragraphs may be used, rather than the haircut requirements of SEA Rule 15c3-1.

    (ii) A participating broker-dealer must:

        a. be a registered broker-dealer subject to the SEC's net capital requirements and, if applicable, Rule 4110(a);

        b. maintain an ownership interest in the carrying/clearing member pursuant to Regulation T of the Federal Reserve Board, Section 220.7; and

        c. maintain a minimum liquidating equity of $1 million in the JBO arrangement exclusive of the ownership interest established in subparagraph (ii)b. above. When the minimum liquidating equity decreases below the $1 million requirement, the participant must deposit a sufficient amount to eliminate this deficiency within 5 business days or be subject to margin account requirements prescribed for customers in Regulation T, and the margin requirements pursuant to the other provisions of this Rule.

(7) Nonpurpose Credit

In a nonsecurities credit account, a member may extend and maintain nonpurpose credit to or for any customer without collateral or on any collateral whatever, provided:

  (A) the account is recorded separately and confined to the transactions and relations specifically authorized by Regulation T;

  (B) the account is not used in any way for the purpose of evading or circumventing any regulation of FINRA or of the Board of Governors of the Federal Reserve System and Rules 400 through 406 of SEC Customer Margin Requirements for Security Futures and Rules 41.42 through 41.49 under the CEA; and

  (C) the amount of any deficiency between the equity in the account and the margin required by the other provisions of this Rule shall be charged against the member's net capital as provided in SEA Rule 15c3-1 and, if applicable, Rule 4110(a).

The term "nonpurpose credit" means an extension of credit other than "purpose credit" as defined in Section 220.2 of Regulation T.

(8) Shelf-Registered and Other Control and Restricted Securities

  (A) Shelf-Registered Securities — The equity to be maintained in margin accounts of customers for securities which are the subject of a current and effective registration for a continuous or delayed offering (shelf-registered securities) shall be at least the amount of margin required by paragraph (c) of this Rule, provided the member:

    (i) obtains a current prospectus in effect with the SEC, meeting the requirements of Section 10 of the Securities Act, covering such securities;

    (ii) has no reason to believe the Registration Statement is not in effect or that the issuer has been delinquent in filing such periodic reports as may be required of it with the SEC and is satisfied that such registration will be kept in effect and that the prospectus will be maintained on a current basis; and

    (iii) retains a copy of such Registration Statement, including the prospectus, in an easily accessible place in its files. Shelf-registered securities which do not meet all the conditions prescribed above shall have no value for purposes of this Rule. Also see subparagraph (C) below.

  (B) Other Control and Restricted Securities — Except as provided in subparagraph (D) below, the equity in accounts of customers for other control and restricted securities of issuers that are subject to Securities Act Rule 144 or 145(c), shall be 40 percent of the current market value of such securities "long" in the account, provided the member:

(i) in computing net capital under SEA Rule 15c3-1 and, if applicable, Rule 4110(a), deducts any margin deficiencies in customers' accounts based upon a margin requirement as specified in subparagraph (C)(iv) below for such securities and values only that amount of such securities which are then saleable under Securities Act Rule 144(b)(2) or 145(d)(2)(i) in conformity with all of the applicable terms and conditions thereof, for purposes of determining such deficiencies; and

(ii) makes volume computations necessary to determine the amount of securities then saleable under Securities Act Rule 144(b)(2) or 145(d)(2)(i) on a weekly basis or at such frequency as the member and/or FINRA may deem appropriate under the circumstances. See also subparagraph (C).

(C) Additional Requirements on Shelf-Registered Securities and Other Control and Restricted Securities — Except as provided in subparagraph (D) below, a member extending credit on shelf-registered and other control and restricted securities in margin accounts of customers shall be subject to the following additional requirements:

(i) FINRA may at any time require reports from members showing relevant information as to the amount of credit extended on shelf-registered, and other control and restricted securities and the amount, if any, deducted from net capital due to such security positions.

(ii) The greater of the aggregate credit agreed to be extended in writing or the aggregate credit that is actually extended to all customers on control and restricted securities of any one issue that exceeds 10 percent of the member's excess net capital shall be deducted from net capital for purposes of determining a member's status under Rule 4120. The amount of such aggregate credit extended, which has been deducted in computing net capital under SEA Rule 15c3-1 and, if applicable, Rule 4110(a), need not be included in this calculation. FINRA, upon written application, may reduce the deduction to net capital under Rule 4120 to 25 percent of such aggregate credit extended that exceeds 10 percent but is less than 15 percent of the member's excess net capital.

(iii) The aggregate credit extended to all customers on all control and restricted securities (reduced by the amount of such aggregate credit which has been deducted in computing net capital under SEA Rule 15c3-1 and, if applicable, Rule 4110(a)), shall be deducted from net capital on the following basis for purposes of determining a member's status under Rule 4120.

   a. To the extent such net amount of credit extended does not exceed 50 percent of a member's excess net capital, 25 percent of such net amount of credit extended shall be deducted, and

   b. 100 percent of such net amount of credit extended which exceeds 50 percent of a member's excess net capital shall be deducted.

(iv) Concentration Reduction. A concentration exists whenever the aggregate position in control and restricted securities of any one issue, excluding excess securities (as defined below), exceeds:

   a. 10 percent of the outstanding shares of such issue, or

   b. 100 percent of the average weekly volume for such issue during the preceding three-month period. Where a concentration exists, for purposes of computing subparagraph (B)(i) above, the margin requirement on such securities shall be, based on the greater of subparagraph (iv)a. or b., above, as specified below:

Percent of Outstanding Shares	or Percent of Average Weekly Volume	Margin Requirement
Up to 10 percent	Up to 100 percent	25 percent
Over 10 percent and under 15 percent	Over 100 percent and under 200 percent	30 percent
15 percent and under 20 percent	200 percent and under 300 percent	45 percent
20 percent and under 25 percent	300 percent and under 400 percent	60 percent
25 percent and under 30 percent	400 percent and under 500 percent	75 percent
30 percent and above	500 percent and above	100 percent

For purposes of this paragraph (e)(8)(C)(iv), "excess securities" shall mean the amount of securities, if any, by which the aggregate position in control and restricted securities of any one issue exceeds the aggregate amount of securities that would be required to support the aggregate credit extended on such control and restricted securities if the applicable margin requirement were 50 percent.

(v) The amount to be deducted from net capital for purposes of determining a member's status under Rule 4120, pursuant to paragraph (e)(8)(C) shall not exceed 100 percent of the aggregate credit extended reduced by any amount deducted in computing net capital under SEA Rule 15c3-1 and, if applicable, Rule 4110(a).

(D) Certain Restricted Securities — Securities either:

(i) then saleable pursuant to the terms and conditions of Securities Act Rule 144(b)(1), or

(ii) then saleable pursuant to the terms and conditions of Securities Act Rule 145(d)(2), shall not be subject to the provisions of paragraph (e)(8) of this Rule.

(f) Other Provisions

(1) Determination of Value for Margin Purposes

Active securities dealt in on a national securities exchange shall, for margin purposes, be valued at current market prices provided that only those options contracts on a stock or stock index, or a stock index warrant, having an expiration that exceeds nine months and that are listed or OTC (as defined in this Rule), may be deemed to have market value for the purposes of this Rule. Other securities shall be valued conservatively in view of current market prices and the amount that might be realized upon liquidation. Substantial additional margin must be required in all cases where the securities carried in "long" or "short" positions are subject to unusually rapid or violent changes in value, or do not have an active market on a national securities exchange, or where the amount carried is such that the position(s) cannot be liquidated promptly.

(2) Puts, Calls and Other Options, Currency Warrants, Currency Index Warrants and Stock Index Warrants

(A) Definitions

Except where the context otherwise requires or as defined below, the definitions contained in paragraph (a) of Rule 2360, "Options," shall apply to the terms used in this Rule.

(i) The term "aggregate discount amount" as used with reference to a Treasury bill option contract means the principal amount of the underlying Treasury bill (A) multiplied by the annualized discount (i.e., 100 percent minus the exercise price of the option contract) and (B) further multiplied by a fraction having a numerator equal to the number of days to maturity of the underlying Treasury bill on the earliest date on which it could be delivered pursuant to the rules of The Options Clearing Corporation in connection with the exercise of the option (normally 91 or 182 days) and a denominator of 360.

(ii) The term "aggregate exercise price" as used with reference to an option contract means:

a. if a single stock underlies the option contract, the exercise price of the option contract multiplied by the number of shares of the underlying stock covered by such option contract;

b. if a Treasury bond or Treasury note underlies the option contract,

1. the exercise price of the option contract multiplied by the principal amount of the underlying security covered by such option contract, plus

2. accrued interest:

A. on bonds (except bonds issued or guaranteed by the United States Government), that portion of the interest on the bonds for a full year, computed for the number of days elapsed since the previous interest date on the basis of a 360-day-year. Each calendar month shall be considered to be 1/12 of 360 days, or 30 days, and each period from a date in one month to the same date in the following month shall be considered to be 30 days.

    B. on bonds issued or guaranteed by the United States Government, that portion of the interest on the bonds for the current full interest period, computed for the actual number of days elapsed since the previous interest date on the basis of actual number of calendar days in the current full interest period. The actual elapsed days in each calendar month shall be used in determining the number of days in a period.

  c. if a Treasury bill underlies the option contract, the difference between the principal amount of such Treasury bill and the aggregate discount amount;

  d. if an index stock group underlies the option contract, the exercise price of the option contract times the index multiplier; or

  e. if a GNMA underlies the option contract, the exercise price of the option contract multiplied by the nominal principal amount of the underlying GNMA covered by such option contract. In the case of an underlying GNMA, if the remaining unpaid principal balance of a GNMA delivered upon exercise of an option contract is a permissible variant of, rather than equal to, the nominal principal amount, the aggregate exercise price shall be adjusted to equal the product of the exercise price and such remaining unpaid principal balance, plus in each case the appropriate differential.

(iii) The term "American-style option" means an option contract that can be exercised at any time prior to its expiration pursuant to the rules of The Options Clearing Corporation.

(iv) The term "annualized discount" as used with reference to a Treasury bill means the percent discount from principal amount at which the Treasury bill may be purchased or sold, expressed as a discount for a term to maturity of 360 days.

(v) The term "appropriate differential" as used with reference to a GNMA option contract means a positive or negative amount equal to the product of (A) the difference between the remaining unpaid principal balance of a GNMA delivered upon exercise of that contract and the nominal principal amount, and (B) the difference between the current cash market price of GNMAs bearing the same stated rate of interest as that borne by the GNMA delivered upon exercise and the exercise price.

(vi) The term "box spread" means an aggregation of positions in a long call and short put with the same exercise price ("buy side") coupled with a long put and short call with the same exercise price ("sell side") structured as: (A) a "long box spread" in which the sell side exercise price exceeds the buy side exercise price or, (B) a "short box spread" in which the buy side exercise price exceeds the sell side exercise price, all of which have the same contract size, underlying component or index and time of expiration, and are based on the same aggregate current underlying value.

(vii) The term "broad index stock group" means an index stock group of 25 or more stocks whose inclusion and relative representation in the group are determined by the inclusion and relative representation of their current market prices in a widely disseminated stock index reflecting the stock market as a whole or an inter-industry sector of the stock market.

(viii) The terms "call" and "put":

  a. as used in connection with a currency, currency index or stock index warrant mean a warrant structured as a "call" or "put" (as appropriate) on the underlying currency, index currency group or stock index group (as the case may be) or

  b. as used in connection with an option contract means an option under which the holder has the right, in accordance with the terms of the option, to purchase from (in the case of a call), or sell to (in the case of a put), The Options Clearing Corporation:

    1. the number of shares of the underlying stock (if a single stock underlies the option contract);

    2. the principal amount of the underlying security (if a Government security underlies the option contract);

3. the multiple of the index group value of the underlying group (if an index stock group underlies the option contract); or

4. the nominal principal amount or any permissible variant of the underlying GNMA (if a GNMA underlies the option contract) covered by the option contract.

(ix) The term "class (of options)" means all option contracts of the same type and kind covering the same underlying security or underlying stock group.

(x) The term "covered" has the same meaning as defined in Rule 2360(a).

(xi) The terms "currency warrant," "currency index" and "currency index warrant" have the same meanings as defined in Rule 2351(b).

(xii) The term "current cash market price" as used with reference to GNMAs means the prevailing price in the cash market for GNMAs bearing a particular stated rate of interest to be delivered on the next applicable monthly settlement date determined in the manner specified in the rules of The Options Clearing Corporation.

(xiii) The terms "current market value" or "current market price" of an option, currency warrant, currency index warrant, or stock index warrant are as defined in Section 220.2 of Regulation T.

(xiv) The term "escrow agreement," when used in connection with cash settled calls, puts, currency warrants, currency index warrants or stock index warrants, carried "short", means any agreement issued in a form acceptable to FINRA under which a bank holding cash, cash equivalents, one or more qualified equity securities or a combination thereof in the case of a call or warrants, or cash, cash equivalents or a combination thereof in the case of a put or warrant is obligated (in the case of an option) to pay the creditor the exercise settlement amount in the event an option is assigned an exercise notice or, (in the case of a warrant) the sufficient funds to purchase a warrant sold "short" in the event of a buy-in.

(xv) The term "European-style option" means an option contract that can be exercised only at its expiration pursuant to the rules of The Options Clearing Corporation.

(xvi) The term "exercise price" in respect of an option or warrant contract means the stated price per unit at which the underlying security may be purchased (in the case of a call) or sold (in the case of a put) upon the exercise of such option contract.

(xvii) The term "exercise settlement amount" shall mean the difference between the "aggregate exercise price" and the "aggregate current index value" (as such terms are defined in the pertinent By-Laws of The Options Clearing Corporation).

(xviii) The term "expiration date" in respect of an option contract means the date and time fixed by the rules of The Options Clearing Corporation for the expiration of all option contracts covering the same underlying security or underlying index stock group and having the same expiration month as such option contract.

(xix) The term "expiration month" in respect of an option contract means the month and year in which such option contract expires.

(xx) The term "index currency group" means a group of currencies whose inclusion and relative representation in the group is determined by the inclusion and relative representation of the current market prices of the currencies in a currency index.

(xxi) The term "index group value," when used in respect of a currency index warrant or a stock index warrant, shall mean $1.00 (1) multiplied by the numerical value reported for the index that is derived from the market prices of the currencies in the index currency group or the stocks in the stock index group and (2) divided by the applicable divisor in the prospectus (if any). When used with reference to the exercise of a stock index group option, the value is the last one reported on the day of exercise or, if the day of exercise is not a trading day, on the last trading day before exercise.

(xxii) The term "index multiplier" as used in reference to an index option contract means the amount specified in the contract by which the index value is to be multiplied to arrive at the value required to be delivered to the holder of a call or by the holder of a put upon valid exercise of the contract.

(xxiii) The term "industry stock index group" means an index stock group of six or more stocks whose inclusion and relative representation in the group are determined by the inclusion and relative representation of their current market prices in a widely disseminated stock index reflecting a particular industry or closely related industries.

(xxiv) The term "listed" as used with reference to a call or put option contract means an option contract that is traded on a national securities exchange or issued and guaranteed by a registered clearing agency and shall include an OCC Cleared OTC Option (as defined in Rule 2360).

(xxv) The term "nominal principal amount" as used with reference to a GNMA option means the remaining unpaid principal balance of GNMAs required to be delivered to the holder of a call or by the holder of a put upon exercise of an option without regard to any variance in the remaining unpaid principal balance permitted to be delivered upon such exercise and shall be $100,000 in the case of a single call or put.

(xxvi) The term "numerical index value," when used in respect of a currency index warrant or stock index warrant, shall mean the level of a particular currency index or stock index as reported by the reporting authority for the index.

(xxvii) The term "OTC" as used with reference to a call or put option contract means an over-the-counter option contract that is not traded on a national securities exchange and is issued and guaranteed by the carrying broker-dealer and shall not include OCC Cleared OTC Option (as defined in Rule 2360).

(xxviii) A "registered clearing agency" shall mean a clearing agency as defined in Section 3(a)(23) of the Exchange Act that is registered with the SEC pursuant to Section 17A(b)(2) of the Exchange Act.

(xxix) The term "reporting authority," when used in respect of a currency index warrant or a stock index warrant, shall mean the institution or reporting service specified in the prospectus as the official source for calculating and reporting the level of such currency index or stock index.

(xxx) The term "series (of options)" means all option contracts of the same class of options having the same expiration date, exercise price and unit of trading.

(xxxi) The term "spot price" in respect of a currency warrant on a particular business day means the noon buying rate in U.S. dollars on such day in New York City for cable transfers of the particular underlying currency as certified for customs purposes by the Federal Reserve Bank of New York.

(xxxii) The term "spread" means a "long" and "short" position in different call option series, different put option series, or a combination of call and put option series, that collectively have a limited risk / reward profile, and meet the following conditions;
  a. all options must have the same underlying security or instrument;
  b. all "long" and "short" option contracts must be either all American-style or all European-style;
  c. all "long" and "short" option contracts must be either all listed or all OTC;
  d. the aggregate underlying contract value of "long" versus "short" contracts within option type(s) must be equal; and
  e. the "short" option(s) must expire on or before the expiration date of the "long" option(s).

(xxxiii) The term "stock index group" has the same meaning as defined in Rule 2351(b).

(xxxiv) The term "stock index warrant" shall mean a put or call warrant that overlies a broad stock index group or an industry stock index group.

(xxxv) The term "underlying component" shall mean in the case of stock, the equivalent number of shares; industry and broad index stock groups, the index group value and the applicable index multiplier; U.S. Treasury bills, notes and bonds, the underlying principal amount; foreign currencies, the units per foreign currency contract; and interest rate contracts, the interest rate measure based on the yield of U.S. Treasury bills, notes or bonds and the applicable multiplier. The term "interest rate measure" represents, in the case of short term U.S. Treasury bills, the annualized discount yield of a specific issue multiplied by ten or, in the case of long term U.S. Treasury notes and bonds, the average of the yield to maturity of the specific multiplied by ten.

(xxxvi) The term "unit of underlying currency" in respect of a currency warrant means a single unit of the currency covered by the warrant.

(B) Except as provided below, and in the case of a put, call, index stock group option, or stock index warrant with a remaining period to expiration exceeding nine months, no put, call, currency warrant, currency index warrant or stock index warrant carried for a customer shall be considered of any value for the purpose of computing the margin to be maintained in the account of such customer.

(C) The issuance, guarantee or sale (other than a "long" sale) for a customer of a put, a call, a currency warrant, a currency index warrant or a stock index warrant shall be considered a security transaction subject to paragraphs (b) and (c).

(D) For purposes of this paragraph (f)(2), obligations issued by the United States Government shall be referred to as United States Government obligations. Mortgage pass-through obligations guaranteed as to timely payment of principal and interest by the Government National Mortgage Association shall be referred to as GNMA obligations.

In the case of any put, call, currency warrant, currency index warrant, or stock index warrant carried "long" in a customer's account that expires in nine months or less, initial margin must be deposited and maintained equal to at least 100 percent of the purchase price of the option or warrant.

"Long" Listed Option or Warrant With An Expiration Exceeding Nine Months. In the case of a listed put, call, index stock group option, or stock index warrant carried "long", margin must be deposited and maintained equal to at least 75 percent of the current market value of the option or warrant; provided that the option or warrant has a remaining period to expiration exceeding nine months.

"Long" OTC Option or Warrant With An Expiration Exceeding Nine Months. In the case of an OTC put, call, index stock group option, or stock index warrant carried "long", margin must be deposited and maintained equal to at least 75 percent of the option's or warrant's "in-the-money" amount plus 100 percent of the amount, if any, by which the current market value of the option or warrant exceeds its "in-the-money" amount provided the option or warrant:

(i) is guaranteed by the carrying broker-dealer,

(ii) has an American-style exercise provision, and

(iii) has a remaining period to expiration exceeding nine months.

(E) The margin required on any listed or OTC put, call, currency warrant, currency index warrant, or stock index warrant carried "short" in a customer's account shall be:

(i) In the case of listed puts and calls, 100 percent of the current market value of the option plus the percentage of the current market value of the underlying component specified in column II of the chart below. In the case of currency warrants, currency index warrants and stock index warrants, 100 percent of the current market value of each such warrant plus the percentage of the warrant's current "underlying component value" (as column IV of the chart below describes) specified in column II of the chart below.

The margin on any listed put, call, currency warrant, currency index warrant, or stock index warrant carried "short" in a customer's account may be reduced by any "out-of-the-money amount" (as defined below), but shall not be less than 100 percent of the current market value of the option or warrant plus the percentage of the current market value of the underlying component specified in column III, except in the case of any listed put carried "short" in a customer's account. Margin on such put option contracts shall not be less than the current value of the put option plus the percentage of the put option's aggregate exercise price as specified in column III.

I Type of Option	II Initial and/or Maintenance Margin Required	III Minimum Margin Required	IV Underlying Component Value
Stock	20%	10%	The equivalent number of shares at current market prices.
Industry index stock group	20%	10%	The product of the index group value and the applicable index multiplier.
Broad index stock group	15%	10%	The product of the index group value and the applicable index multiplier.
U.S. Treasury bills — 95 days or less to maturity	.35%	.05%	The underlying principal amount.
U.S. Treasury notes	3%	.5%	The underlying principal amount.
U.S. Treasury bonds	3.5%	.5%	The underlying principal amount.
Foreign Currency Options and Warrants*	4%	.75%	The product of units per foreign currency contract and the closing spot price.
Interest Rate contracts	10%	5%	The product of the current interest rate measure and the applicable multiplier.
Currency Index Warrants	**	**	The product of the index group value and the applicable index multiplier.
Stock Index Warrant on Broad Index Stock Group	15%	10%	The product of the index group value and the applicable index multiplier.
Stock Index Warrant on Industry Index Stock Group	20%	10%	The product of the index group value and the applicable index multiplier.

* Does not include Canadian dollars, for which the initial requirement is 1 percent.

** Subject to the approval of the SEC, FINRA shall determine applicable initial, maintenance and minimum margin requirements for currency index warrants on a case-by-case basis.

For purposes hereof, "out-of-the-money amounts" are determined as follows:

Option or Warrant Issue	Call	Put
Stock Options	Any excess of the aggregate exercise price of the option over the current market value of the equivalent number of shares of the underlying security.	Any excess of the current market value of the equivalent number of shares of the underlying security over the aggregate exercise price of the option.
U.S. Treasury Options	Any excess of the aggregate exercise price of the option over the current market value of the underlying principal amount.	Any excess of the current market value of the underlying principal amount over the aggregate exercise price of the option.
Index Stock Group Options, Currency Index Warrants, and Stock Index Warrants	Any excess of the aggregate exercise price of the option or warrant over the product of the index group value and the applicable multiplier.	Any excess of the product of the index group value and the applicable multiplier over the aggregate exercise price of the option or warrant.
Foreign Currency Options and Warrants	Any excess of the aggregate exercise price of the option or warrant over the product of units per foreign currency contract and the closing spot prices.	The product of units per foreign currency contract and the closing spot prices over the aggregate price of the option or warrant.
Interest Rate Options	Any excess of the aggregate exercise price of the option over the product of the current interest rate measure value and the applicable multiplier.	Any excess of the product of the current interest rate measure value and the applicable multiplier over the aggregate exercise price of the option.

If the option or warrant contract provides for the delivery of obligations with different maturity dates or coupon rates, the computation of the "out-of-the-money amount," if any, where required by this Rule, shall be made in such a manner as to result in the highest margin requirement on the short option or warrant position.

(ii) In the case of listed puts and calls which represent options on GNMA obligations in the principal amount of $100,000, 130 percent of the current market value of the option plus $1,500, except that the margin required need not exceed $5,000 plus the current market value of the option.

(iii) In the case of OTC puts and calls, the percentage of the current value of the underlying component and the applicable multiplier, if any, specified in column II below, plus any "in-the-money amount" (as defined in this paragraph (f)(2)(E)(iii)).

In the case of OTC options, the margin on any put or call carried "short" in a customer's account may be reduced by any "out-of-the-money amount" (as defined in paragraph (f)(2)(E)(i)), but shall not be less than the percentage of the current value of the underlying component and the applicable multiplier, if any, specified in column III below, except in the case of any OTC put carried "short" in a customer's account. Margin on such put option contracts shall not be less than the percentage of the put option's exercise price as specified in column III that follows.

I Type of Option	II Initial and/or Maintenance Margin Required	III Minimum Margin Required	IV Underlying Component Value
Stock and convertible corporate debt securities	30%	10%	The equivalent number of shares at current market prices for stocks or the underlying principal amount for convertible corporate debt securities.
Industry Index stock group	30%	10%	The product of the index group value and The applicable index multiplier.
Broad index stock group	20%	10%	The product of the index group value and the applicable index multiplier.
U.S. Government or U.S. Government Agency debt securities other than those exempted by SEA Rule 3a12-7	5%	3%	The underlying principal amount.
Listed non-equity securities and other margin eligible non-equity securities as defined in paragraphs (a)(15) and (a)(16).	15%	5%	The underlying principal amount.
All other OTC options not covered above	45%	20%	The underlying principal amount.

For the purpose of this paragraph (f)(2)(E)(iii), "in-the-money amounts" are determined as follows:

Option Issue	Call	Put
Stock options	Any excess of the current market value of the equivalent number of shares of the underlying security over the aggregate exercise price of the option.	Any excess of the aggregate exercise price of the option over the current market value of the equivalent number of shares of the underlying security.
Index stock group options	Any excess of the product of the index group value and the applicable multiplier over the aggregate exercise price of the option.	Any excess of the aggregate exercise price of the option over the product of the index group value and the applicable multiplier.
U.S. Government mortgage related or corporate debt securities options	Any excess of the current value of the underlying principal amount over the aggregate exercise price of the option.	Any excess of the aggregate exercise price of the option over the current value of the underlying principal amount.

(iv) OTC puts and calls representing options on U.S. Government and U.S. Government Agency debt securities that qualify for exemption pursuant to SEA Rule 3a12-7, must be for a principal amount of not less than $500,000, and shall be subject to the following requirements:

    a. For exempt accounts, as defined in paragraph (a)(13), 3 percent of the current value of the underlying principal amount on thirty (30) year U.S. Treasury bonds and non-mortgage backed U.S. Government agency debt securities; and 2 percent of the current value of the underlying principal amount on all other U.S. Government and U.S. Government agency debt securities, plus any "in-the-money amount" (as defined in paragraph (f)(2)(E)(iii)) or minus any "out-of-the-money amount" (as defined in paragraph (f)(2)(E)(i)). The amount of any deficiency between the equity in the account and the margin required shall be deducted in computing the net capital of the member under SEA Rule 15c3-1 and, if applicable, Rule 4110(a), on the following basis:

1. On any one account or group of commonly controlled accounts to the extent such deficiency exceeds 5 percent of a member's tentative net capital (as such term is defined in SEA Rule 15c3-1), 100 percent of such excess amount, and

2. On all accounts combined to the extent such deficiency exceeds 25 percent of a member's tentative net capital (as such term is defined in SEA Rule 15c3-1), 100 percent of such excess amount, reduced by any amount already deducted pursuant to subparagraph (a) above.

b. For non-exempt accounts, 5 percent of the current value of the underlying principal amount on thirty (30) year U.S. Treasury bonds and non-mortgage backed U.S. Government agency debt securities; and 3 percent of the current value of the underlying principal amount on all other U.S. Government and U.S. Government agency debt securities, plus any "in-the-money amount" or minus any "out-of-the-money amount," provided the minimum margin shall not be less than 1 percent of the current value of the underlying principal amount.

(F)(i) Each put or call shall be margined separately and any difference between the current market value of the underlying component and the exercise price of a put or call shall be considered to be of value only in providing the amount of margin required on that particular put or call. Substantial additional margin must be required on listed or OTC options carried "short" with an unusually long period of time to expiration, or written on securities which are subject to unusually rapid or violent changes in value, or which do not have an active market, or where the securities subject to the option cannot be liquidated promptly.

(ii) No margin need be required on any "covered" put or call.

(G)(i) Where both a listed put and call specify the same underlying component and are carried "short" for a customer, the amount of margin required shall be the margin on the put or call, whichever is greater, as required pursuant to paragraph (f)(2)(E)(i) above, plus the current market value on the other option.

When:

a. a currency call warrant position is carried "short" for a customer account and is offset by a "short" currency put warrant and/or currency put option position;

b. a currency put warrant position is carried "short" for a customer account and is offset by a "short" currency call warrant and/or currency put option position;

c. a currency index call warrant position is carried "short" for a customer account and is offset by a "short" currency index put warrant and/or currency put option position;

d. a currency index put warrant position is carried "short" for a customer account and is offset by a "short" currency index call warrant and/or currency index call option position;

e. a stock index call warrant position is carried "short" for a customer account and is offset by a "short" stock index put warrant and/or stock index put option position;

f. a stock index put warrant position is carried "short" for a customer account and is offset by a "short" stock index call warrant and/or stock index call option position;

g. an index call warrant position is carried "short" for a customer account and is offset by a "short" index put warrant and/or index put option position;

h. an index put warrant position is carried "short" for a customer account and is offset by a "short" index call warrant and/or index call option position;

i. a broad index stock group call option position is carried "short" for a customer account and is offset by a "short" broad index stock group put option position; or

j. a broad index stock group put option position is carried "short" for a customer account and is offset by a "short" broad index stock group call option position and the offset position is of equivalent underlying value on the same currency, currency index or index stock group, as appropriate, then the amount of margin required shall be the margin on the put position or the call position, whichever is greater, as required pursuant to subparagraph (E)(i), plus the current market value of the other warrant and/or option position.

(ii) Where either or both the put and call specifying the same underlying component are not listed and are OTC and carried "short" for a customer by the same carrying broker-dealer (as defined in paragraph (f)(2)(H) below), the amount of margin required shall be the margin on the put or call, whichever is greater, as required pursuant to paragraphs (f)(2)(E)(iii) and (E)(iv) above, plus any unrealized loss on the other option. Where either or both the put or call are not listed or OTC and are carried by the same carrying broker-dealer then the put and call must be margined separately pursuant to paragraphs (f)(2)(E)(iii) and (E)(iv) above, however, the minimum margin shall not apply to the other option.

(iii) If both a put and call for the same GNMA obligation in the principal amount of $100,000 are listed or OTC and are carried "short" for a customer, the amount of margin required shall be the margin on the put or call, whichever is greater, as required pursuant to paragraph (f)(2)(E)(ii) above, plus the current market value of the other option.

(H)(i) For spreads as defined in paragraph (f)(2)(A)(xxxii) of this Rule, the margin required on the "short" options shall be the lesser of:

a. The margin required pursuant to paragraph (f)(2)(E); or

b. The maximum potential loss. The maximum potential loss is determined by computing the intrinsic value of the options at price points for the underlying security or instrument that are set to correspond to every exercise price present in the spread. The intrinsic values are netted at each price point. The maximum potential loss is the greatest loss, if any.

"Long" options must be paid for in full. The proceeds of the "short" options may be applied towards the cost of the "long" options and/or any margin requirement.

(ii) Where a call warrant issued on an underlying currency, index currency group or index stock group is carried "long" for a customer's account and the account is also "short" a listed call option, or index stock group, which "short" call position(s) expire on or before the date of expiration of the "long" call position and specify the same number of units of the same underlying currency or the same index multiplier for the same index currency group or index stock group, as the case may be, the margin required on the "short" call(s) shall be the requirement pursuant to paragraph (f)(2)(H)(i) above.

Where a put warrant issued on an underlying currency, index currency group or index stock group is carried "long" for a customer's account and the account is also "short" a listed put option, and/or a put warrant, on the same underlying currency, index currency group, or index stock group, which "short" put position(s) expire on or before the date of expiration of the "long" put position and specify the same number of units of the same underlying currency or the same index multiplier for the same index currency group or index stock group, the margin required on the "short" put(s) shall be the requirement pursuant to paragraph (f)(2)(H)(i) above.

(iii)a. For spreads as defined in paragraph (f)(2)(A)(xxxii) of this Rule, that are written on the same GNMA obligation in the principal amount of $100,000, the margin required on the "short" options shall be the lower of:

1. the margin required pursuant to paragraph (f)(2)(E)(ii) above; or

2. the maximum potential loss, as described in paragraph (f)(2)(H)(i)b. of this Rule, multiplied by the appropriate multiplier factor set forth below.

"Long" options must be paid for in full. The proceeds of the "short" options may be applied towards the cost of the "long" options and/or any margin requirement.

b. For purposes of this paragraph (f)(2)(H)(iii) the multiplier factor to be applied shall depend on the then current highest qualifying rate as defined by the rules of the national securities exchange on or through which the option is listed or traded. If the then current highest qualifying rate is less than 8 percent, the multiplier factor shall be 1; if the then current highest qualifying rate is greater than or equal to 8 percent but less than 10 percent, the multiplier factor shall be 1.2; if the then current highest qualifying rate is greater than or equal to 10 percent but less than 12 percent, the multiplier factor shall be 1.4; if the then current highest qualifying rate is greater than or equal to 12 percent but less than 14 percent, the multiplier factor shall be 1.5; if the then current highest qualifying rate is greater than or equal to 14 percent but less than 16 percent, the multiplier factor shall be 1.6; and if the then current highest qualifying rate is greater than or equal to 16 percent but less than or equal to 18 percent, the multiplier factor shall be 1.7. The multiplier factor or factors for higher qualifying rates shall be established by FINRA as required.

(iv) The "long" and "short" OTC option contracts that comprise a spread as defined in paragraph (f)(2)(A)(xxxii) must be issued and guaranteed by the same carrying broker-dealer and the carrying broker-dealer must also be a FINRA member. If the "long" and "short" OTC option contracts are not issued and guaranteed by the same carrying broker-dealer, or if the carrying broker-dealer is not a FINRA member, then the "short" option contracts must be margined separately pursuant to paragraph (f)(2)(E)(iii) or (E)(iv) above.

(v) The following requirements set forth the minimum amount of margin that must be maintained in margin accounts of customers having positions in components underlying options, and stock index warrants, when such components are held in conjunction with certain positions in the overlying option or warrant. The option or warrant must be listed or OTC (as defined in this Rule). In the case of a call or warrant carried in a short position, a related long position in the underlying component shall be valued at no more than the call/warrant exercise price for margin equity purposes.

a. "Long" Option or Warrant Offset. When a component underlying an option or warrant is carried "long" ("short") in an account in which there is also carried a "long" put (call) or warrant specifying equivalent units of the underlying component, the minimum amount of margin that must be maintained on the underlying component is 10 percent of the aggregate option/warrant exercise price plus the "out-of-the-money" amount, not to exceed the minimum maintenance required pursuant to paragraph (c) of this Rule.

b. Conversions. When a call or warrant carried in a "short" position is covered by a "long" position in equivalent units of the underlying component and is also carried with a "long" put or warrant specifying equivalent units of the same underlying component and having the same exercise price and expiration date as the short call or warrant, the minimum amount of margin that must be maintained for the underlying component shall be 10 percent of the aggregate exercise price.

c. Reverse Conversions. When a put or warrant carried in a "short" position is covered by a "short" position in equivalent units of the underlying component and is also carried with a "long" call or warrant specifying equivalent units of the same underlying component and having the same exercise price and expiration date as the "short" put or warrant, the minimum amount of margin that must be maintained for the underlying component shall be 10 percent of the aggregate exercise price plus the amount by which the exercise price of the put exceeds the current market value of the underlying, if any.

d. Collars. When a call or warrant carried in a "short" position is covered by a "long" position in equivalent units of the underlying component and is also carried with a "long" put or warrant specifying equivalent units of the same underlying component and having a lower exercise price and the same expiration date as the "short" call/warrant, the minimum amount of margin that must be maintained for the underlying component shall be the lesser of 10 percent of the aggregate exercise price of the put plus the put "out-of-the-money" amount or 25 percent of the call aggregate exercise price.

e. "Long" Box Spread in European-Style Options. With respect to a "long" box spread as defined in paragraph (f)(2)(A) of this Rule, in which all component options have a European-style exercise provision and are listed or OTC (as defined in this Rule), margin must be deposited and maintained equal to at least 50 percent of the aggregate difference in the exercise prices. The net proceeds from the sale of "short" option components may be applied to the requirement. For margin purposes, the "long" box spread may be valued at an amount not to exceed 100 percent of the aggregate difference in the exercise prices.

(I)(i) Where a listed or OTC call is carried "short" against an existing net "long" position in the security underlying the option or in any security immediately exchangeable or convertible, other than warrants, without restriction including the payment of money into the security underlying the option, no margin need be required on the call, provided:

a. such net "long" position is adequately margined in accordance with this Rule; and

b. the right to exchange or convert the net "long" position does not expire on or before the date of expiration of the "short" call. Where a listed or OTC put is carried "short" against an existing net "short" position in the security underlying the option, no margin need be required on the put, provided such net "short" position is adequately margined in accordance with this Rule.

(ii) Where a listed or OTC call is carried "short" against an existing net "long" position in a warrant convertible into the security underlying the option, margin shall be required on the call equal to any amount by which the conversion price of the "long" warrant exceeds the exercise price of the call, provided:

a. such net "long" position is adequately margined in accordance with this Rule; and

b. the right to convert the net "long" position does not expire on or before the date of expiration of the "short" call. However, when a payment of money is required to convert the "long" warrant such warrant shall have no value for purposes of this Rule.

(iii) In determining net "long" and net "short" positions, for purposes of paragraphs (f)(2)(I)(i) and (ii) above, offsetting "long" and "short" positions in exchangeable or convertible securities (including warrants) or in the same security, as discussed in paragraph (e)(1), shall be deducted. In computing margin on such an existing net security position carried against a put or call, the current market price to be used shall not be greater than the exercise price in the case of a call or less than the current market price in the case of a put and the required margin shall be increased by any unrealized loss.

(iv) Where a listed or OTC put or call option or stock index warrant is carried "short" in the account of a customer, against an escrow agreement, that is in a form satisfactory to FINRA, is issued by a third party custodian bank or trust company (the "custodian"), either is held in the account at the time the put or call is written, or is received in the account promptly thereafter, and is in compliance with the requirements of Rule 610 of The Options Clearing Corporation, no margin need be required on the put or call.

In the case of a call option or warrant on a broad index stock group, the escrow agreement must certify that the custodian holds for the account of the customer as security for the agreement either cash, cash equivalents, one or more qualified securities, or any combination thereof, having an aggregate market value, computed as at the close of business on the day the call is written, of not less than 100 percent of the aggregate index value computed as at the same time and that the custodian will promptly pay the member the exercise settlement amount in the event the account is assigned an exercise notice. The escrow agreement may provide for substitution of qualified securities held as collateral provided that the substitution shall not cause the value of the qualified securities held to be diminished. A qualified security means an equity security, other than a warrant, right or option, that is registered on any national securities exchange.

In the case of a call on any other option contract, the escrow agreement must certify that the custodian holds for the account of the customer as security for the agreement, the underlying security (or a security immediately convertible into the underlying security without the payment of money) or foreign currency and that the custodian will promptly deliver to the member the underlying security or foreign currency in the event the account is assigned an exercise notice.

In the case of a put on an option contract (including a put on a broad index stock group) or stock index warrant, the escrow agreement must certify that the custodian holds for the account of the customer as security for the agreement, cash or cash equivalents which have an aggregate market value, computed as at the close of business on the day the put is written, of not less than 100 percent of the aggregate exercise price of the put and that the custodian will promptly pay the member the exercise settlement amount (in the case of a put on a broad index stock group) or the aggregate exercise price (in the case of any other put on an option contract) in the event the account is assigned an exercise notice. Cash equivalents shall mean those securities referred to in Section 220.2 of Regulation T.

(J) When a member guarantees an option or stock index warrant to receive or deliver securities or foreign currencies for a customer, such option or stock index warrant shall be margined as if it were a put or call.

(K)(i) Registered specialists, market makers or traders — Notwithstanding the other provisions of this paragraph (f)(2), a member may clear and carry the listed option transactions of one or more registered specialists, registered market makers or registered traders in options (whereby registered traders are deemed specialists for all purposes under the Exchange Act, pursuant to the rules of a national securities exchange) (hereinafter referred to as "specialist(s)"), upon a "Good Faith" margin basis satisfactory to the concerned parties, provided the "Good Faith" margin requirement is not less than the net capital haircut deduction of the member carrying the transaction pursuant to SEA Rule 15c3-1 and, if applicable, Rule 4110(a). In lieu of collecting the "Good Faith" margin requirement, a carrying member may elect to deduct in computing its net capital the amount of any deficiency between the equity maintained in the account and the "Good Faith" margin required.

For purposes of this paragraph (f)(2)(K), a permitted offset position means, in the case of an option in which a specialist or market maker makes a market, a position in the underlying asset or other related assets, and in the case of other securities in which a specialist or market maker makes a market, a position in options overlying the securities in which a specialist or market maker makes a market. Accordingly, a specialist or market maker in options may establish, on a share-for-share basis, a long or short position in the securities underlying the options in which the specialist or market maker makes a market, and a specialist or market maker in securities other than options may purchase or write options overlying the securities in which the specialist or market maker makes a market, if the account holds the following permitted offset positions:

    a. A "short" option position which is not offset by a "long" or "short" option position for an equal or greater number of shares of the same underlying security which is "in the money";

    b. A "long" option position which is not offset by a "long" or "short" option position for an equal or greater number of shares of the same underlying security which is "in the money";

    c. A "short" option position against which an exercise notice was tendered;

    d. A "long" option position which was exercised;

    e. A net "long" position in a security (other than an option) in which a specialist or market maker makes a market;

    f. A net "short" position in a security (other than an option) in which the specialist or market maker makes a market; or

g. A specified portfolio type as referred to in SEA Rule 15c3-1, including its appendices, or any applicable SEC staff interpretation or no-action position.

Permitted offset transactions must be effected for specialist or market making purposes such as hedging, risk reduction, rebalancing of positions, liquidation, or accommodation of customer orders, or other similar specialist or market maker purpose. The specialist or market maker must be able to demonstrate compliance with this provision.

For purposes of this paragraph (f)(2)(K), the term "in the money" means the current market price of the underlying asset or index is not below (with respect to a call option) or above (with respect to a put option) the exercise price of the option; and, the term "overlying option" means a put option purchased or a call option written against a "long" position in an underlying asset; or a call option purchased or a put option written against a "short" position in an underlying asset.

(ii) Securities, including options, in such accounts shall be valued conservatively in the light of current market prices and the amount which might be realized upon liquidation. Substantial additional margin must be required or excess net capital maintained in all cases where the securities carried:

a. are subject to unusually rapid or violent changes in value including volatility in the expiration months of options;

b. do not have an active market; or

c. in one or more or all accounts, including proprietary accounts combined, are such that they cannot be liquidated promptly or represent undue concentration of risk in view of the carrying member's net capital and its overall exposure to material loss.

(L) FINRA may at any time impose higher margin requirements with respect to any option or warrant position(s) when it deems such higher margin requirements are appropriate.

(M) Exclusive designation — A customer may designate at the time an option order is entered which security position held in the account is to serve in lieu of the required margin, if such service is offered by the member; or the customer may have a standing agreement with the member as to the method to be used for determining on any given day which security position will be used in lieu of the margin to support an option transaction. Any security held in the account which serves in lieu of the required margin for a short put or short call shall be unavailable to support any other option transaction in the account.

(N) Cash account transactions — A member may make option transactions in a customer's cash account, provided that:

(i) The transaction is permissible under Regulation T, Section 220.8; or

(ii) A spread, as defined in paragraph (f)(2)(A)(xxxii) of this Rule, comprised of European-style cash-settled index stock group options, or a "short" stock index warrant and a "long" stock index warrant, having the same underlying component or index that is based on the same aggregate current underlying value, that is held in or purchased for the account on the same day, is deemed a covered position and eligible for the cash account provided that:

a. the "long" positions and the "short" positions expire concurrently;

b. the "long" positions are paid in full; and

c. there is held in the account at the time the positions are established, or received into the account promptly thereafter:

1. cash or cash equivalents of not less than the maximum loss, as described in paragraph (f)(2)(H)(i)b. of this Rule, to which net proceeds from the sale of the "short" positions may be applied, or

2. an escrow agreement.

The escrow agreement must certify that the bank holds for the account of the customer as security for the agreement i. cash, ii. cash equivalents, or iii. a combination thereof having an aggregate market value at the time the positions are established of not less than the maximum loss, as described in paragraph (f)(2)(H)(i)b. of this Rule and that the bank will promptly pay the member such amount in the event the account is assigned an exercise notice or that the bank will promptly pay the member sufficient funds to purchase a warrant sold "short" in the event of a buy-in.

    d. A "long" warrant may offset a "short" option contract and a "long" option contract may offset a "short" warrant provided that they have the same underlying component or index and equivalent aggregate current underlying value. In the event that the "long" position is not listed, it must be guaranteed by the carrying broker-dealer; otherwise the "short" position is not eligible for the cash account and must be margined separately pursuant to paragraph (f)(2)(E).

(3) "When Issued" and "When Distributed" Securities

  (A) Margin Accounts

The margin to be maintained on any transaction or net position in each "when issued" security shall be the same as if such security were issued.

Each position in a "when issued" security shall be margined separately and any unrealized profit shall be of value only in providing the amount of margin required on that particular position.

When an account has a "short" position in a "when issued" security and there are held in the account securities upon which the "when issued" security may be issued, such "short" position shall be marked to the market and the balance in the account shall for the purpose of this Rule be adjusted for any unrealized loss in such "short" position.

  (B) Cash Accounts

On any transaction or net position resulting from contracts for a "when issued" security in an account other than that of a member, non-member broker-dealer, or a "designated account," equity must be maintained equal to the margin required were such transaction or position in a margin account.

On any net position resulting from contracts for a "when issued" security made for or with a non-member broker-dealer, no margin need be required, but such net position must be marked to the market.

On any net position resulting from contracts for a "when issued" security made for a member or a "designated account," no margin need be required and such net position need not be marked to the market. However, where such net position is not marked to the market, an amount equal to the loss at the market in such position shall be charged against the member's net capital as provided in SEA Rule 15c3-1 and, if applicable, Rule 4110(a).

The provisions of this paragraph (f)(3) shall not apply to any position resulting from contracts on a "when issued" basis in a security:

    (i) which is the subject of a primary distribution in connection with a bona fide offering by the issuer to the general public for "cash," or

    (ii) which is exempt by FINRA as involving a primary distribution. The term "when issued" as used herein also means "when distributed."

(4) Guaranteed Accounts

Any account guaranteed by another account may be consolidated with such other account and the margin to be maintained may be determined on the net position of both accounts, provided the guarantee is in writing and permits the member carrying the account, without restriction, to use the money and securities in the guaranteeing account to carry the guaranteed account or to pay any deficit therein; and provided further that such guaranteeing account is not owned directly or indirectly by (i) a member, or any stockholder (other than a holder of freely transferable stock only) in the member carrying such account, or (ii) a member, or any stockholder (other than a holder of freely transferable stock only) therein having a definite arrangement for participating in the commissions earned on the guaranteed account. However, the guarantee of a limited partner or of a holder of non-voting stock, if based upon his resources other than his capital contribution to or other than his interest in a member, is not affected by the foregoing prohibition, and such a guarantee may be taken into consideration in computing margin to be maintained in the guaranteed account.

When one or more accounts are guaranteed by another account and the total margin deficiencies guaranteed by any guarantor exceeds 10 percent of the member's excess net capital, the amount of the margin deficiency being guaranteed in excess of 10 percent of excess net capital shall be charged against the member's net capital when computing net capital under SEA Rule 15c3-1 and, if applicable, Rule 4110(a).

(5) Consolidation of Accounts

When two or more accounts are carried for a customer, the margin to be maintained may be determined on the net position of said accounts, provided the customer has consented that the money and securities in each of such accounts may be used to carry or pay any deficit in all such accounts.

(6) Time Within Which Margin or "Mark to Market" Must Be Obtained

The amount of margin or "mark to market" required by any provision of this Rule shall be obtained as promptly as possible and in any event within 15 business days from the date such deficiency occurred, unless FINRA has specifically granted the member additional time.

(7) Practice of Meeting Regulation T Margin Calls by Liquidation Prohibited

When a "margin call," as defined in Section 220.2 of Regulation T, is required in a customer's account, no member shall permit a customer to make a practice of either deferring the deposit of cash or securities beyond the time when such transactions would ordinarily be settled or cleared, or meeting the margin required by the liquidation of the same or other commitments in the account.

This prohibition on liquidations shall not apply (i) to those accounts that, at the time of liquidation, are in compliance with the equity to be maintained pursuant to the provisions of this Rule or (ii) to any account carried on an omnibus basis as prescribed by Regulation T.

(8) Special Initial and Maintenance Margin Requirements

(A) Notwithstanding the other provisions of this Rule, FINRA may, whenever it shall determine that market conditions so warrant, prescribe:

(i) higher initial margin requirements for the purpose of effecting new securities transactions and commitments in accounts of customers with respect to specific securities;

(ii) higher maintenance margin requirements for accounts of customers with respect to any securities; and

(iii) such other terms and conditions as FINRA shall deem appropriate relating to initial and/or maintenance margin requirements for accounts of customers with respect to any securities.

(B) Day Trading

(i) The term "day trading" means the purchasing and selling or the selling and purchasing of the same security on the same day in a margin account except for:

a. a "long" security position held overnight and sold the next day prior to any new purchase of the same security, or

b. a "short" security position held overnight and purchased the next day prior to any new sale of the same security.

(ii) The term "pattern day trader" means any customer who executes four or more day trades within five business days. However, if the number of day trades is 6 percent or less of total trades for the five business day period, the customer will not be considered a pattern day trader and the special requirements under paragraph (f)(8)(B)(iv) of this Rule will not apply. In the event that the member at which a customer seeks to open an account or to resume day trading knows or has a reasonable basis to believe that the customer will engage in pattern day trading, then the special requirements under paragraph (f)(8)(B)(iv) of this Rule will apply.

(iii) The term "day-trading buying power" means the equity in a customer's account at the close of business of the previous day, less any maintenance margin requirement as prescribed in paragraph (c) of this Rule, multiplied by four for equity securities.

The day-trading buying power for non-equity securities may be computed using the applicable special maintenance margin requirements pursuant to other provisions of this Rule.

Whenever day trading occurs in a customer's margin account the special maintenance margin required, based on the cost of all the day trades made during the day, shall be 25 percent for margin eligible equity securities, and 100 percent for non-margin eligible equity securities. For non-equity securities, the special maintenance margin shall be as required pursuant to the other provisions of this Rule. Alternatively, when two or more day trades occur on the same day in the same customer's account, the margin required may be computed utilizing the highest (dollar amount) open position during that day. To utilize the highest open position computation method, a record showing the "time and tick" of each trade must be maintained to document the sequence in which each day trade was completed.

When the equity in a customer's account, after giving consideration to the other provisions of this Rule, is not sufficient to meet the day trading requirements of this paragraph, additional cash or securities must be received into the account to meet any deficiency within five business days of the trade date.

(iv) Special Requirements for Pattern Day Traders

    a. Minimum Equity Requirement for Pattern Day Traders — The minimum equity required for the accounts of customers deemed to be pattern day traders shall be $25,000. This minimum equity must be deposited in the account before such customer may continue day trading and must be maintained in the customer's account at all times.

    b. In the event that the member at which a customer seeks to open an account or resume day trading in an existing account, knows or has a reasonable basis to believe that the customer will engage in pattern day trading, then the minimum equity required under subparagraph (iv)a. above ($25,000) must be deposited in the account prior to commencement of day trading.

    c. Pattern day traders cannot trade in excess of their day-trading buying power as defined in paragraph (f)(8)(B)(iii) above. In the event a pattern day trader exceeds its day-trading buying power, which creates a special maintenance margin deficiency, the following actions will be taken by the member:

        1. The account will be margined based on the cost of all the day trades made during the day,

        2. The customer's day-trading buying power will be limited to the equity in the customer's account at the close of business of the previous day, less the maintenance margin required in paragraph (c) of this Rule, multiplied by two for equity securities, and

        3. "time and tick" (i.e., calculating margin using each trade in the sequence that it is executed, using the highest open position during the day) may not be used.

    d. Pattern day traders who fail to meet their special maintenance margin calls as required within five business days from the date the margin deficiency occurs will be permitted to execute transactions only on a cash available basis for 90 days or until the special maintenance margin call is met.

    e. Pattern day traders are restricted from using the guaranteed account provision pursuant to paragraph (f)(4) of this Rule for meeting the requirements of paragraph (f)(8)(B).

    f. Funds deposited into a pattern day trader's account to meet the minimum equity or maintenance margin requirements of paragraph (f)(8)(B) of this Rule cannot be withdrawn for a minimum of two business days following the close of business on the day of deposit.

(v) In the event a customer does not meet a special margin maintenance call by the fifth business day, then on the sixth business day only, members are required to deduct from net capital the amount of the unmet special margin maintenance call pursuant to SEA Rule 15c3-1 and, if applicable, Rule 4110(a).

(9) Free-Riding in Cash Accounts Prohibited

No member shall permit a customer (other than a broker-dealer) to make a practice, directly or indirectly, of effecting transactions in a cash account where the cost of securities purchased is met by the sale of the securities. No member shall permit a customer to make a practice of selling securities with them in a cash account which are to be received against payment from another broker-dealer where securities were purchased and are not yet paid for. A member transferring an account which is subject to a Regulation T 90-day freeze to another member shall inform the receiving member of such 90-day freeze.

(10) Customer Margin Rules Relating to Security Futures

(A) Applicability

No member may effect a transaction involving, or carry an account containing, a security futures contract with or for a customer in a margin account, without obtaining proper and adequate margin as set forth in this subparagraph.

(B) Amount of customer margin

(i) General Rule. As set forth in paragraphs (b) and (c) of this Rule, the minimum initial and maintenance margin levels for each security futures contract, long and short, shall be 20 percent of the current market value of such contract.

(ii) Excluded from the Rule's requirements are arrangements between a member and a customer with respect to the customer's financing of proprietary positions in security futures, based on the member's good faith determination that the customer is an "Exempted Person," as defined in Rule 401(a)(9) of SEC Customer Margin Requirements for Security Futures, and Rule 41.43(a)(9) under the CEA, except for the proprietary account of a broker-dealer carried by a member pursuant to paragraph (e)(6)(A) of this Rule. Once a registered broker or dealer, or member of a national securities exchange ceases to qualify as an "Exempted Person," it shall notify the member of this fact before establishing any new security futures positions. Any new security futures positions will be subject to the provisions of this subparagraph.

(iii) Permissible Offsets.

Notwithstanding the minimum margin levels specified in paragraph (f)(10)(B)(i) of this Rule, customers with offset positions involving security futures and related positions may have initial or maintenance margin levels (pursuant to the offset table below) that are lower than the levels specified in paragraph (f)(10)(B)(i) of this Rule.

Description of Offset	Security Underlying the Security Future	Initial Margin Requirement	Maintenance Margin Requirement
"Long" security future (or Basket of security futures representing each component of a narrow-based securities index) and "long" put option on the same underlying security (or index).	Individual stock or narrow-based security index.	20 percent of the current market value of the "long" security future, plus pay for the "long" put in full.	The lower of: (1) 10 percent of the aggregate exercise price of the put plus the aggregate put out-of-the-money amount, if any; or (2) 20 percent of the current market value of the "long" security future.
"Short" security future (or basket of security futures representing each component of a narrow-based securities index) and "short" put option on the same underlying security (or index).	Individual stock or narrow-based security index.	20 percent of the current market value of the "short" security future, plus aggregate put in-the-money amount, if any. Proceeds from the put sale may be applied.	20 percent of the current market value of the "short" security future, plus the aggregate put in-the-money amount, if any.

Description of Offset	Security Underlying the Security Future	Initial Margin Requirement	Maintenance Margin Requirement
"Long" security future and "short" position in the same security (or securities basket) underlying the security future.	Individual stock or narrow-based security index.	The initial margin required under Regulation T for the "short" stock or stocks.	5 percent of the current Market value as defined in Regulation T of the stock or stocks underlying the security future.
"Long" security future (or basket of security futures representing each component of a narrow-based securities index) and "short" call option on the same underlying security (or index).	Individual stock or narrow-based security index.	20 percent of the current market value of the "long" security future, plus the aggregate call in-the-money amount, if any. Proceeds from the call sale may be applied.	20 percent of the current market value of the "long" security future, plus the aggregate call in-the-money amount, if any.
"Long" a basket of narrow-based security futures that together tracks a broad based index and "short" a broad-based security index call option contract on the same index.	Narrow-based security index.	20 percent of the current market value of the "long" basket of narrow-based security futures, plus the aggregate call in-the-money amount, if any. Proceeds from the call sale may be applied.	20 percent of the current market value of the "long" basket of narrow-based security futures, plus the aggregate call in-the-money amount, if any.
"Short" a basket of narrow-based security futures that together tracks a broad-based security index and "short" a broad-based security index put option contract on the same index.	Narrow-based security index.	20 percent of the current market value of the "short" basket of narrow-based security futures, plus the aggregate put in--the-money amount. Proceeds from the put sale may be applied.	20 percent of the current market value of the "short" basket of narrow-based security futures, plus the aggregate put in-the-money amount, if any.
"Long" a basket of narrow-based security futures that together tracks a broad-based security index and "long" a broad-based security index put option contract on the same index.	Narrow-based security index.	20 percent of the current market value of the long basket of narrow-based security futures, plus pay for the long put in full.	The lower of: (1) 10 percent of the aggregate exercise price of the put, plus the aggregate put out-of-the-money amount, if any; or (2) 20 percent of the current market value of the long basket of security futures.
"Short" a basket of narrow-based security futures that together tracks a broad-based security index and "long" a broad-based security index call option contract on the same index.	Narrow-based security index.	20 percent of the current market value of the "short" basket of narrow-based security futures, plus pay for the "long" call in full.	The lower of: (1) 10 percent of the aggregate exercise price of the call, plus the aggregate call out-of-the-money amount, if any; or (2) 20 percent of the current market value of the "short" basket of security futures.

Description of Offset	Security Underlying the Security Future	Initial Margin Requirement	Maintenance Margin Requirement
"Long" security future and "short" security future on the same underlying security (or index).	Individual stock or narrow-based security index.	The greater of: (1) 5 percent of the current market value of the "long" security future; or (2) 5 percent of the current market value of the "short" security future.	The greater of: (1) 5 percent of the current market value of the "long" security future; or (2) 5 percent of the current market value of the "short" security future.
"Long" security future, "long" put option and "short" call option. The "long" security future, "long" put and "short" call must be on the same underlying security and the put and call must have the same exercise price. (Conversion)	Individual stock or narrow-based security index.	20 percent of the current market value of the "long" security future, plus the aggregate call in-the-money amount, if any, plus pay for the put in full. Proceeds from the call sale may be applied.	10 percent of the aggregate exercise price, plus the aggregate call in-the-money amount, if any.
"Long" security future, "long" put option and "short" call option. The "long" security future, "long" put and "short" call must be on the same underlying security and the put exercise price must be below the call exercise price. (Collar)	Individual stock or narrow-based security index.	20 percent of the current market value of the long security future, plus the aggregate call in-the-money amount, if any, plus pay for the put in full. Proceeds from call sale may be applied.	The lower of: (1) 10 percent of the aggregate exercise price of the put plus the aggregate put out-of-the-money amount, if any; or (2) 20 percent of the aggregate exercise price of the call, plus the aggregate call in-the-money amount, if any.
"Short" security future and "long" position in the same security (or securities basket) underlying the security future.	Individual stock or narrow-based security index.	The initial margin required under Regulation T for the "long" security or securities.	5 percent of the current Market value, as defined in Regulation T, of the long stock or stocks.
"Short" security future and "long" position in a security immediately convertible into the same security underlying the security future, without restriction, including the payment of money.	Individual stock or narrow-based security index.	The initial margin required under Regulation T for the "long" security or securities.	10 percent of the current market value, as defined in Regulation T, of the long stock or stocks.
"Short" security future (or basket of security futures representing each component of a narrow-based securities index) and "long" call option or warrant on the same underlying security (or index).	Individual stock or narrow-based security index.	20 percent of the current market value of the short security future, plus pay for the call in full.	The lower of: (1) 10 percent of the aggregate exercise price of the put plus the aggregate put out-of-the-money amount, if any; or (2) 20 percent of the current market value of the short security future.

Description of Offset	Security Underlying the Security Future	Initial Margin Requirement	Maintenance Margin Requirement
"Short" security future, "short" put option and "long" call option. The "short" security future, "short" put and "long" call must be on the same underlying security and the put and call must have the same exercise price. (Reverse Conversion)	Individual stock or narrow-based security index.	20 percent of the current market value of the "short" security future, plus the aggregate put in-the-money amount, if any, plus pay for the call in full. Proceeds from put sale may be applied.	10 percent of the aggregate exercise price, plus the aggregate put in-the-money amount, if any.
"Long" ("short") a security future and short ("long") an identical security future traded on a different market.	Individual stock and narrow-based security index.	The greater of: (1) 3 percent of the current market value of the "long" security future(s); or (2) 3 percent of the current market value of the short security future(s).	The greater of: (1) 3 percent of the current market value of the "long" security future(s); or (2) 3 percent of the current market value of the "short" security future(s).
"Long" ("short") a basket of security futures that together tracks a narrow-based index and "short" ("long") a narrow-based index future.	Individual stock and narrow-based security index.	The greater of: (1) 5 percent of the current market value of the "long" security future(s); or (2) 5 percent of the current market value of the "short" security future(s).	The greater of: (1) 5 percent of the current market value of the "long" security future(s); or (2) 5 percent of the current market value of the "short" security future(s).

(C) Definitions

For the purposes of paragraph (f)(10) of this Rule and the offset table noted above, with respect to the term "security futures contracts," the following terms shall have the meanings specified below:

(i) The term "security futures contract" means a "security future" as defined in Section 3(a)(55) of the Exchange Act.

(ii) The term "current market value" has the same meaning as defined in Rule 401(a)(4) of SEC Customer Margin Requirements for Security Futures and Rule 41.43(a)(4) under the CEA.

(iii) The term "underlying security" means, in the case of physically settled security futures contracts, the security that is delivered upon expiration of the contract, and, in the case of cash settled security futures contracts, the security or securities index the price or level of which determines the final settlement price for the security futures contract upon its expiration.

(iv) The term "underlying basket" means, in the case of a securities index, a group of security futures contracts where the underlying securities as defined in subparagraph (iii) above include each of the component securities of the applicable index and that meets the following conditions: (1) the quantity of each underlying security is proportional to its representation in the index, (2) the total market value of the underlying securities is equal to the aggregate value of the applicable index, (3) the basket cannot be used to offset more than the number of contracts or warrants represented by its total market value, and (4) the security futures contracts shall be unavailable to support any other contract or warrant transaction in the account.

(v) The term "underlying stock basket" means a group of securities that includes each of the component securities of the applicable index and that meets the following conditions: (1) the quantity of each stock in the basket is proportional to its representation in the index, (2) the total market value of the basket is equal to the underlying index value of the index options or warrants to be covered, (3) the securities in the basket cannot be used to cover more than the number of index options or warrants represented by that value, and (4) the securities in the basket shall be unavailable to support any other option or warrant transaction in the account.

(vi) The term "variation settlement" has the same meaning as defined in Rule 401(a) of SEC Customer Margin Requirements for Security Futures and Rule 41.43(a)(32) under the CEA.

(D) Security Futures Dealers' Accounts

(i) Notwithstanding the other provisions of this paragraph (f)(10), a member may carry and clear the market maker permitted offset positions (as defined below) of one or more security futures dealers in an account that is limited to market maker transactions, upon a "Good Faith" margin basis that is satisfactory to the concerned parties, provided the "Good Faith" margin requirement is not less than the net capital haircut deduction of the member carrying the transaction pursuant to SEA Rule 15c3-1 and, if applicable, Rule 4110(a). In lieu of collecting the "Good Faith" margin requirement, a carrying member may elect to deduct in computing its net capital the amount of any deficiency between the equity maintained in the account and the "Good Faith" margin required.

For the purpose of this paragraph (f)(10)(D), the term "security futures dealer" means (1) a member of a national securities exchange or a national securities association registered pursuant to Section 15A(a) of the Exchange Act; (2) is registered with such exchange or association as a security futures dealer pursuant to rules that are effective in accordance with Section 19(b)(2) of the Exchange Act and, as applicable Section 5c(c) of the CEA, that: (a) requires such member to be registered as a floor trader or a floor broker with the CFTC under Section 4f(a)(1) of the CEA, or as a dealer with the SEC under Section 15(b) of the Exchange Act; (b) requires such member to maintain sufficient records to prove compliance with the rules of the exchange or association of which it is a member; (c) requires such member to hold itself out as being willing to buy and sell security futures for its own account on a regular and continuous basis; and (d) provides for disciplinary action, including revocation of such member's registration as a security futures dealer, for such member's failure to comply with Rules 400 through 406 of SEC Customer Margin Requirements for Security Futures and Rules 41.42 through 41.49 of the CEA or the rules of the exchange or association of which the security futures dealer is a member.

(ii) For purposes of this paragraph (f)(10)(D), a permitted offset position means in the case of a security futures contract in which a security futures dealer makes a market, a position in the underlying asset or other related assets, or positions in options overlying the asset or related assets. Accordingly, a security futures dealer may establish a long or short position in the assets underlying the security futures contracts in which the security futures dealer makes a market, and may purchase or write options overlying those assets if the account holds the following permitted offset positions:

a. A "long" position in the security futures contract or underlying asset offset by a "short" option position that is "in or at the money";

b. A "short" position in the security futures contract or underlying asset offset by a "long" option position that is "in or at the money";

c. A position in the underlying asset resulting from the assignment of a market-maker "short" option position or making delivery in respect of a short security futures contract;

d. A position in the underlying asset resulting from the assignment of a market-maker "long" option position or taking delivery in respect of a long security futures contract;

e. A net "long" position in a security futures contract in which a security futures dealer makes a market or the underlying asset;

f. A net "short" position in a security futures contract in which a security futures dealer makes a market or the underlying asset; or

g. An offset position as defined in SEA Rule 15c3-1, including its appendices, or any applicable SEC staff interpretation or no-action position.

(E) Approved Options Specialists' or Approved Market Makers' Accounts

(i) Notwithstanding the other provisions of paragraphs (f)(10) and (f)(2)(K), a member may carry and clear the market maker permitted offset positions (as defined below) of one or more approved options specialists or approved market makers in an account that is limited to bona fide approved options specialist or approved market maker transactions, upon a "Good Faith" margin basis that is satisfactory to the concerned parties, provided the "Good Faith" margin requirement is not less than the net capital haircut deduction of the member carrying the transaction pursuant to SEA Rule 15c3-1 and, if applicable, Rule 4110(a). In lieu of collecting the "Good Faith" margin requirement, a carrying member may elect to deduct in computing its net capital the amount of any deficiency between the equity maintained in the account and the "Good Faith" margin required. For the purpose of this paragraph (f)(10)(E), the term "approved options specialist" or "approved market maker" means a specialist, market maker, or registered trader in options as referenced in paragraph (f)(2)(K) of this Rule, who is deemed a specialist for all purposes under the Exchange Act and who is registered pursuant to the rules of a national securities exchange.

(ii) For purposes of this paragraph (f)(10)(E), a permitted offset position means a position in the underlying asset or other related assets. Accordingly, a specialist or market maker may establish a long or short position in the assets underlying the options in which the specialist or market maker makes a market, or a security futures contract thereon, if the account holds the following permitted offset positions:

a. A "long" position in the underlying instrument or security futures contract offset by a "short" option position that is "in or at the money";

b. A "short" position in the underlying instrument or security futures contract offset by a "long" option position that is "in or at the money";

c. A stock position resulting from the assignment of a market-maker short option position or delivery in respect of a "short" security futures contract;

d. A stock position resulting from the exercise of a market maker "long" option position or taking delivery in respect of a long security futures contract;

e. A net "long" position in a security (other than an option) in which the market maker makes a market;

f. A net "short" position in a security (other than an option) in which the market maker makes a market; or

g. An offset position as defined in SEA Rule 15c3-1, including its appendices, or any applicable SEC staff interpretation or no-action position.

(iii) For purposes of paragraphs (f)(10)(D) and (E), the term "in or at the money" means that the current market price of the underlying security is not more than two standard exercise intervals below (with respect to a call option) or above (with respect to a put option) the exercise price of the option; the term "in the money" means that the current market price of the underlying asset or index is not below (with respect to a call option) or above (with respect to a put option) the exercise price of the option; the term "overlying option" means a put option purchased or a call option written against a "long" position in an underlying asset; or a call option purchased, or a put option written against a "short" position in an underlying asset.

(iv) Securities, including options and security futures contracts, in such accounts shall be valued conservatively in light of current market prices and the amount that might be realized upon liquidation. Substantial additional margin must be required or excess net capital maintained in all cases where the securities carried: (a) are subject to unusually rapid or violent changes in value including volatility in the expiration months of options or security futures contracts, (b) do not have an active market, or (c) in one or more or all accounts, including proprietary accounts combined, are such that they cannot be liquidated promptly or represent undue concentration of risk in view of the carrying member's net capital and its overall exposure to material loss.

(F) Approved Specialists' and Approved Market Makers' Accounts — Others

(i) Notwithstanding the other provisions of paragraphs (f)(10) and (f)(2)(K), a member may carry the account of an "approved specialist" or "approved market maker" which account is limited to bona fide specialist or market making transactions including hedge transactions with security futures contracts upon a margin basis that is satisfactory to both parties. The amount of any deficiency between the equity in the account and haircut requirement pursuant to SEA Rule 15c3-1 and, if applicable, Rule 4110(a), shall be charged against the member's net capital when computing net capital under SEA Rule 15c3-1 and Rule 4110(a).

(ii) For purposes of this paragraph (f)(10)(F), the term "approved specialist" or "approved market maker" means a specialist or market maker who is deemed a specialist or market maker for all purposes under the Exchange Act and who is registered pursuant to the rules of a national securities exchange.

(G) Additional Requirements

(i) Money market mutual funds, as defined in Rule 2a-7 under the Investment Company Act, can be used for satisfying margin requirements under this paragraph (f)(10), provided that the requirements of Rule 404(b) of SEC Customer Margin Requirements for Security Futures and Rule 41.46(b)(2) under the CEA are satisfied.

(ii) Day trading of security futures is subject to the minimum requirements of this Rule. If deemed a pattern day trader, the customer must maintain equity of $25,000. The 20 percent requirement, for security futures contracts, should be calculated based on the greater of the initial or closing transaction and any amount exceeding FINRA excess must be collected. The creation of a customer call subjects the account to all the restrictions contained in paragraph (f)(8)(B) of this Rule.

(iii) The use of the "time and tick" method is based on the member's ability to substantiate the validity of the system used. Lacking this ability dictates the use of the aggregate method.

(iv) Security futures contracts transacted or held in a futures account shall not be subject to any provision of this Rule.

(g) Portfolio Margin

As an alternative to the "strategy-based" margin requirements set forth in paragraphs (a) through (f) of this Rule, members may elect to apply the portfolio margin requirements set forth in this paragraph (g) to all margin equity securities, listed options, security futures products (as defined in Section 3(a)(56) of the Exchange Act), unlisted derivatives, warrants, stock index warrants, and related instruments (as defined in paragraph (g)(2)(D)), provided that the requirements of paragraph (g)(6)(B)(i) of this Rule are met.

In addition, a member, provided that it is a Futures Commission Merchant ("FCM") and is either a clearing member of a futures clearing organization or has an affiliate that is a clearing member of a futures clearing organization, is permitted under this paragraph (g) to combine an eligible participant's related instruments with listed index options, unlisted derivatives, options on exchange traded funds ("ETF"), stock index warrants and underlying instruments and compute a margin requirement for such combined products on a portfolio margin basis.

The portfolio margin provisions of this Rule shall not apply to Individual Retirement Accounts ("IRAs").

(1) Monitoring

Members must monitor the risk of portfolio margin accounts and maintain a comprehensive written risk analysis methodology for assessing the potential risk to the member's capital over a specified range of possible market movements of positions maintained in such accounts. The risk analysis methodology shall specify the computations to be made, the frequency of computations, the records to be reviewed and maintained, and the person(s) within the organization responsible for the risk function. This risk analysis methodology must be filed with FINRA, or the member's designated examining authority ("DEA") if other than FINRA, and submitted to the SEC prior to the implementation of portfolio margining. In performing the risk analysis of portfolio margin accounts required by this Rule, each member shall include in the written risk analysis methodology procedures and guidelines for:

(A) obtaining and reviewing the appropriate account documentation and financial information necessary for assessing the amount of credit to be extended to eligible participants;

(B) the determination, review and approval of credit limits to each eligible participant, and across all eligible participants, utilizing a portfolio margin account;

(C) monitoring credit risk exposure to the member from portfolio margin accounts, on both an intra-day and end of day basis, including the type, scope and frequency of reporting to senior management;

(D) the use of stress testing of portfolio margin accounts in order to monitor market risk exposure from individual accounts;

(E) the regular review and testing of these risk analysis procedures by an independent unit such as internal audit or other comparable group;

(F) managing the impact of credit extended related to portfolio margin accounts on the member's overall risk exposure;

(G) the appropriate response by management when limits on credit extensions related to portfolio margin accounts have been exceeded;

(H) determining the need to collect additional margin from a particular eligible participant, including whether that determination was based upon the creditworthiness of the participant and/or the risk of the eligible product; and

(I) monitoring the credit exposure resulting from concentrated positions within both individual portfolio margin accounts and across all portfolio margin accounts.

Moreover, management must periodically review, in accordance with written procedures, the member's credit extension activities for consistency with these guidelines. Management must periodically determine if the data necessary to apply this paragraph (g) is accessible on a timely basis and information systems are available to adequately capture, monitor, analyze and report relevant data.

(2) Definitions — For purposes of this paragraph (g), the following terms shall have the meanings specified below:

(A) The term "listed option" means any equity-based or equity index-based option traded on a registered national securities exchange or issued and guaranteed by a registered clearing agency and shall include an OCC Cleared OTC Option (as defined in Rule 2360).

(B) The term "portfolio" means any eligible product, as defined in paragraph (g)(6)(B)(i), grouped with its underlying instruments and related instruments.

(C) The term "product group" means two or more portfolios of the same type (see table in paragraph (g)(2)(F) below) for which it has been determined by SEA Rule 15c3-1a that a percentage of offsetting profits may be applied to losses at the same valuation point.

(D) The term "related instrument" within a security class or product group means broad-based index futures and options on broad-based index futures covering the same underlying instrument. The term "related instrument" does not include security futures products.

(E) The term "security class" refers to all listed options, security futures products, unlisted derivatives, and related instruments covering the same underlying instrument and the underlying instrument itself.

(F) The term "theoretical gains and losses" means the gain and loss in the value of individual eligible products and related instruments at ten equidistant intervals (valuation points) ranging from an assumed movement (both up and down) in the current market value of the underlying instrument. The magnitude of the valuation point range shall be as follows:

Portfolio Type	Up / Down Market Move (High & Low Valuation Points)
High Capitalization, Broad-based Market Index	+6% / -8%
Non-High Capitalization, Broad-based Market Index	+/- 10%
Any other eligible product that is, or is based on, an equity security or a narrow-based index	+/- 15%

(G) The term "underlying instrument" means a security or security index upon which any listed option, unlisted derivative, security future, or broad-based index future is based.

(H) The term "unlisted derivative" means any equity-based or equity index-based option, forward contract, or security-based swap that can be valued by a theoretical pricing model approved by the SEC and that is neither traded on a national securities exchange, nor issued and guaranteed by a registered clearing agency and shall not include an OCC Cleared OTC Option (as defined in Rule 2360).

(3) Approved Theoretical Pricing Models — Theoretical pricing models must be approved by the SEC.

(4) Eligible Participants — The application of the portfolio margin provisions of this paragraph (g) is limited to the following:

(A) any broker or dealer registered pursuant to Section 15 of the Exchange Act;

(B) any member of a national futures exchange to the extent that listed index options, unlisted derivatives, options on ETFs, stock index warrants or underlying instruments hedge the member's index futures; and

(C) any person or entity not included in paragraphs (g)(4)(A) and (g)(4)(B) above approved for uncovered options and, if transactions in security futures are to be included in the account, approval for such transactions is also required. However, an eligible participant under this paragraph (g)(4)(C) may not establish or maintain positions in unlisted derivatives unless minimum equity of at least $5 million is established and maintained with the member. For purposes of this minimum equity requirement, all securities and futures accounts carried by the member for the same eligible participant may be combined provided ownership across the accounts is identical. A guarantee pursuant to paragraph (f)(4) of this Rule is not permitted for purposes of the minimum equity requirement.

(5) Opening of Accounts

(A) Members must notify and receive approval from FINRA, or the member's DEA if other than FINRA, prior to establishing a portfolio margin methodology for eligible participants.

(B) Only eligible participants that have been approved to engage in uncovered short option contracts pursuant to Rule 2360, or the rules of the member's DEA if other than FINRA, are permitted to utilize a portfolio margin account. If eligible participants engage in security futures products transactions, approval from the member will also be required pursuant to Rule 2370.

(C) On or before the date of the initial transaction in a portfolio margin account, a member shall:

(i) furnish the eligible participant with a special written disclosure statement describing the nature and risks of portfolio margining which includes an acknowledgement for all portfolio margin account owners to sign, attesting that they have read and understood the disclosure statement, and agree to the terms under which a portfolio margin account is provided (see Rule 2360(c)); and

(ii) obtain the signed acknowledgement noted above from the eligible participant and record the date of receipt.

(6) Establishing Account and Eligible Positions

(A) For purposes of applying the portfolio margin requirements prescribed in this paragraph (g), members are to establish and utilize a specific securities margin account, or sub-account of a margin account, clearly identified as a portfolio margin account that is separate from any other securities account carried for an eligible participant.

A margin deficit in the portfolio margin account of an eligible participant may not be considered as satisfied by excess equity in another account. Funds and/or securities must be transferred to the deficient account and a written record created and maintained. However, if a portfolio margin account is carried as a sub-account of a margin account, excess equity in the margin account (determined in accordance with the rules applicable to a margin account other than a portfolio margin account) may be used to satisfy a margin deficit in the portfolio margin sub-account without having to transfer any funds and/or securities.

(B) Eligible Products

(i) For eligible participants as described in paragraphs (g)(4)(A) through (g)(4)(C), a transaction in, or transfer of, an eligible product may be effected in the portfolio margin account. Eligible products under this paragraph (g) consist of:

a. a margin equity security (including a foreign equity security and option on a foreign equity security, provided the foreign equity security is deemed to have a "ready market" under SEA Rule 15c3-1 or a "no-action" position issued thereunder, and a control or restricted security, provided the security has met the requirements in a manner consistent with Securities Act Rule 144 or an SEC "no-action" position issued thereunder, sufficient enough to permit the sale of the security, upon exercise or assignment of any listed option or unlisted derivative written or held against it, without restriction);

b. a listed option on an equity security or index of equity securities;

c. a security futures product;

d. an unlisted derivative on an equity security or index of equity securities;

e. a warrant on an equity security or index of equity securities; and

f. a related instrument as defined in paragraph (g)(2)(D).

(7) Margin Required

The amount of margin required under this paragraph (g) for each portfolio shall be the greater of:

(A) the amount for any of the ten equidistant valuation points representing the largest theoretical loss as calculated pursuant to paragraph (g)(8) below; or

(B) for eligible participants as described in paragraph (g)(4)(A) through (g)(4)(C), $.375 for each listed option, unlisted derivative, security future product, and related instrument, multiplied by the contract's or instrument's multiplier, not to exceed the market value in the case of long contracts in eligible products.

(C) Account guarantees pursuant to paragraph (f)(4) of this Rule are not permitted for purposes of meeting margin requirements.

(D) Positions other than those listed in paragraph (g)(6)(B)(i) above are not eligible for portfolio margin treatment. However, positions not eligible for portfolio margin treatment (except for ineligible related instruments) may be carried in a portfolio margin account, provided the member has the ability to apply the applicable strategy-based margin requirements promulgated under this Rule, with the exception of securities subject to other provisions of paragraph (g). Shares of a money market mutual fund may be carried in a portfolio margin account, also subject to the applicable strategy-based margin requirement under this Rule provided that:

(i) the customer waives any right to redeem shares without the member's consent;

(ii) the member (or, if the shares are deposited with a clearing organization, the clearing organization) obtains the right to redeem shares in cash upon request;

> (iii) the fund agrees to satisfy any conditions necessary or appropriate to ensure that the shares may be redeemed in cash, promptly upon request; and
>
> (iv) the member complies with the requirements of Section 11(d)(1) of the Exchange Act and SEA Rule 11d1-2.

(E) Non-margin eligible equity securities held "long" in a portfolio margin account shall be maintained at 100 percent of the current market value at all times. Non-margin eligible equity securities held "short" in a portfolio margin account shall be maintained at 50 percent of the current market value at all times.

(8) Method of Calculation

(A) Long and short positions in eligible products, including underlying instruments and related instruments, are to be grouped by security class; each security class group being a "portfolio." Each portfolio is categorized as one of the portfolio types specified in paragraph (g)(2)(F) above, as applicable.

(B) For each portfolio, theoretical gains and losses are calculated for each position as specified in paragraph (g)(2)(F) above. For purposes of determining the theoretical gains and losses at each valuation point, members shall obtain and utilize the theoretical values of eligible products as described in this paragraph (g) rendered by an approved theoretical pricing model.

(C) Offsets. Within each portfolio, theoretical gains and losses may be netted fully at each valuation point. Offsets between portfolios within the eligible product groups, as described in paragraph (g)(2)(F), may then be applied as permitted by SEA Rule 15c3-1a.

(D) After applying the offsets above, the sum of the greatest loss from each portfolio is computed to arrive at the total margin required for the account (subject to the per contract minimum).

(E) In addition, if a security that is convertible, exchangeable, or exercisable into a security that is an underlying instrument requires the payment of money or would result in a loss if converted, exchanged, or exercised at the time when the security is deemed an underlying instrument, the full amount of the conversion loss is required.

(9) Portfolio Margin Minimum Equity Deficiency

(A) If, as of the close of business, the equity in the portfolio margin account of an eligible participant as described in paragraph (g)(4)(C), declines below the $5 million minimum equity required, if applicable, and is not restored to at least $5 million within three business days by a deposit of funds and/or securities or through favorable market action, members are prohibited from accepting new opening orders beginning on the fourth business day, except that new opening orders entered for the purpose of reducing market risk may be accepted if the result would be to lower margin requirements. This prohibition shall remain in effect until,

> (i) equity of $5 million is established, or
>
> (ii) all unlisted derivatives are liquidated or transferred from the portfolio margin account to the appropriate securities account.

(B) Members will not be permitted to deduct any portfolio margin minimum equity deficiency amount from net capital in lieu of collecting the minimum equity required.

(10) Portfolio Margin Deficiency

(A) If, as of the close of business, the equity in the portfolio margin account of an eligible participant, as described in paragraph (g)(4)(A) through (g)(4)(C), is less than the margin required, the eligible participant may deposit additional funds and/or securities or establish a hedge to meet the margin requirement within three business days. After the three business day period, members are prohibited from accepting new opening orders, except that new opening orders entered for the purpose of reducing market risk may be accepted if the result would be to lower margin requirements. In the event an eligible participant fails to hedge existing positions or deposit additional funds and/or securities in an amount sufficient to eliminate any margin deficiency after three business days, the member must liquidate positions in an amount sufficient to, at a minimum, lower the total margin required to an amount less than or equal to the account equity.

(B) If the portfolio margin deficiency is not met by the close of business on the next business day after the business day on which such deficiency arises, members will be required to deduct the amount of the deficiency from net capital until such time the deficiency is satisfied or positions are liquidated pursuant to paragraph (g)(10)(A) above.

(C) Members will not be permitted to deduct any portfolio margin deficiency amount from net capital in lieu of collecting the margin required.

(D) FINRA, or the member's DEA if other than FINRA, may grant additional time for an eligible participant to meet a portfolio margin deficiency upon written request, which is expected to be granted in extraordinary circumstances only.

(E) Notwithstanding the provisions of subparagraph (A) above, members should not permit an eligible participant to make a practice of meeting a portfolio margin deficiency by liquidation. Members must have procedures in place to identify accounts that periodically liquidate positions to eliminate margin deficiencies, and the member is expected to take appropriate action when warranted. Liquidation to eliminate margin deficiencies that are caused solely by adverse price movements may be disregarded.

(11) Determination of Value for Margin Purposes

For the purposes of this paragraph (g), all eligible products shall be valued at current market prices. Account equity for the purposes of paragraphs (g)(9)(A) and (g)(10)(A) shall be calculated separately for each portfolio margin account by adding the current market value of all long positions, subtracting current market value of all short positions, and adding the credit (or subtracting the debit) balance in the account.

(12) Net Capital Treatment of Portfolio Margin Accounts

(A) No member that requires margin in any portfolio account pursuant to paragraph (g) of this Rule shall permit the aggregate portfolio margin requirements to exceed ten times its net capital for any period exceeding three business days. The member shall, beginning on the fourth business day, cease opening new portfolio margin accounts until compliance is achieved.

(B) If, at any time, a member's aggregate portfolio margin requirements exceed ten times its net capital, the member shall immediately transmit telegraphic or facsimile notice of such deficiency to the principal office of the SEC in Washington, D.C., the district or regional office of the SEC for the district or region in which the member maintains its principal place of business; and to FINRA, or the member's DEA if other than FINRA. The notice to FINRA shall be in such form as FINRA may prescribe.

(13) Day Trading Requirements — The day trading restrictions promulgated under paragraph (f)(8)(B) of this Rule shall not apply to portfolio margin accounts that establish and maintain at least $5 million in equity, provided that a member has the ability to monitor the intra-day risk associated with day trading. Portfolio margin accounts that do not establish and maintain at least $5 million in equity will be subject to the day trading restrictions under paragraph (f)(8)(B) of this Rule, provided the member has the ability to apply the applicable day trading requirement under this Rule. However, if the position or positions day traded were part of a hedge strategy, the day trading restrictions will not apply. A "hedge strategy" for purposes of this Rule means a transaction or a series of transactions that reduces or offsets a material portion of the risk in a portfolio. Members are expected to monitor these portfolio margin accounts to detect and prevent circumvention of the day trading requirements. In the event day trades executed in a portfolio margin account exceed the day-trading buying power, the day trade margin deficiency that is created must be met by the deposit of cash and/or securities within three business days.

(14) Requirements to Liquidate

(A) A member is required immediately either to liquidate, or transfer to another broker-dealer eligible to carry portfolio margin accounts, all portfolio margin accounts with positions in related instruments if the member is:

(i) insolvent as defined in Section 101 of Title 11 of the United States Code, or is unable to meet its obligations as they mature;

      (ii) the subject of a proceeding pending in any court or before any agency of the United States or any State in which a receiver, trustee, or liquidator for such debtor has been appointed;

      (iii) not in compliance with applicable requirements under the Exchange Act or rules of the SEC or any self-regulatory organization with respect to financial responsibility or hypothecation of eligible participant's securities; or

      (iv) unable to make such computations as may be necessary to establish compliance with such financial responsibility or hypothecation rules.

    (B) Nothing in this paragraph (g)(14) shall be construed as limiting or restricting in any way the exercise of any right of a registered clearing agency to liquidate or cause the liquidation of positions in accordance with its by-laws and rules.

  (15) Members must ensure that portfolio accounts are in compliance with Rule 2360.

(h) Margin Requirement Exception for Certain Members.

Any member designated to another self-regulatory organization for oversight of the member's compliance with applicable securities laws, rules and regulations, and self-regulatory organization rules under SEA Rule 17d-1 is exempt from the provisions of Rule 4210.

---

22. FINRA Rules: 4370 – Business Continuity Plans and Emergency Contact Information

(a) Each member must create and maintain a written business continuity plan identifying procedures relating to an emergency or significant business disruption. Such procedures must be reasonably designed to enable the member to meet its existing obligations to customers. In addition, such procedures must address the member's existing relationships with other broker-dealers and counter-parties. The business continuity plan must be made available promptly upon request to FINRA staff.

(b) Each member must update its plan in the event of any material change to the member's operations, structure, business or location. Each member must also conduct an annual review of its business continuity plan to determine whether any modifications are necessary in light of changes to the member's operations, structure, business, or location.

(c) The elements that comprise a business continuity plan are flexible and may be tailored to the size and needs of a member. Each plan, however, must at a minimum, address:

  (1) Data back-up and recovery (hard copy and electronic);

  (2) All mission critical systems;

  (3) Financial and operational assessments;

  (4) Alternate communications between customers and the member;

  (5) Alternate communications between the member and its employees;

  (6) Alternate physical location of employees;

  (7) Critical business constituent, bank, and counter-party impact;

  (8) Regulatory reporting;

  (9) Communications with regulators; and

  (10) How the member will assure customers' prompt access to their funds and securities in the event that the member determines that it is unable to continue its business.

Each member must address the above-listed categories to the extent applicable and necessary. If any of the above-listed categories is not applicable, the member's business continuity plan need not address the category. The member's business continuity plan, however, must document the rationale for not including such category in its plan. If a member relies on another entity for any one of the above-listed categories or any mission critical system, the member's business continuity plan must address this relationship.

(d) Members must designate a member of senior management to approve the plan and he or she shall be responsible for conducting the required annual review. The member of senior management must also be a registered principal.

(e) Each member must disclose to its customers how its business continuity plan addresses the possibility of a future significant business disruption and how the member plans to respond to events of varying scope. At a minimum, such disclosure must be made in writing to customers at account opening, posted on the member's Web site (if the member maintains a Web site), and mailed to customers upon request.

(f)(1) Each member shall report to FINRA, via such electronic or other means as FINRA may specify, prescribed emergency contact information for the member. The emergency contact information for the member includes designation of two associated persons as emergency contact persons. At least one emergency contact person shall be a member of senior management and a registered principal of the member. If a member designates a second emergency contact person who is not a registered principal, such person shall be a member of senior management who has knowledge of the member's business operations. A member with only one associated person shall designate as a second emergency contact person an individual, either registered with another firm or nonregistered, who has knowledge of the member's business operations (e.g., the member's attorney, accountant, or clearing firm contact).

(2) Each member must promptly update its emergency contact information, via such electronic or other means as FINRA may specify, in the event of any material change. With respect to the designated emergency contact persons, each member must identify, review, and, if necessary, update such designations in the manner prescribed by Rule 4517.

(g) For purposes of this Rule, the following terms shall have the meanings specified below:

(1) "Mission critical system" means any system that is necessary, depending on the nature of a member's business, to ensure prompt and accurate processing of securities transactions, including, but not limited to, order taking, order entry, execution, comparison, allocation, clearance and settlement of securities transactions, the maintenance of customer accounts, access to customer accounts and the delivery of funds and securities.

(2) "Financial and operational assessment" means a set of written procedures that allow a member to identify changes in its operational, financial, and credit risk exposures.

---

23. FINRA Rules: 4511 – General Requirements

(a) Members shall make and preserve books and records as required under the FINRA rules, the Exchange Act and the applicable Exchange Act rules.

(b) Members shall preserve for a period of at least six years those FINRA books and records for which there is no specified period under the FINRA rules or applicable Exchange Act rules.

(c) All books and records required to be made pursuant to the FINRA rules shall be preserved in a format and media that complies with SEA Rule 17a-4.

---

24. FINRA Rules: 4512 – Customer Account Information

(a) Each member shall maintain the following information:

    (1) for each account:

        (A) customer's name and residence;

        (B) whether customer is of legal age;

        (C) name(s) of the associated person(s), if any, responsible for the account, and if multiple individuals are assigned responsibility for the account, a record indicating the scope of their responsibilities with respect to the account, provided, however, that this requirement shall not apply to an institutional account;

        (D) signature of the partner, officer or manager denoting that the account has been accepted in accordance with the member's policies and procedures for acceptance of accounts;

        (E) if the customer is a corporation, partnership or other legal entity, the names of any persons authorized to transact business on behalf of the entity; and

        (F) subject to Supplementary Material .06, name of and contact information for a trusted contact person age 18 or older who may be contacted about the customer's account; provided, however, that this requirement shall not apply to an institutional account.

    (2) for each account other than an institutional account, and accounts in which investments are limited to transactions in open-end investment company shares that are not recommended by the member or its associated persons, each member shall also make reasonable efforts to obtain, prior to the settlement of the initial transaction in the account, the following information to the extent it is applicable to the account:

        (A) customer's tax identification or Social Security number;

        (B) occupation of customer and name and address of employer; and

        (C) whether customer is an associated person of another member; and

    (3) for discretionary accounts maintained by a member, in addition to compliance with subparagraph (1) and, to the extent applicable, subparagraph (2) above, and Rule 3260, the member shall maintain a record of the dated, signature of each named, associated person of the member authorized to exercise discretion in the account. This recordkeeping requirement shall not apply to investment discretion granted by a customer as to the price at which or the time to execute an order given by a customer for the purchase or sale of a definite dollar amount or quantity of a specified security. Nothing in this Rule shall be construed as allowing members to maintain discretionary accounts or exercise discretion in such accounts except to the extent permitted under the federal securities laws.

(b) A member need not meet the requirements of this Rule with respect to any account that was opened pursuant to a prior FINRA rule until such time as the member updates the information for the account either in the course of the member's routine and customary business or as otherwise required by applicable laws or rules.

(c) For purposes of this Rule, the term "institutional account" shall mean the account of:

    (1) a bank, savings and loan association, insurance company or registered investment company;

    (2) an investment adviser registered either with the SEC under Section 203 of the Investment Advisers Act or with a state securities commission (or any agency or office performing like functions); or

    (3) any other person (whether a natural person, corporation, partnership, trust or otherwise) with total assets of at least $50 million.

25. FINRA Rules: 4514 – Authorization Records for Negotiable Instruments Drawn From a Customer's Account

No member or person associated with a member shall obtain from a customer or submit for payment a check, draft or other form of negotiable paper drawn on a customer's checking, savings, share or similar account, without that person's express written authorization, which may include the customer's signature on the negotiable instrument. Where the written authorization is separate from the negotiable instrument, the member shall preserve the authorization for a period of three years following the date the authorization expires. This provision shall not, however, require members to preserve copies of negotiable instruments signed by customers.

---

26. FINRA Rules: 5130 – Restrictions on the Purchase and Sale of Initial Equity Public Offerings

(a) General Prohibitions
  (1) A member or a person associated with a member may not sell, or cause to be sold, a new issue to any account in which a restricted person has a beneficial interest, except as otherwise permitted herein.
  (2) A member or a person associated with a member may not purchase a new issue in any account in which such member or person associated with a member has a beneficial interest, except as otherwise permitted herein.
  (3) A member may not continue to hold new issues acquired by the member as an underwriter, selling group member or otherwise, except as otherwise permitted herein.
  (4) Nothing in this paragraph (a) shall prohibit:
    (A) sales or purchases from one member of the selling group to another member of the selling group that are incidental to the distribution of a new issue to a non-restricted person at the public offering price;
    (B) sales or purchases by a broker-dealer of a new issue at the public offering price as part of an accommodation to a non-restricted person customer of the broker-dealer; or
    (C) purchases by a broker-dealer (or owner of a broker-dealer), organized as an investment partnership, of a new issue at the public offering price, provided such purchases are credited to the capital accounts of its partners in accordance with paragraph (c)(4).
(b) Preconditions for Sale
  Before selling a new issue to any account, a member must in good faith have obtained within the twelve months prior to such sale, a representation from:
  (1) Beneficial Owners
    the account holder(s), or a person authorized to represent the beneficial owners of the account, that the account is eligible to purchase new issues in compliance with this Rule; or
  (2) Conduits
    a bank, foreign bank, broker-dealer, or investment adviser or other conduit that all purchases of new issues are in compliance with this Rule.
  A member may not rely upon any representation that it believes, or has reason to believe, is inaccurate. A member shall maintain a copy of all records and information relating to whether an account is eligible to purchase new issues in its files for at least three years following the member's last sale of a new issue to that account.

(c) General Exemptions

The general prohibitions in paragraph (a) of this Rule shall not apply to sales to and purchases by the following accounts or persons, whether directly or through accounts in which such persons have a beneficial interest:

(1) An investment company registered under the Investment Company Act;

(2) A common trust fund or similar fund as described in Section 3(a)(12)(A)(iii) of the Exchange Act, provided that:

(A) the fund has investments from 1,000 or more accounts; and

(B) the fund does not limit beneficial interests in the fund principally to trust accounts of restricted persons;

(3) An insurance company general, separate or investment account, provided that:

(A) the account is funded by premiums from 1,000 or more policyholders, or, if a general account, the insurance company has 1,000 or more policyholders; and

(B) the insurance company does not limit the policyholders whose premiums are used to fund the account principally to restricted persons, or, if a general account, the insurance company does not limit its policyholders principally to restricted persons;

(4) An account if the beneficial interests of restricted persons do not exceed in the aggregate 10% of such account;

(5) A publicly traded entity (other than a broker-dealer or an affiliate of a broker-dealer where such broker-dealer is authorized to engage in the public offering of new issues either as a selling group member or underwriter) that:

(A) is listed on a national securities exchange; or

(B) is a foreign issuer whose securities meet the quantitative designation criteria for listing on a national securities exchange;

(6) An investment company organized under the laws of a foreign jurisdiction, provided that:

(A) the investment company is listed on a foreign exchange for sale to the public or authorized for sale to the public by a foreign regulatory authority; and

(B) no person owning more than 5% of the shares of the investment company is a restricted person;

(7) An Employee Retirement Income Security Act benefits plan that is qualified under Section 401(a) of the Internal Revenue Code, provided that such plan is not sponsored solely by a broker-dealer;

(8) A state or municipal government benefits plan that is subject to state and/or municipal regulation;

(9) A tax exempt charitable organization under Section 501(c)(3) of the Internal Revenue Code; or

(10) A church plan under Section 414(e) of the Internal Revenue Code.

(d) Issuer-Directed Securities

The prohibitions on the purchase and sale of new issues in this Rule shall not apply to securities that:

(1) are specifically directed by the issuer to persons that are restricted under the Rule; provided, however, that securities directed by an issuer may not be sold to or purchased by:

(A) a broker-dealer; or

(B) an account in which any restricted person specified in paragraphs (i)(10)(B) or (i)(10)(C) of this Rule has a beneficial interest, unless such person, or a member of his or her immediate family, is an employee or director of the issuer, the issuer's parent, or a subsidiary of the issuer or the issuer's parent. Also, for purposes of this paragraph (d)(1) only, a parent/subsidiary relationship is established if the parent has the right to vote 50% or more of a class of voting security of the subsidiary, or has the power to sell or direct 50% or more of a class of voting security of the subsidiary;

(2) are specifically directed by the issuer and are part of an offering in which no broker-dealer:

(A) underwrites any portion of the offering;

(B) solicits or sells any new issue securities in the offering; and

(C) has any involvement or influence, directly or indirectly, in the issuer's allocation decisions with respect to any of the new issue securities in the offering;

(3) are part of a program sponsored by the issuer or an affiliate of the issuer that meets the following criteria:

(A) the opportunity to purchase a new issue under the program is offered to at least 10,000 participants;

(B) every participant is offered an opportunity to purchase an equivalent number of shares, or will receive a specified number of shares under a predetermined formula applied uniformly across all participants;

(C) if not all participants receive shares under the program, the selection of the participants eligible to purchase shares is based upon a random or other non-discretionary allocation method; and

(D) the class of participants does not contain a disproportionate number of restricted persons as compared to the investing public generally; or

(4) are directed to eligible purchasers who are otherwise restricted under the Rule as part of a conversion offering in accordance with the standards of the governmental agency or instrumentality having authority to regulate such conversion offering.

(e) Anti-Dilution Provisions

The prohibitions on the purchase and sale of new issues in this Rule shall not apply to an account in which a restricted person has a beneficial interest that meets the following conditions:

(1) the account has held an equity ownership interest in the issuer, or a company that has been acquired by the issuer in the past year, for a period of one year prior to the effective date of the offering;

(2) the sale of the new issue to the account shall not increase the account's percentage equity ownership in the issuer above the ownership level as of three months prior to the filing of the registration statement in connection with the offering;

(3) the sale of the new issue to the account shall not include any special terms; and

(4) the new issue purchased pursuant to this paragraph (e) shall not be sold, transferred, assigned, pledged or hypothecated for a period of three months following the effective date of the offering.

(f) Stand-by Purchasers

The prohibitions on the purchase and sale of new issues in this Rule shall not apply to the purchase and sale of securities pursuant to a stand-by agreement that meets the following conditions:

(1) the stand-by agreement is disclosed in the prospectus;

(2) the stand-by agreement is the subject of a formal written agreement;

(3) the managing underwriter(s) represents in writing that it was unable to find any other purchasers for the securities; and

(4) the securities sold pursuant to the stand-by agreement shall not be sold, transferred, assigned, pledged or hypothecated for a period of three months following the effective date of the offering.

(g) Under-Subscribed Offerings

Nothing in this Rule shall prohibit an underwriter, pursuant to an underwriting agreement, from placing a portion of a public offering in its investment account when it is unable to sell that portion to the public.

(h) Exemptive Relief

Pursuant to the Rule 9600 Series, the staff, for good cause shown after taking into consideration all relevant factors, may conditionally or unconditionally exempt any person, security or transaction (or any class or classes of persons, securities or transactions) from this Rule to the extent that such exemption is consistent with the purposes of the Rule, the protection of investors and the public interest.

(i) Definitions

(1) "Beneficial interest" means any economic interest, such as the right to share in gains or losses. The receipt of a management or performance based fee for operating a collective investment account, or other fees for acting in a fiduciary capacity, shall not be considered a beneficial interest in the account.

(2) "Collective investment account" means any hedge fund, investment partnership, investment corporation or any other collective investment vehicle that is engaged primarily in the purchase and/or sale of securities. A "collective investment account" does not include a "family investment vehicle" or an "investment club."

(3) "Conversion offering" means any offering of securities made as part of a plan by which a savings and loan association, insurance company or other organization converts from a mutual to a stock form of ownership.

(4) "Family investment vehicle" means a legal entity that is beneficially owned solely by immediate family members.

(5) "Immediate family member" means a person's parents, mother-in-law or father-in-law, spouse, brother or sister, brother-in-law or sister-in-law, son-in-law or daughter-in-law, and children, and any other individual to whom the person provides material support.

(6) "Investment club" means a group of friends, neighbors, business associates or others that pool their money to invest in stock or other securities and are collectively responsible for making investment decisions.

(7) "Limited business broker-dealer" means any broker-dealer whose authorization to engage in the securities business is limited solely to the purchase and sale of investment company/variable contracts securities and direct participation program securities.

(8) "Material support" means directly or indirectly providing more than 25% of a person's income in the prior calendar year. Members of the immediate family living in the same household are deemed to be providing each other with material support.

(9) "New issue" means any initial public offering of an equity security as defined in Section 3(a)(11) of the Exchange Act, made pursuant to a registration statement or offering circular. New issue shall not include:

(A) offerings made pursuant to an exemption under Section 4(1), 4(2) or 4(6) of the Securities Act, or Securities Act Rule 504 if the securities are "restricted securities" under Securities Act Rule 144(a)(3), or Rule 144A or Rule 505 or Rule 506 adopted thereunder;

(B) offerings of exempted securities as defined in Section 3(a)(12) of the Exchange Act, and rules promulgated thereunder;

(C) offerings of securities of a commodity pool operated by a commodity pool operator as defined under Section 1a(5) of the Commodity Exchange Act;

(D) rights offerings, exchange offers, or offerings made pursuant to a merger or acquisition;

(E) offerings of investment grade asset-backed securities;

(F) offerings of convertible securities;

(G) offerings of preferred securities;

(H) offerings of an investment company registered under the Investment Company Act;

(I) offerings of securities (in ordinary share form or ADRs registered on Form F-6) that have a pre-existing market outside of the United States; and

(J) offerings of a business development company as defined in Section 2(a)(48) of the Investment Company Act, a direct participation program as defined in Rule 2310(a) or a real estate investment trust as defined in Section 856 of the Internal Revenue Code.

(10) "Restricted person" means:

(A) Members or other broker-dealers

(B) Broker-Dealer Personnel

(i) Any officer, director, general partner, associated person or employee of a member or any other broker-dealer (other than a limited business broker-dealer);

(ii) Any agent of a member or any other broker-dealer (other than a limited business broker-dealer) that is engaged in the investment banking or securities business; or

(iii) An immediate family member of a person specified in subparagraph (B)(i) or (ii) if the person specified in subparagraph (B)(i) or (ii):

a. materially supports, or receives material support from, the immediate family member;

b. is employed by or associated with the member, or an affiliate of the member, selling the new issue to the immediate family member; or

c. has an ability to control the allocation of the new issue.

(C) Finders and Fiduciaries

    (i) With respect to the security being offered, a finder or any person acting in a fiduciary capacity to the managing underwriter, including, but not limited to, attorneys, accountants and financial consultants; and

    (ii) An immediate family member of a person specified in subparagraph (C)(i) if the person specified in subparagraph (C)(i) materially supports, or receives material support from, the immediate family member.

(D) Portfolio Managers

    (i) Any person who has authority to buy or sell securities for a bank, savings and loan institution, insurance company, investment company, investment advisor or collective investment account.

    (ii) An immediate family member of a person specified in subparagraph (D)(i) that materially supports, or receives material support from, such person.

(E) Persons Owning a Broker-Dealer

    (i) Any person listed, or required to be listed, in Schedule A of a Form BD (other than with respect to a limited business broker-dealer), except persons identified by an ownership code of less than 10%;

    (ii) Any person listed, or required to be listed, in Schedule B of a Form BD (other than with respect to a limited business broker-dealer), except persons whose listing on Schedule B relates to an ownership interest in a person listed on Schedule A identified by an ownership code of less than 10%;

    (iii) Any person listed, or required to be listed, in Schedule C of a Form BD that meets the criteria of subparagraphs (E)(i) and (E)(ii) above;

    (iv) Any person that directly or indirectly owns 10% or more of a public reporting company listed, or required to be listed, in Schedule A of a Form BD (other than a reporting company that is listed on a national securities exchange or other than with respect to a limited business broker-dealer);

    (v) Any person that directly or indirectly owns 25% or more of a public reporting company listed, or required to be listed, in Schedule B of a Form BD (other than a reporting company that is listed on a national securities exchange or other than with respect to a limited business broker-dealer);

    (vi) An immediate family member of a person specified in subparagraphs (E)(i) through (v) unless the person owning the broker-dealer:

        a. does not materially support, or receive material support from, the immediate family member;

        b. is not an owner of the member, or an affiliate of the member, selling the new issue to the immediate family member; and

        c. has no ability to control the allocation of the new issue.

(j) Information Required to be Filed

The book-running managing underwriter of a new issue shall be required to file the following information in the time and manner specified by FINRA with respect to new issues:

  (1) the initial list of distribution participants and their underwriting commitment and retention amounts on or before the offering date; and

  (2) the final list of distribution participants and their underwriting commitment and retention amounts no later than three business days after the offering date.

_____

27. FINRA Rules: 5210 – Publication of Transactions and Quotations

No member shall publish or circulate, or cause to be published or circulated, any notice, circular, advertisement, newspaper article, investment service, or communication of any kind which purports to report any transaction as a purchase or sale of any security unless such member believes that such transaction was a bona fide purchase or sale of such security; or which purports to quote the bid price or asked price for any security, unless such member believes that such quotation represents a bona fide bid for, or offer of, such security.

---

28. FINRA Rules: 5220 – Offers at Stated Prices

No member shall make an offer to buy from or sell to any person any security at a stated price unless such member is prepared to purchase or sell, as the case may be, at such price and under such conditions as are stated at the time of such offer to buy or sell.

---

29. FINRA Rules: 5230 – Payments Involving Publications that Influence the Market Price of a Security

(a) Except as provided in paragraph (b), no member shall, directly or indirectly, give, permit to be given, or offer to give, anything of value to any person for the purpose of influencing or rewarding the action of such person in connection with the publication or circulation in any electronic or other public media, including any investment service or similar publication, Web site, newspaper, magazine or other periodical, radio, or television program of any matter that has, or is intended to have, an effect upon the market price of any security.

(b) The prohibitions in paragraph (a) shall not apply to compensation paid to a person in connection with the publication or circulation of:

(1) a communication that is clearly distinguishable as paid advertising;

(2) a communication that discloses the receipt of compensation and the amount thereof in accordance with Section 17(b) of the Securities Act; or

(3) a research report, as that term is defined in Rule 2241.

---

30. FINRA Rules: 5240 – Anti-intimidation/Coordination

(a) No member or person associated with a member shall:

    (1) coordinate the prices (including quotations), trades or trade reports of such member with any other member or person associated with a member, or any other person;

    (2) direct or request another member to alter a price (including a quotation); or

    (3) engage, directly or indirectly, in any conduct that threatens, harasses, coerces, intimidates or otherwise attempts improperly to influence another member, a person associated with a member, or any other person.

    This includes, but is not limited to, any attempt to influence another member or person associated with a member to adjust or maintain a price or quotation, whether displayed on any facility operated by FINRA or otherwise, or refusals to trade or other conduct that retaliates against or discourages the competitive activities of another market maker or market participant.

(b) Provided that the conduct in subparagraphs (1) through (7) below is otherwise in compliance with all applicable law, nothing in this Rule respecting coordination of quotes, trades or trade reports shall be deemed to limit, constrain or otherwise inhibit the freedom of a member or person associated with a member to:

    (1) set unilaterally its own bid or ask in any security, the prices at which it is willing to buy or sell any security, and the quantity of shares of any security that it is willing to buy or sell;

    (2) set unilaterally its own dealer spread, quote increment or quantity of shares for its quotations (or set any relationship between or among its dealer spread, inside spread, or the size of any quote increment) in any security;

    (3) communicate its own bid or ask, or the prices at or the quantity of shares in which it is willing to buy or sell any security to any person, for the purpose of exploring the possibility of a purchase or sale of that security, and to negotiate for or agree to such purchase or sale;

    (4) communicate its own bid or ask, or the price at or the quantity of shares in which it is willing to buy or sell any security, to any person for the purpose of retaining such person as an agent or subagent for the member or for a customer of the member (or for the purpose of seeking to be retained as an agent or subagent), and to negotiate for or agree to such purchase or sale;

    (5) engage in any underwriting (or any syndicate for the underwriting) of securities to the extent permitted by the federal securities laws;

    (6) take any unilateral action or make any unilateral decision regarding the market makers with which it will trade and the terms on which it will trade unless such action is prohibited by paragraph (a) of this Rule; and

    (7) deliver an order to another member for handling.

---

31. FINRA Rules: 5270 – Front Running of Block Transactions

(a) No member or person associated with a member shall cause to be executed an order to buy or sell a security or a related financial instrument when such member or person associated with a member causing such order to be executed has material, non-public market information concerning an imminent block transaction in that security, a related financial instrument or a security underlying the related financial instrument prior to the time information concerning the block transaction has been made publicly available or has otherwise become stale or obsolete.

(b) This Rule applies to orders caused to be executed for any account in which such member or person associated with the member has an interest, any account with respect to which such member or person associated with a member exercises investment discretion, or for accounts of customers or affiliates of the member when the customer or affiliate has been provided such material, non-public market information by the member or any person associated with the member.

(c) For purposes of this Rule, the term "related financial instrument" shall mean any option, derivative, security-based swap, or other financial instrument overlying a security, the value of which is materially related to, or otherwise acts as a substitute for, such se

---

32. FINRA Rules: 5280 – Trading Ahead of Research Reports

(a) No member shall establish, increase, decrease or liquidate an inventory position in a security or a derivative of such security based on non-public advance knowledge of the content or timing of a research report in that security.

(b) A member must establish, maintain and enforce policies and procedures reasonably designed to restrict or limit the information flow between research department personnel, or other persons with knowledge of the content or timing of a research report, and trading department personnel, so as to prevent trading department personnel from utilizing non-public advance knowledge of the issuance or content of a research report for the benefit of the member or any other person.

---

33. FINRA Rules: 5290 – Order Entry and Execution Practices

No member or associated person shall engage in conduct that has the intent or effect of splitting any order into multiple smaller orders for execution or any execution into multiple smaller executions for transaction reporting for the primary purpose of maximizing a monetary or in-kind amount to be received by the member or associated person as a result of the execution of such orders or the transaction reporting of such executions. For purposes of this Rule, "monetary or in-kind amount" shall be defined to include, but not be limited to, any credits, commissions, gratuities, payments for or rebates of fees, or any other payments of value to the member or associated person.

---

34. FINRA Rules: 5310 – Best Execution and Interpositioning

(a)(1) In any transaction for or with a customer or a customer of another broker-dealer, a member and persons associated with a member shall use reasonable diligence to ascertain the best market for the subject security and buy or sell in such market so that the resultant price to the customer is as favorable as possible under prevailing market conditions. Among the factors that will be considered in determining whether a member has used "reasonable diligence" are:

    (A) the character of the market for the security (e.g., price, volatility, relative liquidity, and pressure on available communications);

    (B) the size and type of transaction;

    (C) the number of markets checked;

    (D) accessibility of the quotation; and

    (E) the terms and conditions of the order which result in the transaction, as communicated to the member and persons associated with the member.

    (2) In any transaction for or with a customer or a customer of another broker-dealer, no member or person associated with a member shall interject a third party between the member and the best market for the subject security in a manner inconsistent with paragraph (a)(1) of this Rule.

(b) When a member cannot execute directly with a market but must employ a broker's broker or some other means in order to ensure an execution advantageous to the customer, the burden of showing the acceptable circumstances for doing so is on the member.

(c) Failure to maintain or adequately staff an over-the-counter order room or other department assigned to execute customers' orders cannot be considered justification for executing away from the best available market; nor can channeling orders through a third party as described above as reciprocation for service or business operate to relieve a member of its obligations under this Rule.

(d) A member through which an order is channeled and that knowingly is a party to an arrangement whereby the initiating member has not fulfilled its obligations, will also be deemed to have violated this Rule.

(e) The obligations described in paragraphs (a) through (d) above exist not only where the member acts as agent for the account of its customer but also where transactions are executed as principal. Such obligations are distinct from the reasonableness of commission rates, markups or markdowns, which are governed by Rule 2121 and its Supplementary Material.

----

35. FINRA Rules: 5320 – Prohibition Against Trading Ahead of Customer Orders

(a) Except as provided herein, a member that accepts and holds an order in an equity security from its own customer or a customer of another broker-dealer without immediately executing the order is prohibited from trading that security on the same side of the market for its own account at a price that would satisfy the customer order, unless it immediately thereafter executes the customer order up to the size and at the same or better price at which it traded for its own account.

(b) A member must have a written methodology in place governing the execution and priority of all pending orders that is consistent with the requirements of this Rule and Rule 5310. A member also must ensure that this methodology is consistently applied.

----

36. FINRA Rules: 6438 – Displaying Priced Quotations in Multiple Quotation Mediums

Members that display priced quotations on a real-time basis for an OTC Equity Security in two or more quotation mediums that permit quotation updates on a real-time basis must display the same priced quotations for the security in each medium, except with respect to a price quotation that represents a customer limit order displayed on an electronic communications network in conformance with the exception to Rule 6460 provided in paragraph (b)(5) of that rule.

---

37. MSRB Rules: G-8 – Books and Records to be Made by Brokers, Dealers, Municipal Securities Dealers, and Municipal Advisors

Summary: Requires dealers and municipal advisors to make and keep current certain specified records.

(a) Description of Books and Records Required to be Made. Except as otherwise specifically indicated in this rule, every broker, dealer and municipal securities dealer shall make and keep current the following books and records, to the extent applicable to the business of such broker, dealer or municipal securities dealer:

  (i) Records of Original Entry. "Blotters" or other records of original entry containing an itemized daily record of all purchases and sales of municipal securities, all receipts and deliveries of municipal securities (including certificate numbers and, if the securities are in registered form, an indication to such effect), all receipts and disbursement of cash with respect to transactions in municipal securities, all other debits and credits pertaining to transactions in municipal securities, and in the case of brokers, dealers and municipal securities dealers other than bank dealers, all other cash receipts and disbursements if not contained in the records required by any other provision of this rule. The records of original entry shall show the name or other designation of the account for which each such transaction was effected (whether effected for the account of such broker, dealer or municipal securities dealer, the account of a customer, or otherwise), the description of the securities, the aggregate par value of the securities, the dollar price or yield and aggregate purchase or sale price of the securities, accrued interest, the trade date, and the name or other designation of the person from whom purchased or received or to whom sold or delivered. With respect to accrued interest and information relating to "when issued' transactions which may not be available at the time a transaction is effected, entries setting forth such information shall be made promptly as such information becomes available. Dollar price, yield and accrued interest relating to any transaction shall be required to be shown only to the extent required to be included in the confirmation delivered by the broker, dealer or municipal securities dealer in connection with such transaction under rule G-12 or rule G-15.

  (ii) Account Records. Account records for each customer account and account of such broker, dealer or municipal securities dealer. Such records shall reflect all purchases and sales of municipal securities, all receipts and deliveries of municipal securities, all receipts and disbursements of cash, and all other debits and credits relating to such account. A bank dealer shall not be required to maintain a record of a customer's bank credit or bank debit balances for purposes of this subparagraph.

  (iii) Securities Records. Records showing separately for each municipal security all positions (including, in the case of a broker, dealer or municipal securities dealer other than a bank dealer, securities in safekeeping) carried by such broker, dealer or municipal securities dealer for its account or for the account of a customer (with all "short" trading positions so designated), the location of all such securities long and the offsetting position to all such securities short, and the name or other designation of the account in which each position is carried. Such records shall also show all long security count differences and short count differences classified by the date of physical count and verification on which they were discovered. Such records shall consist of a single record system. With respect to purchases or sales, such records may be posted on either a settlement date basis or a trade date basis, consistent with the manner of posting the records of original entry of such broker, dealer or municipal securities dealer. For purposes of this subparagraph, multiple maturities of the same issue of municipal securities, as well as multiple coupons of the same maturity, may be shown on the same record, provided that adequate secondary records exist to identify separately such maturities and coupons. With respect to securities which are received in and delivered out by such broker, dealer or municipal securities dealer the same day on or before the settlement date, no posting to such records shall be required. Anything herein to the contrary notwithstanding, a non-clearing broker, dealer or municipal securities dealer which effects transactions for the account of customers on a delivery against payment basis may keep the records of location required by this subparagraph in the form of an alphabetical list or lists of securities showing the location of such securities rather than a record of location separately for each security. Anything herein to the contrary notwithstanding, a bank dealer shall maintain records of the location of securities in its own trading account.

(iv) Subsidiary Records. Ledgers or other records reflecting the following information:

(A) Municipal securities in transfer. With respect to municipal securities which have been sent out for transfer, the description and the aggregate par value of the securities, the name in which registered, the name in which the securities are to be registered, the date sent out for transfer, the address to which sent for transfer, former certificate numbers, the date returned from transfer, and new certificate numbers.

(B) Municipal securities to be validated. With respect to municipal securities which have been sent out for validation, the description and the aggregate par value of the securities, the date sent out for validation, the address to which sent for validation, the certificate numbers, and the date returned from validation.

(C) Municipal securities borrowed or loaned. With respect to municipal securities borrowed or loaned, the date borrowed or loaned, the name of the person from whom borrowed or to whom loaned, the description and the aggregate par value of the securities borrowed or loaned, the value at which the securities were borrowed or loaned, and the date returned.

(D) Municipal securities transactions not completed on settlement date. With respect to municipal securities transactions not completed on the settlement date, the description and the aggregate par value of the securities which are the subject of such transactions, the purchase price (with respect to a purchase transaction not completed on the settlement date), the sale price (with respect to a sale transaction not completed on the settlement date), the name of the customer, broker, dealer or municipal securities dealer from whom delivery is due or to whom delivery is to be made, and the date on which the securities are received or delivered. All municipal securities transactions with brokers, dealers and municipal securities dealers not completed on the settlement date shall be separately identifiable as such. For purposes of this rule, the term "settlement date" means the date upon which delivery of the securities is due in a purchase or sale transaction.

Such records shall be maintained as subsidiary records to the general ledger maintained by such broker, dealer or municipal securities dealer. Anything herein to the contrary notwithstanding, the requirements of this subparagraph will be satisfied if the information described is readily obtainable from other records maintained by such broker, dealer or municipal securities dealer.

(v) Put Options and Repurchase Agreements. Records of all options (whether written or oral) to sell municipal securities (i.e., put options) and of all repurchase agreements (whether written or oral) with respect to municipal securities, in which such broker, dealer or municipal securities dealer has any direct or indirect interest or which such broker, dealer or municipal securities dealer has granted or guaranteed, showing the description and aggregate par value of the securities, and the terms and conditions of the option, agreement or guarantee.

(vi) Records for Agency Transactions. A memorandum of each agency order and any instructions given or received for the purchase or sale of municipal securities pursuant to such order, showing the terms and conditions of the order and instructions, and any modification thereof, the account for which entered, the date and time of receipt of the order by such broker, dealer or municipal securities dealer, the price at which executed, the date of execution and, to the extent feasible, the time of execution and, if such order is entered pursuant to a power of attorney or on behalf of a joint account, corporation or partnership, the name and address (if other than that of the account) of the person who entered the order. If an agency order is canceled by a customer, such records shall also show the terms, conditions and date of cancellation, and, to the extent feasible, the time of cancellation. Orders entered pursuant to the exercise of discretionary power by such broker, dealer or municipal securities dealer shall be designated as such. For purposes of this subparagraph, the term "agency order" shall mean an order given to a broker, dealer or municipal securities dealer to buy a specific security from another person or to sell a specific security to another person, in either case without such broker, dealer or municipal securities dealer acquiring ownership of the security. Customer inquiries of a general nature concerning the availability of securities for purchase or opportunities for sale shall not be considered to be orders. For purposes of this subparagraph and subparagraph (vii) below, the term "memorandum" shall mean a trading ticket or other similar record. For purposes of this subparagraph, the term "instructions" shall mean instructions transmitted within an office with respect to the execution of an agency order, including, but not limited to, instructions transmitted from a sales desk to a trading desk.

(vii) Records for Transactions as Principal. A memorandum of each transaction in municipal securities (whether purchase or sale) for the account of such broker, dealer or municipal securities dealer, showing the price and date of execution and, to the extent feasible, the time of execution; and in the event such purchase or sale is with a customer, a record of the customer's order, showing the date and time of receipt, the terms and conditions of the order, and the name or other designation of the account in which it was entered and, if such order is entered pursuant to a power of attorney or on behalf of a joint account, corporation, or partnership, the name and address (if other than that of the account) of the person who entered the order.

(viii) Records Concerning Primary Offerings.

(A) For each primary offering for which a syndicate has been formed for the purchase of municipal securities, records shall be maintained by the syndicate manager showing the description and aggregate par value of the securities; the name and percentage of participation of each member of the syndicate; the terms and conditions governing the formation and operation of the syndicate; a statement of all terms and conditions required by the issuer (including, those of any retail order period, if applicable); all orders received for the purchase of the securities from the syndicate and selling group, if any; the information required to be submitted pursuant to Rule G-11(k); all pricing information required to be distributed pursuant to Rule G-11(f); all allotments of securities and the price at which sold; those instances in which the syndicate manager allocated securities in a manner other than in accordance with the priority provisions, including those instances in which the syndicate manager accorded equal or greater priority over other orders to orders by syndicate members for their own accounts or their respective related accounts; and the specific reasons for doing so; the date and amount of any good faith deposit made to the issuer; the date of settlement with the issuer; the date of closing of the account; and a reconciliation of profits and expenses of the account.

(B) For each primary offering for which a syndicate has not been formed for the purchase of municipal securities, records shall be maintained by the sole underwriter showing the description and aggregate par value of the securities; all terms and conditions required by the issuer (including, those of any retail order period, if applicable); all orders received for the purchase of the securities from the underwriter; the information required to be submitted pursuant to Rule G-11(k); all allotments of securities and the price at which sold; those instances in which the underwriter accorded equal or greater priority over other orders to orders for its own account or its related accounts, and the specific reasons for doing so; the date and amount of any good faith deposit made to the issuer; and the date of settlement with the issuer.

(ix) Copies of Confirmations, Periodic Statements and Certain Other Notices to Customers. A copy of all confirmations of purchase or sale of municipal securities, of all periodic written statements disclosing purchases, sales or redemptions of municipal fund securities pursuant to rule G-15(a)(viii), of written disclosures to customers, if any, as required under rule G-15(f)(iii) and, in the case of a broker, dealer or municipal securities dealer other than a bank dealer, of all other notices sent to customers concerning debits and credits to customer accounts or, in the case of a bank dealer, notices of debits and credits for municipal securities, cash and other items with respect to transactions in municipal securities.

(x) Financial Records. Every broker, dealer and municipal securities dealer subject to the provisions of rule 15c3-1 under the Act shall make and keep current the books and records described in subparagraphs (a)(2), (a)(4)(iv) and (vi), and (a)(11) of rule 17a-3 under the Act.

(xi) Customer Account Information. A record for each customer, other than an institutional account, setting forth the following information to the extent applicable to such customer:

  (A) customer's name and residence or principal business address;

  (B) whether customer is of legal age;

  (C) tax identification or social security number;

  (D) occupation;

  (E) name and address of employer;

  (F) information about the customer obtained pursuant to rule G-19;

  (G) name and address of beneficial owner or owners of such account if other than the customer and transactions are to be confirmed to such owner or owners;

  (H) signature of municipal securities representative, general securities representative or limited representative -- investment company and variable contracts products introducing the account and signature of a municipal securities principal, municipal securities sales principal or general securities principal indicating acceptance of the account;

  (I) with respect to discretionary accounts, customer's written authorization to exercise discretionary power or authority with respect to the account, written approval of municipal securities principal or municipal securities sales principal who supervises the account, and written approval of municipal securities principal or municipal securities sales principal with respect to each transaction in the account, indicating the time and date of approval;

  (J) whether customer is employed by another broker, dealer or municipal securities dealer;

  (K) in connection with the hypothecation of the customer's securities, the written authorization of, or the notice provided to, the customer in accordance with Commission rules 8c-1 and 15c2-1; and

  (L) with respect to official communications, customer's written authorization, if any, that the customer does not object to the disclosure of its name, security position(s) and contact information to a party identified in G-15(g)(iii)(A)(1) for purposes of transmitting official communications under G-15(g).

  (M) Predispute Arbitration Agreements with Customers.

    (1) Any predispute arbitration clause shall be highlighted and shall be immediately preceded by the following language in outline form:

    This agreement contains a predispute arbitration clause. By signing an arbitration agreement the parties agree as follows:

      (a) All parties to this agreement are giving up the right to sue each other in court, including the right to a trial by jury, except as provided by the rules of the arbitration forum in which a claim is filed.

    (b) Arbitration awards are generally final and binding; a party's ability to have a court reverse or modify an arbitration award is very limited.

    (c) The ability of the parties to obtain documents, witness statements and other discovery is generally more limited in arbitration than in court proceedings.

    (d) The arbitrators do not have to explain the reason(s) for their award.

    (e) The panel of arbitrators will typically include a minority of arbitrators who were or are affiliated with the securities industry.

    (f) The rules of some arbitration forums may impose time limits for bringing a claim in arbitration. In some cases, a claim that is ineligible for arbitration may be brought in court.

    (g) The rules of the arbitration forum in which the claim is filed, and any amendments thereto, shall be incorporated into this agreement.

(2)(a) In any agreement containing a predispute arbitration agreement, there shall be a highlighted statement immediately preceding any signature line or other place for indicating agreement that states that the agreement contains a predispute arbitration clause. The statement shall also indicate at what page and paragraph the arbitration clause is located.

    (b) Within thirty days of signing, a copy of the agreement containing any such clause shall be given to the customer who shall acknowledge receipt thereof on the agreement or on a separate document.

(3)(a) A broker, dealer or municipal securities dealer shall provide a customer with a copy of any predispute arbitration clause or customer agreement executed between the customer and the broker, dealer or municipal securities dealer, or inform the customer that the broker, dealer or municipal securities dealer does not have a copy thereof, within ten business days of receipt of the customer's request. If a customer requests such a copy before the broker, dealer or municipal securities dealer has provided the customer with a copy pursuant to subparagraph (2)(b) above, the broker, dealer or municipal securities dealer must provide a copy to the customer by the earlier date required by this subparagraph (3)(a) or by subparagraph (2)(b) above.

    (b) Upon request by a customer, a broker, dealer or municipal securities dealer shall provide the customer with the names of, and information on how to contact or obtain the rules of, all arbitration forums in which a claim may be filed under the agreement.

(4) No predispute arbitration agreement shall include any condition that: (i) limits or contradicts the rules of any self-regulatory organization; (ii) limits the ability of a party to file any claim in arbitration; (iii) limits the ability of a party to file any claim in court permitted to be filed in court under the rules of the forums in which a claim may be filed under the agreement; (iv) limits the ability of arbitrators to make any award.

(5) If a customer files a complaint in court against a broker, dealer or municipal securities dealer that contains claims that are subject to arbitration pursuant to a predispute arbitration agreement between the broker, dealer or municipal securities dealer and the customer, the broker, dealer or municipal securities dealer may seek to compel arbitration of the claims that are subject to arbitration. If the broker, dealer or municipal securities dealer seeks to compel arbitration of such claims, the broker, dealer or municipal securities dealer must agree to arbitrate all of the claims contained in the complaint if the customer so requests.

(6) All agreements shall include a statement that "No person shall bring a putative or certified class action to arbitration, nor seek to enforce any predispute arbitration agreement against any person who has initiated in court a putative class action; who is a member of a putative class who has not opted out of the class with respect to any claims encompassed by the putative class action until: (i) the class certification is denied; or (ii) the class is decertified; or (iii) the customer is excluded from the class by the court. Such forbearance to enforce an agreement to arbitrate shall not constitute a waiver of any rights under this agreement except to the extent stated herein."

(7) These provisions of Rule G-8(a)(xi)(M) are effective as of May 1, 2005.

For purposes of this subparagraph, the terms "general securities representative," "general securities principal" and "limited representative - investment company and variable contracts products" shall mean such persons as so defined by the rules of a national securities exchange or registered securities association. For purposes of this subparagraph, the term "institutional account" shall mean the account of (i) a bank, savings and loan association, insurance company, or registered investment company; (ii) an investment adviser registered either with the Commission under Section 203 of the Investment Advisers Act of 1940 or with a state securities commission (or any agency or office performing like functions); or (iii) any other entity (whether a natural person, corporation, partnership, trust, or otherwise) with total assets of at least $50 million. Anything in this subparagraph to the contrary notwithstanding, every broker, dealer and municipal securities dealer shall maintain a record of the information required by items (A), (C), (F), (H), (I) and (K) of this subparagraph with respect to each customer which is an institutional account.

(xii) Customer Complaints. A record of all written complaints of customers, and persons acting on behalf of customers that are received by the broker, dealer or municipal securities dealer. This record must include the complainant's name, address, and account number; the date the complaint was received; the date of the activity that gave rise to the complaint; the name of each associated person of the broker, dealer or municipal securities dealer identified in the complaint; a description of the nature of the complaint; and what action, if any, has been taken by such broker, dealer or municipal securities dealer in connection with each such complaint. In addition, this record must be kept in an electronic format using the complaint product and problem codes set forth in the Municipal Securities Rulemaking Board Rule G-8 Customer and Municipal Advisory Client Complaint Product and Problem Codes Guide.

The term "written," for the purposes of this paragraph, shall include electronic correspondence. The term "complaint" shall mean any written statement alleging a grievance involving the activities of the broker, dealer or municipal securities dealer or any associated persons of such broker, dealer or municipal securities dealer with respect to any matter involving a customer's account.

(xiii) Records Concerning Disclosures in Connection With Primary Offerings Pursuant to Rule G-32. A record:

(A) of all documents, notices or written disclosures provided by the broker, dealer or municipal securities dealer to purchasers of offered municipal securities under Rule G-32(a);

(B) if applicable, evidencing compliance with subsection (a)(v) of Rule G-32; and

(C) of all documents, notices and information required to be submitted to the Board by the broker, dealer or municipal securities dealer, in the capacity of underwriter in a primary offering of municipal securities (or, in the event a syndicate or similar account has been formed for the purpose of underwriting the issue, the managing underwriter), under Rule G-32(b), to the extent that any such information is not included in the information submitted through NIIDS (as defined in Rule G-34(a)(ii)(C)(3)(b)) in satisfaction of the requirements of Rule G-32(b) and maintained pursuant to subsection (a)(xxiii) of this rule.

(xiv) Designation of Persons Responsible for Recordkeeping. A record of all designations of persons responsible for the maintenance and preservation of books and records as required by rule G-27(b)(ii).

(xv) Records Concerning Delivery of Official Statements, Advance Refunding Documents and Forms G-36(OS) and G-36(ARD) to the Board or its Designee Pursuant to Former Rule G-36. In connection with each primary offering of municipal securities subject to former Rule G-36 for which a broker, dealer or municipal securities dealer acted as an underwriter (or, in the event a syndicate or similar account has been formed for the purpose of underwriting the issue, the managing underwriter) and was required under the provisions of former Rule G-36 to send to the Board an official statement prior to June 1, 2009, such underwriter shall maintain, to the extent not maintained pursuant to subsection (a)(xiii) of this Rule G-8:

(A) a record of the name, par amount and CUSIP number or numbers for all such primary offerings of municipal securities; the dates that the documents and written information referred to in former Rule G-36 were received from the issuer and were sent to the Board or its designee; the date of delivery of the issue to the underwriters; and, for issues subject to Securities Exchange Act Rule 15c2-12, the date of the final agreement to purchase, offer or sell the municipal securities; and

(B) copies of the Forms G-36(OS) and G-36(ARD) and documents submitted to the Board or its designee along with the certified or registered mail receipt or other record of sending such forms and documents to the Board or its designee.

For purposes of this subsection (a)(xv), the term "former Rule G-36" means Rule G-36 of the Board in effect on May 31, 2009.

(xvi) Records Concerning Political Contributions and Prohibitions on Municipal Securities Business Pursuant to Rule G-37. Records reflecting:

(A) a listing of the names, titles, city/county and state of residence of all municipal finance professionals;

(B) a listing of the names, titles, city/county and state of residence of all non-MFP executive officers;

(C) the states in which the broker, dealer or municipal securities dealer is engaging or is seeking to engage in municipal securities business;

(D) a listing of municipal entities with which the broker, dealer or municipal securities dealer has engaged in municipal securities business, along with the type of municipal securities business engaged in, during the current year and separate listings for each of the previous two calendar years;

(E) the contributions, direct or indirect, to officials of a municipal entity and payments, direct or indirect, made to political parties of states and political subdivisions, by the broker, dealer or municipal securities dealer and each political action committee controlled by the broker, dealer or municipal securities dealer for the current year and separate listings for each of the previous two calendar years, which records shall include: (i) the identity of the contributors, (ii) the names and titles (including any city/county/state or other political subdivision) of the recipients of such contributions and payments, and (iii) the amounts and dates of such contributions and payments;

(F) the contributions, direct or indirect, to officials of a municipal entity made by each municipal finance professional, any political action committee controlled by a municipal finance professional, and non-MFP executive officer for the current year, which records shall include: (i) the names, titles, city/county and state of residence of contributors, (ii) the names and titles (including any city/county/state or other political subdivision) of the recipients of such contributions, (iii) the amounts and dates of such contributions; and (iv) whether any such contribution was the subject of an automatic exemption, pursuant to Rule G-37(j), including the amount of the contribution, the date the broker, dealer or municipal securities dealer discovered the contribution, the name of the contributor, and the date the contributor obtained a return of the contribution; provided, however, that such records need not reflect any contribution made by a municipal finance professional or non-MFP executive officer to officials of a municipal entity for whom such person is entitled to vote if the contributions made by such person, in total, are not in excess of $250 to any official of a municipal entity, per election. In addition, brokers, dealers and municipal securities dealers shall maintain separate listings for each of the previous two calendar years containing the information required pursuant to this subparagraph (F) for each municipal finance representative and each dealer solicitor as defined in Rule G-37(g)(ii) and for any political action committee controlled by such individuals, and separate listings for the previous six months containing the information required pursuant to this subparagraph (F) for each municipal finance principal, dealer supervisory chain person and dealer executive officer as defined in Rule G-37(g)(ii) and for any political action committee controlled by such individuals and for any non-MFP executive officers;

(G) the payments, direct or indirect, to political parties of states and political subdivisions made by all municipal finance professionals, any political action committee controlled by a municipal finance professional, and non-MFP executive officers for the current year, which records shall include: (i) the names, titles, city/county and state of residence of contributors, (ii) the names, and titles (including any city/county/state or other political subdivision) of the recipients of such payments and (iii) the amounts and dates of such payments; provided, however, that such records need not reflect those payments made by any municipal finance professional or non-MFP executive officer to a political party of a state or political subdivision in which such persons are entitled to vote if the payments made by such person, in total, are not in excess of $250 per political party, per year. In addition, brokers, dealers and municipal securities dealers shall maintain separate listings for each of the previous two calendar years containing the information required pursuant to this subparagraph (G) for each municipal finance representative and each dealer solicitor as defined in Rule G-37(g)(ii) and for any political action committee controlled by such individuals, and separate listings for the previous six months containing the information required pursuant to this subparagraph (G) for each municipal finance principal, dealer supervisory chain person and dealer executive officer as defined in Rule G-37(g)(ii) and for any political action committee controlled by such individuals and for any non-MFP executive officers;

(H) the contributions, direct or indirect, to bond ballot campaigns made by the broker, dealer or municipal securities dealer and each political action committee controlled by the broker, dealer or municipal securities dealer for the current year, which records shall include: (i) the identity of the contributors, (ii) the official name of each bond ballot campaign receiving such contributions, and the jurisdiction (including city/county/state or political subdivision) by or for which municipal securities, if approved, would be issued, (iii) the amounts (which, in the case of in-kind contributions, must include both the value and the nature of the goods or services provided, including any ancillary services provided to, on behalf of, or in furtherance of the bond ballot campaign) and the specific dates of such contributions, (iv) the full name of the municipal entity and full issue description of any primary offering resulting from the bond ballot campaign to which the broker, dealer or municipal securities dealer or political action committee controlled by the broker, dealer or municipal securities dealer has made a contribution and the reportable date of selection on which the broker, dealer or municipal securities dealer was selected to engage in the municipal securities business, and (v) the payments or reimbursements, related to any bond ballot contribution, received by the broker, dealer or municipal securities dealer from any third party that are required to be disclosed under Rule G-37(e)(i)(B), including the amount paid and the name of the third party making such payment; and

(I) the contributions, direct or indirect, to bond ballot campaigns made by each municipal finance professional, any political action committee controlled by a municipal finance professional, and non-MFP executive officer for the current year, which records shall include: (i) the names, titles, city/county and state of residence of contributors, (ii) the official name of each bond ballot campaign receiving such contributions, and the jurisdiction (including city/county/state or political subdivision) by or for which municipal securities, if approved, would be issued, (iii) the amounts (which, in the case of in-kind contributions, must include both the value and the nature of the goods or services provided, including any ancillary services provided to, on behalf of, or in furtherance of the bond ballot campaign) and the specific dates of such contributions, (iv) the full name of the municipal entity and full issue description of any primary offering resulting from the bond ballot campaign to which the municipal finance professional, political action committee controlled by the municipal finance professional or non-MFP executive officer has made a contribution required to be disclosed under Rule G-37(e)(i)(B), or to which a contribution has been made by a municipal finance professional or a non-MFP executive officer during the period beginning two years prior to such individual becoming a municipal finance professional or a non-MFP executive officer that would have been required to be disclosed if such individual had been a municipal finance professional or a non-MFP executive officer at the time of such contribution and the reportable date of selection on which the broker, dealer or municipal securities dealer was selected to engage in the municipal securities business, and (v) the payments or reimbursements, related to any bond ballot contribution, received by the municipal finance professional or non-MFP executive officer from any third party that are required to be disclosed by Rule G-37(e)(i)(B), including the amount paid and the name of the third party making such payment or reimbursement; provided, however, that such records need not reflect any contribution made by a municipal finance professional or non-MFP executive officer to a bond ballot campaign for a ballot initiative with respect to which such person is entitled to vote if the contributions made by such person, in total, are not in excess of $250 to any bond ballot campaign, per ballot initiative.

(J) Brokers, dealers and municipal securities dealers shall maintain copies of the Forms G-37 and G-37x submitted to the Board along with a record of submitting such forms to the Board.

(K) Terms used in this paragraph (xvi) have the same meaning as in Rule G-37.

(L) No record is required by this paragraph (a)(xvi) of (i) any municipal securities business done or contribution to officials of issuers or political parties of states or political subdivisions made prior to April 25, 1994 or (ii) any payment to political parties of states or political subdivisions made prior to March 6, 1995.

(M) No broker, dealer or municipal securities dealer shall be subject to the requirements of this paragraph (a)(xvi) during any period that such broker, dealer or municipal securities dealer has qualified for and invoked the exemption set forth in clause (B) of paragraph (e)(ii) of Rule G-37; provided, however, that such broker, dealer or municipal securities dealer shall remain obligated to comply with clause (H) of this paragraph (a)(xvi) during such period of exemption. At such time as a broker, dealer or municipal securities dealer that has been exempted by this clause (M) from the requirements of this paragraph (a)(xvi) engages in any municipal securities business, all requirements of this paragraph (a)(xvi) covering the periods of time set forth herein (beginning with the then current calendar year and the two preceding calendar years) shall become applicable to such broker, dealer or municipal securities dealer.

(xvii) Records Concerning Compliance with Rule G-20. Each broker, dealer and municipal securities dealer shall maintain:

(A) a separate record of any gift or gratuity subject to the general limitation of Rule G-20(c);

(B) all agreements referred to in Rule G-20(f) and records of all compensation paid as a result of those agreements; and

(C) records of all non-cash compensation referred to in Rule G-20(g). The records shall include the name of the person or entity making the payment, the name(s) of the associated person(s) receiving the payments (if applicable), and the nature (including the location of meetings described in Rule G-20(g)(iii), if applicable) and value of non-cash compensation received.

(xviii) Records Concerning Consultants Pursuant to Former Rule G-38. Each broker, dealer and municipal securities dealer shall maintain:

(A) a listing of the name of the consultant pursuant to the Consultant Agreement, business address, role (including the state or geographic area in which the consultant is working on behalf of the broker, dealer or municipal securities dealer) and compensation arrangement of each consultant;

(B) a copy of each Consultant Agreement referred to in former rule G-38(b);

(C) a listing of the compensation paid in connection with each such Consultant Agreement;

(D) where applicable, a listing of the municipal securities business obtained or retained through the activities of each consultant;

(E) a listing of issuers and a record of disclosures made to such issuers, pursuant to former rule G-38(d), concerning each consultant used by the broker, dealer or municipal securities dealer to obtain or retain municipal securities business with each such issuer;

(F) records of each reportable political contribution (as defined in former rule G-38(a)(vi)), which records shall include:

(1) the names, city/county and state of residence of contributors;

(2) the names and titles (including any city/county/state or other political subdivision) of the recipients of such contributions; and

(3) the amounts and dates of such contributions;

(G) records of each reportable political party payment (as defined in former rule G-38(a)(vii)), which records shall include:

(1) the names, city/county and state of residence of contributors;

(2) the names and titles (including any city/county/state or other political subdivision) of the recipients of such payments; and

(3) the amounts and dates of such payments;

(H) records indicating, if applicable, that a consultant made no reportable political contributions (as defined in former rule G-38(a)(vi)) or no reportable political party payments (as defined in former rule G-38(a)(vii));

(I) a statement, if applicable, that a consultant failed to provide any report of information to the dealer concerning reportable political contributions or reportable political party payments;

(J) the date of termination of any consultant arrangement; and

(K) copies of the Forms G-38t sent to the Board along with the certified or registered mail receipt or other record of sending such forms to the Board.

For purposes of this clause (xviii), the term "former rule G-38" shall have the meaning set forth in Rule G-38(c)(ii).

(xix) Negotiable Instruments Drawn From a Customer's Account. No broker, dealer or municipal securities dealer or person associated with such broker, dealer or municipal securities dealer shall obtain from a customer or submit for payment a check, draft or other form of negotiable paper drawn on a customer's checking, savings, share, or similar account, without that person's express written authorization, which may include the customer's signature on the negotiable instrument.

(xx) Records Concerning Compliance with Rule G-27. Each broker, dealer and municipal securities dealer shall maintain the records required under G-27(c), G-27(d) and G-27(e).

(xxi) Records Concerning Sign-in Logs for In-Firm Delivery of the Regulatory Element Continuing Education. If applicable, each broker, dealer and municipal securities dealer shall maintain the records required by rule G-3(h)(i)(G)(6)(c).

(xxii) Records Concerning Compliance with Rule G-34(c).

(A) A broker, dealer or municipal securities dealer that acts as a Program Dealer, as defined in Rule G-34(c)(i)(A)(1), for an Auction Rate Security shall maintain:

(1) a record of the name of and CUSIP number or numbers for all such Auction Rate Securities for which the broker, dealer or municipal securities dealer acts as a Program Dealer;

(2) a record of all information submitted to and received from an Auction Agent as defined in Rule G-34(c)(i) with respect to an auction; and

(3) all information and documents required to be submitted to the Board by the broker, dealer or municipal securities dealer under Rule G-34(c)(i).

(B) A broker, dealer or municipal securities dealer that acts as a Remarketing Agent, as defined in Rule G-34(c)(ii), for a Variable Rate Demand Obligation shall maintain:

(1) a record of the name of and CUSIP number or numbers for all such Variable Rate Demand Obligations for which the broker, dealer or municipal securities dealer acts as a Remarketing Agent; and

(2) all information and documents required to be submitted to the Board by the broker, dealer or municipal securities dealer under Rule G-34(c)(ii); and

(3) for documents detailing provisions of liquidity facilities identified in Rule G-34(c)(ii)(B)(1) associated with the Variable Rate Demand Obligation for which the broker, dealer or municipal securities dealer acts as a Remarketing Agent that are unable to be obtained through best efforts, a record of such efforts undertaken.

(xxiii) Records Concerning Compliance with Rule G-34(a)(ii)(C). A broker, dealer or municipal securities dealer that acts as an underwriter in a primary offering of municipal securities subject to Rule G-34(a)(ii)(C)(1) shall maintain:

(A) a record of the Time of Formal Award;

(B) a record of the Time of First Execution; and

(C) a record of all information submitted to NIIDS (as defined in Rule G-34(a)(ii)(C)(3)(b)) as required elements for "Trade Eligibility" and of the time the new issue received "Trade Eligibility" status in NIIDS.

(xxiv) Records of Secondary Market Trading Account Transactions. With respect to each secondary market trading account formed for the purchase of municipal securities, records shall be maintained by the broker, dealer, or municipal securities dealer designated by the account to maintain the books and records of the account, showing the description and aggregate par value of the securities; the name and percentage of participation of each member of the account; the terms and conditions governing the formation and operation of the account; all orders received for the purchase of the securities from the account; all allotments of securities and the price at which sold; the date of closing of the account; and a reconciliation of profits and expenses of the account.

(xxv) Broker's Brokers. A broker's broker (as defined in Rule G-43(d)(iii)) shall maintain the following records with respect to its municipal securities activities:

(A) all bids to purchase municipal securities, together with the time of receipt;

(B) all offers to sell municipal securities, together with the time the broker's broker first receives the offering and the time the offering is updated for display or distribution;

(C) the time that the high bid is provided to the seller; the time that the seller notifies the broker's broker that it will sell the securities at the high bid; and the time of execution of the trade;

(D) for each communication with a seller or bidder pursuant to Rule G-43(b)(iv), the date and time of the communication; whether the bid deviated from the predetermined parameters and, if so, the amount of the deviation; the full name of the person contacted at the bidder; the full name of the person contacted at the seller, if applicable; the direction provided by the bidder to the broker's broker following the communication; the direction provided by the seller to the broker's broker following the communication, if applicable; and the full name of the person at the bidder, or seller if applicable, who provided that direction;

(E) for each communication with a seller pursuant to Rule G-43(b)(v), the date and time of the communication; the amount by which the bid deviated from the predetermined parameters; the full name of the person contacted at the seller; the direction provided by the seller to the broker's broker following the communication; and the full name of the person at the seller who provided that direction;

(F) for all changed bids, the full name of the person at the bidder that authorized the change and the full name of the person at the broker's broker at whose direction the change was made;

(G) for all changes in offering prices, the full name of the person at the seller that authorized the change and the full name of the person at the broker's broker at whose direction the change was made;

(H) a copy of any writings by which the seller and bidders agreed that the broker's broker represents either the bidders or both seller and bidders, rather than the seller alone, which writings shall include the dates and times such writings were executed; and the full names of the signatories to such writings;

(I) a copy of the policies and procedures required by Rule G-43(c);

(J) a copy of its predetermined parameters (as defined in Rule G-43(d)(viii)), its analysis of why those predetermined parameters were reasonably designed to identify most bids that might not represent the fair market value of municipal securities that were the subject of bid-wanteds to which the parameters were applied, and the results of the periodic tests of such predetermined parameters required by Rule G-43(c)(i)(F); and

(K) if a broker's broker trading system is a separately operated and supervised division or unit of a broker, dealer or municipal securities dealer, there must be separately maintained in or separately extractable from such division's or unit's own facilities or the facilities of the broker, dealer or municipal securities dealer, all of the records relating to the activities of the broker's broker or alternative trading system, and such records shall be so maintained or otherwise accessible as to permit independent examination thereof and enforcement of applicable provisions of the Act, the rules and regulations thereunder, and the rules of the Board.

(xxvi) Alternative Trading Systems. An alternative trading system registered as such with the Commission shall maintain the following records with respect to its municipal securities activities:

(A) for all changed bids, the full name of the person at the bidder firm that authorized the change and the full name of the person at the alternative trading system at whose direction the change was made;

(B) for all changes in offering prices, the full name of the person at the seller firm that authorized the change and the full name of the person at the alternative trading system at whose direction the change was made;

(C) a copy of the policies and procedures required by Rule G-43(d)(iii)(C); and

(D) if the alternative trading system is a separately operated and supervised division or unit of a broker, dealer or municipal securities dealer, there must be separately maintained in or separately extractable from such division's or unit's own facilities or the facilities of the broker, dealer or municipal securities dealer, all of the records relating to the municipal securities activities of the alternative trading system, and such records shall be so maintained or otherwise accessible as to permit independent examination thereof and enforcement of applicable provisions of the Act, the rules and regulations thereunder, and the rules of the Board.

(b) Manner in which Books and Records are to be Maintained. Nothing herein contained shall be construed to require a broker, dealer or municipal securities dealer to maintain the books and records required by this rule in any given manner, provided that the information required to be shown is clearly and accurately reflected thereon and provides an adequate basis for the audit of such information, nor to require a broker, dealer or municipal securities dealer to maintain its books and records relating to transactions in municipal securities separate and apart from books and records relating to transactions in other types of securities; provided, however, that in the case of a bank dealer, all records relating to transactions in municipal securities effected by such bank dealer must be separately extractable from all other records maintained by the bank.

(c) Non-Clearing Brokers, Dealers and Municipal Securities Dealers. A broker, dealer or municipal securities dealer which executes transactions in municipal securities but clears such transactions through a clearing broker, dealer, or bank, or through a clearing agency, shall not be required to make and keep such books and records prescribed in this rule as are customarily made and kept by a clearing broker, dealer, bank or clearing agency; provided that, in the case of a broker, dealer or municipal securities dealer other than a bank dealer, the arrangements with such clearing broker, dealer or bank meet all applicable requirements prescribed in subparagraph (b) of rule 17a-3 under the Act, or the arrangements with such clearing agency have been approved by the Commission or, in the case of a bank dealer, such arrangements have been approved by the appropriate regulatory agency for such bank dealer; and further provided that such broker, dealer or municipal securities dealer shall remain responsible for the accurate maintenance and preservation of such books and records if they are maintained by a clearing agent other than a clearing broker or dealer.

(d) Introducing Brokers, Dealers and Municipal Securities Dealers. A broker, dealer or municipal securities dealer which, as an introducing broker, dealer or municipal securities dealer, clears all transactions with and for customers on a fully disclosed basis with a clearing broker, dealer or municipal securities dealer, and which promptly transmits all customer funds and securities to the clearing broker, dealer or municipal securities dealer which carries all of the accounts of such customers, shall not be required to make and keep such books and records prescribed in this rule as are customarily made and kept by a clearing broker, dealer or municipal securities dealer and which are so made and kept; and such clearing broker, dealer or municipal securities dealer shall be responsible for the accurate maintenance and preservation of such books and records.

(e) Definitions.

(i) Customer. For purposes of this rule, the term "customer" shall not include a broker, dealer, municipal securities dealer or municipal advisor acting in its capacity as such or the issuer of the securities which are the subject of the transaction in question.

(ii) Municipal Advisory Client. For the purposes of paragraph (h)(vi) of this rule, the term "municipal advisory client" shall include either a municipal entity or obligated person for whom the municipal advisor engages in municipal advisory activities as defined in Rule G-42(f)(iv), or a broker, dealer, municipal securities dealer, municipal advisor, or investment adviser (as defined in section 202 of the Investment Advisers Act of 1940) on behalf of whom the municipal advisor undertakes a solicitation of a municipal entity or obligated person, as defined in Rule 15Ba1-1(n), 17 CFR 240.15Ba1-1(n), under the Act.

(f) Compliance with Rule 17a-3. Brokers, dealers and municipal securities dealers other than bank dealers which are in compliance with rule 17a-3 of the Commission will be deemed to be in compliance with the requirements of this rule, provided that the information required by subparagraph (a)(iv)(D) of this rule as it relates to uncompleted transactions involving customers; paragraph (a)(viii); and paragraphs (a)(xi) through (a)(xxvi) shall in any event be maintained.

(g) Transactions in Municipal Fund Securities.

(i) Books and Records Maintained by Transfer Agents. Books and records required to be maintained by a broker, dealer or municipal securities dealer under this rule solely with respect to transactions in municipal fund securities may be maintained by a transfer agent registered under Section 17A(c)(2) of the Act used by such broker, dealer or municipal securities dealer in connection with such transactions; provided that such broker, dealer or municipal securities dealer shall remain responsible for the accurate maintenance and preservation of such books and records.

(ii) Price Substituted for Par Value of Municipal Fund Securities. For purposes of this rule, each reference to the term "par value," when applied to a municipal fund security, shall be substituted with (A) in the case of a purchase of a municipal fund security by a customer, the purchase price paid by the customer, exclusive of any commission, and (B) in the case of a sale or tender for redemption of a municipal fund security by a customer, the sale price or redemption amount paid to the customer, exclusive of any commission or other charge imposed upon redemption or sale.

(iii) Underwriters of Municipal Fund Securities That Are Not Local Government Investment Pools. An underwriter, defined in Rule G-45(d)(xiv), shall maintain the information required to be reported on Form G-45.

(h) Municipal Advisor Records. Every municipal advisor that is registered or required to be registered under Section 15B of the Act and the rules and regulations thereunder shall make and keep current the following books and records:

(i) General Business Records. All books and records described in Rule 15Ba1-8(a)(1)-(8) under the Act.

(ii) Records Concerning Compliance with Rule G-20.

(A) a separate record of any gift or gratuity subject to the general limitation of Rule G-20(c); and

(B) all agreements referred to in Rule G-20(f) and records of all compensation paid as a result of those agreements.

(iii) Records Concerning Political Contributions and Prohibitions on Municipal Advisory Business Pursuant to Rule G-37. Records reflecting:

(A) a listing of the names, titles, city/county and state of residence of all municipal advisor professionals;

(B) a listing of the names, titles, city/county and state of residence of all non-MAP executive officers;

(C) states in which the municipal advisor is engaging or seeks to engage in municipal advisory business;

(D) a listing of municipal entities with which the municipal advisor has engaged in municipal advisory business, along with the type of municipal advisory business engaged in, during the current year and separate listings for each of the previous two calendar years;

(E) the contributions, direct or indirect, to officials of a municipal entity and payments, direct or indirect, made to political parties of states and political subdivisions, by the municipal advisor and each political action committee controlled by the municipal advisor for the current year and separate listings for each of the previous two calendar years, which records shall include: (i) the identity of the contributors, (ii) the names and titles (including any city/county/state or other political subdivision) of the recipients of such contributions and payments, and (iii) the amounts and dates of such contributions and payments;

(F) the contributions, direct or indirect, to officials of a municipal entity made by each municipal advisor professional, any political action committee controlled by a municipal advisor professional, and non-

MAP executive officer for the current year, which records shall include: (i) the names, titles, city/county and state of residence of contributors, (ii) the names and titles (including any city/county/state or other political subdivision) of the recipients of such contributions, (iii) the amounts and dates of such contributions; and (iv) whether any such contribution was the subject of an automatic exemption, pursuant to Rule G-37(j), including the amount of the contribution, the date the municipal advisor discovered the contribution, the name of the contributor, and the date the contributor obtained a return of the contribution; provided, however, that such records need not reflect any contribution made by a municipal advisor professional or non-MAP executive officer to officials of a municipal entity for whom such person is entitled to vote if the contributions made by such person, in total, are not in excess of $250 to any official of a municipal entity, per election. In addition, municipal advisors shall maintain separate listings for each of the previous two calendar years containing the information required pursuant to this subparagraph (F) for each municipal advisor representative and each municipal advisor solicitor as defined in Rule G-37(g)(iii) and for any political action committee controlled by such individuals, and separate listings for the previous six months containing the information required pursuant to this subparagraph (F) for each municipal advisor principal, municipal advisor supervisory chain person and municipal advisor executive officer as defined in Rule G-37(g)(iii) and for any political action committee controlled by such individuals and for any non-MAP executive officers;

(G) the payments, direct or indirect, to political parties of states and political subdivisions made by all municipal advisor professionals, any political action committee controlled by a municipal advisor professional, and non-MAP executive officers for the current year, which records shall include: (i) the names, titles, city/county and state of residence of contributors, (ii) the names, and titles (including any city/county/state or other political subdivision) of the recipients of such payments and (iii) the amounts and dates of such payments; provided, however, that such records need not reflect those payments made by any municipal advisor professional or non-MAP executive officer to a political party of a state or political subdivision in which such persons are entitled to vote if the payments made by such person, in total, are not in excess of $250 per political party, per year. In addition, municipal advisors shall maintain separate listings for each of the previous two calendar years containing the information required pursuant to this subparagraph (G) for each municipal advisor representative and each municipal advisor solicitor as defined in Rule G-37(g)(iii) and for any political action committee controlled by such individuals, and separate listings for the previous six months containing the information required pursuant to this subparagraph (G) for each municipal advisor principal, municipal advisor supervisory chain person and municipal advisor executive officer as defined in Rule G-37(g)(iii) and for any political action committee controlled by such individuals and for any non-MAP executive officers;

(H) the contributions, direct or indirect, to bond ballot campaigns made by the municipal advisor and each political action committee controlled by the municipal advisor for the current year, which records shall include: (i) the identity of the contributors, (ii) the official name of each bond ballot campaign receiving such contributions, and the jurisdiction by or for which municipal securities, if approved, would be issued, (iii) the amounts (which, in the case of in-kind contributions, must include both the value and the nature of the goods or services provided, including any ancillary services provided to, on behalf of, or in furtherance of the bond ballot campaign) and the specific dates of such contributions, (iv) the full name of the municipal entity and full issue description of any primary offering resulting from the bond ballot campaign to which the municipal advisor or political action committee controlled by the municipal advisor has made a contribution and the reportable date of selection on which the municipal advisor was selected to engage in the municipal advisory business, and (v) the payments or reimbursements, related to any bond ballot contribution, received by the municipal advisor from any third party that are required to be disclosed under Rule G-37(e)(i)(B), including the amount paid and the name of the third party making such payment; and

(I) the contributions, direct or indirect, to bond ballot campaigns made by each municipal advisor professional, any political action committee controlled by a municipal advisor professional, and non-MAP executive officer for the current year, which records shall include: (i) the names, titles, city/county and state of residence of contributors, (ii) the official name of each bond ballot campaign receiving such contributions, and the jurisdiction (including city/county/state or political subdivision) by or for which municipal securities, if approved, would be issued, (iii) the amounts (which, in the case of in-kind contributions, must include both the value and the nature of the goods or services provided, including any ancillary services provided to, on behalf of, or in furtherance of the bond ballot campaign) and the specific dates of such contributions, (iv) the full name of the municipal entity and full issue description of any primary offering resulting from the bond ballot campaign to which the municipal advisor professional, political action committee controlled by the municipal advisor professional or non-MAP executive officer has made a contribution required to be disclosed under Rule G-37(e)(i)(B), or to which a contribution has been made by a municipal advisor professional or a non-MAP executive officer during the period beginning two years prior to such individual becoming a municipal advisor professional or a non-MAP executive officer that would have been required to be disclosed if such individual had been a municipal advisor professional or a non-MAP executive officer at the time of such contribution and the reportable date of selection on which the municipal advisor was selected to engage in the municipal advisory business, and (v) the payments or reimbursements, related to any bond ballot contribution, received by the municipal advisor professional or non-MAP executive officer from any third party that are required to be disclosed by Rule G-37(e)(i)(B), including the amount paid and the name of the third party making such payment or reimbursement; provided, however, that such records need not reflect any contribution made by a municipal advisor professional or non-MAP executive officer to a bond ballot campaign for a ballot initiative with respect to which such person is entitled to vote if the contributions made by such person, in total, are not in excess of $250 to any bond ballot campaign, per ballot initiative.

(J) Municipal advisors shall maintain copies of the Forms G-37 and G-37x submitted to the Board along with a record of submitting such forms to the Board.

(K) Terms used in this paragraph (iii) have the same meaning as in Rule G-37.

(L) No record is required by this paragraph (h)(iii) of:

(i) any municipal advisory business done or contribution to officials of municipal entities or political parties of states or political subdivisions; or

(ii) any payment to political parties of states or political subdivisions if such municipal advisory business, contribution, or payment was made prior to August 17, 2016.

(M) No municipal advisor shall be subject to the requirements of this paragraph (h)(iii) during any period that such municipal advisor has qualified for and invoked the exemption set forth in clause (B) of paragraph (e)(ii) of Rule G-37; provided, however, that such municipal advisor shall remain obligated to comply with clause (H) of this paragraph (h)(iii) during such period of exemption. At such time as a municipal advisor that has been exempted by this clause (M) from the requirements of this paragraph (h)(iii) engages in any municipal advisory business, all requirements of this paragraph (h)(iii) covering the periods of time set forth herein (beginning with the then current calendar year and the two preceding calendar years) shall become applicable to such municipal advisor.

(iv) Records Concerning Duties of Non-Solicitor Municipal Advisors pursuant to Rule G-42.

(A) A copy of any document created by a municipal advisor that was material to its review of a recommendation by another party or that memorializes the basis for any determination as to suitability.

(v) Records Concerning Compliance with Rule G-44.

(A) The written supervisory procedures required by Rule G-44(a)(i);

(B) A record of all designations of persons responsible for supervision as required by Rule G-44(a)(ii);

(C) Records of the reviews of written compliance policies and written supervisory procedures as required by Rule G-44(a) and (b);

(D) A record of all designations of persons as chief compliance officer as required by Rule G-44(c);

(E) The annual certifications as to compliance processes required by Rule G-44(d); and

(F) Any certifications made as to substantially equivalent supervisory and compliance obligations and books and records requirements pursuant to Rule G-44(e).

(vi) Municipal Advisory Client Complaints. A record of all written complaints of municipal advisory clients or persons acting on behalf of municipal advisory clients that are received by the municipal advisor. This record must include the complainant's name, address, and municipal advisory client number or code, if any; the date the complaint was received; the date of the activity that gave rise to the complaint; the name of each associated person of the municipal advisor identified in the complaint; a description of the nature of the complaint; and what action, if any, has been taken by such municipal advisor in connection with each such complaint. In addition, this record must be kept in an electronic format using the complaint product and problem codes set forth in the Municipal Securities Rulemaking Board Rule G-8 Customer and Municipal Advisory Client Complaint Product and Problem Codes Guide.

The term "written," for the purposes of this paragraph, shall include electronic correspondence. The term "complaint" shall mean any written statement alleging a grievance involving the municipal advisory activities of the municipal advisor or any associated person of such municipal advisor.

(vii) Records Concerning Compliance with Continuing Education Requirements

(A) Copies of the municipal advisor's needs analysis and written training plan as required by subparagraphs (i)(ii)(B)(1) and (i)(ii)(E)(1) of Rule G-3; and

(B) Records documenting the content of the training programs and completion of the programs by each covered person as required by Rule G-3(i)(ii)(B)(3).

---

38. MSRB Rules: G-9 – Preservation of Records

Summary: Prescribes the periods of time that records must be preserved and requires that records be accessible for inspection by appropriate regulatory agencies.

(a) Records to be Preserved for Six Years. Every broker, dealer and municipal securities dealer shall preserve the following records for a period of not less than six years:

(i) the records of original entry described in rule G-8(a)(i);

(ii) the account records described in rule G-8(a)(ii);

(iii) the securities records described in rule G-8(a)(iii);

(iv) the records concerning primary offerings described in rule G-8(a)(viii), provided, however, that such records need not be preserved for a syndicate or by a sole underwriter that, in either case, is not successful in purchasing an issue of municipal securities;

(v) the customer complaint records described in rule G-8(a)(xii);

(vi) if such broker, dealer or municipal securities dealer is subject to rule 15c3-1 under the Act, the general ledgers described in paragraph (a)(2) of rule 17a-3 under the Act;

(vii) the record, described in rule G-27(b)(ii), of each person designated as responsible for supervision of the municipal securities activities of the broker, dealer, or municipal securities dealer and the designated principal's supervisory responsibilities, provided that such record shall be preserved for the period of designation of each person designated and for at least six years following any change in such designation;

(viii) the records to be maintained pursuant to rule G-8(a)(xvi); provided, however, that copies of Forms G-37x shall be preserved for the period during which such Forms G-37x are effective and for at least six years following the end of such effectiveness;

(ix) the records regarding information on gifts and gratuities and employment agreements required to be maintained pursuant to rule G-8(a)(xvii);

(x) the records required to be maintained pursuant to rule G-8(a)(xviii);

(xi) the records concerning secondary market trading account transactions described in rule G-8(a)(xxiv), provided, however, that such records need not be preserved for a secondary market trading account which is not successful in purchasing municipal securities;

(xii) the records required to be maintained pursuant to rule G-8(a)(xxv);

(xiii) the records required to be maintained pursuant to rule G-8(a)(xxvi); and

(xiv) the records required to be maintained pursuant to Rule G-8(g)(iii).

(b) Records to be Preserved for Four Years. Every broker, dealer and municipal securities dealer shall preserve the following records for a period of not less than four years; provided, however, that each municipal securities dealer that is a bank or subsidiary or department or division of a bank shall preserve the following records for a period of not less than three years:

(i) the subsidiary records described in rule G-8(a)(iv);

(ii) the records of put options and repurchase agreements described in rule G-8(a)(v);

(iii) the records relating to agency transactions described in rule G-8(a)(vi);

(iv) the records of transactions as principal described in rule G-8(a)(vii);

(v) the copies of confirmations and other notices described in rule G-8(a)(ix);

(vi) the customer account information described in rule G-8(a)(xi), provided that records showing the terms and conditions relating to the opening and maintenance of an account shall be preserved for a period of at least six years following the closing of such account;

(vii) if such broker, dealer or municipal securities dealer is subject to rule 15c3-1 under the Act, the records described in subparagraphs (a)(4)(iv) and (vi) and (a)(11) of rule 17a-3 and subparagraphs (b)(5) and (b)(8) of rule 17a-4 under the Act;

(viii) the following records, to the extent made or received by such broker, dealer or municipal securities dealer in connection with its business as such broker, dealer or municipal securities dealer and not otherwise described in this rule:

(A) check books, bank statements, canceled checks, cash reconciliations and wire transfers;

(B) bills receivable or payable;

(C) all written and electronic communications received and sent, including inter-office memoranda, relating to the conduct of the activities of such municipal securities broker or municipal securities dealer with respect to municipal securities;

(D) all written agreements entered into by such broker, dealer or municipal securities dealer, including agreements with respect to any account; and

(E) all powers of attorney and other evidence of the granting of any authority to act on behalf of any account, and copies of resolutions empowering an agent to act on behalf of a corporation.

(ix) all records relating to fingerprinting which are required pursuant to paragraph (e) of rule 17f-2 under the Act;

(x) all records relating to Rule G-32 required to be retained as described in rule G-8(a)(xiii);

(xi) the records to be maintained pursuant to rule G-8(a)(xv);

(xii) the authorization required by rule G-8(a)(xix)(B); however, this provision shall not require maintenance of copies of negotiable instruments signed by customers;

(xiii) each advertisement from the date of each use.

(xiv) the records required to be maintained pursuant to rule G-8(a)(xx);

(xv) the records to be maintained pursuant to rule G-8(a)(xxi);

(xvi) the records to be maintained pursuant to rule G-8(a)(xxii); and

(xvii) the records to be maintained pursuant to Rule G-8(a)(xxiii).

(c) Records to be Preserved for Life of Enterprise. Every broker, dealer and municipal securities dealer other than a bank dealer shall preserve during the life of such broker, dealer or municipal securities dealer and of any successor broker, dealer or municipal securities dealer all partnership articles or, in the case of a corporation, all articles of incorporation or charter, minute books and stock certificate books.

(d) Accessibility and Availability of Records. All books and records required to be preserved pursuant to this rule shall be available for ready inspection by each regulatory authority having jurisdiction under the Act to inspect such records, shall be maintained and preserved in an easily accessible place for a period of at least two years and thereafter shall be maintained and preserved in such manner as to be accessible to each such regulatory authority within a reasonable period of time, taking into consideration the nature of the record and the amount of time expired since the record was made.

(e) Method of Record Retention. Whenever a record is required to be preserved by this rule, such record may be retained either as an original or as a copy or other reproduction thereof, or on microfilm, magnetic tape, electronic storage media, or by the other similar medium of record retention, provided that such broker, dealer, municipal securities dealer, or municipal advisor shall have available adequate facilities for ready retrieval and inspection of any such record and for production of easily readable facsimile copies thereof and, in the case of records retained on microfilm, magnetic tape, electronic storage media, or other similar medium of record retention, duplicates of such records shall be stored separately from each other for the periods of time required by this rule.

(f) Effect of Lapse of Registration. The requirements of this rule shall continue to apply, for the periods of time specified, to any broker, dealer, municipal securities dealer, or municipal advisor which ceases to be registered with the Commission, except in the event a successor registrant shall undertake to maintain and preserve the books and records described herein for the required periods of time.

(g) Compliance with Rules 17a-3 and 17a-4. Brokers, dealers and municipal securities dealers other than bank dealers that are in compliance with rules 17a-3 and 17a-4 under the Act will be deemed to be in compliance with the requirements of this rule, provided that the records enumerated in section (f) of Rule G-8 of the Board and section (b) of this rule shall in any event be preserved for the applicable time periods specified in this rule.

(h) Municipal Advisor Records.

(i) Subject to subsections (ii) and (iii) of this section, every municipal advisor shall preserve the books and records described in Rule G-8(h) for a period of not less than five years.

(ii) The records described in Rule G-8(h)(v)(B) and (D) shall be preserved for the period of designation of each person designated and for at least six years following any change in such designation.

(iii) The records described in Rule G-8(h)(iii) and (vi) shall be preserved for at least six years; provided, however, that copies of Forms G-37x shall be preserved for the period during which such Forms G-37x are effective and for at least six years following the end of such effectiveness.

(i) Municipal Advisor Records Related to Formation and Cessation of its Business. Every municipal advisor shall comply with the provisions of Rule 15Ba1-8(b)(2) and (c) under the Act.

(j) Records of Non-Resident Municipal Advisors. Every non-resident municipal advisor shall comply with the provisions of Rule 15Ba1-8(f) under the Act.

(k) Electronic Storage of Municipal Advisor Records Permitted. Whenever a record is required to be preserved by this rule by a municipal advisor, such record may be preserved on electronic storage media in accordance with section (e). Electronic preservation of any record in a manner that complies with Rule 15Ba1-8(d) under the Act will be deemed to be in compliance with the requirements of this rule.

---

39. MSRB Rules: G-13 – Quotations

Summary: Requires quotations distributed or published by a dealer to represent bona fide bids or offers of municipal securities, based upon the dealer's best judgment of the fair market value of the securities, and prohibits misrepresentation of another dealer's quotations.

(a) General. The provisions of this rule shall apply to all quotations relating to municipal securities which are distributed or published, or caused to be distributed or published, by any broker, dealer or municipal securities dealer or any person associated with and acting on behalf of a broker, dealer or municipal securities dealer. For purposes of this rule, the term "quotation" shall mean any bid for, or offer of, municipal securities, or any request for bids for or offers of municipal securities, including indications of "bid wanted" or "offer wanted." The terms "distributed" or "published" shall mean the dissemination of quotations by any means of communication. Reference in this rule to a broker, dealer or municipal securities dealer shall be deemed to include reference to any person associated with a broker, dealer or municipal securities dealer.

(b) Bona Fide Quotations.

   (i) Except as provided below, no broker, dealer or municipal securities dealer shall distribute or publish, or cause to be distributed or published, any quotation relating to municipal securities, unless the quotation represents a bona fide bid for, or offer of, municipal securities by such broker, dealer or municipal securities dealer, provided, however, that all quotations, unless otherwise indicated at the time made, shall be subject to prior purchase or sale and to subsequent change in price. If such broker, dealer or municipal securities dealer is distributing or publishing the quotation on behalf of another broker, dealer, or municipal securities dealer, such broker, dealer or municipal securities dealer shall have no reason to believe that such quotation does not represent a bona fide bid for, or offer of, municipal securities. Nothing in this paragraph shall be construed to prohibit requests for bids or offers, including indications of "bid wanted" or "offer wanted," or shall be construed to prohibit nominal quotations, if such quotations are, at the time made, clearly stated or indicated to be such. For purposes of this paragraph, a "nominal quotation" shall mean an indication of the price given solely for informational purposes.

   (ii) No broker, dealer or municipal securities dealer shall distribute or publish, or cause to be distributed or published, any quotation relating to municipal securities, unless the price stated in the quotation is based on the best judgment of such broker, dealer or municipal securities dealer of the fair market value of the securities which are the subject of the quotation at the time the quotation is made. If a broker, dealer or municipal securities dealer is distributing or publishing a quotation on behalf of another broker, dealer, or municipal securities dealer, such broker, dealer or municipal securities dealer shall have no reason to believe that the price stated in the quotation is not based on the best judgment of the fair market value of the securities of the broker, dealer or municipal securities dealer on whose behalf such broker, dealer or municipal securities dealer is distributing or publishing the quotation.

   (iii) For purposes of subparagraph (i), a quotation shall be deemed to represent a "bona fide bid for, or offer of, municipal securities" if the broker, dealer or municipal securities dealer making the quotation is prepared to purchase or sell the security which is the subject of the quotation at the price stated in the quotation and under such conditions, if any, as are specified at the time the quotation is made.

   (iv) No broker, dealer or municipal securities dealer shall knowingly misrepresent a quotation relating to municipal securities made by any other broker, dealer, or municipal securities dealer.

(c) Multiple Markets in the Same Securities. No broker, dealer or municipal securities dealer participating in a joint account shall, together with one or more other participants in such account, distribute or publish, or cause to be distributed or published, quotations relating to the municipal securities which are the subject of such account if such quotations indicate more than one market for the same securities.

40. MSRB Rules: G-14 – Reports of Sales or Purchases

Summary: Prohibits dealers from distributing or publishing reports of purchases or sales of municipal securities unless the report is made with knowledge or reason to believe that the transaction was effected, and without any reason to believe that the reported transaction is fictitious, or in furtherance of any fraudulent, deceptive or manipulative purpose, and establishes transaction reporting requirements and procedures.

(a) General. No broker, dealer or municipal securities dealer or person associated with a broker, dealer or municipal securities dealer shall distribute or publish, or cause to be distributed or published, any report of a purchase or sale of municipal securities, unless such broker, dealer or municipal securities dealer or associated person knows or has reason to believe that the purchase or sale was actually effected and has no reason to believe that the reported transaction is fictitious or in furtherance of any fraudulent, deceptive or manipulative purpose. For purposes of this rule, the terms "distributed" or "published" shall mean the dissemination of a report by any means of communication.

(b) Transaction Reporting Requirements.

   (i) Each broker, dealer or municipal securities dealer ("dealer") shall report to the Board or its designee information about each purchase and sale transaction effected in municipal securities to the Real-time Transaction Reporting System ("RTRS") in the manner prescribed by Rule G-14 RTRS Procedures and the RTRS Users Manual. Transaction information collected by the Board under this rule will be used to make public reports of market activity and prices and to assess transaction fees. The transaction information will be made available by the Board to the Commission, securities associations registered under Section 15A of the Act and other appropriate regulatory agencies defined in Section 3(a)(34)(A) of the Act to assist in the inspection for compliance with and the enforcement of Board rules.

   (ii) The information specified in the Rule G-14 RTRS Procedures is critical to public reporting of prices for transparency purposes and to the compilation of an audit trail for regulatory purposes. All dealers have an ongoing obligation to report this information promptly, accurately and completely. The dealer may employ an agent for the purpose of submitting transaction information; however the primary responsibility for the timely and accurate submission remains with the dealer that effected the transaction. A dealer that acts as a submitter for another dealer has specific responsibility to ensure that transaction reporting requirements are met with respect to those aspects of the reporting process that are under the Submitter's control. A dealer that submits inter-dealer municipal securities transactions for comparison, either for itself or on behalf of another dealer, has specific responsibility to ensure that transaction reporting requirements are met with respect to those aspects of the comparison process that are under the Submitter's control.

   (iii) To identify its transactions for reporting purposes, each dealer shall obtain a unique broker symbol from NASDAQ Subscriber Services.

   (iv) The provisions of this section (b) shall not apply to a dealer if such dealer does not effect any transactions in municipal securities or if such dealer's transactions in municipal securities are limited exclusively to transactions described in subsection (b)(v) of this rule and the dealer has confirmed that it is qualified for this exemption as provided in Rule A-12(g).

   (v) The following transactions shall not be reported under Rule G-14:

     (A) Transactions in securities without assigned CUSIP numbers;

     (B) Transactions in Municipal Fund Securities; and

     (C) Inter-dealer transactions for principal movement of securities between dealers that are not inter-dealer transactions eligible for comparison in a clearing agency registered with the Commission.

Rule G-14 RTRS Procedures

(a) General Procedures.

(i) The Board has designated three RTRS Portals for dealers to use in the submission of transaction information. Transaction data submissions must conform to the formats specified for the RTRS Portal used for the trade submission. The RTRS Portals may be used as follows:

(A) The message-based trade input RTRS Portal operated by National Securities Clearing Corporation (NSCC) ("Message Portal") may be used for any trade record submission or trade record modification.

(B) The RTRS Web-based trade input method ("RTRS Web Portal" or "RTRS Web") operated by the MSRB may be used for low volume transaction submissions and for modifications of trade records, but cannot be used for submitting or amending inter-dealer transaction data that is used in the comparison process. Comparison data instead must be entered into the comparison system using a method authorized by the registered clearing agency.

(C) The NSCC Real-Time Trade Matching ("RTTM") Web-based trade input method ("RTTM Web Portal" or "RTTM Web") may be used only for submitting or modifying data with respect to Inter-Dealer Transactions Eligible for Comparison.

(ii) Transactions effected with a Time of Trade during the hours of the RTRS Business Day shall be reported within 15 minutes of Time of Trade to an RTRS Portal except in the following situations:

(A) "List Offering Price/Takedown Transaction," as defined in paragraph (d)(vii) of Rule G-14 RTRS Procedures, shall be reported by the end of the day on which the trade is executed.

(B) A dealer effecting trades in short-term instruments maturing in nine months or less, variable rate instruments that may be tendered for purchase at least as frequently as every nine months, auction rate products for which auctions are scheduled to occur at least as frequently as every nine months, and commercial paper maturing or rolling-over in nine months or less shall report such trades by the end of the RTRS Business Day on which the trades were executed.

(C) A dealer reporting an "away from market" trade as described in Section 4.3.2 of the Specifications for Real-Time Reporting of Municipal Securities Transactions shall report such trade by the end of the day on which the trade is executed.

(D) A dealer reporting an inter-dealer "VRDO ineligible on trade date" as described in Section 4.3.2 of the Specifications for Real-Time Reporting of Municipal Securities Transactions shall report such trade by the end of the day on which the trade becomes eligible for automated comparison by a clearing agency registered with the Commission.

(E) A dealer reporting an inter-dealer "resubmission of an RTTM cancel" as described in Section 4.3.2 of the Specifications for Real-Time Reporting of Municipal Securities Transactions shall resubmit identical information about the trade cancelled by the end of the RTRS Business Day following the day the trade was cancelled.

(iii) Transactions effected with a Time of Trade outside the hours of the RTRS Business Day shall be reported no later than 15 minutes after the beginning of the next RTRS Business Day.

(iv) Transaction data that is not submitted in a timely and accurate manner in accordance with these Procedures shall be submitted or corrected as soon as possible.

(v) Information on the status of trade reports in RTRS is available through the Message Portal, through the RTRS Web Portal, or via electronic mail. Trade status information from RTRS indicating a problem or potential problem with reported trade data must be reviewed and addressed promptly to ensure that the information being disseminated by RTRS is as accurate and timely as possible.

(vi) RTRS Portals will be open for transmission of transaction data and status of trade reports beginning 30 minutes prior to the beginning of the RTRS Business Day and ending 90 minutes after the end of the RTRS Business Day.

(b) Reporting Requirements for Specific Types of Transactions.

(i) Inter-Dealer Transactions Eligible for Comparison by a Clearing Agency Registered with the Commission.

(A) Bilateral Submissions: Inter-Dealer Transactions Eligible for Trade Comparison at a Clearing Agency

Registered with the Commission (registered clearing agency) shall be reported by each dealer submitting, or causing to be submitted, such transaction records required by the registered clearing agency to achieve comparison of the transaction. The transaction records also shall include the additional trade information for such trades listed in the Specifications for Real-Time Reporting of Municipal Securities Transactions contained in the RTRS Users Manual.

(B) Unilateral Submissions: For transactions that, under the rules of the registered clearing agency, are deemed compared upon submission by one side of the transaction (unilateral submissions), a submission is not required by the contra-side of the transaction. The contra-side, however, must monitor such submissions to ensure that data representing its side of the trade is correct and use procedures of the registered clearing agency to correct the trade data if it is not.

(ii) Customer Transactions. Reports of transactions with customers shall include the specific items of information listed for such transactions in the Specifications for Real-Time Reporting of Municipal Securities Transactions.

(iii) Agency Transactions With Customers Effected By An Introducing Broker Against Principal Account of its Clearing Broker. Reports of agency transactions effected by an introducing broker for a customer against the principal account of its clearing broker shall include the specific items of information listed in the Specifications for Real-Time Reporting of Municipal Securities Transactions for "Inter-Dealer Regulatory-Only" trades.

(iv) Transactions with Special Conditions. Reports of transactions affected by the special conditions described in the RTRS Users Manual in Section 4.3.2 of the Specifications for Real-Time Reporting of Municipal Securities Transactions shall be reported with the "special condition indicators" shown and in the manner specified. Special condition indicators designated as "optional" in these Specifications are required for the Submitter to obtain an extended reporting deadline under paragraphs (a)(ii)(B)-(C) of Rule G-14 RTRS Procedures, but may be omitted if a deadline extension is not claimed. All other special condition indicators are mandatory, including the List Offering Price/Takedown Transaction indicator for transactions identified in paragraph (a)(ii)(A) of Rule G-14 RTRS Procedures, alternative trading system transaction indicator for transactions defined in paragraph (d)(ix) of Rule G-14 RTRS Procedures, and non-transaction-based compensation arrangement indicator for transactions defined in paragraph (d)(x) of Rule G-14 RTRS Procedures.

(c) RTRS Users Manual. The RTRS Users Manual is comprised of the Specifications for Real-Time Reporting of Municipal Securities Transactions, the Users Guide for RTRS Web, guidance on how to report specific types of transactions and other information relevant to transaction reporting under Rule G-14. The RTRS Users Manual is located at www.msrb.org and may be updated from time to time with additional guidance or revisions to existing documents.

(d) Definitions.

(i) "RTRS" or "Real-Time Transaction Reporting System" is a facility operated by the MSRB. RTRS receives municipal securities transaction reports submitted by dealers pursuant to Rule G-14, disseminates price and volume information in real time for transparency purposes, and otherwise processes information pursuant to Rule G-14.

(ii) The "RTRS Business Day" is 7:30 a.m. to 6:30 p.m., Eastern Time, Monday through Friday, unless otherwise announced by the Board.

(iii) "Time of Trade" is the time at which a contract is formed for a sale or purchase of municipal securities at a set quantity and set price.

(iv) "Submitter" means a dealer, or service bureau acting on behalf of a dealer, that has been authorized to interface with RTRS for the purposes of entering transaction data into the system.

(v) "Inter-Dealer Transaction Eligible for Automated Comparison by a Clearing Agency Registered with the Commission" is defined in MSRB Rule G-12(f)(iv).

(vi) "Municipal Fund Securities" is defined in Rule D-12.

(vii) "List Offering Price/Takedown Transaction" means a primary market sale transaction executed on the first day of trading of a new issue:

    (A) by a sole underwriter, syndicate manager, syndicate member, selling group member, or distribution participant to a customer at the published list offering price for the security ("List Offering Price Transaction"); or

    (B) by a sole underwriter or syndicate manager to a syndicate member, selling group member, or distribution participant ("RTRS Takedown Transaction").

(viii) "Distribution participant" means for the purposes of this rule a dealer that has agreed to assist an underwriter in selling a new issue at the list offering price.

(ix) "Alternative trading system transaction" means for the purposes of this rule an inter-dealer transaction with or executed using the services of an alternative trading system with Form ATS on file with the Securities and Exchange Commission.

(x) "Non-transaction-based compensation arrangement transaction" means for the purposes of this rule a transaction with a customer that does not include a mark-up, mark-down or commission.

---

41. MSRB Rules: G-15 – Confirmation, Clearance, Settlement and Other Uniform Practice Requirements with Respect to Transactions with Customers

Summary: Requires dealers to provide customers with written confirmations of transactions, containing specified information, including mark-ups and mark-downs, and prescribes certain uniform practice procedures for dealers that transact municipal securities business with customers.

(a) Customer Confirmations.

    (i) At or before the completion of a transaction in municipal securities with or for the account of a customer, each broker, dealer or municipal securities dealer shall give or send to the customer a written confirmation that complies with the requirements of this paragraph (i):

        (A) Transaction information. The confirmation shall include information regarding the terms of the transaction as set forth in this subparagraph (A):

            (1) The parties, their capacities, and any remuneration from other parties. The following information regarding the parties to the transaction and their relationship shall be included:

                (a) name, address, and telephone number of the broker, dealer, or municipal securities dealer, provided, however, that the address and telephone number need not be stated on a confirmation sent through the automated confirmation facilities of a clearing agency registered with the Securities and Exchange Commission;

                (b) name of customer;

                (c) designation of whether the transaction was a purchase from or sale to the customer;

                (d) the capacity in which the broker, dealer or municipal securities dealer effected the transaction, whether acting:

                    (i) as principal for its own account,

                    (ii) as agent for the customer,

                    (iii) as agent for a person other than the customer, or

                    (iv) as agent for both the customer and another person;

(e) if the broker, dealer or municipal securities dealer is effecting a transaction as agent for the customer or as agent for both the customer and another person, the confirmation shall include: (i) either (A) the name of the person from whom the securities were purchased or to whom the securities were sold for the customer, or (B) a statement that this information will be furnished upon the written request of the customer; and (ii) either (A) the source and amount of any remuneration received or to be received (shown in aggregate dollar amount) by the broker, dealer or municipal securities dealer in connection with the transaction from any person other than the customer, or (B) a statement indicating whether any such remuneration has been or will be received and that the source and amount of such other remuneration will be furnished upon written request of the customer. In applying the terms of this subparagraph (A)(1)(e), if a security is acquired at a discount (e.g., "net" price less concession) and is sold at a "net" price to a customer, the discount must be disclosed as remuneration received from the customer pursuant to subparagraph (A)(6)(f) of this paragraph rather than as remuneration received from "a person other than the customer."

(2) Trade date and time of execution.

    (a) The trade date shall be shown.

    (b) The time of execution shall be shown; provided that, for a transaction for an institutional account as defined in Rule G-8(a)(xi) or a transaction in municipal fund securities, a statement that the time of execution will be furnished upon written request of the customer may be shown in satisfaction of the obligation to disclose the time of execution on the confirmation.

(3) Par value. The par value of the securities shall be shown, with special requirements for the following securities:

    (a) Zero coupon securities. For zero coupon securities, the maturity value of the securities must be shown if it differs from the par value.

    (b) Municipal fund securities. For municipal fund securities, in place of par value, the confirmation shall show (i) in the case of a purchase of a municipal fund security by a customer, the total purchase price paid by the customer, exclusive of any commission, and (ii) in the case of a sale or tender for redemption of a municipal fund security by a customer, the total sale price or redemption amount paid to the customer, exclusive of any commission or other charge imposed upon redemption or sale.

(4) Settlement date. The settlement date as defined in section (b) of this rule shall be shown.

(5) Yield and dollar price. Yields and dollar prices shall be computed and shown in the following manner, subject to the exceptions stated in subparagraph (A)(5)(d) of this paragraph:

    (a) For transactions that are effected on the basis of a yield to maturity, yield to a call date, or yield to a put date:

        (i) The yield at which the transaction was effected shall be shown and, if that yield is to a call date or to a put date, this shall be noted, along with the date and dollar price of the call or put.

        (ii) A dollar price shall be computed and shown in accordance with the rules in subparagraph (A)(5)(c) of this paragraph, and such dollar price shall be used in computations of extended principal and final monies shown on the confirmation.

    (b) For transactions that are effected on the basis of a dollar price:

        (i) The dollar price at which the transaction was effected shall be shown.

        (ii) A yield shall be computed and shown in accordance with subparagraph (A)(5)(c) of this paragraph, unless the transaction was effected at "par."

    (c) In computing yield and dollar price, the following rules shall be observed:

        (i) The yield or dollar price computed and shown shall be computed to the lower of call or nominal maturity date, with the exceptions noted in this subparagraph (A)(5)(c).

(ii) For purposes of computing yield to call or dollar price to call, only those call features that represent "in whole calls" of the type that may be used by the issuer without restriction in a refunding ("pricing calls") shall be considered in computations made under this subparagraph (A)(5).

(iii) Yield computations shall take into account dollar price concessions granted to the customer, commissions charged to the customer and adjustable tender fees applicable to puttable securities, but shall not take into account incidental transaction fees or miscellaneous charges, provided, however, that as specified in subparagraph (A)(6)(e) of this paragraph, such fees or charges must be indicated on the confirmation.

(iv) With respect to the following specific situations, these additional rules shall be observed:

(A) Declining premium calls. For those securities subject to a series of pricing calls at declining premiums, the call date resulting in the lowest yield or dollar price shall be considered the yield to call or dollar price to call.

(B) Continuously callable securities. For those securities that, at the time of trade, are subject to a notice of a pricing call at any time, the yield to call or dollar price to call shall be computed based upon the assumption that a notice of call may be issued on the day after trade date or on any subsequent date.

(C) Mandatory tender dates. For those securities subject to a mandatory tender date, the mandatory tender date and dollar price of redemption shall be used in computations in lieu of nominal maturity date and maturity value.

(D) Securities sold on basis of yield to put. For those transactions effected on the basis of a yield to put date, the put date and dollar price of redemption shall be used in computations in lieu of maturity date and maturity value.

(E) Prerefunded or called securities. For those securities that are prerefunded or called to a call date prior to maturity, the date and dollar price of redemption set by the prerefunding shall be used in computations in lieu of maturity date and maturity value.

(v) Computations shall be made in accordance with the requirements of rule G-33.

(vi) If the computed yield or dollar price shown on the confirmation is not based upon the nominal maturity date, then the date used in the computation shall be identified and stated. If the computed yield or dollar price is not based upon a redemption value of par, the dollar price used in the computation shall be shown (e.g., 5.00% yield to call on 1/1/99 at 103).

(vii) If the computed yield required by this paragraph (5) is different than the yield at which the transaction was effected, the computed yield must be shown in addition to the yield at which the transaction was effected.

(d) Notwithstanding the requirements noted in subparagraphs (A)(5)(a) through (c) of this paragraph above:

(i) Securities that prepay principal. For securities that prepay principal periodically, a yield computation and display of yield is not required, provided, however, that if a yield is displayed, there shall be included a statement describing how the yield was computed.

(ii) Municipal Collateralized Mortgage Obligations. For municipal collateralized mortgage obligations, a yield computation and display of yield is not required, provided however, that if a yield is displayed, there shall be included a statement describing how the yield was computed.

(iii) Defaulted securities. For securities that have defaulted in the payment of interest or principal, a yield shall not be shown.

(iv) Variable rate securities. For municipal securities with a variable interest rate, a yield shall not be shown unless the transaction was effected on the basis of yield to put.

(v) Securities traded on a discounted basis. For securities traded on a discounted basis, a yield shall not be shown.

(vi) Municipal fund securities. For municipal fund securities, neither yield nor dollar price shall be shown.

(6) Final Monies. The following information relating to the calculation and display of final monies shall be shown:

(a) total dollar amount of transaction;

(b) amount of accrued interest, with special requirements for the following securities:

(i) Zero coupon securities. For zero coupon securities, no figure for accrued interest shall be shown;

(ii) Securities traded on discounted basis. For securities traded on a discounted basis (other than discounted securities traded on a yield-equivalent basis), no figure for accrued interest shall be shown;

(iii) Municipal fund securities. For municipal fund securities, no figure for accrued interest shall be shown;

(c) if the securities pay interest on a current basis but are traded without interest, a notation of "flat;"

(d) extended principal amount, with special requirements for the following securities:

(i) Securities traded on discounted basis. For securities traded on a discounted basis (other than discounted securities sold on a yield-equivalent basis) total dollar amount of discount may be shown in lieu of the resulting dollar price and extended principal amount;

(ii) Municipal fund securities. For municipal fund securities, no extended principal amount shall be shown;

(e) the nature and amount of miscellaneous fees, such as special delivery arrangements or a "per transaction" fee, or if agreed to, any fees for converting registered certificates to or from bearer form;

(f) if the broker, dealer or municipal securities dealer is effecting the transaction as agent for the customer or as agent for both the customer and another person, the amount of any remuneration received or to be received (shown in aggregate dollar amount) by the broker, dealer or municipal securities dealer from the customer in connection with the transaction unless remuneration paid by the customer is determined, pursuant to a written agreement with the customer, other than on a transaction basis;

(g) the first interest payment date if other than semi-annual, but only if necessary for the calculation of final money;

(h) for callable zero coupon securities, if applicable, the percentage of the purchase price at risk due to the lowest possible call, which shall be calculated based upon the ratio between (i) the difference between the price paid by the customer and the lowest possible call price, and (ii) the price paid by the customer.

(7) Delivery of securities. The following information regarding the delivery of securities shall be shown:

(a) Securities other than bonds or municipal fund securities. For securities other than bonds or municipal fund securities, denominations to be delivered;

(b) Bond certificates delivered in non-standard denominations. For bonds, denominations of certificates to be delivered shall be stated if:

(i) for bearer bonds, denominations are other than $1,000 or $5,000 in par value, and

(ii) for registered bonds, denominations are other than multiples of $1,000 par value, or exceed $100,000 par value;

(c) Municipal fund securities. For municipal fund securities, the purchase price, exclusive of commission, of each share or unit and the number of shares or units to be delivered;

(d) Delivery instructions. Instructions, if available, regarding receipt or delivery of securities and form of payment, if other than as usual and customary between the parties.

(8) Additional information about the transaction. In addition to the transaction information required above, such other information as may be necessary to ensure that the parties agree to details of the transaction also shall be shown.

(B) Securities identification information. The confirmation shall include a securities identification which includes, at a minimum:

(1) the name of the issuer, with special requirements for the following securities:

(a) For stripped coupon securities, the trade name and series designation assigned to the stripped coupon municipal security by the broker, dealer or municipal securities dealer sponsoring the program must be shown;

(b) Municipal fund securities. For municipal fund securities, the name used by the issuer to identify such securities and, to the extent necessary to differentiate the securities from other municipal fund securities of the issuer, any separate program series, portfolio or fund designation for such securities must be shown;

(2) CUSIP number, if any, assigned to the securities;

(3) maturity date, if any, with special requirements for the following securities:

(a) Stripped coupon securities. For stripped coupon securities, the maturity date of the instrument must be shown in lieu of the maturity date of the underlying securities;

(b) Municipal fund securities. For municipal fund securities, no maturity date shall be shown;

(4) interest rate, if any, with special requirements for the following securities:

(a) Zero coupon securities. For zero coupon securities, the interest rate must be shown as 0%;

(b) Variable rate securities. For securities with a variable or floating interest rate, the interest rate must be shown as "variable;" provided however if the yield is computed to put date or to mandatory tender date, the interest rate used in that calculation shall be shown.

(c) Securities with adjustable tender fees. If the net interest rate paid on a tender option security is affected by an adjustable "tender fee," the stated interest rate must be shown as that of the underlying security with the phrase "less fee for put;"

(d) Stepped coupon securities. For stepped coupon securities, the interest rate currently being paid must be shown;

(e) Stripped coupon securities. For stripped coupon securities, the interest rate actually paid on the instrument must be shown in lieu of interest rate on underlying security;

(f) Municipal fund securities. For municipal fund securities, no interest rate shall be shown;

(5) the dated date if it affects the price or interest calculation, with special requirements for the following securities:

(a) Stripped coupon securities. For stripped coupon securities, the date that interest begins accruing to the custodian for payment to the beneficial owner shall be shown in lieu of the dated date of the underlying securities. This date, along with the first date that interest will be paid to the owner, must be stated on the confirmation whenever it is necessary for calculation of price or accrued interest.

(C) Securities descriptive information. The confirmation shall include descriptive information about the securities which includes, at a minimum:

(1) Credit backing. The following information regarding the credit backing of the security:

(a) Revenue securities. For revenue securities, a notation of that fact, and a notation of the primary source of revenue (e.g., project name). This subparagraph will be satisfied if these designations appear on the confirmation in the formal title of the security or elsewhere in the securities description.

    (b) Securities with additional credit backing. The name of any company or other person in addition to the issuer obligated, directly or indirectly, with respect to debt service or, if there is more than one such obligor, the statement "multiple obligors" may be shown and, if a letter of credit is used, the identity of the bank issuing the letter of credit must be noted.

(2) Features of the securities. The following information, if applicable, regarding features of the securities:

    (a) Callable securities. If the securities are subject to call prior to maturity through any means, a notation of "callable" shall be included. This shall not be required if the only call feature applicable to the securities is a "catastrophe" or "calamity" call feature, such as one relating to an event such as an act of God or eminent domain, and which event is beyond the control of the issuer of the securities. The date and price of the next pricing call shall be included and so designated. Other specific call features are not required to be listed unless required by subparagraph (A)(5)(c)(ii) of this paragraph on computation and display of price and yield. If any specific call feature is listed even though not required by this rule, it shall be identified. If there are any call features in addition to the next pricing call, disclosure must be made on the confirmation that "additional call features exist that may affect yield; complete information will be provided upon request;"

    (b) Puttable securities. If the securities are puttable by the customer, a designation to that effect;

    (c) Stepped coupon securities. If stepped coupon securities, a designation to that effect;

    (d) Book-entry only securities. If the securities are available only in book entry form, a designation to that effect;

    (e) Periodic interest payment. With respect to securities that pay interest on other than a semiannual basis, a statement of the basis on which interest is paid;

(3) Information on status of securities. The following information, as applicable, regarding the status of the security shall be included:

    (a) Prerefunded and called securities. If the securities are called or "prerefunded," a designation to such effect, the date of maturity which has been fixed by the call notice, and the amount of the call price.

    (b) Escrowed to maturity securities. If the securities are advance refunded to maturity date and no call feature (with the exception of a sinking fund call) is explicitly reserved by the issuer, the securities must be described as "escrowed to maturity" and, if a sinking fund call is operable with respect to the securities, additionally described as "callable."

    (c) Advanced refunded/callable securities. If advanced refunded securities have an explicitly reserved call feature other than a sinking fund call, the securities shall be described as "escrowed to [redemption date]—callable."

    (d) Advanced refunded/stripped coupon securities. If the municipal securities underlying stripped coupon securities are advance-refunded, the stripped coupon securities shall be described as "escrowed-to-maturity," or "pre-refunded" as applicable.

    (e) Securities in default. If the securities are in default as to the payment of interest or principal, they shall be described as "in default;"

    (f) Unrated securities. If the security is unrated by a nationally recognized statistical rating organization, a disclosure to such effect.

(4) Tax information. The following information that may be related to the tax treatment of the security:

    (a) Taxable securities. If the securities are identified by the issuer or sold by the underwriter as subject to federal taxation, a designation to that effect.

    (b) Alternative minimum tax securities. If interest on the securities is identified by the issuer or underwriter as subject to the alternative minimum tax, a designation to that effect.

      (c) Original issue discount securities. If the securities pay periodic interest and are sold by the underwriter as original issue discount securities, a designation that they are "original issue discount" securities and a statement of the initial public offering price of the securities, expressed as a dollar price.

   (5) Municipal fund securities. For municipal fund securities, the information described in clauses (1) through (4) of this subparagraph (C) is not required to be shown.

(D) Disclosure statements:

   (1) The confirmation for zero coupon securities shall include a statement to the effect that "No periodic payments," and, if applicable, "callable below maturity value," and, if callable and available in bearer form, "callable without notice by mail to holder unless registered."

   (2) The confirmation for municipal collateralized mortgage obligations shall include a statement indicating that the actual yield of such security may vary according to the rate at which the underlying receivables or other financial assets are prepaid and a statement that information concerning the factors that affect yield (including at a minimum estimated yield, weighted average life, and the prepayment assumptions underlying yield) will be furnished upon written request.

   (3) The confirmation for securities for which a deferred commission or other charge is imposed upon redemption or as a condition for payment of principal or interest thereon shall include a statement that the customer may be required to make a payment of such deferred commission or other charge upon redemption of such securities or as a condition for payment of principal or interest thereon, as appropriate, and that information concerning such deferred commission or other charge will be furnished upon written request.

   (4) The confirmation for a transaction (other than a transaction in municipal fund securities) executed for or with a non-institutional customer shall include, in a format specified by the MSRB, a reference and, if the confirmation is electronic, a hyperlink to a webpage on EMMA that contains publicly available trading data for the specific security that was traded, along with a brief description of the type of information available on that page.

(E) Confirmation format. All requirements must be clearly and specifically indicated on the front of the confirmation, except that the following statements may be on the reverse side of the confirmation:

   (1) The disclosure statements required in subparagraph (D)(1), (D)(2) or (D)(3) of this paragraph, provided that their specific applicability is noted on the front of the confirmation.

   (2) The statement concerning the person from whom the securities were purchased or to whom the securities were sold that can be provided in satisfaction of subparagraph (A)(1)(e)(i) of this paragraph.

(F) Mark-ups and Mark-downs.

   (1) General. A confirmation shall include the dealer's mark-up or mark-down for the transaction, to be calculated in compliance with Rule G-30, Supplementary Material .06 and expressed as a total dollar amount and as a percentage of the prevailing market price if:

      (a) the broker, dealer or municipal securities dealer ("dealer") is effecting a transaction in a principal capacity with a non-institutional customer, and

      (b) the broker, dealer or municipal securities dealer purchased (sold) the security in one or more offsetting transactions in an aggregate trading size meeting or exceeding the size of such sale to (purchase from) the non-institutional customer on the same trading day as the non-institutional customer transaction. If any such transaction occurs with an affiliate of the dealer and is not an arms-length transaction, the dealer is required to "look through" to the time and terms of the affiliate's transaction(s) with third parties in the security in determining whether the conditions of this paragraph have been met.

   (2) Exceptions. A dealer shall not be required to include the disclosure specified in paragraph (F)(1) above if:

(a) the non-institutional customer transaction was executed by a principal trading desk that is functionally separate from the principal trading desk within the same dealer that executed the dealer purchase (in the case of a sale to a customer) or dealer sale (in the case of a purchase from a customer) of the security, and the dealer had in place policies and procedures reasonably designed to ensure that the functionally separate principal trading desk through which the dealer purchase or dealer sale was executed had no knowledge of the customer transaction;

(b) the customer transaction is a "list offering price transaction" as defined in paragraph (d)(vii) of Rule G-14 RTRS Procedures; or

(c) the customer transaction is for the purchase or sale of municipal fund securities.

(ii) Separate confirmation for each transaction. Each broker, dealer or municipal securities dealer for each transaction in municipal securities shall give or send to the customer a separate written confirmation in accordance with the requirements of (i) above. Multiple confirmations may be printed on one page, provided that each transaction is clearly segregated and the information provided for each transaction complies with the requirements of (i) above; provided, however, that if multiple confirmations are printed in a continuous manner within a single document, it is permissible for the name and address of the broker, dealer or municipal securities dealer and the customer to appear once at the beginning of the document, rather than being included in the confirmation information for each transaction.

(iii) "When, as and if issued" transactions. A confirmation meeting the requirements of this rule shall be sent in all "when, as and if issued" transactions. In addition, a broker, dealer or municipal securities dealer may send a confirmation for a "when, as and if issued" transaction executed prior to determination of settlement date and may be required to do so for delivery vs. payment and receipt vs. payment ("DVP/RVP") accounts under paragraph (d)(i)(C) of this rule. If such a confirmation is sent, it shall include all information required by this section with the exception of settlement date, dollar price for transactions executed on a yield basis, yield for transactions executed on a dollar price, total monies, accrued interest, extended principal and delivery instructions.

(iv) Confirmation to customers who tender put option bonds or municipal fund securities. A broker, dealer, or municipal securities dealer that has an interest in put option bonds (including acting as remarketing agent) and accepts for tender put option bonds from a customer, or that has an interest in municipal fund securities (including acting as agent for the issuer thereof) and accepts for redemption municipal fund securities tendered by a customer, is engaging in a transaction in such municipal securities and shall send a confirmation under paragraph (i) of this section.

(v) Timing for providing information. Information requested by a customer pursuant to statements required on the confirmation shall be given or sent to the customer within five business days following the date of receipt of a request for such information; provided however, that in the case of information relating to a transaction executed more than 30 calendar days prior to the date of receipt of a request, the information shall be given or sent to the customer within 15 business days following the date of receipt of the request.

(vi) Definitions. For purposes of this rule, the following terms shall have the following meanings:

(A) Execution of a transaction. The term "the time of execution of a transaction" shall be the time of execution reflected in the records of the broker, dealer or municipal securities dealer pursuant to rule G-8 or Rule 17a-3 under the Act.

(B) Completion of transaction. The term "completion of transaction" shall have the same meaning as provided in Rule 15c1-1 under the Act.

(C) Stepped coupon securities. The term "stepped coupon securities" shall mean securities with the interest rate periodically changing on a pre-established schedule.

(D) Zero coupon securities. The term "zero coupon securities" shall mean securities maturing in more than two years and paying investment return solely at redemption.

(E) Stripped coupon securities. The term "stripped coupon securities" shall have the same meaning as in SEC staff letter dated January 19, 1989 (Stripped Coupon Municipal Securities, SEC No-Action Letter, Fed. Sec. L. Rep. (CCH) ¶ 78,949 (Jan. 19, 1989)), reprinted in MSRB Reports, Vol. 9, No. 1 (March 1989) at 6-7.

(F) The term "pricing call" shall mean a call feature that represents "an in whole call" of the type that may be used by the issuer without restriction in a refunding.

(G) The term "periodic municipal fund security plan" shall mean any written authorization or arrangement for a broker, dealer or municipal securities dealer, acting as agent, to purchase, sell or redeem for a customer or group of customers one or more specific municipal fund securities, in specific amounts (calculated in security units or dollars), at specific time intervals and setting forth the commissions or charges to be paid by the customer in connection therewith (or the manner of calculating them).

(H) The term "non-periodic municipal fund security program" shall mean any written authorization or arrangement for a broker, dealer or municipal securities dealer, acting as agent, to purchase, sell or redeem for a customer or group of customers one or more specific municipal fund securities, setting forth the commissions or charges to be paid by the customer in connection therewith (or the manner of calculating them) and either (1) providing for the purchase, sale or redemption of such municipal fund securities at the direction of the customer or customers or (2) providing for the purchase, sale or redemption of such municipal fund securities at the direction of the customer or customers as well as authorizing the purchase, sale or redemption of such municipal fund securities in specific amounts (calculated in security units or dollars) at specific time intervals.

(I) The term "arms-length transaction" shall mean a transaction that was conducted through a competitive process in which non-affiliate firms could also participate, and where the affiliate relationship did not influence the price paid or proceeds received by the dealer.

(J) The term "non-institutional customer" shall mean a customer with an account that is not an institutional account, as defined in Rule G-8(a)(xi).

(vii) Price substituted for par value of municipal fund securities. For purposes of this rule, each reference to the term "par value," when applied to a municipal fund security, shall be substituted with (i) in the case of a purchase of a municipal fund security by a customer, the purchase price paid by the customer, exclusive of any commission, and (ii) in the case of a sale or tender for redemption of a municipal fund security by a customer, the sale price or redemption amount paid to the customer, exclusive of any commission or other charge imposed upon redemption or sale.

(viii) Alternative periodic reporting for certain transactions in municipal fund securities. Notwithstanding any other provision of this section (a), a broker, dealer or municipal securities dealer may effect transactions in municipal fund securities with customers without giving or sending to such customer the written confirmation required by paragraph (i) of this section (a) at or before completion of each such transaction if:

(A) such transactions are effected pursuant to a periodic municipal fund security plan or a non-periodic municipal fund security program; and

(B) such broker, dealer or municipal securities dealer gives or sends to such customer within five business days after the end of each quarterly period, in the case of a customer participating in a periodic municipal fund security plan, or each monthly period, in the case of a customer participating in a non-periodic municipal fund security program, a written statement disclosing, for each purchase, sale or redemption effected for or with, and each payment of investment earnings credited to or reinvested for, the account of such customer during the reporting period, the information required to be disclosed to customers pursuant to subparagraphs (A) through (D) of paragraph (i) of this section (a), with the information regarding each transaction clearly segregated; provided that it is permissible:

(1) for the name and address of the broker, dealer or municipal securities dealer and the customer to appear once at the beginning of the periodic statement; and

(2) for information required to be included pursuant to subparagraph (A)(1)(d), (A)(2)(a) or (D)(3) of paragraph (i) of this section (a) to:

(a) appear once in the periodic statement if such information is identical for all transactions disclosed in such statement; or

(b) be omitted from the periodic statement, but only if such information previously has been delivered to the customer in writing and the periodic statement includes a statement indicating that such information has been provided to the customer and identifying the document in which such information appears; and

(C) in the case of a periodic municipal fund security plan that consists of an arrangement involving a group of two or more customers and contemplating periodic purchases of municipal fund securities by each customer through a person designated by the group, such broker, dealer or municipal securities dealer:

(1) gives or sends to the designated person, at or before the completion of the transaction for the purchase of such municipal fund securities, a written notification of the receipt of the total amount paid by the group;

(2) sends to anyone in the group who was a customer in the prior quarter and on whose behalf payment has not been received in the current quarter a quarterly written statement reflecting that a payment was not received on such customer's behalf; and

(3) advises each customer in the group if a payment is not received from the designated person on behalf of the group within 10 days of a date certain specified in the arrangement for delivery of that payment by the designated person and either (a) thereafter sends to each customer the written confirmation described in paragraph (i) of this section (a) for the next three succeeding payments, or (b) includes in the quarterly statement referred to in subparagraph (B) of this paragraph (viii) each date certain specified in the arrangement for delivery of a payment by the designated person and each date on which a payment received from the designated person is applied to the purchase of municipal fund securities; and

(D) such customer is provided with prior notification in writing disclosing the intention to send the written information referred to in subparagraph (B) of this paragraph (viii) on a periodic basis in lieu of an immediate confirmation for each transaction; and

(E) such customer has consented in writing to receipt of the written information referred to in subparagraph (B) of this paragraph (viii) on a periodic basis in lieu of an immediate confirmation for each transaction; provided, however, that such customer consent shall not be required if:

(1) the customer is not a natural person;

(2) the customer is a natural person who participates in a periodic municipal fund security plan described in subparagraph (C) of this paragraph (viii); or

(3) the customer is a natural person who participates in a periodic municipal fund security plan (other than a plan described in subparagraph (C) of this paragraph (viii)) or a non-periodic municipal fund security program and the issuer has consented in writing to the use by the broker, dealer or municipal securities dealer of the periodic written information referred to in subparagraph (B) of this paragraph (viii) in lieu of an immediate confirmation for each transaction with each customer participating in such plan or program.

(b) Settlement Dates.

(i) Definitions. For purposes of this rule, the following terms shall have the following meanings:

(A) Settlement Date. The term "settlement date" shall mean the day used in price and interest computations, which shall also be the day delivery is due unless otherwise agreed by the parties.

(B) Business Day. The term "business day" shall mean a day recognized by the Financial Industry Regulatory Authority as a day on which securities transactions may be settled.

(ii) Settlement Dates. Settlement dates shall be as follows:

(A) for "cash" transactions, the trade date;

(B) for "regular way" transactions, the second business day following the trade date;

(C) for all other transactions, a date agreed upon by both parties; provided, however, that a broker, dealer or municipal securities dealer shall not effect or enter into a transaction for the purchase or sale of a municipal security (other than a "when, as and if issued" transaction) that provides for payment of funds and delivery of securities later than the second business day after the date of the transaction unless expressly agreed to by the parties, at the time of the transaction.

(c) Deliveries to Customers. Except as provided in section (d) below, a delivery of securities by a broker, dealer, or municipal securities dealer to a customer or to another person acting as agent for the customer shall, unless otherwise agreed by the parties or otherwise specified by the customer, be made in accordance with the following provisions:

(i) Securities Delivered.

(A) All securities delivered on a transaction shall be identical as to the applicable information set forth in section (a) of this rule. All securities delivered shall also be identical as to the call provisions and the dated date of such securities.

(B) CUSIP Numbers.

(1) The securities delivered on a transaction shall have the same CUSIP number as that set forth on the confirmation of such transaction pursuant to the requirements of section (a) of this rule; provided, however, that for purposes of this item (1), a security shall be deemed to have the same CUSIP number as that specified on the confirmation (a) if the number assigned to the security and the number specified on the confirmation differ only as a result of a transposition or other transcription error, or (b) if the number specified on the confirmation has been assigned as a substitute or alternative number for the number reflected on the security.

(2) A new issue security delivered by an underwriter who is subject to the provisions of rule G-34 shall have the CUSIP number assigned to the security imprinted on or otherwise affixed to the security.

(ii) Delivery Ticket. A delivery ticket shall accompany the delivery of securities. Such ticket shall contain the information set forth in section (a) of this rule.

(iii) Units of Delivery. Delivery of bonds shall be made in the following denominations:

(A) for bearer bonds, in denominations of $1,000 or $5,000 par value; and

(B) for registered bonds, in denominations which are multiples of $1,000 par value, up to $100,000 par value.

Delivery of other municipal securities shall be made in the denominations specified on the confirmation as required pursuant to section (a) of this rule.

(iv) Form of Securities.

(A) Bearer and Registered Form. Delivery of securities which are issuable in both bearer and registered form may be in bearer form unless otherwise agreed by the parties; provided, however, that delivery of securities which are required to be in registered form in order for interest thereon to be exempted from Federal income taxation shall be in registered form.

(B) Book-Entry Form. Notwithstanding the other provisions of this section (c), a delivery of a book-entry form security shall be made only by a book-entry transfer of the ownership of the security to the purchasing customer or a person designated by the purchasing customer. For purposes of this subparagraph a "book-entry form" security shall mean a security which may be transferred only by bookkeeping entry, without the issuance or physical delivery of securities certificates, on books maintained for this purpose by a registered clearing agency or by the issuer or a person acting on behalf of the issuer.

(v) Mutilated Certificates. Delivery of a certificate which is damaged to the extent that any of the following is not ascertainable:

(A) name of issuer;

(B) par value;

(C) signature;

(D) coupon rate;

(E) maturity date;

(F) seal of the issuer; or

(G) certificate number

shall not constitute good delivery unless validated by the trustee, registrar, transfer agent, paying agent or issuer of the securities or by an authorized agent or official of the issuer.

(vi) Coupon Securities.

(A) Coupon securities shall have securely attached to the certificate in the correct sequence all appropriate coupons, including supplemental coupons if specified at the time of trade, which in the case of securities upon which interest is in default shall include all unpaid or partially paid coupons. All coupons attached to the certificates must have the same serial number as the certificate.

(B) Anything herein to the contrary notwithstanding, if securities are traded "and interest" and the settlement date is on or after the interest payment date, such securities shall be delivered without the coupon payable on such interest payment date.

(C) If delivery of securities is made on or after the thirtieth calendar day prior to an interest payment date, the seller may deliver to the purchaser a draft or bank check of the seller or its agent, payable not later than the interest payment date or the delivery date, whichever is later, in an amount equal to the interest due, in lieu of the coupon.

(vii) Mutilated or Cancelled Coupons. Delivery of a certificate which bears a coupon which is damaged to the extent that any one of the following cannot be ascertained from the coupon:

(A) title of the issuer;

(B) certificate number;

(C) coupon number or payment date (if either the coupon number or the payment date is ascertainable from the coupon, the coupon will not be considered mutilated); or

(D) the fact that there is a signature;

or which coupon has been cancelled, shall not constitute good delivery unless the coupon is endorsed or guaranteed. In the case of damaged coupons, such endorsement or guarantee must be by the issuer or by a commercial bank. In the case of cancelled coupons, such endorsement or guarantee must be by the issuer or an authorized agent or official of the issuer, or by the trustee or paying agent.

(viii) Delivery of Certificates Called for Redemption.

(A) A certificate for which a notice of call applicable to less than the entire issue of securities has been published on or prior to the delivery date shall not constitute good delivery unless the securities are identified as "called" at the time of trade.

(B) A certificate for which a notice of call applicable to the entire issue of securities has been published on or prior to the trade date shall not constitute good delivery unless the securities are identified as "called" at the time of trade.

(C) For purposes of this paragraph (viii) the term "entire issue of securities" shall mean securities of the same issuer having the same date of issue, maturity date and interest rate.

(ix) Delivery Without Legal Opinions or Other Documents. Delivery of certificates without legal opinions or other documents legally required to accompany the certificates shall not constitute good delivery unless identified as "ex legal" at the time of trade.

(x) Insured Securities. Delivery of certificates for securities traded as insured securities shall be accompanied by evidence of such insurance, either on the face of the certificate or document attached to certificate.

(xi) Endorsements for Banking or Insurance Requirements. A security bearing an endorsement indicating that it was deposited in accordance with legal requirements applicable to banking institutions or insurance companies shall not constitute good delivery unless it bears a release acknowledged before an officer authorized to take such acknowledgments and was designated as a released endorsed security at the time of trade.

(xii) Delivery of Registered Securities.

    (A) Delivery to the Customer. Registered securities delivered directly to a customer shall be registered in the customer's name or in such name as the customer shall direct.

    (B) Delivery to an Agent of the Customer. Registered securities delivered to an agent of a customer may be registered in the customer's name or as otherwise directed by the customer. If such securities are not so registered, such securities shall be delivered in accordance with the following provisions:

        (1) Assignments. Delivery of a certificate in registered form must be accompanied by an assignment on the certificate or on a separate bond power for such certificate, containing a signature or signatures which correspond in every particular with the name or names written upon the certificate, except that the following shall be interchangeable: "and" or "&"; "Company" or "Co."; "Incorporated" or "Inc."; and "Limited" or "Ltd."

        (2) Detached Assignment Requirements. A detached assignment shall provide for the irrevocable appointment of an attorney, with power of substitution, a full description of the security, including the name of the issuer, the maturity date and interest date, the bond or note number, and the par value (expressed in words and numerals).

        (3) Power of Substitution. When the name of an individual or firm has been inserted in an assignment as attorney, a power of substitution shall be executed in blank by such individual or firm. When the name of an individual or firm has been inserted in a power of substitution as a substitute attorney, a new power of substitution shall be executed in blank by such substitute attorney.

        (4) Guarantee. Each assignment, endorsement, alteration and erasure shall bear a guarantee acceptable to the transfer agent or registrar.

        (5) Form of Registration. Delivery of a certificate accompanied by the documentation required in this subparagraph (B) shall constitute good delivery if the certificate is registered in the name of:

            (a) an individual or individuals;

            (b) a nominee;

            (c) a member of a national securities exchange whose specimen signature is on file with the transfer agent or any other broker, dealer or municipal securities dealer who has filed specimen signatures with the transfer agent and places a statement to this effect on the assignment; or

            (d) an individual or individuals acting in a fiduciary capacity.

        (6) Certificate in Legal Form. Good transfer of a security in legal form shall be determined only by the transfer agent for the security. Delivery of a certificate in legal form shall not constitute good delivery unless the certificate is identified as being in such form at the time of trade. A certificate shall be considered to be in legal form if documentation in addition to that specified in this subparagraph (B) is required to complete a transfer of the securities.

    (C) Payment of Interest. If a registered security is traded "and interest" and transfer of record ownership cannot be or has not been accomplished on or before the record date for the determination of registered holders for the payment of interest, delivery shall be accompanied by a draft or bank check of the seller or its agent, payable not later than the interest payment date or the delivery date, whichever is later, for the amount of the interest.

    (D) Registered Securities In Default. If a registered security is in default (i.e., is in default in the payment of principal or interest) and transfer of record ownership cannot be or has not been accomplished on or before the record date for the determination of registered holders for the payment of interest, an interest payment date having been established on or after the trade date, delivery shall be accompanied by a draft or bank check of the seller or its agent, payable not later than the interest payment date or the delivery date, whichever is later, for the amount of the payment to be made by the issuer, unless the security is traded "ex-interest."

(d) Delivery/Receipt vs. Payment Transactions.

(i) No broker, dealer or municipal securities dealer shall execute a transaction with a customer pursuant to an arrangement whereby payment for securities received (RVP) or delivery against payment of securities sold (DVP) is to be made to or by an agent of the customer unless all of the following procedures are followed:

(A) the broker, dealer or municipal securities dealer shall have received from the customer prior to or at the time of accepting such order, the name and address of the agent and the name and account number of the customer on file with the agent;

(B) the memorandum of such order made in accordance with the requirements of paragraph (a)(vi) or (a)(vii) of rule G-8 shall include a designation of the fact that it is a delivery vs. payment (DVP) or receipt vs. payment (RVP) transaction;

(C) the broker, dealer or municipal securities dealer shall give or send to the customer a confirmation in accordance with the requirements of section (a) of this rule with respect to the execution of the order not later than the day of such execution; and

(D) the broker, dealer or municipal securities dealer shall have obtained a representation from the customer (1) that the customer will furnish the agent instructions with respect to the receipt or delivery of the securities involved in the transaction promptly and in a manner to assure that settlement will occur on settlement date, and (2) that, with respect to a transaction subject to the provisions of paragraph (ii) below, the customer will furnish the agent such instructions in accordance with the rules of the registered clearing agency through whose facilities the transaction has been or will be confirmed.

(ii) Requirement for Confirmation/Acknowledgment.

(A) Use of Registered Clearing Agency or Qualified Vendor. Except as provided in this paragraph (ii) of rule G-15(d), no broker, dealer or municipal securities dealer shall effect a customer transaction for settlement on a delivery vs. payment or receipt vs. payment (DVP/RVP) basis unless the facilities of a Clearing Agency or Qualified Vendor are used for automated confirmation and acknowledgment of the transaction. Each broker, dealer and municipal securities dealer executing a customer transaction on a DVP/RVP basis shall:

(1) ensure that the customer has the capability, either directly or through its clearing agent, to acknowledge transactions in an automated confirmation/acknowledgment system operated by a Clearing Agency or Qualified Vendor;

(2) submit or cause to be submitted to a Clearing Agency or Qualified Vendor all information and instructions required by the Clearing Agency or Qualified Vendor for the production of a confirmation that can be acknowledged by the customer or the customer's clearing agent; and

(3) submit such transaction information to the automated confirmation/acknowledgment system on the date of execution of such transaction; provided that a transaction that is not eligible for automated confirmation and acknowledgment through the facilities of a Clearing Agency shall not be subject to this paragraph (ii).

(B) Definitions for Rule G-15(d)(ii).

(1) "Clearing Agency" shall mean a clearing agency as defined in Section 3(a)(23) of the Act that is registered with the Commission pursuant to Section 17A(b)(2) of the Act or has obtained from the Commission an exemption from registration granted specifically to allow the clearing agency to provide confirmation/acknowledgment services.

(2) "Qualified Vendor" shall mean a vendor of electronic confirmation and acknowledgment services that:

(a) for each transaction subject to this rule:

(i) delivers a trade record to a Clearing Agency in the Clearing Agency's format;

(ii) obtains a control number for the trade record from the Clearing Agency;

(iii) cross-references the control number to the confirmation and subsequent acknowledgment of the trade; and

        (iv) electronically delivers any acknowledgment received on the trade to the Clearing Agency and includes the control number when delivering the acknowledgment of the trade to the Clearing Agency;

   (b) certifies to its customers:

        (i) with respect to its electronic trade confirmation/acknowledgment system, that it has a capacity requirements evaluation and monitoring process that allows the vendor to formulate current and anticipated estimated capacity requirements;

        (ii) that its electronic trade confirmation/acknowledgment system has sufficient capacity to process the volume of data that it reasonably anticipates to be entered into its electronic trade confirmation/acknowledgment service during the upcoming year;

        (iii) that its electronic trade confirmation/acknowledgment system has formal contingency procedures, that the entity has followed a formal process for reviewing the likelihood of contingency occurrences, and that the contingency protocols are reviewed, tested, and updated on a regular basis;

        (iv) that its electronic confirmation/acknowledgment system has a process for preventing, detecting, and controlling any potential or actual systems or computer operations failures, including any failure to interface with a Clearing Agency as described in rule G-15(d)(ii)(B)(2)(a), above, and that its procedures designed to protect against security breaches are followed; and

        (v) that its current assets exceed its current liabilities by at least five hundred thousand dollars;

   (c) when it begins providing such services, and annually thereafter, submits an Auditor's Report to the Commission staff which is not deemed unacceptable by the Commission staff. (An Auditor's Report will be deemed unacceptable if it contains any findings of material weakness.);

   (d) notifies the Commission staff immediately in writing of any material change to its confirmation/affirmation systems. (For purposes of this subparagraph (d) "material change" means any changes to the vendor's systems that significantly affect or have the potential to significantly affect its electronic trade confirmation/acknowledgment systems, including: changes that:

        (i) affect or potentially affect the capacity or security of its electronic trade confirmation/acknowledgment system;

        (ii) rely on new or substantially different technology;

        (iii) provide a new service as part of the Qualified Vendor's electronic trade confirmation/acknowledgment system; or

        (iv) affect or have the potential to adversely affect the vendor's confirmation/acknowledgment system's interface with a Clearing Agency.);

   (e) notifies the Commission staff in writing if it intends to cease providing services;

   (f) provides the Board with copies of any submissions to the Commission staff made pursuant to subparagraphs (c), (d), and (e) of this rule G-15(d)(ii)(B)(2) within ten business days; and

   (g) promptly supplies supplemental information regarding its confirmation/acknowledgment system when requested by the Commission staff or the Board.

  (3) "Auditor's Report" shall mean a written report which is prepared by competent, independent, external audit personnel in accordance with the standards of the American Institute of Certified Public Accountants and the Information Systems Audit and Control Association and which:

   (a) verifies the certifications described in subparagraph (d)(ii)(B)(2)(b) of this rule G-15;

   (b) contains a risk analysis of all aspects of the entity's information technology systems including, computer operations, telecommunications, data security, systems development, capacity planning and testing, and contingency planning and testing; and

(c) contains the written response of the entity's management to the information provided pursuant to (a) and (b) of this subparagraph (d)(ii)(B)(3) of rule G-15.

(C) Disqualification of Vendor. A broker, dealer or municipal securities dealer using a Qualified Vendor that ceases to be qualified under the definition in rule G-15(d)(ii)(B)(2) shall not be deemed in violation of this rule G-15(d)(ii) if it ceases using such vendor promptly upon receiving notice that the vendor is no longer qualified.

(iii) Notwithstanding the provisions of section (c) of this rule, no broker, dealer or municipal securities dealer shall effect a delivery vs. payment or receipt vs. payment (DVP/RVP) customer transaction that is eligible for book-entry settlement in a depository registered with the Securities and Exchange Commission (depository) unless the transaction is settled through the facilities of a depository or through the interface between the two depositories. Each broker, dealer and municipal securities dealer settling such a customer transaction on a DVP/RVP basis shall:

(A) ensure that the customer has the capability, either directly or through its clearing agent, to settle transactions in a depository; and

(B) submit or cause to be submitted to a depository all information and instructions required from the broker, dealer or municipal securities dealer by the depository for book-entry settlement of the transaction to occur; provided that, if a party to a DVP/RVP customer transaction has made arrangements, through its clearing agent or otherwise, to use one or more depositories exclusively, a transaction by that party shall not be subject to the requirements of this paragraph (iii) if the transaction is ineligible for settlement at all such depositories with which such arrangements have been made; and further provided that purchases made by trustees or issuers to retire securities shall not be subject to this paragraph (iii).

(e) Interest Payment Claims. A broker, dealer or municipal securities dealer that receives from a customer a claim for the payment of interest due the customer on securities previously delivered to (or by) the customer shall respond to the claim no later than 10 business days following the date of the receipt of the claim or 20 business days in the case of a claim involving an interest payment scheduled to be made more than 60 days prior to the date of the claim.

(f) Minimum Denominations.

(i) Except as provided in this section (f), a broker, dealer or municipal securities dealer shall not effect a customer transaction in municipal securities issued after June 1, 2002 in an amount lower than the minimum denomination of the issue.

(ii) The prohibition in subsection (f)(i) of this rule shall not apply to the purchase of securities from a customer in an amount below the minimum denomination if the broker, dealer or municipal securities dealer determines that the customer's position in the issue already is below the minimum denomination and that the entire position would be liquidated by the transaction. In determining whether this is the case, a broker, dealer or municipal securities dealer may rely either upon customer account information in its possession or upon a written statement by the customer as to its position in an issue.

(iii) The prohibition in subsection (f)(i) of this rule shall not apply to the sale of securities to a customer in an amount below the minimum denomination if the broker, dealer or municipal securities dealer determines that the securities position being sold is the result of a customer liquidating a position below the minimum denomination, as described in subsection (f)(ii). In determining whether this is the case, a broker, dealer or municipal securities dealer may rely upon customer account records in its possession or upon a written statement provided by the party from which the securities are purchased. A broker, dealer or municipal securities dealer effecting a sale to a customer under this subsection (iii) shall at or before the completion of the transaction, give or send to the customer a written statement informing the customer that the quantity of securities being sold is below the minimum denomination for the issue and that this may adversely affect the liquidity of the position unless the customer has other securities from the issue that can be combined to reach the minimum denomination. Such written statement may be included on the customer's confirmation or may be provided on a document separate from the confirmation.

(g) Forwarding Official Communications.

    (i) If a broker, dealer or municipal securities dealer receives an official communication to beneficial owners applicable to an issue of municipal securities that the broker, dealer or municipal securities dealer has in safekeeping along with a request to forward such official communication to the applicable beneficial owners, the broker, dealer or municipal securities dealer shall use reasonable efforts to promptly retransmit the official communication to the parties for whom it is safekeeping the issue.

    (ii) In determining whether reasonable efforts have been made to retransmit official communications, the following considerations are relevant:

        (A) CUSIP Numbers. If CUSIP numbers are included on or with the official communication to beneficial owners, the broker, dealer or municipal securities dealer shall use such CUSIP numbers in determining the issue(s) to which the official communication applies. If CUSIP numbers are not included on or with the official communication, the broker, dealer or municipal securities dealer shall use reasonable efforts to determine the issue(s) to which the official communication applies; provided however, that it shall not be a violation of this rule if, after reasonable efforts are made, the issue(s) to which the official communication applies are not correctly identified by the broker, dealer or municipal securities dealer.

        (B) Compensation. A broker, dealer or municipal securities dealer shall not be required by this rule to retransmit official communications without an offer of adequate compensation. If compensation is explicitly offered in or with the official communication, the broker, dealer or municipal securities dealer shall effect the retransmission and seek compensation concurrently; provided, however, that if total compensation would be more than $500.00, the broker, dealer or municipal securities dealer may, in lieu of this procedure, promptly contact the party offering compensation, inform it of the amount of compensation required, obtain specific agreement on the amount of compensation and wait for receipt of such compensation prior to proceeding with the retransmission. In determining whether compensation is adequate, the broker, dealer or municipal securities dealer shall make reference to the suggested rates for similar document transmission services found in "Suggested Rates of Reimbursement" for expenses incurred in forwarding proxy material, annual reports, information statements and other material referenced in FINRA Rule 2251(g), taking into account revisions or amendments to such suggested rates as may be made from time to time.

        (C) Sufficient Copies of Official Communications. A broker, dealer or municipal securities dealer is not required to provide duplication services for official communications but may elect to do so. If sufficient copies of official communications are not received, and the broker, dealer or municipal securities dealer elects not to offer duplication services, the broker, dealer or municipal securities dealer shall promptly request from the party requesting the forwarding of the official communication the correct number of copies of the official communication.

        (D) Non-Objecting Beneficial Owners. In lieu of retransmitting official communications to beneficial owners who have indicated in writing that they do not object to the disclosure of their names and security positions, a broker, dealer or municipal securities dealer may instead promptly provide a list of such non-objecting beneficial owners and their addresses.

        (E) Beneficial Owners Residing Outside of the United States. A broker, dealer or municipal securities dealer shall not be required to send official communications to persons outside of the United States of America, although brokers, dealers and municipal securities dealers may voluntarily do so.

        (F) Investment Advisors. A broker, dealer or municipal securities dealer shall send official communications to the investment advisor for a beneficial owner, rather than to the beneficial owner, when the broker, dealer or municipal securities dealer has on file a written authorization for such documents to be sent to the investment advisor in lieu of the beneficial owner.

(iii) Definitions

   (A) The terms "official communication to beneficial owners" and "official communication," as used in this section (g), mean any document or collection of documents pertaining to a specific issue or issues of municipal securities that both:

      (1) is addressed to beneficial owners and was prepared or authorized by: (a) an issuer of municipal securities; (b) a trustee for an issue of municipal securities in its capacity as trustee; (c) a state or federal tax authority; or (d) a custody agent for a stripped coupon municipal securities program in its capacity as custody agent; and

      (2) contains official information about such issue or issues including, but not limited to, notices concerning monetary or technical defaults, financial reports, material event notices, information statements, or status or review of status as to taxability.

----

42. MSRB Rules: G-18 – Best Execution

Summary: Requires dealers to use reasonable diligence to ascertain the best market for the subject security and buy or sell in that market so that the resultant price to the customer is as favorable as possible under prevailing market conditions.

(a) In any transaction in a municipal security for or with a customer or a customer of another broker, dealer, or municipal securities dealer ("dealer"), a dealer must use reasonable diligence to ascertain the best market for the subject security and buy or sell in that market so that the resultant price to the customer is as favorable as possible under prevailing market conditions. Among the factors that will be considered in determining whether a dealer has used "reasonable diligence," with no single factor being determinative, are:

   (1) the character of the market for the security (e.g., price, volatility, and relative liquidity);

   (2) the size and type of transaction;

   (3) the number of markets checked;

   (4) the information reviewed to determine the current market for the subject security or similar securities;

   (5) the accessibility of quotations; and

   (6) the terms and conditions of the customer's inquiry or order, including any bids or offers, that result in the transaction, as communicated to the dealer.

(b) In any transaction for or with a customer, a dealer must not interject a third party between itself and the best market for the subject security in a manner inconsistent with paragraph (a) of this rule.

(c) The obligations described in paragraphs (a) and (b) above apply to transactions in which the dealer is acting as agent and transactions in which the dealer is acting as principal. These obligations are distinct from the fairness and reasonableness of commissions, markups or markdowns, which are governed by Rule G-30.

----

43. MSRB Rules: G-21 – Advertising

Summary: Prohibits dealers from publishing false or misleading advertisements relating to municipal securities or concerning the facilities, services or skills of any dealer; establishes specific requirements for advertisements of new issues and municipal fund securities; and requires a municipal securities or general securities principal to approve in writing advertisements prior to first use.

(a) General Provisions.

    (i) Definition of "Advertisement." For purposes of this rule, the term "advertisement" means any material (other than listings of offerings) published or used in any electronic or other public media, or any written or electronic promotional literature distributed or made generally available to customers or the public, including any notice, circular, report, market letter, form letter, telemarketing script, seminar text, press release concerning the products or services of the broker, dealer or municipal securities dealer, or re-print, or any excerpt of the foregoing or of a published article. The term does not apply to preliminary official statements or official statements, but does apply to abstracts or summaries of the foregoing and other such similar documents prepared by brokers, dealers or municipal securities dealers.

    (ii) Definition of "Form Letter." For purposes of this rule, the term "form letter" means any written letter or electronic mail message distributed to more than 25 persons within any period of 90 consecutive days.

    (iii) Content Standards.

        (A) All advertisements by a broker, dealer or municipal securities dealer must be based on the principles of fair dealing and good faith, must be fair and balanced, and must provide a sound basis for evaluating the facts in regard to any particular municipal security or type of municipal security, industry or service. No broker, dealer or municipal securities dealer may omit any material fact or qualification if the omission, in light of the context of the material presented, would cause the advertisements to be misleading.

        (B) No broker, dealer or municipal securities dealer may make any false, exaggerated, unwarranted, promissory or misleading statement or claim in any advertisement.

        (C) A broker, dealer or municipal securities dealer may place information in a legend or footnote only in the event that such placement would not inhibit a customer's or a potential customer's understanding of the advertisement.

        (D) A broker, dealer or municipal securities dealer must ensure that statements are clear and not misleading within the context in which they are made, and that they provide balanced treatment of risks and potential benefits. An advertisement must be consistent with the risks inherent to the investment.

        (E) A broker, dealer or municipal securities dealer must consider the nature of the audience to which the advertisement will be directed and must provide details and explanations appropriate to the audience.

        (F) An advertisement may not predict or project performance, imply that past performance will recur or make any exaggerated or unwarranted claim, opinion or forecast; provided, however, that this paragraph (a)(iii)(F) does not prohibit:

            (1) A hypothetical illustration of mathematical principles, provided that it does not predict or project the performance of an investment; and

            (2) An investment analysis tool, or a written report produced by an investment analysis tool.

        (G)(1) If an advertisement contains a testimonial about a technical aspect of investing, the person making the testimonial must have the knowledge and experience to form a valid opinion;

            (2) If an advertisement contains a testimonial about the investment advice or investment performance of a broker, dealer or municipal securities dealer or its products, that advertisement must prominently disclose the following:

                (a) The fact that the testimonial may not be representative of the experience of other customers.

(b) The fact that the testimonial is no guarantee of future performance or success.

(c) If more than $100 in value is paid for the testimonial, the fact that it is a paid testimonial.

(H) A broker, dealer or municipal securities dealer may indicate registration with the Municipal Securities Rulemaking Board in any advertisement that complies with the applicable standards of all other Board rules and that neither states nor implies that the Municipal Securities Rulemaking Board or any other corporate name or facility owned by the Municipal Securities Rulemaking Board, or any other regulatory organization endorses, indemnifies, or guarantees the broker, dealer or municipal securities dealer's business practices, selling methods, the class or type of securities offered, or any specific security.

(iv) General Standard for Advertisements. Subject to the further requirements of this rule relating to professional advertisements and product advertisements, no broker, dealer or municipal securities dealer shall publish or disseminate, or cause to be published or disseminated, any advertisement relating to municipal securities that such broker, dealer or municipal securities dealer knows or has reason to know contains any untrue statement of material fact or is otherwise false or misleading.

(b) Professional Advertisements.

(i) Definition of "Professional Advertisement." The term "professional advertisement" means any advertisement concerning the facilities, services or skills with respect to municipal securities of such broker, dealer or municipal securities dealer or of another broker, dealer, or municipal securities dealer.

(ii) Standard for Professional Advertisements. No broker, dealer or municipal securities dealer shall publish or disseminate, or cause to be published or disseminated, any professional advertisement that contains any untrue statement of material fact or is otherwise false or misleading.

(c) Product Advertisements.

(i) Definition of "Product Advertisement." The term "product advertisement" means any advertisement concerning one or more specific municipal securities, one or more specific issues of municipal securities, the municipal securities of one or more specific issuers, or the specific features of municipal securities.

(ii) Standard for Product Advertisements. No broker, dealer or municipal securities dealer shall publish or disseminate, or cause to be published or disseminated, any product advertisement that such broker, dealer, or municipal securities dealer knows or has reason to know contains any untrue statement of material fact or is otherwise false or misleading and, to the extent applicable, that is not in compliance with section (d) or (e) hereof.

(d) New Issue Product Advertisements. In addition to the requirements of section (c), all product advertisements for new issue municipal securities (other than municipal fund securities) shall be subject to the following requirements:

(i) Accuracy at Time of Sale. A syndicate or syndicate member which publishes or causes to be published any advertisement regarding the offering by the syndicate of a new issue of municipal securities, or any part thereof, may show the initial reoffering prices or yields for the securities, even if the price or yield for a maturity or maturities may have changed, provided that the advertisement contains the date of sale of the securities by the issuer to the syndicate. In the event that the prices or yields shown in a new issue advertisement are other than the initial reoffering prices or yields, such an advertisement must show the prices or yields of the securities as of the time the advertisement is submitted for publication. For purposes of this rule, the date of sale shall be deemed to be, in the case of competitive sales, the date on which bids are required to be submitted to an issuer and, in the case of negotiated sales, the date on which a contract to purchase securities from an issuer is executed.

(ii) Accuracy at Time of Publication. Each advertisement relating to a new issue of municipal securities shall also indicate, if applicable, that the securities shown as available from the syndicate may no longer be available from the syndicate at the time of publication or may be available from the syndicate at a price or yield different from that shown in the advertisement.

(e) Municipal Fund Security Product Advertisements. In addition to the requirements of section (c), all product advertisements for municipal fund securities shall be subject to the following requirements:

(i) Required Disclosures.

    (A) Substance and Format of Disclosure. Except as described in paragraph (B) of this subsection (i), each product advertisement for municipal fund securities:

        (1) basic disclosure – must include a statement to the effect that:

            (a) an investor should consider the investment objectives, risks, and charges and expenses associated with municipal fund securities before investing;

            (b) more information about municipal fund securities is available in the issuer's official statement;

            (c) if the advertisement identifies a source from which an investor may obtain an official statement and the broker, dealer or municipal securities dealer that publishes the advertisement is the underwriter for one or more of the issues of municipal fund securities for which any such official statement may be supplied, such broker, dealer or municipal securities dealer is the underwriter for one or more issues (as appropriate) of such municipal fund securities; and

            (d) the official statement should be read carefully before investing.

        (2) additional disclosures for identified products – that refers by name (including marketing name) to any municipal fund security, issuer of municipal fund securities, state or other governmental entity that sponsors the issuance of municipal fund securities, or to any securities held as assets of municipal fund securities or to any issuer thereof, must include the following disclosures, as applicable:

            (a) unless the offer of such municipal fund securities is exempt from Exchange Act Rule 15c2-12 and the issuer thereof has not produced an official statement, a source from which an investor may obtain an official statement;

            (b) if the advertisement relates to municipal fund securities issued by a qualified tuition program under Internal Revenue Code Section 529, a statement to the effect that an investor should consider, before investing, whether the investor's or designated beneficiary's home state offers any state tax or other state benefits such as financial aid, scholarship funds, and protection from creditors that are only available for investments in such state's qualified tuition program; provided, however, that this statement shall not be required for any advertisement relating to municipal fund securities of a specific state if such advertisement is sent to, or is otherwise distributed through means that are reasonably likely to result in the advertisement being received by, only residents of such state and is not otherwise published or disseminated by the broker, dealer or municipal securities dealer, or made available by the broker, dealer or municipal securities dealer to any of its affiliates, the issuer or any of the issuer's agents with the expectation or understanding that such other parties will otherwise publish or disseminate such advertisement; and

            (c) if the advertisement is for a municipal fund security that has an investment option that invests solely in a money market fund:

                (i) and that money market fund is not a government money market fund, as defined in Rule 2a-7(a)(14), 17 CFR 270.2a-7(a)(14), under the Investment Company Act of 1940 or a retail money market fund, as defined in Rule 2a-7(a)(21), 17 CFR 270.2a-7(a)(21), under the Investment Company Act of 1940, statements to the effect that:

You could lose money by investing in this investment option. Because the share price of the money market fund in which your investment option invests (the "underlying fund") will fluctuate, when you redeem your units in that investment option, those units may be worth more or less than what you originally paid for them. The underlying fund may impose a fee upon sale of those shares or may temporarily suspend the ability of the investment option to redeem shares if the underlying fund's liquidity falls below required minimums because of market conditions or other factors. An investment in the investment option is not insured or guaranteed by the Federal Deposit Insurance Corporation or any other government agency. The underlying fund's sponsor has no legal obligation to provide financial support to the underlying fund, and you should not expect that the sponsor will provide financial support to the underlying fund at any time.

(ii) and that money market fund is a government money market fund, as defined in Rule 2a-7(a)(14), 17 CFR 270.2a-7(a)(14), under the Investment Company Act of 1940 or a retail money market fund, as defined in Rule 2a-7(a)(21), 17 CFR 270.2a-7(a)(21), under the Investment Company Act of 1940, and that is subject to the requirements of Rule 2a-7(c)(2)(i) and/or (ii), 17 CFR 270.2a-7(c)(2)(i) and/or (ii), under the Investment Company Act of 1940 (or is not subject to the requirements of Rule 2a-7(c)(2)(i) and/or (ii), 17 CFR 270.2a-7(c)(2)(i) and/or (ii), pursuant to Rule 2a-7(c)(2)(iii), 17 CFR 270.2a-7(c)(2)(iii), under the Investment Company Act of 1940, but has chosen to rely on the ability to impose liquidity fees and suspend redemptions consistent with the requirements of Rule 2a-7(c)(2)(i) and/or (ii), 17 CFR 270.2a-7(c)(2)(i) and/or (ii), under the Investment Company Act of 1940), statements to the effect that:

You could lose money by investing in this investment option. Although the money market fund in which your investment option invests (the "underlying fund") seeks to preserve the value of its shares at $1.00 per share, the underlying fund cannot guarantee it will do so. The underlying fund may impose a fee upon the investment option's redemption of the underlying fund's shares or the underlying fund may temporarily suspend the investment option's ability to redeem its shares if the underlying fund's liquidity falls below required minimums because of market conditions or other factors. An investment in the investment option is not insured or guaranteed by the Federal Deposit Insurance Corporation or any other government agency. The underlying fund's sponsor has no legal obligation to provide financial support to the underlying fund, and you should not expect that the sponsor will provide financial support to the underlying fund at any time.

(iii) and that money market fund is a government money market fund, as defined in Rule 2a-7(a)(14), 17 CFR 270.2a-7(a)(14), under the Investment Company Act of 1940, that is not subject to the requirements of Rule 2a-7(c)(2)(i) and/or (ii), 17 CFR 270.2a-7(c)(2)(i) and/or (ii), under the Investment Company Act of 1940, pursuant to Rule 2a-7(c)(2)(iii), 17 CFR 270.2a-7(c)(2)(iii), under the Investment Company Act of 1940, and that has not chosen to rely on the ability to impose liquidity fees and suspend redemptions consistent with the requirements of Rule 2a-7(c)(2)(i) and/or (ii), 17 CFR 270.2a-7(c)(2)(i) and/or (ii), under the Investment Company Act of 1940, a statement to the effect that:

You could lose money by investing in this investment option. Although the money market fund in which your investment option invests (the "underlying fund") seeks to preserve its value at $1.00 per share, the underlying fund cannot guarantee it will do so. An investment in this investment option is not insured or guaranteed by the Federal Deposit Insurance Corporation or any other government agency. The underlying fund's sponsor has no legal obligation to provide financial support to the underlying fund, and you should not expect that the sponsor will provide financial support to the underlying fund at any time.

(3) additional disclosures concerning performance – that includes performance data must include:

(a) a legend disclosing that the performance data included in the advertisement represents past performance; that past performance does not guarantee future results; that the investment return and the value of the investment will fluctuate so that an investor's units, when redeemed, may be worth more or less than their original cost; and that current performance may be lower or higher than the performance data included in the advertisement. Unless the advertisement includes total return quotations current to the most recent month ended seven business days prior to the date of any use of the advertisement, the legend must also identify either a toll-free (or collect) telephone number or website (that may be hyperlinked) where an investor may obtain total return quotations current to the most recent month-end for which such total return, or all information required for the calculation of such total return, is available, however an investment option that invests in a money market fund that is a government money market fund, as defined in Rule 2a-7(a)(14), 17 CFR 270.2a-7(a)(14), under the Investment Company Act of 1940 or a retail money market fund, as defined in Rule 2a-7(a)(21), 17 CFR 270.2a-7(a)(21), under the Investment Company Act of 1940 may omit the disclosure about principal value fluctuation;

(b) if a sales load or any other nonrecurring fee is charged, the maximum amount of the load or fee (current as of the date such advertisement is submitted for publication or otherwise disseminated) and, if the sales load or fee is not reflected in the performance data included in the advertisement, a statement that the performance data does not reflect the deduction of the sales load or fee and that the performance data would be lower if such load or fee were included; and

(c) to the extent that such performance data relates to municipal fund security investment options that are not held out as having the characteristics of a money market fund and to the extent applicable, the total annual operating expense ratio of such municipal fund security investment options (calculated in the same manner as the total annual fund operating expenses required to be included in the registration statement for a registered investment company, subject to paragraph (e)(ii)(A) hereof), gross of any fee waivers or expense reimbursements.

(4) format of disclosure – must meet the following requirements:

(a) for a print advertisement:

(i) the statements required by subparagraphs (1), (2) and (3) of this paragraph (A) must be presented in a type size at least as large as and of a style different from, but at least as prominent as, that used in the major portion of the advertisement, provided that when performance data is presented in a type size smaller than that of the major portion of the advertisement, the statements required by subparagraph (3) of this paragraph may appear in a type size no smaller than that of the performance data;

(ii) the statements required by subparagraph (3) of this paragraph must be presented in close proximity to the performance data; provided that such statements must be presented in the body of the advertisement and not in a footnote unless the performance data appears only in such footnote; and

(iii) the maximum amount of the sales load required to be disclosed pursuant to clause (3)(b) and the information required to be disclosed pursuant to clause (3)(c), along with the standardized performance information mandated by Securities Act Rule 482 as applicable by virtue of subsection (e)(ii) of this rule, must be presented in a prominent text box that contains only such information but which may also contain comparative performance and fee data and disclosures required under this section (e).

(b) for an advertisement delivered through an electronic medium:

(i) the legibility requirements for the statements required by subparagraphs (1), (2) and (3) of this paragraph relating to type size and style may be satisfied by presenting the statements in any manner reasonably calculated to draw investor attention to them;

(ii) if such advertisement is a radio or television advertisement, the statements required by subparagraphs (1), (2) and (3) of this paragraph must be given emphasis equal to that used in the major portion of the advertisement; and

(iii) the statements required by subparagraph (3) of this paragraph must be presented in close proximity to the performance data.

(B) Exceptions from Certain Disclosure Requirements. Notwithstanding any other provision of this rule, the following advertisements relating to municipal fund securities shall not be subject to the provisions of subparagraphs (1) and (2) of paragraph (e)(i)(A):

    (1) generic advertisements – any advertisement that does not refer by name to any specific investment option or portfolio offered by an issuer of municipal fund securities, but includes the name and address of the broker, dealer or municipal securities dealer or other person sponsoring the advertisement, and that is limited to any one or more of the following:

        (a) explanatory information relating to municipal fund securities generally or the nature of the issuers thereof or of the programs through which they are issued, or to services offered in connection with the ownership of such securities; or

        (b) the mention or explanation of municipal fund securities of different generic types or having various investment objectives; or

        (c) offers, descriptions, and explanations of various products and services not constituting a municipal fund security, provided that such offers, descriptions, and explanations do not relate directly to the desirability of owning or purchasing a municipal fund security; or

        (d) invitation to inquire for further information; provided that if an official statement for municipal fund securities is to be sent or delivered in response to such inquiries and if the sponsor of the advertisement is the underwriter for one or more of the issues of municipal fund securities for which such official statement may be supplied, the advertisement must state that such broker, dealer or municipal securities dealer is the underwriter for one or more issues (as appropriate) of such municipal fund securities.

    (2) certain blind advertisements – any advertisement that does not identify a broker, dealer or municipal securities dealer or any affiliate of a broker, dealer or municipal securities dealer and that is limited to any one or more of the following:

        (a) the name of an issuer of municipal fund securities; or

        (b) contact information for an issuer of municipal fund securities or for any agent of such issuer to obtain an official statement or other information; provided that, if any such agent of the issuer is a broker, dealer or municipal securities dealer or an affiliate of a broker, dealer or municipal securities dealer, no orders for municipal fund securities shall be accepted through such source unless initiated by the customer; or

        (c) a logo or other graphic design of an issuer of municipal fund securities that does not directly or indirectly identify the broker, dealer or municipal securities dealer or any affiliate of the broker, dealer or municipal securities dealer; or

        (d) a service mark, trademark or short slogan of the issuer's general objectives that does not constitute a call to invest in municipal fund securities.

    (3) certain form letters to existing customers – any form letter relating to municipal fund securities distributed solely to existing customers of the broker, dealer or municipal securities dealer to whom the broker, dealer or municipal securities dealer has previously sent or caused to be sent an official statement for:

        (a) any municipal fund securities of the issuer of such municipal fund securities; or

        (b) any municipal fund securities of a different issuer of municipal fund securities, provided that the advertisement includes the applicable disclosures under clause (e)(i)(A)(1)(c) and subparagraph (e)(i)(A)(2) of this rule.

(ii) Performance Data. Each product advertisement that includes performance data relating to municipal fund securities must present performance data in the format, and calculated pursuant to the methods, prescribed in paragraph (d) of Securities Act Rule 482 (or, in the case of a municipal fund security that the issuer holds out as having the characteristics of a money market fund, paragraph (e) of Securities Act Rule 482) and, to the extent applicable, subparagraph (e)(i)(A)(4) of this rule, provided that:

(A) source of data – to the extent that information necessary to calculate performance data or to determine loads, fees and expenses for purposes of clause (e)(i)(A)(3)(b) or (c) is not available from an applicable balance sheet included in a registration statement, or from a prospectus, the broker, dealer or municipal securities dealer shall use information derived from the issuer's official statement, otherwise made available by the issuer or its agents, or (when unavailable from the official statement, the issuer or the issuer's agents) derived from such other sources which the broker, dealer or municipal securities dealer reasonably believes are reliable;

(B) period of calculation – if the issuer first began issuing the municipal fund securities fewer than one, five, or ten years prior to the date of the submission of the advertisement for publication, such shorter period shall be substituted for any otherwise prescribed longer period in connection with the calculation of average annual total return or any similar returns;

(C) currentness of calculation – performance data and total annual operating expense ratio shall be calculated as of the most recent practicable date considering the type of municipal fund securities and the media through which data will be conveyed, except that any advertisement containing total return quotations will be considered to have complied with this paragraph provided that:

  (1)(a) the total return quotations are current to the most recent calendar quarter ended prior to the submission of the advertisement for publication for which such performance data, or all information required for the calculation of such performance data, is available to the broker, dealer or municipal securities dealer as described in paragraph (A) of this subsection (e)(ii); and

    (b) total return quotations (current to the most recent month ended seven business days prior to the date of any use of the advertisement for which such total return, or all information required for the calculation of such total return, is available to the broker, dealer or municipal securities dealer as described in paragraph (A) of this subsection (e)(ii)) are provided at the toll-free (or collect) telephone number or website identified pursuant to clause (i)(A)(3)(a) of this section (e) and the month to which such information is current is identified; or

  (2) the total return quotations are current to the most recent month ended seven business days prior to the date of any use of the advertisement for which such total return, or all information required for the calculation of such total return, is available to the broker, dealer or municipal securities dealer and the month to which such information is current is identified.

(D) 12b-1-type plans – where such calculation is required to include expenses accrued under a plan adopted under Investment Company Act Rule 12b-1, the broker, dealer or municipal securities dealer shall include all such expenses as well as any expenses having the same characteristics as expenses under such a plan where such a plan is not required to be adopted under said Rule 12b-1 as a result of Section 2(b) of the Investment Company Act of 1940;

(E) tax-adjusted calculations – in calculating tax-equivalent yields or after-tax returns, the broker, dealer or municipal securities dealer shall assume that any unreinvested distributions are used in the manner intended with respect to such municipal fund securities in order to qualify for any federal tax-exemption or other federally tax-advantaged treatment with respect to such distributions, provided that the advertisement must also provide a general description of how federal law intends that such distributions be used and disclose that such yield or return would be lower if distributions are not used in this manner.

(F) applicability with respect to underlying assets – notwithstanding any of the foregoing, this subsection (e)(ii) shall apply solely to the calculation of performance relating to municipal fund securities and does not apply to, or limit the applicability of any rule of the Commission or any other regulatory body relating to, the calculation of performance for any security held as an underlying asset of the municipal fund securities.

(iii) Nature of Issuer and Security. An advertisement for a specific municipal fund security must provide sufficient information to identify such specific security in a manner that is not false or misleading. An advertisement that identifies a specific municipal fund security must include the name of the issuer (or the issuer's marketing name for its issuance of municipal fund securities, together with the state of the issuer), presented in a manner no less prominent than any other entity identified in the advertisement, and must not imply that a different entity is the issuer of the municipal fund security. An advertisement must not raise an inference that, because municipal fund securities are issued under a government-sponsored plan, investors are guaranteed against investment losses if no such guarantee exists. If an advertisement concerns a specific class or category of an issuer's municipal fund securities (e.g., A shares versus B shares; direct sale shares versus advisor shares; in-state shares versus national shares; etc.), this must clearly be disclosed in a manner no less prominent than the information provided with respect to such class or category.

(iv) Capacity of Dealer and Other Parties. An advertisement that relates to or describes services provided with respect to municipal fund securities must clearly indicate the entity providing those services. If any person or entity other than the broker, dealer or municipal securities dealer is named in the advertisement, the advertisement must reflect any relationship between the broker, dealer or municipal securities dealer and such other person or entity. An advertisement soliciting purchases of municipal fund securities that would be effected by a broker, dealer or municipal securities dealer or any other entity other than the broker, dealer or municipal securities dealer that publishes the advertisement must identify which entity would effect the transaction, provided that the advertisement may identify one or more such entities in general descriptive terms but must specifically name any such other entity if it is the issuer, an affiliate of the issuer, or an affiliate of the broker, dealer or municipal securities dealer that publishes the advertisement. This subsection (iv) shall not apply to any advertisement described in subparagraph (e)(i)(B)(2) of this rule.

(v) Tax Consequences and Other Features. Any discussion of tax implications or other benefits or features of investments in municipal fund securities included in an advertisement must not be false or misleading. In the case of an advertisement that includes generalized statements regarding tax or other benefits offered in connection with such municipal fund securities or otherwise offered under state or federal law, the advertisement also must include a generalized statement that the availability of such tax or other benefits may be conditioned on meeting certain requirements. If the advertisement describes the nature of specific benefits, such advertisement must also briefly list the substantive factors that may materially limit the availability of such benefits (such as residency, purpose for or timing of distributions, or other factors, as applicable). Such statements of conditions or limitations must be presented in close proximity to, and in a manner no less prominent than, the description of such benefits.

(vi) Underlying Registered Securities. If an advertisement for a municipal fund security provides specific details of a security held as an underlying asset of the municipal fund security, the details included in the advertisement relating to such underlying security must be presented in a manner that would be in compliance with any Commission or other advertising rules that would be applicable if the advertisement related solely to such underlying security; provided that details of the underlying security must be accompanied by any further statements relating to such details as are necessary to ensure that the inclusion of such details does not cause the advertisement to be false or misleading with respect to the municipal fund securities advertised. This subsection does not limit the applicability of any rule of the Commission or any other regulatory body relating to advertisements of securities other than municipal fund securities, including advertisements that contain information about such other securities together with information about municipal securities.

(vii) Correspondence Presenting Performance Data. Notwithstanding other provisions of this rule, all correspondence with the public that includes performance data relating to municipal fund securities must comply with provisions of subparagraph (e)(i)(A)(3) (presented in the manner provided in subparagraph (e)(i)(A)(4)) and subsection (e)(ii) as if correspondence were a product advertisement under the rule.

(f) Approval by Principal. Each advertisement subject to the requirements of this rule must be approved in writing by a municipal securities principal or general securities principal prior to first use.

(g) Interactive Content. Interactive content that is an advertisement and that would be posted or disseminated in an interactive electronic forum is exempt from the requirement to be approved in writing by a municipal securities principal or general securities principal prior to first use.

(h) Records. Each broker, dealer and municipal securities dealer shall make and keep current in a separate file records of all advertisements.

---

44. MSRB Rules: G-25 – Improper Use of Assets

Summary: Prohibits dealers from improperly using municipal securities or funds held on behalf of another person, guaranteeing customers against loss in customer accounts and transactions, and sharing in profits and losses of customer accounts and transactions by any dealer.

(a) Improper Use. No broker, dealer, or municipal securities dealer shall make improper use of municipal securities or funds held on behalf of another person.

(b) Guaranties. No broker, dealer, or municipal securities dealer shall guarantee or offer to guarantee a customer against loss in
  (i) an account carried or introduced by such broker, dealer, or municipal securities dealer in which municipal securities are held or for which municipal securities are purchased, sold or exchanged or
  (ii) a transaction in municipal securities with or for a customer.
  Put options and repurchase agreements shall not be deemed to be guaranties against loss if their terms are provided in writing to the customer with or on the confirmation of the transaction and recorded in accordance with rule G-8(a)(v).

(c) Sharing Account. No broker, dealer, or municipal securities dealer shall share, directly or indirectly, in the profits or losses of
  (i) an account of a customer carried or introduced by such broker, dealer, or municipal securities dealer in which municipal securities are held or for which municipal securities are purchased or sold or
  (ii) a transaction in municipal securities with or for a customer.
  Nothing herein contained shall be construed to prohibit an associated person of a broker, dealer, or municipal securities dealer from participating in his or her private capacity in an investment partnership or joint account, provided that such participation is solely in direct proportion to the financial contribution made by such person to the partnership or account.

---

45. MSRB Rules: G-39 – Telemarketing

Summary: Establishes telemarketing requirements with respect to the municipal securities activities of dealers.

(a) General Telemarketing Requirements. No broker, dealer or municipal securities dealer shall initiate any outbound telephone call to:

  (i) Time of Day Restriction. Any residence of a person before the hour of 8:00 a.m. or after 9:00 p.m. (local time at the called party's location), unless

    (A) the broker, dealer or municipal securities dealer has an established business relationship with the person pursuant to paragraph (n)(xii)(A),

    (B) the broker, dealer or municipal securities dealer has received that person's express prior consent, or

    (C) the person called is a broker, dealer or municipal securities dealer;

  (ii) Firm-Specific Do-Not-Call List. Any person that previously has stated that he or she does not wish to receive any outbound telephone calls made by or on behalf of the broker, dealer or municipal securities dealer; or

  (iii) National Do-Not-Call List. Any person who has registered his or her telephone number on the Federal Trade Commission's national do-not-call registry.

  (iv) Compliance with Other Requirements. This rule does not affect the obligation of any broker, dealer or municipal securities dealer that engages in telemarketing to comply with relevant state and federal laws and rules, including, but not limited to, the Telemarketing and Consumer Fraud and Abuse Prevention Act codified at 15 U.S.C. 6101 – 6108, as amended, the Telephone Consumer Protection Act codified at 47 U.S.C. 227, and the rules of the Federal Communications Commission relating to telemarketing practices and the rights of telephone consumers codified at 47 CFR 64.1200.

(b) National Do-Not-Call List Exceptions. A broker, dealer or municipal securities dealer making outbound telephone calls will not be liable for violating paragraph (a)(iii) if:

  (i) Established Business Relationship Exception. The broker, dealer or municipal securities dealer has an established business relationship with the recipient of the call. A person's request to be placed on the broker, dealer or municipal securities dealer's firm-specific do-not-call list terminates the established business relationship exception to the national do-not-call list provision for that broker, dealer or municipal securities dealer even if the person continues to do business with the broker, dealer or municipal securities dealer;

  (ii) Prior Express Written Consent Exception. The broker, dealer or municipal securities dealer has obtained the person's prior express written consent. Such consent must be clearly evidenced by a signed, written agreement (which may be obtained electronically under the Electronic Signatures in Global and National Commerce Act, 15 U.S.C. 7001, et seq. ("E-Sign Act")) between the person and the broker, dealer or municipal securities dealer, which states that the person agrees to be contacted by the broker, dealer or municipal securities dealer and includes the telephone number to which the calls may be placed; or

  (iii) Personal Relationship Exception. The broker, dealer or municipal securities dealer making the call has a personal relationship with the recipient of the call.

(c) Safe Harbor Provision. A broker, dealer or municipal securities dealer making outbound telephone calls will not be liable for violating paragraph (a)(iii) if the broker, dealer or municipal securities dealer demonstrates that the violation is the result of an error and that as part of the broker, dealer or municipal securities dealer's routine business practice, it meets the following standards:

  (i) Written procedures. The broker, dealer or municipal securities dealer has established and implemented written procedures to comply with the national do-not-call rules;

  (ii) Training of personnel. The broker, dealer or municipal securities dealer has trained its personnel, and any entity assisting in its compliance, in the procedures established pursuant to the national do-not-call rules;

  (iii) Recording. The broker, dealer or municipal securities dealer has maintained and recorded a list of telephone numbers that it may not contact; and

(iv) Accessing the national do-not-call database. The broker, dealer or municipal securities dealer uses a process to prevent outbound telephone calls to any telephone number on any list established pursuant to the do-not-call rules, employing a version of the national do-not-call registry obtained from the administrator of the registry no more than 31 days prior to the date any call is made, and maintains records documenting this process.

(d) Procedures. Prior to engaging in telemarketing, a broker, dealer or municipal securities dealer must institute procedures to comply with paragraph (a). Such procedures must meet the following minimum standards:

(i) Written policy. Brokers, dealers and municipal securities dealers must have a written policy for maintaining a do-not-call list.

(ii) Training of personnel engaged in telemarketing. Personnel engaged in any aspect of telemarketing must be informed and trained in the existence and use of the do-not-call list.

(iii) Recording, disclosure of do-not-call requests. If a broker, dealer or municipal securities dealer receives a request from a person not to receive calls from that broker, dealer or municipal securities dealer, the broker, dealer or municipal securities dealer must record the request and place the person's name, if provided, and telephone number on the firm's do-not-call list at the time the request is made. Brokers, dealers and municipal securities dealers must honor a person's do-not-call request within a reasonable time from the date such request is made. This period may not exceed 30 days from the date of such request. If such requests are recorded or maintained by a party other than the broker, dealer or municipal securities dealer on whose behalf the outbound telephone call is made, the broker, dealer or municipal securities dealer on whose behalf the outbound telephone call is made will be liable for any failures to honor the do-not-call request.

(iv) Identification of sellers and telemarketers. A broker, dealer or municipal securities dealer making an outbound telephone call must provide the called party with the name of the individual caller, the name of the broker, dealer or municipal securities dealer, an address or telephone number at which the broker, dealer or municipal securities dealer may be contacted, and that the purpose of the call is to solicit the purchase of securities or related service. The telephone number provided may not be a 900 number or any other number for which charges exceed local or long distance transmission charges.

(v) Affiliated persons or entities. In the absence of a specific request by the person to the contrary, a person's do-not-call request shall apply to the broker, dealer or municipal securities dealer making the call, and will not apply to affiliated entities unless the consumer reasonably would expect them to be included given the identification of the caller and the product being advertised.

(vi) Maintenance of do-not-call lists. A broker, dealer or municipal securities dealer making outbound telephone calls must maintain a permanent record of a person's request not to receive further calls.

(e) Wireless Communications. The provisions set forth in this rule are applicable to brokers, dealers and municipal securities dealers making outbound telephone calls to wireless telephone numbers.

(f) Outsourcing Telemarketing. If a broker, dealer or municipal securities dealer uses another appropriately registered or licensed entity or person to perform telemarketing services on its behalf, the broker, dealer or municipal securities dealer remains responsible for ensuring compliance with all provisions contained in this rule.

(g) Caller Identification Information.

(i) Any broker, dealer or municipal securities dealer that engages in telemarketing must transmit or cause to be transmitted the telephone number, and, when made available by the broker, dealer or municipal securities dealer's telephone carrier, the name of the broker, dealer or municipal securities dealer, to any caller identification service in use by a recipient of an outbound telephone call.

(ii) The telephone number so provided must permit any person to make a do-not-call request during regular business hours.

(iii) Any broker, dealer or municipal securities dealer that engages in telemarketing is prohibited from blocking the transmission of caller identification information.

(h) Unencrypted Consumer Account Numbers. No broker, dealer or municipal securities dealer shall disclose or receive, for consideration, unencrypted consumer account numbers for use in telemarketing. The term "unencrypted" means not only complete, visible account numbers, whether provided in lists or singly, but also encrypted information with a key to its decryption. This paragraph shall not apply to the disclosure or receipt of a customer's billing information to process a payment pursuant to a telemarketing transaction.

(i) Submission of Billing Information. For any telemarketing transaction, a broker, dealer or municipal securities dealer must obtain the express informed consent of the person to be charged and to be charged using the identified account.

    (i) In any telemarketing transaction involving preacquired account information and a free-to-pay conversion feature, the broker, dealer or municipal securities dealer must:

        (A) obtain from the customer, at a minimum, the last four digits of the account number to be charged;

        (B) obtain from the customer an express agreement to be charged and to be charged using the account number pursuant to paragraph (i)(i)(A); and

        (C) make and maintain an audio recording of the entire telemarketing transaction.

    (ii) In any other telemarketing transaction involving preacquired account information not described in paragraph (i)(i), the broker, dealer or municipal securities dealer must:

        (A) identify the account to be charged with sufficient specificity for the customer to understand what account will be charged; and

        (B) obtain from the customer an express agreement to be charged and to be charged using the account number identified pursuant to paragraph (i)(ii)(A).

(j) Abandoned Calls.

    (i) No broker, dealer or municipal securities dealer shall "abandon" any outbound telephone call. An outbound call is "abandoned" if a called person answers it and the call is not connected to a broker, dealer or municipal securities dealer within two seconds of the called person's completed greeting.

    (ii) A broker, dealer or municipal securities dealer shall not be liable for violating paragraph (j)(i) if:

        (A) the broker, dealer or municipal securities dealer employs technology that ensures abandonment of no more than three percent of all outbound telephone calls answered by a person, measured over the duration of a single calling campaign, if less than 30 days, or separately over each successive 30-day period or portion thereof that the campaign continues;

        (B) the broker, dealer or municipal securities dealer, for each outbound telephone call placed, allows the telephone to ring for at least 15 seconds or four rings before disconnecting an unanswered call;

        (C) whenever a broker, dealer or municipal securities dealer is not available to speak with the person answering the outbound telephone call within two seconds after the person's completed greeting, the broker, dealer or municipal securities dealer promptly plays a recorded message that states the name and telephone number of the broker, dealer or municipal securities dealer on whose behalf the call was placed; and

        (D) the broker, dealer or municipal securities dealer retains records establishing compliance with paragraph (j)(ii).

(k) Prerecorded Messages.

    (i) No broker, dealer or municipal securities dealer shall initiate any outbound telephone call that delivers a prerecorded message other than a prerecorded message permitted for compliance with the call abandonment safe harbor in paragraph (j)(ii)(C) unless:

        (A) the broker, dealer or municipal securities dealer has obtained from the recipient of the call an express agreement, in writing, that:

            (1) the broker, dealer or municipal securities dealer obtained only after a clear and conspicuous disclosure that the purpose of the agreement is to authorize the broker, dealer or municipal securities dealer to place prerecorded calls to such person;

            (2) the broker, dealer or municipal securities dealer obtained without requiring that the agreement be executed as a condition of opening an account or purchasing any good or service;

      (3) evidences the willingness of the recipient of the call to receive calls that deliver prerecorded messages by or on behalf of a specific broker, dealer or municipal securities dealer; and

      (4) includes such person's telephone number and signature (which may be obtained electronically under the E-Sign Act);

    (B) the broker, dealer or municipal securities dealer allows the telephone to ring for at least 15 seconds or four rings before disconnecting an unanswered call; and within two seconds after the completed greeting of the person called, plays a prerecorded message that promptly provides the disclosures in paragraph (d)(iv), followed immediately by a disclosure of one or both of the following:

      (1) for a call that could be answered by a person, that the person called can use an automated interactive voice and/or keypress-activated opt-out mechanism to assert a firm-specific do-not-call request pursuant to the broker, dealer or municipal securities dealer's procedures instituted under paragraph (d)(iii) at any time during the message. The mechanism must:

         (a) automatically add the number called to the broker, dealer or municipal securities dealer's firm-specific do-not-call list;

         (b) once invoked, immediately disconnect the call; and

         (c) be available for use at any time during the message;

      (2) for a call that could be answered by an answering machine or voicemail service, that the person called can use a toll-free telephone number to assert a firm-specific do-not-call request pursuant to the broker, dealer or municipal securities dealer's procedures instituted under paragraph (d)(iii). The number provided must connect directly to an automated interactive voice or keypress-activated opt-out mechanism that:

         (a) automatically adds the number called to the broker, dealer or municipal securities dealer's firm-specific do-not-call list;

         (b) immediately thereafter disconnects the call; and

         (c) is accessible at any time throughout the duration of the telemarketing campaign; and

    (C) the broker, dealer or municipal securities dealer complies with all other requirements of this rule and other applicable federal and state laws.

  (ii) Any call that complies with all applicable requirements of paragraph (k) shall not be deemed to violate paragraph (j).

(l) Credit Card Laundering. Except as expressly permitted by the applicable credit card system, no broker, dealer or municipal securities dealer shall:

  (i) present to or deposit into, the credit card system for payment, a credit card sales draft generated by a telemarketing transaction that is not the result of a telemarketing credit card transaction between the cardholder and the broker, dealer or municipal securities dealer;

  (ii) employ, solicit, or otherwise cause a merchant, or an employee, representative or agent of the merchant, to present to or to deposit into the credit card system for payment, a credit card sales draft generated by a telemarketing transaction that is not the result of a telemarketing credit card transaction between the cardholder and the merchant; or

  (iii) obtain access to the credit card system through the use of a business relationship or an affiliation with a merchant, when such access is not authorized by the merchant agreement or the applicable credit card system.

(m) Exemption. Outbound telephone calls from a broker, dealer, or municipal securities dealer to a business entity, government, or political subdivision, agency, or instrumentality of a government are exempt from this rule, other than sections (a)(ii) and (d)(i)-(iii), (v) and (vi).

(n) Definitions.

  For purposes of this rule:

  (i) The term "account activity" shall include, but not be limited to, purchases, sales, interest credits or debits, charges or credits, dividend payments, transfer activity, securities receipts or deliveries, and/or journal entries relating to securities or funds in the possession or control of the broker, dealer or municipal securities dealer.

(ii) The term "acquirer" means a business organization, financial institution, or an agent of a business organization or financial institution that has authority from an organization that operates or licenses a credit card system to authorize merchants to accept, transmit, or process payment by credit card through the credit card system for money, goods or services, or anything else of value.

(iii) The term "billing information" means any data that enables any person to access a customer's or donor's account, such as a credit or debit card number, a brokerage, checking, or savings account number, or a mortgage loan account number. A "donor" means any person solicited to make a charitable contribution. A "charitable contribution" means any donation or gift of money or any other thing of value, for example a transfer to a pooled income fund.

(iv) The term "broker, dealer or municipal securities dealer of record" refers to the broker, dealer or municipal securities dealer identified on a customer's account application for accounts held by the issuer's agent for municipal fund securities.

(v) The term "caller identification service" means a service that allows a telephone subscriber to have the telephone number, and, where available, name of the calling party transmitted contemporaneously with the telephone call, and displayed on a device in or connected to the subscriber's telephone.

(vi) The term "cardholder" means a person to whom a credit card is issued or who is authorized to use a credit card on behalf of or in addition to the person to whom the credit card is issued.

(vii) The term "credit" means the right granted by a creditor to a debtor to defer payment of debt or to incur debt and defer its payment.

(viii) The term "credit card" means any card, plate, coupon book, or other credit device existing for the purpose of obtaining money, property, labor, or services on credit.

(ix) The term "credit card sales draft" means any record or evidence of a credit card transaction.

(x) The term "credit card system" means any method or procedure used to process credit card transactions involving credit cards issued or licensed by the operator of that system.

(xi) The term "customer" means any person who is or may be required to pay for goods or services offered through telemarketing.

(xii) The term "established business relationship" means a relationship between a broker, dealer or municipal securities dealer and a person if:

(A) the person has made a financial transaction or has a security position, a money balance, or account activity with the broker, dealer or municipal securities dealer or at a clearing firm that provides clearing services to such broker, dealer or municipal securities dealer within the eighteen months immediately preceding the date of an outbound telephone call;

(B) the broker, dealer or municipal securities dealer is the broker, dealer or municipal securities dealer of record for an account of the person within the eighteen months immediately preceding the date of an outbound telephone call; or

(C) the person has contacted the broker, dealer or municipal securities dealer to inquire about a product or service offered by the broker, dealer or municipal securities dealer within the three months immediately preceding the date of an outbound telephone call.

A person's established business relationship with a broker, dealer or municipal securities dealer does not extend to the broker, dealer or municipal securities dealer's affiliated entities unless the person would reasonably expect them to be included. Similarly, a person's established business relationship with a broker, dealer or municipal securities dealer's affiliate does not extend to the broker, dealer or municipal securities dealer unless the person would reasonably expect the broker, dealer or municipal securities dealer to be included.

(xiii) The term "free-to-pay conversion" means, in an offer or agreement to sell or provide any goods or services, a provision under which a customer receives a product or service for free for an initial period and will incur an obligation to pay for the product or service if he or she does not take affirmative action to cancel before the end of that period.

(xiv) The term "merchant" means a person who is authorized under a written contract with an acquirer to honor or accept credit cards, or to transmit or process for payment credit card payments, for the purchase of goods or services or a charitable contribution.

(xv) The term "merchant agreement" means a written contract between a merchant and an acquirer to honor or accept credit cards, or to transmit or process for payment credit card payments, for the purchase of goods or services or a charitable contribution.

(xvi) The term "outbound telephone call" means a telephone call initiated by a telemarketer to induce the purchase of goods or services or to solicit a charitable contribution from a donor.

(xvii) The term "person" means any individual, group, unincorporated association, limited or general partnership, corporation, other business entity, government, or political subdivision, agency, or instrumentality of a government.

(xviii) The term "personal relationship" means any family member, friend, or acquaintance of the broker, dealer or municipal securities dealer making an outbound telephone call.

(xix) The term "preacquired account information" means any information that enables a broker, dealer or municipal securities dealer to cause a charge to be placed against a customer's or donor's account without obtaining the account number directly from the customer or donor during the telemarketing transaction pursuant to which the account will be charged.

(xx) The term "telemarketer" means any person who, in connection with telemarketing, initiates or receives telephone calls to or from a customer or donor.

(xxi) The term "telemarketing" means consisting of or relating to a plan, program, or campaign involving at least one outbound telephone call pertaining to municipal securities or municipal financial products, for example cold-calling. The term does not include the solicitation of sales through the mailing of written marketing materials, when the person making the solicitation does not solicit customers by telephone but only receives calls initiated by customers in response to the marketing materials and during those calls takes orders only without further solicitation. For purposes of the previous sentence, the term "further solicitation" does not include providing the customer with information about, or attempting to sell, anything promoted in the same marketing materials that prompted the customer's call.

---

46. MSRB Rules: G-41 – Anti-money Laundering Compliance Program

Summary: Requires a dealer to establish and implement an anti-money laundering program that complies with the rules and regulations governing anti-money laundering programs of either its registered securities association or its appropriate banking regulator.

Every broker, dealer or municipal securities dealer shall establish and implement an anti-money laundering compliance program reasonably designed to achieve and monitor ongoing compliance with the requirements of the Bank Secrecy Act, 31 U.S.C. 5311, et seq. ("BSA"), and the regulations thereunder. A broker, dealer or municipal securities dealer that establishes and implements an anti-money laundering compliance program that is in compliance with the rules, regulations or requirements governing the establishment and maintenance of anti-money laundering programs of the registered securities association of which the broker, dealer or municipal securities dealer is a member (e.g., FINRA Rule 3310) or the appropriate regulatory agency as defined in Section 3(a)(34) of the Act (e.g., 12 C.F.R. 21.21 (OCC); 12 C.F.R. 208.63 (FRB); 12 C.F.R. 326.8 (FDIC)) or, if applicable, the Office of Thrift Supervision (12 C.F.R. 563.177) will be deemed to be in compliance with Section 5318(h)(1) of the BSA and the regulations promulgated thereunder for purposes of this Rule.

---

47. MSRB Rules: G-47 – Time of Trade Disclosure

Summary: Requires dealers to disclose to customers at or prior to the time of trade all material information known or available publicly through established industry sources.

(a) No broker, dealer, or municipal securities dealer shall sell a municipal security to a customer, or purchase a municipal security from a customer, whether unsolicited or recommended, and whether in a primary offering or secondary market transaction, without disclosing to the customer, orally or in writing, at or prior to the time of trade, all material information known about the transaction, as well as material information about the security that is reasonably accessible to the market.

(b) Definitions.

   (i) "Established industry sources" shall include the MSRB's Electronic Municipal Market Access ("EMMA"®) system, rating agency reports, and other sources of information relating to municipal securities transactions generally used by brokers, dealers, and municipal securities dealers that effect transactions in the type of municipal securities at issue.

   (ii) "Material information": Information is considered to be material if there is a substantial likelihood that the information would be considered important or significant by a reasonable investor in making an investment decision.

   (iii) "Reasonably accessible to the market" shall mean that the information is made available publicly through established industry sources.

---

48. SEC Rules and Regulations: Regulation M

Rule 100 — Preliminary note; definitions.

(a) Preliminary note: Any transaction or series of transactions, whether or not effected pursuant to the provisions of Regulation M (§§ 242.100-242.105 of this chapter), remain subject to the antifraud and antimanipulation provisions of the securities laws, including, without limitation, Section 17(a) of the Securities Act of 1933 [15 U.S.C. 77q(a)] and Sections 9, 10(b), and 15(c) of the Securities Exchange Act of 1934 [15 U.S.C. 78i, 78j(b), and 78o(c)].

(b) For purposes of regulation M (§§ 242.100 through 242.105 of this chapter) the following definitions shall apply:

ADTV means the worldwide average daily trading volume during the two full calendar months immediately preceding, or any 60 consecutive calendar days ending within the 10 calendar days preceding, the filing of the registration statement; or, if there is no registration statement or if the distribution involves the sale of securities on a delayed basis pursuant to § 230.415 of this chapter, two full calendar months immediately preceding, or any consecutive 60 calendar days ending within the 10 calendar days preceding, the determination of the offering price.

Affiliated purchaser means:

(1) A person acting, directly or indirectly, in concert with a distribution participant, issuer, or selling security holder in connection with the acquisition or distribution of any covered security; or

(2) An affiliate, which may be a separately identifiable department or division of a distribution participant, issuer, or selling security holder, that, directly or indirectly, controls the purchases of any covered security by a distribution participant, issuer, or selling security holder, whose purchases are controlled by any such person, or whose purchases are under common control with any such person; or

(3) An affiliate, which may be a separately identifiable department or division of a distribution participant, issuer, or selling security holder, that regularly purchases securities for its own account or for the account of others, or that recommends or exercises investment discretion with respect to the purchase or sale of securities; Provided, however, That this paragraph (3) shall not apply to such affiliate if the following conditions are satisfied:

  (i) The distribution participant, issuer, or selling security holder:

    (A) Maintains and enforces written policies and procedures reasonably designed to prevent the flow of information to or from the affiliate that might result in a violation of §§ 242.101, 242.102, and 242.104; and

    (B) Obtains an annual, independent assessment of the operation of such policies and procedures; and

  (ii) The affiliate has no officers (or persons performing similar functions) or employees (other than clerical, ministerial, or support personnel) in common with the distribution participant, issuer, or selling security holder that direct, effect, or recommend transactions in securities; and

  (iii) The affiliate does not, during the applicable restricted period, act as a market maker (other than as a specialist in compliance with the rules of a national securities exchange), or engage, as a broker or a dealer, in solicited transactions or proprietary trading, in covered securities.

Agent independent of the issuer means a trustee or other person who is independent of the issuer. The agent shall be deemed to be independent of the issuer only if:

- The agent is not an affiliate of the issuer; and

- Neither the issuer nor any affiliate of the issuer exercises any direct or indirect control or influence over the prices or amounts of the securities to be purchased, the timing of, or the manner in which, the securities are to be purchased, or the selection of a broker or dealer (other than the independent agent itself) through which purchases may be executed; Provided, however, That the issuer or its affiliate will not be deemed to have such control or influence solely because it revises not more than once in any three-month period the source of the shares to fund the plan the basis for determining the amount of its contributions to a plan, or the basis for determining the frequency of its allocations to a plan, or any formula specified in a plan that determines the amount or timing of securities to be purchased by the agent.

Asset-backed security has the meaning contained in § 229.1101 of this chapter.

At-the-market offering means an offering of securities at other than a fixed price.

Business day refers to a 24 hour period determined with reference to the principal market for the securities to be distributed, and that includes a complete trading session for that market.

Completion of participation in a distribution. Securities acquired in the distribution for investment by any person participating in a distribution, or any affiliated purchaser of such person, shall be deemed to be distributed. A person shall be deemed to have completed its participation in a distribution as follows:

- An issuer or selling security holder, when the distribution is completed;

- An underwriter, when such person's participation has been distributed, including all other securities of the

same class that are acquired in connection with the distribution, and any stabilization arrangements and trading restrictions in connection with the distribution have been terminated; Provided, however, That an underwriter's participation will not be deemed to have been completed if a syndicate overallotment option is exercised in an amount that exceeds the net syndicate short position at the time of such exercise; and
- Any other person participating in the distribution, when such person's participation has been distributed.

Covered security means any security that is the subject of a distribution, or any reference security.

Current exchange rate means the current rate of exchange between two currencies, which is obtained from at least one independent entity that provides or disseminates foreign exchange quotations in the ordinary course of its business.

Distribution means an offering of securities, whether or not subject to registration under the Securities Act, that is distinguished from ordinary trading transactions by the magnitude of the offering and the presence of special selling efforts and selling methods.

Distribution participant means an underwriter, prospective underwriter, broker, dealer, or other person who has agreed to participate or is participating in a distribution.

Electronic communications network has the meaning provided in § 242.600.

Employee has the meaning contained in Form S-8 (§ 239.16b of this chapter) relating to employee benefit plans.

Exchange Act means the Securities Exchange Act of 1934 (15 U.S.C. 78aet seq.).

Independent bid means a bid by a person who is not a distribution participant, issuer, selling security holder, or affiliated purchaser.

NASD means the National Association of Securities Dealers, Inc. or any of its subsidiaries.

Nasdaq means the electronic dealer quotation system owned and operated by The Nasdaq Stock Market, Inc.

Nasdaq security means a security that is authorized for quotation on Nasdaq, and such authorization is not suspended, terminated, or prohibited.

Net purchases means the amount by which a passive market maker's purchases exceed its sales.

Offering price means the price at which the security is to be or is being distributed.

Passive market maker means a market maker that effects bids or purchases in accordance with the provisions of § 242.103.

Penalty bid means an arrangement that permits the managing underwriter to reclaim a selling concession from a syndicate member in connection with an offering when the securities originally sold by the syndicate member are purchased in syndicate covering transactions.

Plan means any bonus, profit-sharing, pension, retirement, thrift, savings, incentive, stock purchase, stock option, stock ownership, stock appreciation, dividend reinvestment, or similar plan; or any dividend or interest reinvestment plan or employee benefit plan as defined in § 230.405 of this chapter.

Principal market means the single securities market with the largest aggregate reported trading volume for the class of securities during the 12 full calendar months immediately preceding the filing of the registration statement; or, if there is no registration statement or if the distribution involves the sale of securities on a delayed basis pursuant to § 230.415 of this chapter, during the 12 full calendar months immediately preceding the determination of the offering price. For the purpose of determining the aggregate trading volume in a security, the trading volume of depositary shares representing such security shall be included, and shall be multiplied by the multiple or fraction of the security represented by the depositary share. For purposes of this paragraph, depositary share means a security, evidenced by a depositary receipt, that represents another security, or a multiple or fraction thereof, deposited with a depositary.

Prospective underwriter means a person:
- Who has submitted a bid to the issuer or selling security holder, and who knows or is reasonably certain that such bid will be accepted, whether or not the terms and conditions of the underwriting have been agreed upon; or
- Who has reached, or is reasonably certain to reach, an understanding with the issuer or selling security holder, or managing underwriter that such person will become an underwriter, whether or not the terms and conditions of the underwriting have been agreed upon.

Public float value shall be determined in the manner set forth on the front page of Form 10-K (§ 249.310 of this chapter), even if the issuer of such securities is not required to file Form 10-K, relating to the aggregate market value of common equity securities held by non-affiliates of the issuer.

Reference period means the two full calendar months immediately preceding the filing of the registration statement or, if there is no registration statement or if the distribution involves the sale of securities on a delayed basis pursuant to § 230.415 of this chapter, the two full calendar months immediately preceding the determination of the offering price.

Reference security means a security into which a security that is the subject of a distribution ("subject security") may be converted, exchanged, or exercised or which, under the terms of the subject security, may in whole or in significant part determine the value of the subject security.

Restricted period means:
- For any security with an ADTV value of $100,000 or more of an issuer whose common equity securities have a public float value of $25 million or more, the period beginning on the later of one business day prior to the determination of the offering price or such time that a person becomes a distribution participant, and ending upon such person's completion of participation in the distribution; and
- For all other securities, the period beginning on the later of five business days prior to the determination of the offering price or such time that a person becomes a distribution participant, and ending upon such person's completion of participation in the distribution.
- In the case of a distribution involving a merger, acquisition, or exchange offer, the period beginning on the day proxy solicitation or offering materials are first disseminated to security holders, and ending upon the completion of the distribution.

Securities Act means the Securities Act of 1933 (15 U.S.C. 77aet seq.).

Selling security holder means any person on whose behalf a distribution is made, other than an issuer.

Stabilize or stabilizing means the placing of any bid, or the effecting of any purchase, for the purpose of pegging, fixing, or maintaining the price of a security.

Syndicate covering transaction means the placing of any bid or the effecting of any purchase on behalf of the sole distributor or the underwriting syndicate or group to reduce a short position created in connection with the offering.

30% ADTV limitation means 30 percent of the market maker's ADTV in a covered security during the reference period, as obtained from the NASD.

Underwriter means a person who has agreed with an issuer or selling security holder:
- To purchase securities for distribution; or
- To distribute securities for or on behalf of such issuer or selling security holder; or
- To manage or supervise a distribution of securities for or on behalf of such issuer or selling security holder.

Rule 101 — Activities by distribution participants.

(a) Unlawful Activity. In connection with a distribution of securities, it shall be unlawful for a distribution participant or an affiliated purchaser of such person, directly or indirectly, to bid for, purchase, or attempt to induce any person to bid for or purchase, a covered security during the applicable restricted period; Provided, however, That if a distribution participant or affiliated purchaser is the issuer or selling security holder of the securities subject to the distribution, such person shall be subject to the provisions of § 242.102, rather than this section.

(b) Excepted Activity. The following activities shall not be prohibited by paragraph (a) of this section:
(1) Research. The publication or dissemination of any information, opinion, or recommendation, if the conditions of § 230.138, § 230.139, or § 230.139b of this chapter are met; or
(2) Transactions complying with certain other sections. Transactions complying with §§ 242.103 or 242.104; or
(3) Odd-lot transactions. Transactions in odd-lots; or transactions to offset odd-lots in connection with an odd-lot tender offer conducted pursuant to § 240.13e-4(h)(5) of this chapter; or

(4) Exercises of securities. The exercise of any option, warrant, right, or any conversion privilege set forth in the instrument governing a security; or

(5) Unsolicited transactions. Unsolicited brokerage transactions; or unsolicited purchases that are not effected from or through a broker or dealer, on a securities exchange, or through an inter-dealer quotation system or electronic communications network; or

(6) Basket transactions.

    (i) Bids or purchases, in the ordinary course of business, in connection with a basket of 20 or more securities in which a covered security does not comprise more than 5% of the value of the basket purchased; or

    (ii) Adjustments to such a basket in the ordinary course of business as a result of a change in the composition of a standardized index; or

(7) De minimis transactions. Purchases during the restricted period, other than by a passive market maker, that total less than 2% of the ADTV of the security being purchased, or unaccepted bids; Provided, however, That the person making such bid or purchase has maintained and enforces written policies and procedures reasonably designed to achieve compliance with the other provisions of this section; or

(8) Transactions in connection with a distribution. Transactions among distribution participants in connection with a distribution, and purchases of securities from an issuer or selling security holder in connection with a distribution, that are not effected on a securities exchange, or through an inter-dealer quotation system or electronic communications network; or

(9) Offers to sell or the solicitation of offers to buy. Offers to sell or the solicitation of offers to buy the securities being distributed (including securities acquired in stabilizing), or securities offered as principal by the person making such offer or solicitation; or

(10) Transactions in Rule 144A securities. Transactions in securities eligible for resale under § 230.144A(d)(3) of this chapter, or any reference security, if the Rule 144A securities are sold in the United States solely to:

    (i) Qualified institutional buyers, as defined in § 230.144A(a)(1) of this chapter, or to purchasers that the seller and any person acting on behalf of the seller reasonably believes are qualified institutional buyers, in transactions exempt from registration under section 4(2) of the Securities Act (15 U.S.C. 77d(2)) or §§ 230.144A or § 230.500 et seq of this chapter; or

    (ii) Persons not deemed to be "U.S. persons" for purposes of §§ 230.902(o)(2) or 230.902(o)(7) of this chapter, during a distribution qualifying under paragraph (b)(10)(i) of this section.

(c) Excepted Securities. The provisions of this section shall not apply to any of the following securities:

(1) Actively-traded securities. Securities that have an ADTV value of at least $1 million and are issued by an issuer whose common equity securities have a public float value of at least $150 million; Provided, however, That such securities are not issued by the distribution participant or an affiliate of the distribution participant; or

(2) Investment grade nonconvertible and asset-backed securities. Nonconvertible debt securities, nonconvertible preferred securities, and asset-backed securities, that are rated by at least one nationally recognized statistical rating organization, as that term is used in § 240.15c3-1 of this chapter, in one of its generic rating categories that signifies investment grade; or

(3) Exempted securities. "Exempted securities" as defined in section 3(a)(12) of the Exchange Act (15 U.S.C. 78c(a)(12)); or

(4) Face-amount certificates or securities issued by an open-end management investment company or unit investment trust. Face-amount certificates issued by a face-amount certificate company, or redeemable securities issued by an open-end management investment company or a unit investment trust. Any terms used in this paragraph (c)(4) that are defined in the Investment Company Act of 1940 (15 U.S.C. 80a-1et seq.) shall have the meanings specified in such Act.

(d) Exemptive authority. Upon written application or upon its own motion, the Commission may grant an exemption from the provisions of this section, either unconditionally or on specified terms and conditions, to any transaction or class of transactions, or to any security or class of securities.

Rule 102 — Activities by issuers and selling security holders during a distribution.

(a) Unlawful Activity. In connection with a distribution of securities effected by or on behalf of an issuer or selling security holder, it shall be unlawful for such person, or any affiliated purchaser of such person, directly or indirectly, to bid for, purchase, or attempt to induce any person to bid for or purchase, a covered security during the applicable restricted period; Except That if an affiliated purchaser is a distribution participant, such affiliated purchaser may comply with § 242.101, rather than this section.

(b) Excepted Activity. The following activities shall not be prohibited by paragraph (a) of this section:

　(1) Odd-lot transactions. Transactions in odd-lots, or transactions to offset odd-lots in connection with an odd-lot tender offer conducted pursuant to § 240.13e-4(h)(5) of this chapter; or

　(2) Transactions by closed-end investment companies.

　　(i) Transactions complying with § 270.23c-3 of this chapter; or

　　(ii) Periodic tender offers of securities, at net asset value, conducted pursuant to § 240.13e-4 of this chapter by a closed-end investment company that engages in a continuous offering of its securities pursuant to § 230.415 of this chapter; Provided, however, That such securities are not traded on a securities exchange or through an inter-dealer quotation system or electronic communications network; or

　(3) Redemptions by commodity pools or limited partnerships. Redemptions by commodity pools or limited partnerships, at a price based on net asset value, which are effected in accordance with the terms and conditions of the instruments governing the securities; Provided, however, That such securities are not traded on a securities exchange, or through an inter-dealer quotation system or electronic communications network; or

　(4) Exercises of securities. The exercise of any option, warrant, right, or any conversion privilege set forth in the instrument governing a security; or

　(5) Offers to sell or the solicitation of offers to buy. Offers to sell or the solicitation of offers to buy the securities being distributed; or

　(6) Unsolicited purchases. Unsolicited purchases that are not effected from or through a broker or dealer, on a securities exchange, or through an inter-dealer quotation system or electronic communications network; or

　(7) Transactions in Rule 144A securities. Transactions in securities eligible for resale under § 230.144A(d)(3) of this chapter, or any reference security, if the Rule 144A securities are sold in the United States solely to:

　　(i) Qualified institutional buyers, as defined in § 230.144A(a)(1) of this chapter, or to purchasers that the seller and any person acting on behalf of the seller reasonably believes are qualified institutional buyers, in transactions exempt from registration under section 4(2) of the Securities Act (15 U.S.C. 77d(2)) or §§ 230.144A or § 230.500 et seq of this chapter; or

　　(ii) Persons not deemed to be "U.S. persons" for purposes of §§ 230.902(o)(2) or 230.902(o)(7) of this chapter, during a distribution qualifying under paragraph (b)(7)(i) of this section.

(c) Plans.

　(1) Paragraph (a) of this section shall not apply to distributions of securities pursuant to a plan, which are made:

　　(i) Solely to employees or security holders of an issuer or its subsidiaries, or to a trustee or other person acquiring such securities for the accounts of such persons; or

　　(ii) To persons other than employees or security holders, if bids for or purchases of securities pursuant to the plan are effected solely by an agent independent of the issuer and the securities are from a source other than the issuer or an affiliated purchaser of the issuer.

(2) Bids for or purchases of any security made or effected by or for a plan shall be deemed to be a purchase by the issuer unless the bid is made, or the purchase is effected, by an agent independent of the issuer.

(d) Excepted Securities. The provisions of this section shall not apply to any of the following securities:

(1) Actively-traded reference securities. Reference securities with an ADTV value of at least $1 million that are issued by an issuer whose common equity securities have a public float value of at least $150 million; Provided, however, That such securities are not issued by the issuer, or any affiliate of the issuer, of the security in distribution.

(2) Investment grade nonconvertible and asset-backed securities. Nonconvertible debt securities, nonconvertible preferred securities, and asset-backed securities, that are rated by at least one nationally recognized statistical rating organization, as that term is used in § 240.15c3-1 of this chapter, in one of its generic rating categories that signifies investment grade; or

(3) Exempted securities. "Exempted securities" as defined in section 3(a)(12) of the Exchange Act (15 U.S.C. 78c(a)(12)); or

(4) Face-amount certificates or securities issued by an open-end management investment company or unit investment trust. Face-amount certificates issued by a face-amount certificate company, or redeemable securities issued by an open-end management investment company or a unit investment trust. Any terms used in this paragraph (d)(4) that are defined in the Investment Company Act of 1940 (15 U.S.C. 80a-1et seq.) shall have the meanings specified in such Act.

(e) Exemptive Authority. Upon written application or upon its own motion, the Commission may grant an exemption from the provisions of this section, either unconditionally or on specified terms and conditions, to any transaction or class of transactions, or to any security or class of securities.

Rule 103 — Nasdaq passive market making.

(a) Scope of section. This section permits broker-dealers to engage in market making transactions in covered securities that are Nasdaq securities without violating the provisions of § 242.101; Except That this section shall not apply to any security for which a stabilizing bid subject to § 242.104 is in effect, or during any at-the-market offering or best efforts offering.

(b) Conditions to be met -

(1) General limitations. A passive market maker must effect all transactions in the capacity of a registered market maker on Nasdaq. A passive market maker shall not bid for or purchase a covered security at a price that exceeds the highest independent bid for the covered security at the time of the transaction, except as permitted by paragraph (b)(3) of this section or required by a rule promulgated by the Commission or the NASD governing the handling of customer orders.

(2) Purchase limitation. On each day of the restricted period, a passive market maker's net purchases shall not exceed the greater of its 30% ADTV limitation or 200 shares (together, "purchase limitation"); Provided, however, That a passive market maker may purchase all of the securities that are part of a single order that, when executed, results in its purchase limitation being equalled or exceeded. If a passive market maker's net purchases equal or exceed its purchase limitation, it shall withdraw promptly its quotations from Nasdaq. If a passive market maker withdraws its quotations pursuant to this paragraph, it may not effect any bid or purchase in the covered security for the remainder of that day, irrespective of any later sales during that day, unless otherwise permitted by § 242.101.

(3) Requirement to lower the bid. If all independent bids for a covered security are reduced to a price below the passive market maker's bid, the passive market maker must lower its bid promptly to a level not higher than the then highest independent bid; Provided, however, That a passive market maker may continue to bid and effect purchases at its bid at a price exceeding the then highest independent bid until the passive market maker purchases an aggregate amount of the covered security that equals or, through the purchase of all securities that are part of a single order, exceeds the lesser of two times the minimum quotation size for the security, as determined by NASD rules, or the passive market maker's remaining purchasing capacity under paragraph (b)(2) of this section.

(4) Limitation on displayed size. At all times, the passive market maker's displayed bid size may not exceed the lesser of the minimum quotation size for the covered security, or the passive market maker's remaining purchasing capacity under paragraph (b)(2); Provided, however, That a passive market maker whose purchasing capacity at any time is between one and 99 shares may display a bid size of 100 shares.

(5) Identification of a passive market making bid. The bid displayed by a passive market maker shall be designated as such.

(6) Notification and reporting to the NASD. A passive market maker shall notify the NASD in advance of its intention to engage in passive market making, and shall submit to the NASD information regarding passive market making purchases, in such form as the NASD shall prescribe.

(7) Prospectus disclosure. The prospectus for any registered offering in which any passive market maker intends to effect transactions in any covered security shall contain the information required in §§ 228.502, 228.508, 229.502, and 229.508 of this chapter.

(c) Transactions at prices resulting from unlawful activity. No transaction shall be made at a price that the passive market maker knows or has reason to know is the result of activity that is fraudulent, manipulative, or deceptive under the securities laws, or any rule or regulation thereunder.

Rule 104 — Stabilizing and other activities in connection with an offering.

(a) Unlawful activity. It shall be unlawful for any person, directly or indirectly, to stabilize, to effect any syndicate covering transaction, or to impose a penalty bid, in connection with an offering of any security, in contravention of the provisions of this section. No stabilizing shall be effected at a price that the person stabilizing knows or has reason to know is in contravention of this section, or is the result of activity that is fraudulent, manipulative, or deceptive under the securities laws, or any rule or regulation thereunder.

(b) Purpose. Stabilizing is prohibited except for the purpose of preventing or retarding a decline in the market price of a security.

(c) Priority. To the extent permitted or required by the market where stabilizing occurs, any person stabilizing shall grant priority to any independent bid at the same price irrespective of the size of such independent bid at the time that it is entered.

(d) Control of stabilizing. No sole distributor or syndicate or group stabilizing the price of a security or any member or members of such syndicate or group shall maintain more than one stabilizing bid in any one market at the same price at the same time.

(e) At-the-market offerings. Stabilizing is prohibited in an at-the-market offering.

(f) Stabilizing levels -

(1) Maximum stabilizing bid. Notwithstanding the other provisions of this paragraph (f), no stabilizing shall be made at a price higher than the lower of the offering price or the stabilizing bid for the security in the principal market (or, if the principal market is closed, the stabilizing bid in the principal market at its previous close).

(2) Initiating stabilizing -

(i) Initiating stabilizing when the principal market is open. After the opening of quotations for the security in the principal market, stabilizing may be initiated in any market at a price no higher than the last independent transaction price for the security in the principal market if the security has traded in the principal market on the day stabilizing is initiated or on the most recent prior day of trading in the principal market and the current asked price in the principal market is equal to or greater than the last independent transaction price. If both conditions of the preceding sentence are not satisfied, stabilizing may be initiated in any market after the opening of quotations in the principal market at a price no higher than the highest current independent bid for the security in the principal market.

(ii) Initiating stabilizing when the principal market is closed.

(A) When the principal market for the security is closed, but immediately before the opening of quotations for the security in the market where stabilizing will be initiated, stabilizing may be initiated at a price no higher than the lower of:

(1) The price at which stabilizing could have been initiated in the principal market for the security at its previous close; or

(2) The most recent price at which an independent transaction in the security has been effected in any market since the close of the principal market, if the person stabilizing knows or has reason to know of such transaction.

(B) When the principal market for the security is closed, but after the opening of quotations in the market where stabilizing will be initiated, stabilizing may be initiated at a price no higher than the lower of:

(1) The price at which stabilization could have been initiated in the principal market for the security at its previous close; or

(2) The last independent transaction price for the security in that market if the security has traded in that market on the day stabilizing is initiated or on the last preceding business day and the current asked price in that market is equal to or greater than the last independent transaction price. If both conditions of the preceding sentence are not satisfied, under this paragraph (f)(2)(ii)(B)(2), stabilizing may be initiated at a price no higher than the highest current independent bid for the security in that market.

(iii) Initiating stabilizing when there is no market for the security or before the offering price is determined. If no bona fide market for the security being distributed exists at the time stabilizing is initiated, no stabilizing shall be initiated at a price in excess of the offering price. If stabilizing is initiated before the offering price is determined, then stabilizing may be continued after determination of the offering price at the price at which stabilizing then could be initiated.

(3) Maintaining or carrying over a stabilizing bid. A stabilizing bid initiated pursuant to paragraph (f)(2) of this section, which has not been discontinued, may be maintained, or carried over into another market, irrespective of changes in the independent bids or transaction prices for the security.

(4) Increasing or reducing a stabilizing bid. A stabilizing bid may be increased to a price no higher than the highest current independent bid for the security in the principal market if the principal market is open, or, if the principal market is closed, to a price no higher than the highest independent bid in the principal market at the previous close thereof. A stabilizing bid may be reduced, or carried over into another market at a reduced price, irrespective of changes in the independent bids or transaction prices for the security. If stabilizing is discontinued, it shall not be resumed at a price higher than the price at which stabilizing then could be initiated.

(5) Initiating, maintaining, or adjusting a stabilizing bid to reflect the current exchange rate. If a stabilizing bid is expressed in a currency other than the currency of the principal market for the security, such bid may be initiated, maintained, or adjusted to reflect the current exchange rate, consistent with the provisions of this section. If, in initiating, maintaining, or adjusting a stabilizing bid pursuant to this paragraph (f)(5), the bid would be at or below the midpoint between two trading differentials, such stabilizing bid shall be adjusted downward to the lower differential.

(6) Adjustments to stabilizing bid. If a security goes ex-dividend, ex-rights, or ex-distribution, the stabilizing bid shall be reduced by an amount equal to the value of the dividend, right, or distribution. If, in reducing a stabilizing bid pursuant to this paragraph (f)(6), the bid would be at or below the midpoint between two trading differentials, such stabilizing bid shall be adjusted downward to the lower differential.

(7) Stabilizing of components. When two or more securities are being offered as a unit, the component securities shall not be stabilized at prices the sum of which exceeds the then permissible stabilizing price for the unit.

(8) Special prices. Any stabilizing price that otherwise meets the requirements of this section need not be adjusted to reflect special prices available to any group or class of persons (including employees or holders of warrants or rights).

(g) Offerings with no U.S. stabilizing activities.
  (1) Stabilizing to facilitate an offering of a security in the United States shall not be deemed to be in violation of this section if all of the following conditions are satisfied:
    (i) No stabilizing is made in the United States;
    (ii) Stabilizing outside the United States is made in a jurisdiction with statutory or regulatory provisions governing stabilizing that are comparable to the provisions of this section; and
    (iii) No stabilizing is made at a price above the offering price in the United States, except as permitted by paragraph (f)(5) of this section.
  (2) For purposes of this paragraph (g), the Commission by rule, regulation, or order may determine whether a foreign statute or regulation is comparable to this section considering, among other things, whether such foreign statute or regulation: specifies appropriate purposes for which stabilizing is permitted; provides for disclosure and control of stabilizing activities; places limitations on stabilizing levels; requires appropriate recordkeeping; provides other protections comparable to the provisions of this section; and whether procedures exist to enable the Commission to obtain information concerning any foreign stabilizing transactions.
(h) Disclosure and notification.
  (1) Any person displaying or transmitting a bid that such person knows is for the purpose of stabilizing shall provide prior notice to the market on which such stabilizing will be effected, and shall disclose its purpose to the person with whom the bid is entered.
  (2) Any person effecting a syndicate covering transaction or imposing a penalty bid shall provide prior notice to the self-regulatory organization with direct authority over the principal market in the United States for the security for which the syndicate covering transaction is effected or the penalty bid is imposed.
  (3) Any person subject to this section who sells to, or purchases for the account of, any person any security where the price of such security may be or has been stabilized, shall send to the purchaser at or before the completion of the transaction, a prospectus, offering circular, confirmation, or other document containing a statement similar to that comprising the statement provided for in Item 502(d) of Regulation S-B (§ 228.502(d) of this chapter) or Item 502(d) of Regulation S-K (§ 229.502(d) of this chapter).
(i) Recordkeeping requirements. A person subject to this section shall keep the information and make the notification required by § 240.17a-2 of this chapter.
(j) Excepted securities. The provisions of this section shall not apply to:
  (1) Exempted securities. "Exempted securities," as defined in section 3(a)(12) of the Exchange Act (15 U.S.C. 78c(a)(12)); or
  (2) Transactions of Rule 144A securities. Transactions in securities eligible for resale under § 230.144A(d)(3) of this chapter, if such securities are sold in the United States solely to:
    (i) Qualified institutional buyers, as defined in § 230.144A(a)(1) of this chapter, or to purchasers that the seller and any person acting on behalf of the seller reasonably believes are qualified institutional buyers, in a transaction exempt from registration under section 4(2) of the Securities Act (15 U.S.C. 77d(2)) or §§ 230.144A or § 230.500 et seq of this chapter; or
    (ii) Persons not deemed to be "U.S. persons" for purposes of §§ 230.902(o)(2) or 230.902(o)(7) of this chapter, during a distribution qualifying under paragraph (j)(2)(i) of this section.
(k) Exemptive authority. Upon written application or upon its own motion, the Commission may grant an exemption from the provisions of this section, either unconditionally or on specified terms and conditions, to any transaction or class of transactions, or to any security or class of securities.

Rule 105 — Short selling in connection with a public offering.
(a) Unlawful activity. In connection with an offering of equity securities for cash pursuant to a registration statement or a notification on Form 1-A (§ 239.90 of this chapter) or Form 1-E (§ 239.200 of this chapter) filed under the Securities Act of 1933 ("offered securities"), it shall be unlawful for any person to sell short (as defined in § 242.200(a)) the security that is the subject of the offering and purchase the offered securities from

an underwriter or broker or dealer participating in the offering if such short sale was effected during the period ("Rule 105 restricted period") that is the shorter of the period:

(1) Beginning five business days before the pricing of the offered securities and ending with such pricing; or

(2) Beginning with the initial filing of such registration statement or notification on Form 1-A or Form 1-E and ending with the pricing.

(b) Excepted activity -

(1) Bona fide purchase. It shall not be prohibited for such person to purchase the offered securities as provided in paragraph (a) of this section if:

(i) Such person makes a bona fide purchase(s) of the security that is the subject of the offering that is:

(A) At least equivalent in quantity to the entire amount of Rule 105 restricted period short sale(s);

(B) Effected during regular trading hours;

(C) Reported to an "effective transaction reporting plan" (as defined in § 242.600(b)(23)); and

(D) Effected after the last Rule 105 restricted period short sale, and no later than the business day prior to the day of pricing; and

(ii) Such person did not effect a short sale, that is reported to an effective transaction reporting plan, within the 30 minutes prior to the close of regular trading hours (as defined in § 242.600(b)(68)) on the business day prior to the day of pricing.

(2) Separate accounts. Paragraph (a) of this section shall not prohibit the purchase of the offered security in an account of a person where such person sold short during the Rule 105 restricted period in a separate account, if decisions regarding securities transactions for each account are made separately and without coordination of trading or cooperation among or between the accounts.

(3) Investment companies. Paragraph (a) of this section shall not prohibit an investment company (as defined by Section 3 of the Investment Company Act) that is registered under Section 8 of the Investment Company Act, or a series of such company (investment company) from purchasing an offered security where any of the following sold the offered security short during the Rule 105 restricted period:

(i) An affiliated investment company, or any series of such a company; or

(ii) A separate series of the investment company.

(c) Excepted offerings. This section shall not apply to offerings that are not conducted on a firm commitment basis.

(d) Exemptive authority. Upon written application or upon its own motion, the Commission may grant an exemption from the provisions of this section, either unconditionally or on specified terms and conditions, to any transaction or class of transactions, or to any security or class of securities.

---

49. SEC Rules and Regulations: Regulation S-P – Privacy of Consumer Financial Information and Safeguarding Personal Information

(a) Purpose. This subpart governs the treatment of nonpublic personal information about consumers by the financial institutions listed in paragraph (b) of this section. This subpart:

(1) Requires a financial institution to provide notice to customers about its privacy policies and practices;

(2) Describes the conditions under which a financial institution may disclose nonpublic personal information about consumers to nonaffiliated third parties; and

(3) Provides a method for consumers to prevent a financial institution from disclosing that information to most nonaffiliated third parties by "opting out" of that disclosure, subject to the exceptions in §§ 248.13, 248.14, and 248.15.

(b) Scope. Except with respect to § 248.30(b), this subpart applies only to nonpublic personal information about individuals who obtain financial products or services primarily for personal, family, or household purposes from the institutions listed below. This subpart does not apply to information about companies or about individuals who obtain financial products or services primarily for business, commercial, or agricultural purposes. This part applies to brokers, dealers, and investment companies, as well as to investment advisers that are registered with the Commission. It also applies to foreign (non-resident) brokers, dealers, investment companies and investment advisers that are registered with the Commission. These entities are referred to in this subpart as "you." This subpart does not apply to foreign (non-resident) brokers, dealers, investment companies and investment advisers that are not registered with the Commission. Nothing in this subpart modifies, limits, or supersedes the standards governing individually identifiable health information promulgated by the Secretary of Health and Human Services under the authority of sections 262 and 264 of the Health Insurance Portability and Accountability Act of 1996 (42 U.S.C. 1320d-1320d-8).

---

50. SEC Rules and Regulations, Securities Exchange Act of 1934: Section 10 – Regulation of the Use of Manipulative and Deceptive Devices

It shall be unlawful for any person, directly or indirectly, by the use of any means or instrumentality of interstate commerce or of the mails, or of any facility of any national securities exchange—

(a)(1) To effect a short sale, or to use or employ any stop-loss order in connection with the purchase or sale, of any security other than a government security, in contravention of such rules and regulations as the Commission may prescribe as necessary or appropriate in the public interest or for the protection of investors.

(2) Paragraph (1) of this subsection shall not apply to security futures products.

(b) To use or employ, in connection with the purchase or sale of any security registered on a national securities exchange or any security not so registered, or any securities-based swap agreement [1] any manipulative or deceptive device or contrivance in contravention of such rules and regulations as the Commission may prescribe as necessary or appropriate in the public interest or for the protection of investors.

(c)(1) To effect, accept, or facilitate a transaction involving the loan or borrowing of securities in contravention of such rules and regulations as the Commission may prescribe as necessary or appropriate in the public interest or for the protection of investors.

(2) Nothing in paragraph (1) may be construed to limit the authority of the appropriate Federal banking agency (as defined in section 1813(q) of title 12), the National Credit Union Administration, or any other Federal department or agency having a responsibility under Federal law to prescribe rules or regulations restricting transactions involving the loan or borrowing of securities in order to protect the safety and soundness of a financial institution or to protect the financial system from systemic risk.

Rules promulgated under subsection (b) that prohibit fraud, manipulation, or insider trading (but not rules imposing or specifying reporting or recordkeeping requirements, procedures, or standards as prophylactic measures against fraud, manipulation, or insider trading), and judicial precedents decided under subsection (b) and rules promulgated thereunder that prohibit fraud, manipulation, or insider trading, shall apply to security-based swap agreements to the same extent as they apply to securities. Judicial precedents decided under section 77q(a) of this title and sections 78i, 78o, 78p, 78t, and 78u–1 of this title, and judicial precedents decided under applicable rules promulgated under such sections, shall apply to security-based swap agreements to the same extent as they apply to securities.

---

51. SEC Rules and Regulations, Securities Exchange Act of 1934: Section 11(d) – Trading by Members of Exchanges, Brokers and Dealers – "Prohibition on Extension of Credit by Broker-Dealer"

(a) Trading for own account or account of associated person; exceptions

   (1) It shall be unlawful for any member of a national securities exchange to effect any transaction on such exchange for its own account, the account of an associated person, or an account with respect to which it or an associated person thereof exercises investment discretion: Provided, however, That this paragraph shall not make unlawful—

      (A) any transaction by a dealer acting in the capacity of market maker;

      (B) any transaction for the account of an odd-lot dealer in a security in which he is so registered;

      (C) any stabilizing transaction effected in compliance with rules under section 78j(b) of this title to facilitate a distribution of a security in which the member effecting such transaction is participating;

      (D) any bona fide arbitrage transaction, any bona fide hedge transaction involving a long or short position in an equity security and a long or short position in a security entitling the holder to acquire or sell such equity security, or any risk arbitrage transaction in connection with a merger, acquisition, tender offer, or similar transaction involving a recapitalization;

      (E) any transaction for the account of a natural person, the estate of a natural person, or a trust created by a natural person for himself or another natural person;

      (F) any transaction to offset a transaction made in error;

      (G) any other transaction for a member's own account provided that (i) such member is primarily engaged in the business of underwriting and distributing securities issued by other persons, selling securities to customers, and acting as broker, or any one or more of such activities, and whose gross income normally is derived principally from such business and related activities and (ii) such transaction is effected in compliance with rules of the Commission which, as a minimum, assure that the transaction is not inconsistent with the maintenance of fair and orderly markets and yields priority, parity, and precedence in execution to orders for the account of persons who are not members or associated with members of the exchange;

      (H) any transaction for an account with respect to which such member or an associated person thereof exercises investment discretion if such member—

        (i) has obtained, from the person or persons authorized to transact business for the account, express authorization for such member or associated person to effect such transactions prior to engaging in the practice of effecting such transactions;

        (ii) furnishes the person or persons authorized to transact business for the account with a statement at least annually disclosing the aggregate compensation received by the exchange member in effecting such transactions; and

        (iii) complies with any rules the Commission has prescribed with respect to the requirements of clauses (i) and (ii); and

      (I) any other transaction of a kind which the Commission, by rule, determines is consistent with the purposes of this paragraph, the protection of investors, and the maintenance of fair and orderly markets.

   (2) The Commission, by rule, as it deems necessary or appropriate in the public interest and for the protection of investors, to maintain fair and orderly markets, or to assure equal regulation of exchange markets and markets occurring otherwise than on an exchange, may regulate or prohibit:

      (A) transactions on a national securities exchange not unlawful under paragraph (1) of this subsection effected by any member thereof for its own account (unless such member is acting in the capacity of market maker or odd-lot dealer), the account of an associated person, or an account with respect to which such member or an associated person thereof exercises investment discretion;

      (B) transactions otherwise than on a national securities exchange effected by use of the mails or any means or instrumentality of interstate commerce by any member of a national securities exchange, broker, or dealer for the account of such member, broker, or dealer (unless such member, broker, or dealer is acting in the capacity of a market maker) [1] the account of an associated person, or an account with respect to which such member, broker, or dealer or associated person thereof exercises investment discretion; and

   (C) transactions on a national securities exchange effected by any broker or dealer not a member thereof for the account of such broker or dealer (unless such broker or dealer is acting in the capacity of market maker), the account of an associated person, or an account with respect to which such broker or dealer or associated person thereof exercises investment discretion.

  (3) The provisions of paragraph (1) of this subsection insofar as they apply to transactions on a national securities exchange effected by a member thereof who was a member on February 1, 1978 shall not become effective until February 1, 1979. Nothing in this paragraph shall be construed to impair or limit the authority of the Commission to regulate or prohibit such transactions prior to February 1, 1979, pursuant to paragraph (2) of this subsection.

(b) Registration of members as odd-lot dealers and specialists

When not in contravention of such rules and regulations as the Commission may prescribe as necessary or appropriate in the public interest and for the protection of investors, to maintain fair and orderly markets, or to remove impediments to and perfect the mechanism of a national market system, the rules of a national securities exchange may permit (1) a member to be registered as an odd-lot dealer and as such to buy and sell for his own account so far as may be reasonably necessary to carry on such odd-lot transactions, and (2) a member to be registered as a specialist. Under the rules and regulations of the Commission a specialist may be permitted to act as a broker and dealer or limited to acting as a broker or dealer. It shall be unlawful for a specialist or an official of the exchange to disclose information in regard to orders placed with such specialist which is not available to all members of the exchange, to any person other than an official of the exchange, a representative of the Commission, or a specialist who may be acting for such specialist: Provided, however, That the Commission, by rule, may require disclosure to all members of the exchange of all orders placed with specialists, under such rules and regulations as the Commission may prescribe as necessary or appropriate in the public interest or for the protection of investors. It shall also be unlawful for a specialist permitted to act as a broker and dealer to effect on the exchange as broker any transaction except upon a market or limited price order.

(c) Exemptions from provisions of section and rules and regulations

If because of the limited volume of transactions effected on an exchange, it is in the opinion of the Commission impracticable and not necessary or appropriate in the public interest or for the protection of investors to apply any of the foregoing provisions of this section or the rules and regulations thereunder, the Commission shall have power, upon application of the exchange and on a showing that the rules of such exchange are otherwise adequate for the protection of investors, to exempt such exchange and its members from any such provision or rules and regulations.

(d) Prohibition on extension of credit by broker-dealer

It shall be unlawful for a member of a national securities exchange who is both a dealer and a broker, or for any person who both as a broker and a dealer transacts a business in securities through the medium of a member or otherwise, to effect through the use of any facility of a national securities exchange or of the mails or of any means or instrumentality of interstate commerce, or otherwise in the case of a member, (1) any transaction in connection with which, directly or indirectly, he extends or maintains or arranges for the extension or maintenance of credit to or for a customer on any security (other than an exempted security) which was a part of a new issue in the distribution of which he participated as a member of a selling syndicate or group within thirty days prior to such transaction: Provided, That credit shall not be deemed extended by reason of a bona fide delayed delivery of (i) any such security against full payment of the entire purchase price thereof upon such delivery within thirty-five days after such purchase or (ii) any mortgage related security or any small business related security against full payment of the entire purchase price thereof upon such delivery within one hundred and eighty days after such purchase, or within such shorter period as the Commission may prescribe by rule or regulation, or (2) any transaction with respect to any security (other than an exempted security) unless, if the transaction is with a customer, he discloses to such customer in writing at or before the completion of the transaction whether he is acting as a dealer for his own account, as a broker for such customer, or as a broker for some other person.

---

52. SEC Rules and Regulations, Securities Exchange Act of 1934: Section 14 – Proxies

(a) Solicitation of proxies in violation of rules and regulations
  (1) It shall be unlawful for any person, by the use of the mails or by any means or instrumentality of interstate commerce or of any facility of a national securities exchange or otherwise, in contravention of such rules and regulations as the Commission may prescribe as necessary or appropriate in the public interest or for the protection of investors, to solicit or to permit the use of his name to solicit any proxy or consent or authorization in respect of any security (other than an exempted security) registered pursuant to section 78l of this title.
  (2) The rules and regulations prescribed by the Commission under paragraph (1) may include—
    (A) a requirement that a solicitation of proxy, consent, or authorization by (or on behalf of) an issuer include a nominee submitted by a shareholder to serve on the board of directors of the issuer; and
    (B) a requirement that an issuer follow a certain procedure in relation to a solicitation described in subparagraph (A).
(b) Giving or refraining from giving proxy in respect of any security carried for account of customer
  (1) It shall be unlawful for any member of a national securities exchange, or any broker or dealer registered under this chapter, or any bank, association, or other entity that exercises fiduciary powers, in contravention of such rules and regulations as the Commission may prescribe as necessary or appropriate in the public interest or for the protection of investors, to give, or to refrain from giving a proxy, consent, authorization, or information statement in respect of any security registered pursuant to section 78l of this title, or any security issued by an investment company registered under the Investment Company Act of 1940 [15 U.S.C. 80a–1 et seq.], and carried for the account of a customer.
  (2) With respect to banks, the rules and regulations prescribed by the Commission under paragraph (1) shall not require the disclosure of the names of beneficial owners of securities in an account held by the bank on December 28, 1985, unless the beneficial owner consents to the disclosure. The provisions of this paragraph shall not apply in the case of a bank which the Commission finds has not made a good faith effort to obtain such consent from such beneficial owners.
(c) Information to holders of record prior to annual or other meeting
  Unless proxies, consents, or authorizations in respect of a security registered pursuant to section 78l of this title, or a security issued by an investment company registered under the Investment Company Act of 1940 [15 U.S.C. 80a–1 et seq.], are solicited by or on behalf of the management of the issuer from the holders of record of such security in accordance with the rules and regulations prescribed under subsection (a) of this section, prior to any annual or other meeting of the holders of such security, such issuer shall, in accordance with rules and regulations prescribed by the Commission, file with the Commission and transmit to all holders of record of such security information substantially equivalent to the information which would be required to be transmitted if a solicitation were made, but no information shall be required to be filed or transmitted pursuant to this subsection before July 1, 1964.

(d) Tender offer by owner of more than five per centum of class of securities; exceptions

(1) It shall be unlawful for any person, directly or indirectly, by use of the mails or by any means or instrumentality of interstate commerce or of any facility of a national securities exchange or otherwise, to make a tender offer for, or a request or invitation for tenders of, any class of any equity security which is registered pursuant to section 78l of this title, or any equity security of an insurance company which would have been required to be so registered except for the exemption contained in section 78l(g)(2)(G) of this title, or any equity security issued by a closed-end investment company registered under the Investment Company Act of 1940 [15 U.S.C. 80a–1 et seq.], if, after consummation thereof, such person would, directly or indirectly, be the beneficial owner of more than 5 per centum of such class, unless at the time copies of the offer or request or invitation are first published or sent or given to security holders such person has filed with the Commission a statement containing such of the information specified in section 78m(d) of this title, and such additional information as the Commission may by rules and regulations prescribe as necessary or appropriate in the public interest or for the protection of investors. All requests or invitations for tenders or advertisements making a tender offer or requesting or inviting tenders of such a security shall be filed as a part of such statement and shall contain such of the information contained in such statement as the Commission may by rules and regulations prescribe. Copies of any additional material soliciting or requesting such tender offers subsequent to the initial solicitation or request shall contain such information as the Commission may by rules and regulations prescribe as necessary or appropriate in the public interest or for the protection of investors, and shall be filed with the Commission not later than the time copies of such material are first published or sent or given to security holders. Copies of all statements, in the form in which such material is furnished to security holders and the Commission, shall be sent to the issuer not later than the date such material is first published or sent or given to any security holders.

(2) When two or more persons act as a partnership, limited partnership, syndicate, or other group for the purpose of acquiring, holding, or disposing of securities of an issuer, such syndicate or group shall be deemed a "person" for purposes of this subsection.

(3) In determining, for purposes of this subsection, any percentage of a class of any security, such class shall be deemed to consist of the amount of the outstanding securities of such class, exclusive of any securities of such class held by or for the account of the issuer or a subsidiary of the issuer.

(4) Any solicitation or recommendation to the holders of such a security to accept or reject a tender offer or request or invitation for tenders shall be made in accordance with such rules and regulations as the Commission may prescribe as necessary or appropriate in the public interest or for the protection of investors.

(5) Securities deposited pursuant to a tender offer or request or invitation for tenders may be withdrawn by or on behalf of the depositor at any time until the expiration of seven days after the time definitive copies of the offer or request or invitation are first published or sent or given to security holders, and at any time after sixty days from the date of the original tender offer or request or invitation, except as the Commission may otherwise prescribe by rules, regulations, or order as necessary or appropriate in the public interest or for the protection of investors.

(6) Where any person makes a tender offer, or request or invitation for tenders, for less than all the outstanding equity securities of a class, and where a greater number of securities is deposited pursuant thereto within ten days after copies of the offer or request or invitation are first published or sent or given to security holders than such person is bound or willing to take up and pay for, the securities taken up shall be taken up as nearly as may be pro rata, disregarding fractions, according to the number of securities deposited by each depositor. The provisions of this subsection shall also apply to securities deposited within ten days after notice of an increase in the consideration offered to security holders, as described in paragraph (7), is first published or sent or given to security holders.

(7) Where any person varies the terms of a tender offer or request or invitation for tenders before the expiration thereof by increasing the consideration offered to holders of such securities, such person shall pay

the increased consideration to each security holder whose securities are taken up and paid for pursuant to the tender offer or request or invitation for tenders whether or not such securities have been taken up by such person before the variation of the tender offer or request or invitation.

(8) The provisions of this subsection shall not apply to any offer for, or request or invitation for tenders of, any security—

    (A) if the acquisition of such security, together with all other acquisitions by the same person of securities of the same class during the preceding twelve months, would not exceed 2 per centum of that class;

    (B) by the issuer of such security; or

    (C) which the Commission, by rules or regulations or by order, shall exempt from the provisions of this subsection as not entered into for the purpose of, and not having the effect of, changing or influencing the control of the issuer or otherwise as not comprehended within the purposes of this subsection.

(e) Untrue statement of material fact or omission of fact with respect to tender offer

It shall be unlawful for any person to make any untrue statement of a material fact or omit to state any material fact necessary in order to make the statements made, in the light of the circumstances under which they are made, not misleading, or to engage in any fraudulent, deceptive, or manipulative acts or practices, in connection with any tender offer or request or invitation for tenders, or any solicitation of security holders in opposition to or in favor of any such offer, request, or invitation. The Commission shall, for the purposes of this subsection, by rules and regulations define, and prescribe means reasonably designed to prevent, such acts and practices as are fraudulent, deceptive, or manipulative.

(f) Election or designation of majority of directors of issuer by owner of more than five per centum of class of securities at other than meeting of security holders

If, pursuant to any arrangement or understanding with the person or persons acquiring securities in a transaction subject to subsection (d) of this section or subsection (d) of section 78m of this title, any persons are to be elected or designated as directors of the issuer, otherwise than at a meeting of security holders, and the persons so elected or designated will constitute a majority of the directors of the issuer, then, prior to the time any such person takes office as a director, and in accordance with rules and regulations prescribed by the Commission, the issuer shall file with the Commission, and transmit to all holders of record of securities of the issuer who would be entitled to vote at a meeting for election of directors, information substantially equivalent to the information which would be required by subsection (a) or (c) of this section to be transmitted if such person or persons were nominees for election as directors at a meeting of such security holders.

(g) Filing fees

  (1)

    (A) At the time of filing such preliminary proxy solicitation material as the Commission may require by rule pursuant to subsection (a) of this section that concerns an acquisition, merger, consolidation, or proposed sale or other disposition of substantially all the assets of a company, the person making such filing, other than a company registered under the Investment Company Act of 1940 [15 U.S.C. 80a–1 et seq.], shall pay to the Commission the following fees:

      (i) for preliminary proxy solicitation material involving an acquisition, merger, or consolidation, if there is a proposed payment of cash or transfer of securities or property to shareholders, a fee at a rate that, subject to paragraph (4), is equal to $92 [1] per $1,000,000 of such proposed payment, or of the value of such securities or other property proposed to be transferred; and

      (ii) for preliminary proxy solicitation material involving a proposed sale or other disposition of substantially all of the assets of a company, a fee at a rate that, subject to paragraph (4), is equal to $92 1 per $1,000,000 of the cash or of the value of any securities or other property proposed to be received upon such sale or disposition.

(B) The fee imposed under subparagraph (A) shall be reduced with respect to securities in an amount equal to any fee paid to the Commission with respect to such securities in connection with the proposed transaction under section 77f(b) of this title, or the fee paid under that section shall be reduced in an amount equal to the fee paid to the Commission in connection with such transaction under this subsection. Where two or more companies involved in an acquisition, merger, consolidation, sale, or other disposition of substantially all the assets of a company must file such proxy material with the Commission, each shall pay a proportionate share of such fee.

(2) At the time of filing such preliminary information statement as the Commission may require by rule pursuant to subsection (c) of this section, the issuer shall pay to the Commission the same fee as required for preliminary proxy solicitation material under paragraph (1) of this subsection.

(3) At the time of filing such statement as the Commission may require by rule pursuant to subsection (d)(1) of this section, the person making the filing shall pay to the Commission a fee at a rate that, subject to paragraph (4), is equal to $92 1 per $1,000,000 of the aggregate amount of cash or of the value of securities or other property proposed to be offered. The fee shall be reduced with respect to securities in an amount equal to any fee paid with respect to such securities in connection with the proposed transaction under section 6(b) of the Securities Act of 1933 (15 U.S.C. 77f(b)), or the fee paid under that section shall be reduced in an amount equal to the fee paid to the Commission in connection with such transaction under this subsection.

(4) Annual adjustment.— For each fiscal year, the Commission shall by order adjust the rate required by paragraphs (1) and (3) for such fiscal year to a rate that is equal to the rate (expressed in dollars per million) that is applicable under section 6(b) of the Securities Act of 1933 (15 U.S.C. 77f(b)) for such fiscal year.

(5) Fee collection.— Fees collected pursuant to this subsection for fiscal year 2012 and each fiscal year thereafter shall be deposited and credited as general revenue of the Treasury and shall not be available for obligation.

(6) Review; effective date; publication.— In exercising its authority under this subsection, the Commission shall not be required to comply with the provisions of section 553 of title 5. An adjusted rate prescribed under paragraph (4) shall be published and take effect in accordance with section 6(b) of the Securities Act of 1933 (15 U.S.C. 77f(b)).

(7) Pro rata application.— The rates per $1,000,000 required by this subsection shall be applied pro rata to amounts and balances of less than $1,000,000.

(8) Notwithstanding any other provision of law, the Commission may impose fees, charges, or prices for matters not involving any acquisition, merger, consolidation, sale, or other disposition of assets described in this subsection, as authorized by section 9701 of title 31, or otherwise.

(h) Proxy solicitations and tender offers in connection with limited partnership rollup transactions

(1) Proxy rules to contain special provisions.

It shall be unlawful for any person to solicit any proxy, consent, or authorization concerning a limited partnership rollup transaction, or to make any tender offer in furtherance of a limited partnership rollup transaction, unless such transaction is conducted in accordance with rules prescribed by the Commission under subsections (a) and (d) as required by this subsection. Such rules shall—

(A) permit any holder of a security that is the subject of the proposed limited partnership rollup transaction to engage in preliminary communications for the purpose of determining whether to solicit proxies, consents, or authorizations in opposition to the proposed limited partnership rollup transaction, without regard to whether any such communication would otherwise be considered a solicitation of proxies, and without being required to file soliciting material with the Commission prior to making that determination, except that—

(i) nothing in this subparagraph shall be construed to limit the application of any provision of this chapter prohibiting, or reasonably designed to prevent, fraudulent, deceptive, or manipulative acts or practices under this chapter; and

(ii) any holder of not less than 5 percent of the outstanding securities that are the subject of the proposed limited partnership rollup transaction who engages in the business of buying and selling limited partnership interests in the secondary market shall be required to disclose such ownership interests and any potential conflicts of interests in such preliminary communications;

(B) require the issuer to provide to holders of the securities that are the subject of the limited partnership rollup transaction such list of the holders of the issuer's securities as the Commission may determine in such form and subject to such terms and conditions as the Commission may specify;

(C) prohibit compensating any person soliciting proxies, consents, or authorizations directly from security holders concerning such a limited partnership rollup transaction—

(i) on the basis of whether the solicited proxy, consent, or authorization either approves or disapproves the proposed limited partnership rollup transaction; or

(ii) contingent on the approval, disapproval, or completion of the limited partnership rollup transaction;

(D) set forth disclosure requirements for soliciting material distributed in connection with a limited partnership rollup transaction, including requirements for clear, concise, and comprehensible disclosure with respect to—

(i) any changes in the business plan, voting rights, form of ownership interest, or the compensation of the general partner in the proposed limited partnership rollup transaction from each of the original limited partnerships;

(ii) the conflicts of interest, if any, of the general partner;

(iii) whether it is expected that there will be a significant difference between the exchange values of the limited partnerships and the trading price of the securities to be issued in the limited partnership rollup transaction;

(iv) the valuation of the limited partnerships and the method used to determine the value of the interests of the limited partners to be exchanged for the securities in the limited partnership rollup transaction;

(v) the differing risks and effects of the limited partnership rollup transaction for investors in different limited partnerships proposed to be included, and the risks and effects of completing the limited partnership rollup transaction with less than all limited partnerships;

(vi) the statement by the general partner required under subparagraph (E);

(vii) such other matters deemed necessary or appropriate by the Commission;

(E) require a statement by the general partner as to whether the proposed limited partnership rollup transaction is fair or unfair to investors in each limited partnership, a discussion of the basis for that conclusion, and an evaluation and a description by the general partner of alternatives to the limited partnership rollup transaction, such as liquidation;

(F) provide that, if the general partner or sponsor has obtained any opinion (other than an opinion of counsel), appraisal, or report that is prepared by an outside party and that is materially related to the limited partnership rollup transaction, such soliciting materials shall contain or be accompanied by clear, concise, and comprehensible disclosure with respect to—

(i) the analysis of the transaction, scope of review, preparation of the opinion, and basis for and methods of arriving at conclusions, and any representations and undertakings with respect thereto;

(ii) the identity and qualifications of the person who prepared the opinion, the method of selection of such person, and any material past, existing, or contemplated relationships between the person or any of its affiliates and the general partner, sponsor, successor, or any other affiliate;

(iii) any compensation of the preparer of such opinion, appraisal, or report that is contingent on the transaction's approval or completion; and

(iv) any limitations imposed by the issuer on the access afforded to such preparer to the issuer's personnel, premises, and relevant books and records;

(G) provide that, if the general partner or sponsor has obtained any opinion, appraisal, or report as described in subparagraph (F) from any person whose compensation is contingent on the transaction's approval or completion or who has not been given access by the issuer to its personnel and premises and relevant books and records, the general partner or sponsor shall state the reasons therefor;

(H) provide that, if the general partner or sponsor has not obtained any opinion on the fairness of the proposed limited partnership rollup transaction to investors in each of the affected partnerships, such soliciting materials shall contain or be accompanied by a statement of such partner's or sponsor's reasons for concluding that such an opinion is not necessary in order to permit the limited partners to make an informed decision on the proposed transaction;

(I) require that the soliciting material include a clear, concise, and comprehensible summary of the limited partnership rollup transaction (including a summary of the matters referred to in clauses (i) through (vii) of subparagraph (D) and a summary of the matter referred to in subparagraphs (F), (G), and (H)), with the risks of the limited partnership rollup transaction set forth prominently in the fore part thereof;

(J) provide that any solicitation or offering period with respect to any proxy solicitation, tender offer, or information statement in a limited partnership rollup transaction shall be for not less than the lesser of 60 calendar days or the maximum number of days permitted under applicable State law; and

(K) contain such other provisions as the Commission determines to be necessary or appropriate for the protection of investors in limited partnership rollup transactions.

(2) Exemptions

The Commission may, consistent with the public interest, the protection of investors, and the purposes of this chapter, exempt by rule or order any security or class of securities, any transaction or class of transactions, or any person or class of persons, in whole or in part, conditionally or unconditionally, from the requirements imposed pursuant to paragraph (1) or from the definition contained in paragraph (4).

(3) Effect on Commission authority

Nothing in this subsection limits the authority of the Commission under subsection (a) or (d) or any other provision of this chapter or precludes the Commission from imposing, under subsection (a) or (d) or any other provision of this chapter, a remedy or procedure required to be imposed under this subsection.

(4) "Limited partnership rollup transaction" defined.

Except as provided in paragraph (5), as used in this subsection, the term "limited partnership rollup transaction" means a transaction involving the combination or reorganization of one or more limited partnerships, directly or indirectly, in which—

(A) some or all of the investors in any of such limited partnerships will receive new securities, or securities in another entity, that will be reported under a transaction reporting plan declared effective before December 17, 1993, by the Commission under section 78k–1 of this title;

(B) any of the investors' limited partnership securities are not, as of the date of filing, reported under a transaction reporting plan declared effective before December 17, 1993, by the Commission under section 78k–1 of this title;

(C) investors in any of the limited partnerships involved in the transaction are subject to a significant adverse change with respect to voting rights, the term of existence of the entity, management compensation, or investment objectives; and

(D) any of such investors are not provided an option to receive or retain a security under substantially the same terms and conditions as the original issue.

(5) Exclusions from definition.

Notwithstanding paragraph (4), the term "limited partnership rollup transaction" does not include—

(A) a transaction that involves only a limited partnership or partnerships having an operating policy or practice of retaining cash available for distribution and reinvesting proceeds from the sale, financing, or refinancing of assets in accordance with such criteria as the Commission determines appropriate;

(B) a transaction involving only limited partnerships wherein the interests of the limited partners are repurchased, recalled, or exchanged in accordance with the terms of the preexisting limited partnership agreements for securities in an operating company specifically identified at the time of the formation of the original limited partnership;

(C) a transaction in which the securities to be issued or exchanged are not required to be and are not registered under the Securities Act of 1933 [15 U.S.C. 77a et seq.];

(D) a transaction that involves only issuers that are not required to register or report under section 78l of this title, both before and after the transaction;

(E) a transaction, except as the Commission may otherwise provide by rule for the protection of investors, involving the combination or reorganization of one or more limited partnerships in which a non-affiliated party succeeds to the interests of a general partner or sponsor, if—

    (i) such action is approved by not less than 66⅔ percent of the outstanding units of each of the participating limited partnerships; and

    (ii) as a result of the transaction, the existing general partners will receive only compensation to which they are entitled as expressly provided for in the preexisting limited partnership agreements; or

(F) a transaction, except as the Commission may otherwise provide by rule for the protection of investors, in which the securities offered to investors are securities of another entity that are reported under a transaction reporting plan declared effective before December 17, 1993, by the Commission under section 78k–1 of this title, if—

    (i) such other entity was formed, and such class of securities was reported and regularly traded, not less than 12 months before the date on which soliciting material is mailed to investors; and

    (ii) the securities of that entity issued to investors in the transaction do not exceed 20 percent of the total outstanding securities of the entity, exclusive of any securities of such class held by or for the account of the entity or a subsidiary of the entity.

(i) Disclosure of pay versus performance

The Commission shall, by rule, require each issuer to disclose in any proxy or consent solicitation material for an annual meeting of the shareholders of the issuer a clear description of any compensation required to be disclosed by the issuer under section 229.402 of title 17, Code of Federal Regulations (or any successor thereto), including, for any issuer other than an emerging growth company, information that shows the relationship between executive compensation actually paid and the financial performance of the issuer, taking into account any change in the value of the shares of stock and dividends of the issuer and any distributions. The disclosure under this subsection may include a graphic representation of the information required to be disclosed.

(j) Disclosure of hedging by employees and directors.

The Commission shall, by rule, require each issuer to disclose in any proxy or consent solicitation material for an annual meeting of the shareholders of the issuer whether any employee or member of the board of directors of the issuer, or any designee of such employee or member, is permitted to purchase financial instruments (including prepaid variable forward contracts, equity swaps, collars, and exchange funds) that are designed to hedge or offset any decrease in the market value of equity securities—

    (1) granted to the employee or member of the board of directors by the issuer as part of the compensation of the employee or member of the board of directors; or

    (2) held, directly or indirectly, by the employee or member of the board of directors.

53. SEC Rules and Regulations, Securities Exchange Act of 1934: Section 15 – Rules Relating to Over-the-Counter Markets

Also see 15c1-2, 15c1-3, 15c2-12 referenced later in this section.

<u>240.15c2-11 Initiation or resumption of quotations without specific information.</u>
Preliminary Note: Brokers and dealers may wish to refer to Securities Exchange Act Release No. 29094 (April 17, 1991), for a discussion of procedures for gathering and reviewing the information required by this rule and the requirement that a broker or dealer have a reasonable basis for believing that the information is accurate and obtained from reliable sources.

(a) As a means reasonably designed to prevent fraudulent, deceptive, or manipulative acts or practices, it shall be unlawful for a broker or dealer to publish any quotation for a security or, directly or indirectly, to submit any such quotation for publication, in any quotation medium (as defined in this section) unless such broker or dealer has in its records the documents and information required by this paragraph (for purposes of this section, "paragraph (a) information"), and, based upon a review of the paragraph (a) information together with any other documents and information required by paragraph (b) of this section, has a reasonable basis under the circumstances for believing that the paragraph (a) information is accurate in all material respects, and that the sources of the paragraph (a) information are reliable. The information required pursuant to this paragraph is:

 (1) A copy of the prospectus specified by section 10(a) of the Securities Act of 1933 for an issuer that has filed a registration statement under the Securities Act of 1933, other than a registration statement on Form F-6, which became effective less than 90 calendar days prior to the day on which such broker or dealer publishes or submits the quotation to the quotation medium, Provided That such registration statement has not thereafter been the subject of a stop order which is still in effect when the quotation is published or submitted; or

 (2) A copy of the offering circular provided for under Regulation A under the Securities Act of 1933 for an issuer that has filed a notification under Regulation A and was authorized to commence the offering less than 40 calendar days prior to the day on which such broker or dealer publishes or submits the quotation to the quotation medium, Provided That the offering circular provided for under Regulation A has not thereafter become the subject of a suspension order which is still in effect when the quotation is published or submitted; or

 (3) A copy of the issuer's most recent annual report filed pursuant to section 13 or 15(d) of the Act or pursuant to Regulation A ((§§ 230.251 through 230.263 of this chapter), or a copy of the annual statement referred to in section 12(g)(2)(G)(i) of the Act in the case of an issuer required to file reports pursuant to section 13 or 15(d) of the Act or an issuer of a security covered by section 12(g)(2)(B) or (G) of the Act, together with any semiannual, quarterly and current reports that have been filed under the provisions of the Act or Regulation A by the issuer after such annual report or annual statement; provided, however, that until such issuer has filed its first annual report pursuant to section 13 or 15(d) of the Act or pursuant to Regulation A, or annual statement referred to in section 12(g)(2)(G)(i) of the Act, the broker or dealer has in its records a copy of the prospectus specified by section 10(a) of the Securities Act of 1933 included in a registration statement filed by the issuer under the Securities Act of 1933, other than a registration statement on Form F-6, or a copy of the offering circular specified by Regulation A included in an offering statement filed by the issuer under Regulation A, that became effective or was qualified within the prior 16 months, or a copy of any registration statement filed by the issuer under section 12 of the Act that became effective within the prior 16 months, together with any semiannual, quarterly and current reports filed thereafter under section 13 or 15(d) of the Act or Regulation A; and provided further, that the broker or dealer has a reasonable basis under the circumstances for believing that the issuer is current in filing annual, semiannual, quarterly, and current reports filed pursuant to section 13 or 15(d) of

the Act or Regulation A, or, in the case of an insurance company exempted from section 12(g) of the Act by reason of section 12(g)(2)(G) thereof, the annual statement referred to in section 12(g)(2)(G)(i) of the Act; or

(4) The information that, since the beginning of its last fiscal year, the issuer has published pursuant to § 240.12g3-2(b), and which the broker or dealer shall make reasonably available upon the request of a person expressing an interest in a proposed transaction in the issuer's security with the broker or dealer, such as by providing the requesting person with appropriate instructions regarding how to obtain the information electronically; or

(5) The following information, which shall be reasonably current in relation to the day the quotation is submitted and which the broker or dealer shall make reasonably available upon request to any person expressing an interest in a proposed transaction in the security with such broker or dealer:

(i) The exact name of the issuer and its predecessor (if any);

(ii) The address of its principal executive offices;

(iii) The state of incorporation, if it is a corporation;

(iv) The exact title and class of the security;

(v) The par or stated value of the security;

(vi) The number of shares or total amount of the securities outstanding as of the end of the issuer's most recent fiscal year;

(vii) The name and address of the transfer agent;

(viii) The nature of the issuer's business;

(ix) The nature of products or services offered;

(x) The nature and extent of the issuer's facilities;

(xi) The name of the chief executive officer and members of the board of directors;

(xii) The issuer's most recent balance sheet and profit and loss and retained earnings statements;

(xiii) Similar financial information for such part of the 2 preceding fiscal years as the issuer or its predecessor has been in existence;

(xiv) Whether the broker or dealer or any associated person is affiliated, directly or indirectly with the issuer;

(xv) Whether the quotation is being published or submitted on behalf of any other broker or dealer, and, if so, the name of such broker or dealer; and

(xvi) Whether the quotation is being submitted or published directly or indirectly on behalf of the issuer, or any director, officer or any person, directly or indirectly the beneficial owner of more than 10 percent of the outstanding units or shares of any equity security of the issuer, and, if so, the name of such person, and the basis for any exemption under the federal securities laws for any sales of such securities on behalf of such person.

If such information is made available to others upon request pursuant to this paragraph, such delivery, unless otherwise represented, shall not constitute a representation by such broker or dealer that such information is accurate, but shall constitute a representation by such broker or dealer that the information is reasonably current in relation to the day the quotation is submitted, that the broker or dealer has a reasonable basis under the circumstances for believing the information is accurate in all material respects, and that the information was obtained from sources which the broker or dealer has a reasonable basis for believing are reliable. This paragraph (a)(5) shall not apply to any security of an issuer included in paragraph (a)(3) of this section unless a report or statement of such issuer described in paragraph (a)(3) of this section is not reasonably available to the broker or dealer. A report or statement of an issuer described in paragraph (a)(3) of this section shall be "reasonably available" when such report or statement is filed with the Commission.

(b) With respect to any security the quotation of which is within the provisions of this section, the broker or dealer submitting or publishing such quotation shall have in its records the following documents and information:

(1) A record of the circumstances involved in the submission of publication of such quotation, including the identity of the person or persons for whom the quotation is being submitted or published and any information regarding the transactions provided to the broker or dealer by such person or persons;

(2) A copy of any trading suspension order issued by the Commission pursuant to section 12(k) of the Act respecting any securities of the issuer or its predecessor (if any) during the 12 months preceding the date of the publication or submission of the quotation, or a copy of the public release issued by the Commission announcing such trading suspension order; and

(3) A copy or a written record of any other material information (including adverse information) regarding the issuer which comes to the broker's or dealer's knowledge or possession before the publication or submission of the quotation.

(c) The broker or dealer shall preserve the documents and information required under paragraphs (a) and (b) of this section for a period of not less than three years, the first two years in an easily accessible place.

(d)

(1) For any security of an issuer included in paragraph (a)(5) of this section, the broker or dealer submitting the quotation shall furnish to the interdealer quotation system (as defined in paragraph (e)(2) of this section), in such form as such system shall prescribe, at least 3 business days before the quotation is published or submitted, the information regarding the security and the issuer which such broker or dealer is required to maintain pursuant to said paragraph (a)(5) of this section.

(2) For any security of an issuer included in paragraph (a)(3) of this section,

(i) A broker-dealer shall be in compliance with the requirement to obtain current reports filed by the issuer if the broker-dealer obtains all current reports filed with the Commission by the issuer as of a date up to five business days in advance of the earlier of the date of submission of the quotation to the quotation medium and the date of submission of the information in paragraph (a) of this section pursuant to the applicable rule of the Financial Industry Regulatory Authority, Inc. or its successor organization; and

(ii) A broker-dealer shall be in compliance with the requirement to obtain the annual, quarterly, and current reports filed by the issuer, if the broker-dealer has made arrangements to receive all such reports when filed by the issuer and it has regularly received reports from the issuer on a timely basis, unless the broker-dealer has a reasonable basis under the circumstances for believing that the issuer has failed to file a required report or has filed a report but has not sent it to the broker-dealer.

(e) For purposes of this section:

(1) Quotation medium shall mean any "interdealer quotation system" or any publication or electronic communications network or other device which is used by brokers or dealers to make known to others their interest in transactions in any security, including offers to buy or sell at a stated price or otherwise, or invitations of offers to buy or sell.

(2) Interdealer quotation system shall mean any system of general circulation to brokers or dealers which regularly disseminates quotations of identified brokers or dealers.

(3) Except as otherwise specified in this rule, quotation shall mean any bid or offer at a specified price with respect to a security, or any indication of interest by a broker or dealer in receiving bids or offers from others for a security, or any indication by a broker or dealer that he wishes to advertise his general interest in buying or selling a particular security.

(4) Issuer, in the case of quotations for American Depositary Receipts, shall mean the issuer of the deposited shares represented by such American Depositary Receipts.

(f) The provisions of this section shall not apply to:

(1) The publication or submission of a quotation respecting a security admitted to trading on a national securities exchange and which is traded on such an exchange on the same day as, or on the business day next preceding, the day the quotation is published or submitted.

(2) The publication or submission by a broker or dealer, solely on behalf of a customer (other than a person acting as or for a dealer), of a quotation that represents the customer's indication of interest and does

not involve the solicitation of the customer's interest; Provided, however, That this paragraph (f)(2) shall not apply to a quotation consisting of both a bid and an offer, each of which is at a specified price, unless the quotation medium specifically identifies the quotation as representing such an unsolicited customer interest.

(3)

(i) The publication or submission, in an interdealer quotation system that specifically identifies as such unsolicited customer indications of interest of the kind described in paragraph (f)(2) of this section, of a quotation respecting a security which has been the subject of quotations (exclusive of any identified customer interests) in such a system on each of at least 12 days within the previous 30 calendar days, with no more than 4 business days in succession without a quotation; or

(ii) The publication or submission, in an interdealer quotation system that does not so identify any such unsolicited customer indications of interest, of a quotation respecting a security which has been the subject of both bid and ask quotations in an interdealer quotation system at specified prices on each of at least 12 days within the previous 30 calendar days, with no more than 4 business days in succession without such a two-way quotation;

(iii) A dealer acting in the capacity of market maker, as defined in section 3(a)(38) of the Act, that has published or submitted a quotation respecting a security in an interdealer quotation system and such quotation has qualified for an exception provided in this paragraph (f)(3), may continue to publish or submit quotations for such security in the interdealer quotation system without compliance with this section unless and until such dealer ceases to submit or publish a quotation or ceases to act in the capacity of market maker respecting such security.

(4) The publication or submission of a quotation respecting a municipal security.

(5) The publication or submission of a quotation respecting a Nasdaq security (as defined in § 242.600 of this chapter), and such security's listing is not suspended, terminated, or prohibited.

(g) The requirement in paragraph (a)(5) of this section that the information with respect to the issuer be "reasonably current" will be presumed to be satisfied, unless the broker or dealer has information to the contrary, if:

(1) The balance sheet is as of a date less than 16 months before the publication or submission of the quotation, the statements of profit and loss and retained earnings are for the 12 months preceding the date of such balance sheet, and if such balance sheet is not as of a date less than 6 months before the publication or submission of the quotation, it shall be accompanied by additional statements of profit and loss and retained earnings for the period from the date of such balance sheet to a date less than 6 months before the publication or submission of the quotation.

(2) Other information regarding the issuer specified in paragraph (a)(5) of this section is as of a date within 12 months prior to the publication or submission of the quotation.

(h) This section shall not prohibit any publication or submission of any quotation if the Commission, upon written request or upon its own motion, exempts such quotation either unconditionally or on specified terms and conditions, as not constituting a fraudulent, manipulative or deceptive practice comprehended within the purpose of this section.

---

54. SEC Rules and Regulations, Securities Exchange Act of 1934:
Section 20A – Liability to Contemporaneous Traders for Insider Trading

(a) Private rights of action based on contemporaneous trading

Any person who violates any provision of this chapter or the rules or regulations thereunder by purchasing or selling a security while in possession of material, nonpublic information shall be liable in an action in any court of competent jurisdiction to any person who, contemporaneously with the purchase or sale of securities that is the subject of such violation, has purchased (where such violation is based on a sale of securities) or sold (where such violation is based on a purchase of securities) securities of the same class.

(b) Limitations on liability

(1) Contemporaneous trading actions limited to profit gained or loss avoided

The total amount of damages imposed under subsection (a) shall not exceed the profit gained or loss avoided in the transaction or transactions that are the subject of the violation.

(2) Offsetting disgorgements against liability

The total amount of damages imposed against any person under subsection (a) shall be diminished by the amounts, if any, that such person may be required to disgorge, pursuant to a court order obtained at the instance of the Commission, in a proceeding brought under section 78u(d) of this title relating to the same transaction or transactions.

(3) Controlling person liability

No person shall be liable under this section solely by reason of employing another person who is liable under this section, but the liability of a controlling person under this section shall be subject to section 78t(a) of this title.

(4) Statute of limitations

No action may be brought under this section more than 5 years after the date of the last transaction that is the subject of the violation.

(c) Joint and several liability for communicating

Any person who violates any provision of this chapter or the rules or regulations thereunder by communicating material, nonpublic information shall be jointly and severally liable under subsection (a) with, and to the same extent as, any person or persons liable under subsection (a) to whom the communication was directed.

(d) Authority not to restrict other express or implied rights of action

Nothing in this section shall be construed to limit or condition the right of any person to bring an action to enforce a requirement of this chapter or the availability of any cause of action implied from a provision of this chapter.

(e) Provisions not to affect public prosecutions

This section shall not be construed to bar or limit in any manner any action by the Commission or the Attorney General under any other provision of this chapter, nor shall it bar or limit in any manner any action to recover penalties, or to seek any other order regarding penalties.

———————————————————————

55. SEC Rules and Regulations, Securities Exchange Act of 1934: Section 21A – Civil Penalties for Insider Trading

(a) Authority to impose civil penalties

(1) Judicial actions by Commission authorized

Whenever it shall appear to the Commission that any person has violated any provision of this chapter or the rules or regulations thereunder by purchasing or selling a security or security-based swap agreement while in possession of material, nonpublic information in, or has violated any such provision by communicating such information in connection with, a transaction on or through the facilities of a national securities exchange or from or through a broker or dealer, and which is not part of a public offering by an issuer of securities other than standardized options or security futures products, the Commission—

(A) may bring an action in a United States district court to seek, and the court shall have jurisdiction to impose, a civil penalty to be paid by the person who committed such violation; and

(B) may, subject to subsection (b)(1), bring an action in a United States district court to seek, and the court shall have jurisdiction to impose, a civil penalty to be paid by a person who, at the time of the violation, directly or indirectly controlled the person who committed such violation.

(2) Amount of penalty for person who committed violation

The amount of the penalty which may be imposed on the person who committed such violation shall be determined by the court in light of the facts and circumstances, but shall not exceed three times the profit gained or loss avoided as a result of such unlawful purchase, sale, or communication.

(3) Amount of penalty for controlling person

The amount of the penalty which may be imposed on any person who, at the time of the violation, directly or indirectly controlled the person who committed such violation, shall be determined by the court in light of the facts and circumstances, but shall not exceed the greater of $1,000,000, or three times the amount of the profit gained or loss avoided as a result of such controlled person's violation. If such controlled person's violation was a violation by communication, the profit gained or loss avoided as a result of the violation shall, for purposes of this paragraph only, be deemed to be limited to the profit gained or loss avoided by the person or persons to whom the controlled person directed such communication.

(b) Limitations on liability

(1) Liability of controlling persons

No controlling person shall be subject to a penalty under subsection (a)(1)(B) unless the Commission establishes that—

(A) such controlling person knew or recklessly disregarded the fact that such controlled person was likely to engage in the act or acts constituting the violation and failed to take appropriate steps to prevent such act or acts before they occurred; or

(B) such controlling person knowingly or recklessly failed to establish, maintain, or enforce any policy or procedure required under section 78o(f) [1] of this title or section 80b–4a of this title and such failure substantially contributed to or permitted the occurrence of the act or acts constituting the violation.

(2) Additional restrictions on liability

No person shall be subject to a penalty under subsection (a) solely by reason of employing another person who is subject to a penalty under such subsection, unless such employing person is liable as a controlling person under paragraph (1) of this subsection. Section 78t(a) of this title shall not apply to actions under subsection (a) of this section.

(c) Authority of Commission

The Commission, by such rules, regulations, and orders as it considers necessary or appropriate in the public interest or for the protection of investors, may exempt, in whole or in part, either unconditionally or upon specific terms and conditions, any person or transaction or class of persons or transactions from this section.

(d) Procedures for collection

    (1) Payment of penalty to Treasury

        A penalty imposed under this section shall be payable into the Treasury of the United States, except as otherwise provided in section 7246 of this title and section 78u–6 of this title.

    (2) Collection of penalties

        If a person upon whom such a penalty is imposed shall fail to pay such penalty within the time prescribed in the court's order, the Commission may refer the matter to the Attorney General who shall recover such penalty by action in the appropriate United States district court.

    (3) Remedy not exclusive

        The actions authorized by this section may be brought in addition to any other actions that the Commission or the Attorney General are entitled to bring.

    (4) Jurisdiction and venue

        For purposes of section 78aa of this title, actions under this section shall be actions to enforce a liability or a duty created by this chapter.

    (5) Statute of limitations

        No action may be brought under this section more than 5 years after the date of the purchase or sale. This section shall not be construed to bar or limit in any manner any action by the Commission or the Attorney General under any other provision of this chapter, nor shall it bar or limit in any manner any action to recover penalties, or to seek any other order regarding penalties, imposed in an action commenced within 5 years of such transaction.

(e) Definition

    For purposes of this section, "profit gained" or "loss avoided" is the difference between the purchase or sale price of the security and the value of that security as measured by the trading price of the security a reasonable period after public dissemination of the nonpublic information.

(f) Limitation on Commission authority

    The authority of the Commission under this section with respect to security-based swap agreements shall be subject to the restrictions and limitations of section 78c–1(b) of this title.

(g) Duty of Members and employees of Congress

    (1) In general

        Subject to the rule of construction under section 10 of the STOCK Act and solely for purposes of the insider trading prohibitions arising under this chapter, including section 78j(b) of this title and Rule 10b–5 thereunder, each Member of Congress or employee of Congress owes a duty arising from a relationship of trust and confidence to the Congress, the United States Government, and the citizens of the United States with respect to material, nonpublic information derived from such person's position as a Member of Congress or employee of Congress or gained from the performance of such person's official responsibilities.

    (2) Definitions

        In this subsection—

        (A) the term "Member of Congress" means a member of the Senate or House of Representatives, a Delegate to the House of Representatives, and the Resident Commissioner from Puerto Rico; and

        (B) the term "employee of Congress" means—

            (i) any individual (other than a Member of Congress), whose compensation is disbursed by the Secretary of the Senate or the Chief Administrative Officer of the House of Representatives; and

            (ii) any other officer or employee of the legislative branch (as defined in section 109(11) of the Ethics in Government Act of 1978 (5 U.S.C. App. 109(11))).

    (3) Rule of construction

        Nothing in this subsection shall be construed to impair or limit the construction of the existing antifraud provisions of the securities laws or the authority of the Commission under those provisions.

(h) Duty of other Federal officials

    (1) In general, Subject to the rule of construction under section 10 of the STOCK Act and solely for purposes of the insider trading prohibitions arising under this chapter, including section 78j(b) of this title, and Rule 10b–5 thereunder, each executive branch employee, each judicial officer, and each judicial employee owes a duty arising from a relationship of trust and confidence to the United States Government and the citizens of the United States with respect to material, nonpublic information derived from such person's position as an executive branch employee, judicial officer, or judicial employee or gained from the performance of such person's official responsibilities.

    (2) Definitions

        In this subsection—

        (A) the term "executive branch employee"—

            (i) has the meaning given the term "employee" under section 2105 of title 5;

            (ii) includes—

                (I) the President;

                (II) the Vice President; and

                (III) an employee of the United States Postal Service or the Postal Regulatory Commission;

        (B) the term "judicial employee" has the meaning given that term in section 109(8) of the Ethics in Government Act of 1978 (5 U.S.C. App. 109(8)); and

        (C) the term "judicial officer" has the meaning given that term under section 109(10) of the Ethics in Government Act of 1978 (5 U.S.C. App. 109(10)).

    (3) Rule of construction

        Nothing in this subsection shall be construed to impair or limit the construction of the existing antifraud provisions of the securities laws or the authority of the Commission under those provisions.

        (i) Participation in initial public offerings

            An individual described in section 101(f) of the Ethics in Government Act of 1978 may not purchase securities that are the subject of an initial public offering (within the meaning given such term in section 78l(f)(1)(G)(i) of this title) in any manner other than is available to members of the public generally.

---

56. SEC Rules and Regulations, Securities Exchange Act of 1934: 10b-1 – Prohibition of Use of Manipulative or Deceptive Devices or Contrivances with Respect to Certain Securities Exempted from Registration

The term manipulative or deceptive device or contrivance, as used in section 10(b) (48 Stat. 891; 15 U.S.C. 78j(b)), is hereby defined to include any act or omission to act with respect to any security exempted from the operation of section 12(a) (48 Stat. 892; 15 U.S.C. 78l(a)) pursuant to any section in this part which specifically provides that this section shall be applicable to such security if such act or omission to act would have been unlawful under section 9(a) (48 Stat. 889; 15 U.S.C. 78i(a)), or any rule or regulation heretofore or hereafter prescribed thereunder, if done or omitted to be done with respect to a security registered on a national securities exchange, and the use of any means or instrumentality of interstate commerce or of the mails or of any facility of any national securities exchange to use or employ any such device or contrivance in connection with the purchase or sale of any such security is hereby prohibited.

---

57. SEC Rules and Regulations, Securities Exchange Act of 1934: 10b-3 – Employment of Manipulative and Deceptive Devices by Brokers or Dealers

(a) It shall be unlawful for any broker or dealer, directly or indirectly, by the use of any means or instrumentality of interstate commerce, or of the mails, or of any facility of any national securities exchange, to use or employ, in connection with the purchase or sale of any security otherwise than on a national securities exchange, any act, practice, or course of business defined by the Commission to be included within the term "manipulative, deceptive, or other fraudulent device or contrivance", as such term is used in section 15(c)(1) of the act.

(b) It shall be unlawful for any municipal securities dealer directly or indirectly, by the use of any means or instrumentality of interstate commerce, or of the mails, or of any facility of any national securities exchange, to use or employ, in connection with the purchase or sale of any municipal security, any act, practice, or course of business defined by the Commission to be included within the term "manipulative, deceptive, or other fraudulent device or contrivance," as such term is used in section 15(c)(1) of the act.

_____

58. SEC Rules and Regulations, Securities Exchange Act of 1934: 10b-5 – Employment of Manipulative and Deceptive Devices

It shall be unlawful for any person, directly or indirectly, by the use of any means or instrumentality of interstate commerce, or of the mails or of any facility of any national securities exchange,

(a) To employ any device, scheme, or artifice to defraud,

(b) To make any untrue statement of a material fact or to omit to state a material fact necessary in order to make the statements made, in the light of the circumstances under which they were made, not misleading, or

(c) To engage in any act, practice, or course of business which operates or would operate as a fraud or deceit upon any person,

in connection with the purchase or sale of any security.

_____

59. SEC Rules and Regulations, Securities Exchange Act of 1934: 10b5-1 – Trading on Material Nonpublic Information in Insider Trading Cases

Preliminary Note: This provision defines when a purchase or sale constitutes trading "on the basis of" material nonpublic information in insider trading cases brought under Section 10(b) of the Act and Rule 10b-5 thereunder. The law of insider trading is otherwise defined by judicial opinions construing Rule 10b-5, and Rule 10b5-1 does not modify the scope of insider trading law in any other respect.

(a) General. The "manipulative and deceptive devices" prohibited by Section 10(b) of the Act (15 U.S.C. 78j) and § 240.10b-5 thereunder include, among other things, the purchase or sale of a security of any issuer, on the basis of material nonpublic information about that security or issuer, in breach of a duty of trust or confidence that is owed directly, indirectly, or derivatively, to the issuer of that security or the shareholders of that issuer, or to any other person who is the source of the material nonpublic information.

(b) Definition of "on the basis of." Subject to the affirmative defenses in paragraph (c) of this section, a purchase or sale of a security of an issuer is "on the basis of" material nonpublic information about that security or issuer if the person making the purchase or sale was aware of the material nonpublic information when the person made the purchase or sale.

(c) Affirmative defenses.

   (1)(i) Subject to paragraph (c)(1)(ii) of this section, a person's purchase or sale is not "on the basis of" material nonpublic information if the person making the purchase or sale demonstrates that:

   (A) Before becoming aware of the information, the person had:

       (1) Entered into a binding contract to purchase or sell the security,

       (2) Instructed another person to purchase or sell the security for the instructing person's account, or

       (3) Adopted a written plan for trading securities;

   (B) The contract, instruction, or plan described in paragraph (c)(1)(i)(A) of this Section:

       (1) Specified the amount of securities to be purchased or sold and the price at which and the date on which the securities were to be purchased or sold;

       (2) Included a written formula or algorithm, or computer program, for determining the amount of securities to be purchased or sold and the price at which and the date on which the securities were to be purchased or sold; or

       (3) Did not permit the person to exercise any subsequent influence over how, when, or whether to effect purchases or sales; provided, in addition, that any other person who, pursuant to the contract, instruction, or plan, did exercise such influence must not have been aware of the material nonpublic information when doing so; and

   (C) The purchase or sale that occurred was pursuant to the contract, instruction, or plan. A purchase or sale is not "pursuant to a contract, instruction, or plan" if, among other things, the person who entered into the contract, instruction, or plan altered or deviated from the contract, instruction, or plan to purchase or sell securities (whether by changing the amount, price, or timing of the purchase or sale), or entered into or altered a corresponding or hedging transaction or position with respect to those securities.

   (ii) Paragraph (c)(1)(i) of this section is applicable only when the contract, instruction, or plan to purchase or sell securities was given or entered into in good faith and not as part of a plan or scheme to evade the prohibitions of this section.

   (iii) This paragraph (c)(1)(iii) defines certain terms as used in paragraph (c) of this Section.

   (A) "Amount" means either a specified number of shares or other securities or a specified dollar value of securities.

   (B) "Price" means the market price on a particular date or a limit price, or a particular dollar price.

   (C) "Date" means, in the case of a market order, the specific day of the year on which the order is to be executed (or as soon thereafter as is practicable under ordinary principles of best execution). "Date" means, in the case of a limit order, a day of the year on which the limit order is in force.

   (2) A person other than a natural person also may demonstrate that a purchase or sale of securities is not "on the basis of" material nonpublic information if the person demonstrates that:

   (i) The individual making the investment decision on behalf of the person to purchase or sell the securities was not aware of the information; and

   (ii) The person had implemented reasonable policies and procedures, taking into consideration the nature of the person's business, to ensure that individuals making investment decisions would not violate the laws prohibiting trading on the basis of material nonpublic information. These policies and procedures may include those that restrict any purchase, sale, and causing any purchase or sale of any security as to which the person has material nonpublic information, or those that prevent such individuals from becoming aware of such information.

---

60. SEC Rules and Regulations, Securities Exchange Act of 1934: 10b5-2 – Duties of Trust or Confidence in Misappropriation Insider Trading Cases

Preliminary Note: This section provides a non-exclusive definition of circumstances in which a person has a duty of trust or confidence for purposes of the "misappropriation" theory of insider trading under Section 10(b) of the Act and Rule 10b-5. The law of insider trading is otherwise defined by judicial opinions construing Rule 10b-5, and Rule 10b5-2 does not modify the scope of insider trading law in any other respect.

(a) Scope of Rule. This section shall apply to any violation of Section 10(b) of the Act (15 U.S.C. 78j(b)) and § 240.10b-5 thereunder that is based on the purchase or sale of securities on the basis of, or the communication of, material nonpublic information misappropriated in breach of a duty of trust or confidence.

(b) Enumerated "duties of trust or confidence." For purposes of this section, a "duty of trust or confidence" exists in the following circumstances, among others:

(1) Whenever a person agrees to maintain information in confidence;

(2) Whenever the person communicating the material nonpublic information and the person to whom it is communicated have a history, pattern, or practice of sharing confidences, such that the recipient of the information knows or reasonably should know that the person communicating the material nonpublic information expects that the recipient will maintain its confidentiality; or

(3) Whenever a person receives or obtains material nonpublic information from his or her spouse, parent, child, or sibling; provided, however, that the person receiving or obtaining the information may demonstrate that no duty of trust or confidence existed with respect to the information, by establishing that he or she neither knew nor reasonably should have known that the person who was the source of the information expected that the person would keep the information confidential, because of the parties' history, pattern, or practice of sharing and maintaining confidences, and because there was no agreement or understanding to maintain the confidentiality of the information.

---

61. SEC Rules and Regulations, Securities Exchange Act of 1934: 10b-10 – Confirmation of Transactions

Preliminary Note: This section requires broker-dealers to disclose specified information in writing to customers at or before completion of a transaction. The requirements under this section that particular information be disclosed is not determinative of a broker-dealer's obligation under the general antifraud provisions of the federal securities laws to disclose additional information to a customer at the time of the investment decision.

(a) Disclosure requirement. It shall be unlawful for any broker or dealer to effect for or with an account of a customer any transaction in, or to induce the purchase or sale by such customer of, any security (other than U.S. Savings Bonds or municipal securities) unless such broker or dealer, at or before completion of such transaction, gives or sends to such customer written notification disclosing:

   (1) The date and time of the transaction (or the fact that the time of the transaction will be furnished upon written request to such customer) and the identity, price, and number of shares or units (or principal amount) of such security purchased or sold by such customer; and

   (2) Whether the broker or dealer is acting as agent for such customer, as agent for some other person, as agent for both such customer and some other person, or as principal for its own account; and if the broker or dealer is acting as principal, whether it is a market maker in the security (other than by reason of acting as a block positioner); and

      (i) If the broker or dealer is acting as agent for such customer, for some other person, or for both such customer and some other person:

         (A) The name of the person from whom the security was purchased, or to whom it was sold, for such customer or the fact that the information will be furnished upon written request of such customer; and

         (B) The amount of any remuneration received or to be received by the broker from such customer in connection with the transaction unless remuneration paid by such customer is determined pursuant to written agreement with such customer, otherwise than on a transaction basis; and

         (C) For a transaction in any NMS stock as defined in § 242.600 of this chapter or a security authorized for quotation on an automated interdealer quotation system that has the characteristics set forth in section 17B of the Act (15 U.S.C. 78q-2), a statement whether payment for order flow is received by the broker or dealer for transactions in such securities and the fact that the source and nature of the compensation received in connection with the particular transaction will be furnished upon written request of the customer; provided, however, that brokers or dealers that do not receive payment for order flow in connection with any transaction have no disclosure obligations under this paragraph; and

         (D) The source and amount of any other remuneration received or to be received by the broker in connection with the transaction: Provided, however, that if, in the case of a purchase, the broker was not participating in a distribution, or in the case of a sale, was not participating in a tender offer, the written notification may state whether any other remuneration has been or will be received and the fact that the source and amount of such other remuneration will be furnished upon written request of such customer; or

      (ii) If the broker or dealer is acting as principal for its own account:

         (A) In the case where such broker or dealer is not a market maker in an equity security and, if, after having received an order to buy from a customer, the broker or dealer purchased the equity security from another person to offset a contemporaneous sale to such customer or, after having received an order to sell from a customer, the broker or dealer sold the security to another person to offset a contemporaneous purchase from such customer, the difference between the price to the customer and the dealer's contemporaneous purchase (for customer purchases) or sale price (for customer sales); or

(B) In the case of any other transaction in an NMS stock as defined by § 242.600 of this chapter, or an equity security that is traded on a national securities exchange and that is subject to last sale reporting, the reported trade price, the price to the customer in the transaction, and the difference, if any, between the reported trade price and the price to the customer.

(3) Whether any odd-lot differential or equivalent fee has been paid by such customer in connection with the execution of an order for an odd-lot number of shares or units (or principal amount) of a security and the fact that the amount of any such differential or fee will be furnished upon oral or written request: Provided, however, that such disclosure need not be made if the differential or fee is included in the remuneration disclosure, or exempted from disclosure, pursuant to paragraph (a)(2)(i)(B) of this section; and

(4) In the case of any transaction in a debt security subject to redemption before maturity, a statement to the effect that such debt security may be redeemed in whole or in part before maturity, that such a redemption could affect the yield represented and the fact that additional information is available upon request; and

(5) In the case of a transaction in a debt security effected exclusively on the basis of a dollar price:
(i) The dollar price at which the transaction was effected, and
(ii) The yield to maturity calculated from the dollar price: Provided, however, that this paragraph (a)(5)(ii) shall not apply to a transaction in a debt security that either:
(A) Has a maturity date that may be extended by the issuer thereof, with a variable interest payable thereon; or
(B) Is an asset-backed security, that represents an interest in or is secured by a pool of receivables or other financial assets that are subject continuously to prepayment; and

(6) In the case of a transaction in a debt security effected on the basis of yield:
(i) The yield at which the transaction was effected, including the percentage amount and its characterization (e.g., current yield, yield to maturity, or yield to call) and if effected at yield to call, the type of call, the call date and call price; and
(ii) The dollar price calculated from the yield at which the transaction was effected; and
(iii) If effected on a basis other than yield to maturity and the yield to maturity is lower than the represented yield, the yield to maturity as well as the represented yield; Provided, however, that this paragraph (a)(6)(iii) shall not apply to a transaction in a debt security that either:
(A) Has a maturity date that may be extended by the issuer thereof, with a variable interest rate payable thereon; or
(B) Is an asset-backed security, that represents an interest in or is secured by a pool of receivables or other financial assets that are subject continuously to prepayment; and

(7) In the case of a transaction in a debt security that is an asset-backed security, which represents an interest in or is secured by a pool of receivables or other financial assets that are subject continuously to prepayment, a statement indicating that the actual yield of such asset-backed security may vary according to the rate at which the underlying receivables or other financial assets are prepaid and a statement of the fact that information concerning the factors that affect yield (including at a minimum estimated yield, weighted average life, and the prepayment assumptions underlying yield) will be furnished upon written request of such customer; and

(8) That the broker or dealer is not a member of the Securities Investor Protection Corporation (SIPC), or that the broker or dealer clearing or carrying the customer account is not a member of SIPC, if such is the case: Provided, however, that this paragraph (a)(9) shall not apply in the case of a transaction in shares of a registered open-end investment company or unit investment trust if:
(i) The customer sends funds or securities directly to, or receives funds or securities directly from, the registered open-end investment company or unit investment trust, its transfer agent, its custodian, or other designated agent, and such person is not an associated person of the broker or dealer required by paragraph (a) of this section to send written notification to the customer; and

(ii) The written notification required by paragraph (a) of this section is sent on behalf of the broker or dealer to the customer by a person described in paragraph (a)(9)(i) of this section.

(b) Alternative periodic reporting. A broker or dealer may effect transactions for or with the account of a customer without giving or sending to such customer the written notification described in paragraph (a) of this section if:

    (1) Such transactions are effected pursuant to a periodic plan or an investment company plan, or effected in shares of any open-end management investment company registered under the Investment Company Act of 1940 that holds itself out as a money market fund and attempts to maintain a stable net asset value per share: Provided, however, that no sales load is deducted upon the purchase or redemption of shares in the money market fund; and

    (2) Such broker or dealer gives or sends to such customer within five business days after the end of each quarterly period, for transactions involving investment company and periodic plans, and after the end of each monthly period, for other transactions described in paragraph (b)(1) of this section, a written statement disclosing each purchase or redemption, effected for or with, and each dividend or distribution credited to or reinvested for, the account of such customer during the month; the date of such transaction; the identity, number, and price of any securities purchased or redeemed by such customer in each such transaction; the total number of shares of such securities in such customer's account; any remuneration received or to be received by the broker or dealer in connection therewith; and that any other information required by paragraph (a) of this section will be furnished upon written request: Provided, however, that the written statement may be delivered to some other person designated by the customer for distribution to the customer; and

    (3) Such customer is provided with prior notification in writing disclosing the intention to send the written information referred to in paragraph (b)(1) of this section in lieu of an immediate confirmation.

(c) A broker or dealer shall give or send to a customer information requested pursuant to this rule within 5 business days of receipt of the request: Provided, however, That in the case of information pertaining to a transaction effected more than 30 days prior to receipt of the request, the information shall be given or sent to the customer within 15 business days.

(d) Definitions. For the purposes of this section:

    (1) Customer shall not include a broker or dealer;

    (2) Completion of the transaction shall have the meaning provided in rule 15c1-1 under the Act;

    (3) Time of the transaction means the time of execution, to the extent feasible, of the customer's order;

    (4) Debt security as used in paragraphs (a)(3), (4), and (5) only, means any security, such as a bond, debenture, note, or any other similar instrument which evidences a liability of the issuer (including any such security that is convertible into stock or a similar security) and fractional or participation interests in one or more of any of the foregoing: Provided, however, That securities issued by an investment company registered under the Investment Company Act of 1940 shall not be included in this definition;

    (5) Periodic plan means any written authorization for a broker acting as agent to purchase or sell for a customer a specific security or securities (other than securities issued by an open end investment company or unit investment trust registered under the Investment Company Act of 1940), in specific amounts (calculated in security units or dollars), at specific time intervals and setting forth the commissions or charges to be paid by the customer in connection therewith (or the manner of calculating them); and

    (6) Investment company plan means any plan under which securities issued by an open-end investment company or unit investment trust registered under the Investment Company Act of 1940 are purchased by a customer (the payments being made directly to, or made payable to, the registered investment company, or the principal underwriter, custodian, trustee, or other designated agent of the registered investment company), or sold by a customer pursuant to:

        (i) An individual retirement or individual pension plan qualified under the Internal Revenue Code;

        (ii) A contractual or systematic agreement under which the customer purchases at the applicable public offering price, or redeems at the applicable redemption price, such securities in specified amounts (calculated in security units or dollars) at specified time intervals and setting forth the commissions or charges to be paid by such customer in connection therewith, or

(iii) Any other arrangement involving a group of two or more customers and contemplating periodic purchases of such securities by each customer through a person designated by the group: Provided, That such arrangement requires the registered investment company or its agent –

(A) To give or send to the designated person, at or before the completion of the transaction for the purchase of such securities, a written notification of the receipt of the amount paid by the group;

(B) To send to anyone in the group who was a customer in the prior quarter and on whose behalf payment has not been received in the current quarter a quarterly written statement reflecting that a payment was not received on his behalf; and

(C) To advise each customer in the group if a payment is not received from the designated person on behalf of the group within 10 days of a date certain specified in the arrangement for delivery of that payment by the designated person and thereafter to send to each such customer the written notification described in paragraph (a) of this section for the next three succeeding payments.

(7) NMS stock shall have the meaning provided in § 242.600 of this chapter.

(8) Payment for order flow shall mean any monetary payment, service, property, or other benefit that results in remuneration, compensation, or consideration to a broker or dealer from any broker or dealer, national securities exchange, registered securities association, or exchange member in return for the routing of customer orders by such broker or dealer to any broker or dealer, national securities exchange, registered securities association, or exchange member for execution, including but not limited to: research, clearance, custody, products or services; reciprocal agreements for the provision of order flow; adjustment of a broker or dealer's unfavorable trading errors; offers to participate as underwriter in public offerings; stock loans or shared interest accrued thereon; discounts, rebates, or any other reductions of or credits against any fee to, or expense or other financial obligation of, the broker or dealer routing a customer order that exceeds that fee, expense or financial obligation.

(9) Asset-backed security means a security that is primarily serviced by the cashflows of a discrete pool of receivables or other financial assets, either fixed or revolving, that by their terms convert into cash within a finite time period plus any rights or other assets designed to assure the servicing or timely distribution of proceeds to the security holders.

(e) Security futures products. The provisions of paragraphs (a) and (b) of this section shall not apply to a broker or dealer registered pursuant to section 15(b)(11)(A) of the Act (15 U.S.C. 78o(b)(11)(A)) to the extent that it effects transactions for customers in security futures products in a futures account (as that term is defined in § 240.15c3-3(a)(15)) and a broker or dealer registered pursuant to section 15(b)(1) of the Act (15 U.S.C. 78o(b)(1)) that is also a futures commission merchant registered pursuant to section 4f(a)(1) of the Commodity Exchange Act (7 U.S.C. 6f(a)(1)), to the extent that it effects transactions for customers in security futures products in a futures account (as that term is defined in § 240.15c3-3(a)(15)), Provided that:

(1) The broker or dealer that effects any transaction for a customer in security futures products in a futures account gives or sends to the customer no later than the next business day after execution of any futures securities product transaction, written notification disclosing:

(i) The date the transaction was executed, the identity of the single security or narrow-based security index underlying the contract for the security futures product, the number of contracts of such security futures product purchased or sold, the price, and the delivery month;

(ii) The source and amount of any remuneration received or to be received by the broker or dealer in connection with the transaction, including, but not limited to, markups, commissions, costs, fees, and other charges incurred in connection with the transaction, provided, however, that if no remuneration is to be paid for an initiating transaction until the occurrence of the corresponding liquidating transaction, that the broker or dealer may disclose the amount of remuneration only on the confirmation for the liquidating transaction;

(iii) The fact that information about the time of the execution of the transaction, the identity of the other party to the contract, and whether the broker or dealer is acting as agent for such customer, as agent for some other person, as agent for both such customer and some other person, or as principal for its own account, and if the broker or dealer is acting as principal, whether it is engaging in a block transaction or an exchange of security futures products for physical securities, will be available upon written request of the customer; and

(iv) Whether payment for order flow is received by the broker or dealer for such transactions, the amount of this payment and the fact that the source and nature of the compensation received in connection with the particular transaction will be furnished upon written request of the customer; provided, however, that brokers or dealers that do not receive payment for order flow have no disclosure obligation under this paragraph.

(2) Transitional provision.

(i) Broker-dealers are not required to comply with paragraph (e)(1)(iii) of this section until June 1, 2003, Provided that, if, not withstanding the absence of the disclosure required in that paragraph, the broker-dealer receives a written request from a customer for the information described in paragraph (e)(1)(iii) of this section, the broker-dealer must make the information available to the customer; and

(ii) Broker-dealers are not required to comply with paragraph (e)(1)(iv) of this section until June 1, 2003.

(f) The Commission may exempt any broker or dealer from the requirements of paragraphs (a) and (b) of this section with regard to specific transactions of specific classes of transactions for which the broker or dealer will provide alternative procedures to effect the purposes of this section; any such exemption may be granted subject to compliance with such alternative procedures and upon such other stated terms and conditions as the Commission may impose.

----

62. SEC Rules and Regulations, Securities Exchange Act of 1934: 15c1-2 – Fraud and Misrepresentation

(a) The term manipulative, deceptive, or other fraudulent device or contrivance, as used in section 15(c)(1) of the Act (section 2, 52 Stat. 1075; 15 U.S.C. 78o(c)(1), is hereby defined to include any act, practice, or course of business which operates or would operate as a fraud or deceit upon any person.

(b) The term manipulative, deceptive, or other fraudulent device or contrivance, as used in section 15(c)(1) of the Act, is hereby defined to include any untrue statement of a material fact and any omission to state a material fact necessary in order to make the statements made, in the light of the circumstances under which they are made, not misleading, which statement or omission is made with knowledge or reasonable grounds to believe that it is untrue or misleading.

(c) The scope of this section shall not be limited by any specific definitions of the term "manipulative, deceptive, or other fraudulent device or contrivance" contained in other rules adopted pursuant to section 15(c)(1) of the act.

----

63. SEC Rules and Regulations, Securities Exchange Act of 1934:
15c1-3 – Misrepresentation by Brokers, Dealers and
Municipal Securities Dealers as to Registration

The term manipulative, deceptive, or other fraudulent device or contrivance, as used in section 15(c)(1) of the Act, is hereby defined to include any representation by a broker, dealer or municipal securities dealer that the registration of a broker or dealer, pursuant to section 15(b) of the Act, or the registration of a municipal securities dealer pursuant to section 15B(a) of the Act, or the failure of the Commission to deny or revoke such registration, indicates in any way that the Commission has passed upon or approved the financial standing, business, or conduct of such registered broker, dealer or municipal securities dealer or the merits of any security or any transaction or transactions therein.

---

64. SEC Rules and Regulations, Securities Exchange Act of 1934:
15c2-12 – Municipal Securities Disclosure

Preliminary Note: For a discussion of disclosure obligations relating to municipal securities, issuers, brokers, dealers, and municipal securities dealers should refer to Securities Act Release No. 7049, Securities Exchange Act Release No. 33741, FR-42 (March 9, 1994). For a discussion of the obligations of underwriters to have a reasonable basis for recommending municipal securities, brokers, dealers, and municipal securities dealers should refer to Securities Exchange Act Release No. 26100 (Sept. 22, 1988) and Securities Exchange Act Release No. 26985 (June 28, 1989).

(a) General. As a means reasonably designed to prevent fraudulent, deceptive, or manipulative acts or practices, it shall be unlawful for any broker, dealer, or municipal securities dealer (a "Participating Underwriter" when used in connection with an Offering) to act as an underwriter in a primary offering of municipal securities with an aggregate principal amount of $1,000,000 or more (an "Offering") unless the Participating Underwriter complies with the requirements of this section or is exempted from the provisions of this section.

(b) Requirements.

(1) Prior to the time the Participating Underwriter bids for, purchases, offers, or sells municipal securities in an Offering, the Participating Underwriter shall obtain and review an official statement that an issuer of such securities deems final as of its date, except for the omission of no more than the following information: The offering price(s), interest rate(s), selling compensation, aggregate principal amount, principal amount per maturity, delivery dates, any other terms or provisions required by an issuer of such securities to be specified in a competitive bid, ratings, other terms of the securities depending on such matters, and the identity of the underwriter(s).

(2) Except in competitively bid offerings, from the time the Participating Underwriter has reached an understanding with an issuer of municipal securities that it will become a Participating Underwriter in an Offering until a final official statement is available, the Participating Underwriter shall send no later than the next business day, by first-class mail or other equally prompt means, to any potential customer, on request, a single copy of the most recent preliminary official statement, if any.

(3) The Participating Underwriter shall contract with an issuer of municipal securities or its designated agent to receive, within seven business days after any final agreement to purchase, offer, or sell the municipal securities in an Offering and in sufficient time to accompany any confirmation that requests payment

from any customer, copies of a final official statement in sufficient quantity to comply with paragraph (b)(4) of this rule and the rules of the Municipal Securities Rulemaking Board.

(4) From the time the final official statement becomes available until the earlier of –

(i) Ninety days from the end of the underwriting period or

(ii) The time when the official statement is available to any person from the Municipal Securities Rulemaking Board, but in no case less than twenty-five days following the end of the underwriting period, the Participating Underwriter in an Offering shall send no later than the next business day, by first-class mail or other equally prompt means, to any potential customer, on request, a single copy of the final official statement.

(5)

(i) A Participating Underwriter shall not purchase or sell municipal securities in connection with an Offering unless the Participating Underwriter has reasonably determined that an issuer of municipal securities, or an obligated person for whom financial or operating data is presented in the final official statement has undertaken, either individually or in combination with other issuers of such municipal securities or obligated persons, in a written agreement or contract for the benefit of holders of such securities, to provide the following to the Municipal Securities Rulemaking Board in an electronic format as prescribed by the Municipal Securities Rulemaking Board, either directly or indirectly through an indenture trustee or a designated agent:

(A) Annual financial information for each obligated person for whom financial information or operating data is presented in the final official statement, or, for each obligated person meeting the objective criteria specified in the undertaking and used to select the obligated persons for whom financial information or operating data is presented in the final official statement, except that, in the case of pooled obligations, the undertaking shall specify such objective criteria;

(B) If not submitted as part of the annual financial information, then when and if available, audited financial statements for each obligated person covered by paragraph (b)(5)(i)(A) of this section;

(C) In a timely manner not in excess of ten business days after the occurrence of the event, notice of any of the following events with respect to the securities being offered in the Offering:

(1) Principal and interest payment delinquencies;

(2) Non-payment related defaults, if material;

(3) Unscheduled draws on debt service reserves reflecting financial difficulties;

(4) Unscheduled draws on credit enhancements reflecting financial difficulties;

(5) Substitution of credit or liquidity providers, or their failure to perform;

(6) Adverse tax opinions, the issuance by the Internal Revenue Service of proposed or final determinations of taxability, Notices of Proposed Issue (IRS Form 5701-TEB) or other material notices or determinations with respect to the tax status of the security, or other material events affecting the tax status of the security;

(7) Modifications to rights of security holders, if material;

(8) Bond calls, if material, and tender offers;

(9) Defeasances;

(10) Release, substitution, or sale of property securing repayment of the securities, if material;

(11) Rating changes;

(12) Bankruptcy, insolvency, receivership or similar event of the obligated person;

(13) The consummation of a merger, consolidation, or acquisition involving an obligated person or the sale of all or substantially all of the assets of the obligated person, other than in the ordinary course of business, the entry into a definitive agreement to undertake such an action or the termination of a definitive agreement relating to any such actions, other than pursuant to its terms, if material;

(14) Appointment of a successor or additional trustee or the change of name of a trustee, if material;

(15) Incurrence of a financial obligation of the obligated person, if material, or agreement to covenants, events of default, remedies, priority rights, or other similar terms of a financial obligation of the obligated person, any of which affect security holders, if material; and

(16) Default, event of acceleration, termination event, modification of terms, or other similar events under the terms of a financial obligation of the obligated person, any of which reflect financial difficulties; and

(D) In a timely manner, notice of a failure of any person specified in paragraph (b)(5)(i)(A) of this section to provide required annual financial information, on or before the date specified in the written agreement or contract.

(ii) The written agreement or contract for the benefit of holders of such securities also shall identify each person for whom annual financial information and notices of material events will be provided, either by name or by the objective criteria used to select such persons, and, for each such person shall:

(A) Specify, in reasonable detail, the type of financial information and operating data to be provided as part of annual financial information;

(B) Specify, in reasonable detail, the accounting principles pursuant to which financial statements will be prepared, and whether the financial statements will be audited; and

(C) Specify the date on which the annual financial information for the preceding fiscal year will be provided.

(iii) Such written agreement or contract for the benefit of holders of such securities also may provide that the continuing obligation to provide annual financial information and notices of events may be terminated with respect to any obligated person, if and when such obligated person no longer remains an obligated person with respect to such municipal securities.

(iv) Such written agreement or contract for the benefit of holders of such securities also shall provide that all documents provided to the Municipal Securities Rulemaking Board shall be accompanied by identifying information as prescribed by the Municipal Securities Rulemaking Board.

(c) Recommendations. As a means reasonably designed to prevent fraudulent, deceptive, or manipulative acts or practices, it shall be unlawful for any broker, dealer, or municipal securities dealer to recommend the purchase or sale of a municipal security unless such broker, dealer, or municipal securities dealer has procedures in place that provide reasonable assurance that it will receive prompt notice of any event disclosed pursuant to paragraph (b)(5)(i)(C), paragraph (b)(5)(i)(D), and paragraph (d)(2)(ii)(B) of this section with respect to that security.

(d) Exemptions.

(1) This section shall not apply to a primary offering of municipal securities in authorized denominations of $100,000 or more, if such securities:

(i) Are sold to no more than thirty-five persons each of whom the Participating Underwriter reasonably believes:

(A) Has such knowledge and experience in financial and business matters that it is capable of evaluating the merits and risks of the prospective investment; and

(B) Is not purchasing for more than one account or with a view to distributing the securities; or

(ii) Have a maturity of nine months or less.

(2) Paragraph (b)(5) of this section shall not apply to an Offering of municipal securities if, at such time as an issuer of such municipal securities delivers the securities to the Participating Underwriters:

(i) No obligated person will be an obligated person with respect to more than $10,000,000 in aggregate amount of outstanding municipal securities, including the offered securities and excluding municipal securities that were offered in a transaction exempt from this section pursuant to paragraph (d)(1) of this section;

(ii) An issuer of municipal securities or obligated person has undertaken, either individually or in combination with other issuers of municipal securities or obligated persons, in a written agreement or contract for the benefit of holders of such municipal securities, to provide the following to the Municipal

Securities Rulemaking Board in an electronic format as prescribed by the Municipal Securities Rulemaking Board:

    (A) At least annually, financial information or operating data regarding each obligated person for which financial information or operating data is presented in the final official statement, as specified in the undertaking, which financial information and operating data shall include, at a minimum, that financial information and operating data which is customarily prepared by such obligated person and is publicly available; and

    (B) In a timely manner not in excess of ten business days after the occurrence of the event, notice of events specified in paragraph (b)(5)(i)(C) of this section with respect to the securities that are the subject of the Offering; and

    (C) Such written agreement or contract for the benefit of holders of such securities also shall provide that all documents provided to the Municipal Securities Rulemaking Board shall be accompanied by identifying information as prescribed by the Municipal Securities Rulemaking Board; and

  (iii) The final official statement identifies by name, address, and telephone number the persons from which the foregoing information, data, and notices can be obtained.

(3) The provisions of paragraph (b)(5) of this section, other than paragraph (b)(5)(i)(C) of this section, shall not apply to an Offering of municipal securities, if such municipal securities have a stated maturity of 18 months or less.

(4) The provisions of paragraph (c) of this section shall not apply to municipal securities:

  (i) Sold in an Offering to which paragraph (b)(5) of this section did not apply, other than Offerings exempt under paragraph (d)(2)(ii) of this section; or

  (ii) Sold in an Offering exempt from this section under paragraph (d)(1) of this section.

(5) With the exception of paragraphs (b)(1) through (b)(4), this section shall apply to a primary offering of municipal securities in authorized denominations of $100,000 or more if such securities may, at the option of the holder thereof, be tendered to an issuer of such securities or its designated agent for redemption or purchase at par value or more at least as frequently as every nine months until maturity, earlier redemption, or purchase by an issuer or its designated agent; provided, however, that paragraphs (b)(5) and (c) of this section shall not apply to such securities outstanding on November 30, 2010, for so long as they continuously remain in authorized denominations of $100,000 or more and may, at the option of the holder thereof, be tendered to an issuer of such securities or its designated agent for redemption or purchase at par value or more at least as frequently as every nine months until maturity, earlier redemption, or purchase by an issuer or its designated agent.

(e) Exemptive authority. The Commission, upon written request, or upon its own motion, may exempt any broker, dealer, or municipal securities dealer, whether acting in the capacity of a Participating Underwriter or otherwise, that is a participant in a transaction or class of transactions from any requirement of this section, either unconditionally or on specified terms and conditions, if the Commission determines that such an exemption is consistent with the public interest and the protection of investors.

(f) Definitions. For the purposes of this rule -

(1) The term authorized denominations of $100,000 or more means municipal securities with a principal amount of $100,000 or more and with restrictions that prevent the sale or transfer of such securities in principal amounts of less than $100,000 other than through a primary offering; except that, for municipal securities with an original issue discount of 10 percent or more, the term means municipal securities with a minimum purchase price of $100,000 or more and with restrictions that prevent the sale or transfer of such securities, in principal amounts that are less than the original principal amount at the time of the primary offering, other than through a primary offering.

(2) The term end of the underwriting period means the later of such time as

  (i) The issuer of municipal securities delivers the securities to the Participating Underwriters or

  (ii) The Participating Underwriter does not retain, directly or as a member or an underwriting syndicate, an unsold balance of the securities for sale to the public.

(3) The term final official statement means a document or set of documents prepared by an issuer of municipal securities or its representatives that is complete as of the date delivered to the Participating Underwriter(s) and that sets forth information concerning the terms of the proposed issue of securities; information, including financial information or operating data, concerning such issuers of municipal securities and those other entities, enterprises, funds, accounts, and other persons material to an evaluation of the Offering; and a description of the undertakings to be provided pursuant to paragraph (b)(5)(i), paragraph (d)(2)(ii), and paragraph (d)(2)(iii) of this section, if applicable, and of any instances in the previous five years in which each person specified pursuant to paragraph (b)(5)(ii) of this section failed to comply, in all material respects, with any previous undertakings in a written contract or agreement specified in paragraph (b)(5)(i) of this section. Financial information or operating data may be set forth in the document or set of documents, or may be included by specific reference to documents available to the public on the Municipal Securities Rulemaking Board's Internet Web site or filed with the Commission.

(4) The term issuer of municipal securities means the governmental issuer specified in section 3(a)(29) of the Act and the issuer of any separate security, including a separate security as defined in rule 3b-5(a) under the Act.

(5) The term potential customer means (i) Any person contacted by the Participating Underwriter concerning the purchase of municipal securities that are intended to be offered or have been sold in an offering, (ii) Any person who has expressed an interest to the Participating Underwriter in possibly purchasing such municipal securities, (iii) Any person who has a customer account with the Participating Underwriter.

(6) The term preliminary official statement means an official statement prepared by or for an issuer of municipal securities for dissemination to potential customers prior to the availability of the final official statement.

(7) The term primary offering means an offering of municipal securities directly or indirectly by or on behalf of an issuer of such securities, including any remarketing of municipal securities.
   (i) That is accompanied by a change in the authorized denomination of such securities from $100,000 or more to less than $100,000, or
   (ii) That is accompanied by a change in the period during which such securities may be tendered to an issuer of such securities or its designated agent for redemption or purchase from a period of nine months or less to a period of more than nine months.

(8) The term underwriter means any person who has purchased from an issuer of municipal securities with a view to, or offers or sells for an issuer of municipal securities in connection with, the offering of any municipal security, or participates or has a direct or indirect participation in any such undertaking, or participates or has a participation in the direct or indirect underwriting of any such undertaking; except, that such term shall not include a person whose interest is limited to a commission, concession, or allowance from an underwriter, broker, dealer, or municipal securities dealer not in excess of the usual and customary distributors' or sellers' commission, concession, or allowance.

(9) The term annual financial information means financial information or operating data, provided at least annually, of the type included in the final official statement with respect to an obligated person, or in the case where no financial information or operating data was provided in the final official statement with respect to such obligated person, of the type included in the final official statement with respect to those obligated persons that meet the objective criteria applied to select the persons for which financial information or operating data will be provided on an annual basis. Financial information or operating data may be set forth in the document or set of documents, or may be included by specific reference to documents available to the public on the Municipal Securities Rulemaking Board's Internet Web site or filed with the Commission.

(10) The term obligated person means any person, including an issuer of municipal securities, who is generally or through an enterprise, fund, or account of such person committed by contract or other arrangement to support payment of all, or part of the obligations on the municipal securities to be sold in the Offering (other than providers of municipal bond insurance, letters of credit, or other liquidity facilities).

(11)(i) The term financial obligation means a:
    (A) Debt obligation;
    (B) Derivative instrument entered into in connection with, or pledged as security or a source of payment for, an existing or planned debt obligation; or
    (C) Guarantee of paragraph (f)(11)(i)(A) or (B).
  (ii) The term financial obligation shall not include municipal securities as to which a final official statement has been provided to the Municipal Securities Rulemaking Board consistent with this rule.
(g) Transitional provision. If on July 28, 1989, a Participating Underwriter was contractually committed to act as underwriter in an Offering of municipal securities originally issued before July 29, 1989, the requirements of paragraphs (b)(3) and (b)(4) shall not apply to the Participating Underwriter in connection with such an Offering. Paragraph (b)(5) of this section shall not apply to a Participating Underwriter that has contractually committed to act as an underwriter in an Offering of municipal securities before July 3, 1995; except that paragraph (b)(5)(i)(A) and paragraph (b)(5)(i)(B) shall not apply with respect to fiscal years ending prior to January 1, 1996. Paragraph (c) shall become effective on January 1, 1996. Paragraph (d)(2)(ii) and paragraph (d)(2)(iii) of this section shall not apply to an Offering of municipal securities commencing prior to January 1, 1996.

-----

65. SEC Rules and Regulations, Securities Exchange Act of 1934: 17a-3 – Records to be Made by Certain Exchange Members, Brokers and Dealers

(a) Every member of a national securities exchange who transacts a business in securities directly with others than members of a national securities exchange, and every broker or dealer who transacts a business in securities through the medium of any such member, and every broker or dealer registered pursuant to section 15 of the Securities Exchange Act of 1934, as amended, (48 Stat. 895, 49 Stat. 1377, 52 Stat. 1075; 15 U.S.C. 78o) shall make and keep current the following books and records relating to its business:
  (1) Blotters (or other records of original entry) containing an itemized daily record of all purchases and sales of securities, all receipts and deliveries of securities (including certificate numbers), all receipts and disbursements of cash and all other debits and credits. Such records shall show the account for which each such transaction was effected, the name and amount of securities, the unit and aggregate purchase or sale price (if any), the trade date, and the name or other designation of the person from whom purchased or received or to whom sold or delivered.
  (2) Ledgers (or other records) reflecting all assets and liabilities, income and expense and capital accounts.
  (3) Ledger accounts (or other records) itemizing separately as to each cash and margin account of every customer and of such member, broker or dealer and partners thereof, all purchases, sales, receipts and deliveries of securities and commodities for such account and all other debits and credits to such account.
  (4) Ledgers (or other records) reflecting the following:
    (i) Securities in transfer;
    (ii) Dividends and interest received;
    (iii) Securities borrowed and securities loaned;
    (iv) Moneys borrowed and moneys loaned (together with a record of the collateral therefor and any substitutions in such collateral);
    (v) Securities failed to receive and failed to deliver;
    (vi) All long and all short securities record differences arising from the examination, count, verification and comparison pursuant to §§ 240.17a-5, 240.17a-12, and 240.17a-13 (by date of examination,

count, verification and comparison showing for each security the number of long or short count differences);

(vii) Repurchase and reverse repurchase agreements;

(5) A securities record or ledger reflecting separately for each security as of the clearance dates all "long" or "short" positions (including securities in safekeeping and securities that are the subjects of repurchase or reverse repurchase agreements) carried by such member, broker or dealer for its account of for the account of its customers or partners or others and showing the location of all securities long and the offsetting position to all securities short, including long security count differences and short security count differences classified by the date of the physical count and verification in which they were discovered, and in all cases the name or designation of the account in which each position is carried.

(6)

(i) A memorandum of each brokerage order, and of any other instruction, given or received for the purchase or sale of securities, whether executed or unexecuted. The memorandum shall show the terms and conditions of the order or instructions and of any modification or cancellation thereof; the account for which entered; the time the order was received; the time of entry; the price at which executed; the identity of each associated person, if any, responsible for the account; the identity of any other person who entered or accepted the order on behalf of the customer or, if a customer entered the order on an electronic system, a notation of that entry; and, to the extent feasible, the time of execution or cancellation. The memorandum need not show the identity of any person, other than the associated person responsible for the account, who may have entered or accepted the order if the order is entered into an electronic system that generates the memorandum and if that system is not capable of receiving an entry of the identity of any person other than the responsible associated person; in that circumstance, the member, broker or dealer shall produce upon request by a representative of a securities regulatory authority a separate record which identifies each other person. An order entered pursuant to the exercise of discretionary authority by the member, broker or dealer, or associated person thereof, shall be so designated. The term instruction shall include instructions between partners and employees of a member, broker or dealer. The term time of entry shall mean the time when the member, broker or dealer transmits the order or instruction for execution.

(ii) This memorandum need not be made as to a purchase, sale or redemption of a security on a subscription way basis directly from or to the issuer, if the member, broker or dealer maintains a copy of the customer's subscription agreement regarding a purchase, or a copy of any other document required by the issuer regarding a sale or redemption.

(7) A memorandum of each purchase and sale for the account of the member, broker, or dealer showing the price and, to the extent feasible, the time of execution; and, in addition, where the purchase or sale is with a customer other than a broker or dealer, a memorandum of each order received, showing the time of receipt; the terms and conditions of the order and of any modification thereof; the account for which it was entered; the identity of each associated person, if any, responsible for the account; the identity of any other person who entered or accepted the order on behalf of the customer or, if a customer entered the order on an electronic system, a notation of that entry. The memorandum need not show the identity of any person other than the associated person responsible for the account who may have entered the order if the order is entered into an electronic system that generates the memorandum and if that system is not capable of receiving an entry of the identity of any person other than the responsible associated person: in that circumstance, the member, broker or dealer shall produce upon request by a representative of a securities regulatory authority a separate record which identifies each other person. An order with a customer other than a member, broker or dealer entered pursuant to the exercise of discretionary authority by the member, broker or dealer, or associated person thereof, shall be so designated.

(8) Copies of confirmations of all purchases and sales of securities, including all repurchase and reverse repurchase agreements, and copies of notices of all other debits and credits for securities, cash and other items for the account of customers and partners of such member, broker or dealer.

(9) A record in respect of each cash and margin account with such member, broker or dealer indicating

    (i) The name and address of the beneficial owner of such account, and

    (ii) Except with respect to exempt employee benefit plan securities as defined in § 240.14a-1(d), but only to the extent such securities are held by employee benefit plans established by the issuer of the securities, whether or not the beneficial owner of securities registered in the name of such members, brokers or dealers, or a registered clearing agency or its nominee objects to disclosure of his or her identity, address and securities positions to issuers, and

    (iii) In the case of a margin account, the signature of such owner; Provided, That, in the case of a joint account or an account of a corporation, such records are required only in respect of the person or persons authorized to transact business for such account.

(10) A record of all puts, calls, spreads, straddles and other options in which such member, broker or dealer has any direct or indirect interest or which such members, broker or dealer has granted or guaranteed, containing, at least, an identification of the security and the number of units involved. An OTC derivatives dealer shall also keep a record of all eligible OTC derivative instruments as defined in § 240.3b-13 in which the OTC derivatives dealer has any direct or indirect interest or which it has written or guaranteed, containing, at a minimum, an identification of the security or other instrument, the number of units involved, and the identity of the counterparty.

(11) A record of the proof of money balances of all ledger accounts in the form of trial balances, and a record of the computation of aggregate indebtedness and net capital, as of the trial balance date, pursuant to § 240.15c3-1; Provided, however, (i) That such computation need not be made by any member, broker or dealer unconditionally exempt from § 240.15c3-1 by paragraph (b)(1) or (b)(3), thereof; and (ii) that any member of an exchange whose members are exempt from § 240.15c3-1 by paragraph (b)(2) thereof shall make a record of the computation of aggregate indebtedness and net capital as of the trial balance date in accordance with the capital rules of at least one of the exchanges therein listed of which it is a member. Such trial balances and computations shall be prepared currently at least once a month.

(12)

    (i) A questionnaire or application for employment executed by each "associated person" (as defined in paragraph (h)(4) of this section) of the member, broker or dealer, which questionnaire or application shall be approved in writing by an authorized representative of the member, broker or dealer and shall contain at least the following information with respect to the associated person:

        (A) The associated person's name, address, social security number, and the starting date of the associated person's employment or other association with the member, broker or dealer;

        (B) The associated person's date of birth;

        (C) A complete, consecutive statement of all the associated person's business connections for at least the preceding ten years, including whether the employment was part-time or full-time;

        (D) A record of any denial of membership or registration, and of any disciplinary action taken, or sanction imposed, upon the associated person by any federal or state agency, or by any national securities exchange or national securities association, including any finding that the associated person was a cause of any disciplinary action or had violated any law;

        (E) A record of any denial, suspension, expulsion or revocation of membership or registration of any member, broker or dealer with which the associated person was associated in any capacity when such action was taken;

        (F) A record of any permanent or temporary injunction entered against the associated person or any member, broker or dealer with which the associated person was associated in any capacity at the time such injunction was entered;

        (G) A record of any arrest or indictment for any felony, or any misdemeanor pertaining to securities, commodities, banking, insurance or real estate (including, but not limited to, acting or being associated with a broker-dealer, investment company, investment adviser, futures sponsor, bank, or savings and loan association), fraud, false statements or omissions, wrongful taking of property or bribery, forgery, counterfeiting or extortion, and the disposition of the foregoing.

(H) A record of any other name or names by which the associated person has been known or which the associated person has used;

Provided, however, That if such associated person has been registered as a registered representative of such member, broker or dealer with, or the associated person's employment has been approved by, the Financial Industry Regulatory Authority, Inc., the American Stock Exchange LLC, the Boston Stock Exchange, Inc., the Chicago Stock Exchange, Inc., New York Stock Exchange LLC, NYSE Arca, Inc., the Philadelphia Stock Exchange, Inc., the Chicago Board Options Exchange, Incorporated, the National Stock Exchange, Inc. or the International Securities Exchange, LLC, then retention of a full, correct, and complete copy of any and all applications for such registration or approval shall be deemed to satisfy the requirements of this paragraph.

(ii) A record listing every associated person of the member, broker or dealer which shows, for each associated person, every office of the member, broker or dealer where the associated person regularly conducts the business of handling funds or securities or effecting any transactions in, or inducing or attempting to induce the purchase or sale of any security for the member, broker or dealer, and the Central Registration Depository number, if any, and every internal identification number or code assigned to that person by the member, broker or dealer.

(13) Records required to be maintained pursuant to paragraph (d) of § 240.17f-2.

(14) Copies of all Forms X-17F-1A filed pursuant to § 240.17f-1, all agreements between reporting institutions regarding registration or other aspects of § 240.17f-1, and all confirmations or other information received from the Commission or its designee as a result of inquiry.

(15) Records required to be maintained pursuant to paragraph (e) of § 240.17f-2.

(16)

(i) The following records regarding any internal broker-dealer system of which such a broker or dealer is the sponsor:

(A) A record of the broker's or dealer's customers that have access to an internal broker-dealer system sponsored by such broker or dealer (identifying any affiliations between such customers and the broker or dealer);

(B) Daily summaries of trading in the internal broker-dealer system, including:

(1) Securities for which transactions have been executed through use of such system; and

(2) Transaction volume (separately stated for trading occurring during hours when consolidated trade reporting facilities are and are not in operation):

(i) With respect to equity securities, stated in number of trades, number of shares, and total U.S. dollar value;

(ii) With respect to debt securities, stated in total settlement value in U.S. dollars; and

(iii) With respect to other securities, stated in number of trades, number of units of securities, and in dollar value, or other appropriate commonly used measure of value of such securities; and

(C) Time-sequenced records of each transaction effected through the internal broker-dealer system, including date and time executed, price, size, security traded, counterparty identification information, and method of execution (if internal broker-dealer system allows alternative means or locations for execution, such as routing to another market, matching with limit orders, or executing against the quotations of the broker or dealer sponsoring the system).

(ii) For purposes of paragraph (a) of this section, the term:

(A) Internal broker-dealer system shall mean any facility, other than a national securities exchange, an exchange exempt from registration based on limited volume, or an alternative trading system as defined in Regulation ATS, §§ 242.300 through 242.303 of this chapter, that provides a mechanism, automated in full or in part, for collecting, receiving, disseminating, or displaying system orders and facilitating agreement to the basic terms of a purchase or sale of a security between a customer and the sponsor, or between two customers of the sponsor, through use of the internal broker-dealer system or through the broker or dealer sponsor of such system;

(B) Sponsor shall mean any broker or dealer that organizes, operates, administers, or otherwise directly controls an internal broker-dealer trading system or, if the operator of the internal broker-dealer system is not a registered broker or dealer, any broker or dealer that, pursuant to contract, affiliation, or other agreement with the system operator, is involved on a regular basis with executing transactions in connection with use of the internal broker-dealer system, other than solely for its own account or as a customer with access to the internal broker-dealer system; and

(C) System order means any order or other communication or indication submitted by any customer with access to the internal broker-dealer system for entry into a trading system announcing an interest in purchasing or selling a security. The term "system order" does not include inquiries or indications of interest that are not entered into the internal broker-dealer system.

(17) For each account with a natural person as a customer or owner:

(i)

(A) An account record including the customer's or owner's name, tax identification number, address, telephone number, date of birth, employment status (including occupation and whether the customer is an associated person of a member, broker or dealer), annual income, net worth (excluding value of primary residence), and the account's investment objectives. In the case of a joint account, the account record must include personal information for each joint owner who is a natural person; however, financial information for the individual joint owners may be combined. The account record shall indicate whether it has been signed by the associated person responsible for the account, if any, and approved or accepted by a principal of the member, broker or dealer. For accounts in existence on the effective date of this section, the member, broker or dealer must obtain this information within three years of the effective date of the section.

(B) A record indicating that:

(1) The member, broker or dealer has furnished to each customer or owner within three years of the effective date of this section, and to each customer or owner who opened an account after the effective date of this section within thirty days of the opening of the account, and thereafter at intervals no greater than thirty-six months, a copy of the account record or an alternate document with all information required by paragraph (a)(17)(i)(A) of this section. The member, broker or dealer may elect to send this notification with the next statement mailed to the customer or owner after the opening of the account. The member, broker or dealer may choose to exclude any tax identification number and date of birth from the account record or alternative document furnished to the customer or owner. The member, broker or dealer shall include with the account record or alternative document provided to each customer or owner an explanation of any terms regarding investment objectives. The account record or alternate document furnished to the customer or owner shall include or be accompanied by prominent statements that the customer or owner should mark any corrections and return the account record or alternate document to the member, broker or dealer, and that the customer or owner should notify the member, broker or dealer of any future changes to information contained in the account record.

(2) For each account record updated to reflect a change in the name or address of the customer or owner, the member, broker or dealer furnished a notification of that change to the customer's old address, or to each joint owner, and the associated person, if any, responsible for that account, on or before the 30th day after the date the member, broker or dealer received notice of the change.

(3) For each change in the account's investment objectives the member, broker or dealer has furnished to each customer or owner, and the associated person, if any, responsible for that

account a copy of the updated customer account record or alternative document with all information required to be furnished by paragraph (a)(17)(i)(B)(1) of this section, on or before the 30th day after the date the member, broker or dealer received notice of any change, or, if the account was updated for some reason other than the firm receiving notice of a change, after the date the account record was updated. The member, broker or dealer may elect to send this notification with the next statement scheduled to be mailed to the customer or owner.

(C) For purposes of this paragraph (a)(17), the neglect, refusal, or inability of a customer or owner to provide or update any account record information required under paragraph (a)(17)(i)(A) of this section shall excuse the member, broker or dealer from obtaining that required information.

(D) The account record requirements in paragraph (a)(17)(i)(A) of this section shall only apply to accounts for which the member, broker or dealer is, or has within the past 36 months been, required to make a suitability determination under the federal securities laws or under the requirements of a self-regulatory organization of which it is a member. Additionally, the furnishing requirement in paragraph (a)(17)(i)(B)(1) of this section shall not be applicable to an account for which, within the last 36 months, the member, broker or dealer has not been required to make a suitability determination under the federal securities laws or under the requirements of a self-regulatory organization of which it is a member. This paragraph (a)(17)(i)(D) does not relieve a member, broker or dealer from any obligation arising from the rules of a self-regulatory organization of which it is a member regarding the collection of information from a customer or owner.

(ii) If an account is a discretionary account, a record containing the dated signature of each customer or owner granting the authority and the dated signature of each natural person to whom discretionary authority was granted.

(iii) A record for each account indicating that each customer or owner was furnished with a copy of each written agreement entered into on or after the effective date of this paragraph pertaining to that account and that, if requested by the customer or owner, the customer or owner was furnished with a fully executed copy of each agreement.

(18) A record:

(i) As to each associated person of each written customer complaint received by the member, broker or dealer concerning that associated person. The record shall include the complainant's name, address, and account number; the date the complaint was received; the name of any other associated person identified in the complaint; a description of the nature of the complaint; and the disposition of the complaint. Instead of the record, a member, broker or dealer may maintain a copy of each original complaint in a separate file by the associated person named in the complaint along with a record of the disposition of the complaint.

(ii) Indicating that each customer of the member, broker or dealer has been provided with a notice containing the address and telephone number of the department of the member, broker or dealer to which any complaints as to the account may be directed.

(19) A record:

(i) As to each associated person listing each purchase and sale of a security attributable, for compensation purposes, to that associated person. The record shall include the amount of compensation if monetary and a description of the compensation if non-monetary. In lieu of making this record, a member, broker or dealer may elect to produce the required information promptly upon request of a representative of a securities regulatory authority.

(ii) Of all agreements pertaining to the relationship between each associated person and the member, broker or dealer including a summary of each associated person's compensation arrangement or plan with the member, broker or dealer, including commission and concession schedules and, to the extent that compensation is based on factors other than remuneration per trade, the method by which the compensation is determined.

(20) A record, which need not be separate from the advertisements, sales literature, or communications, documenting that the member, broker or dealer has complied with, or adopted policies and procedures reasonably designed to establish compliance with, applicable federal requirements and rules of a self-regulatory organization of which the member, broker or dealer is a member which require that advertisements, sales literature, or any other communications with the public by a member, broker or dealer or its associated persons be approved by a principal.

(21) A record for each office listing, by name or title, each person at that office who, without delay, can explain the types of records the firm maintains at that office and the information contained in those records.

(22) A record listing each principal of a member, broker or dealer responsible for establishing policies and procedures that are reasonably designed to ensure compliance with any applicable federal requirements or rules of a self-regulatory organization of which the member, broker or dealer is a member that require acceptance or approval of a record by a principal.

(23) A record documenting the credit, market, and liquidity risk management controls established and maintained by the broker or dealer to assist it in analyzing and managing the risks associated with its business activities, Provided, that the records required by this paragraph (a)(23) need only be made if the broker or dealer has more than:

(i) $1,000,000 in aggregate credit items as computed under § 240.15c3-3a; or

(ii) $20,000,000 in capital, which includes debt subordinated in accordance with § 240.15c3-1d.

(24) A record of the date that each Form CRS was provided to each retail investor, including any Form CRS provided before such retail investor opens an account.

(25)-(34) [Reserved].

(35) For each retail customer to whom a recommendation of any securities transaction or investment strategy involving securities is or will be provided:

(i) A record of all information collected from and provided to the retail customer pursuant to § 240.15l-1, as well as the identity of each natural person who is an associated person, if any, responsible for the account.

(ii) For purposes of this paragraph (a)(35), the neglect, refusal, or inability of the retail customer to provide or update any information described in paragraph (a)(35)(i) of this section shall excuse the broker, dealer, or associated person from obtaining that required information.

(b)

(1) This section shall not be deemed to require a member of a national securities exchange, a broker, or dealer who transacts a business in securities through the medium of any such member, or a broker or dealer registered pursuant to section 15 of the Act, to make or keep such records of transactions cleared for such member, broker, or dealer as are customarily made and kept by a clearing broker or dealer pursuant to the requirements of §§ 240.17a-3 and 240.17a-4: Provided, That the clearing broker or dealer has and maintains net capital of not less than $25,000 and is otherwise in compliance with § 240.15c3-1 or the capital rules of the exchange of which such clearing broker or dealer is a member if the members of such exchange are exempt from § 240.15c3-1 by paragraph (b)(2) thereof.

(2) This section shall not be deemed to require a member of a national securities exchange, a broker, or dealer who transacts a business in securities through the medium of any such member, or a broker or dealer registered pursuant to section 15 of the Act, to make or keep such records of transactions cleared for such member, broker or dealer by a bank as are customarily made and kept by a clearing broker or dealer pursuant to the requirements of §§ 240.17a-3 and 240.17a-4: Provided, That such member, broker, or dealer obtains from such bank an agreement in writing to the effect that the records made and kept by such bank are the property of the member, broker, or dealer: And provided further, That such bank files with the Commission a written undertaking in form acceptable to the Commission and signed by a duly authorized person, that such books and records are available for examination by representatives of the Commission as specified in section 17(a) of the Act, and that it will furnish to the Commission,

upon demand, at its principal office in Washington, DC, or at any regional office of the Commission designated in such demand, true, correct, complete, and current copies of any or all of such records. Such undertaking shall include the following provisions:

The undersigned hereby undertakes to maintain and preserve on behalf of [BD] the books and records required to be maintained and preserved by [BD] pursuant to Rules 17a-3 and 17a-4 under the Securities Exchange Act of 1934 and to permit examination of such books and records at any time or from time to time during business hours by examiners or other representatives of the Securities and Exchange Commission, and to furnish to said Commission at its principal office in Washington, DC, or at any regional office of said Commission specified in a demand made by or on behalf of said Commission for copies of books and records, true, correct, complete, and current copies of any or all, or any part, of such books and records. This undertaking shall be binding upon the undersigned, and the successors and assigns of the undersigned.

Nothing herein contained shall be deemed to relieve such member, broker, or dealer from the responsibility that such books and records be accurately maintained and preserved as specified in §§ 240.17a-3 and 240.17a-4.

(c) This section shall not be deemed to require a member of a national securities exchange, or a broker or dealer registered pursuant to section 15 of the Securities Exchange Act of 1934 (48 Stat. 895, 49 Stat. 1377; 15 U.S.C. 78o) as amended, to make or keep such records as are required by paragraph (a) reflecting the sale of United States Tax Savings Notes, United States Defense Savings Stamps, or United States Defense Savings Bonds, Series E, F and G.

(d) The records specified in paragraph (a) of this section shall not be required with respect to any cash transaction of $100 or less involving only subscription rights or warrants which by their terms expire within 90 days after the issuance thereof.

(e) For purposes of transactions in municipal securities by municipal securities brokers and municipal securities dealers, compliance with Rule G-8 of the Municipal Securities Rulemaking Board will be deemed to be in compliance with this section.

(f) Security futures products. The provisions of this section shall not apply to security futures product transactions and positions in a futures account (as that term is defined in § 240.15c3-3(a)(15)); provided, that the Commodity Futures Trading Commission's recordkeeping rules apply to those transactions and positions.

(g) Every member, broker or dealer shall make and keep current, as to each office, the books and records described in paragraphs (a)(1), (a)(6), (a)(7), (a)(12), (a)(17), (a)(18)(i), (a)(19), (a)(20), (a)(21), and (a)(22) of this section.

(h) When used in this section:
   (1) The term office means any location where one or more associated persons regularly conduct the business of handling funds or securities or effecting any transactions in, or inducing or attempting to induce the purchase or sale of, any security.
   (2) The term principal means any individual registered with a registered national securities association as a principal or branch manager of a member, broker or dealer or any other person who has been delegated supervisory responsibility over associated persons by the member, broker or dealer.
   (3) The term securities regulatory authority means the Commission, any self-regulatory organization, or any securities commission (or any agency or office performing like functions) of the States.
   (4) The term associated person means an "associated person of a member" or "associated person of a broker or dealer" as defined in sections 3(a)(21) and 3(a)(18) of the Act (15 U.S.C. 78c(a)(21) and (a)(18)) respectively, but shall not include persons whose functions are solely clerical or ministerial.

66. SEC Rules and Regulations, Securities Exchange Act of 1934:
17a-4 – Records to be Preserved by Certain Exchange Members, Brokers and Dealers

(a) Every member, broker and dealer subject to § 240.17a-3 shall preserve for a period of not less than six years, the first two years in an easily accessible place, all records required to be made pursuant to paragraphs § 240.17a-3(a)(1), (a)(2), (a)(3), (a)(5), (a)(21), (a)(22), and analogous records created pursuant to paragraph § 240.17a-3(f).

(b) Every member, broker and dealer subject to § 240.17a-3 shall preserve for a period of not less than three years, the first two years in an easily accessible place:

(1) All records required to be made pursuant to § 240.17a-3(a)(4), (a)(6), (a)(7), (a)(8), (a)(9), (a)(10), (a)(16), (a)(18), (a)(19), (a)(20), and analogous records created pursuant to § 240.17a-3(g).

(2) All check books, bank statements, cancelled checks and cash reconciliations.

(3) All bills receivable or payable (or copies thereof), paid or unpaid, relating to the business of such member, broker or dealer, as such.

(4) Originals of all communications received and copies of all communications sent (and any approvals thereof) by the member, broker or dealer (including inter-office memoranda and communications) relating to its business as such, including all communications which are subject to rules of a self-regulatory organization of which the member, broker or dealer is a member regarding communications with the public. As used in this paragraph (b)(4), the term communications includes sales scripts.

(5) All trial balances, computations of aggregate indebtedness and net capital (and working papers in connection therewith), financial statements, branch office reconciliations, and internal audit working papers, relating to the business of such member, broker or dealer, as such.

(6) All guarantees of accounts and all powers of attorney and other evidence of the granting of any discretionary authority given in respect of any account, and copies of resolutions empowering an agent to act on behalf of a corporation.

(7) All written agreements (or copies thereof) entered into by such member, broker or dealer relating to its business as such, including agreements with respect to any account.

(8) Records which contain the following information in support of amounts included in the report prepared as of the audit date on Form X-17A-5 (§ 249.617 of this chapter) Part II or Part IIA or Part IIB and in annual audited financial statements required by § 240.17a-5(d) and § 240.17a-12(b):

(i) Money balance position, long or short, including description, quantity, price and valuation of each security including contractual commitments in customers' accounts, in cash and fully secured accounts, partly secured accounts, unsecured accounts, and in securities accounts payable to customers;

(ii) Money balance and position, long or short, including description, quantity, price and valuation of each security including contractual commitments in non-customers' accounts, in cash and fully secured accounts, partly secured and unsecured accounts, and in securities accounts payable to non-customers;

(iii) Position, long or short, including description, quantity, price and valuation of each security including contractual commitments included in the Computation of Net Capital as commitments, securities owned, securities owned not readily marketable, and other investments owned not readily marketable;

(iv) Amount of secured demand note, description of collateral securing such secured demand note including quantity, price and valuation of each security and cash balance securing such secured demand note;

(v) Description of futures commodity contracts, contract value on trade date, market value, gain or loss, and liquidating equity or deficit in customers' and non-customers' accounts;

(vi) Description of futures commodity contracts, contract value on trade date, market value, gain or loss and liquidating equity or deficit in trading and investment accounts;

(vii) Description, money balance, quantity, price and valuation of each spot commodity position or commitments in customers' and non-customers' accounts;

(viii) Description, money balance, quantity, price and valuation of each spot commodity position or commitments in trading and investment accounts;

(ix) Number of shares, description of security, exercise price, cost and market value of put and call options including short out of the money options having no market or exercise value, showing listed and unlisted put and call options separately;

(x) Quantity, price, and valuation of each security underlying the haircut for undue concentration made in the Computation for Net Capital;

(xi) Description, quantity, price and valuation of each security and commodity position or contractual commitment, long or short, in each joint account in which the broker or dealer has an interest, including each participant's interest and margin deposit;

(xii) Description, settlement date, contract amount, quantity, market price, and valuation for each aged failed to deliver requiring a charge in the Computation of Net Capital pursuant to § 240.15c3-1;

(xiii) Detail relating to information for possession or control requirements under § 240.15c3-3 and reported on the schedule in Part II or IIA of Form X-17A-5 (§ 249.617 of this chapter);

(xiv) Detail of all items, not otherwise substantiated, which are charged or credited in the Computation of Net Capital pursuant to § 240.15c3-1, such as cash margin deficiencies, deductions related to securities values and undue concentration, aged securities differences and insurance claims receivable; and

(xv) Other schedules which are specifically prescribed by the Commission as necessary to support information reported as required by § 240.17a-5 and § 240.17a-12.

(9) The records required to be made pursuant to § 240.15c3-3(d)(5) and (o).

(10) The records required to be made pursuant to § 240.15c3-4 and the results of the periodic reviews conducted pursuant to § 240.15c3-4(d).

(11) All notices relating to an internal broker-dealer system provided to the customers of the broker or dealer that sponsors such internal broker-dealer system, as defined in paragraph (a)(16)(ii)(A) of § 240.17a-3. Notices, whether written or communicated through the internal broker-dealer trading system or other automated means, shall be preserved under this paragraph (b)(11) if they are provided to all customers with access to an internal broker-dealer system, or to one or more classes of customers. Examples of notices to be preserved under this paragraph (b)(11) include, but are not limited to, notices addressing hours of system operations, system malfunctions, changes to system procedures, maintenance of hardware and software, and instructions pertaining to access to the internal broker-dealer system.

(12) The records required to be made pursuant to § 240.15c3-1e(c)(4)(vi).

(13) The written policies and procedures the broker-dealer establishes, documents, maintains, and enforces to assess creditworthiness for the purpose of § 240.15c3-1(c)(2)(vi)(E), (c)(2)(vi)(F)(1), (c)(2)(vi)(F)(2), and (c)(2)(vi)(H).

(c) Every member, broker and dealer subject to § 240.17a-3 shall preserve for a period of not less than six years after the closing of any customer's account any account cards or records which relate to the terms and conditions with respect to the opening and maintenance of the account.

(d) Every member, broker and dealer subject to § 240.17a-3 shall preserve during the life of the enterprise and of any successor enterprise all partnership articles or, in the case of a corporation, all articles of incorporation or charter, minute books and stock certificate books (or, in the case of any other form of legal entity, all records such as articles of organization or formation, and minute books used for a purpose similar to those records required for corporations or partnerships), all Forms BD (§ 249.501 of this chapter), all Forms BDW (§ 249.501a of this chapter), all amendments to these forms, all licenses or other documentation showing the registration of the member, broker or dealer with any securities regulatory authority.

(e) Every member, broker and dealer subject to § 240.17a-3 shall maintain and preserve in an easily accessible place:

(1) All records required under paragraph (a)(12) of § 240.17a-3 until at least three years after the associated person's employment and any other connection with the member, broker or dealer has terminated.

(2) All records required under paragraph (a)(13) of § 240.17a-3 until at least three years after the termination of employment or association of those persons required by § 240.17f-2 to be fingerprinted; and

(3) All records required pursuant to paragraph (a)(15) of § 240.17a-3 for the life of the enterprise.

(4) All records required pursuant to paragraph (a)(14) of § 240.17a-3 for three years.

(5) All account record information required pursuant to § 240.17a-3(a)(17) and all records required pursuant to § 240.17a-3(a)(35), in each case until at least six years after the earlier of the date the account was closed or the date on which the information was collected, provided, replaced, or updated.

(6) Each report which a securities regulatory authority has requested or required the member, broker or dealer to make and furnish to it pursuant to an order or settlement, and each securities regulatory authority examination report until three years after the date of the report.

(7) Each compliance, supervisory, and procedures manual, including any updates, modifications, and revisions to the manual, describing the policies and practices of the member, broker or dealer with respect to compliance with applicable laws and rules, and supervision of the activities of each natural person associated with the member, broker or dealer until three years after the termination of the use of the manual.

(8) All reports produced to review for unusual activity in customer accounts until eighteen months after the date the report was generated. In lieu of maintaining the reports, a member, broker or dealer may produce promptly the reports upon request by a representative of a securities regulatory authority. If a report was generated in a computer system that has been changed in the most recent eighteen month period in a manner such that the report cannot be reproduced using historical data in the same format as it was originally generated, the report may be produced by using the historical data in the current system, but must be accompanied by a record explaining each system change which affected the reports. If a report is generated in a computer system that has been changed in the most recent eighteen month period in a manner such that the report cannot be reproduced in any format using historical data, the member, broker or dealer shall promptly produce upon request a record of the parameters that were used to generate the report at the time specified by a representative of a securities regulatory authority, including a record of the frequency with which the reports were generated.

(9) All records required pursuant to § 240.17a-3(a)(23) until three years after the termination of the use of the risk management controls documented therein.

(10) All records required pursuant to § 240.17a-3(a)(24), as well as a copy of each Form CRS, until at least six years after such record or Form CRS is created.

(f) The records required to be maintained and preserved pursuant to §§ 240.17a-3 and 240.17a-4 may be immediately produced or reproduced on "micrographic media" (as defined in this section) or by means of "electronic storage media" (as defined in this section) that meet the conditions set forth in this paragraph and be maintained and preserved for the required time in that form.

(1) For purposes of this section:

(i) The term micrographic media means microfilm or microfiche, or any similar medium; and

(ii) The term electronic storage media means any digital storage medium or system and, in the case of both paragraphs (f)(1)(i) and (f)(1)(ii) of this section, that meets the applicable conditions set forth in this paragraph (f).

(2) If electronic storage media is used by a member, broker, or dealer, it shall comply with the following requirements:

(i) The member, broker, or dealer must notify its examining authority designated pursuant to section 17(d) of the Act (15 U.S.C. 78q(d)) prior to employing electronic storage media. If employing any electronic storage media other than optical disk technology (including CD-ROM), the member, broker, or dealer must notify its designated examining authority at least 90 days prior to employing such storage media. In either case, the member, broker, or dealer must provide its own representation or one from the storage medium vendor or other third party with appropriate expertise that the selected storage media meets the conditions set forth in this paragraph (f)(2).

(ii) The electronic storage media must:

    (A) Preserve the records exclusively in a non-rewriteable, non-erasable format;

    (B) Verify automatically the quality and accuracy of the storage media recording process;

    (C) Serialize the original and, if applicable, duplicate units of storage media, and time-date for the required period of retention the information placed on such electronic storage media; and

    (D) Have the capacity to readily download indexes and records preserved on the electronic storage media to any medium acceptable under this paragraph (f) as required by the Commission or the self-regulatory organizations of which the member, broker, or dealer is a member.

(3) If a member, broker, or dealer uses micrographic media or electronic storage media, it shall:

(i) At all times have available, for examination by the staffs of the Commission and self-regulatory organizations of which it is a member, facilities for immediate, easily readable projection or production of micrographic media or electronic storage media images and for producing easily readable images.

(ii) Be ready at all times to provide, and immediately provide, any facsimile enlargement which the staffs of the Commission, any self-regulatory organization of which it is a member, or any State securities regulator having jurisdiction over the member, broker or dealer may request.

(iii) Store separately from the original, a duplicate copy of the record stored on any medium acceptable under § 240.17a-4 for the time required.

(iv) Organize and index accurately all information maintained on both original and any duplicate storage media.

    (A) At all times, a member, broker, or dealer must be able to have such indexes available for examination by the staffs of the Commission and the self- regulatory organizations of which the broker or dealer is a member.

    (B) Each index must be duplicated and the duplicate copies must be stored separately from the original copy of each index.

    (C) Original and duplicate indexes must be preserved for the time required for the indexed records.

(v) The member, broker, or dealer must have in place an audit system providing for accountability regarding inputting of records required to be maintained and preserved pursuant to §§ 240.17a-3 and 240.17a-4 to electronic storage media and inputting of any changes made to every original and duplicate record maintained and preserved thereby.

    (A) At all times, a member, broker, or dealer must be able to have the results of such audit system available for examination by the staffs of the Commission and the self-regulatory organizations of which the broker or dealer is a member.

    (B) The audit results must be preserved for the time required for the audited records.

(vi) The member, broker, or dealer must maintain, keep current, and provide promptly upon request by the staffs of the Commission or the self-regulatory organizations of which the member, broker, or broker-dealer is a member all information necessary to access records and indexes stored on the electronic storage media; or place in escrow and keep current a copy of the physical and logical file format of the electronic storage media, the field format of all different information types written on the electronic storage media and the source code, together with the appropriate documentation and information necessary to access records and indexes.

(vii) For every member, broker, or dealer exclusively using electronic storage media for some or all of its record preservation under this section, at least one third party ("the undersigned"), who has access to and the ability to download information from the member's, broker's, or dealer's electronic storage media to any acceptable medium under this section, shall file with the designated examining authority for the member, broker, or dealer the following undertakings with respect to such records:

The undersigned hereby undertakes to furnish promptly to the U.S. Securities and Exchange Commission ("Commission"), its designees or representatives, any self-regulatory organization of which it is a member, or any State securities regulator having jurisdiction over the member, broker or dealer, upon reasonable request, such information as is deemed necessary by the staffs of the Commission, any self-regulatory organization of which it is a member, or any State securities regulator having jurisdiction over the member, broker or dealer to download information kept on the broker's or dealer's electronic storage media to any medium acceptable under Rule 17a-4.

Furthermore, the undersigned hereby undertakes to take reasonable steps to provide access to information contained on the broker's or dealer's electronic storage media, including, as appropriate, arrangements for the downloading of any record required to be maintained and preserved by the broker or dealer pursuant to Rules 17a-3 and 17a-4 under the Securities Exchange Act of 1934 in a format acceptable to the staffs of the Commission, any self-regulatory organization of which it is a member, or any State securities regulator having jurisdiction over the member, broker or dealer. Such arrangements will provide specifically that in the event of a failure on the part of a broker or dealer to download the record into a readable format and after reasonable notice to the broker or dealer, upon being provided with the appropriate electronic storage medium, the undersigned will undertake to do so, as the staffs of the Commission, any self-regulatory organization of which it is a member, or any State securities regulator having jurisdiction over the member, broker or dealer may request.

(g) If a person who has been subject to § 240.17a-3 ceases to transact a business in securities directly with others than members of a national securities exchange, or ceases to transact a business in securities through the medium of a member of a national securities exchange, or ceases to be registered pursuant to section 15 of the Securities Exchange Act of 1934 as amended (48 Stat. 895, 49 Stat. 1377; 15 U.S.C. 78o), such person shall, for the remainder of the periods of time specified in this section, continue to preserve the records which he theretofore preserved pursuant to this section.

(h) For purposes of transactions in municipal securities by municipal securities brokers and municipal securities dealers, compliance with Rule G-9 of the Municipal Securities Rulemaking Board will be deemed to be in compliance with this section.

(i) If the records required to be maintained and preserved pursuant to the provisions of §§ 240.17a-3 and 240.17a-4 are prepared or maintained by an outside service bureau, depository, bank which does not operate pursuant to § 240.17a-3(b)(2), or other recordkeeping service on behalf of the member, broker or dealer required to maintain and preserve such records, such outside entity shall file with the Commission a written undertaking in form acceptable to the Commission, signed by a duly authorized person, to the effect that such records are the property of the member, broker or dealer required to maintain and preserve such records and will be surrendered promptly on request of the member, broker or dealer and including the following provision:

With respect to any books and records maintained or preserved on behalf of [BD], the undersigned hereby undertakes to permit examination of such books and records at any time or from time to time during business hours by representatives or designees of the Securities and Exchange Commission, and to promptly furnish to said Commission or its designee true, correct, complete and current hard copy of any or all or any part of such books and records.

Agreement with an outside entity shall not relieve such member, broker or dealer from the responsibility to prepare and maintain records as specified in this section or in § 240.17a-3.

(j) Every member, broker and dealer subject to this section shall furnish promptly to a representative of the Commission legible, true, complete, and current copies of those records of the member, broker or dealer that are required to be preserved under this section, or any other records of the member, broker or dealer subject to examination under section 17(b) of the Act (15 U.S.C. 78q(b)) that are requested by the representative of the Commission.

(k) Exchanges of futures for physical.

(1) Except as provided in paragraph (k)(2) of this section, upon request of any designee or representative of

the Commission or of any self-regulatory organization of which it is a member, every member, broker or dealer subject to this section shall request and obtain from its customers documentation regarding an exchange of security futures products for physical securities, including documentation of underlying cash transactions and exchanges. Upon receipt of such documentation, the member, broker or dealer shall promptly provide that documentation to the requesting designee or representative.

    (2) This paragraph (k) does not apply to an underlying cash transaction(s) or exchange(s) that was effected through a member, broker or dealer registered with the Commission and is of a type required to be recorded pursuant to § 240.17a-3.

(l) Records for the most recent two year period required to be made pursuant to § 240.17a-3(g) and paragraphs (b)(4) and (e)(7) of this section which relate to an office shall be maintained at the office to which they relate. If an office is a private residence where only one associated person (or multiple associated persons who reside at that location and are members of the same immediate family) regularly conducts business, and it is not held out to the public as an office nor are funds or securities of any customer of the member, broker or dealer handled there, the member, broker or dealer need not maintain records at that office, but the records must be maintained at another location within the same State as the member, broker or dealer may select. Rather than maintain the records at each office, the member, broker or dealer may choose to produce the records promptly at the request of a representative of a securities regulatory authority at the office to which they relate or at another location agreed to by the representative

(m) When used in this section:

    (1) The term office shall have the meaning set forth in § 240.17a-3(h)(1).

    (2) The term principal shall have the meaning set forth in § 240.17a-3(h)(2).

    (3) The term securities regulatory authority shall have the meaning set forth in § 240.17a-3(h)(3).

    (4) The term associated person shall have the meaning set forth in § 240.17a-3(h)(4).

67: SEC Rules and Regulations, Investment Company Act of 1940:
17a-6 – Exemption for Transactions with Portfolio Affiliates

(a) Exemption for transactions with portfolio affiliates. A transaction to which a fund, or a company controlled by a fund, and a portfolio affiliate of the fund are parties is exempt from the provisions of section 17(a) of the Act (15 U.S.C. 80a-17(a)), provided that none of the following persons is a party to the transaction, or has a direct or indirect financial interest in a party to the transaction other than the fund:

    (1) An officer, director, employee, investment adviser, member of an advisory board, depositor, promoter of or principal underwriter for the fund;

    (2) A person directly or indirectly controlling the fund;

    (3) A person directly or indirectly owning, controlling or holding with power to vote five percent or more of the outstanding voting securities of the fund;

    (4) A person directly or indirectly under common control with the fund, other than:

        (i) A portfolio affiliate of the fund; or

        (ii) A fund whose sole interest in the transaction or a party to the transaction is an interest in the portfolio affiliate; or

    (5) An affiliated person of any of the persons mentioned in paragraphs (a)(1)-(4) of this section, other than the fund or a portfolio affiliate of the fund.

(b) Definitions -
  (1) Financial interest.
    (i) The term financial interest as used in this section does not include:
      (A) Any interest through ownership of securities issued by the fund;
      (B) Any interest of a wholly-owned subsidiary of a fund;
      (C) Usual and ordinary fees for services as a director;
      (D) An interest of a non-executive employee;
      (E) An interest of an insurance company arising from a loan or policy made or issued by it in the ordinary course of business to a natural person;
      (F) An interest of a bank arising from a loan or account made or maintained by it in the ordinary course of business to or with a natural person, unless it arises from a loan to a person who is an officer, director or executive of a company which is a party to the transaction, or from a loan to a person who directly or indirectly owns, controls, or holds with power to vote, five percent or more of the outstanding voting securities of a company which is a party to the transaction;
      (G) An interest acquired in a transaction described in paragraph (d)(3) of § 270.17d-1; or
      (H) Any other interest that the board of directors of the fund, including a majority of the directors who are not interested persons of the fund, finds to be not material, provided that the directors record the basis for that finding in the minutes of their meeting.
    (ii) A person has a financial interest in any party in which it has a financial interest, in which it had a financial interest within six months prior to the transaction, or in which it will acquire a financial interest pursuant to an arrangement in existence at the time of the transaction.
  (2) Fund means a registered investment company or separate series of a registered investment company.
  (3) Portfolio affiliate of a fund means a person that is an affiliated person (or an affiliated person of an affiliated person) of a fund solely because the fund, a fund under common control with the fund, or both:
    (i) Controls such person (or an affiliated person of such person); or
    (ii) Owns, controls, or holds with power to vote five percent or more of the outstanding voting securities of such person (or an affiliated person of such person).

68: SEC Rules and Regulations, Investment Company Act of 1940: 17a-7 – Exemption of Certain Purchase or Sale Transactions Between an Investment Company and Certain Affiliated Persons Thereof

A purchase or sale transaction between registered investment companies or separate series of registered investment companies, which are affiliated persons, or affiliated persons of affiliated persons, of each other, between separate series of a registered investment company, or between a registered investment company or a separate series of a registered investment company and a person which is an affiliated person of such registered investment company (or affiliated person of such person) solely by reason of having a common investment adviser or investment advisers which are affiliated persons of each other, common directors, and/or common officers, is exempt from section 17(a) of the Act; Provided, That:
(a) The transaction is a purchase or sale, for no consideration other than cash payment against prompt delivery of a security for which market quotations are readily available;
(b) The transaction is effected at the independent current market price of the security. For purposes of this paragraph the "current market price" shall be:
  (1) If the security is an "NMS stock" as that term is defined in 17 CFR 242.600, the last sale price with respect

to such security reported in the consolidated transaction reporting system ("consolidated system") or the average of the highest current independent bid and lowest current independent offer for such security (reported pursuant to 17 CFR 242.602) if there are no reported transactions in the consolidated system that day; or

(2) If the security is not a reported security, and the principal market for such security is an exchange, then the last sale on such exchange or the average of the highest current independent bid and lowest current independent offer on such exchange if there are no reported transactions on such exchange that day; or

(3) If the security is not a reported security and is quoted in the NASDAQ System, then the average of the highest current independent bid and lowest current independent offer reported on Level 1 of NASDAQ; or

(4) For all other securities, the average of the highest current independent bid and lowest current independent offer determined on the basis of reasonable inquiry;

(c) The transaction is consistent with the policy of each registered investment company and separate series of a registered investment company participating in the transaction, as recited in its registration statement and reports filed under the Act;

(d) No brokerage commission, fee (except for customary transfer fees), or other remuneration is paid in connection with the transaction;

(e) The board of directors of the investment company, including a majority of the directors who are not interested persons of such investment company,

(1) Adopts procedures pursuant to which such purchase or sale transactions may be effected for the company, which are reasonably designed to provide that all of the conditions of this section in paragraphs (a) through (d) have been complied with,

(2) Makes and approves such changes as the board deems necessary, and

(3) Determines no less frequently than quarterly that all such purchases or sales made during the preceding quarter were effected in compliance with such procedures;

(f) The board of directors of the investment company satisfies the fund governance standards defined in § 270.0-1(a)(7); and

(g) The investment company (1) maintains and preserves permanently in an easily accessible place a written copy of the procedures (and any modifications thereto) described in paragraph (e) of this section, and (2) maintains and preserves for a period not less than six years from the end of the fiscal year in which any transactions occurred, the first two years in an easily accessible place, a written record of each such transaction setting forth a description of the security purchased or sold, the identity of the person on the other side of the transaction, the terms of the purchase or sale transaction, and the information or materials upon which the determinations described in paragraph (e)(3) of this section were made.

---

69. Insider Trading & Securities Fraud Enforcement Act of 1988 (ITSFEA)

Passed House amended (09/14/1988)
(Measure passed House, amended, roll call #314 (410-0))

Insider Trading and Securities Fraud Enforcement Act of 1988 - Amends the Securities Exchange Act of 1934 to revise the authority of the Securities and Exchange Commission (SEC) to seek civil penalties against persons who participate in illegal insider trading. Authorizes the SEC to seek to impose civil penalties upon any person who, at the time of the violation, directly or indirectly controlled the person who committed the illegal insider trading. Limits the civil liability of a controlled person to the greater of $1,000,000 or three times the amount of the profit gained or loss avoided as a result of the controlled person's violation. Specifies that a controlling person shall not be subject to civil penalties unless the SEC establishes that: (1) such controlling person knew or recklessly disregarded the fact that the controlled person was likely to engage in prohibited acts and failed to take appropriate steps to prevent such prohibited acts; or (2) such controlling person knowingly or recklessly failed to establish or enforce any policy or procedure required under provisions of the Securities Exchange Act and of the Investment Advisers Act of 1940. Sets forth procedures for the collection of any such civil penalty imposed. Specifies a statute of limitations of five years for any such action brought by the SEC.

Authorizes the SEC to award a bounty of up to ten percent of any civil penalty imposed to the person or persons who provide information leading to the imposition of such penalty.

Requires every registered broker or dealer to establish, maintain, and enforce written policies and procedures to prevent the misuse of material, nonpublic information by such broker or dealer or any person associated with such broker or dealer. Amends the Investment Advisers Act of 1940 to require every investment adviser subject to such Act to establish, maintain, and enforce written policies and procedures to prevent the misuse of material, nonpublic information by such investment adviser.

Requires the SEC to make recommendations to the Congress with respect to the extension of its authority to impose civil penalties or administrative fines to other violations of the Securities Exchange Act of 1934.

Increases the monetary penalties for any criminal violations of the Securities Exchange Act of 1934 from an individual maximum of $100,000 to $1,000,000 and a maximum for non-natural persons from $500,000 to $2,500,000. Makes all non-natural persons subject to the higher penalty. (Current law imposes the higher penalty only on exchanges.) Increases the maximum prison term for securities law violations from five years to ten years.

Allows a private right of action against any person who violates insider trading rules to be brought by anyone who, contemporaneously with the purchase or sale of securities that form the basis of such violation, purchased or sold securities of the same class. Limits the total amount of damages in such a contemporaneous trading action to any profit gained or loss avoided and reduces any such damages by the amounts the violating person is required to disgorge pursuant to a court order obtained by the SEC. Specifies that a person may not be held liable solely by reason of employing another person who is liable. Specifies a statute of limitations of five years for any such private right of action. Imposes joint and several liability on anyone who communicates insider information to the same extent as those who directly profit from the insider trading. Specifies that the authority to bring such an action shall not be construed to: (1) limit or condition any implied private rights of action; or (2) bar or limit any action by the SEC or the Attorney General.

Authorizes the SEC to provide investigatory assistance to foreign securities authorities.

Directs the SEC to make a study and investigation of the adequacy of the Federal securities laws for the protection of the public interest and the interests of investors. Requires the SEC to report to the Congress concerning the results of such study and investigation. Authorizes appropriations to carry out such study and investigation.

Authorizes appropriations to the SEC for: (1) official reception and representation expenses; and (2) maintaining membership in, and contributing to, the operating expenses of the International Organization of Securities Commissions.

70. Federal Reserve Board: Regulation T

§ 220.1 Authority, purpose, and scope.

(a) Authority and purpose.

Regulation T (this part) is issued by the Board of Governors of the Federal Reserve System (the Board) pursuant to the Securities Exchange Act of 1934 (the Act) (15 U.S.C. 78a et seq.). Its principal purpose is to regulate extensions of credit by brokers and dealers; it also covers related transactions within the Board's authority under the Act. It imposes, among other obligations, initial margin requirements and payment rules on certain securities transactions.

(b) Scope.

(1) This part provides a margin account and four special purpose accounts in which to record all financial relations between a customer and a creditor. Any transaction not specifically permitted in a special purpose account shall be recorded in a margin account.

(2) This part does not preclude any exchange, national securities association, or creditor from imposing additional requirements or taking action for its own protection.

(3) This part does not apply to:

(i) Financial relations between a customer and a creditor to the extent that they comply with portfolio margining system under rules approved or amended by the SEC;

(ii) Credit extended by a creditor based on a good faith determination that the borrower is an exempted borrower;

(iii) Financial relations between a customer and a broker or dealer registered only under section 15C of the Act; and

(iv) Financial relations between a foreign branch of a creditor and a foreign person involving foreign securities.

§ 220.2 Definitions.

The terms used in this part have the meanings given them in section 3(a) of the Act or as defined in this section as follows:

Affiliated corporation means a corporation of which all common stock is owned directly or indirectly by the firm or general partners and employees of the firm, or by the corporation or holders of the controlling stock and employees of the corporation, and the affiliation has been approved by the creditor's examining authority.

Cash equivalent means securities issued or guaranteed by the United States or its agencies, negotiable bank certificates of deposit, bankers acceptances issued by banking institutions in the United States and payable in the United States, or money market mutual funds.

Covered option transaction means any transaction involving options or warrants in which the customer's risk is limited and all elements of the transaction are subject to contemporaneous exercise if:

(1) The amount at risk is held in the account in cash, cash equivalents, or via an escrow receipt; and

(2) The transaction is eligible for the cash account by the rules of the registered national securities exchange authorized to trade the option or warrant or by the rules of the creditor's examining authority in the case of an unregistered option, provided that all such rules have been approved or amended by the SEC.

Credit balance means the cash amount due the customer in a margin account after debiting amounts transferred to the special memorandum account.

Creditor means any broker or dealer (as defined in sections 3(a)(4) and 3(a)(5) of the Act), any member of a national securities exchange, or any person associated with a broker or dealer (as defined in section 3(a)(18) of the Act), except for business entities controlling or under common control with the creditor.

Current market value of:

(1) A security means:

(i) Throughout the day of the purchase or sale of a security, the security's total cost of purchase or the net proceeds of its sale including any commissions charged; or

      (ii) At any other time, the closing sale price of the security on the preceding business day, as shown by any regularly published reporting or quotation service. If there is no closing sale price, the creditor may use any reasonable estimate of the market value of the security as of the close of business on the preceding business day.

    (2) Any other collateral means a value determined by any reasonable method.

Customer excludes an exempted borrower and includes:

    (1) Any person or persons acting jointly:

      (i) To or for whom a creditor extends, arranges, or maintains any credit; or

      (ii) Who would be considered a customer of the creditor according to the ordinary usage of the trade;

    (2) Any partner in a firm who would be considered a customer of the firm absent the partnership relationship; and

    (3) Any joint venture in which a creditor participates and which would be considered a customer of the creditor if the creditor were not a participant.

Debit balance means the cash amount owed to the creditor in a margin account after debiting amounts transferred to the special memorandum account.

Delivery against payment, Payment against delivery, or a C.O.D. transaction refers to an arrangement under which a creditor and a customer agree that the creditor will deliver to, or accept from, the customer, or the customer's agent, a security against full payment of the purchase price.

Equity means the total current market value of security positions held in the margin account plus any credit balance less the debit balance in the margin account.

Escrow agreement means any agreement issued in connection with a call or put option under which a bank or any person designated as a control location under paragraph (c) of SEC Rule 15c3--3 (17 CFR 240.15c3--3(c)), holding the underlying asset or required cash or cash equivalents, is obligated to deliver to the creditor (in the case of a call option) or accept from the creditor (in the case of a put option) the underlying asset or required cash or cash equivalent against payment of the exercise price upon exercise of the call or put.

Examining authority means:

    (1) The national securities exchange or national securities association of which a creditor is a member; or

    (2) If a member of more than one self-regulatory organization, the organization designated by the SEC as the examining authority for the creditor.

Exempted borrower means a member of a national securities exchange or a registered broker or dealer, a substantial portion of whose business consists of transactions with persons other than brokers or dealers, and includes a borrower who:

    (1) Maintains at least 1000 active accounts on an annual basis for persons other than brokers, dealers, and persons associated with a broker or dealer;

    (2) Earns at least $10 million in gross revenues on an annual basis from transactions with persons other than brokers, dealers, and persons associated with a broker or dealer; or

    (3) Earns at least 10 percent of its gross revenues on an annual basis from transactions with persons other than brokers, dealers, and persons associated with a broker or dealer.

Exempted securities mutual fund means any security issued by an investment company registered under section 8 of the Investment Company Act of 1940 (15 U.S.C. 80a-8), provided the company has at least 95 percent of its assets continuously invested in exempted securities (as defined in section 3(a)(12) of the Act).

Foreign margin stock means a foreign security that is an equity security that:

    (1) Appears on the Board's periodically published List of Foreign Margin Stocks; or

    (2) Is deemed to have a "ready market" under SEC Rule 15c3--1 (17 CFR 240.15c3--1) or a "no-action" position issued thereunder.

Foreign person means a person other than a United States person as defined in section 7(f) of the Act.

Foreign security means a security issued in a jurisdiction other than the United States.

Good faith with respect to:

    (1) Margin means the amount of margin which a creditor would require in exercising sound credit judgment;

(2) Making a determination or accepting a statement concerning a borrower means that the creditor is alert to the circumstances surrounding the credit, and if in possession of information that would cause a prudent person not to make the determination or accept the notice or certification without inquiry, investigates and is satisfied that it is correct.

Margin call means a demand by a creditor to a customer for a deposit of additional cash or securities to eliminate or reduce a margin deficiency as required under this part.

Margin deficiency means the amount by which the required margin exceeds the equity in the margin account.

Margin equity security means a margin security that is an equity security (as defined in section 3(a)(11) of the Act).

Margin excess means the amount by which the equity in the margin account exceeds the required margin. When the margin excess is represented by securities, the current value of the securities is subject to the percentages set forth in § 220.12 (the Supplement).

Margin security means:

(1) Any security registered or having unlisted trading privileges on a national securities exchange;

(2) After January 1, 1999, any security listed on the Nasdaq Stock Market;

(3) Any non-equity security;

(4) Any security issued by either an open-end investment company or unit investment trust which is registered under section 8 of the Investment Company Act of 1940 (15 U.S.C. 80a--8);

(5) Any foreign margin stock;

(6) Any debt security convertible into a margin security;

(7) Until January 1, 1999, any OTC margin stock; or

(8) Until January 1, 1999, any OTC security designated as qualified for trading in the national market system under a designation plan approved by the Securities and Exchange Commission (NMS security).

Money market mutual fund means any security issued by an investment company registered under section 8 of the Investment Company Act of 1940 (15 U.S.C. 80a--8) that is considered a money market fund under SEC Rule 2a--7 (17 CFR 270.2a--7).

Non-equity security means a security that is not an equity security (as defined in section 3(a)(11) of the Act).

Nonexempted security means any security other than an exempted security (as defined in section 3(a)(12) of the Act).

OTC margin stock means any equity security traded over the counter that the Board has determined has the degree of national investor interest, the depth and breadth of market, the availability of information respecting the security and its issuer, and the character and permanence of the issuer to warrant being treated like an equity security treaded on a national securities exchange. An OTC stock is not considered to be an OTC margin stock unless it appears on the Board's periodically published list of OTC margin stocks.

Payment period means the number of business days in the standard securities settlement cycle in the United States, as defined in paragraph (a) of SEC Rule 15c6--1 (17 CFR 240.15c6--1(a)), plus two business days.

Purpose credit means credit for the purpose of:

(1) Buying, carrying, or trading in securities; or

(2) Buying or carrying any part of an investment contract security which shall be deemed credit for the purpose of buying or carrying the entire security.

Short call or short put means a call option or a put option that is issued, endorsed, or guaranteed in or for an account.

(1) A short call that is not cash-settled obligates the customer to sell the underlying asset at the exercise price upon receipt of a valid exercise notice or as otherwise required by the option contract.

(2) A short put that is not cash-settled obligates the customer to purchase the underlying asset at the exercise price upon receipt of a valid exercise notice or as otherwise required by the option contract.

(3) A short call or a short put that is cash-settled obligates the customer to pay the holder of an in the money long put or long call who has, or has been deemed to have, exercised the option the cash differ-

ence between the exercise price and the current assigned value of the option as established by the option contract.

Underlying asset means:

(1) The security or other asset that will be delivered upon exercise of an option; or

(2) In the case of a cash-settled option, the securities or other assets which comprise the index or other measure from which the option's value is derived.

§ 220.3 General provisions.

(a) Records. The creditor shall maintain a record for each account showing the full details of all transactions.

(b) Separation of accounts—

(1) In general. The requirements of one account may not be met by considering items in any other account. If withdrawals of cash or securities are permitted under this part, written entries shall be made when cash or securities are used for purposes of meeting requirements in another account.

(2) Exceptions. Notwithstanding paragraph (b)(1) of this section:

(i) For purposes of calculating the required margin for a security in a margin account, assets held in the good faith account pursuant to § 220.6(e)(1)(i) or (ii) may serve in lieu of margin;

(ii) Transfers may be effected between the margin account and the special memorandum account pursuant to §§ 220.4 and 220.5.

(c) Maintenance of credit. Except as prohibited by this part, any credit initially extended in compliance with this part may be maintained regardless of:

(1) Reductions in the customer's equity resulting from changes in market prices;

(2) Any security in an account ceasing to be margin or exempted; or

(3) Any change in the margin requirements prescribed under this part.

(d) Guarantee of accounts. No guarantee of a customer's account shall be given any effect for purposes of this part.

(e) Receipt of funds or securities.

(1) A creditor, acting in good faith, may accept as immediate payment:

(i) Cash or any check, draft, or order payable on presentation; or

(ii) Any security with sight draft attached.

(2) A creditor may treat a security, check or draft as received upon written notification from another creditor that the specified security, check, or draft has been sent.

(3) Upon notification that a check, draft, or order has been dishonored or when securities have not been received within a reasonable time, the creditor shall take the action required by this part when payment or securities are not received on time.

(4) To temporarily finance a customer's receipt of securities pursuant to an employee benefit plan registered on SEC Form S--8 or the withholding taxes for an employee stock award plan, a creditor may accept, in lieu of the securities, a properly executed exercise notice, where applicable, and instructions to the issuer to deliver the stock to the creditor. Prior to acceptance, the creditor must verify that the issuer will deliver the securities promptly and the customer must designate the account into which the securities are to be deposited.

(f) Exchange of securities.

(1) To enable a customer to participate in an offer to exchange securities which is made to all holders of an issue of securities, a creditor may submit for exchange any securities held in a margin account, without regard to the other provisions of this part, provided the consideration received is deposited into the account.

(2) If a nonmargin, nonexempted security is acquired in exchange for a margin security, its retention, withdrawal, or sale within 60 days following its acquisition shall be treated as if the security is a margin security.

(g) Arranging for loans by others. A creditor may arrange for the extension or maintenance of credit to or for any customer by any person, provided the creditor does not willfully arrange credit that violates parts 221 or 224 of this chapter.

(h) Innocent mistakes. If any failure to comply with this part results from a mistake made in good faith in executing a transaction or calculating the amount of margin, the creditor shall not be deemed in violation of this part if, promptly after the discovery of the mistake, the creditor takes appropriate corrective action.

(i) Foreign currency.

    (1) Freely convertible foreign currency may be treated at its U.S. dollar equivalent, provided the currency is marked-to-market daily.

    (2) A creditor may extend credit denominated in any freely convertible foreign currency.

(j) Exempted borrowers.

    (1) A member of a national securities exchange or a registered broker or dealer that has been in existence for less than one year may meet the definition of exempted borrower based on a six-month period.

    (2) Once a member of a national securities exchange or registered broker or dealer ceases to qualify as an exempted borrower, it shall notify its lender of this fact before obtaining additional credit. Any new extensions of credit to such a borrower; including rollovers, renewals, and additional draws on existing lines of credit, are subject to the provisions of this part.

(k) 220.4 Margin account.

(a) Margin transactions.

    (1) All transactions not specifically authorized for inclusion in another account shall be recorded in the margin account.

    (2) A creditor may establish separate margin accounts for the same person to:

        (i) Clear transactions for other creditors where the transactions are introduced to the clearing creditor by separate creditors; or

        (ii) Clear transactions through other creditors if the transactions are cleared by separate creditors; or

        (iii) Provide one or more accounts over which the creditor or a third party investment adviser has investment discretion.

(b) Required margin—

    (1) Applicability. The required margin for each long or short position in securities is set forth in § 220.12 (the Supplement) and is subject to the following exceptions and special provisions.

    (2) Short sale against the box. A short sale "against the box" shall be treated as a long sale for the purpose of computing the equity and the required margin.

    (3) When-issued securities. The required margin on a net long or net short commitment in a when-issued security is the margin that would be required if the security were an issued margin security, plus any unrealized loss on the commitment or less any unrealized gain.

    (4) Stock used as cover.

        (i) When a short position held in the account serves in lieu of the required margin for a short put, the amount prescribed by paragraph (b)(1) of this section as the amount to be added to the required margin in respect of short sales shall be increased by any unrealized loss on the position.

        (ii) When a security held in the account serves in lieu of the required margin for a short call, the security shall be valued at no greater than the exercise price of the short call.

    (5) Accounts of partners. If a partner of the creditor has a margin account with the creditor, the creditor shall disregard the partner's financial relations with the firm (as shown in the partner's capital and ordinary drawing accounts) in calculating the margin or equity of the partner's margin account.

    (6) Contribution to joint venture. If a margin account is the account of a joint venture in which the creditor participates, any interest of the creditor in the joint account in excess of the interest which the creditor

would have on the basis of its right to share in the profits shall be treated as an extension of credit to the joint account and shall be margined as such.

(7) Transfer of accounts.

(i) A margin account that is transferred from one creditor to another may be treated as if it had been maintained by the transferee from the date of its origin, if the transferee accepts, in good faith, a signed statement of the transferor (or, if that is not practicable, of the customer), that any margin call issued under this part has been satisfied.

(ii) A margin account that is transferred from one customer to another as part of a transaction, not undertaken to avoid the requirements of this part, may be treated as if it had been maintained for the transferee from the date of its origin, if the creditor accepts in good faith and keeps with the transferee account a signed statement of the transferor describing the circumstances for the transfer.

(8) Sound credit judgment. In exercising sound credit judgment to determine the margin required in good faith pursuant to § 220.12 (the Supplement), the creditor shall make its determination for a specified security position without regard to the customer's other assets or securities positions held in connection with unrelated transactions.

(c) When additional margin is required—

(1) Computing deficiency. All transactions on the same day shall be combined to determine whether additional margin is required by the creditor. For the purpose of computing equity in an account, security positions are established or eliminated and a credit or debit created on the trade date of a security transaction. Additional margin is required on any day when the day's transactions create or increase a margin deficiency in the account and shall be for the amount of the margin deficiency so created or increased.

(2) Satisfaction of deficiency. The additional required margin may be satisfied by a transfer from the special memorandum account or by a deposit of cash, margin securities, exempted securities, or any combination thereof.

(3) Time limits.

(i) A margin call shall be satisfied within one payment period after the margin deficiency was created or increased.

(ii) The payment period may be extended for one or more limited periods upon application by the creditor to its examining authority unless the examining authority believes that the creditor is not acting in good faith or that the creditor has not sufficiently determined that exceptional circumstances warrant such action. Applications shall be filed and acted upon prior to the end of the payment period or the expiration of any subsequent extension.

(4) Satisfaction restriction. Any transaction, position, or deposit that is used to satisfy one requirement under this part shall be unavailable to satisfy any other requirement.

(d) Liquidation in lieu of deposit. If any margin call is not met in full within the required time, the creditor shall liquidate securities sufficient to meet the margin call or to eliminate any margin deficiency existing on the day such liquidation is required, whichever is less. If the margin deficiency created or increased is $1000 or less, no action need be taken by the creditor.

(e) Withdrawals of cash or securities.

(1) Cash or securities may be withdrawn from an account, except if:

(i) Additional cash or securities are required to be deposited into the account for a transaction on the same or a previous day; or

(ii) The withdrawal, together with other transactions, deposits, and withdrawals on the same day, would create or increase a margin deficiency.

(2) Margin excess may be withdrawn or may be transferred to the special memorandum account (§ 220.5) by making a single entry to that account which will represent a debit to the margin account and a credit to the special memorandum account.

(3) If a creditor does not receive a distribution of cash or securities which is payable with respect to any security in a margin account on the day it is payable and withdrawal would not be permitted under this paragraph (e), a withdrawal transaction shall be deemed to have occurred on the day the distribution is payable.

(f) Interest, service charges, etc.

(1) Without regard to the other provisions of this section, the creditor, in its usual practice, may debit the following items to a margin account if they are considered in calculating the balance of such account:

(i) Interest charged on credit maintained in the margin account;

(ii) Premiums on securities borrowed in connection with short sales or to effect delivery;

(iii) Dividends, interest, or other distributions due on borrowed securities;

(iv) Communication or shipping charges with respect to transactions in the margin account; and

(v) Any other service charges which the creditor may impose.

(2) A creditor may permit interest, dividends, or other distributions credited to a margin account to be withdrawn from the account if:

(i) The withdrawal does not create or increase a margin deficiency in the account; or

(ii) The current market value of any securities withdrawn does not exceed 10 percent of the current market value of the security with respect to which they were distributed.

§ 220.5 Special memorandum account.

(a) A special memorandum account (SMA) may be maintained in conjunction with a margin account. A single entry amount may be used to represent both a credit to the SMA and a debit to the margin account. A transfer between the two accounts may be effected by an increase or reduction in the entry. When computing the equity in a margin account, the single entry amount shall be considered as a debit in the margin account. A payment to the customer or on the customer's behalf or a transfer to any of the customer's other accounts from the SMA reduces the single entry amount.

(b) The SMA may contain the following entries:

(1) Dividend and interest payments;

(2) Cash not required by this part, including cash deposited to meet a maintenance margin call or to meet any requirement of a self-regulatory organization that is not imposed by this part;

(3) Proceeds of a sale of securities or cash no longer required on any expired or liquidated security position that may be withdrawn under § 220.4(e); and

(4) Margin excess transferred from the margin account under § 220.4(e)(2).

§ 220.6 Good faith account.

In a good faith account, a creditor may effect or finance customer transactions in accordance with the following provisions:

(a) Securities entitled to good faith margin—

(1) Permissible transactions. A creditor may effect and finance transactions involving the buying, carrying, or trading of any security entitled to "good faith" margin as set forth in § 220.12 (the Supplement).

(2) Required margin. The required margin is set forth in § 220.12 (the Supplement).

(3) Satisfaction of margin. Required margin may be satisfied by a transfer from the special memorandum account or by a deposit of cash, securities entitled to "good faith" margin as set forth in § 220.12 (the Supplement), any other asset that is not a security, or any combination thereof. An asset that is not a security shall have a margin value determined by the creditor in good faith.

(b) Arbitrage. A creditor may effect and finance for any customer bona fide arbitrage transactions. For the purpose of this section, the term "bona fide arbitrage" means:

(1) A purchase or sale of a security in one market together with an offsetting sale or purchase of the same security in a different market at as nearly the same time as practicable for the purpose of taking advantage of a difference in prices in the two markets; or

(2) A purchase of a security which is, without restriction other than the payment of money, exchangeable or convertible within 90 calendar days of the purchase into a second security together with an offsetting sale of the second security at or about the same time, for the purpose of taking advantage of a concurrent disparity in the prices of the two securities.

(c) "Prime broker" transactions. A creditor may effect transactions for a customer as part of a "prime broker" arrangement in conformity with SEC guidelines.

(d) Credit to ESOPs. A creditor may extend and maintain credit to employee stock ownership plans without regard to the other provisions of this part.

(e) Nonpurpose credit.

(1) A creditor may:

(i) Effect and carry transactions in commodities;

(ii) Effect and carry transactions in foreign exchange;

(iii) Extend and maintain secured or unsecured nonpurpose credit, subject to the requirements of paragraph (e)(2) of this section.

(2) Every extension of credit, except as provided in paragraphs (e)(1)(i) and (e)(1)(ii) of this section, shall be deemed to be purpose credit unless, prior to extending the credit, the creditor accepts in good faith from the customer a written statement that it is not purpose credit. The statement shall conform to the requirements established by the Board.

§ 220.7 Broker-dealer credit account.

(a) Requirements. In a broker-dealer credit account, a creditor may effect or finance transactions in accordance with the following provisions.

(b) Purchase or sale of security against full payment. A creditor may purchase any security from or sell any security to another creditor or person regulated by a foreign securities authority under a good faith agreement to promptly deliver the security against full payment of the purchase price.

(c) Joint back office. A creditor may effect or finance transactions of any of its owners if the creditor is a clearing and servicing broker or dealer owned jointly or individually by other creditors.

(d) Capital contribution. A creditor may extend and maintain credit to any partner or stockholder of the creditor for the purpose of making a capital contribution to, or purchasing stock of, the creditor, affiliated corporation or another creditor.

(e) Emergency and subordinated credit. A creditor may extend and maintain, with the approval of the appropriate examining authority:

(1) Credit to meet the emergency needs of any creditor; or

(2) Subordinated credit to another creditor for capital purposes, if the other creditor:

(i) Is an affiliated corporation or would not be considered a customer of the lender apart from the subordinated loan; or

(ii) Will not use the proceeds of the loan to increase the amount of dealing in securities for the account of the creditor, its firm or corporation or an affiliated corporation.

(f) Omnibus credit.

(1) A creditor may effect and finance transactions for a broker or dealer who is registered with the SEC under section 15 of the Act and who gives the creditor written notice that:

(i) All securities will be for the account of customers of the broker or dealer; and

(ii) Any short sales effected will be short sales made on behalf of the customers of the broker or dealer other than partners.

(2) The written notice required by paragraph (f)(1) of this section shall conform to any SEC rule on the hypothecation of customers' securities by brokers or dealers.

(g) Special purpose credit. A creditor may extend the following types of credit with good faith margin:

(1) Credit to finance the purchase or sale of securities for prompt delivery, if the credit is to be repaid upon completion of the transaction.

(2) Credit to finance securities in transit or surrendered for transfer, if the credit is to be repaid upon completion of the transaction.

(3) Credit to enable a broker or dealer to pay for securities, if the credit is to be repaid on the same day it is extended.

(4) Credit to an exempted borrower.

(5) Credit to a member of a national securities exchange or registered broker or dealer to finance its activities as a market maker or specialist.

(6) Credit to a member of a national securities exchange or registered broker or dealer to finance its activities as an underwriter.

§ 220.8 Cash account.

(a) Permissible transactions. In a cash account, a creditor, may:

(1) Buy for or sell to any customer any security or other asset if:

(i) There are sufficient funds in the account; or

(ii) The creditor accepts in good faith the customer's agreement that the customer will promptly make full cash payment for the security or asset before selling it and does not contemplate selling it prior to making such payment;

(2) Buy from or sell for any customer any security or other asset if:

(i) The security is held in the account; or

(ii) The creditor accepts in good faith the customer's statement that the security is owned by the customer or the customer's principal, and that it will be promptly deposited in the account;

(3) Issue, endorse, or guarantee, or sell an option for any customer as part of a covered option transaction; and

(4) Use an escrow agreement in lieu of the cash, cash equivalents or underlying asset position if:

(i) In the case of a short call or a short put, the creditor is advised by the customer that the required securities, assets or cash are held by a person authorized to issue an escrow agreement and the creditor independently verifies that the appropriate escrow agreement will be delivered by the person promptly; or

(ii) In the case of a call issued, endorsed, guaranteed, or sold on the same day the underlying asset is purchased in the account and the underlying asset is to be delivered to a person authorized to issue an escrow agreement, the creditor verifies that the appropriate escrow agreement will be delivered by the person promptly.

(b) Time periods for payment; cancellation or liquidation.

(1) Full cash payment. A creditor shall obtain full cash payment for customer purchases:

(i) Within one payment period of the date:

(A) Any nonexempted security was purchased;

(B) Any when-issued security was made available by the issuer for delivery to purchasers;

(C) Any "when distributed" security was distributed under a published plan;

(D) A security owned by the customer has matured or has been redeemed and a new refunding security of the same issuer has been purchased by the customer, provided:

(1) The customer purchased the new security no more than 35 calendar days prior to the date of maturity or redemption of the old security;

(2) The customer is entitled to the proceeds of the redemption; and

(3) The delayed payment does not exceed 103 percent of the proceeds of the old security.

(ii) In the case of the purchase of a foreign security, within one payment period of the trade date or within one day after the date on which settlement is required to occur by the rules of the foreign securities market, provided this period does not exceed the maximum time permitted by this part for delivery against payment transactions.

(2) Delivery against payment. If a creditor purchases for or sells to a customer a security in a delivery against payment transaction, the creditor shall have up to 35 calendar days to obtain payment if delivery of the security is delayed due to the mechanics of the transaction and is not related to the customer's willingness or ability to pay.

(3) Shipment of securities, extension. If any shipment of securities is incidental to consummation of a transaction, a creditor may extend the payment period by the number of days required for shipment, but not by more than one additional payment period.

(4) Cancellation; liquidation; minimum amount. A creditor shall promptly cancel or otherwise liquidate a transaction or any part of a transaction for which the customer has not made full cash payment within the required time. A creditor may, at its option, disregard any sum due from the customer not exceeding $1000.

(c) 90 day freeze.

(1) If a nonexempted security in the account is sold or delivered to another broker or dealer without having been previously paid for in full by the customer, the privilege of delaying payment beyond the trade date shall be withdrawn for 90 calendar days following the date of sale of the security. Cancellation of the transaction other than to correct an error shall constitute a sale.

(2) The 90 day freeze shall not apply if:

(i) Within the period specified in paragraph (b)(1) of this section, full payment is received or any check or draft in payment has cleared and the proceeds from the sale are not withdrawn prior to such payment or check clearance; or

(ii) The purchased security was delivered to another broker or dealer for deposit in a cash account which holds sufficient funds to pay for the security. The creditor may rely on a written statement accepted in good faith from the other broker or dealer that sufficient funds are held in the other cash account.

(d) Extension of time periods; transfers.

(1) Unless the creditor's examining authority believes that the creditor is not acting in good faith or that the creditor has not sufficiently determined that exceptional circumstances warrant such action, it may upon application by the creditor:

(i) Extend any period specified in paragraph (b) of this section;

(ii) Authorize transfer to another account of any transaction involving the purchase of a margin or exempted security; or

(iii) Grant a waiver from the 90 day freeze.

(2) Applications shall be filed and acted upon prior to the end of the payment period, or in the case of the purchase of a foreign security within the period specified in paragraph (b)(1)(ii) of this section, or the expiration of any subsequent extension.

§ 220.9 Clearance of securities, options, and futures.

(a) Credit for clearance of securities. The provisions of this part shall not apply to the extension or maintenance of any credit that is not for more than one day if it is incidental to the clearance of transactions in securities directly between members of a national securities exchange or association or through any clearing agency registered with the SEC.

(b) Deposit of securities with a clearing agency. The provisions of this part shall not apply to the deposit of securities with an option or futures clearing agency for the purpose of meeting the deposit requirements of the agency if:

(1) The clearing agency:

(i) Issues, guarantees performance on, or clears transactions in, any security (including options on any security, certificate of deposit, securities index or foreign currency); or

(ii) Guarantees performance of contracts for the purchase or sale of a commodity for future delivery or options on such contracts;

(2) The clearing agency is registered with the Securities and Exchange Commission or is the clearing agency for a contract market regulated by the Commodity Futures Trading Commission; and

(3) The deposit consists of any margin security and complies with the rules of the clearing agency that have been approved by the Securities and Exchange Commission or the Commodity Futures Trading Commission.

§ 220.10 Borrowing and lending securities.

(a) Without regard to the other provisions of this part, a creditor may borrow or lend securities for the purpose of making delivery of the securities in the case of short sales, failure to receive securities required to be delivered, or other similar situations. If a creditor reasonably anticipates a short sale or fail transaction, such borrowing may be made up to one standard settlement cycle in advance of trade date.

(b) A creditor may lend foreign securities to a foreign person (or borrow such securities for the purpose of re-lending them to a foreign person) for any purpose lawful in the country in which they are to be used.

(c) A creditor that is an exempted borrower may lend securities without regard to the other provisions of this part and a creditor may borrow securities from an exempted borrower without regard to the other provisions of this part.

§ 220.11 Requirements for the list of marginable OTC stocks and the list of foreign margin stocks.

(a) Requirements for inclusion on the list of marginable OTC stocks. Except as provided in paragraph (f) of this section, OTC margin stock shall meet the following requirements:

(1) Four or more dealers stand willing to, and do in fact, make a market in such stock and regularly submit bona fide bids and offers to an automated quotations system for their own accounts;

(2) The minimum average bid price of such stock, as determined by the Board, is at least $5 per share;

(3) The stock is registered under section 12 of the Act, is issued by an insurance company subject to section 12(g)(2)(G) of the Act, is issued by a closed-end investment management company subject to registration pursuant to section 8 of the Investment Company Act of 1940 (15 U.S.C. 80a--8), is an American Depository Receipt (ADR) of a foreign issuer whose securities are registered under section 12 of the Act, or is a stock of an issuer required to file reports under section 15(d) of the Act;

(4) Daily quotations for both bid and asked prices for the stock are continuously available to the general public;

(5) The stock has been publicly traded for at least six months;

(6) The issuer has at least $4 million of capital, surplus, and undivided profits;

(7) There are 400,000 or more shares of such stock outstanding in addition to shares held beneficially by officers, directors or beneficial owners of more than 10 percent of the stock;

(8) There are 1,200 or more holders of record, as defined in SEC Rule 12g5--1 (17 CFR 240.12g5--1), of the stock who are not officers, directors or beneficial owners of 10 percent or more of the stock, or the average daily trading volume of such stock as determined by the Board, is at least 500 shares; and

(9) The issuer or a predecessor in interest has been in existence for at least three years.

(b) Requirements for continued inclusion on the list of marginable OTC stocks. Except as provided in paragraph (f) of this section, OTC margin stock shall meet the following requirements:

(1) Three or more dealers stand willing to, and do in fact, make a market in such stock and regularly submit bona fide bids and offers to an automated quotations system for their own accounts;

(2) The minimum average bid price of such stocks, as determined by the Board, is at least $2 per share;

(3) The stock is registered as specified in paragraph (a)(3) of this section;

(4) Daily quotations for both bid and asked prices for the stock are continuously available to the general public;

(5) The issuer has at least $1 million of capital, surplus, and undivided profits;

(6) There are 300,000 or more shares of such stock outstanding in addition to shares held beneficially by officers, directors, or beneficial owners of more than 10 percent of the stock; and

(7) There continue to be 800 or more holders of record, as defined in SEC Rule 12g5--1 (17 CFR 240.12g5--1), of the stock who are not officers, directors, or beneficial owners of 10 percent or more of the stock, or the average daily trading volume of such stock, as determined by the Board, is at least 300 shares.

(c) Requirements for inclusion on the list of foreign margin stocks. Except as provided in paragraph (f) of this section, a foreign security shall meet the following requirements before being placed on the List of Foreign Margin Stocks:

    (1) The security is an equity security that is listed for trading on or through the facilities of a foreign securities exchange or a recognized foreign securities market and has been trading on such exchange or market for at least six months;

    (2) Daily quotations for both bid and asked or last sale prices for the security provided by the foreign securities exchange or foreign securities market on which the security is traded are continuously available to creditors in the United States pursuant to an electronic quotation system;

    (3) The aggregate market value of shares, the ownership of which is unrestricted, is not less than $1 billion;

    (4) The average weekly trading volume of such security during the preceding six months is either at least 200,000 shares or $1 million; and

    (5) The issuer or a predecessor in interest has been in existence for at least five years.

(d) Requirements for continued inclusion on the list of foreign margin stocks. Except as provided in paragraph (f) of this section, a foreign security shall meet the following requirements to remain on the List of Foreign Margin Stocks:

    (1) The security continues to meet the requirements specified in paragraphs (c)(1) and (2) of this section;

    (2) The aggregate market value of shares, the ownership of which is unrestricted, is not less than $500 million; and

    (3) The average weekly trading volume of such security during the preceding six months is either at least 100,000 shares or $500,000.

(e) Removal from the list. The Board shall periodically remove from the lists any stock that:

    (1) Ceases to exist or of which the issuer ceases to exist; or

    (2) No longer substantially meets the provisions of paragraphs (b) or (d) of this section or the definition of OTC margin stock.

(f) Discretionary authority of Board. Without regard to other paragraphs of this section, the Board may add to, or omit or remove from the list of marginable OTC stocks and the list of foreign margin stocks and equity security, if in the judgment of the Board, such action is necessary or appropriate in the public interest.

(g) Unlawful representations. It shall be unlawful for any creditor to make, or cause to be made, any representation to the effect that the inclusion of a security on the list of marginable OTC stocks or the list of foreign margin stocks is evidence that the Board or the SEC has in any way passed upon the merits of, or given approval to, such security or any transactions therein. Any statement in an advertisement or other similar communication containing a reference to the Board in connection with the lists or stocks on those lists shall be an unlawful representation.

§ 220.12 Supplement: Margin requirements.

The required margin for each security position held in a margin account shall be as follows:

(a) Margin equity security, except for an exempted security, money market mutual fund or exempted securities mutual fund, warrant on a securities index or foreign currency or a long position in an option: 50 percent of the current market value of the security or the percentage set by the regulatory authority where the trade occurs, whichever is greater.

(b) Exempted security, non-equity security, money market mutual fund or exempted securities mutual fund: The margin required by the creditor in good faith or the percentage set by the regulatory authority where the trade occurs, whichever is greater.

(c) Short sale of a nonexempted security, except for a non-equity security:

    (1) 150 percent of the current market value of the security; or

    (2) 100 percent of the current market value if a security exchangeable or convertible within 90 calendar days without restriction other than the payment of money into the security sold short is held in the account, provided that any long call to be used as margin in connection with a short sale of the underlying security is an American-style option issued by a registered clearing corporation and listed or traded on a registered national securities exchange with an exercise price that does not exceed the price at which the underlying security was sold short.

(d) Short sale of an exempted security or non-equity security: 100 percent of the current market value of the security plus the margin required by the creditor in good faith.

(e) Nonmargin, nonexempted equity security: 100 percent of the current market value.

(f) Put or call on a security, certificate of deposit, securities index or foreign currency or a warrant on a securities index or foreign currency:

    (1) In the case of puts and calls issued by a registered clearing corporation and listed or traded on a registered national securities exchange or a registered securities association and registered warrants on a securities index or foreign currency, the amount, or other position specified by the rules of the registered national securities exchange or the registered securities association authorized to trade the option or warrant, provided that all such rules have been approved or amended by the SEC; or

    (2) In the case of all other puts and calls, the amount, or other position, specified by the maintenance rules of the creditor's examining authority.

---

71. Federal Trade Commission: Telemarketing Sales Rule

§ 310.1 Scope of regulations in this part.
This part implements the Telemarketing and Consumer Fraud and Abuse Prevention Act, 15 U.S.C. 6101-6108, as amended.

§ 310.2 Definitions.

(a) *Acquirer* means a business organization, financial institution, or an agent of a business organization or financial institution that has authority from an organization that operates or licenses a credit card system to authorize merchants to accept, transmit, or process payment by credit card through the credit card system for money, goods or services, or anything else of value.

(b) *Attorney General* means the chief legal officer of a state.

(c) *Billing information* means any data that enables any person to access a customer's or donor's account, such as a credit card, checking, savings, share or similar account, utility bill, mortgage loan account, or debit card.

(d) *Caller identification service* means a service that allows a telephone subscriber to have the telephone number, and, where available, name of the calling party transmitted contemporaneously with the telephone call, and displayed on a device in or connected to the subscriber's telephone.

(e) *Cardholder* means a person to whom a credit card is issued or who is authorized to use a credit card on behalf of or in addition to the person to whom the credit card is issued.

(f) *Cash-to-cash money transfer* means the electronic (as defined in section 106(2) of the Electronic Signatures in Global and National Commerce Act (15 U.S.C. 7006(2))) transfer of the value of cash received from one person to another person in a different location that is sent by a money transfer provider and received in the form of cash. For purposes of this definition, money transfer provider means any person or financial institution that provides cash-to-cash money transfers for a person in the normal course of its business, whether or not the person holds an account with such person or financial institution. The term cash-to-cash money transfer includes a remittance transfer, as defined in section 919(g)(2) of the Electronic Fund Transfer Act ("EFTA"), 15 U.S.C. 1693a, that is a cash-to-cash transaction; however it does not include any transaction that is:

(1) An electronic fund transfer as defined in section 903 of the EFTA;

(2) Covered by Regulation E, 12 CFR 1005.20, pertaining to gift cards; or

(3) Subject to the Truth in Lending Act, 15 U.S.C. 1601et seq.

(g) *Cash reload mechanism* is a device, authorization code, personal identification number, or other security measure that makes it possible for a person to convert cash into an electronic (as defined in section 106(2) of the Electronic Signatures in Global and National Commerce Act (15 U.S.C. 7006(2)) form that can be used to add funds to a general-use prepaid card, as defined in Regulation E, 12 CFR 1005.2, or an account with a payment intermediary. For purposes of this definition, a cash reload mechanism is not itself a general-use prepaid debit card or a swipe reload process or similar method in which funds are added directly onto a person's own general-use prepaid card or account with a payment intermediary.

(h) *Charitable contribution* means any donation or gift of money or any other thing of value.

(i) *Commission* means the Federal Trade Commission.

(j) *Credit* means the right granted by a creditor to a debtor to defer payment of debt or to incur debt and defer its payment.

(k) *Credit card* means any card, plate, coupon book, or other credit device existing for the purpose of obtaining money, property, labor, or services on credit.

(l) *Credit card sales draft* means any record or evidence of a credit card transaction.

(m) *Credit card system* means any method or procedure used to process credit card transactions involving credit cards issued or licensed by the operator of that system.

(n) *Customer* means any person who is or may be required to pay for goods or services offered through telemarketing.

(o) *Debt relief service* means any program or service represented, directly or by implication, to renegotiate, settle, or in any way alter the terms of payment or other terms of the debt between a person and one or more unsecured creditors or debt collectors, including, but not limited to, a reduction in the balance, interest rate, or fees owed by a person to an unsecured creditor or debt collector.

(p) *Donor* means any person solicited to make a charitable contribution.

(q) *Established business relationship* means a relationship between a seller and a consumer based on:

(1) the consumer's purchase, rental, or lease of the seller's goods or services or a financial transaction between the consumer and seller, within the eighteen (18) months immediately preceding the date of a telemarketing call; or

(2) the consumer's inquiry or application regarding a product or service offered by the seller, within the three (3) months immediately preceding the date of a telemarketing call.

(r) *Free-to-pay conversion* means, in an offer or agreement to sell or provide any goods or services, a provision under which a customer receives a product or service for free for an initial period and will incur an obligation to pay for the product or service if he or she does not take affirmative action to cancel before the end of that period.

(s) *Investment opportunity* means anything, tangible or intangible, that is offered, offered for sale, sold, or traded based wholly or in part on representations, either express or implied, about past, present, or future income, profit, or appreciation.

(t) *Material* means likely to affect a person's choice of, or conduct regarding, goods or services or a charitable contribution.

(u) *Merchant* means a person who is authorized under a written contract with an acquirer to honor or accept credit cards, or to transmit or process for payment credit card payments, for the purchase of goods or services or a charitable contribution.

(v) *Merchant agreement* means a written contract between a merchant and an acquirer to honor or accept credit cards, or to transmit or process for payment credit card payments, for the purchase of goods or services or a charitable contribution.

(w) *Negative option feature* means, in an offer or agreement to sell or provide any goods or services, a provision under which the customer's silence or failure to take an affirmative action to reject goods or services or to cancel the agreement is interpreted by the seller as acceptance of the offer.

(x) *Outbound telephone call* means a telephone call initiated by a telemarketer to induce the purchase of goods or services or to solicit a charitable contribution.

(y) *Person* means any individual, group, unincorporated association, limited or general partnership, corporation, or other business entity.

(z) *Preacquired account information* means any information that enables a seller or telemarketer to cause a charge to be placed against a customer's or donor's account without obtaining the account number directly from the customer or donor during the telemarketing transaction pursuant to which the account will be charged.

(aa) *Prize* means anything offered, or purportedly offered, and given, or purportedly given, to a person by chance. For purposes of this definition, chance exists if a person is guaranteed to receive an item and, at the time of the offer or purported offer, the telemarketer does not identify the specific item that the person will receive.

(bb) *Prize promotion* means:
   (1) A sweepstakes or other game of chance; or
   (2) An oral or written express or implied representation that a person has won, has been selected to receive, or may be eligible to receive a prize or purported prize.

(cc) *Remotely created payment order* means any payment instruction or order drawn on a person's account that is created by the payee or the payee's agent and deposited into or cleared through the check clearing system. The term includes, without limitation, a "remotely created check," as defined in Regulation CC, Availability of Funds and Collection of Checks, 12 CFR 229.2(fff), but does not include a payment order cleared through an Automated Clearinghouse (ACH) Network or subject to the Truth in Lending Act, 15 U.S.C. 1601et seq., and Regulation Z, 12 CFR part 1026.

(dd) *Seller* means any person who, in connection with a telemarketing transaction, provides, offers to provide, or arranges for others to provide goods or services to the customer in exchange for consideration.

(ee) *State* means any state of the United States, the District of Columbia, Puerto Rico, the Northern Mariana Islands, and any territory or possession of the United States.

(ff) *Telemarketer* means any person who, in connection with telemarketing, initiates or receives telephone calls to or from a customer or donor.

(gg) *Telemarketing* means a plan, program, or campaign which is conducted to induce the purchase of goods or services or a charitable contribution, by use of one or more telephones and which involves more than one interstate telephone call. The term does not include the solicitation of sales through the mailing of a catalog which: contains a written description or illustration of the goods or services offered for sale; includes the business address of the seller; includes multiple pages of written material or illustrations; and has been issued not less frequently than once a year, when the person making the solicitation does not solicit customers by telephone but only receives calls initiated by customers in response to the catalog and during those calls takes orders only without further solicitation. For purposes of the previous sentence, the term "further solicitation" does not include providing the customer with information about, or attempting to sell, any other item included in the same catalog which prompted the customer's call or in a substantially similar catalog.

(hh) *Upselling* means soliciting the purchase of goods or services following an initial transaction during a single telephone call. The upsell is a separate telemarketing transaction, not a continuation of the initial transaction. An "external upsell" is a solicitation made by or on behalf of a seller different from the seller in the initial transaction, regardless of whether the initial transaction and the subsequent solicitation are made by the same telemarketer. An "internal upsell" is a solicitation made by or on behalf of the same seller as in the initial transaction, regardless of whether the initial transaction and subsequent solicitation are made by the same telemarketer.

§ 310.3 Deceptive telemarketing acts or practices.

(a) Prohibited deceptive telemarketing acts or practices. It is a deceptive telemarketing act or practice and a violation of this Rule for any seller or telemarketer to engage in the following conduct:

(1) Before a customer consents to pay for goods or services offered, failing to disclose truthfully, in a clear and conspicuous manner, the following material information:

(i) The total costs to purchase, receive, or use, and the quantity of, any goods or services that are the subject of the sales offer;

(ii) All material restrictions, limitations, or conditions to purchase, receive, or use the goods or services that are the subject of the sales offer;

(iii) If the seller has a policy of not making refunds, cancellations, exchanges, or repurchases, a statement informing the customer that this is the seller's policy; or, if the seller or telemarketer makes a representation about a refund, cancellation, exchange, or repurchase policy, a statement of all material terms and conditions of such policy;

(iv) In any prize promotion, the odds of being able to receive the prize, and, if the odds are not calculable in advance, the factors used in calculating the odds; that no purchase or payment is required to win a prize or to participate in a prize promotion and that any purchase or payment will not increase the person's chances of winning; and the no-purchase/no-payment method of participating in the prize promotion with either instructions on how to participate or an address or local or toll-free telephone number to which customers may write or call for information on how to participate;

(v) All material costs or conditions to receive or redeem a prize that is the subject of the promotion;

(vi) In the sale of any goods or services represented to protect, insure, or otherwise limit a customer's liability in the event of unauthorized use of the customer's credit card, the limits on a cardholder's liability for unauthorized use of a credit card pursuant to 15 U.S.C. 1643;

(vii) If the offer includes a negative option feature, all material terms and conditions of the negative option feature, including, but not limited to, the fact that the customer's account will be charged unless the customer takes an affirmative action to avoid the charge(s), the date(s) the charge(s) will be submitted for payment, and the specific steps the customer must take to avoid the charge(s); and

(viii) In the sale of any debt relief service:

(A) the amount of time necessary to achieve the represented results, and to the extent that the service may include a settlement offer to any of the customer's creditors or debt collectors, the time by which the debt relief service provider will make a bona fide settlement offer to each of them;

(B) to the extent that the service may include a settlement offer to any of the customer's creditors or debt collectors, the amount of money or the percentage of each outstanding debt that the customer must accumulate before the debt relief service provider will make a bona fide settlement offer to each of them;

(C) to the extent that any aspect of the debt relief service relies upon or results in the customer's failure to make timely payments to creditors or debt collectors, that the use of the debt relief service will likely adversely affect the customer's creditworthiness, may result in the customer being subject to collections or sued by creditors or debt collectors, and may increase the amount of money the customer owes due to the accrual of fees and interest; and

(D) to the extent that the debt relief service requests or requires the customer to place funds in an account at an insured financial institution, that the customer owns the funds held in the account, the customer may withdraw from the debt relief service at any time without penalty, and, if the customer withdraws, the customer must receive all funds in the account, other than funds earned by the debt relief service in compliance with § 310.4(a)(5)(i)(A) through (C).

(2) Misrepresenting, directly or by implication, in the sale of goods or services any of the following material information:

    (i) The total costs to purchase, receive, or use, and the quantity of, any goods or services that are the subject of a sales offer;

    (ii) Any material restriction, limitation, or condition to purchase, receive, or use goods or services that are the subject of a sales offer;

    (iii) Any material aspect of the performance, efficacy, nature, or central characteristics of goods or services that are the subject of a sales offer;

    (iv) Any material aspect of the nature or terms of the seller's refund, cancellation, exchange, or repurchase policies;

    (v) Any material aspect of a prize promotion including, but not limited to, the odds of being able to receive a prize, the nature or value of a prize, or that a purchase or payment is required to win a prize or to participate in a prize promotion;

    (vi) Any material aspect of an investment opportunity including, but not limited to, risk, liquidity, earnings potential, or profitability;

    (vii) A seller's or telemarketer's affiliation with, or endorsement or sponsorship by, any person or government entity;

    (viii) That any customer needs offered goods or services to provide protections a customer already has pursuant to 15 U.S.C. 1643;

    (ix) Any material aspect of a negative option feature including, but not limited to, the fact that the customer's account will be charged unless the customer takes an affirmative action to avoid the charge(s), the date(s) the charge(s) will be submitted for payment, and the specific steps the customer must take to avoid the charge(s); or

    (x) Any material aspect of any debt relief service, including, but not limited to, the amount of money or the percentage of the debt amount that a customer may save by using such service; the amount of time necessary to achieve the represented results; the amount of money or the percentage of each outstanding debt that the customer must accumulate before the provider of the debt relief service will initiate attempts with the customer's creditors or debt collectors or make a bona fide offer to negotiate, settle, or modify the terms of the customer's debt; the effect of the service on a customer's creditworthiness; the effect of the service on collection efforts of the customer's creditors or debt collectors; the percentage or number of customers who attain the represented results; and whether a debt relief service is offered or provided by a non-profit entity.

(3) Causing billing information to be submitted for payment, or collecting or attempting to collect payment for goods or services or a charitable contribution, directly or indirectly, without the customer's or donor's express verifiable authorization, except when the method of payment used is a credit card subject to protections of the Truth in Lending Act and Regulation Z, or a debit card subject to the protections of the Electronic Fund Transfer Act and Regulation E. Such authorization shall be deemed verifiable if any of the following means is employed:

    (i) Express written authorization by the customer or donor, which includes the customer's or donor's signature;

    Express oral authorization which is audio-recorded and made available upon request to the customer or donor, and the customer's or donor's bank or other billing entity, and which evidences clearly both the customer's or donor's authorization of payment for the goods or services or charitable contribution that are the subject of the telemarketing transaction and the customer's or donor's receipt of all of the following information:

        (A) An accurate description, clearly and conspicuously stated, of the goods or services or charitable contribution for which payment authorization is sought;

        (B) The number of debits, charges, or payments (if more than one);

        (C) The date(s) the debit(s), charge(s), or payment(s) will be submitted for payment;

      (D) The amount(s) of the debit(s), charge(s), or payment(s);

      (E) The customer's or donor's name;

      (F) The customer's or donor's billing information, identified with sufficient specificity such that the customer or donor understands what account will be used to collect payment for the goods or services or charitable contribution that are the subject of the telemarketing transaction;

      (G) A telephone number for customer or donor inquiry that is answered during normal business hours; and

      (H) The date of the customer's or donor's oral authorization; or

    (ii) Written confirmation of the transaction, identified in a clear and conspicuous manner as such on the outside of the envelope, sent to the customer or donor via first class mail prior to the submission for payment of the customer's or donor's billing information, and that includes all of the information contained in §§ 310.3(a)(3)(ii)(A)-(G) and a clear and conspicuous statement of the procedures by which the customer or donor can obtain a refund from the seller or telemarketer or charitable organization in the event the confirmation is inaccurate; provided, however, that this means of authorization shall not be deemed verifiable in instances in which goods or services are offered in a transaction involving a free-to-pay conversion and preacquired account information.

  (4) Making a false or misleading statement to induce any person to pay for goods or services or to induce a charitable contribution.

(b) Assisting and facilitating. It is a deceptive telemarketing act or practice and a violation of this Rule for a person to provide substantial assistance or support to any seller or telemarketer when that person knows or consciously avoids knowing that the seller or telemarketer is engaged in any act or practice that violates §§ 310.3(a), (c) or (d), or § 310.4 of this Rule.

(c) Credit card laundering. Except as expressly permitted by the applicable credit card system, it is a deceptive telemarketing act or practice and a violation of this Rule for:

  (1) A merchant to present to or deposit into, or cause another to present to or deposit into, the credit card system for payment, a credit card sales draft generated by a telemarketing transaction that is not the result of a telemarketing credit card transaction between the cardholder and the merchant;

  (2) Any person to employ, solicit, or otherwise cause a merchant, or an employee, representative, or agent of the merchant, to present to or deposit into the credit card system for payment, a credit card sales draft generated by a telemarketing transaction that is not the result of a telemarketing credit card transaction between the cardholder and the merchant; or

  (3) Any person to obtain access to the credit card system through the use of a business relationship or an affiliation with a merchant, when such access is not authorized by the merchant agreement or the applicable credit card system.

(d) Prohibited deceptive acts or practices in the solicitation of charitable contributions. It is a fraudulent charitable solicitation, a deceptive telemarketing act or practice, and a violation of this Rule for any telemarketer soliciting charitable contributions to misrepresent, directly or by implication, any of the following material information:

  (1) The nature, purpose, or mission of any entity on behalf of which a charitable contribution is being requested;

  (2) That any charitable contribution is tax deductible in whole or in part;

  (3) The purpose for which any charitable contribution will be used;

  (4) The percentage or amount of any charitable contribution that will go to a charitable organization or to any particular charitable program;

  (5) Any material aspect of a prize promotion including, but not limited to: the odds of being able to receive a prize; the nature or value of a prize; or that a charitable contribution is required to win a prize or to participate in a prize promotion; or

  (6) A charitable organization's or telemarketer's affiliation with, or endorsement or sponsorship by, any person or government entity.

§ 310.4 Abusive telemarketing acts or practices.

(a) Abusive conduct generally. It is an abusive telemarketing act or practice and a violation of this Rule for any seller or telemarketer to engage in the following conduct:

  (1) Threats, intimidation, or the use of profane or obscene language;

  (2) Requesting or receiving payment of any fee or consideration for goods or services represented to remove derogatory information from, or improve, a person's credit history, credit record, or credit rating until:

   (i) The time frame in which the seller has represented all of the goods or services will be provided to that person has expired; and

   (ii) The seller has provided the person with documentation in the form of a consumer report from a consumer reporting agency demonstrating that the promised results have been achieved, such report having been issued more than six months after the results were achieved. Nothing in this Rule should be construed to affect the requirement in the Fair Credit Reporting Act, 15 U.S.C. 1681, that a consumer report may only be obtained for a specified permissible purpose;

  (3) Requesting or receiving payment of any fee or consideration from a person for goods or services represented to recover or otherwise assist in the return of money or any other item of value paid for by, or promised to, that person in a previous transaction, until seven (7) business days after such money or other item is delivered to that person. This provision shall not apply to goods or services provided to a person by a licensed attorney;

  (4) Requesting or receiving payment of any fee or consideration in advance of obtaining a loan or other extension of credit when the seller or telemarketer has guaranteed or represented a high likelihood of success in obtaining or arranging a loan or other extension of credit for a person;

  (5)
   (i) Requesting or receiving payment of any fee or consideration for any debt relief service until and unless:

    (A) The seller or telemarketer has renegotiated, settled, reduced, or otherwise altered the terms of at least one debt pursuant to a settlement agreement, debt management plan, or other such valid contractual agreement executed by the customer;

    (B) The customer has made at least one payment pursuant to that settlement agreement, debt management plan, or other valid contractual agreement between the customer and the creditor or debt collector; and

    (C) To the extent that debts enrolled in a service are renegotiated, settled, reduced, or otherwise altered individually, the fee or consideration either:

     (1) Bears the same proportional relationship to the total fee for renegotiating, settling, reducing, or altering the terms of the entire debt balance as the individual debt amount bears to the entire debt amount. The individual debt amount and the entire debt amount are those owed at the time the debt was enrolled in the service; or

     (2) Is a percentage of the amount saved as a result of the renegotiation, settlement, reduction, or alteration. The percentage charged cannot change from one individual debt to another. The amount saved is the difference between the amount owed at the time the debt was enrolled in the service and the amount actually paid to satisfy the debt.

   (ii) Nothing in § 310.4(a)(5)(i) prohibits requesting or requiring the customer to place funds in an account to be used for the debt relief provider's fees and for payments to creditors or debt collectors in connection with the renegotiation, settlement, reduction, or other alteration of the terms of payment or other terms of a debt, provided that:

    (A) The funds are held in an account at an insured financial institution;

    (B) The customer owns the funds held in the account and is paid accrued interest on the account, if any;

    (C) The entity administering the account is not owned or controlled by, or in any way affiliated with, the debt relief service;

(D) The entity administering the account does not give or accept any money or other compensation in exchange for referrals of business involving the debt relief service; and

(E) The customer may withdraw from the debt relief service at any time without penalty, and must receive all funds in the account, other than funds earned by the debt relief service in compliance with § 310.4(a)(5)(i)(A) through (C), within seven (7) business days of the customer's request.

(6) Disclosing or receiving, for consideration, unencrypted consumer account numbers for use in telemarketing; provided, however, that this paragraph shall not apply to the disclosure or receipt of a customer's or donor's billing information to process a payment for goods or services or a charitable contribution pursuant to a transaction;

(7) Causing billing information to be submitted for payment, directly or indirectly, without the express informed consent of the customer or donor. In any telemarketing transaction, the seller or telemarketer must obtain the express informed consent of the customer or donor to be charged for the goods or services or charitable contribution and to be charged using the identified account. In any telemarketing transaction involving preacquired account information, the requirements in paragraphs (a)(7)(i) through (ii) of this section must be met to evidence express informed consent.

(i) In any telemarketing transaction involving preacquired account information and a free-to-pay conversion feature, the seller or telemarketer must:

(A) Obtain from the customer, at a minimum, the last four (4) digits of the account number to be charged;

(B) Obtain from the customer his or her express agreement to be charged for the goods or services and to be charged using the account number pursuant to paragraph (a)(7)(i)(A) of this section; and,

(C) Make and maintain an audio recording of the entire telemarketing transaction.

(ii) In any other telemarketing transaction involving preacquired account information not described in paragraph (a)(7)(i) of this section, the seller or telemarketer must:

(A) At a minimum, identify the account to be charged with sufficient specificity for the customer or donor to understand what account will be charged; and

(B) Obtain from the customer or donor his or her express agreement to be charged for the goods or services and to be charged using the account number identified pursuant to paragraph (a)(7)(ii)(A) of this section;

(8) Failing to transmit or cause to be transmitted the telephone number, and, when made available by the telemarketer's carrier, the name of the telemarketer, to any caller identification service in use by a recipient of a telemarketing call; provided that it shall not be a violation to substitute (for the name and phone number used in, or billed for, making the call) the name of the seller or charitable organization on behalf of which a telemarketing call is placed, and the seller's or charitable organization's customer or donor service telephone number, which is answered during regular business hours;

(9) Creating or causing to be created, directly or indirectly, a remotely created payment order as payment for goods or services offered or sold through telemarketing or as a charitable contribution solicited or sought through telemarketing; or

(10) Accepting from a customer or donor, directly or indirectly, a cash-to-cash money transfer or cash reload mechanism as payment for goods or services offered or sold through telemarketing or as a charitable contribution solicited or sought through telemarketing.

(b) Pattern of calls.

(1) It is an abusive telemarketing act or practice and a violation of this Rule for a telemarketer to engage in, or for a seller to cause a telemarketer to engage in, the following conduct:

(i) Causing any telephone to ring, or engaging any person in telephone conversation, repeatedly or continuously with intent to annoy, abuse, or harass any person at the called number;

(ii) Denying or interfering in any way, directly or indirectly, with a person's right to be placed on any registry of names and/or telephone numbers of persons who do not wish to receive outbound telephone calls established to comply with paragraph (b)(1)(iii)(A) of this section, including, but not limited to, harassing any person who makes such a request; hanging up on that person; failing to honor the request; requiring the person to listen to a sales pitch before accepting the request; assessing a charge or fee for honoring the request; requiring a person to call a different number to submit the request; and requiring the person to identify the seller making the call or on whose behalf the call is made;

(iii) Initiating any outbound telephone call to a person when:

    (A) That person previously has stated that he or she does not wish to receive an outbound telephone call made by or on behalf of the seller whose goods or services are being offered or made on behalf of the charitable organization for which a charitable contribution is being solicited; or

    (B) That person's telephone number is on the "do-not-call" registry, maintained by the Commission, of persons who do not wish to receive outbound telephone calls to induce the purchase of goods or services unless the seller or telemarketer:

        (1) Can demonstrate that the seller has obtained the express agreement, in writing, of such person to place calls to that person. Such written agreement shall clearly evidence such person's authorization that calls made by or on behalf of a specific party may be placed to that person, and shall include the telephone number to which the calls may be placed and the signature of that person; or

        (2) Can demonstrate that the seller has an established business relationship with such person, and that person has not stated that he or she does not wish to receive outbound telephone calls under paragraph (b)(1)(iii)(A) of this section; or

(iv) Abandoning any outbound telephone call. An outbound telephone call is "abandoned" under this section if a person answers it and the telemarketer does not connect the call to a sales representative within two (2) seconds of the person's completed greeting.

(v) Initiating any outbound telephone call that delivers a prerecorded message, other than a prerecorded message permitted for compliance with the call abandonment safe harbor in § 310.4(b)(4)(iii), unless:

    (A) In any such call to induce the purchase of any good or service, the seller has obtained from the recipient of the call an express agreement, in writing, that:

        (i) The seller obtained only after a clear and conspicuous disclosure that the purpose of the agreement is to authorize the seller to place prerecorded calls to such person;

        (ii) The seller obtained without requiring, directly or indirectly, that the agreement be executed as a condition of purchasing any good or service;

        (iii) Evidences the willingness of the recipient of the call to receive calls that deliver prerecorded messages by or on behalf of a specific seller; and

        (iv) Includes such person's telephone number and signature; and

    (B) In any such call to induce the purchase of any good or service, or to induce a charitable contribution from a member of, or previous donor to, a non-profit charitable organization on whose behalf the call is made, the seller or telemarketer:

        (i) Allows the telephone to ring for at least fifteen (15) seconds or four (4) rings before disconnecting an unanswered call; and

        (ii) Within two (2) seconds after the completed greeting of the person called, plays a prerecorded message that promptly provides the disclosures required by § 310.4(d) or (e), followed immediately by a disclosure of one or both of the following:

            (A) In the case of a call that could be answered in person by a consumer, that the person called can use an automated interactive voice and/or keypress-activated opt-out mechanism to assert a Do Not Call request pursuant to § 310.4(b)(1)(iii)(A) at any time during the message. The mechanism must:

(1) Automatically add the number called to the seller's entity-specific Do Not Call list;

(2) Once invoked, immediately disconnect the call; and

(3) Be available for use at any time during the message; and

(B) In the case of a call that could be answered by an answering machine or voicemail service, that the person called can use a toll-free telephone number to assert a Do Not Call request pursuant to § 310.4(b)(1)(iii)(A). The number provided must connect directly to an automated interactive voice or keypress-activated opt-out mechanism that:

(1) Automatically adds the number called to the seller's entity-specific Do Not Call list;

(2) Immediately thereafter disconnects the call; and

(3) Is accessible at any time throughout the duration of the telemarketing campaign; and

(iii) Complies with all other requirements of this part and other applicable federal and state laws.

(C) Any call that complies with all applicable requirements of this paragraph (v) shall not be deemed to violate § 310.4(b)(1)(iv) of this part.

(D) This paragraph (v) shall not apply to any outbound telephone call that delivers a prerecorded healthcare message made by, or on behalf of, a covered entity or its business associate, as those terms are defined in the HIPAA Privacy Rule, 45 CFR 160.103.

(2) It is an abusive telemarketing act or practice and a violation of this Rule for any person to sell, rent, lease, purchase, or use any list established to comply with § 310.4(b)(1)(iii)(A), or maintained by the Commission pursuant to § 310.4(b)(1)(iii)(B), for any purpose except compliance with the provisions of this Rule or otherwise to prevent telephone calls to telephone numbers on such lists.

(3) A seller or telemarketer will not be liable for violating § 310.4(b)(1)(ii) and (iii) if it can demonstrate that, as part of the seller's or telemarketer's routine business practice:

(i) It has established and implemented written procedures to comply with § 310.4(b)(1)(ii) and (iii);

(ii) It has trained its personnel, and any entity assisting in its compliance, in the procedures established pursuant to § 310.4(b)(3)(i);

(iii) The seller, or a telemarketer or another person acting on behalf of the seller or charitable organization, has maintained and recorded a list of telephone numbers the seller or charitable organization may not contact, in compliance with § 310.4(b)(1)(iii)(A);

(iv) The seller or a telemarketer uses a process to prevent telemarketing to any telephone number on any list established pursuant to § 310.4(b)(3)(iii) or 310.4(b)(1)(iii)(B), employing a version of the "do-not-call" registry obtained from the Commission no more than thirty-one (31) days prior to the date any call is made, and maintains records documenting this process;

(v) The seller or a telemarketer or another person acting on behalf of the seller or charitable organization, monitors and enforces compliance with the procedures established pursuant to § 310.4(b)(3)(i); and

(vi) Any subsequent call otherwise violating paragraph (b)(1)(ii) or (iii) of this section is the result of error and not of failure to obtain any information necessary to comply with a request pursuant to paragraph (b)(1)(iii)(A) of this section not to receive further calls by or on behalf of a seller or charitable organization.

(4) A seller or telemarketer will not be liable for violating § 310.4(b)(1)(iv) if:

(i) The seller or telemarketer employs technology that ensures abandonment of no more than three (3) percent of all calls answered by a person, measured over the duration of a single calling campaign, if less than 30 days, or separately over each successive 30-day period or portion thereof that the campaign continues.

(ii) The seller or telemarketer, for each telemarketing call placed, allows the telephone to ring for at least fifteen (15) seconds or four (4) rings before disconnecting an unanswered call;

(iii) Whenever a sales representative is not available to speak with the person answering the call within two (2) seconds after the person's completed greeting, the seller or telemarketer promptly plays a recorded message that states the name and telephone number of the seller on whose behalf the call was placed; and

(iv) The seller or telemarketer, in accordance with § 310.5(b)-(d), retains records establishing compliance with § 310.4(b)(4)(i)-(iii).

(c) Calling time restrictions. Without the prior consent of a person, it is an abusive telemarketing act or practice and a violation of this Rule for a telemarketer to engage in outbound telephone calls to a person's residence at any time other than between 8:00 a.m. and 9:00 p.m. local time at the called person's location.

(d) Required oral disclosures in the sale of goods or services. It is an abusive telemarketing act or practice and a violation of this Rule for a telemarketer in an outbound telephone call or internal or external upsell to induce the purchase of goods or services to fail to disclose truthfully, promptly, and in a clear and conspicuous manner to the person receiving the call, the following information:

(1) The identity of the seller;

(2) That the purpose of the call is to sell goods or services;

(3) The nature of the goods or services; and

(4) That no purchase or payment is necessary to be able to win a prize or participate in a prize promotion if a prize promotion is offered and that any purchase or payment will not increase the person's chances of winning. This disclosure must be made before or in conjunction with the description of the prize to the person called. If requested by that person, the telemarketer must disclose the no-purchase/no-payment entry method for the prize promotion; provided, however, that, in any internal upsell for the sale of goods or services, the seller or telemarketer must provide the disclosures listed in this section only to the extent that the information in the upsell differs from the disclosures provided in the initial telemarketing transaction.

(e) Required oral disclosures in charitable solicitations. It is an abusive telemarketing act or practice and a violation of this Rule for a telemarketer, in an outbound telephone call to induce a charitable contribution, to fail to disclose truthfully, promptly, and in a clear and conspicuous manner to the person receiving the call, the following information:

(1) The identity of the charitable organization on behalf of which the request is being made; and

(2) That the purpose of the call is to solicit a charitable contribution.

§ 310.5 Recordkeeping requirements.

(a) Any seller or telemarketer shall keep, for a period of 24 months from the date the record is produced, the following records relating to its telemarketing activities:

(1) All substantially different advertising, brochures, telemarketing scripts, and promotional materials;

(2) The name and last known address of each prize recipient and the prize awarded for prizes that are represented, directly or by implication, to have a value of $25.00 or more;

(3) The name and last known address of each customer, the goods or services purchased, the date such goods or services were shipped or provided, and the amount paid by the customer for the goods or services;

(4) The name, any fictitious name used, the last known home address and telephone number, and the job title(s) for all current and former employees directly involved in telephone sales or solicitations; provided, however, that if the seller or telemarketer permits fictitious names to be used by employees, each fictitious name must be traceable to only one specific employee; and

(5) All verifiable authorizations or records of express informed consent or express agreement required to be provided or received under this Rule.

(b) A seller or telemarketer may keep the records required by § 310.5(a) in any form, and in the same manner, format, or place as they keep such records in the ordinary course of business. Failure to keep all records required by § 310.5(a) shall be a violation of this Rule.

(c) The seller and the telemarketer calling on behalf of the seller may, by written agreement, allocate responsibility between themselves for the recordkeeping required by this Section. When a seller and telemarketer have entered into such an agreement, the terms of that agreement shall govern, and the seller or telemarketer, as the case may be, need not keep records that duplicate those of the other. If the agreement is unclear as to who must maintain any required record(s), or if no such agreement exists, the seller shall be responsible for complying with §§ 310.5(a)(1)-(3) and (5); the telemarketer shall be responsible for complying with § 310.5(a)(4).

(d) In the event of any dissolution or termination of the seller's or telemarketer's business, the principal of that seller or telemarketer shall maintain all records as required under this section. In the event of any sale, assignment, or other change in ownership of the seller's or telemarketer's business, the successor business shall maintain all records required under this section.

§ 310.6 Exemptions.

(a) Solicitations to induce charitable contributions via outbound telephone calls are not covered by § 310.4(b)(1)(iii)(B) of this Rule.

(b) The following acts or practices are exempt from this Rule:

(1) The sale of pay-per-call services subject to the Commission's Rule entitled "Trade Regulation Rule Pursuant to the Telephone Disclosure and Dispute Resolution Act of 1992," 16 CFR part 308, provided, however, that this exemption does not apply to the requirements of §§ 310.4(a)(1), (a)(7), (b), and (c);

(2) The sale of franchises subject to the Commission's Rule entitled "Disclosure Requirements and Prohibitions Concerning Franchising," ("Franchise Rule") 16 CFR part 436, and the sale of business opportunities subject to the Commission's Rule entitled "Disclosure Requirements and Prohibitions Concerning Business Opportunities," ("Business Opportunity Rule") 16 CFR part 437, provided, however, that this exemption does not apply to the requirements of §§ 310.4(a)(1), (a)(7), (b), and (c);

(3) Telephone calls in which the sale of goods or services or charitable solicitation is not completed, and payment or authorization of payment is not required, until after a face-to-face sales or donation presentation by the seller or charitable organization, provided, however, that this exemption does not apply to the requirements of §§ 310.4(a)(1), (a)(7), (b), and (c);

(4) Telephone calls initiated by a customer or donor that are not the result of any solicitation by a seller, charitable organization, or telemarketer, provided, however, that this exemption does not apply to any instances of upselling included in such telephone calls;

(5) Telephone calls initiated by a customer or donor in response to an advertisement through any medium, other than direct mail solicitation, provided, however, that this exemption does not apply to:

(i) Calls initiated by a customer or donor in response to an advertisement relating to investment opportunities, debt relief services, business opportunities other than business arrangements covered by the Franchise Rule or Business Opportunity Rule, or advertisements involving offers for goods or services described in § 310.3(a)(1)(vi) or § 310.4(a)(2) through (4);

(ii) The requirements of § 310.4(a)(9) or (10); or

(iii) Any instances of upselling included in such telephone calls;

(6) Telephone calls initiated by a customer or donor in response to a direct mail solicitation, including solicitations via the U.S. Postal Service, facsimile transmission, electronic mail, and other similar methods of delivery in which a solicitation is directed to specific address(es) or person(s), that clearly, conspicuously, and truthfully discloses all material information listed in § 310.3(a)(1), for any goods or services offered in the direct mail solicitation, and that contains no material misrepresentation regarding any item contained in § 310.3(d) for any requested charitable contribution; provided, however, that this exemption does not apply to:

(i) Calls initiated by a customer in response to a direct mail solicitation relating to prize promotions, investment opportunities, debt relief services, business opportunities other than business arrangements covered by the Franchise Rule or Business Opportunity Rule, or goods or services described in § 310.3(a)(1)(vi) or § 310.4(a)(2) through (4);

(ii) The requirements of § 310.4(a)(9) or (10); or

(iii) Any instances of upselling included in such telephone calls; and

(7) Telephone calls between a telemarketer and any business to induce the purchase of goods or services or a charitable contribution by the business, except calls to induce the retail sale of nondurable office or cleaning supplies; provided, however, that §§ 310.4(b)(1)(iii)(B) and 310.5 shall not apply to sellers or telemarketers of nondurable office or cleaning supplies.

§ 310.7 Actions by states and private persons.

(a) Any attorney general or other officer of a state authorized by the state to bring an action under the Telemarketing and Consumer Fraud and Abuse Prevention Act, and any private person who brings an action under that Act, shall serve written notice of its action on the Commission, if feasible, prior to its initiating an action under this Rule. The notice shall be sent to the Office of the Director, Bureau of Consumer Protection, Federal Trade Commission, Washington, DC 20580, and shall include a copy of the state's or private person's complaint and any other pleadings to be filed with the court. If prior notice is not feasible, the state or private person shall serve the Commission with the required notice immediately upon instituting its action.

(b) Nothing contained in this Section shall prohibit any attorney general or other authorized state official from proceeding in state court on the basis of an alleged violation of any civil or criminal statute of such state.

§ 310.8 Fee for access to the National Do Not Call Registry.

Link to an amendment published at 84 FR 44687, Aug. 27, 2019.

(a) It is a violation of this Rule for any seller to initiate, or cause any telemarketer to initiate, an outbound telephone call to any person whose telephone number is within a given area code unless such seller, either directly or through another person, first has paid the annual fee, required by § 310.8(c), for access to telephone numbers within that area code that are included in the National Do Not Call Registry maintained by the Commission under § 310.4(b)(1)(iii)(B); provided, however, that such payment is not necessary if the seller initiates, or causes a telemarketer to initiate, calls solely to persons pursuant to §§ 310.4(b)(1)(iii)(B)(i) or (ii), and the seller does not access the National Do Not Call Registry for any other purpose.

(b) It is a violation of this Rule for any telemarketer, on behalf of any seller, to initiate an outbound telephone call to any person whose telephone number is within a given area code unless that seller, either directly or through another person, first has paid the annual fee, required by § 310.8(c), for access to the telephone numbers within that area code that are included in the National Do Not Call Registry; provided, however, that such payment is not necessary if the seller initiates, or causes a telemarketer to initiate, calls solely to persons pursuant to §§ 310.4(b)(1)(iii)(B)(i) or (ii), and the seller does not access the National Do Not Call Registry for any other purpose.

(c) The annual fee, which must be paid by any person prior to obtaining access to the National Do Not Call Registry, is $63 for each area code of data accessed, up to a maximum of $17,406; provided, however, that there shall be no charge to any person for accessing the first five area codes of data, and provided further, that there shall be no charge to any person engaging in or causing others to engage in outbound telephone calls to consumers and who is accessing area codes of data in the National Do Not Call Registry if the person is permitted to access, but is not required to access, the National Do Not Call Registry under this Rule, 47 CFR 64.1200, or any other Federal regulation or law. No person may participate in any arrangement to share the cost of accessing the National Do Not Call Registry, including any arrangement with any telemarketer or service provider to divide the costs to access the registry among various clients of that telemarketer or service provider.

(d) Each person who pays, either directly or through another person, the annual fee set forth in paragraph (c) of this section, each person excepted under paragraph (c) from paying the annual fee, and each person excepted from paying an annual fee under § 310.4(b)(1)(iii)(B), will be provided a unique account number that will allow that person to access the registry data for the selected area codes at any time for the twelve month period beginning on the first day of the month in which the person paid the fee ("the annual period"). To obtain access to additional area codes of data during the first six months of the annual period, each person required to pay the fee under paragraph (c) of this section must first pay $63 for each additional area code of data not initially selected. To obtain access to additional area codes of data during the second six months of the annual period, each person required to pay the fee under paragraph (c) of this section must first pay $32 for each additional area code of data not initially selected. The payment of the additional fee will permit the person to access the additional area codes of data for the remainder of the annual period.

(e) Access to the National Do Not Call Registry is limited to telemarketers, sellers, others engaged in or causing others to engage in telephone calls to consumers, service providers acting on behalf of such persons, and any government agency that has law enforcement authority. Prior to accessing the National Do Not Call Registry, a person must provide the identifying information required by the operator of the registry to collect the fee, and must certify, under penalty of law, that the person is accessing the registry solely to comply with the provisions of this Rule or to otherwise prevent telephone calls to telephone numbers on the registry. If the person is accessing the registry on behalf of sellers, that person also must identify each of the sellers on whose behalf it is accessing the registry, must provide each seller's unique account number for access to the national registry, and must certify, under penalty of law, that the sellers will be using the information gathered from the registry solely to comply with the provisions of this Rule or otherwise to prevent telephone calls to telephone numbers on the registry.

§ 310.9 Severability.

The provisions of this Rule are separate and severable from one another. If any provision is stayed or determined to be invalid, it is the Commission's intention that the remaining provisions shall continue in effect.

---

72. USA PATRIOT Act:
Section 314 – Cooperative Efforts to Deter Money Laundering

a. Cooperation among financial institutions, regulatory authorities, and law enforcement authorities

    1. Regulations — The Secretary shall, within 120 days after the date of enactment of this Act, adopt regulations to encourage further cooperation among financial institutions, their regulatory authorities, and law enforcement authorities, with the specific purpose of encouraging regulatory authorities and law enforcement authorities to share with financial institutions information regarding individuals, entities, and organizations engaged in or reasonably suspected based on credible evidence of engaging in terrorist acts or money laundering activities.

    2. Cooperation and information sharing procedures — The regulations adopted under paragraph (1) may include or create procedures for cooperation and information sharing focusing on —

        A. matters specifically related to the finances of terrorist groups, the means by which terrorist groups transfer funds around the world and within the United States, including through the use of charitable organizations, nonprofit organizations, and nongovernmental organizations, and the extent to which financial institutions in the United States are unwittingly involved in such finances and the extent to which such institutions are at risk as a result;

    B. the relationship, particularly the financial relationship, between international narcotics traffickers and foreign terrorist organizations, the extent to which their memberships overlap and engage in joint activities, and the extent to which they cooperate with each other in raising and transferring funds for their respective purposes; and

    C. means of facilitating the identification of accounts and transactions involving terrorist groups and facilitating the exchange of information concerning such accounts and transactions between financial institutions and law enforcement organizations.

3. Contents — The regulations adopted pursuant to paragraph (1) may —

    A. require that each financial institution designate 1 or more persons to receive information concerning, and to monitor accounts of individuals, entities, and organizations identified, pursuant to paragraph (1); and

    B. further establish procedures for the protection of the shared information, consistent with the capacity, size, and nature of the institution to which the particular procedures apply.

4. Rule of constructions — The receipt of information by a financial institution pursuant to this section shall not relieve or otherwise modify the obligations of the financial institution with respect to any other person or account.

5. Use of information — Information received by a financial institution pursuant to this section shall not be used for any purpose other than identifying and reporting on activities that may involve terrorist acts or money laundering activities.

b. Cooperation among financial institutions — Upon notice provided to the Secretary, 2 or more financial institutions and any association of financial institutions may share information with one another regarding individuals, entities, organizations, and countries suspected of possible terrorist or money laundering activities. A financial institution or association that transmits, receives, or shares such information for the purposes of identifying and reporting activities that may involve terrorist acts or money laundering activities shall not be liable to any person under any law or regulation of the United States, any constitution, law, or regulation of any State or political subdivision thereof, or under any contract or other legally enforceable agreement (including any arbitration agreement), for such disclosure or for any failure to provide notice of such disclosure to the person who is the subject of such disclosure, or any other person identified in the disclosure, except where such transmission, receipt, or sharing violates this section or regulations promulgated pursuant to this section.

c. Rule of construction — Compliance with the provisions of this title requiring or allowing financial institutions and any association of financial institutions to disclose or share information regarding individuals, entities, and organizations engaged in or suspected of engaging in terrorist acts or money laundering activities shall not constitute a violation of the provisions of title V of the Gramm-Leach-Bliley Act (Public Law 106-102).

d. Reports to the financial services industry on suspicious financial activities - At least semiannually, the Secretary shall —

1. publish a report containing a detailed analysis identifying patterns of suspicious activity and other investigative insights derived from suspicious activity reports and investigations conducted by Federal, State, and local law enforcement agencies to the extent appropriate; and

2. distribute such report to financial institutions (as defined in section 5312 of title 31, United States Code).

---

73. USA PATRIOT Act: Section 326 – Verification of Identification

a. In general — Section 5318 of title 31, United States Code, as amended by this title, is amended by adding at the end the following:

Identification and verification of accountholders —

1. In general — Subject to the requirements of this subsection, the Secretary of the Treasury shall prescribe regulations setting forth the minimum standards for financial institutions and their customers regarding the identity of the customer that shall apply in connection with the opening of an account at a financial institution.

2. Minimum requirements — The regulations shall, at a minimum, require financial institutions to implement, and customers (after being given adequate notice) to comply with, reasonable procedures for

   A. verifying the identity of any person seeking to open an account to extent reasonable and practicable;

   B. maintaining records of the information used to verify a person's identity, including name, address, and other identifying information; and

   C. consulting lists of known or suspected terrorists or terrorist organizations provided to the financial institution by any government agency to determine whether a person seeking to open an account appears on any such list.

3. Factors to be considered — In prescribing regulations under this subsection, the Secretary shall take into consideration the various types of accounts maintained by various types of financial institutions, the various methods of opening accounts, and the various types of identifying information available.

4. Certain financial institutions — In the case of any financial institution the business of which is engaging in financial activities described in section 4(k) of the Bank Holding Company Act of 1956 (including financial activities subject to the jurisdiction of the Commodity Futures Trading Commission), the regulations prescribed by the Secretary under paragraph (1) shall be prescribed jointly with each Federal functional regulator (as defined in section 509 of the Gramm-Leach-Bliley Act, including the Commodity Futures Trading Commission) appropriate for such financial institution.

5. Exemptions — The Secretary (and, in the case of any financial institution described in paragraph (4), any Federal agency described in such paragraph) may, by regulation or order, exempt any financial institution or type of account from the requirements of any regulation prescribed under this subsection in accordance with such standards and procedures as the Secretary may prescribe.

6. Effective date — Final regulations prescribed under this subsection shall take effect before the end of the 1-year period beginning on the date of enactment of the International Money Laundering Abatement and Financial Anti-Terrorism Act of 2001.

b. Study and report required — Within 6 months after the date of enactment of this Act, the Secretary, in consultation with Federal functional regulators (as defined in section 509 of the Gramm-Leach-Bliley Act) and other appropriate Government agencies, shall submit a report to the Congress containing recommendations for —

1. determining the most timely and effective way to require foreign nationals to provide domestic financial institutions and agencies with appropriate and accurate information, comparable to that which is required of United States nationals, concerning the identity, address, and other related information about such foreign nationals necessary to enable such institutions and agencies to comply with the requirements of this section;

2. requiring foreign nationals to apply for and obtain, before opening an account with a domestic financial institution, an identification number which would function similarly to a Social Security number or tax identification number; and

3. establishing a system for domestic financial institutions and agencies to review information maintained by relevant Government agencies for purposes of verifying the identities of foreign nationals seeking to open accounts at those institutions and agencies.

74. USA PATRIOT Act: Section 352 – Anti-Money Laundering Programs

a. In general — Section 5318(h) of title 31, United States Code, is amended to read as follows:

   h. Anti-money laundering programs

   1. In general — In order to guard against money laundering through financial institutions, each financial institution shall establish anti-money laundering programs, including, at a minimum –

      A. the development of internal policies, procedures, and controls;
      B. the designation of a compliance officer;
      C. an ongoing employee training program; and
      D. an independent audit function to test programs.

   2. Regulations — The Secretary of the Treasury, after consultation with the appropriate Federal functional regulator (as defined in section 509 of the Gramm-Leach-Bliley Act), may prescribe minimum standards for programs established under paragraph (1), and may exempt from the application of those standards any financial institution that is not subject to the provisions of the rules contained in part 103 of title 31, of the Code of Federal Regulations, or any successor rule thereto, for so long as such financial institution is not subject to the provisions of such rules.

   i. Effective date — The amendment made by subsection (a) shall take effect at the end of the 180-day period beginning on the date of enactment of this Act.

   j. Date of application of regulations, factors to be taken into account — Before the end of the 180-day period beginning on the date of enactment of this Act, the Secretary shall prescribe regulations that consider the extent to which the requirements imposed under this section are commensurate with the size, location, and activities of the financial institutions to which such regulations apply.

Section 4

Overview of the Regulatory Framework

1. FINRA By-Laws: Article I – Definitions

When used in these By-Laws, unless the context otherwise requires, the term:

(a) "Act" means the Securities Exchange Act of 1934, as amended;

(b) "bank" means (1) a banking institution organized under the laws of the United States, (2) a member bank of the Federal Reserve System, (3) any other banking institution, whether incorporated or not, doing business under the laws of any State or of the United States, a substantial portion of the business of which consists of receiving deposits or exercising fiduciary powers similar to those permitted to national banks under the authority of the Comptroller of the Currency pursuant to the first section of Public Law 87-722 (12 U.S.C. § 92a), and which is supervised and examined by a State or Federal authority having supervision over banks, and which is not operated for the purpose of evading the provisions of the Act, and (4) a receiver, conservator, or other liquidating agent of any institution or firm included in clauses (1), (2), or (3) of this subsection;

(c) "Board" means the Board of Governors of the Corporation;

(d) "branch office" means an office defined as a branch office in the Rules of the Corporation;

(e) "broker" means any individual, corporation, partnership, association, joint stock company, business trust, unincorporated organization, or other legal entity engaged in the business of effecting transactions in securities for the account of others, but does not include a bank;

(f) "Closing" means the closing of the consolidation of certain member firm regulatory functions of NYSE Regulation, Inc. and the Corporation;

(g) "Commission" means the Securities and Exchange Commission;

(h) "controlling" shall mean the possession, directly or indirectly, of the power to direct or cause the direction of the management and policies of a person, whether through the ownership of voting stock, by contract or otherwise. A person who is the owner of 20% or more of the outstanding voting stock of any corporation, partnership, unincorporated association or other entity shall be presumed to have control of such entity, in the absence of proof by a preponderance of the evidence to the contrary. Notwithstanding the foregoing, a presumption of control shall not apply where such person holds voting stock, in good faith, as an agent, bank, broker, nominee, custodian or trustee for one or more owners who do not individually or as a group have control of such entity;

(i) "Corporation" means the National Association of Securities Dealers, Inc. or any future name of this entity;

(j) "day" means calendar day;

(k) "dealer" means any individual, corporation, partnership, association, joint stock company, business trust, unincorporated organization, or other legal entity engaged in the business of buying and selling securities for such individual's or entity's own account, through a broker or otherwise, but does not include a bank, or any person insofar as such person buys or sells securities for such person's own account, either individually or in some fiduciary capacity, but not as part of a regular business;

(l) "Delegation Plan" means the "Plan of Allocation and Delegation of Functions by NASD to Subsidiaries" as approved by the Commission, and as amended from time to time;

(m) "district" means a district established by the NASD Regulation Board pursuant to NASD Regulation By-Laws;

(n) "Floor Member Governor" means a member of the Board appointed as such who is a person associated with a member (or a firm in the process of becoming a member) which is a specialist or floor broker on the New York Stock Exchange trading floor;

(o) "government securities broker" shall have the same meaning as in Section 3(a)(43) of the Act except that it shall not include financial institutions as defined in Section 3(a)(46) of the Act;

(p) "government securities dealer" shall have the same meaning as in Section 3(a)(44) of the Act except that it shall not include financial institutions as defined in Section 3(a)(46) of the Act;

(q) "Governor" means a member of the Board;

(r) "Independent Dealer/Insurance Affiliate Governor" means a member of the Board appointed as such who is a person associated with a member which is an independent contractor financial planning member firm or an insurance company, or an affiliate of such a member;

(s) "Industry Director" means a Director of the NASD Regulation Board or NASD Dispute Resolution Board (excluding the Presidents) who: (1) is or has served in the prior year as an officer, director (other than as an independent director), employee or controlling person of a broker or dealer, or (2) has a consulting or employment relationship with or provides professional services to a self regulatory organization registered under the Act, or has had any such relationship or provided any such services at any time within the prior year;

(t) "Industry Governor" or "Industry committee member" means the Floor Member Governor, the Independent Dealer/Insurance Affiliate Governor and the Investment Company Affiliate Governor and any other Governor (excluding the Chief Executive Officer of the Corporation and, during the Transitional Period, the Chief Executive Officer of NYSE Regulation, Inc.) or committee member who: (1) is or has served in the prior year as an officer, director (other than as an independent director), employee or controlling person of a broker or dealer, or (2) has a consulting or employment relationship with or provides professional services to a self regulatory organization registered under the Act, or has had any such relationship or provided any such services at any time within the prior year;

(u) "investment banking or securities business" means the business, carried on by a broker, dealer, or municipal securities dealer (other than a bank or department or division of a bank), or government securities broker or dealer, of underwriting or distributing issues of securities, or of purchasing securities and offering the same for sale as a dealer, or of purchasing and selling securities upon the order and for the account of others;

(v) "Investment Company" means an "investment company" as such term is defined in The Investment Company Act of 1940, as amended;

(w) "Investment Company Affiliate Governor" means a member of the Board appointed as such who is a person associated with a member which is an Investment Company or an affiliate of such a member;

(x) "Joint Public Governor" means the one Public Governor to be appointed as such by the Board of Directors of NYSE Group, Inc. and the Board in office prior to the Closing jointly;

(y) "Large Firm" means any broker or dealer admitted to membership in the Corporation which, at the time of determination, has 500 or more registered persons;

(z) "Large Firm Governor" means a member of the Board to be elected by Large Firm members, provided, however, that in order to be eligible to serve, a Large Firm Governor must be an Industry Governor and must be registered with a member which is a Large Firm member;

(aa) "Large Firm Governor Committee" means a committee of the Board comprised of all of the Large Firm Governors;

(bb) "Lead Governor" means a member of the Board elected as such by the Board, provided, however, that any member of the Board who is concurrently serving as a member of the Board of Directors of NYSE Group, Inc. shall not be eligible to serve as the Lead Governor;

(cc) "Mid-Size Firm" means any broker or dealer admitted to membership in the Corporation which, at the time of determination, has at least 151 and no more than 499 registered persons;

(dd) "Mid-Size Firm Governor" means a member of the Board to be elected by Mid-Size Firm members, provided, however, that in order to be eligible to serve, a Mid-Size Firm Governor must be an Industry Governor and must be registered with a member which is a Mid-Size Firm member;

(ee) "member" means any broker or dealer admitted to membership in the Corporation;

(ff) "municipal securities" means securities which are direct obligations of, or obligations guaranteed as to principal or interest by, a State or any political subdivision thereof, or any agency or instrumentality of a State or any political subdivision thereof, or any municipal corporate instrumentality of one or more States, or any security which is an industrial development bond as defined by Section 3(a)(29) of the Act;

(gg) "municipal securities broker" means a broker, except a bank or department or division of a bank, engaged in the business of effecting transactions in municipal securities for the account of others;

(hh) "municipal securities dealer" means any person, except a bank or department or division of a bank, engaged in the business of buying and selling municipal securities for such person's own account, through a broker or otherwise, but does not include any person insofar as such person buys or sells securities for such person's own account either individually or in some fiduciary capacity, but not as a part of a regular business;

(ii) "NASD Dispute Resolution" means NASD Dispute Resolution, Inc. or any future name of this entity;

(jj) "NASD Group Committee" means a committee of the Board comprised of the five Public Governors and the Independent Dealer/Insurance Affiliate Governor appointed as such by the Board in office prior to Closing, and the Small Firm Governors which were nominated for election as such by the Board in office prior to Closing, and in each case their successors;

(kk) "NASD Public Governors" means the five Public Governors to be appointed as such by the Board in office prior to the Closing effective as of Closing;

(ll) "NASD Regulation" means NASD Regulation, Inc. or any future name of this entity;

(mm) "NASD Regulation Board" means the Board of Directors of NASD Regulation;

(nn) "National Adjudicatory Council" means a body appointed pursuant to Article V of the NASD Regulation By-Laws;

(oo) "Nominating Committee" means the Nominating Committee appointed pursuant to Article VII, Section 9 of these By-Laws;

(pp) "NYSE Group Committee" means a committee of the Board comprised of the five Public Governors and the Floor Member Governor appointed as such by the Board of Directors of NYSE Group, Inc., and the Large Firm Governors which were nominated for election as such by the Board of Directors of NYSE Group, Inc., and in each case their successors;

(qq) "NYSE Public Governors" shall mean the five Public Governors to be appointed as such by the Board of Directors of NYSE Group, Inc. effective as of Closing;

(rr) "person associated with a member" or "associated person of a member" means: (1) a natural person who is registered or has applied for registration under the Rules of the Corporation; (2) a sole proprietor, partner, officer, director, or branch manager of a member, or other natural person occupying a similar status or performing similar functions, or a natural person engaged in the investment banking or securities business who is directly or indirectly controlling or controlled by a member, whether or not any such person is registered or exempt from registration with the Corporation under these By-Laws or the Rules of the Corporation; and (3) for purposes of Rule 8210, any other person listed in Schedule A of Form BD of a member;

(ss) "Public Director" means a Director of the NASD Regulation Board or NASD Dispute Resolution Board who is not an Industry Director and who otherwise has no material business relationship with a broker or dealer or a self regulatory organization registered under the Act (other than serving as a public director of such a self regulatory organization);

(tt) "Public Governor" or "Public committee member" means any Governor or committee member who is not the Chief Executive Officer of the Corporation or, during the Transitional Period, the Chief Executive Officer of NYSE Regulation, Inc., who is not an Industry Governor and who otherwise has no material business relationship with a broker or dealer or a self regulatory organization registered under the Act (other than serving as a public director of such a self regulatory organization);

(uu) "registered broker, dealer, municipal securities broker or dealer, or government securities broker or dealer" means any broker, dealer, municipal securities broker or dealer, or government securities broker or dealer which is registered with the Commission under the Act;

(vv) "Rules of the Corporation" or "Rules" means the numbered rules set forth in the manual of the Corporation beginning with the Rule 0100 Series, as adopted by the Board pursuant to these By-Laws, as hereafter amended or supplemented;

(ww) "Small Firm" means any broker or dealer admitted to membership in the Corporation which, at the time of determination, has at least 1 and no more than 150 registered persons;

(xx) "Small Firm Governor" means a member of the Board to be elected by Small Firm members, provided, however, that in order to be eligible to serve, a Small Firm Governor must be registered with a member which is a Small Firm member and must be an Industry Governor;

(yy) "Small Firm Governor Committee" means a committee of the Board comprised of all the Small Firm Governors; and

(zz) "Transitional Period" means the period commencing on the date of the Closing and ending on the third anniversary of the date of the Closing.

---

2. FINRA By-Laws: Article III – Qualifications of Members and Associated Persons

<u>Persons Eligible to Become Members and Associated Persons of Members</u>

Sec. 1. (a) Any registered broker, dealer, municipal securities broker or dealer, or government securities broker or dealer authorized to transact, and whose regular course of business consists in actually transacting, any branch of the investment banking or securities business in the United States, under the laws of the United States, shall be eligible for membership in the Corporation, except such registered brokers, dealers, or municipal securities brokers or dealers, or government securities brokers or dealers which are excluded under the provisions of Section 3.

(b) Any person shall be eligible to become an associated person of a member, except such persons who are excluded under the provisions of Section 3.

<u>Authority of Board to Adopt Qualification Requirements</u>

Sec. 2. (a) The Board shall have authority to adopt rules and regulations applicable to applicants for membership, members, and persons associated with applicants or members establishing specified and appropriate standards with respect to the training, experience, competence, and such other qualifications as the Board finds necessary or desirable, and in the case of an applicant for membership or a member, standards of financial responsibility and operational capability.

(b) In establishing and applying such standards, the Board may classify members and persons associated with such members, taking into account relevant matters, including the nature, extent, and type of business being conducted and of securities sold, dealt in, or otherwise handled. The Board may specify that all or any portion of such standards shall be applicable to any such class and may require the persons in any such class to be registered with the Corporation.

(c) The Board may from time to time make changes in such rules, regulations, and standards as it deems necessary or appropriate.

<u>Ineligibility of Certain Persons for Membership or Association</u>

Sec. 3. (a) No registered broker, dealer, municipal securities broker or dealer, or government securities broker or dealer shall be admitted to membership, and no member shall be continued in membership, if such broker, dealer, municipal securities broker or dealer, government securities broker or dealer, or member fails or ceases to satisfy the qualification requirements established under Section 2, if applicable, or if such broker, dealer, municipal securities broker or dealer, government securities broker or dealer, or member is or becomes subject to a disqualification under Section 4, or if such member fails to comply with the requirement that all forms filed pursuant to these By-Laws be filed via electronic process or such other process as the Corporation may prescribe.

(b) No person shall become associated with a member, continue to be associated with a member, or transfer association to another member, if such person fails or ceases to satisfy the qualification requirements established under Section 2, if applicable, or if such person is or becomes subject to a disqualification under Section 4; and no broker, dealer, municipal securities broker or dealer, or government securities broker or dealer shall be admitted to membership, and no member shall be continued in membership, if any person associated with it is ineligible to be an associated person under this subsection.

(c) If it deems appropriate, the Board, upon notice and opportunity for a hearing, may cancel the membership of a member if it becomes ineligible for continuance in membership under subsection (a), may suspend or bar a person from continuing to be associated with any member if such person is or becomes ineligible for association under subsection (b), and may cancel the membership of any member who continues to be associated with any such ineligible person.

(d) Any member that is ineligible for continuance in membership may file with the Board an application requesting relief from the ineligibility pursuant to the Rules of the Corporation. A member may file such application on its own behalf and on behalf of a current or prospective associated person. The Board may, in its discretion, approve the continuance in membership, and may also approve the association or continuance of association of any person, if the Board determines that such approval is consistent with the public interest and the protection of investors. Any approval hereunder may be granted unconditionally or on such terms and conditions as the Board considers necessary or appropriate. In the exercise of the authority granted hereunder, the Board may conduct such inquiry or investigation into the relevant facts and circumstances as it, in its discretion, considers necessary to its determination, which, in addition to the background and circumstances giving rise to the failure to qualify or disqualification, may include the proposed or present business of a member and the conditions of association of any current or prospective associated person.

(e) An application filed under subsection (d) shall not foreclose any action which the Board is authorized to take under subsection (c) until approval has been granted.

(f) Approval by the Board of an application made under subsection (d) shall be subject to whatever further action the Commission may take pursuant to authority granted to the Commission under the Act.

(g) The Board may delegate its authority under this Section in a manner not inconsistent with the Delegation Plan.

Definition of Disqualification

Sec. 4. A person is subject to a "disqualification" with respect to membership, or association with a member, if such person is subject to any "statutory disqualification" as such term is defined in Section 3(a)(39) of the Act.

---

3. FINRA By-Laws: Article IV – Membership

Application for Membership

Sec. 1. (a) Application for membership in the Corporation, properly signed by the applicant, shall be made to the Corporation via electronic process or such other process as the Corporation may prescribe, on the form to be prescribed by the Corporation, and shall contain:

    (1) an agreement to comply with the federal securities laws, the rules and regulations thereunder, the rules of the Municipal Securities Rulemaking Board and the Treasury Department, the By-Laws of the Corporation, NASD Regulation, or NASD Dispute Resolution, the Rules of the Corporation, and all rulings, orders, directions, and decisions issued and sanctions imposed under the Rules of the Corporation;

    (2) an agreement to pay such dues, assessments, and other charges in the manner and amount as from time to time shall be fixed pursuant to the By-Laws of the Corporation, Schedules to the By-Laws of the Corporation, and the Rules of the Corporation; and

    (3) such other reasonable information with respect to the applicant as the Corporation may require.

  (b) Any application for membership received by the Corporation shall be processed in the manner set forth in the Rules of the Corporation.

  (c) Each applicant and member shall ensure that its membership application with the Corporation is kept current at all times by supplementary amendments via electronic process or such other process as the Corporation may prescribe to the original application. Such amendments to the application shall be filed with the Corporation not later than 30 days after learning of the facts or circumstances giving rise to the amendment.

Similarity of Membership Names

Sec. 2. (a) No person or firm shall be admitted to or continued in membership in the Corporation having a name that is identical to the name of another member appearing on the membership roll of the Corporation or a name so similar to any such name as to tend to confuse or mislead.

  (b) No member may change its name without prior approval of the Corporation.

Executive Representative

Sec. 3. Each member shall appoint and certify to the Secretary of the Corporation one "executive representative" who shall represent, vote, and act for the member in all the affairs of the Corporation, except that other executives of a member may also hold office in the Corporation, serve on the Board or committees appointed under Article IX, Section 1 or otherwise take part in the affairs of the Corporation. A member may change its executive representative upon giving notice thereof via electronic process or such other process as the Corporation may prescribe to the Secretary, or may, when necessary, appoint, by notice via electronic process to the Secretary, a substitute for its executive representative. An executive representative of a member or a substitute shall be a member of senior management and registered principal of the member. Not later than January 1, 1999, each executive representative shall maintain an Internet electronic mail account for communication with the Corporation and shall update firm contact information via the NASD Regulation Web Site or such other means as prescribed by the Corporation.

Membership Roll

Sec. 4. The Secretary of the Corporation shall keep a currently accurate and complete membership roll, containing the name and address of each member, and the name and address of the executive representative of each member. In any case where a membership has been terminated, such fact shall be recorded together with the date on which the membership ceased. The membership roll of the Corporation shall at all times be available to all members of the Corporation, to all governmental authorities, and to the general public.

Resignation of Members

Sec. 5. Membership in the Corporation may be voluntarily terminated only by formal resignation. Resignations of members must be filed via electronic process or such other process as the Corporation may prescribe and addressed to the Corporation. Any member may resign from the Corporation at any time. Such resignation shall not take effect until 30 days after receipt thereof by the Corporation and until all indebtedness due the Corporation from such member shall have been paid in full and so long as any complaint or action is pending against the member under the Rules of the Corporation. The Corporation, however, may in its discretion declare a resignation effective at any time.

Retention of Jurisdiction

Sec. 6. A resigned member or a member that has had its membership canceled or revoked shall continue to be subject to the filing of a complaint under the Rules of the Corporation based upon conduct which commenced prior to the effective date of the member's resignation from the Corporation or the cancellation or revocation of its membership. Any such complaint, however, shall be filed within two years after the effective date of resignation, cancellation, or revocation.

Transfer and Termination of Membership

Sec. 7. (a) Except as provided hereinafter, no member of the Corporation may transfer its membership or any right arising therefrom and the membership of a corporation, partnership, or any other business organization which is a member of the Corporation shall terminate upon its liquidation, dissolution, or winding up, and the membership of a sole proprietor which is a member shall terminate at death, provided that all obligations of membership under the By-Laws and the Rules of the Corporation have been fulfilled.

(b) The consolidation, reorganization, merger, change of name, or similar change in any corporate member shall not terminate the membership of such corporate member provided that the member or surviving organization, if any, shall be deemed a successor to the business of the corporate member, and the member or the surviving organization shall continue in the investment banking and securities business, and shall possess the qualifications for membership in the Corporation. The death, change of name, withdrawal of any partner, the addition of any new partner, reorganization, consolidation, or any change in the legal structure of a partnership member shall not terminate the membership of such partnership member provided that the member or surviving organization, if any, shall be deemed a successor to the business of the partnership member, and the member or surviving organization shall continue in the investment banking and securities business and shall possess the qualifications for membership in the Corporation. If the business of any predecessor member is to be carried on by an organization deemed to be a successor organization by the Corporation, the membership of such predecessor member shall be extended to the successor organization subject to the notice and application requirements of the Rules of the Corporation and the right of the Corporation to place restrictions on the successor organization pursuant to the Rules of the Corporation; otherwise, any surviving organization shall be required to satisfy all of the membership application requirements of these By-Laws and the Rules of the Corporation.

Registration of Branch Offices

Sec. 8. (a) Each branch office of a member of the Corporation shall be registered with and listed upon the membership roll of the Corporation, and shall pay such dues, assessments, and other charges as shall be fixed from time to time by the Board pursuant to Article VI.

(b) Each member of the Corporation shall promptly advise the Corporation via electronic process or such other process as the Corporation may prescribe of the opening, closing, relocation, change in designated supervisor, or change in designated activities of any branch office of such member not later than 30 days after the effective date of such change.

4. FINRA By-Laws: Article V – Registered Representatives and Associated Persons

Qualification Requirements

Sec. 1. No member shall permit any person associated with the member to engage in the investment banking or securities business unless the member determines that such person satisfies the qualification requirements established under Article III, Section 2 and is not subject to a disqualification under Article III, Section 4.

Application for Registration

Sec. 2. (a) Application by any person for registration with the Corporation, properly signed by the applicant, shall be made to the Corporation via electronic process or such other process as the Corporation may prescribe, on the form to be prescribed by the Corporation and shall contain:

(1) an agreement to comply with the federal securities laws, the rules and regulations thereunder, the rules of the Municipal Securities Rulemaking Board and the Treasury Department, the By-Laws of the Corporation, NASD Regulation, and NASD Dispute Resolution, the Rules of the Corporation, and all rulings, orders, directions, and decisions issued and sanctions imposed under the Rules of the Corporation; and

(2) such other reasonable information with respect to the applicant as the Corporation may require.

(b) The Corporation shall not approve an application for registration of any person who is not eligible to be an associated person of a member under the provisions of Article III, Section 3.

(c) Every application for registration filed with the Corporation shall be kept current at all times by supplementary amendments via electronic process or such other process as the Corporation may prescribe to the original application. Such amendment to the application shall be filed with the Corporation not later than 30 days after learning of the facts or circumstances giving rise to the amendment. If such amendment involves a statutory disqualification as defined in Section 3(a)(39) and Section 15(b)(4) of the Act, such amendment shall be filed not later than ten days after such disqualification occurs.

Notification by Member to the Corporation and Associated Person of Termination; Amendments to Notification

Sec. 3. (a) Following the termination of the association with a member of a person who is registered with it, such member shall, not later than 30 days after such termination, give notice of the termination of such association to the Corporation via electronic process or such other process as the Corporation may prescribe on a form designated by the Corporation, and concurrently shall provide to the person whose association has been terminated a copy of said notice as filed with the Corporation. A member that does not submit such notification and provide a copy to the person whose association has been terminated, within the time period prescribed, shall be assessed a late filing fee as specified by the Corporation. Termination of registration of such person associated with a member shall not take effect so long as any complaint or action under the Rules of the Corporation is pending against a member and to which complaint or action such person associated with a member is also a respondent, or so long as any complaint or action is pending against such person individually under the Rules of the Corporation. The Corporation, however, may in its discretion declare the termination effective at any time.

(b) The member shall notify the Corporation via electronic process or such other process as the Corporation may prescribe by means of an amendment to the notice filed pursuant to subsection (a) in the event that the member learns of facts or circumstances causing any information set forth in said notice to become inaccurate or incomplete. Such amendment shall be filed with the Corporation via electronic process or such other process as the Corporation may prescribe and a copy provided to the person whose association with the member has been terminated not later than 30 days after the member learns of the facts or circumstances giving rise to the amendment.

Retention of Jurisdiction

Sec. 4. (a) A person whose association with a member has been terminated and is no longer associated with any member of Corporation or a person whose registration has been revoked or canceled shall continue to be subject to the filing of a complaint under the Corporation Rules based upon conduct that commenced prior to the termination, revocation, or cancellation or upon such person's failure, while subject to the Corporation's jurisdiction as provided herein, to provide information requested by Corporation pursuant to the Corporation's Rules, but any such complaint shall be filed within:

    (i) two years after the effective date of termination of registration pursuant to Section 3, provided, however that any amendment to a notice of termination filed pursuant to Section 3(b) that is filed within two years of the original notice that discloses that such person may have engaged in conduct actionable under any applicable statute, rule, or regulation shall operate to recommence the running of the two-year period under this subsection;

    (ii) two years after the effective date of revocation or cancellation of registration pursuant to the Corporation's Rules; or

    (iii) in the case of an unregistered person, two years after the date upon which such person ceased to be associated with the member.

(b) A person whose association with a member has been terminated and is no longer associated with any member of Corporation shall continue to be subject to a proceeding to suspend, consistent with Article VI, Section 3 of the By-Laws, his or her ability to associate with a member based on such person's failure to comply with an arbitration award or a written and executed settlement agreement obtained in connection with an arbitration or mediation submitted for disposition pursuant to the Corporation's Rules, provided that such proceeding is instituted within two years after the date of entry of such award.

---

5. FINRA By-Laws: Article VI – Dues, Assessments, and Other Charges

Power of the Corporation to Fix and Levy Assessments

Sec. 1. The Corporation shall prepare an estimate of the funds necessary to defray reasonable expenses of administration in carrying on the work of the Corporation each fiscal year, and on the basis of such estimate, shall fix and levy the amount of admission fees, dues, assessments, and other charges to be paid by the members and issuers and any other persons using any facility or system which the Corporation, NASD Regulation, or NASD Dispute Resolution operates or controls. Fees, dues, assessments, and other charges shall be called and payable as determined by the Corporation from time to time; provided, however, that such admission fees, dues, assessments, and other charges shall be equitably allocated among members and issuers and any other persons using any facility or system which the Corporation operates or controls. The Corporation may from time to time make such changes or adjustments in such fees, dues, assessments, and other charges as it deems necessary or appropriate to assure equitable allocation of dues among members. In the event of termination of membership or the extension of any membership to a successor organization during any fiscal year for which an assessment has been levied and become payable, the Corporation may make such adjustment in the fees, dues, assessments, or other charges payable by any such member or successor organization or organizations during such fiscal years as it deems fair and appropriate in the circumstances.

Reports of Members

Sec. 2. Each member, issuer, or other person shall promptly furnish all information or reports requested by the Corporation in connection with the determination of the amount of admission fees, dues, assessments, or other charges.

Suspension or Cancellation

Sec. 3. (a) The Corporation after 15 days notice in writing, may suspend or cancel the membership of any member or the registration of any person in arrears in the payment of any fees, dues, assessments, or other charges or for failure to furnish any information or reports requested pursuant to Section 2.

(b) The Corporation after 15 days notice in writing, may suspend or cancel the membership of any member or suspend from association with any member any person, for failure to comply with an award of arbitrators properly rendered pursuant to the Corporation's Rules, where a timely motion to vacate or modify such award has not been made pursuant to applicable law or where such a motion has been denied, or for failure to comply with a written and executed settlement agreement obtained in connection with an arbitration or mediation submitted for disposition pursuant to the Corporation's Rules.

Reinstatement of Membership or Registration

Sec. 4. Any membership or registration suspended or canceled under this Article may be reinstated by the Corporation upon such terms and conditions as it shall deem just; provided, however, that any applicant for reinstatement of membership or registration shall possess the qualifications required for membership or registration in the Corporation.

Delegation

Sec. 5. The Corporation may delegate its authority in a manner not inconsistent with the Delegation Plan.

---

6. FINRA By-Laws: Article XII – Disciplinary Proceedings

Sec. 1. The Board shall have authority to establish procedures relating to disciplinary proceedings involving members and their associated persons.

Sec. 2. Except as otherwise permitted under these By-Laws or the Act, in any disciplinary proceeding under the Rules of the Corporation, any member or person associated with a member shall be given the opportunity to have a hearing at which such member or person associated with a member shall be entitled to be heard in person or by counsel or by a representative as provided in the Rules of the Corporation. Such persons may present any relevant material in accordance with the Rules of the Corporation. In any such proceeding against a member or against a person associated with a member to determine whether the member or the person associated with a member shall be disciplined:

(a) specific charges shall be brought;

(b) such member or person associated with a member shall be notified of and be given an opportunity to defend against such charges;

(c) a record shall be kept; and

(d) any determination shall include a statement setting forth:

(i) any act or practice, in which such member or person associated with a member may be found to have engaged or which such member or person associated with a member may be found to have omitted;

(ii) the rule, regulation, or statutory provision of which any such act or practice, or omission to act, is deemed to be in violation;

(iii) the basis upon which any findings are made; and

(iv) the sanction imposed.

---

7. FINRA By-Laws: Article XV – Limitations of Power

Prohibitions

Sec. 1. Under no circumstances shall the Board or any officer, employee, or member of the Corporation have the power to:

(a) make any donation or contribution from the funds of the Corporation or to commit the Corporation for the payment of any donations or contributions for political or charitable purposes; or

(b) use the name or the facilities of the Corporation in aid of any political party or candidate for any public office.

Use of Name of the Corporation by Members

Sec. 2. No member shall use the name of the Corporation except to the extent that may be permitted by the Rules of the Corporation.

Unauthorized Expenditures

Sec. 3. No officer, employee, member of the Board or of any committee shall have any power to incur or contract any liability on behalf of the Corporation not authorized by the Board. The Board may delegate to the Chief Executive Officer of the Corporation or the Chief Executive Officer's delegate such authority as it deems necessary to contract on behalf of the Corporation or to satisfy unanticipated liabilities during the period between Board meetings.

Conflicts of Interest

Sec. 4. (a) A Governor or a member of a committee shall not directly or indirectly participate in any adjudication of the interests of any party if such Governor or committee member has a conflict of interest or bias, or if circumstances otherwise exist where his or her fairness might reasonably be questioned. In any such case, the Governor or committee member shall recuse himself or herself or shall be disqualified in accordance with the Rules of the Corporation.

(b) No contract or transaction between the Corporation and one or more of its Governors or officers, or between the Corporation and any other corporation, partnership, association, or other organization in which one or more of its Governors or officers are directors or officers, or have a financial interest, shall be void or voidable solely for this reason if: (i) the material facts pertaining to such Governor's or officer's relationship or interest and the contract or transaction are disclosed or are known to the Board or the committee, and the Board or committee in good faith authorizes the contract or transaction by the affirmative vote of a majority of the disinterested Governors, even though the disinterested governors be less than a quorum; or (ii) the material facts are disclosed or become known to the Board or committee after the contract or transaction is entered into, and the Board or committee in good faith ratifies the contract or transaction by the affirmative vote of a majority of the disinterested Governors even though the disinterested governors be less than a quorum. Only disinterested Governors may be counted in determining the presence of a quorum at the portion of a meeting of the Board or of a committee that authorizes the contract or transaction. This subsection shall not apply to any contract or transaction between the Corporation and NASD Regulation, or NASD Dispute Resolution.

Municipal Securities

Sec. 5. The provisions of the By-Laws conferring rulemaking authority upon the Board shall not be applicable to the municipal securities activities of members or persons associated with members to the extent that the application of such authority would be inconsistent with Section 15B of the Act.

8. FINRA Rules: 0100 Series – General Standards

0110. Adoption of Rules
The Rules are adopted pursuant to Article VII, Section 1, of the FINRA By-Laws.

0120. Effective Date
The Rules shall become effective as provided in Article XI, Section 1, of the FINRA By-Laws.

0130. Interpretation
The Rules shall be interpreted in light of the purposes sought to be achieved by the Rules and to further FINRA's regulatory programs.

0140. Applicability
(a) The Rules shall apply to all members and persons associated with a member. Persons associated with a member shall have the same duties and obligations as a member under the Rules.

(b) A member or person associated with a member, who has been expelled, canceled or revoked from membership or from registration, or who has been barred from being associated with all members, shall cease to have any privileges of membership or registration. A member or person associated with a member who has been suspended from membership or registration shall also cease to have any privileges of membership or registration other than those under the Code of Procedure as set forth in the Rule 9000 Series or insurance programs sponsored by FINRA. In neither case shall such a member or person associated with a member be entitled to recover any admission fees, dues, assessments or other charges paid to FINRA.

(c) A member or person associated with a member who has been suspended from membership or from registration shall be considered as a non-member during the period of suspension for purposes of applying the provisions of the Rules which govern dealings between members and non-members. However, such member or person associated with a member shall have all of the obligations imposed by the Rules.

0150. Application of Rules to Exempted Securities Except Municipal Securities
(a) For purposes of this Rule, the terms "exempted securities" and "municipal securities" shall have the meanings specified in Sections 3(a)(12) and 3(a)(29) of the Exchange Act, respectively.

(b) The Rules are not intended to be, and shall not be construed as, rules concerning transactions in municipal securities.

(c) Unless otherwise indicated within a particular Rule, the following rules are applicable to transactions in, and business activities relating to, exempted securities, except municipal securities, conducted by members and associated persons: Rules 1020, 2010, 2020, 2060, 2111, 2122, 2150, 2210, 2211, 2212, 2231, 2232, 2261, 2268, 2269, 2320(g), 3110, 3210, 3220, 3260, 3270, 3280, 4120, 4130, 4210, 4311, 4330, 4360, 4510 Series, 4530, 5160, 5210, 5220, 5230, 5310, 5340, 6700 Series, 8110, 8120, 8210, 8310, 8311, 8312, 8320, 8330 and 9552.

(d) FINRA Rule 2121 is applicable to transactions in, and business activities relating to, exempted securities that are government securities.

0151. Coordination with the MSRB
(a) FINRA will request guidance from the MSRB in interpretation of the rules of the MSRB. FINRA also will provide information to the MSRB about the enforcement actions and examinations pertaining to municipal securities brokers, municipal securities dealers, and municipal advisors conducted by FINRA regarding the Exchange Act and the rules and regulations thereunder and the rules of the MSRB, so that the MSRB may: (1) assist in such enforcement actions and examinations; and (2) evaluate the ongoing effectiveness of the rules of the MSRB.

0160. Definitions

(a) The terms used in the Rules, if defined in the FINRA By-Laws, shall have the meaning as defined in the FINRA By-Laws, unless a term is defined differently in a Rule, or unless the context of the term within a Rule requires a different meaning.

(b) When used in the Rules, unless the context otherwise requires:

    (1) "By-Laws"

        The term "By-Laws" means the By-Laws of the Corporation or the FINRA By-Laws.

    (2) "Code of Procedure"

        The term "Code of Procedure" means the procedural rules contained in the Rule 9000 Series.

    (3) "Completion of the Transaction"

        The term "completion of the transaction" means:

        (A) In the case of a customer who purchases a security through or from a member, except as provided in subparagraph (B), the time when such customer pays the member any part of the purchase price, or, if payment is effected by a bookkeeping entry, the time when such bookkeeping entry is made by the member for any part of the purchase price;

        (B) In the case of a customer who purchases a security through or from a member and who makes payment therefor prior to the time when payment is requested or notification is given that payment is due, the time when such member delivers, or credits such delivery of, the security to or into the account of such customer;

        (C) In the case of a customer who sells a security through or to a member, except as provided in subparagraph (D), if any security is not in the custody of the member at the time of sale, the time when the security is delivered to the member, and if the security is in the custody of the member at the time of sale, the earlier of when the member transfers the security from the account of such customer or the closing date of the transaction;

        (D) In the case of a customer who sells a security through or to a member and who delivers such security to such member prior to the time when delivery is requested or notification is given that delivery is due, the time when such member makes payment to or into the account of such customer.

    (4) "Customer"

        The term "customer" shall not include a broker or dealer.

    (5) "Exchange Act" or "SEA"

        The term "Exchange Act" or "SEA" means the Securities Exchange Act of 1934, as amended.

    (6) "FINRA"

        The term "FINRA" means, collectively, FINRA, Inc., FINRA Regulation, Inc. and FINRA CAT, LLC.

    (7) "FINRA Regulation"

        The term "FINRA Regulation" means FINRA Regulation, Inc.

    (8) "Investment Advisers Act"

        The term "Investment Advisers Act" means the Investment Advisers Act of 1940, as amended.

    (9) "Investment Company Act"

        The term "Investment Company Act" means the Investment Company Act of 1940, as amended.

    (10) "Member"

        The term "member" means any individual, partnership, corporation or other legal entity admitted to membership in FINRA under the provisions of Articles III and IV of the FINRA By-Laws.

    (11) "Office of Dispute Resolution"

        The term "Office of Dispute Resolution" means the office within FINRA Regulation that assumes the responsibilities and functions relating to dispute resolution programs including, but not limited to, the arbitration, mediation, or other resolution of disputes among and between members, associated persons and customers.

    (12) "Person"

        The term "person" shall include any natural person, partnership, corporation, association, or legal entity.

(13) "SEC"

The term "SEC" means the Securities and Exchange Commission.

(14) "Securities Act"

The term "Securities Act" means the Securities Act of 1933, as amended.

(15) "Selling Group"

The term "selling group" means any group formed in connection with a public offering, to distribute all or part of an issue of securities by sales made directly to the public by or through members of such selling group, under an agreement which imposes no financial commitment on the members of such group to purchase any such securities except as they may elect to do so.

(16) "Selling Syndicate"

The term "selling syndicate" means any syndicate formed in connection with a public offering, to distribute all or part of an issue of securities by sales made directly to the public by or through participants in such syndicate under an agreement which imposes a financial commitment upon participants in such syndicate to purchase any such securities.

(17) "State"

The term "State" shall mean any state of the United States, the District of Columbia, Puerto Rico, the Virgin Islands, or any other possession of the United States.

0170. Delegation, Authority and Access

(a) The Financial Industry Regulatory Authority, Inc. delegates to its subsidiaries, FINRA Regulation, Inc. and FINRA CAT, LLC (hereinafter "Subsidiaries"), the authority to act on behalf of FINRA as set forth in a Plan of Allocation and Delegation adopted by the Board of Governors and approved by the SEC pursuant to its authority under the Exchange Act.

(b) Notwithstanding any delegation of authority to the Subsidiaries pursuant to this Rule, the staff, books, records and premises of the Subsidiaries are the staff, books, records and premises of FINRA subject to oversight pursuant to the Exchange Act, and all officers, directors, employees and agents of the Subsidiaries are the officers, directors, employees and agents of FINRA for purposes of the Exchange Act, subject to applicable provisions of the National Market System Plan Governing the Consolidated Audit Trail.

0180. Application of Rules to Security-Based Swaps

(a) The Rules shall not apply to members' activities and positions with respect to security-based swaps, except for the following:

(1) FINRA Rule 2010;

(2) FINRA Rule 2020;

(3) FINRA Rule 3310; and

(4) FINRA Rule 4240.

(b) The following Rules shall apply to members' activities and positions with respect to security-based swaps only to the extent they would have applied as of July 15, 2011:

(1) NASD Rule 3110 and all successor FINRA Rules to such NASD Rule;

(2) the FINRA Rule 4500 Series; and

(3) the FINRA Rule 4100 Series.

(c) The following Rules shall apply as necessary to effectuate members' compliance with paragraphs (a) and (b) of this Rule:

(1) the FINRA Rule 0100 Series;

(2) the NASD Rule 1000 Series and all successor FINRA Rules to such NASD Rule Series;

(3) the FINRA Rule 1000 and 1100 Series;

(4) NASD Rules 3010 and 3012 and IM-3010-1 and all successor FINRA Rules to such NASD Rules and Interpretive Material;

(5) FINRA Rule 3130;

(6) the FINRA Rule 8000 Series; and

(7) the FINRA Rule 9000 Series.

(d) This Rule shall expire on February 12, 2020.

0190. Effective Date of Revocation, Cancellation, Expulsion, Suspension or Resignation

(a) A member shall be considered as a non-member of FINRA from the effective date of any order or notice from FINRA or the SEC issuing a revocation, cancellation, expulsion or suspension of its membership. In the case of suspension, a member shall be automatically reinstated to membership in FINRA at the termination of the suspension period.

(b) A member shall be considered as a non-member of FINRA from the date of acceptance by FINRA of any resignation of such member.

---

9. FINRA Rules: 1000 Series – Member Application and Associated Person Registration

1010. Electronic Filing Requirements for Uniform Forms

(a) Filing Requirement

Except as provided in Rule 1013(a)(2), all forms required to be filed by Article IV, Sections 1, 7, and 8, and Article V, Sections 2 and 3, of the FINRA By-Laws shall be filed through an electronic process or such other process FINRA may prescribe to the Central Registration Depository.

(b) Supervisory Requirements

(1) In order to comply with the supervisory procedures requirement in Rule 3110, each member shall identify a registered principal(s) or corporate officer(s) who has a position of authority over registration functions, to be responsible for supervising the electronic filing of appropriate forms pursuant to this Rule.

(2) The registered principal(s) or corporate officer(s) who has or have the responsibility to review and approve the forms filed pursuant to this Rule shall be required to acknowledge, electronically, that he is filing this information on behalf of the member and the member's associated persons.

(c) Form U4 Filing Requirements

(1) Except as provided in paragraphs (c)(2) and (c)(3) below, every initial and transfer electronic Form U4 filing and any amendments to the disclosure information on Form U4 shall be based on a manually signed Form U4 provided to the member or applicant for membership by the person on whose behalf the Form U4 is being filed. As part of the member's recordkeeping requirements, it shall retain the person's manually signed Form U4 or amendments to the disclosure information on Form U4 in accordance with SEA Rule 17a-4(e)(1) and make them available promptly upon regulatory request. An applicant for membership also shall retain in accordance with SEA Rule 17a-4(e)(1) every manually signed Form U4 it receives during the application process and make them available promptly upon regulatory request.

(2) A member may file electronically amendments to the disclosure information on Form U4 without obtaining the subject associated person's manual signature on the form, provided that the member shall use reasonable efforts to:

(A) provide the associated person with a copy of the amended disclosure information prior to filing; and

(B) obtain the associated person's written acknowledgment (which may be electronic) prior to filing that the information has been received and reviewed. As part of the member's recordkeeping requirements, the member shall retain this acknowledgment in accordance with SEA Rule 17a-4(e)(1) and make it available promptly upon regulatory request.

(3) In the event a member is not able to obtain an associated person's manual signature or written acknowl-edgement of amended disclosure information on Form U4 prior to filing of such information pursuant to paragraph (c)(1) or (2), the member is obligated to file the disclosure information as to which it has knowledge in accordance with Article V, Section 2 of the FINRA By-Laws. The member shall use reasona-ble efforts to provide the associated person with a copy of the amended disclosure information that was filed.

(4) A member may file electronically amendments to administrative data on Form U4 without obtaining the subject associated person's signature on the form. The member shall use reasonable efforts to provide the associated person with a copy of the amended administrative information that was filed.

(d) Fingerprint Information

Upon filing an electronic Form U4 on behalf of a person applying for registration, a member shall promptly submit fingerprint information for that person. FINRA may make a registration effective pending receipt of the fingerprint information. If a member fails to submit the fingerprint information within 30 days after FINRA receives the electronic Form U4, the person's registration shall be deemed inactive. In such case, FINRA shall notify the member that the person must immediately cease all activities requiring registration and is prohibited from performing any duties and functioning in any capacity requiring registration. FINRA shall administratively terminate a registration that is inactive for a period of two years. A person whose regis-tration is administratively terminated may reactivate the registration only by reapplying for registration and meeting the qualification requirements of the applicable provisions of the Rules 1210 and 1220. Upon appli-cation and a showing of good cause, FINRA may extend the 30-day period.

(e) Form U5 Filing Requirements

Initial filings and amendments of Form U5 shall be submitted electronically. As part of the member's record-keeping requirements, it shall retain such records for a period of not less than three years, the first two years in an easily accessible place, in accordance with SEA Rule 17a-4, and make such records available promptly upon regulatory request.

1011. Definitions

Unless otherwise provided, terms used in the Rule 1000 Series shall have the meaning as defined in Rule 0160.

(a) "Applicant"

The term "Applicant" means a person that applies for membership in FINRA under Rule 1013 or a member that files an application for approval of a change in ownership, control, or business operations under Rule 1017.

(b) "Associated Person"

The term "Associated Person" means: (1) a natural person registered under FINRA rules; or (2) a sole proprie-tor, or any partner, officer, director, branch manager of the Applicant, or any person occupying a similar sta-tus or performing similar functions; (3) any company, government or political subdivision or agency or instru-mentality of a government controlled by or controlling the Applicant; (4) any employee of the Applicant, ex-cept any person whose functions are solely clerical or ministerial; (5) any person directly or indirectly control-ling the Applicant whether or not such person is registered or exempt from registration under the FINRA By-Laws or FINRA rules; (6) any person engaged in investment banking or securities business controlled directly or indirectly by the Applicant whether such person is registered or exempt from registration under the FINRA By-Laws or FINRA rules; or (7) any person who will be or is anticipated to be a person described in (1) through (6) above.

(c) "Department"

The term "Department" means the Department of Member Regulation of FINRA.

(d) "Director"

The term "Director" means a member of the FINRA Regulation Board.

(e) "district"

The term "district" means a district established by the FINRA Regulation Board.

(f) "district office"

The term "district office" means an office of FINRA located in a district.

(g) "FINRA Board"

The term "FINRA Board" means the Board of Governors of FINRA.

(h) "FINRA Regulation Board"

The term "FINRA Regulation Board" means the Board of Directors of FINRA Regulation.

(i) "Governor"

The term "Governor" means a member of the FINRA Board.

(j) "Interested FINRA Staff"

The term "Interested FINRA Staff" means an employee who directly participates in a decision under Rule 1014 or 1017, an employee who directly supervises an employee with respect to such decision, an employee who conducted an investigation or examination of a member that files an application under Rule 1017, the District Director for the relevant district, and the head of the Department.

(k) "material change in business operations"

The term "material change in business operations" includes, but is not limited to:

(1) removing or modifying a membership agreement restriction;

(2) market making, underwriting, or acting as a dealer for the first time; and

(3) adding business activities that require a higher minimum net capital under SEA Rule 15c3-1;

(l) "principal place of business"

The term "principal place of business" means the executive office from which the sole proprietor or the officers, partners, or managers of the Applicant direct, control, and coordinate the activities of the Applicant, unless the Department determines that the principal place of business is where: (1) the largest number of Associated Persons of the Applicant are located; or (2) the books and records necessary to provide information and data to operate the business and comply with applicable rules are located.

(m) "sales practice event"

The term "sales practice event" means any customer complaint, arbitration, or civil litigation that has been reported to the Central Registration Depository, currently is required to be reported to the Central Registration Depository, or otherwise has been reported to FINRA.

(n) "Subcommittee"

The term "Subcommittee" means a subcommittee of the National Adjudicatory Council that is constituted pursuant to Rule 1015 to conduct a review of a Department decision issued under the Rule 1000 Series.

M-1011-1. Safe Harbor for Business Expansions

This interpretive material concerns the types of business expansions that will not require a member to submit a Rule 1017 application to obtain FINRA's approval of the expansion. This safe harbor applies to: (1) firms that do not have a membership agreement, and (2) firms that have a membership agreement that does not contain a restriction on the factors listed below.

The safe harbor is not available to a member that has a membership agreement that contains a specific restriction as to one or more of the factors listed below. In that case, the agreement takes precedence because FINRA has determined that a particular restriction should apply as to one or more of the factors, and FINRA has issued a decision with a rationale for that restriction. Similarly, the safe harbor also does not apply if the member has a membership agreement that permits expansion beyond the limits set forth below (e.g., an Applicant requests and obtains approval for 10 registered representatives in the first six months with an additional 10 registered representatives in the next year); in such case, FINRA has specifically considered the firm's expansion plans and approved them.

The safe harbor is not available to any member that has disciplinary history. For purposes of this Interpretation, "disciplinary history" means a finding of a violation by the member or a principal of the member in the past five years by the SEC, a self-regulatory organization, or a foreign financial regulatory authority of one or more of the following provisions (or a comparable foreign provision) or rules or regulations thereunder: violations of the types enumerated in Section 15(b)(4)(E) and Section 15(c) of the Exchange Act; Section 17(a) of the Securities Act; SEA Rules 10b-5 and 15g-1 through 15g-9; FINRA Rules 2010 (only if the finding of a violation is for unauthorized trading, churning, conversion, material misrepresentations or omissions to a customer, frontrunning, trading ahead of research reports or excessive markups), 2020, 2111, 2150, 4330, 3110 (failure to supervise only), 5210, and 5230; and MSRB Rules G-19, G-30, and G-37(b) and (c), and all predecessor NASD rules to such FINRA rules.

For those firms to which the safe harbor is available, the following types of expansions are presumed not to be a material change in business operations and therefore do not require a Rule 1017 application. For any expansion beyond these limits, a member should contact its district office prior to implementing the change to determine whether the proposed expansion requires an application under Rule 1017. Expansions in each area are measured on a rolling 12-month basis; members are required to keep records of increases in personnel, offices, and markets to determine whether they are within the safe harbor.

"Associated Persons involved in sales" includes all Associated Persons, whether or not registered, who are involved in sales activities with public customers, including sales assistants and cold callers, but excludes clerical, back office, and trading personnel who are not involved in sales activities.

1012. General Provisions
(a) Filing by Applicant or Service by FINRA
(1) An Applicant for membership shall file an application in the manner prescribed in Rule 1013, including the timely submission of an application fee pursuant to Schedule A to the FINRA By-Laws.
(2) An Applicant seeking approval of a change of ownership, control, or business operations shall file an application in the manner prescribed in Rule 1017, including the timely submission of an application fee pursuant to Schedule A to the FINRA By-Laws.
(3) Except where FINRA has otherwise prescribed an electronic or alternative filing process, an Applicant may file an application or any document or information requested under the Rule 1000 Series by first-class mail, overnight courier, or hand delivery. If the Department and the Applicant agree, the Applicant also may file a requested document or information by facsimile.
(4) FINRA shall serve a notice or decision issued under the Rule 1000 Series by first-class mail on the Applicant or its counsel, unless a Rule specifies a different method of service.
(5) For purposes of the Rule 1000 Series, service by FINRA or filing by an Applicant shall be deemed complete as follows:
(A) Service or filing by first-class mail shall be deemed complete on the date of postmark;
(B) Service or filing by overnight courier shall be deemed complete on the date of delivery to the overnight courier as specified in the airbill;
(C) Service or filing by hand delivery shall be deemed complete on the date of receipt as evidenced by a date stamp;
(D) Service or filing by facsimile shall be deemed complete on the date specified in the document and on the written confirmation of transmission; and
(E) Filing by an electronic system shall be deemed complete on the date specified on the confirmation page generated by the electronic filing system.
(b) Lapse of Application
(1) Absent a showing of good cause, an application filed under Rule 1013 or 1017 shall lapse if an Applicant fails to:
(A) respond fully within 60 days after service of an initial written request for information or documents under Rule 1013, within 30 days after service of an initial written request for information or documents under Rule 1017, within 30 days after service of a subsequent written request for information

or documents under Rule 1013 or 1017, or within such other time period agreed to by the Department and the Applicant;

    (B) appear at or otherwise participate in a scheduled membership interview pursuant to Rule 1013(b) or 1017(g); or

    (C) file an executed membership agreement under Rule 1014(d) or Rule 1017(h)(4) within 25 days after service of the agreement, or within other period agreed to by the Department and the Applicant.

  (2) If an Applicant wishes to continue to seek membership or approval of a change in ownership, control, or business operations, then the Applicant shall be required to submit a new application in the manner prescribed in Rule 1013 or 1017, respectively, including the timely submission of an application fee pursuant to Schedule A to the FINRA By-Laws. FINRA shall not refund any fee for a lapsed application.

(c) Ex Parte Communications

  (1) The prohibitions against ex parte communications shall become effective when FINRA staff has knowledge that an Applicant intends to file a written request for review by the National Adjudicatory Council under Rule 1015.

  (2) Unless on notice and opportunity for an Applicant and Interested FINRA Staff to participate, or to the extent required for the disposition of ex parte matters as authorized by FINRA rules:

    (A) an Applicant, a counsel or representative of an Applicant, or an Interested FINRA Staff shall not make or knowingly cause to be made an ex parte communication relevant to the merits of a membership proceeding under the Rule 1000 Series to a Governor, a member of the National Adjudicatory Council or a Subcommittee thereof, or a FINRA employee who is participating or advising in a decision of such a person with respect to that proceeding; and

    (B) a Governor, a member of the National Adjudicatory Council or a Subcommittee thereof, or a FINRA employee who is participating or advising in the decision of such a person with respect to a membership proceeding shall not make or knowingly cause to be made to an Applicant, a counsel or representative of the Applicant, or an Interested FINRA Staff an ex parte communication relevant to the merits of that proceeding.

  (3) A Governor, a member of the National Adjudicatory Council or a Subcommittee thereof, or a FINRA employee participating or advising in the decision of such a person, who receives, makes, or knowingly causes to be made a communication prohibited by this paragraph shall place in the record of the membership proceeding:

    (A) all such written communications;

    (B) memoranda stating the substance of all such oral communications; and

    (C) all written responses and memoranda stating the substance of all oral responses to all such communications.

(d) Recusal or Disqualification

A Governor or a member of the National Adjudicatory Council or a Subcommittee thereof shall not participate in a matter governed by the Rule 1000 Series as to which that person has a conflict of interest or bias, or if circumstances otherwise exist where his or her fairness might reasonably be questioned. In such a case, the person shall recuse himself or shall be disqualified as follows:

  (1) The Chair of the FINRA Board shall have authority to direct the disqualification of a Governor, and a majority of the Governors of the FINRA Board excluding the Chair shall have authority to direct the disqualification of the Chair of the FINRA Board.

  (2) The Chair of the National Adjudicatory Council shall have authority to direct the disqualification of a member of the National Adjudicatory Council or a member of a Subcommittee appointed pursuant to Rule 1015, and the Vice Chair of the National Adjudicatory Council shall have authority to direct the disqualification of the Chair of the National Adjudicatory Council.

(e) Computation of Time

  (1) Calendar Day

    In the Rule 1000 Series, "day" means calendar day.

(2) Formula

In computing a period of time under the Rule 1000 Series, the day of the act, event, default, or lapse from which the period of time designated begins to run shall not be included. The last day of the period so computed shall be included unless it is a Saturday, Sunday, or Federal holiday, in which event the period runs until the end of the next day that is not a Saturday, Sunday, or Federal holiday. Intermediate Saturdays, Sundays, and Federal holidays shall be excluded from the computation when the period prescribed is 10 days or less.

1013. New Member Application and Interview
(a) Filing of Application
   (1) How to File

   An Applicant for FINRA membership shall file its application with the Department in the manner prescribed by FINRA. An Applicant shall submit an application that includes:

   (A) Form NMA;

   (B) an original signed and notarized paper Form BD, with applicable schedules;

   (C) an original FINRA-approved fingerprint card for each Associated Person who will be subject to SEA Rule 17f-2;

   (D) a new member assessment report;

   (E) a detailed business plan that adequately and comprehensively describes all material aspects of the business that will be, or are reasonably anticipated to be, performed at and after the initiation of business operations, including future business expansion plans, if any, and includes:

   (i) a trial balance, balance sheet, supporting schedules, and computation of net capital, each of which has been prepared as of a date that is within 30 days before the filing date of the application;

   (ii) a monthly projection of income and expenses, with a supporting rationale, for the first 12 months of operations;

   (iii) an organizational chart;

   (iv) the intended location of the Applicant's principal place of business and all other offices, if any, whether or not such offices would be required to be registered under FINRA rules, and the names of the persons who will be in charge of each office;

   (v) a list of the types of securities to be offered and sold and the types of retail or institutional customers to be solicited;

   (vi) a description of the methods and media to be employed to develop a customer base and to offer and sell products and services to customers, including the use of the Internet, telephone solicitations, seminars, or mailings;

   (vii) a description of the business facilities and a copy of any proposed or final lease;

   (viii) the number of markets to be made, if any, the type and volatility of the products, and the anticipated maximum inventory positions;

   (ix) any plan to enter into contractual commitments, such as underwritings or other securities-related activities;

   (x) any plan to distribute or maintain securities products in proprietary positions, and the risks, volatility, degree of liquidity, and speculative nature of the products;

   (xi) any other activity that the Applicant may engage in that reasonably could have a material impact on net capital within the first 12 months of business operations; and

   (xii) a description of the communications and operational systems the Applicant will employ to conduct business with customers or other members and the plans and procedures the Applicant will employ to ensure business continuity, including: system capacity to handle the anticipated level of usage; contingency plans in the event of systems or other technological or communications problems or failures that may impede customer usage or firm order entry or execution; system redundancies; disaster recovery plans; system security; disclosures to be made to potential and existing customers who may use such systems; and supervisory or customer protection measures that may apply to customer use of, or access to, such systems;

(F) a copy of any decision or order by a federal or state authority or self-regulatory organization taking permanent or temporary adverse action with respect to a registration or licensing determination regarding the Applicant or an Associated Person;

(G) a list of all Associated Persons;

(H) documentation of any of the following events, unless the event has been reported to the Central Registration Depository:

(i) a regulatory action against or investigation of the Applicant or an Associated Person by the SEC, the Commodity Futures Trading Commission, a federal, state, or foreign regulatory agency, or a self-regulatory organization that is pending, adjudicated, or settled;

(ii) an investment-related civil action for damages or an injunction against the Applicant or an Associated Person that is pending, adjudicated, or settled;

(iii) an investment-related customer complaint or arbitration that is required to be reported on Form U4;

(iv) a criminal action (other than a minor traffic violation) against the Applicant or an Associated Person that is pending, adjudicated, or that has resulted in a guilty or no contest plea; and

(v) a copy of any document evidencing a termination for cause or a permitted resignation after investigation of an alleged violation of a federal or state securities law, a rule or regulation thereunder, a self-regulatory organization rule, or an industry standard of conduct;

(I) a description of any remedial action, such as special training, continuing education requirements, or heightened supervision, imposed on an Associated Person by a state or federal authority or self-regulatory organization;

(J) a written acknowledgment that heightened supervisory procedures and special educational programs may be required pursuant to Notice to Members 97-19 for an Associated Person whose record reflects disciplinary actions or sales practice events;

(K) a copy of final or proposed contracts with banks, clearing entities, or service bureaus, and a general description of any other final or proposed contracts;

(L) a description of the nature and source of Applicant's capital with supporting documentation, including a list of all persons or entities that have contributed or plan to contribute financing to the Applicant's business, the terms and conditions of such financing arrangements, the risk to net capital presented by the Applicant's proposed business activities, and any arrangement for additional capital should a business need arise;

(M) a description of the financial controls to be employed by the Applicant;

(N) a description of the Applicant's supervisory system and a copy of its written supervisory procedures, internal operating procedures (including operational and internal controls), internal inspections plan, written approval process, and qualifications investigations required by Rule 3110;

(O) a description of the number, experience, and qualifications of supervisors and principals and the number, experience, and qualifications of persons to be supervised by such personnel, the other responsibilities of the supervisors and principals with the Applicant, their full-time or part-time status, any business activities that the supervisors or principals may engage in outside of their association with the Applicant, the hours per week devoted to such activities, and an explanation of how a part-time supervisor or principal will be able to discharge his or her designated functions on a part-time basis;

(P) a description of Applicant's proposed recordkeeping system;

(Q) a copy of the Applicant's written training plan to comply with Firm Element continuing education requirements described in Rule 1240(b), including the name of the Associated Person responsible for implementation; and

(R) a FINRA Entitlement Program Agreement and Terms of Use and a FINRA Member Firm Account Administrator Entitlement Form.

(2) Uniform Registration Forms

Upon approval of the Applicant's FINRA Member Firm Account Administrator Entitlement Form, the Applicant shall submit its Forms U4 for each Associated Person who is required to be registered under FINRA rules, any amendments to its Forms BD or U4, and any Form U5 electronically via Web CRD.

(3) Rejection of Application That Is Not Substantially Complete

If the Department determines within 30 days after the filing of an application that the application is not substantially complete, the Department may reject the application and deem it not to have been filed. In such case, within the 30 day period, the Department shall serve a written notice on the Applicant of the Department's determination and the reasons therefor. FINRA shall refund the application fee, less $500, which shall be retained by FINRA as a processing fee. If the Applicant determines to continue to seek membership, the Applicant shall submit a new application under this Rule and fee pursuant to Schedule A to the FINRA By-Laws.

(4) Request For Additional Documents Or Information

Within 30 days after the filing of an application, the Department shall serve an initial request for any additional information or documents necessary to render a decision on the application. The Department may serve subsequent requests for additional information or documents at any time during the membership application process.

Unless otherwise agreed by the Department and the Applicant, the Applicant shall file any additional information and documents with the Department within 60 days after service of the Department's initial request and 30 days after service of any subsequent request.

(5) Withdrawal of Application

If an Applicant withdraws an application within 30 days after filing the application, FINRA shall refund the application fee, less $500, which shall be retained by FINRA as a processing fee. If the Applicant determines to again seek membership, the Applicant shall submit a new application under this Rule and fee pursuant to Schedule A to the FINRA By-Laws.

(b) Membership Interview

(1) Requirement for Interview

Before the Department serves its decision on an application for new membership in FINRA, the Department shall conduct a membership interview with a representative or representatives of the Applicant.

(2) Service of Notice

At least seven days before the membership interview, the Department shall serve on the Applicant a written notice that specifies the date and time of the interview and the representative or representatives of the Applicant who are required to participate in the interview. The Department shall serve the notice by facsimile or overnight courier. The Applicant and the Department may agree to a shorter or longer period for notice or a different method of service under this subparagraph.

(3) Time

Unless the Department directs otherwise for good cause shown, a membership interview shall be scheduled to occur within 90 days after the filing of an application or within 60 days after the filing of all additional information or documents requested, whichever is later.

(4) Place

Unless the Department and the Applicant otherwise agree, the membership interview shall be conducted in the district office for the district in which the Applicant has or intends to have its principal place of business.

(5) Updated Financial Documents

On or before the date of the membership interview, the Applicant shall file an updated trial balance, balance sheet, supporting schedules, and computation of net capital. The Applicant shall prepare such documents as of a date that is within 45 days before the date of the membership interview, unless the Applicant and the Department agree on a longer period. The Applicant shall promptly notify the Department in writing of any material adverse change in its financial condition that occurs before a decision constituting final action of FINRA is served on the Applicant.

(6) Review of Standards for Admission

During the membership interview, the Department shall review the application and the standards for admission to membership with the Applicant's representative or representatives.

(7) Information From Other Sources

During the membership interview, the Department shall provide to the Applicant's representative or representatives any information or document that the Department has obtained from the Central Registration Depository or a source other than the Applicant and upon which the Department intends to base its decision under Rule 1014. If the Department receives such information or document after the membership interview or decides to base its decision on such information after the membership interview, the Department shall promptly serve the information or document and an explanation thereof on the Applicant.

IM-1013-1. Membership Waive-In Process for Certain New York Stock Exchange Member Organizations

This Interpretive Material sets forth a membership waive-in process for certain New York Stock Exchange ("NYSE") member organizations to become members of FINRA as part of the consolidation of the member firm regulatory functions of NASD and NYSE Regulation, Inc. ("NYSE Regulation"). It applies to firms that, as of July 25, 2007, (1) are approved NYSE member organizations or (2) have submitted an application to become an NYSE member organization and are subsequently approved for NYSE membership (together "NYSE-only member organizations"), provided that such firms were not also NASD members as of July 30, 2007. Such firms are eligible to automatically become FINRA members and to automatically register all associated persons whose registrations are approved with NYSE in registration categories recognized by FINRA upon submission to the Department of a signed waive-in membership application ("Waive-In Application") with the following information:

(1) General company information, including Central Registration Depository (CRD®) Number and contact person.

(2) An attestation that all information on the applicant's CRD form, as of the date of submission of the Waive-In Application is accurate and complete and fully reflects all aspects of the applicant's current business, including, but not limited to, ownership structure, management, product lines and disclosures.

(3) The identity of the firm's Executive Representative.

(4) Completed and signed Entitlement Forms.

(5) A signed FINRA Membership Agreement.

(6) Representations that the NYSE applicant's Uniform Application for Broker-Dealer Registration (Form BD) will be amended as needed to keep current and accurate; that all individual and entity registrations with FINRA will be kept current; and that all information and statements contained in the Waive-In Application are current, true and complete.

The Department shall review the Waive-In Application within three business days of receipt and, if complete, issue a letter notifying the applicant that it has been approved for membership. The Membership Agreement shall become effective on the date of such notification letter.

Firms admitted pursuant to this Interpretive Material shall be subject to the FINRA By-Laws and Schedules to By-Laws, including Schedule A, and FINRA rules, other than FINRA Rules 1011 through 1016, 1019 through 1021, 2231, 3260 and 4540, provided that their securities business is limited to floor brokerage on the NYSE, or routing away to other markets orders that are ancillary to their core floor business under NYSE Rule 70.40 ("permitted floor activities"). If an NYSE-only member organization admitted pursuant to this Interpretive Material seeks to expand its business operations to include any activities other than the permitted floor activities, such firm must apply for and receive approval to engage in such business activity pursuant to Rule 1017. Upon approval of such business expansion, the firm shall be subject to the FINRA By-Laws and Schedules to By-Laws, including Schedule A, and all FINRA rules.

Pursuant to IM-Section 4(b)(1) and (e) to Schedule A of the FINRA By-Laws, a firm applying to waive in for membership pursuant to this Interpretive Material shall not be assessed certain registration and application fees set forth in Sections 4(b)(1) and (e) to Schedule A of the FINRA By-Laws.

IM-1013-2. Membership Waive-In Process for Certain NYSE American LLC Member Organizations

This Interpretive Material sets forth a membership waive-in process for certain NYSE American LLC ("NYSE American") member organizations to become members of FINRA as part of the acquisition by NYSE Euronext of the Amex Membership Corporation. It applies to any NYSE American member organization that (i) holds a valid 86 Trinity Permit as of the date such firm transfers its equities operations to the NYSE American Trading Systems and (ii) is not currently a FINRA member. Such firms are eligible to automatically become FINRA members and to automatically register all associated persons whose registrations are approved with NYSE American in registration categories recognized by FINRA upon submission to the Department of a signed waive-in membership application ("Waive-In Application") with the following information:

(1) General company information, including Central Registration Depository (CRD®) Number and contact person;

(2) An attestation that all information on the applicant's® form, as of the date of submission of the Waive-In Application, is accurate and complete and fully reflects all aspects of the applicant's current business, including, but not limited to, ownership structure, management, product lines and disclosures;

(3) The identity of the firm's Executive Representative;

(4) Completed and signed Entitlement Forms (unless previously submitted);

(5) A signed FINRA Membership Agreement; and

(6) Representations that the NYSE American applicant's Uniform Application for Broker-Dealer Registration (Form BD) will be amended as needed to keep current and accurate; that all individual and entity registrations with FINRA will be kept current; and that all information and statements contained in the Waive-In Application are current, true and complete.

The Department shall review the Waive-In Application within three business days of receipt and, if complete, issue a letter notifying the applicant that it has been approved for membership. The Membership Agreement shall become effective on the date of such notification letter.

Firms admitted pursuant to this Interpretive Material shall be member organizations of both NYSE and NYSE American and as such are subject to FINRA rules (provided that firms admitted to FINRA membership under IM-1013-1 also are subject to FINRA rules), other than FINRA Rules 1011 through 1016, 1019 through 1021, 2231, 3260 and 4540, the FINRA By-Laws and Schedules to By-Laws, including Schedule A, and the FINRA Rule 8000 and Rule 9000 Series, provided that their NYSE or NYSE American securities business is limited to floor-based activities in either NYSE-traded or NYSE American-traded securities, or routing away to other markets orders that are ancillary to their core NYSE or NYSE American floor business under NYSE Rule 70.40 or NYSE American Equities Rule 70.40 ("permitted floor activities"). If a firm admitted pursuant to this Interpretive Material seeks to expand its business operations to include any activities other than the permitted floor activities or makes changes to its securities business that would otherwise require FINRA membership, such firm must apply for and receive approval to engage in such business activity pursuant to Rule 1017.

Upon approval of such business expansion, the firm shall be subject to the FINRA By-Laws and Schedule to By-Laws, including Schedule A, and all FINRA rules.

Pursuant to IM-Section 4(b)(1) and (e) to Schedule A of the FINRA By-Laws, a firm applying to waive in for membership pursuant to this Interpretive Material shall not be assessed certain registration and application fees set forth in Sections 4(b)(1) and (e) to Schedule A of the FINRA By-Laws.

1014. Department Decision

(a) Standards for Admission

After considering the application, the membership interview, other information and documents provided by the Applicant, other information and documents obtained by the Department, and the public interest and the protection of investors, the Department shall determine whether the Applicant meets each of the following standards:

(1) The application and all supporting documents are complete and accurate.

(2) The Applicant and its Associated Persons have all licenses and registrations required by state and federal authorities and self-regulatory organizations.

(3) The Applicant and its Associated Persons are capable of complying with the federal securities laws, the rules and regulations thereunder, and FINRA rules, including observing high standards of commercial honor and just and equitable principles of trade. In determining whether this standard is met, the Department shall take into consideration whether:

   (A) a state or federal authority or self-regulatory organization has taken permanent or temporary adverse action with respect to a registration or licensing determination regarding the Applicant or an Associated Person;

   (B) an Applicant's or Associated Person's record reflects a sales practice event, a pending arbitration, or a pending private civil action;

   (C) an Applicant or Associated Person is the subject of a pending, adjudicated, or settled regulatory action or investigation by the SEC, the Commodity Futures Trading Commission, a federal, state, or foreign regulatory agency, or a self-regulatory organization; an adjudicated, or settled investment-related private civil action for damages or an injunction; or a criminal action (other than a minor traffic violation) that is pending, adjudicated, or that has resulted in a guilty or no contest plea or an Applicant, its control persons, principals, registered representatives, other Associated Persons, any lender of 5 percent or more of the Applicant's net capital, and any other member with respect to which these persons were a control person or a 5 percent lender of its net capital is subject to unpaid arbitration awards, other adjudicated customer awards, or unpaid arbitration settlements;

   (D) an Associated Person was terminated for cause or permitted to resign after an investigation of an alleged violation of a federal or state securities law, a rule or regulation thereunder, a self-regulatory organization rule, or industry standard of conduct;

   (E) a state or federal authority or self-regulatory organization has imposed a remedial action, such as special training, continuing education requirements, or heightened supervision, on an Associated Person; and

   (F) a state or federal authority or self-regulatory organization has provided information indicating that the Applicant or an Associated Person otherwise poses a threat to public investors.

(4) The Applicant has established all contractual or other arrangements and business relationships with banks, clearing corporations, service bureaus, or others necessary to:

   (A) initiate the operations described in the Applicant's business plan, considering the nature and scope of operations and the number of personnel; and

   (B) comply with the federal securities laws, the rules and regulations thereunder, and FINRA rules.

(5) The Applicant has or has adequate plans to obtain facilities that are sufficient to:

   (A) initiate the operations described in the Applicant's business plan, considering the nature and scope of operations and the number of personnel; and

   (B) comply with the federal securities laws, the rules and regulations thereunder, and FINRA rules.

(6) The communications and operational systems that the Applicant intends to employ for the purpose of conducting business with customers and other members are adequate and provide reasonably for business continuity in each area set forth in Rule 1013(a)(1)(E)(xii);

(7) The Applicant is capable of maintaining a level of net capital in excess of the minimum net capital re-

quirements set forth in SEA Rule 15c3-1 adequate to support the Applicant's intended business operations on a continuing basis, based on information filed under Rule 1013(b)(5). The Department may impose a reasonably determined higher net capital requirement for the initiation of operations after considering:

(A) the amount of net capital sufficient to avoid early warning level reporting requirements, such as SEA
Rule 17a-11;

(B) the amount of capital necessary to meet expenses net of revenues for at least 12 months, based on
reliable projections agreed to by the Applicant and the Department;

(C) any planned market making activities, the number of markets to be made, the type and volatility of
products, and the anticipated maximum inventory positions;

(D) any plan to enter into other contractual commitments, such as underwritings or other securities-related activities;

(E) any plan to distribute or maintain securities products in proprietary positions, and the risks, volatility,
degree of liquidity, and speculative nature of the products; and

(F) any other activity that the Applicant will engage in that reasonably could have a material impact on
net capital within the first 12 months of business operations.

(8) The Applicant has financial controls to ensure compliance with the federal securities laws, the rules and
regulations thereunder, and FINRA rules.

(9) The Applicant has compliance, supervisory, operational, and internal control practices and standards that
are consistent with practices and standards regularly employed in the investment banking or securities
business, taking into account the nature and scope of Applicant's proposed business.

(10) The Applicant has a supervisory system, including written supervisory procedures, internal operating
procedures (including operational and internal controls), and compliance procedures designed to prevent and detect, to the extent practicable, violations of the federal securities laws, the rules and regulations thereunder, and FINRA rules. In evaluating the adequacy of a supervisory system, the Department
shall consider the overall nature and scope of the Applicant's intended business operations and shall
consider whether:

(A) the number, location, experience, and qualifications of supervisory personnel are adequate in light
of the number, location, experience, and qualifications of persons to be supervised; the Central Registration Depository record or other disciplinary history of supervisory personnel and persons to be
supervised; and the number and locations of the offices that the Applicant intends to open and the
nature and scope of business to be conducted at each office;

(B) the Applicant has identified specific Associated Persons to supervise and discharge each of the functions in the Applicant's business plan, and to supervise each of the Applicant's intended offices,
whether or not such offices are required to be registered under FINRA rules;

(C) the Applicant has identified the functions to be performed by each Associated Person and has
adopted procedures to assure the registration with FINRA and applicable states of all persons whose
functions are subject to such registration requirements;

(D) each Associated Person identified in the business plan to discharge a supervisory function has at
least one year of direct experience or two years of related experience in the subject area to be supervised;

(E) the Applicant will solicit retail or institutional business;

(F) the Applicant will recommend securities to customers;

(G) the location or part-time status of a supervisor or principal will affect such person's ability to be an
effective supervisor;

(H) the Applicant should be required to place one or more Associated Persons under heightened supervision pursuant to Notice to Members 97-19;

(I) any remedial action, such as special training or continuing education requirements or heightened supervision, has been imposed on an Associated Person by a state or federal authority or self-regulatory organization; and

(J) any other condition that will have a material impact on the Applicant's ability to detect and prevent violations of the federal securities laws, the rules and regulations thereunder, and FINRA rules.

(11) The Applicant has a recordkeeping system that enables Applicant to comply with federal, state, and self-regulatory organization recordkeeping requirements and a staff that is sufficient in qualifications and number to prepare and preserve required records.

(12) The Applicant has completed a training needs assessment and has a written training plan that complies with the continuing education requirements imposed by the federal securities laws, the rules and regulations thereunder, and FINRA rules.

(13) FINRA does not possess any information indicating that the Applicant may circumvent, evade, or otherwise avoid compliance with the federal securities laws, the rules and regulations thereunder, or FINRA rules.

(14) The application and all supporting documents otherwise are consistent with the federal securities laws, the rules and regulations thereunder, and FINRA rules.

(b) Granting or Denying Application

(1) In reviewing an application for membership, the Department shall consider whether the Applicant and its Associated Persons meet each of the standards in paragraph (a). Where the Department determines that the Applicant or its Associated Persons are the subject of any of the events set forth in Rule 1014(a)(3)(A) and (C) through (E), a presumption exists that the application should be denied. The Applicant may overcome the presumption by demonstrating that it can meet each of the standards in paragraph (a), notwithstanding the existence of any of the events set forth in Rule 1014(a)(3)(A) and (C) through (E).

(2) If the Department determines that the Applicant meets each of the standards in paragraph (a), the Department shall grant the application for membership.

(3) If the Department determines that the Applicant does not meet one or more of the standards in paragraph (a) in whole or in part, the Department shall:

(A) grant the application subject to one or more restrictions reasonably designed to address a specific financial, operational, supervisory, disciplinary, investor protection, or other regulatory concern based on the standards for admission in Rule 1014(a); or

(B) deny the application.

(c) Decision

(1) Time

The Department shall serve a written decision on the membership application within 30 days after the conclusion of the membership interview or after the filing of additional information or documents, whichever is later.

(2) Content

If the Department denies the application, the decision shall explain in detail the reason for denial, referencing the applicable standard or standards in paragraph (a). If the Department grants the application subject to restrictions, the decision shall explain in detail the reason for each restriction, referencing the applicable standard or standards in paragraph (a) upon which the restriction is based and identify the specific financial, operational, supervisory, disciplinary, investor protection, or other regulatory concern that the restriction is designed to address and the manner in which the restriction is reasonably designed to address the concern.

(3) Failure to Serve Decision

If the Department fails to serve a decision within 180 days after the filing of an application or such later date as the Department and the Applicant have agreed in writing, the Applicant may file a written request with the FINRA Board requesting that the FINRA Board direct the Department to serve a decision. Within seven days after the filing of such a request, the FINRA Board shall direct the Department to serve its written decision immediately or to show good cause for an extension of time. If the Department shows good cause for an extension of time, the FINRA Board may extend the 180 day time limit by not more than 90 days.

(d) Submission of Membership Agreement

If the Department grants an application, with or without restriction, the Applicant's approval for membership shall be contingent upon the Applicant's filing of an executed written membership agreement, satisfactory to the Department, undertaking to:

(1) abide by any restriction specified in the Department's decision; and

(2) obtain the Department's approval of a change in ownership, control, or business operations pursuant to Rule 1017, including the modification or removal of a membership agreement restriction.

The Applicant shall not waive the right to file a written request for review under Rule 1015 by executing a membership agreement under this paragraph.

(e) Service and Effectiveness of Decision

The Department shall serve its decision and the membership agreement on the Applicant in accordance with Rule 1012. The decision shall become effective upon service and shall remain in effect during the pendency of any review until a decision constituting final action of FINRA is issued under Rule 1015 or 1016, unless otherwise directed by the National Adjudicatory Council, the FINRA Board, or the SEC.

(f) Effectiveness of Restriction

A restriction imposed under this Rule shall remain in effect and bind the Applicant and all successors to the ownership or control of the Applicant unless:

(1) removed or modified by a decision constituting final action of FINRA issued under Rule 1015, 1016, or 1017;

(2) stayed by the National Adjudicatory Council, the FINRA Board, or the SEC.

(g) Final Action

Unless the Applicant files a written request for a review under Rule 1015, the Department's decision shall constitute final action by FINRA.

1015. Review by National Adjudicatory Council

(a) Initiation of Review by Applicant

Within 25 days after service of a decision under Rule 1014 or 1017, an Applicant may file a written request for review with the National Adjudicatory Council. A request for review shall state with specificity why the Applicant believes that the Department's decision is inconsistent with the membership standards set forth in Rule 1014, or otherwise should be set aside, and state whether a hearing is requested. The Applicant simultaneously shall file by first-class mail a copy of the request to the district office where the Applicant filed its application.

(b) Transmission of Documents

Within ten days after the filing of a request for review, the Department shall:

(1) transmit to the National Adjudicatory Council copies of all documents that were considered in connection with the Department's decision and an index to the documents; and

(2) serve on the Applicant a copy of such documents (other than those documents originally submitted by Applicant) and a copy of the index.

(c) Membership Application Docket

The Department shall promptly record in FINRA's membership application docket each request for review filed with the National Adjudicatory Council under this Rule and each material subsequent event, filing, and change in the status of a membership proceeding.

(d) Appointment of Subcommittee

The National Adjudicatory Council or the Review Subcommittee defined in Rule 9120 shall appoint a Subcommittee to participate in the review. The Subcommittee shall be composed of two or more persons who shall be current or past members of the National Adjudicatory Council or former Directors or Governors.

(e) Powers of Subcommittee

If a hearing is requested, the Subcommittee shall conduct the hearing. If a hearing is not requested, the Sub-committee may serve a notice directing that a hearing be held. If a hearing is not requested or directed, the Subcommittee shall conduct its review on the basis of the record developed before the Department and any written submissions made by the Applicant or the Department in connection with the request for review.

(f) Hearing

(1) Notice

If a hearing is requested or directed, the hearing shall be held within 45 days after the filing of the re-quest with the National Adjudicatory Council or service of the notice by the Subcommittee. The National Adjudicatory Council shall serve written notice of the date and time of the hearing to the Applicant by facsimile or overnight courier not later than 14 days before the hearing.

(2) Counsel

The Applicant and the Department may be represented by counsel at a hearing conducted pursuant to this Rule.

(3) Evidence

Formal rules of evidence shall not apply to a hearing under this Rule. Not later than five days before the hearing, the Applicant and the Department shall exchange copies of their proposed hearing exhibits and witness lists and provide copies to the National Adjudicatory Council. If the Applicant or the Department fails to provide copies of its proposed hearing exhibits or witness list within such time, the Subcommittee shall exclude the evidence or witnesses from the proceeding, unless the Subcommittee determines that good cause is shown for failure to comply with the production date set forth in this subparagraph.

(4) Transcript

The hearing shall be recorded and a transcript prepared by a court reporter. A transcript of the hearing shall be available for purchase from the court reporter at prescribed rates. The Applicant, the Depart-ment, or a witness may seek to correct the transcript. A proposed correction of the transcript shall be submitted to the Subcommittee within a reasonable period of time prescribed by the Subcommittee. Upon notice to the Applicant and the Department, the Subcommittee may direct the correction to the transcript as requested or sua sponte.

(g) Additional Information, Briefs

At any time during its consideration, the Subcommittee or the National Adjudicatory Council may direct the Applicant or the Department to file additional information or briefs. Any additional information or brief filed shall be provided to all parties before the National Adjudicatory Council renders its decision.

(h) Abandonment of Request for Review

If an Applicant fails to specify the grounds for its request for review under Rule 1015(a)(1), appear at a hear-ing for which it has notice, or file information or briefs as directed, the National Adjudicatory Council or the Review Subcommittee may dismiss the request for review as abandoned, and the decision of the Department shall become the final action of FINRA. Upon a showing of good cause, the National Adjudicatory Council or the Review Subcommittee may withdraw a dismissal entered pursuant to this paragraph.

(i) Subcommittee Recommendation

The Subcommittee shall present a recommended decision in writing to the National Adjudicatory Council within 60 days after the date of the hearing held pursuant to paragraph (f), and not later than seven days be-fore the meeting of the National Adjudicatory Council at which the membership proceeding shall be consid-ered.

(j) Decision

(1) Proposed Written Decision

After considering all matters presented in the review and the Subcommittee's recommended written de-cision, the National Adjudicatory Council may affirm, modify, or reverse the Department's decision or re-mand the membership proceeding with instructions. The National Adjudicatory Council shall prepare a proposed written decision pursuant to subparagraph (2).

(2) Contents

   The decision shall include:

   (A) a description of the Department's decision, including its rationale;

   (B) a description of the principal issues raised in the review;

   (C) a summary of the evidence on each issue; and

   (D) a statement whether the Department's decision is affirmed, modified, or reversed, and a rationale therefor that references the applicable standards in Rule 1014.

(3) Issuance of Decision After Expiration of Call for Review Periods

   The National Adjudicatory Council shall provide its proposed written decision to the FINRA Board. The FINRA Board may call the membership proceeding for review pursuant to Rule 1016. If the FINRA Board does not call the membership proceeding for review, the proposed written decision of the National Adjudicatory Council shall become final. The National Adjudicatory Council shall serve the Applicant with a written notice specifying the date on which the call for review period expired and stating that the final written decision will be served within 15 days after such date. The National Adjudicatory Council shall serve its final written decision within 15 days after the date on which the call for review period expired. The decision shall constitute the final action of FINRA for purposes of SEA Rule 19d-3, unless the National Adjudicatory Council remands the membership proceeding.

(4) Failure to Issue Decision

   If the National Adjudicatory Council fails to serve its final written decision within the time prescribed in subparagraph (3), the Applicant may file a written request with the FINRA Board requesting that the FINRA Board direct the National Adjudicatory Council to serve its decision immediately or to show good cause for an extension of time. Within seven days after the filing of such a request, the FINRA Board shall direct the National Adjudicatory Council to serve its written decision immediately or to show good cause for an extension of time. If the National Adjudicatory Council shows good cause for an extension of time, the FINRA Board may extend the 15 day time limit by not more than 15 days.

1016. Discretionary Review by FINRA Board

(a) Call For Review By Governor

   A Governor may call a membership proceeding for review by the FINRA Board if the call for review is made within the period prescribed in paragraph (b).

(b) 15 Day Period; Waiver

   A Governor shall make his or her call for review at the next meeting of the FINRA Board that is at least 15 days after the date on which the FINRA Board receives the proposed written decision of the National Adjudicatory Council. By unanimous vote of the FINRA Board, the FINRA Board may shorten the period to less than 15 days. By an affirmative vote of the majority of the FINRA Board then in office, the FINRA Board may, during the 15 day period, vote to extend the period to more than 15 days.

(c) Review At Next Meeting

   If a Governor calls a membership proceeding for review within the time prescribed in paragraph (b), the FINRA Board shall review the membership proceeding not later than the next meeting of the FINRA Board. The FINRA Board may order the Applicant and the Department to file briefs in connection with review proceedings pursuant to this paragraph.

(d) Decision of FINRA Board, Including Remand

   After review, the FINRA Board may affirm, modify, or reverse the proposed written decision of the National Adjudicatory Council. Alternatively, the FINRA Board may remand the membership proceeding with instructions. The FINRA Board shall prepare a written decision that includes elements described in Rule 1015(j)(2).

(e) Issuance of Decision

   The FINRA Board shall serve its written decision on the Applicant within 15 days after the meeting at which it conducted its review. The decision shall constitute the final action of FINRA for purposes of SEA Rule 19d-3, unless the FINRA Board remands the membership proceeding.

1017. Application for Approval of Change in Ownership, Control, or Business Operations

(a) Events Requiring Application

A member shall file an application for approval of any of the following changes to its ownership, control, or business operations:

(1) a merger of the member with another member, unless both are members of the New York Stock Exchange, Inc. or the surviving entity will continue to be a member of the New York Stock Exchange, Inc.;

(2) a direct or indirect acquisition by the member of another member, unless the acquiring member is a member of the New York Stock Exchange, Inc.;

(3) direct or indirect acquisitions or transfers of 25 percent or more in the aggregate of the member's assets or any asset, business or line of operation that generates revenues composing 25 percent or more in the aggregate of the member's earnings measured on a rolling 36-month basis, unless both the seller and acquirer are members of the New York Stock Exchange, Inc.;

(4) a change in the equity ownership or partnership capital of the member that results in one person or entity directly or indirectly owning or controlling 25 percent or more of the equity or partnership capital; or

(5) a material change in business operations as defined in Rule 1011(k).

(b) Filing and Content of Application

(1) The member shall file with the Department the application in the manner prescribed by FINRA.

(2) An applicant shall submit an application that includes a Form CMA including a detailed description of the change in ownership, control, or business operations.

(A) If the application requests approval of a change in ownership or control, the application also shall include the names of the new owners, their percentage of ownership, and the sources of their funding for the purchase and recapitalization of the member.

(B) If the application requests the removal or modification of a membership agreement restriction, the application also shall:

(i) present facts showing that the circumstances that gave rise to the restriction have changed; and

(ii) state with specificity why the restriction should be modified or removed in light of the standards set forth in Rule 1014 and the articulated rationale for the imposition of the restriction.

(C) If the application requests approval of an increase in Associated Persons involved in sales, offices, or markets made, the application shall set forth the increases in such areas during the preceding 12 months.

(c) Effecting Change and Imposition of Interim Restrictions

(1) A member shall file an application for approval of a change in ownership or control at least 30 days prior to such change. A member may effect a change in ownership or control prior to the conclusion of the proceeding, but the Department may place new interim restrictions on the member based on the standards in Rule 1014, pending final Department action.

(2) A member may file an application to remove or modify a membership agreement restriction at any time. An existing restriction shall remain in effect during the pendency of the proceeding.

(3) A member may file an application for approval of a material change in business operations, other than the modification or removal of a restriction, at any time, but the member may not effect such change until the conclusion of the proceeding, unless the Department and the member otherwise agree.

(d) Rejection Of Application That Is Not Substantially Complete

If the Department determines within 30 days after the filing of an application that the application is not substantially complete, the Department shall reject the application and deem it not to have been filed. In such case, within the 30 day period, the Department shall serve a written notice on the Applicant of the Department's determination and the reasons therefor. FINRA shall refund the application fee, less $500, which shall be retained by FINRA as a processing fee. If the Applicant determines to continue to apply for approval of a change in ownership, control, or business operations, the Applicant shall submit a new application under this Rule and fee pursuant to Schedule A to the FINRA By-Laws.

(e) Request for Additional Documents and Information

Within 30 days after the filing of an application, the Department shall serve a request for any additional information or documents necessary to render a decision on the application. The Department may request additional information or documents at any time during the application process. Unless otherwise agreed to by the Department and the Applicant, the Applicant shall file such additional information or documents with the Department within 30 days after the Department's request.

(f) Withdrawal of Application

If an Applicant withdraws an application within 30 days after filing the application, FINRA shall refund the application fee, less $500, which shall be retained by FINRA as a processing fee. If the Applicant determines to again apply for approval of a change in ownership, control, or business operations, the Applicant shall submit a new application under this Rule and fee pursuant to Schedule A to the FINRA By-Laws.

(g) Membership Interview

(1) The Department may require the Applicant to participate in a membership interview within 30 days after the filing of the application, or if the Department requests additional information or documents, within 30 days after the filing of the additional information or documents by the Applicant.

(2) At least seven days before the membership interview, the Department shall serve on the Applicant a written notice that specifies the date and time of the interview and persons who are required to participate in the interview. The Department shall serve the notice by facsimile or overnight courier. The Applicant and the Department may agree to a shorter or longer period for notice or a different method of service.

(3) Unless the Department and the Applicant otherwise agree, the membership interview shall be conducted in the district office for the district in which the Applicant has its principal place of business.

(4) During the membership interview, the Department shall review the application and the considerations for the Department's decision set forth in paragraph (h)(1) with the Applicant's representative or representatives. The Department shall provide to the Applicant's representative or representatives any information or document that the Department has obtained from the Central Registration Depository or a source other than the Applicant and upon which the Department intends to base its decision under paragraph (h). If the Department receives such information or document after the membership interview or decides to base its decision on such information after the membership interview, the Department shall promptly serve the information or document and an explanation thereof on the Applicant.

(h) Department Decision

(1) The Department shall consider the application, the membership interview, other information and documents provided by the Applicant or obtained by the Department, the public interest, and the protection of investors. In rendering a decision on an application submitted under Rule 1017(a), the Department shall consider whether the Applicant and its Associated Persons meet each of the standards in Rule 1014(a). Where the Department determines that the Applicant or its Associated Person are the subject of any of the events set forth in Rule 1014(a)(3)(A) and (C) through (E), a presumption exists that the application should be denied. The Applicant may overcome the presumption by demonstrating that it can meet each of the standards in Rule 1014 (a), notwithstanding the existence of any of the events set forth in Rule 1014(a)(3)(A) and (C) through (E).

(A) In rendering a decision on an application for approval of a change in ownership or control, or an application for approval of a material change in business operations that does not involve modification or removal of a membership agreement restriction, the Department shall determine if the Applicant would continue to meet the standards in Rule 1014(a) upon approval of the application.

(B) In rendering a decision on an application requesting the modification or removal of a membership agreement restriction, the Department shall consider whether maintenance of the restriction is appropriate in light of:

(i) the standards set forth in Rule 1014;

(ii) the circumstances that gave rise to the imposition of the restriction;

  (iii) the Applicant's operations since the restriction was imposed;

  (iv) any change in ownership or control or supervisors and principals; and

  (v) any new evidence submitted in connection with the application.

 (2) The Department shall serve a written decision on the application within 30 days after the conclusion of the membership interview or the filing of additional information or documents, whichever is later. If the Department does not require the Applicant to participate in a membership interview or request additional information or documents, the Department shall serve a written decision within 45 days after the filing of the application under paragraph (a). The decision shall state whether the application is granted or denied in whole or in part, and shall provide a rationale for the Department's decision, referencing the applicable standard in Rule 1014.

 (3) If the Department fails to serve a decision within 180 days after filing of an application or such later date as the Department and the Applicant have agreed in writing, the Applicant may file a written request with the FINRA Board requesting that the FINRA Board direct the Department to issue a decision. Within seven days after the filing of such a request, the FINRA Board shall direct the Department to issue a written decision immediately or to show good cause for an extension of time. If the Department shows good cause for an extension of time, the FINRA Board may extend the time limit for issuing a decision by not more than 30 days.

 (4) If the Department approves an application under this Rule in whole or part, the Department may require an Applicant to file an executed membership agreement.

(i) Service and Effectiveness of Decision

The Department shall serve its decision on the Applicant in accordance with Rule 1012. The decision shall become effective upon service and shall remain in effect during the pendency of any review until a decision constituting final action of FINRA is issued under Rule 1015 or 1016, unless otherwise directed by the National Adjudicatory Council, the FINRA Board, or the SEC.

(j) Request for Review; Final Action

An Applicant may file a written request for review of the Department's decision with the National Adjudicatory Council pursuant to Rule 1015. The procedures set forth in Rule 1015 shall apply to such review, and the National Adjudicatory Council's decision shall be subject to discretionary review by the FINRA Board pursuant to Rule 1016. If the Applicant does not file a request for a review, the Department's decision shall constitute final action by FINRA.

(k) Removal or Modification of Restriction on Department's Initiative

The Department shall modify or remove a restriction on its own initiative if the Department determines such action is appropriate in light of the considerations set forth in paragraph (h)(1). The Department shall notify the member in writing of the Department's determination and inform the member that it may apply for further modification or removal of a restriction by filing an application under paragraph (a).

(l) Lapse or Denial of Application for Approval of Change in Ownership

If an application for approval of a change in ownership lapses, or is denied and all appeals are exhausted or waived, the member shall, no more than 60 days after the lapse or exhaustion or waiver of appeal:

 (1) submit a new application under this Rule and fee pursuant to Schedule A to the FINRA By-Laws;

 (2) unwind the transaction; or

 (3) file a Form BDW.

  For the protection of investors, the Department may shorten the 60-day period. For good cause shown by the member, the Department may lengthen the 60-day period. The Department shall serve written notice on the Applicant of any change in the 60-day period and the reasons therefor. During the 60-day or other imposed period, the Department may continue to place interim restrictions on the member for the protection of investors.

1018. Reserved

1019. Application to the SEC for Review

A person aggrieved by final action of FINRA under the Rule 1000 Series may apply for review by the SEC pursuant to Section 19(d)(2) of the Exchange Act. The filing of an application for review shall not stay the effectiveness of a decision constituting final action of FINRA, unless the SEC otherwise orders.

1020. Approval of Change in Exempt Status Under SEA Rule 15c3-3

(a) Application — For the purposes of this Rule, the term "member" shall be limited to any member of FINRA who is subject to SEA Rule 15c3-3 and is not designated to another self-regulatory organization by the Commission for financial responsibility pursuant to Section 17 of the Exchange Act and SEA Rule 17d-1 promulgated thereunder. Further, the term shall not be applicable to any member that is subject to Section 402.2(c) of the rules of the Treasury Department.

(b) A member operating pursuant to any exemptive provision as contained in subparagraph (k) of SEA Rule 15c3-3, shall not change its method of doing business in a manner which will change its exemptive status from that governed by subparagraph (k)(1) or (k)(2)(ii) to that governed by subparagraph (k)(2)(i); or from subparagraph (k)(1), (k)(2)(i) or (k)(2)(ii) to a fully computing firm that is subject to all provisions of SEA Rule 15c3-3; or commence operations that will disqualify it for continued exemption under SEA Rule 15c3-3 without first having obtained the prior written approval of FINRA.

(c) In making the determination as to whether to approve, deny in whole or in part an application made pursuant to paragraph (b), FINRA staff shall consider among other things the type of business in which the member is engaged, the training, experience and qualifications of persons associated with the member, the member's procedures for safeguarding customer funds and securities, the member's overall financial and operational condition and any other information deemed relevant in the particular circumstances and the time these measures would remain in effect.

1021. Foreign Members

A member which does not maintain an office in the United States responsible for preparing and maintaining financial and other reports required to be filed with the SEC and FINRA must:

(a) prepare all such reports, and maintain a general ledger chart of account and any description thereof, in English and U.S. dollars;

(b) reimburse FINRA for any expenses incurred in connection with examinations of the member to the extent that such expenses exceed the cost of examining a member located within the continental United States in the geographic location most distant from the District Office of appropriate jurisdiction;

(c) ensure the availability of an individual fluent in English and knowledgeable in securities and financial matters to assist representatives of FINRA during examinations; and

(d) utilize, either directly or indirectly, the services of a broker-dealer registered with the SEC, a bank or a clearing agency registered with the SEC located in the United States in clearing all transactions involving members of FINRA, except where both parties to a transaction agree otherwise.

1122. Filing of Misleading Information as to Membership or Registration

No member or person associated with a member shall file with FINRA information with respect to membership or registration which is incomplete or inaccurate so as to be misleading, or which could in any way tend to mislead, or fail to correct such filing after notice thereof.

1210. Registration Requirements

Each person engaged in the investment banking or securities business of a member shall be registered with FINRA as a representative or principal in each category of registration appropriate to his or her functions and responsibilities as specified in Rule 1220, unless exempt from registration pursuant to Rule 1230. Such person shall not be qualified to function in any registered capacity other than that for which the person is registered, unless otherwise stated in the rules.

1220. Registration Categories
(a) Definition of Principal and Principal Registration Categories
    (1) Definition of Principal

A "principal" is any person associated with a member, including, but not limited to, sole proprietor, officer, partner, manager of office of supervisory jurisdiction, director or other person occupying a similar status or performing similar functions, who is actively engaged in the management of the member's investment banking or securities business, such as supervision, solicitation, conduct of business in securities or the training of persons associated with a member for any of these functions. Such persons shall include, among other persons, a member's chief executive officer and chief financial officer (or equivalent officers).

A "principal" also includes any other person associated with a member who is performing functions or carrying out responsibilities that are required to be performed or carried out by a principal under the FINRA rules.

The term "actively engaged in the management of the member's investment banking or securities business" includes the management of, and the implementation of corporate policies related to, such business. The term also includes managerial decision-making authority with respect to the member's investment banking or securities business and management-level responsibilities for supervising any aspect of such business, such as serving as a voting member of the member's executive, management or operations committees.

    (2) General Securities Principal

      (A) Requirement

Each principal as defined in paragraph (a)(1) of this Rule shall be required to register with FINRA as a General Securities Principal, subject to the following exceptions:

        (i) if a principal's activities include the functions of a Compliance Officer, a Financial and Operations Principal (or an Introducing Broker-Dealer Financial and Operations Principal, as applicable), a Principal Financial Officer, a Principal Operations Officer, an Investment Banking Principal, a Research Principal, a Securities Trader Principal or a Registered Options Principal as specified in paragraphs (a)(3) through (a)(8) of this Rule, then such person shall appropriately register in one or more of those categories;

        (ii) if a principal's activities are limited solely to the functions of a Government Securities Principal, an Investment Company and Variable Contracts Products Principal, a Direct Participation Programs Principal or a Private Securities Offerings Principal as specified in paragraphs (a)(9), (a)(11), (a)(12) or (a)(13) of this Rule, then such person may appropriately register in one or more of those categories in lieu of registering as a General Securities Principal;

        (iii) if a principal's activities are limited solely to the functions of a General Securities Sales Supervisor as specified in paragraph (a)(10) of this Rule, then such person may appropriately register in that category in lieu of registering as a General Securities Principal, provided, however, that if such person is engaged in options sales activities, such person shall be required to register with FINRA as a Registered Options Principal as specified in paragraph (a)(8) of this Rule or as a General Securities Sales Supervisor as specified in paragraph (a)(10) of this Rule; and

        (iv) if a principal's activities are limited solely to the functions of a Supervisory Analyst as specified in paragraph (a)(14) of this Rule, then such person may appropriately register in that category in lieu of registering as a General Securities Principal, provided, however, that if such person is responsible for approving the content of a member's research report on equity securities, such person shall be required to register with FINRA as a Research Principal as specified in paragraph (a)(6) of this Rule or as a Supervisory Analyst as specified in paragraph (a)(14) of this Rule.

(B) Qualifications

Subject to the lapse of registration provisions in Rule 1210.08, each person registered with FINRA as a Corporate Securities Representative and a General Securities Principal on October 1, 2018 and each person who was registered with FINRA as a Corporate Securities Representative and a General Securities Principal within two years prior to October 1, 2018 shall be qualified to register as a General Securities Principal without passing any additional qualification examinations, provided that his or her supervisory responsibilities in the investment banking or securities business of a member are limited to corporate securities activities of the member.

All other individuals registering as General Securities Principals after October 1, 2018 shall, prior to or concurrent with such registration, become registered pursuant to paragraph (b)(2) of this Rule as a General Securities Representative and either (i) pass the General Securities Principal qualification examination or (ii) register as a General Securities Sales Supervisor and pass the General Securities Principal Sales Supervisor Module qualification examination.

(3) Compliance Officer

(A) Requirement

Subject to the exception in paragraph (a)(3)(C) of this Rule, each person designated as a Chief Compliance Officer on Schedule A of Form BD as specified in Rule 3130(a) shall be required to register with FINRA as a Compliance Officer.

(B) Qualifications

Subject to the lapse of registration provisions in Rule 1210.08, each person registered with FINRA as a General Securities Representative and a General Securities Principal on October 1, 2018 and each person who was registered with FINRA as a General Securities Representative and a General Securities Principal within two years prior to October 1, 2018 shall be qualified to register as a Compliance Officer without passing any additional qualification examinations. In addition, subject to the lapse of registration provisions in Rule 1210.08, each person registered as a Compliance Official in the CRD system on October 1, 2018 and each person who was registered as a Compliance Official in the CRD system within two years prior to October 1, 2018 shall be qualified to register as a Compliance Officer without passing any additional qualification examinations.

All other individuals registering as Compliance Officers after October 1, 2018, shall, prior to or concurrent with such registration: (i) become registered pursuant to paragraph (b)(2) of this Rule as a General Securities Representative and pass the General Securities Principal qualification examination; or (ii) pass the Compliance Official qualification examination.

(C) Exception

An individual designated as a Chief Compliance Officer on Schedule A of Form BD of a member that is engaged in limited investment banking or securities business may be registered in a principal category under Rule 1220(a) that corresponds to the limited scope of the member's business.

(4) Financial and Operations Principal and Introducing Broker-Dealer Financial and Operations Principal

(A) Requirement

Each member that is operating pursuant to the provisions of SEA Rules 15c3-1(a)(1)(ii), (a)(2)(i) or (a)(8), shall designate a Financial and Operations Principal. Each member subject to the requirements of SEA Rule 15c3-1, other than a member operating pursuant to SEA Rules 15c3-1(a)(1)(ii), (a)(2)(i) or (a)(8), shall designate either a Financial and Operations Principal or an Introducing Broker-Dealer Financial and Operations Principal.

A Financial and Operations Principal and an Introducing Broker-Dealer Financial and Operations Principal shall be responsible for performing the following duties:

(i) final approval and responsibility for the accuracy of financial reports submitted to any duly established securities industry regulatory body;

(ii) final preparation of such reports;

(iii) supervision of individuals who assist in the preparation of such reports;

(iv) supervision of and responsibility for individuals who are involved in the actual maintenance of the member's books and records from which such reports are derived;

(v) supervision and performance of the member's responsibilities under all financial responsibility rules promulgated pursuant to the provisions of the Exchange Act;

(vi) overall supervision of and responsibility for the individuals who are involved in the administration and maintenance of the member's back office operations; and

(vii) any other matter involving the financial and operational management of the member.

The requirements of paragraph(a)(4)(A) of this Rule shall not apply to a member that is exempt from the requirement to designate a Financial and Operations Principal or an Introducing Broker-Dealer Financial and Operations Principal.

(B) Designation of Principal Financial Officer and Principal Operations Officer

Each member shall designate a:

(i) Principal Financial Officer with primary responsibility for financial filings and those books and records related to such filings; and

(ii) Principal Operations Officer with primary responsibility for the day-to-day operations of the member's business, including overseeing the receipt and delivery of securities and funds, safeguarding customer and member assets, calculation and collection of margin from customers and processing dividend receivables and payables and reorganization redemptions and those books and records related to such activities.

Each member that self-clears, or that clears for other members, shall be required to designate separate persons to function as Principal Financial Officer and Principal Operations Officer. Such persons may also carry out the other responsibilities of a Financial and Operations Principal and an Introducing Broker-Dealer Financial and Operations Principal as specified in paragraph (a)(4)(A) of this Rule. If such member is limited in size and resources, it may, pursuant to the Rule 9600 Series, request a waiver of the requirement to designate separate persons to function as Principal Financial Officer and Principal Operations Officer.

Each member that is an introducing member may designate the same person to function as Financial and Operations Principal (or Introducing Broker-Dealer Financial and Operations Principal), Principal Financial Officer and Principal Operations Officer.

Each person designated as a Principal Financial Officer or Principal Operations Officer, other than a person associated with a member that is exempt from the requirement to designate a Financial and Operations Principal or an Introducing Broker-Dealer Financial and Operations Principal, shall be required to register as a Financial and Operations Principal or an Introducing Broker-Dealer Financial and Operations Principal pursuant to paragraph (a)(4)(A) of this Rule.

(C) Qualifications

Each person seeking to register as a Financial and Operations Principal shall, prior to or concurrent with such registration, pass the Financial and Operations Principal qualification examination. Each person seeking to register as an Introducing Broker-Dealer Financial and Operations Principal shall, prior to or concurrent with such registration, pass the Financial and Operations Principal qualification examination or the Introducing Broker-Dealer Financial and Operations Principal qualification examination.

(5) Investment Banking Principal

(A) Requirement

Each principal as defined in paragraph (a)(1) of this Rule who is responsible for supervising the investment banking activities specified in paragraph (b)(5) of this Rule shall be required to register with FINRA as an Investment Banking Principal.

(B) Qualifications

Subject to the lapse of registration provisions in Rule 1210.08, each person registered with FINRA as an Investment Banking Representative and a General Securities Principal on October 1, 2018 and each person who was registered with FINRA as an Investment Banking Representative and a General Securities Principal within two years prior to October 1, 2018 shall be qualified to register as an Investment Banking Principal without passing any additional qualification examinations.

All other individuals registering as Investment Banking Principals after October 1, 2018 shall, prior to or concurrent with such registration, become registered pursuant to paragraph (b)(5) of this Rule as an Investment Banking Representative and pass the General Securities Principal qualification examination.

(6) Research Principal

    (A) Requirement

Each principal as defined in paragraph (a)(1) of this Rule who is responsible for approving the content of a member's research reports on equity securities, or who, with respect to equity research, is responsible for supervising the overall conduct of a Research Analyst registered pursuant to paragraph (b)(6) of this Rule or a Supervisory Analyst registered pursuant to paragraph (a)(14) of this Rule shall be required to register with FINRA as a Research Principal, subject to the following exceptions:

    (i) if a principal's activities are limited solely to approving the content of a member's research reports on equity securities, then such person may register as a Supervisory Analyst pursuant to paragraph (a)(14) of this Rule in lieu of registering as a Research Principal;

    (ii) if a principal's activities are limited solely to reviewing a member's research reports on equity securities only for compliance with the disclosure provisions of Rule 2241, then such person may register as a General Securities Principal pursuant to paragraph (a)(2) of this Rule in lieu of registering as a Research Principal; and

    (iii) if a principal's activities are limited solely to approving the content of a member's research reports on debt securities or the content of third-party research reports, then such person may register as a General Securities Principal pursuant to paragraph (a)(2) of this Rule or as a Supervisory Analyst pursuant to paragraph (a)(14) of this Rule in lieu of registering as a Research Principal.

    (B) Qualifications

Subject to the lapse of registration provisions in Rule 1210.08, each person registered with FINRA as a Research Principal on October 1, 2018 and each person who was registered with FINRA as a Research Principal within two years prior to October 1, 2018 shall be qualified to register as a Research Principal without passing any additional qualification examinations.

All other individuals registering as Research Principals after October 1, 2018 shall, prior to or concurrent with such registration: (i) become registered pursuant to paragraph (b)(6) of this Rule as a Research Analyst and pass the General Securities Principal qualification examination; or (ii) become registered pursuant to paragraph (a)(14) of this Rule as a Supervisory Analyst and pass the General Securities Principal qualification examination.

(7) Securities Trader Principal

    (A) Requirement

Each principal as defined in paragraph (a)(1) of this Rule who is responsible for supervising the securities trading activities specified in paragraph (b)(4) of this Rule shall be required to register with FINRA as a Securities Trader Principal.

    (B) Qualifications

Each person seeking to register as a Securities Trader Principal shall, prior to or concurrent with such registration, become registered pursuant to paragraph (b)(4) of this Rule as a Securities Trader and pass the General Securities Principal qualification examination.

(8) Registered Options Principal

    (A) Requirement

Each member that is engaged in transactions in options with the public shall have at least one Registered Options Principal.

In addition, each principal as defined in paragraph (a)(1) of this Rule who is responsible for supervising a member's options sales practices with the public, including a person designated pursuant to Rule 3110(a)(2), shall be required to register with FINRA as a Registered Options Principal, subject to the following exception. If a principal's options activities are limited solely to those activities that may be supervised by a General Securities Sales Supervisor as specified in Rule 2360, then such person may register as a General Securities Sales Supervisor pursuant to paragraph (a)(10) of this Rule in lieu of registering as a Registered Options Principal.

(B) Qualifications

Subject to the lapse of registration provisions in Rule 1210.08, each person registered with FINRA as a Registered Options Principal on October 1, 2018 and each person who was registered with FINRA as a Registered Options Principal within two years prior to October 1, 2018 shall be qualified to register as a Registered Options Principal without passing any additional qualification examinations.

All other individuals registering as Registered Options Principals after October 1, 2018 shall, prior to or concurrent with such registration, become registered pursuant to paragraph (b)(2) of this Rule as a General Securities Representative and pass the Registered Options Principal qualification exam.

(9) Government Securities Principal

(A) Requirement

Each principal as defined in paragraph (a)(1) of this Rule shall be required to register with FINRA as a Government Securities Principal if his or her activities include:

(i) the management or supervision of the member's government securities business, including:

    a. underwriting, trading or sales of government securities;

    b. financial advisory or consultant services for issuers in connection with the issuance of government securities;

    c. research or investment advice, other than general economic information or advice, with respect to government securities in connection with the activities described in subparagraphs a. and b. above;

    d. activities other than those specifically described above that involve communication, directly or indirectly, with public investors in government securities in connection with the activities described in subparagraphs a. and b. above; or

(ii) the supervision of:

    a. the processing and clearance activities with respect to government securities; or

    b. the maintenance of records involving any of the activities described in paragraph (a)(9)(A)(i) of this Rule.

If a principal's functions include the activities specified in paragraph (a)(9)(A) of this Rule, then such person may register as a General Securities Principal pursuant to paragraph (a)(2) of this Rule in lieu of registering as a Government Securities Principal.

(B) Qualifications

Subject to the lapse of registration provisions in Rule 1210.08, each person registered with FINRA as a Government Securities Principal on October 1, 2018 and each person who was registered with FINRA as a Government Securities Principal within two years prior to October 1, 2018 shall be qualified to register as a Government Securities Principal without passing any additional qualification examinations.

All other individuals registering as Government Securities Principals after October 1, 2018 shall, prior to or concurrent with such registration, become registered pursuant to paragraph (b)(2) of this Rule as a General Securities Representative.

(10) General Securities Sales Supervisor

(A) Principals Engaged in Limited Activities

Each principal as defined in paragraph (a)(1) of this Rule may register with FINRA as a General Securities Sales Supervisor if his or her supervisory responsibilities in the investment banking or securities business of a member are limited to the securities sales activities of the member, including the approval of customer accounts, training of sales and sales supervisory personnel and the maintenance of records of original entry or ledger accounts of the member required to be maintained in branch offices by Exchange Act record-keeping rules.

A person registered solely as a General Securities Sales Supervisor shall not be qualified to perform any of the following activities:

(i) supervision of the origination and structuring of underwritings;

(ii) supervision of market making commitments;

(iii) supervision of the custody of broker-dealer or customer funds or securities for purposes of SEA Rule 15c3-3; or

(iv) supervision of overall compliance with financial responsibility rules for broker-dealers promulgated pursuant to the provisions of the Exchange Act.

(B) Qualifications

Each person seeking to register as a General Securities Sales Supervisor shall, prior to or concurrent with such registration become registered pursuant to paragraph (b)(2) of this Rule as a General Securities Representative and pass the General Securities Sales Supervisor qualification examinations

(11) Investment Company and Variable Contracts Products Principal

(A) Principals Engaged in Limited Activities

Each principal as defined in paragraph (a)(1) of this Rule may register with FINRA as an Investment Company and Variable Contracts Products Principal if his or her activities in the investment banking or securities business of a member are limited to the activities specified in paragraph (b)(7) of this Rule.

(B) Qualifications

Each person seeking to register as an Investment Company and Variable Contracts Products Principal shall, prior to or concurrent with such registration: (i) become registered pursuant to paragraph (b)(2) of this Rule as a General Securities Representative and pass the Investment Company and Variable Contracts Products Principal qualification examination; or (ii) become registered pursuant to paragraph (b)(7) of this Rule as an Investment Company and Variable Contracts Products Representative and pass the Investment Company and Variable Contracts Products Principal qualification examination.

(12) Direct Participation Programs Principal

(A) Principals Engaged in Limited Activities

Each principal as defined in paragraph (a)(1) of this Rule may register with FINRA as a Direct Participation Program Principal if his or her activities in the investment banking or securities business of a member are limited to the activities specified in paragraph (b)(8) of this Rule.

(B) Qualifications

Each person seeking to register as a Direct Participation Program Principal shall, prior to or concurrent with such registration: (i) become registered pursuant to paragraph (b)(2) of this Rule as a General Securities Representative and pass the Direct Participation Program Principal qualification examination; or (ii) become registered pursuant to paragraph (b)(8) of this Rule as a Direct Participation Programs Representative and pass the Direct Participation Program Principal qualification examination.

(13) Private Securities Offerings Principal

(A) Principals Engaged in Limited Activities

Each principal as defined in paragraph (a)(1) of this Rule may register with FINRA as a Private Securities Offerings Principal if his or her activities in the investment banking or securities business of a member are limited to the activities specified in paragraph (b)(9) of this Rule.

(B) Qualifications

Subject to the lapse of registration provisions in Rule 1210.08, each person registered with FINRA as a

Private Securities Offerings Representative and a General Securities Principal on October 1, 2018 and each person who was registered with FINRA as a Private Securities Offerings Representative and a General Securities Principal within two years prior to October 1, 2018 shall be qualified to register as a Private Securities Offerings Principal without passing any additional qualification examinations.

All other individuals registering as Private Securities Offerings Principals after October 1, 2018 shall, prior to or concurrent with such registration, become registered pursuant to paragraph (b)(9) of this Rule as a Private Securities Offerings Representative and pass the General Securities Principal qualification examination.

(14) Supervisory Analyst

(A) Principals Engaged in Limited Activities

Each principal as defined in paragraph (a)(1) of this Rule may register with FINRA as a Supervisory Analyst if his or her activities are limited to approving the following: (i) the content of a member's research reports on equity securities; (ii) the content of a member's research reports on debt securities; (iii) the content of third-party research reports; (iv) retail communications as described in Rule 2241(a)(11)(A); or (v) other research communications that do not meet the definition of "research report" under Rule 2241, provided that the Supervisory Analyst has technical expertise in the particular product area.

The activities of a Supervisory Analyst engaged in equity research shall be supervised by a Research Principal registered pursuant to paragraph (a)(6) of this Rule.

(B) Qualifications

Each person seeking to register as a Supervisory Analyst shall, prior to or concurrent with such registration pass the Supervisory Analyst qualification examination.

Upon written request pursuant to the Rule 9600 Series, FINRA shall grant a waiver from the securities analysis portion (Part II) of the Supervisory Analyst qualification examination upon verification that the applicant has passed Level I of the Chartered Financial Analyst ("CFA") Examination.

(b) Definition of Representative and Representative Registration Categories

(1) Definition of Representative

A "representative" is any person associated with a member, including assistant officers other than principals, who is engaged in the member's investment banking or securities business, such as supervision, solicitation, conduct of business in securities or the training of persons associated with a member for any of these functions.

(2) General Securities Representative

(A) Requirement

Each representative as defined in paragraph (b)(1) of this Rule shall be required to register with FINRA as a General Securities Representative, subject to the following exceptions:

(i) if a representative's activities include the functions of an Operations Professional, a Securities Trader, an Investment Banking Representative or a Research Analyst as specified in paragraphs (b)(3) through (b)(6) of this Rule, then such person shall appropriately register in one or more of those categories; and

(ii) if a representative's activities are limited solely to the functions of an Investment Company and Variable Contracts Products Representative, a Direct Participation Programs Representative or a Private Securities Offerings Representative as specified in paragraphs (b)(7) through (b)(9) of this Rule, then such person may appropriately register in one or more of those categories in lieu of registering as a General Securities Representative.

(B) Qualifications

Subject to the lapse of registration provisions in Rule 1210.08, each person registered with FINRA as a General Securities Representative on October 1, 2018 and each person who was registered with FINRA as a General Securities Representative within two years prior to October 1, 2018 shall be qualified to register as a General Securities Representative without passing any additional qualification examinations. All other individuals registering as General Securities Representatives after October 1, 2018 shall, prior to or concurrent with such registration, pass the SIE and the General Securities Representative qualification examination.

(3) Operations Professional

  (A) Requirement

    (i) Covered Persons

Each of the following persons shall be required to register with FINRA as an Operations Professional:

  a. senior management with direct responsibility over the covered functions specified in paragraph (b)(3)(A)(ii) of this Rule;

  b. any person designated by senior management specified in paragraph (b)(3)(A)(i)a. of this Rule as a supervisor, manager or other person responsible for approving or authorizing work, including work of other persons, in direct furtherance of each of the covered functions specified in paragraph (b)(3)(A)(ii) of this Rule, as applicable, provided that there is sufficient designation of such persons by senior management to address each of the applicable covered functions; and

  c. persons with the authority or discretion materially to commit a member's capital in direct furtherance of the covered functions specified in paragraph (b)(3)(A)(ii) of this Rule or to commit a member to any material contract or agreement (written or oral) in direct furtherance of the covered functions specified in paragraph (b)(3)(A)(ii) of this Rule.

    (ii) Covered Functions

For purposes of paragraph (b)(3) of this Rule, the following are the covered functions:

  a. client on-boarding (customer account data and document maintenance);

  b. collection, maintenance, re-investment (i.e., sweeps) and disbursement of funds;

  c. receipt and delivery of securities and funds, account transfers;

  d. bank, custody, depository and firm account management and reconciliation;

  e. settlement, fail control, buy ins, segregation, possession and control;

  f. trade confirmation and account statements;

  g. margin;

  h. stock loan or securities lending;

  i. prime brokerage (services to other broker-dealers and financial institutions);

  j. approval of pricing models used for valuations;

  k. financial control, including general ledger and treasury;

  l. contributing to the process of preparing and filing financial regulatory reports;

  m. defining and approving business requirements for sales and trading systems and any other systems related to the covered functions, and validation that these systems meet such business requirements;

  n. defining and approving business security requirements and policies for information technology, including, but not limited to, systems and data, in connection with the covered functions;

  o. defining and approving information entitlement policies in connection with the covered functions; and

  p. posting entries to a member's books and records in connection with the covered functions to ensure integrity and compliance with the federal securities laws and regulations and FINRA rules.

  (B) Qualifications

Subject to the lapse of registration provisions in Rule 1210.08, each person registered with FINRA as an Investment Company Products and Variable Contracts Representative, a General Securities Representative, a United Kingdom Securities Representative, a Canada Securities Representative, an Operations Professional, a Registered Options Principal, a General Securities Sales Supervisor, a Supervisory Analyst, a General Securities Principal, an Investment Company Products and Variable Products Principal, a Financial and Operations Principal, an Introducing Broker-Dealer Financial and Operations Principal, a Municipal Fund Securities Limited Principal or a Municipal Securities Principal on October 1, 2018 and each person who was registered with FINRA in such registration categories within two years prior to October 1, 2018 shall be qualified to register as an Operations Professional without passing any additional qualification examinations.

Each person who registers with FINRA as an Investment Company Products and Variable Contracts Representative, a General Securities Representative, a Registered Options Principal, a General Securities Sales Supervisor, a Supervisory Analyst, a General Securities Principal, an Investment Company Products and Variable Products Principal, a Financial and Operations Principal, an Introducing Broker-Dealer Financial and Operations Principal, a Municipal Fund Securities Limited Principal or a Municipal Securities Principal after October 1, 2018 shall also be qualified to register as an Operations Professional without passing any additional qualification examinations.

All other individuals registering as Operations Professionals after October 1, 2018 shall, prior to or concurrent with such registration, pass the SIE and the Operations Professional qualification examination.

FINRA may accept as an alternative to the qualification examination requirement in paragraph (b)(3)(B) of this Rule any domestic or foreign qualification if it determines that acceptance of such alternative qualification is consistent with the purposes of paragraph (b)(3) of this Rule, the protection of investors, and the public interest.

A person registering as an Operations Professional shall be allowed a period of 120 days beginning on the date such person requests Operations Professional registration to pass any applicable qualification examination, during which time such person may function as an Operations Professional.

(4) Securities Trader

(A) Requirement

Each representative as defined in paragraph (b)(1) of this Rule shall be required to register with FINRA as a Securities Trader if, with respect to transactions in equity, preferred or convertible debt securities effected otherwise than on a securities exchange, such person is engaged in proprietary trading, the execution of transactions on an agency basis, or the direct supervision of such activities, other than any person associated with a member whose trading activities are conducted principally on behalf of an investment company that is registered with the SEC pursuant to the Investment Company Act and that controls, is controlled by or is under common control, with the member.

In addition, each person associated with a member who is: (i) primarily responsible for the design, development or significant modification of an algorithmic trading strategy relating to equity, preferred or convertible debt securities; or (ii) responsible for the day-to-day supervision or direction of such activities shall be required to register with FINRA as a Securities Trader.

For purposes of paragraph (b)(4) of this Rule, an "algorithmic trading strategy" is an automated system that generates or routes orders (or order-related messages) but shall not include an automated system that solely routes orders received in their entirety to a market center.

(B) Qualifications

Subject to the lapse of registration provisions in Rule 1210.08, each person registered with FINRA as a Securities Trader on October 1, 2018 and each person who was registered with FINRA as a Securities Trader within two years prior to October 1, 2018 shall be qualified to register as a Securities Trader without passing any additional qualification examinations.

All other individuals registering as Securities Traders after October 1, 2018 shall, prior to or concurrent with such registration, pass the SIE and the Securities Trader qualification examination.

(5) Investment Banking Representative

  (A) Requirement

    Each representative as defined in paragraph (b)(1) of this Rule shall be required to register with FINRA as an Investment Banking Representative if his or her activities in the investment banking or securities business of a member involve:

      (i) advising on or facilitating debt or equity securities offerings through a private placement or a public offering, including but not limited to origination, underwriting, marketing, structuring, syndication, and pricing of such securities and managing the allocation and stabilization activities of such offerings, or

      (ii) advising on or facilitating mergers and acquisitions, tender offers, financial restructurings, asset sales, divestitures or other corporate reorganizations or business combination transactions, including but not limited to rendering a fairness, solvency or similar opinion.

  (B) Qualifications

    Subject to the lapse of registration provisions in Rule 1210.08, each person registered with FINRA as an Investment Banking Representative on October 1, 2018 and each person who was registered with FINRA as an Investment Banking Representative within two years prior to October 1, 2018 shall be qualified to register as an Investment Banking Representative without passing any additional qualification examinations.

    All other individuals registering as Investment Banking Representatives after October 1, 2018 shall, prior to or concurrent with such registration, pass the SIE and the Investment Banking Representative qualification examination.

  (C) Exceptions

    (i) Associated Persons Participating in New Employee Training Program

      An associated person who participates in a new employee training program conducted by a member shall not be required to register as an Investment Banking Representative for a period of up to six months from the time the associated person first engages within the program in activities described in paragraph (b)(5) of this Rule, but in no event more than two years after commencing participation in the training program. This exception is conditioned upon the member maintaining records that:

        a. evidence the existence and details of the training program, including but not limited to its scope, length, eligible participants and administrator; and

        b. identify those participants whose activities otherwise would require registration as an Investment Banking Representative and the date on which each participant commenced such activities.

    (ii) Associated Persons Engaged in Limited Activities

      An associated person shall not be required to register as an Investment Banking Representative if his or her activities in the investment banking or securities business of a member are limited solely to:

        a. advising on or facilitating the placement of direct participation program securities as defined in paragraph (b)(8)(A) of this Rule;

        b. effecting private securities offerings as specified in paragraph (b)(9) of this Rule; or c. retail or institutional sales and trading activities.

        c. retail or institutional sales and trading activities.

(6) Research Analyst

  (A) Requirement

    Each person associated with a member who is to function as a research analyst shall be required to register with FINRA as a Research Analyst.

    For purposes of paragraph (b)(6) of this Rule, "research analyst" shall mean an associated person whose primary job function is to provide investment research and who is primarily responsible for the preparation of the substance of an equity research report or whose name appears on an equity research report, and "research report" shall have the same meaning as in Rule 2241.

The requirements of paragraph (b)(6) of this Rule shall not apply to an associated person who:

(i) is an employee of a non-member foreign affiliate of a member ("foreign research analyst");

(ii) resides outside the United States; and

(iii) contributes, partially or entirely, to the preparation of globally branded or foreign affiliate research reports but does not contribute to the preparation of a member's research, including a mixed-team report, that is not globally branded.

Provided that the following conditions are satisfied:

a. a member that publishes or otherwise distributes globally branded research reports partially or entirely prepared by a foreign research analyst must subject such research to pre-use review and approval by a Research Principal registered pursuant to paragraph (a)(6) of this Rule or a Supervisory Analyst registered pursuant to paragraph (a)(14) of this Rule. In addition, the member must ensure that such research reports comply with Rule 2241, as applicable;

b. in publishing or otherwise distributing globally branded research reports partially or entirely prepared by a foreign research analyst, a member must prominently disclose:

1. each affiliate contributing to the research report;

2. the names of the foreign research analysts employed by each contributing affiliate;

3. that such research analysts are not registered as Research Analysts with FINRA; and

4. that such research analysts may not be associated persons of the member and therefore may not be subject to Rule 2241 restrictions on communications with a subject company, public appearances and trading securities held by a research analyst account;

c. the disclosures required by paragraph (b)(6)(A)(iii)b. of this Rule shall be presented on the front page of the research report or the front page shall refer to the page on which the disclosures can be found. In electronic research reports, a member may hyperlink to the disclosures. References and disclosures shall be clear, comprehensive and prominent;

d. members shall establish and maintain records that identify those individuals who have availed themselves of this exemption, the basis for such exemption, and evidence of compliance with the conditions of the exemption. Failure to establish and maintain such records shall create an inference of a violation of paragraph (b)(6) of this Rule. Members shall also establish and maintain records that evidence compliance with the applicable content, disclosure and supervision provisions of Rule 2241. Members shall maintain these records in accordance with the supervisory requirements of Rule 3110, and in addition to such requirement, the failure to establish and maintain such records shall create an inference of a violation of the applicable content, disclosure and supervision provisions of Rule 2241;

e. nothing in paragraph (b)(6) of this Rule shall affect the obligation of any person or broker-dealer, including a foreign broker-dealer, to comply with the applicable provisions of the federal securities laws, rules and regulations and any self-regulatory organization rules;

f. the fact that a foreign research analyst avails himself or herself of the exemption in paragraph (b)(6) of this Rule shall not be probative of whether that individual is an associated person of the member for other purposes, including whether the foreign research analyst is subject to the Rule 2241 restrictions on communications with a subject company, public appearances and trading securities held by a research analyst account;

g. a member that distributes non-member foreign affiliate research reports that are clearly and prominently labeled as such must comply with the third-party research report requirements in Rule 2241; and

h. for purposes of the exemption in paragraph (b)(6) of this Rule, the terms "affiliate," "globally branded research report" and "mixed-team research report" shall have the following meanings:

1. "affiliate" shall mean a person that directly or indirectly controls, is controlled by, or is under common control with, a member;
2. "globally branded research report" refers to the use of a single marketing identity that encompasses the member and one or more of its affiliates; and
3. "mixed-team research report" refers to any member research report that is not globally branded and includes a contribution by a research analyst who is not an associated person of the member.

(B) Qualifications

Subject to the lapse of registration provisions in Rule 1210.08, each person registered with FINRA as a Research Analyst on October 1, 2018 and each person who was registered with FINRA as a Research Analyst within two years prior to October 1, 2018 shall be qualified to register as a Research Analyst without passing any additional qualification examinations.

All other individuals registering as Research Analysts after October 1, 2018 shall, prior to or concurrent with such registration, pass the SIE and the Research Analyst qualification examinations.

Upon written request pursuant to the Rule 9600 Series, FINRA shall grant a waiver from the analytical portion of the Research Analyst qualification examinations (Series 86) upon verification that the applicant has passed:

(i) Levels I and II of the CFA Examination; or

(ii) if the applicant functions as a research analyst who prepares only technical research reports as defined in paragraph (b)(6) of this Rule, Levels I and II of the Chartered Market Technician ("CMT") Examination; and

(iii) has either functioned as a research analyst continuously since having passed the Level II CFA or CMT Examination or applied for registration as a Research Analyst within two years of having passed the Level II CFA or CMT Examination.

For purposes of paragraph (b)(6) of this Rule, a "technical research report" shall mean a research report, as that term is defined in Rule 2241, that is based solely on stock price movement and trading volume and not on the subject company's financial information, business prospects, contact with subject company's management, or the valuation of a subject company's securities.

An applicant who has been granted an exemption pursuant to paragraph (b)(6)(B) of this Rule still must pass the regulatory portion of the Research Analyst qualification examinations (Series 87) before that applicant can be registered as a Research Analyst.

(7) Investment Company and Variable Contracts Products Representative

(A) Representatives Engaged in Limited Activities

Each representative as defined in paragraph (b)(1) of this Rule may register with FINRA as an Investment Company and Variable Contracts Products Representative if his or her activities in the investment banking or securities business of a member are limited to the solicitation, purchase or sale of:

(i) redeemable securities of companies registered pursuant to the Investment Company Act;

(ii) securities of closed-end companies registered pursuant to the Investment Company Act during the period of original distribution only;

(iii) variable contracts and insurance premium funding programs and other contracts issued by an insurance company except contracts that are exempt securities pursuant to Section 3(a)(8) of the Securities Act; or

(iv) municipal fund securities as defined under MSRB Rule D-12.

(B) Qualifications

Subject to the lapse of registration provisions in Rule 1210.08, each person registered with FINRA as an Investment Company and Variable Contracts Products Representative on October 1, 2018 and each person who was registered with FINRA as an Investment Company and Variable Contracts Products Representative within two years prior to October 1, 2018 shall be qualified to register as an Investment Company and Variable Contracts Products Representative without passing any additional qualification examinations. All other individuals registering as Investment Company and Variable Contracts Products Representatives after October 1, 2018 shall, prior to or concurrent with such registration, pass the SIE and the Investment Company and Variable Contracts Products Representative qualification examination.

(8) Direct Participation Programs Representative

(A) Representatives Engaged in Limited Activities

Each representative as defined in paragraph (b)(1) of this Rule may register with FINRA as a Direct Participation Programs Representative if his or her activities in the investment banking or securities business of a member are limited to the solicitation, purchase or sale of equity interests in or the debt of direct participation programs as defined in paragraph (b)(8)(A) of this Rule.

"Direct participation programs" shall mean programs that provide for flow-through tax consequences regardless of the structure of the legal entity or vehicle for distribution including, but not limited to, oil and gas programs, cattle programs, condominium securities, Subchapter S corporate offerings and all other programs of a similar nature, regardless of the industry represented by the program, or any combination thereof. Excluded from this definition are real estate investment trusts, tax qualified pension and profit sharing plans pursuant to Sections 401 and 403(a) of the Internal Revenue Code ("Code") and individual retirement plans under Section 408 of the Code, tax sheltered annuities pursuant to the provisions of Section 403(b) of the Code and any company including separate accounts registered pursuant to the Investment Company Act. Also excluded from this definition is any program that is listed on a national securities exchange or any program for which an application for listing on a national securities exchange has been made.

(B) Qualifications

Subject to the lapse of registration provisions in Rule 1210.08, each person registered with FINRA as a Direct Participation Programs Representative on October 1, 2018 and each person who was registered with FINRA as a Direct Participation Programs Representative within two years prior to October 1, 2018 shall be qualified to register as a Direct Participation Programs Representative without passing any additional qualification examinations.

All other individuals registering as Direct Participation Programs Representatives after October 1, 2018 shall, prior to or concurrent with such registration, pass the SIE and the Direct Participation Programs Representative qualification examination.

(9) Private Securities Offerings Representative

(A) Representatives Engaged in Limited Activities

Each representative as defined in paragraph (b)(1) of this Rule may register with FINRA as a Private Securities Offerings Representative if his or her activities in the investment banking or securities business of a member are limited to effecting sales as part of a primary offering of securities not involving a public offering, pursuant to Sections 3(b), 4(2) or 4(6) of the Securities Act and the Securities Act rules and regulations, provided, however, that such person shall not effect sales of municipal or government securities, or equity interests in or the debt of direct participation programs as defined in paragraph (b)(8)(A) of this Rule.

(B) Qualifications

Subject to the lapse of registration provisions in Rule 1210.08, each person registered with FINRA as a Private Securities Offerings Representative on October 1, 2018 and each person who was registered with FINRA as a Private Securities Offerings Representative within two years prior to October 1, 2018 shall be qualified to register as a Private Securities Offerings Representative without passing any additional qualification examinations.

All other individuals registering as Private Securities Offerings Representatives after October 1, 2018 shall, prior to or concurrent with such registration, pass the SIE and the Private Securities Offerings Representative qualification examination. However, FINRA shall, upon such evidence as it determines to be appropriate, deem any person who while employed by a bank, engaged in effecting sales of private securities offerings as described in paragraph (b)(9) of this Rule, during the period from May 12, 1999 to November 12, 1999, as qualified to register as a Private Securities Offerings Representative without the need to pass the SIE and the Private Securities Offerings Representative qualification examination.

1230. Associated Persons Exempt from Registration

The following persons associated with a member are not required to be registered with FINRA:

(a) persons associated with a member whose functions are solely and exclusively clerical or ministerial; and

(b) persons associated with a member whose functions are related solely and exclusively to:

    (1) effecting transactions on the floor of a national securities exchange and who are appropriately registered with such exchange;

    (2) transactions in municipal securities;

    (3) transactions in commodities; or

    (4) transactions in security futures, provided that any such person is registered with a registered futures association.

1240. Continuing Education Requirements

This Rule prescribes requirements regarding the continuing education of specified persons subsequent to their initial registration with FINRA. The requirements shall consist of a Regulatory Element and a Firm Element as set forth below.

(a) Regulatory Element

    (1) Requirements

    All covered persons shall comply with the requirement to complete the Regulatory Element.

    Each covered person shall complete the Regulatory Element on the occurrence of their second registration anniversary date and every three years thereafter, or as otherwise prescribed by FINRA. On each occasion, the Regulatory Element must be completed within 120 days after the person's registration anniversary date. A person's initial registration date, also known as the "base date," shall establish the cycle of anniversary dates for purposes of this Rule. The content of the Regulatory Element shall be appropriate to either the registered representative or principal status of persons subject to the Rule. The content of the Regulatory Element for a person designated as eligible for a waiver pursuant to Rule 1210.09 shall be determined based on the person's most recent registration status, and the Regulatory Element shall be completed based on the same cycle had the person remained registered.

    (2) Failure to Complete

    Unless otherwise determined by FINRA, any covered persons who have not completed the Regulatory Element within the prescribed time frames will have their registrations deemed inactive until such time as the requirements of the program have been satisfied. Any person whose registration has been deemed inactive under this Rule shall cease all activities as a registered person and is prohibited from performing any duties and functioning in any capacity requiring registration. Further, such person may not accept or solicit business or receive any compensation for the purchase or sale of securities. However, such person may receive trail or residual commissions resulting from transactions completed before the inactive status, unless the member with which such person is associated has a policy prohibiting such trail or residual commissions. A registration that is inactive for a period of two years will be administratively terminated. A person whose registration is so terminated may reactivate the registration only by reapplying for registration and meeting the qualification requirements of the applicable provisions of Rules 1210 and 1220. FINRA may, upon application and a showing of good cause, allow for additional time for a covered person to satisfy the program requirements. If a person designated as eligible for a waiver pursuant to Rule 1210.09 fails to complete the Regulatory Element within the prescribed time frames, the person shall no longer be eligible for such a waiver.

(3) Disciplinary Actions

Unless otherwise determined by FINRA, a covered person, other than a person designated as eligible for a waiver pursuant to Rule 1210.09, will be required to retake the Regulatory Element and satisfy all of its requirements in the event such person:

(A) is subject to any statutory disqualification as defined in Section 3(a)(39) of the Exchange Act;

(B) is subject to suspension or to the imposition of a fine of $5,000 or more for violation of any provision of any securities law or regulation, or any agreement with or rule or standard of conduct of any securities governmental agency, securities self-regulatory organization, or as imposed by any such regulatory or self-regulatory organization in connection with a disciplinary proceeding; or

(C) is ordered as a sanction in a disciplinary action to retake the Regulatory Element by any securities governmental agency or self-regulatory organization.

The retaking of the Regulatory Element shall commence with participation within 120 days of the covered person becoming subject to the statutory disqualification, in the case of (A) above, or the disciplinary action becoming final, in the case of (B) and (C) above. The date of the disciplinary action shall be treated as such person's new base date with FINRA.

(4) Reassociation in a Registered Capacity

Any covered person who has terminated association with a member and who has, within two years of the date of termination, become reassociated in a registered capacity with a member shall participate in the Regulatory Element at such intervals that may apply (second anniversary and every three years thereafter) based on the initial registration anniversary date rather than based on the date of reassociation in a registered capacity.

(5) Definition of Covered Person

For purposes of this Rule, the term "covered person" means any person, other than a Foreign Associate, registered with FINRA pursuant to Rule 1210, including any person who is permissively registered pursuant to Rule 1210.02, and any person who is designated as eligible for a waiver pursuant to Rule 1210.09.

(6) Delivery of the Regulatory Element

The continuing education Regulatory Element program will be administered through Web-based delivery or such other technological manner and format as specified by FINRA.

(7) Regulatory Element Contact Person

Each member shall designate and identify to FINRA (by name and e-mail address) an individual or individuals responsible for receiving e-mail notifications provided via the Central Registration Depository regarding when a covered person is approaching the end of his or her Regulatory Element time frame and when a covered person is deemed inactive due to failure to complete the requirements of the Regulatory Element program. Each member shall identify, review, and, if necessary, update the information regarding its Regulatory Element contact person(s) in the manner prescribed by Rule 4517.

(b) Firm Element

(1) Persons Subject to the Firm Element

The requirements of this subparagraph shall apply to any person registered with a member who has direct contact with customers in the conduct of the member's securities sales, trading and investment banking activities, any person registered as an operations professional pursuant to Rule 1220(b)(3) or a research analyst pursuant to Rule 1220(b)(6), and to the immediate supervisors of such persons (collectively, "covered registered persons"). "Customer" shall mean any natural person and any organization, other than another broker or dealer, executing securities transactions with or through or receiving investment banking services from a member.

(2) Standards for the Firm Element

(A) Each member must maintain a continuing and current education program for its covered registered persons to enhance their securities knowledge, skill, and professionalism. At a minimum, each member shall at least annually evaluate and prioritize its training needs and develop a written training plan. The plan must take into consideration the member's size, organizational structure, and scope of business activities, as well as regulatory developments and the performance of covered registered persons in the Regulatory Element. If a member's analysis establishes the need for supervisory training for persons with supervisory responsibilities, such training must be included in the member's training plan.

(B) Minimum Standards for Training Programs — Programs used to implement a member's training plan must be appropriate for the business of the member and, at a minimum must cover training in ethics and professional responsibility and the following matters concerning securities products, services, and strategies offered by the member:

(i) General investment features and associated risk factors;

(ii) Suitability and sales practice considerations; and

(iii) Applicable regulatory requirements.

(C) Administration of Continuing Education Program — A member must administer its continuing education programs in accordance with its annual evaluation and written plan and must maintain records documenting the content of the programs and completion of the programs by covered registered persons.

(3) Participation in the Firm Element

Covered registered persons included in a member's plan must take all appropriate and reasonable steps to participate in continuing education programs as required by the member.

(4) Specific Training Requirements

FINRA may require a member, individually or as part of a larger group, to provide specific training to its covered registered persons in such areas as FINRA deems appropriate. Such a requirement may stipulate the class of covered registered persons for which it is applicable, the time period in which the requirement must be satisfied and, where appropriate, the actual training content.

---

10. FINRA Rules: 1122 – Filing of Misleading Information as to Membership or Registration

No member or person associated with a member shall file with FINRA information with respect to membership or registration which is incomplete or inaccurate so as to be misleading, or which could in any way tend to mislead, or fail to correct such filing after notice thereof.

---

11. FINRA Rules: 1250 – Continuing Education Requirements
(FINRA renumbered the revised rule as Rule 1240)

This Rule prescribes requirements regarding the continuing education of specified persons subsequent to their initial registration with FINRA. The requirements shall consist of a Regulatory Element and a Firm Element as set forth below.

(a) Regulatory Element

(1) Requirements

All covered persons shall comply with the requirement to complete the Regulatory Element.

Each covered person shall complete the Regulatory Element on the occurrence of their second registration anniversary date and every three years thereafter, or as otherwise prescribed by FINRA. On each occasion, the Regulatory Element must be completed within 120 days after the person's registration anniversary date. A person's initial registration date, also known as the "base date," shall establish the cycle of anniversary dates for purposes of this Rule. The content of the Regulatory Element shall be appropriate to either the registered representative or principal status of persons subject to the Rule. The content of the Regulatory Element for a person designated as eligible for a waiver pursuant to Rule 1210.09 shall be determined based on the person's most recent registration status, and the Regulatory Element shall be completed based on the same cycle had the person remained registered.

(2) Failure to Complete

Unless otherwise determined by FINRA, any covered persons who have not completed the Regulatory Element within the prescribed time frames will have their registrations deemed inactive until such time as the requirements of the program have been satisfied. Any person whose registration has been deemed inactive under this Rule shall cease all activities as a registered person and is prohibited from performing any duties and functioning in any capacity requiring registration. Further, such person may not accept or solicit business or receive any compensation for the purchase or sale of securities. However, such person may receive trail or residual commissions resulting from transactions completed before the inactive status, unless the member with which such person is associated has a policy prohibiting such trail or residual commissions. A registration that is inactive for a period of two years will be administratively terminated. A person whose registration is so terminated may reactivate the registration only by reapplying for registration and meeting the qualification requirements of the applicable provisions of Rules 1210 and 1220. FINRA may, upon application and a showing of good cause, allow for additional time for a covered person to satisfy the program requirements. If a person designated as eligible for a waiver pursuant to Rule 1210.09 fails to complete the Regulatory Element within the prescribed time frames, the person shall no longer be eligible for such a waiver.

(3) Disciplinary Actions

Unless otherwise determined by FINRA, a covered person, other than a person designated as eligible for a waiver pursuant to Rule 1210.09, will be required to retake the Regulatory Element and satisfy all of its requirements in the event such person:

(A) is subject to any statutory disqualification as defined in Section 3(a)(39) of the Exchange Act;

(B) is subject to suspension or to the imposition of a fine of $5,000 or more for violation of any provision of any securities law or regulation, or any agreement with or rule or standard of conduct of any securities governmental agency, securities self-regulatory organization, or as imposed by any such regulatory or self-regulatory organization in connection with a disciplinary proceeding; or

(C) is ordered as a sanction in a disciplinary action to retake the Regulatory Element by any securities governmental agency or self-regulatory organization.

The retaking of the Regulatory Element shall commence with participation within 120 days of the covered person becoming subject to the statutory disqualification, in the case of (A) above, or the disciplinary action becoming final, in the case of (B) and (C) above. The date of the disciplinary action shall be treated as such person's new base date with FINRA.

(4) Reassociation in a Registered Capacity

Any covered person who has terminated association with a member and who has, within two years of the date of termination, become reassociated in a registered capacity with a member shall participate in the Regulatory Element at such intervals that may apply (second anniversary and every three years thereafter) based on the initial registration anniversary date rather than based on the date of reassociation in a registered capacity.

(5) Definition of Covered Person

For purposes of this Rule, the term "covered person" means any person, other than a Foreign Associate, registered with FINRA pursuant to Rule 1210, including any person who is permissively registered pursuant to Rule 1210.02, and any person who is designated as eligible for a waiver pursuant to Rule 1210.09.

(6) Delivery of the Regulatory Element

The continuing education Regulatory Element program will be administered through Web-based delivery or such other technological manner and format as specified by FINRA.

(7) Regulatory Element Contact Person

Each member shall designate and identify to FINRA (by name and e-mail address) an individual or individuals responsible for receiving e-mail notifications provided via the Central Registration Depository regarding when a covered person is approaching the end of his or her Regulatory Element time frame and when a covered person is deemed inactive due to failure to complete the requirements of the Regulatory Element program. Each member shall identify, review, and, if necessary, update the information regarding its Regulatory Element contact person(s) in the manner prescribed by Rule 4517.

(b) Firm Element

(1) Persons Subject to the Firm Element

The requirements of this subparagraph shall apply to any person registered with a member who has direct contact with customers in the conduct of the member's securities sales, trading and investment banking activities, any person registered as an operations professional pursuant to Rule 1220(b)(3) or a research analyst pursuant to Rule 1220(b)(6), and to the immediate supervisors of such persons (collectively, "covered registered persons"). "Customer" shall mean any natural person and any organization, other than another broker or dealer, executing securities transactions with or through or receiving investment banking services from a member.

(2) Standards for the Firm Element

(A) Each member must maintain a continuing and current education program for its covered registered persons to enhance their securities knowledge, skill, and professionalism. At a minimum, each member shall at least annually evaluate and prioritize its training needs and develop a written training plan. The plan must take into consideration the member's size, organizational structure, and scope of business activities, as well as regulatory developments and the performance of covered registered persons in the Regulatory Element. If a member's analysis establishes the need for supervisory training for persons with supervisory responsibilities, such training must be included in the member's training plan.

(B) Minimum Standards for Training Programs — Programs used to implement a member's training plan must be appropriate for the business of the member and, at a minimum must cover training in ethics and professional responsibility and the following matters concerning securities products, services, and strategies offered by the member:

(i) General investment features and associated risk factors;

(ii) Suitability and sales practice considerations; and

(iii) Applicable regulatory requirements.

(C) Administration of Continuing Education Program — A member must administer its continuing education programs in accordance with its annual evaluation and written plan and must maintain records documenting the content of the programs and completion by covered registered persons.

(3) Participation in the Firm Element

Covered registered persons included in a member's plan must take all appropriate and reasonable steps to participate in continuing education programs as required by the member.

(4) Specific Training Requirements

FINRA may require a member, individually or as part of a larger group, to provide specific training to its covered registered persons in such areas as FINRA deems appropriate. Such a requirement may stipulate the class of covered registered persons for which it is applicable, the time period in which the requirement must be satisfied and, where appropriate, the actual training content.

---

12. FINRA Rules: 2060 – Use of Information Obtained in Fiduciary Capacity

A member who in the capacity of paying agent, transfer agent, trustee, or in any other similar capacity, has received information as to the ownership of securities, shall under no circumstances make use of such information for the purpose of soliciting purchases, sales or exchanges except at the request and on behalf of the issuer.

---

13. FINRA Rules: 2263 – Arbitration Disclosure to Associated Persons Signing or Acknowledging Form U4

A member shall provide an associated person with the following written statement whenever the associated person is asked, pursuant to FINRA Rule 1010, to manually sign an initial or amended Form U4, or otherwise provide written (which may be electronic) acknowledgment of an amendment to the Form U4:

The Form U4 contains a predispute arbitration clause. It is in item 5 of Section 15A of the Form U4. You should read that clause now. Before signing the Form U4, you should understand the following:

(1) You are agreeing to arbitrate any dispute, claim or controversy that may arise between you and your firm, or a customer, or any other person that is required to be arbitrated under the rules of the self-regulatory organizations with which you are registering. This means you are giving up the right to sue a member, customer, or another associated person in court, including the right to a trial by jury, except as provided by the rules of the arbitration forum in which a claim is filed.

(2) A claim alleging employment discrimination, including a sexual harassment claim, in violation of a statute is not required to be arbitrated under FINRA rules. Such a claim may be arbitrated at FINRA only if the parties have agreed to arbitrate it, either before or after the dispute arose. The rules of other arbitration forums may be different.

(3) A dispute arising under a whistleblower statute that prohibits the use of predispute arbitration agreements is not required to be arbitrated under FINRA rules. Such a dispute may be arbitrated only if the parties have agreed to arbitrate it after the dispute arose.

(4) Arbitration awards are generally final and binding; a party's ability to have a court reverse or modify an arbitration award is very limited.

(5) The ability of the parties to obtain documents, witness statements and other discovery is generally more limited in arbitration than in court proceedings.

(6) The arbitrators do not have to explain the reason(s) for their award unless, in an eligible case, a joint request for an explained decision has been submitted by all parties to the panel at least 20 days prior to the first scheduled hearing date.

(7) The panel of arbitrators may include arbitrators who were or are affiliated with the securities industry or public arbitrators, as provided by the rules of the arbitration forum in which a claim is filed.

(8) The rules of some arbitration forums may impose time limits for bringing a claim in arbitration. In some cases, a claim that is ineligible for arbitration may be brought in court.

---

14. FINRA Rules: 2267 – Investor Education and Protection

(a) Except as otherwise provided in this Rule, each member shall once every calendar year provide in writing (which may be electronic) to each customer the following items of information:

    (1) FINRA BrokerCheck Hotline Number;

    (2) FINRA Web site address; and

    (3) A statement as to the availability to the customer of an investor brochure that includes information describing FINRA BrokerCheck.

(b) Notwithstanding the requirement in paragraph (a) of this Rule,

    (1) any member whose contact with customers is limited to introducing customer accounts to be held directly at an entity other than a FINRA member and thereafter does not carry customer accounts or hold customer funds and securities may furnish a customer with the information required by paragraph (a) of this Rule at or prior to the time of the customer's initial purchase, in lieu of once every calendar year; and

    (2) any member that does not have customers or is a party to a carrying agreement where the carrying firm member complies with paragraph (a) of this Rule is exempt from the requirements of this Rule.

---

15. FINRA Rules: 2310(c) – Non-cash Compensation

(c) Non-Cash Compensation

    (1) Definitions

        The terms "compensation," "non-cash compensation" and "offeror" for the purposes of this paragraph (c) shall have the following meanings:

        (A) "Compensation" shall mean cash compensation and non-cash compensation.

        (B) "Non-cash compensation" shall mean any form of compensation received in connection with the sale and distribution of direct participation securities that is not cash compensation, including but not limited to merchandise, gifts and prizes, travel expenses, meals and lodging.

        (C) "Offeror" shall mean an issuer, sponsor, an adviser to an issuer or sponsor, an underwriter and any affiliated person of such entities.

(2) Restriction on Non-Cash Compensation

In connection with the sale and distribution of direct participation program or REIT securities, no member or person associated with a member shall directly or indirectly accept or make payments or offers of payments of any non-cash compensation, except as provided in this provision. Non-cash compensation arrangements are limited to the following:

(A) Gifts that do not exceed an annual amount per person fixed periodically by the Board of Governors and are not conditioned on achievement of a sales target.

(B) An occasional meal, a ticket to a sporting event or the theater, or comparable entertainment which is neither so frequent nor so extensive as to raise any question of propriety and is not preconditioned on achievement of a sales target.

(C) Payment or reimbursement by offerors in connection with meetings held by an offeror or by a member for the purpose of training or education of associated persons of a member, provided that:

(i) associated persons obtain the member's prior approval to attend the meeting and attendance by a member's associated persons is not conditioned by the member on the achievement of a sales target or any other incentives pursuant to a non-cash compensation arrangement permitted by paragraph (c)(2)(D);

(ii) the location is appropriate to the purpose of the meeting, which shall mean a United States office of the offeror or the member holding the meeting, or a facility located in the vicinity of such office, or a United States regional location with respect to meetings of associated persons who work within that region or, with respect to meetings with direct participation programs or REITs, a United States location at which a significant or representative asset of the program or REIT is located;

(iii) the payment or reimbursement is not applied to the expenses of guests of the associated person; and

(iv) the payment or reimbursement by the offeror is not conditioned by the offeror on the achievement of a sales target or any other non-cash compensation arrangement permitted by paragraph (c)(2)(D).

(D) Non-cash compensation arrangements between a member and its associated persons or a company that controls a member company and the member's associated persons, provided that no unaffiliated non-member company or other unaffiliated member directly or indirectly participates in the member's or non-member's organization of a permissible non-cash compensation arrangement; and

(E) Contributions by a non-member company or other member to a non-cash compensation arrangement between a member and its associated persons, provided that the arrangement meets the criteria in paragraph (c)(2)(D).

A member shall maintain records of all non-cash compensation received by the member or its associated persons in arrangements permitted by paragraphs (c)(2)(C) through (E). The records shall include: the names of the offerors, non-members or other members making the non-cash compensation contributions; the names of the associated persons participating in the arrangements; the nature and value of non-cash compensation received; the location of training and education meetings; and any other information that proves compliance by the member and its associated persons with paragraph (c)(2)(C) through (E).

---

16. FINRA Rules: 2320(g)(4) – Non-cash Compensation

(g)(4) No member or person associated with a member shall directly or indirectly accept or make payments or offers of payments of any non-cash compensation, except as provided in this provision. Notwithstanding the provisions of paragraph (g)(1), the following non-cash compensation arrangements are permitted:

(A) Gifts that do not exceed an annual amount per person fixed periodically by FINRA and are not preconditioned on achievement of a sales target.

(B) An occasional meal, a ticket to a sporting event or the theater, or comparable entertainment which is neither so frequent nor so extensive as to raise any question of propriety and is not preconditioned on achievement of a sales target.

(C) Payment or reimbursement by offerors in connection with meetings held by an offeror or by a member for the purpose of training or education of associated persons of a member, provided that:

(i) the record keeping requirement in paragraph (g)(3) is satisfied;

(ii) associated persons obtain the member's prior approval to attend the meeting and attendance by a member's associated persons is not preconditioned by the member on the achievement of a sales target or any other incentives pursuant to a non-cash compensation arrangement permitted by paragraph (g)(4)(D);

(iii) the location is appropriate to the purpose of the meeting, which shall mean an office of the offeror or the member, or a facility located in the vicinity of such office, or a regional location with respect to regional meetings;

(iv) the payment or reimbursement is not applied to the expenses of guests of the associated person; and

(v) the payment or reimbursement by the offeror is not preconditioned by the offeror on the achievement of a sales target or any other non-cash compensation arrangement permitted by paragraph (g)(4)(D).

(D) Non-cash compensation arrangements between a member and its associated persons or a non-member company and its sales personnel who are associated persons of an affiliated member, provided that:

(i) the member's or non-member's non-cash compensation arrangement, if it includes variable contract securities, is based on the total production of associated persons with respect to all variable contract securities distributed by the member;

(ii) the non-cash compensation arrangement requires that the credit received for each variable contract security is equally weighted;

(iii) no unaffiliated non-member company or other unaffiliated member directly or indirectly participates in the member's or non-member's organization of a permissible non-cash compensation arrangement; and

(iv) the record keeping requirement in paragraph (g)(3) is satisfied.

(E) Contributions by a non-member company or other member to a non-cash compensation arrangement between a member and its associated persons, provided that the arrangement meets the criteria in paragraph (g)(4)(D).

---

17. FINRA Rules: 2341(l)(5) – Non-cash Compensation

(l)(5) No member or person associated with a member shall directly or indirectly accept or make payments or offers of payments of any non-cash compensation, except as provided in this provision. Notwithstanding the provisions of paragraph (l)(1), the following non-cash compensation arrangements are permitted:

(A) Gifts that do not exceed an annual amount per person fixed periodically by FINRA and are not preconditioned on achievement of a sales target.

(B) An occasional meal, a ticket to a sporting event or the theater, or comparable entertainment which is neither so frequent nor so extensive as to raise any question of propriety and is not preconditioned on achievement of a sales target.

(C) Payment or reimbursement by offerors in connection with meetings held by an offeror or by a member for the purpose of training or education of associated persons of a member, provided that:

  (i) the recordkeeping requirement in paragraph (l)(3) is satisfied;

  (ii) associated persons obtain the member's prior approval to attend the meeting and attendance by a member's associated persons is not preconditioned by the member on the achievement of a sales target or any other incentives pursuant to a non-cash compensation arrangement permitted by paragraph (l)(5)(D);

  (iii) the location is appropriate to the purpose of the meeting, which shall mean an office of the offeror or the member, or a facility located in the vicinity of such office, or a regional location with respect to regional meetings;

  (iv) the payment or reimbursement is not applied to the expenses of guests of the associated person; and

  (v) the payment or reimbursement by the offeror is not preconditioned by the offeror on the achievement of a sales target or any other non-cash compensation arrangement permitted by paragraph (l)(5)(D).

(D) Non-cash compensation arrangements between a member and its associated persons or a non-member company and its sales personnel who are associated persons of an affiliated member, provided that:

  (i) the member's or non-member's non-cash compensation arrangement, if it includes investment company securities, is based on the total production of associated persons with respect to all investment company securities distributed by the member;

  (ii) the non-cash compensation arrangement requires that the credit received for each investment company security is equally weighted;

  (iii) no unaffiliated non-member company or other unaffiliated member directly or indirectly participates in the member's or non-member's organization of a permissible non-cash compensation arrangement; and

  (iv) the recordkeeping requirement in paragraph (l)(3) is satisfied.

(E) Contributions by a non-member company or other member to a non-cash compensation arrangement between a member and its associated persons, provided that the arrangement meets the criteria in paragraph (l)(5)(D).

18. FINRA Rules: 3110(e) – Responsibility of Member to Investigate Applicants for Registration

(e) Responsibility of Member to Investigate Applicants for Registration

Each member shall ascertain by investigation the good character, business reputation, qualifications and experience of an applicant before the member applies to register that applicant with FINRA and before making a representation to that effect on the application for registration.

If the applicant previously has been registered with FINRA or another self-regulatory organization, the member shall review a copy of the applicant's most recent Form U5, including any amendments thereto, within 60 days of the filing date of an application for registration, or demonstrate to FINRA that it has made reasonable efforts to do so. In conducting its review of the Form U5, the member shall take such action as may be deemed appropriate.

The member shall also review an applicant's employment experience to determine if the applicant has been recently employed by a Futures Commission Merchant or an Introducing Broker that is notice-registered with the SEC pursuant to Section 15(b)(11) of the Exchange Act. In such a case, the member shall also review a copy of the applicant's most recent CFTC Form 8-T, including any amendments thereto, within 60 days of the filing date of an application for registration, or demonstrate to FINRA that it has made reasonable efforts to do so. In conducting its review of a Form 8-T, the member shall take such action as may be deemed appropriate.

In addition, each member shall establish and implement written procedures reasonably designed to verify the accuracy and completeness of the information contained in an applicant's initial or transfer Form U4 no later than 30 calendar days after the form is filed with FINRA. Such procedures shall, at a minimum, provide for a search of reasonably available public records to be conducted by the member, or a third-party service provider, to verify the accuracy and completeness of the information contained in the applicant's initial or transfer Form U4.

---

19. FINRA Rules: 3220 – Influencing or Rewarding the Employees of Others

(a) No member or person associated with a member shall, directly or indirectly, give or permit to be given anything of value, including gratuities, in excess of one hundred dollars per individual per year to any person, principal, proprietor, employee, agent or representative of another person where such payment or gratuity is in relation to the business of the employer of the recipient of the payment or gratuity. A gift of any kind is considered a gratuity.

(b) This Rule shall not apply to contracts of employment with or to compensation for services rendered by persons enumerated in paragraph (a) provided that there is in existence prior to the time of employment or before the services are rendered, a written agreement between the member and the person who is to be employed to perform such services. Such agreement shall include the nature of the proposed employment, the amount of the proposed compensation, and the written consent of such person's employer or principal.

(c) A separate record of all payments or gratuities in any amount known to the member, the employment agreement referred to in paragraph (b) and any employment compensation paid as a result thereof shall be retained by the member for the period specified by SEA Rule 17a-4.

---

20. FINRA Rules: 3270 – Outside Business Activities of Registered Persons

No registered person may be an employee, independent contractor, sole proprietor, officer, director or partner of another person, or be compensated, or have the reasonable expectation of compensation, from any other person as a result of any business activity outside the scope of the relationship with his or her member firm, unless he or she has provided prior written notice to the member, in such form as specified by the member. Passive investments and activities subject to the requirements of Rule 3280 shall be exempted from this requirement.

---

21. FINRA Rules: 3280 – Private Securities Transactions of an Associated Person

(a) Applicability

No person associated with a member shall participate in any manner in a private securities transaction except in accordance with the requirements of this Rule.

(b) Written Notice

Prior to participating in any private securities transaction, an associated person shall provide written notice to the member with which he is associated describing in detail the proposed transaction and the person's proposed role therein and stating whether he has received or may receive selling compensation in connection with the transaction; provided however that, in the case of a series of related transactions in which no selling compensation has been or will be received, an associated person may provide a single written notice.

(c) Transactions for Compensation

(1) In the case of a transaction in which an associated person has received or may receive selling compensation, a member which has received notice pursuant to paragraph (b) shall advise the associated person in writing stating whether the member:

(A) approves the person's participation in the proposed transaction; or

(B) disapproves the person's participation in the proposed transaction.

(2) If the member approves a person's participation in a transaction pursuant to paragraph (c)(1), the transaction shall be recorded on the books and records of the member and the member shall supervise the person's participation in the transaction as if the transaction were executed on behalf of the member.

(3) If the member disapproves a person's participation pursuant to paragraph (c)(1), the person shall not participate in the transaction in any manner, directly or indirectly.

(d) Transactions Not for Compensation

In the case of a transaction or a series of related transactions in which an associated person has not and will not receive any selling compensation, a member which has received notice pursuant to paragraph (b) shall provide the associated person prompt written acknowledgment of said notice and may, at its discretion, require the person to adhere to specified conditions in connection with his participation in the transaction.

(e) Definitions

For purposes of this Rule, the following terms shall have the stated meanings:

(1) "Private securities transaction" shall mean any securities transaction outside the regular course or scope of an associated person's employment with a member, including, though not limited to, new offerings of securities which are not registered with the Commission, provided however that transactions subject to the notification requirements of Rule 3210, transactions among immediate family members (as defined

in FINRA Rule 5130), for which no associated person receives any selling compensation, and personal transactions in investment company and variable annuity securities, shall be excluded.

(2) "Selling compensation" shall mean any compensation paid directly or indirectly from whatever source in connection with or as a result of the purchase or sale of a security, including, though not limited to, commissions; finder's fees; securities or rights to acquire securities; rights of participation in profits, tax benefits, or dissolution proceeds, as a general partner or otherwise; or expense reimbursements.

---

22. FINRA Rules: 4513 – Written Customer Complaints

(a) Each member shall keep and preserve in each office of supervisory jurisdiction either a separate file of all written customer complaints that relate to that office (including complaints that relate to activities supervised from that office) and action taken by the member, if any, or a separate record of such complaints and a clear reference to the files in that office containing the correspondence connected with such complaints. Rather than keep and preserve the customer complaint records required under this Rule at the office of supervisory jurisdiction, the member may choose to make them promptly available at that office, upon request of FINRA. Customer complaint records shall be preserved for a period of at least four years.

(b) For purposes of this Rule, "customer complaint" means any grievance by a customer or any person authorized to act on behalf of the customer involving the activities of the member or a person associated with the member in connection with the solicitation or execution of any transaction or the disposition of securities or funds of that customer.

---

23. FINRA Rules: 4330 – Customer Protection – Permissible Use of Customers' Securities

(a) Authorization to Lend Customers' Margin Securities
No member shall lend securities that are held on margin for a customer and that are eligible to be pledged or loaned, unless such member shall first have obtained a written authorization from such customer permitting the lending of such securities.

(b) Requirements for Borrowing of Customers' Fully Paid or Excess Margin Securities
(1) A member that borrows fully paid or excess margin securities carried for the account of any customer shall:
(A) comply with the requirements of SEA Rule 15c3-3;
(B) comply with the requirements of Section 15(e) of the Exchange Act; and
(C) notify FINRA, in such manner and format as FINRA may require, at least 30 days prior to first engaging in such securities borrows.
(2) Prior to first entering into securities borrows with a customer pursuant to paragraph (b)(1) of this Rule, a member shall:

(A) have reasonable grounds for believing that the customer's loan(s) of securities are appropriate for the customer. In making this determination, the member shall exercise reasonable diligence to ascertain the essential facts relative to the customer, including, but not limited to, the customer's financial situation and needs, tax status, investment objectives, investment time horizon, liquidity needs, risk tolerance and any other information the customer may disclose to the member or associated person in connection with entering such securities loans.

(B) provide the customer, in writing (which may be electronic), with the following:

(i) clear and prominent notice stating that the provisions of the Securities Investor Protection Act of 1970 may not protect the customer with respect to the customer's securities loan transaction and that the collateral delivered to the customer may constitute the only source of satisfaction of the member's obligation in the event the member fails to return the securities; and

(ii) disclosures regarding the customer's rights with respect to the loaned securities, and the risks and financial impact associated with the customer's loan(s) of securities, including, but not limited to:

a. loss of voting rights;

b. the customer's right to sell the loaned securities and any limitations on the customer's ability to do so, if applicable;

c. the factors that determine the amount of compensation received by the member and its associated persons in connection with the use of the securities borrowed from the customer;

d. the factors that determine the amount of compensation (e.g., interest rate) to be paid to the customer and whether or not such compensation can be changed by the member under the terms of the borrow agreement;

e. the risks associated with each type of collateral provided to the customer;

f. that the securities may be "hard-to-borrow" because of short-selling or may be used to satisfy delivery requirements resulting from short sales;

g. potential tax implications, including payments deemed cash-in-lieu of dividend paid on securities while on loan; and

h. the member's right to liquidate the transaction because of a condition of the kind specified in Rule 4314(b).

(3) A member that is subject to paragraph (b)(1) of this Rule shall create and maintain records evidencing the member's compliance with the requirements of paragraph (b)(2) of this Rule. Such records shall be maintained in accordance with the requirements of SEA Rule 17a-4(a).

---

24. FINRA Rules: 4530 – Reporting Requirements

(a) Each member shall promptly report to FINRA, but in any event not later than 30 calendar days, after the member knows or should have known of the existence of any of the following:

(1) the member or an associated person of the member:

(A) has been found to have violated any securities-, insurance-, commodities-, financial- or investment-related laws, rules, regulations or standards of conduct of any domestic or foreign regulatory body, self-regulatory organization or business or professional organization;

(B) is the subject of any written customer complaint involving allegations of theft or misappropriation of funds or securities or of forgery;

(C) is named as a defendant or respondent in any proceeding brought by a domestic or foreign regulatory body or self-regulatory organization alleging the violation of any provision of the Exchange Act, or of any other federal, state or foreign securities, insurance or commodities statute, or of any rule or regulation thereunder, or of any provision of the by-laws, rules or similar governing instruments of any securities, insurance or commodities domestic or foreign regulatory body or self-regulatory organization;

(D) is denied registration or is expelled, enjoined, directed to cease and desist, suspended or otherwise disciplined by any securities, insurance or commodities industry domestic or foreign regulatory body or self-regulatory organization or is denied membership or continued membership in any such self-regulatory organization; or is barred from becoming associated with any member of any such self-regulatory organization;

(E) is indicted, or convicted of, or pleads guilty to, or pleads no contest to, any felony; or any misdemeanor that involves the purchase or sale of any security, the taking of a false oath, the making of a false report, bribery, perjury, burglary, larceny, theft, robbery, extortion, forgery, counterfeiting, fraudulent concealment, embezzlement, fraudulent conversion, or misappropriation of funds, or securities, or a conspiracy to commit any of these offenses, or substantially equivalent activity in a domestic, military or foreign court;

(F) is a director, controlling stockholder, partner, officer or sole proprietor of, or an associated person with, a broker, dealer, investment company, investment advisor, underwriter or insurance company that was suspended, expelled or had its registration denied or revoked by any domestic or foreign regulatory body, jurisdiction or organization or is associated in such a capacity with a bank, trust company or other financial institution that was convicted of or pleaded no contest to, any felony or misdemeanor in a domestic or foreign court;

(G) is a defendant or respondent in any securities- or commodities-related civil litigation or arbitration, is a defendant or respondent in any financial-related insurance civil litigation or arbitration, or is the subject of any claim for damages by a customer, broker or dealer that relates to the provision of financial services or relates to a financial transaction, and such civil litigation, arbitration or claim for damages has been disposed of by judgment, award or settlement for an amount exceeding $15,000. However, when the member is the defendant or respondent or is the subject of any claim for damages by a customer, broker or dealer, then the reporting to FINRA shall be required only when such judgment, award or settlement is for an amount exceeding $25,000; or

(H)(i) is subject to a "statutory disqualification" as that term is defined in the Exchange Act; or (ii) is involved in the sale of any financial instrument, the provision of any investment advice or the financing of any such activities with any person that is subject to a "statutory disqualification" as that term is defined in the Exchange Act, provided, however, that this requirement shall not apply to activities with a member or an associated person that has been approved (or is otherwise permitted pursuant to FINRA rules and the federal securities laws) to be a member or to be associated with a member. The report shall include the name of the person subject to the statutory disqualification and details concerning the disqualification; or

(2) an associated person of the member is the subject of any disciplinary action taken by the member involving suspension, termination, the withholding of compensation or of any other remuneration in excess of $2,500, the imposition of fines in excess of $2,500 or is otherwise disciplined in any manner that would have a significant limitation on the individual's activities on a temporary or permanent basis.

(b) Each member shall promptly report to FINRA, but in any event not later than 30 calendar days, after the member has concluded or reasonably should have concluded that an associated person of the member or the member itself has violated any securities-, insurance-, commodities-, financial- or investment-related laws, rules, regulations or standards of conduct of any domestic or foreign regulatory body or self-regulatory organization.

(c) Each person associated with a member shall promptly report to the member the existence of any of the events set forth in paragraph (a)(1) of this Rule.

(d) Each member shall report to FINRA statistical and summary information regarding written customer complaints in such detail as FINRA shall specify by the 15th day of the month following the calendar quarter in which customer complaints are received by the member.

(e) Nothing contained in this Rule shall eliminate, reduce or otherwise abrogate the responsibilities of a member to promptly disclose required information on the Forms BD, U4 or U5, as applicable, to make any other required filings or to respond to FINRA with respect to any customer complaint, examination or inquiry. In addition, members are required to comply with the reporting obligations under paragraphs (a), (b) and (d) of this Rule, regardless of whether the information is reported or disclosed pursuant to any other rule or requirement, including the requirements of the Form BD. However, a member need not report: (1) an event otherwise required to be reported under paragraph (a)(1) of this Rule if the member discloses the event on the Form U4, consistent with the requirements of that form, and indicates, in such manner and format that FINRA may require, that such disclosure satisfies the requirements of paragraph (a)(1) of this Rule, as applicable; or (2) an event otherwise required to be reported under paragraphs (a) or (b) of this Rule if the member discloses the event on the Form U5, consistent with the requirements of that form.

(f) Each member shall promptly file with FINRA copies of:

  (1) any indictment, information or other criminal complaint or plea agreement for conduct reportable under paragraph (a)(1)(E) of this Rule;

  (2) any complaint in which a member is named as a defendant or respondent in any securities- or commodities-related private civil litigation, or is named as a defendant or respondent in any financial-related insurance private civil litigation;

  (3) any securities- or commodities-related arbitration claim, or financial-related insurance arbitration claim, filed against a member in any forum other than the FINRA Dispute Resolution forum;

  (4) any indictment, information or other criminal complaint, any plea agreement, or any private civil complaint or arbitration claim against a person associated with a member that is reportable under question 14 on Form U4, irrespective of any dollar thresholds Form U4 imposes for notification, unless, in the case of an arbitration claim, the claim has been filed in the FINRA Dispute Resolution forum.

(g) Members may file electronically, in such manner and format as specified by FINRA, the documents required by paragraph (f); provided, however, that the filings shall be accompanied by summary information regarding the documents in such detail as specified by FINRA.

(h) Members shall not be required to comply separately with paragraph (f) in the event that any of the documents required by paragraph (f) have been the subject of a request by FINRA's Registration and Disclosure staff, provided that the member produces those requested documents to the Registration and Disclosure staff not later than 30 days after receipt of such request. This paragraph does not supersede any FINRA rule or policy that requires production of documents specified in paragraph (f) sooner than 30 days after receipt of a request by the Registration and Disclosure staff.

25. FINRA Rules: 5110(h) – Non-cash Compensation

(h) Non-Cash Compensation
  (1) Definitions. The terms "compensation," "non-cash compensation" and "offeror" as used in this paragraph
    (i) shall have the following meanings:
      (A) "Compensation" shall mean cash compensation and non-cash compensation.
      (B) "Non-cash compensation" shall mean any form of compensation received in connection with the sale and distribution of securities that is not cash compensation, including but not limited to merchandise, gifts and prizes, travel expenses, meals and lodging.
      (C) "Offeror" shall mean an issuer, an adviser to an issuer, an underwriter and any affiliated person of such entities.
  (2) Restrictions on Non-Cash Compensation. In connection with the sale and distribution of a public offering of securities, no member or person associated with a member shall directly or indirectly accept or make payments or offers of payments of any non-cash compensation, except as provided in this provision. Non-cash compensation arrangements are limited to the following:
      (A) Gifts that do not exceed an annual amount per person fixed periodically by the Board of Governors and are not preconditioned on achievement of a sales target.
      (B) An occasional meal, a ticket to a sporting event or the theater, or comparable entertainment which is neither so frequent nor so extensive as to raise any question of propriety and is not preconditioned on achievement of a sales target.
      (C) Payment or reimbursement by offerors in connection with meetings held by an offeror or by a member for the purpose of training or education of associated persons of a member, provided that:
        (i) associated persons obtain the member's prior approval to attend the meeting and attendance by a member's associated persons is not conditioned by the member on the achievement of a sales target or any other incentives pursuant to a non-cash compensation arrangement permitted by paragraph (h)(2)(D);
        (ii) the location is appropriate to the purpose of the meeting, which shall mean an office of the issuer or affiliate thereof, the office of the member, or a facility located in the vicinity of such office, or a regional location with respect to regional meetings;
        (iii) the payment or reimbursement is not applied to the expenses of guests of the associated person; and
        (iv) the payment or reimbursement by the issuer or affiliate of the issuer is not conditioned by the issuer or an affiliate of the issuer on the achievement of a sales target or any other non-cash compensation arrangement permitted by paragraph (h)(2)(D).
      (D) Non-cash compensation arrangements between a member and its associated persons or a company that controls a member company and the member's associated persons, provided that no unaffiliated non-member company or other unaffiliated member directly or indirectly participates in the member's or non-member's organization of a permissible non-cash compensation arrangement; and
      (E) Contributions by a non-member company or other member to a non-cash compensation arrangement between a member and its associated persons, provided that the arrangement meets the criteria in paragraph (h)(2)(D).
  A member shall maintain records of all non-cash compensation received by the member or its associated persons in arrangements permitted by paragraphs (h)(2)(C) through (E). The records shall include: the names of the offerors, non-members or other members making the non-cash compensation contributions; the names of the associated persons participating in the arrangements; the nature and value of non-cash compensation received; the location of training and education meetings; and any other information that proves compliance by the member and its associated persons with paragraphs (h)(2)(C) through (E).

26. FINRA Rules: 8312 – FINRA's BrokerCheck Disclosure

(a) In response to a written inquiry, electronic inquiry, or telephonic inquiry via a toll-free telephone listing, FINRA shall release through FINRA BrokerCheck information regarding:

    (1) a current or former FINRA member or a current or former member of a registered national securities exchange that uses the Central Registration Depository ("CRD") for registration purposes ("CRD Exchange") (collectively, "BrokerCheck Firms"); or

    (2) a current or former associated person of a BrokerCheck Firm.

(b)(1) Except as otherwise provided in paragraph (d) below, FINRA shall release the information specified in sub-paragraph (2) below for inquiries regarding a current or former BrokerCheck Firm, a person currently associated with a BrokerCheck Firm, or a person who was associated with a BrokerCheck Firm within the preceding ten years.

    (2) The following information shall be released pursuant to this paragraph (b):

        (A) any information reported on the most recently filed Form U4, Form U5, Form U6, Form BD, and Form BDW (collectively "Registration Forms");

        (B) currently approved registrations;

        (C) summary information about certain arbitration awards against a BrokerCheck Firm involving a securities or commodities dispute with a public customer;

        (D) the most recently submitted comment, if any, provided to FINRA by the person who is covered by BrokerCheck, in the form and in accordance with the procedures established by FINRA, for inclusion with the information provided through BrokerCheck. Only comments that relate to the information provided through BrokerCheck will be included;

        (E) information as to qualifications examinations passed by the person and date passed. FINRA will not release information regarding examination scores or failed examinations;

        (F) in response to telephonic inquiries via the BrokerCheck toll-free telephone listing, whether a particular member is subject to the provisions of Rule 3170 ("Taping Rule");

        (G) Historic Complaints (i.e., the information last reported on Registration Forms relating to customer complaints that are more than two (2) years old and that have not been settled or adjudicated, and customer complaints, arbitrations or litigations that have been settled for an amount less than $10,000 prior to May 18, 2009 or an amount less than $15,000 on or after May 18, 2009 and are no longer reported on a Registration Form), provided that any such matter became a Historic Complaint on or after August 16, 1999; and

        (H) the name and succession history for current or former BrokerCheck Firms.

(c)(1) Except as otherwise provided in paragraph (d) below, FINRA shall release the information specified in sub-paragraph (2) below for inquiries regarding a person who was formerly associated with a BrokerCheck Firm, but who has not been associated with a BrokerCheck Firm within the preceding ten years, and:

        (A) was ever the subject of a final regulatory action as defined in Form U4 that has been reported to the CRD system on a Registration Form; or

        (B) was registered with FINRA or a CRD Exchange on or after August 16, 1999, and any of the following applies, as reported to the CRD system on a Registration Form:

            (i) was convicted of or pled guilty or nolo contendere to a crime;

            (ii) was the subject of a civil injunction in connection with investment-related activity, a civil court finding of involvement in a violation of any investment-related statute or regulation, or an investment-related civil action brought by a state or foreign financial regulatory authority that was dismissed pursuant to a settlement agreement; or

            (iii) was named as a respondent or defendant in an investment-related, consumer-initiated arbitration or civil litigation which alleged that the person was involved in a sales practice violation and which resulted in an arbitration award or civil judgment against the person.

(2) The following information shall be released pursuant to this paragraph (c):

    (A) information regarding the event(s) enumerated in paragraph (c)(1)(A) or (B) as reported on a Registration Form;

    (B) administrative information, including employment history and registration history derived from information reported on a Registration Form;

    (C) the most recently submitted comment, if any, provided to FINRA by the person who is covered by BrokerCheck, in the form and in accordance with the procedures established by FINRA, for inclusion with the information provided through BrokerCheck. Only comments that relate to the information provided through BrokerCheck will be included; and

    (D) information as to qualifications examinations passed by the person and date passed. FINRA will not release information regarding examination scores or failed examinations.

For purposes of this paragraph (c), a final regulatory action as defined in Form U4 may include any final action, including any action that is on appeal, by the SEC, the Commodity Futures Trading Commission, a federal banking agency, the National Credit Union Administration, another federal regulatory agency, a state regulatory agency, a foreign financial regulatory authority, or a self-regulatory organization (as those terms are used in Form U4).

(d) FINRA shall not release:

    (1) information reported as a Social Security number, residential history, or physical description, information that FINRA is otherwise prohibited from releasing under Federal law, or information that is provided solely for use by regulators. FINRA reserves the right to exclude, on a case-by-case basis, information that contains confidential customer information, offensive or potentially defamatory language or information that raises significant identity theft, personal safety or privacy concerns that are not outweighed by investor protection concerns;

    (2) information reported on Registration Forms relating to regulatory investigations or proceedings if the reported regulatory investigation or proceeding was vacated or withdrawn by the instituting authority;

    (3) "Internal Review Disclosure" information reported on Section 7 of the Form U5;

    (4) "Reason for Termination" information reported on Section 3 of the Form U5;

    (5) events reported on Section 7 of the Form U5 (other than an "Internal Review Disclosure" event) for three business days after FINRA's processing of the filing. However, if an event is reported on Form U5 and the same event is thereafter reported on Form U4 prior to the expiration of the three-business-day period, FINRA will release the Forms U4 and U5 information simultaneously upon processing. Under such circumstances, the three-business-day period may be curtailed;

    (6) the most recent information reported on a Registration Form, if:

        (A) FINRA has determined that the information was reported in error by a BrokerCheck Firm, regulator or other appropriate authority;

        (B) the information has been determined by regulators, through amendments to the uniform Registration Forms, to be no longer relevant to securities registration or licensure, regardless of the disposition of the event or the date the event occurred;

    (7) information provided on Schedule E of Form BD.

(e) Eligible parties may dispute the accuracy of certain information disclosed through FINRA BrokerCheck pursuant to the administrative process described below:

    (1) Initiation of a Dispute

        (A) The following persons (each an "eligible party") may initiate a dispute regarding the accuracy of information disclosed in that eligible party's BrokerCheck report:

            (i) any current BrokerCheck Firm;

            (ii) any former BrokerCheck Firm, provided that the dispute is submitted by a natural person who served as the former BrokerCheck Firm's Chief Executive Officer, Chief Financial Officer, Chief Operating Officer, Chief Legal Officer or Chief Compliance Officer, or individual with similar status or function, as identified on Schedule A of Form BD at the time the former BrokerCheck Firm ceased being registered with FINRA or a CRD Exchange; or

(iii) any associated person of a BrokerCheck Firm or person formerly associated with a BrokerCheck Firm for whom a BrokerCheck report is available.

(B) To initiate a dispute, an eligible party must submit a written notice to FINRA, in such manner and format that FINRA may require, identifying the alleged inaccurate factual information and explaining the reason that such information is allegedly inaccurate. The eligible party must submit with the written notice all available supporting documentation.

(2) Determination of Disputes Eligible for Investigation

(A) FINRA will presume that a dispute of factual information is eligible for investigation unless FINRA reasonably determines that the facts and circumstances involving the dispute suggest otherwise.

(B) If FINRA determines that a dispute is eligible for investigation, FINRA will, except in circumstances involving court-ordered expungement, add a notation to the eligible party's BrokerCheck report stating that the eligible party has disputed certain information included in the report. The notation will be removed from the eligible party's BrokerCheck report upon resolution of the dispute by FINRA. In disputes involving a court order to expunge information from BrokerCheck, FINRA will prevent the disputed information from being displayed via BrokerCheck while FINRA evaluates the matter.

(C) If FINRA determines that a dispute is not eligible for investigation, it will notify the eligible party of this determination in writing, including a brief description of the reason for the determination. A determination by FINRA that a dispute is not eligible for investigation is not subject to appeal.

(3) Investigation and Resolution of Disputes

(A) If FINRA determines that the written notice and supporting documentation submitted by the eligible party is sufficient to update, modify or remove the information that is the subject of the request, FINRA will make the appropriate change. If the written notice and supporting documentation do not include sufficient information upon which FINRA can make a determination, FINRA, under most circumstances, will contact the entity that reported the disputed information (the "reporting entity") to the CRD system and request that the reporting entity verify that the information, as disclosed through BrokerCheck, is accurate in content and presentation. If a reporting entity other than FINRA is involved, FINRA will defer to the reporting entity about whether the information received is accurate. If the reporting entity acknowledges that the information is not accurate, FINRA will update, modify or remove the information, as appropriate, based on the information provided by the reporting entity. If the reporting entity confirms that the information is accurate in content and presentation or the reporting entity no longer exists or is otherwise unable to verify the accuracy of the information, FINRA will not change the information.

(B) FINRA will notify the eligible party that the investigation has resulted in a determination that:

(i) the information is inaccurate or not accurately presented and has been updated, modified or deleted;

(ii) the information is accurate in content and presentation and no changes have been made; or

(iii) the accuracy of the information or its presentation could not be verified and no changes have been made.

(C) A determination by FINRA, including a determination to leave unchanged or to modify or delete disputed information, is not subject to appeal.

(f) Upon written request, FINRA may provide a compilation of information about FINRA members, subject to terms and conditions established by FINRA and after execution of a licensing agreement prepared by FINRA. FINRA may charge commercial users of such information reasonable fees as determined by FINRA. Such compilations shall consist solely of information selected by FINRA from Forms BD and BDW and shall be limited to information that is otherwise publicly available from the SEC.

27. CBOE Rule: 7.10 – Fingerprint-based Background Checks of Exchange Directors, Officers, Employees and Others

(a) In order to enhance the security of the facilities, systems, data, and records of the Exchange (collectively, "facilities and records"), the Exchange conducts fingerprint-based criminal records checks of (i) directors, officers and employees of the Exchange, and (ii) temporary personnel, independent contractors, consultants, vendors and service providers who have or are anticipated to have access to its facilities and records (collectively, "contractors"). The Exchange also conducts fingerprint-based criminal records checks of Exchange director candidates that are not already serving on the Exchange's Board before they are formally nominated and of employee candidates after an offer of employment has been made by the Exchange. The Exchange may choose to not obtain fingerprints from, or to seek fingerprint-based information with respect to, any contractor due to that contractor's limited, supervised, or restricted access to facilities and records, or the nature or location of his or her work or services, or if the contractor's employer conducts fingerprint based criminal records checks of its personnel.

(b) The Exchange shall submit fingerprints obtained pursuant to this rule to the Attorney General of the United States or his or her designee for identification and processing. The Exchange shall at all times maintain the security of all fingerprints provided to, and all criminal history record information received from, the Attorney General or his or her designee. The Exchange shall redisseminate fingerprints and criminal history record information only to the extent permitted by applicable law.

(c) The Exchange shall evaluate information received from the Attorney General or his or her designee and otherwise administer this rule in accordance with Exchange fingerprint procedures as in effect from time to time and the provisions of applicable law. Fingerprint-based criminal record information that reflects felony or misdemeanor convictions will be a factor in making employment decisions; engaging or retaining any contractors; or permitting any fingerprinted person access to facilities and records.

(d) Any employee who refuses to submit to fingerprinting will be subject to progressive discipline up to and including the termination of employment. Any person who is given an offer of employment with the Exchange who refuses to submit to fingerprinting will have the offer withdrawn. A contractor who refuses to submit to fingerprinting will be denied access to facilities and records.

---

28. MSRB Rules: G-2 – Standards of Professional Qualifications

Summary: Prohibits dealers from effecting transactions in municipal securities and municipal advisors from engaging in municipal advisory activities unless they and their associated personnel are qualified in accordance with MSRB rules.

No broker, dealer or municipal securities dealer shall effect any transaction in, or induce or attempt to induce the purchase or sale of, any municipal security, and no municipal advisor shall engage in municipal advisory activities, unless such broker, dealer, municipal securities dealer or municipal advisor and every natural person associated with such broker, dealer, municipal securities dealer or municipal advisor is qualified in accordance with the rules of the Board.

---

29. MSRB Rules: G-3 – Professional Qualification Requirements

Summary: Establishes professional qualification and continuing education requirements for, and specifies the number of supervisory personnel who must be associated with, dealers and municipal advisors.

No broker, dealer, municipal securities dealer, municipal advisor or person who is a municipal securities representative, municipal securities sales limited representative, limited representative - investment company and variable contracts products, municipal securities principal, municipal fund securities limited principal, municipal securities sales principal, municipal advisor representative or municipal advisor principal (as hereafter defined) shall be qualified for purposes of Rule G-2 unless such broker, dealer, municipal securities dealer, municipal advisor or person meets the requirements of this rule.

(a) Municipal Securities Representative, Municipal Securities Sales Limited Representative and Limited Representative - Investment Company and Variable Contracts Products.

  (i) Definitions.

    (A) The term "municipal securities representative" means a natural person associated with a broker, dealer or municipal securities dealer, other than a person whose functions are solely clerical or ministerial, whose activities include one or more of the following:

      (1) underwriting, trading or sales of municipal securities;

      (2) financial advisory or consultant services for issuers in connection with the issuance of municipal securities;

      (3) research or investment advice with respect to municipal securities; or

      (4) any other activities which involve communication, directly or indirectly, with public investors in municipal securities;

      provided, however, that the activities enumerated in subparagraphs (3) and (4) above shall be limited to such activities as they relate to the activities enumerated in subparagraphs (1) and (2) above.

    (B) The term "municipal securities sales limited representative" means a municipal securities representative whose activities with respect to municipal securities are limited exclusively to sales to and purchases from customers of municipal securities.

    (C) The term "limited representative – investment company and variable contracts products" means a municipal securities representative whose activities with respect to municipal securities are limited exclusively to sales to and purchases from customers of municipal fund securities.

  (ii) Qualification Requirements.

    (A) Except as otherwise provided in this paragraph (a)(ii), any person seeking to become qualified as a municipal securities representative, in accordance with the requirements under this subparagraph, shall take and pass the Securities Industry Essentials Examination ("SIE") and the Municipal Securities Representative Qualification Examination prior to being qualified as a municipal securities representative.

    (B) The requirements of subparagraph (a)(ii)(A) of this rule shall not apply to:

      (1) any person who is duly qualified as a general securities representative by reason of having taken and passed the General Securities Registered Representative Examination before November 7, 2011, and

      (2) a municipal securities sales limited representative who is duly qualified as a general securities representative by reason of having taken and passed the General Securities Registered Representative Examination.

      (3) any person who is duly qualified as a limited representative - investment company and variable contracts products by reason of having taken and passed the Limited Representative - Investment Company and Variable Contracts Products Examination.

(C) Any person who ceases to be associated with a broker, dealer or municipal securities dealer (whether as a municipal securities representative or otherwise) for two or more years at any time after having qualified as a municipal securities representative in accordance with subparagraph (a)(ii)(A) or (B) shall again meet the requirements of subparagraph (a)(ii)(A) or (B) prior to being qualified as a municipal securities representative.

(b) Municipal Securities Principal; Municipal Fund Securities Limited Principal.

(i) Definition. The term "municipal securities principal" means a natural person (other than a municipal securities sales principal), associated with a broker, dealer or municipal securities dealer who is directly engaged in the management, direction or supervision of one or more of the following activities:

(A) underwriting, trading or sales of municipal securities;

(B) financial advisory or consultant services for issuers in connection with the issuance of municipal securities;

(C) processing, clearance, and, in the case of brokers, dealers and municipal securities dealers other than bank dealers, safekeeping of municipal securities;

(D) research or investment advice with respect to municipal securities;

(E) any other activities which involve communication, directly or indirectly, with public investors in municipal securities;

(F) maintenance of records with respect to the activities described in subparagraphs (A) through (E); or

(G) training of municipal securities principals or municipal securities representatives.

provided, however, that the activities enumerated in subparagraphs (D) and (E) above shall be limited to such activities as they relate to the activities enumerated in subparagraphs (A) or (B) above.

(ii) Qualification Requirements.

(A) Every municipal securities principal shall take and pass the Municipal Securities Principal Qualification Examination prior to being qualified as a municipal securities principal. The passing grade shall be determined by the Board.

(B) Any person seeking to become qualified as a municipal securities principal in accordance with subparagraph (b)(ii)(A) of this rule must, prior to being qualified as a municipal securities principal:

(1) have been duly qualified as either a municipal securities representative or a general securities representative; provided, however, that any person who qualifies as a municipal securities representative solely by reason of subparagraph (a)(ii)(C) shall not be qualified to take the Municipal Securities Principal Qualification Examination on or after October 1, 2002, and any person who qualifies as a municipal securities representative solely by reason of clause (a)(ii)(B)(2) shall not be qualified to take the Municipal Securities Principal Qualification Examination on or after November 7, 2011; or

(2) have taken and passed either the Municipal Securities Representative Qualification Examination or, in the case of persons described in clause (a)(ii)(B)(1), the General Securities Registered Representative Examination.

(C) Any person who ceases to act as a municipal securities principal for two or more years at any time after having qualified as such shall meet the requirements of subparagraphs (b)(ii)(A) and (B) prior to being qualified as a municipal securities principal.

(D) For the first 120 calendar days after becoming a municipal securities principal, the requirements of subparagraph (b)(ii)(A) shall not apply to any person who is qualified as a municipal securities representative or general securities representative, provided that such qualified representative has at least 18 months of experience functioning as a representative within the five-year period immediately preceding the principal designation, or as a general securities principal, provided, however, that each such person shall take and pass the Municipal Securities Principal Qualification Examination within that period.

(iii) Numerical Requirements. Every broker, dealer and municipal securities dealer shall have at least two municipal securities principals, except:

(A) every broker, dealer or municipal securities dealer which is a member of a registered securities association and which conducts a general securities business, or

(B) every broker, dealer or municipal securities dealer having fewer than eleven persons associated with it in whatever capacity on a full-time or full-time equivalent basis who are engaged in the performance of its municipal securities activities, or, in the case of a bank dealer, in the performance of its municipal securities dealer activities, shall have at least one municipal securities principal.

(iv) Municipal Fund Securities Limited Principal.

(A) Definition. The term "municipal fund securities limited principal" means a natural person (other than a municipal securities principal or municipal securities sales principal), associated with a broker, dealer or municipal securities dealer that has filed with the Board in compliance with rule A-12, who is directly engaged in the functions of a municipal securities principal as set forth in paragraph (b)(i), but solely as such activities relate to transactions in municipal fund securities.

(B) Qualification Requirements.

(1) Every municipal fund securities limited principal shall take and pass the Municipal Fund Securities Limited Principal Qualification Examination prior to being qualified as a municipal fund securities limited principal. The passing grade shall be determined by the Board.

(2) Any person seeking to become qualified as a municipal fund securities limited principal in accordance with clause (b)(iv)(B)(1) of this rule must, as a condition to being qualified as a municipal fund securities limited principal:

(a) have been duly qualified as either a general securities principal or an investment company/variable contracts limited principal; or

(b) have taken and passed either the General Securities Principal Qualification Examination or the Investment Company and Annuity Principal Qualification Examination.

(3) Any person who ceases to act as a municipal fund securities limited principal for two or more years at any time after having qualified as such shall meet the requirements of clauses (b)(iv)(B)(1) and (2) prior to being qualified as a municipal fund securities limited principal.

(4) For the first 120 calendar days after becoming a municipal fund securities limited principal, the requirements of clauses (b)(iv)(B)(1) and (2) shall not apply to any person who is qualified as a general securities representative or investment company/variable contracts limited representative, provided that such qualified representative has at least 18 months of experience functioning as a representative within the five-year period immediately preceding the principal designation, or as a general securities principal or investment company/variable contracts limited principal, provided, however, that each such person shall meet the requirements of clauses (b)(iv)(B)(1) and (2) within that period.

(C) Actions as Municipal Securities Principal. Any municipal fund securities limited principal may undertake all actions required or permitted under any Board rule to be taken by a municipal securities principal, but solely with respect to activities related to municipal fund securities, and shall be subject to all provisions of Board rules applicable to municipal securities principals except to the extent inconsistent with this paragraph (b)(iv).

(D) Numerical Requirements. Any broker, dealer or municipal securities dealer whose municipal securities activities are limited exclusively to municipal fund securities may count any municipal fund securities limited principal toward the numerical requirement for municipal securities principal set forth in paragraph (b)(iii).

(c) Municipal Securities Sales Principal.

(i) Definition. The term "municipal securities sales principal" means a natural person (other than a municipal securities principal) associated with a broker, dealer or municipal securities dealer (other than a bank dealer) whose supervisory activities with respect to municipal securities are limited exclusively to supervising sales to and purchases from customers of municipal securities.

(ii) Qualification Requirements.

    (A) Every municipal securities sales principal shall take and pass the General Securities Sales Supervisor Qualification Examination prior to acting in such capacity. The passing grade shall be determined by the Board.

    (B) Any person seeking to become qualified as a municipal securities sales principal in accordance with subparagraph (c)(ii)(A) of this rule, must, prior to being qualified as a municipal securities sales principal:

        (1) have been duly qualified as either a municipal securities representative or a general securities representative; or

        (2) have taken and passed either the Municipal Securities Representative Qualification Examination or the General Securities Registered Representative Examination.

    (C) Any person who ceases to act as a municipal securities sales principal for two or more years at any time after having qualified as such shall meet the requirements of subparagraphs (c)(ii)(A) and (B) prior to being qualified as a municipal securities sales principal.

    (D) For the first 120 calendar days after becoming a municipal securities sales principal, the requirements of subparagraph (c)(ii)(A) shall not apply to any person who is qualified as a municipal securities representative or general securities representative, provided that such qualified representative has at least 18 months of experience functioning as a representative within the five-year period immediately preceding the principal designation, or as a general securities principal, provided, however, that each such person shall take and pass the General Securities Sales Supervisory Qualification Examination within that period.

(d) Municipal Advisor Representative

  (i) Definition.

    (A) The term "municipal advisor representative" means a natural person associated with a municipal advisor who engages in municipal advisory activities on the municipal advisor's behalf, other than a person performing only clerical, administrative, support or similar functions.

  (ii) Qualification Requirements.

    (A) Every municipal advisor representative shall take and pass the Municipal Advisor Representative Qualification Examination prior to being qualified as a municipal advisor representative. The passing grade shall be determined by the Board.

    (B) Any person who ceases to be associated with a municipal advisor for two or more years at any time after having qualified as a municipal advisor representative in accordance with subparagraph (d)(ii)(A) shall take and pass the Municipal Advisor Representative Qualification Examination prior to being qualified as a municipal advisor representative, unless a waiver is granted pursuant to subparagraph (h)(ii) of this rule.

(e) Municipal Advisor Principal

  (i) Definition. The term "municipal advisor principal" means a natural person associated with a municipal advisor who is directly engaged in the management, direction or supervision of the municipal advisory activities of the municipal advisor and its associated persons.

  (ii) Qualification Requirements.

    (A) To become qualified as a municipal advisor principal a person must:

        (1) As a pre-requisite take and pass the Municipal Advisor Representative Qualification Examination; and

        (2) Take and pass the Municipal Advisor Principal Qualification Examination.

      The passing score shall be determined by the Board.

    (B) Any person qualified as a municipal advisor principal who ceases to be associated with a municipal advisor for two or more years at any time after having qualified as a municipal advisor principal in accordance with subparagraph (e)(ii)(A) shall take and pass the Municipal Advisor Representative

Qualification Examination and the Municipal Advisor Principal Qualification Examination prior to being qualified as a municipal advisor principal, unless a waiver is granted pursuant to subparagraph (h)(ii) of this rule.

(C) For the first 120 calendar days after becoming a municipal advisor principal, the requirements of subparagraph (e)(ii)(A)(2) shall not apply to any person who is qualified as a municipal advisor representative, provided, however, that such person shall take and pass the Municipal Advisor Principal Qualification Examination within that period.

(iii) Numerical Requirements. Every municipal advisor shall have at least one municipal advisor principal.

(f) Confidentiality of Qualification Examinations. No associated person of a broker, dealer, municipal securities dealer or municipal advisor shall:

(i) in the course of taking a qualification examination required by this rule receive or give assistance of any nature;

(ii) disclose to any person questions, or answers to any questions, on any qualification examination required by this rule;

(iii) engage in any activity inconsistent with the confidential nature of any qualification examination required by this rule, or with its purpose as a test of the qualification of persons taking such examinations; or

(iv) knowingly sign a false certification concerning any such qualification examination.

(g) Retaking of Qualification Examinations. Any associated person of a broker, dealer, municipal securities dealer or municipal advisor who fails to pass a qualification examination prescribed by the Board shall be permitted to take the examination again after a period of 30 days has elapsed from the date of the prior examination, except that any person who fails to pass an examination three or more times in succession within a two-year period shall be prohibited from again taking the examination until a period of 180 calendar days has elapsed from the date of such person's last attempt to pass the examination.

(h) Waiver of Qualification Requirements.

(i) The requirements of paragraphs (a)(ii), (a)(iii), (b)(ii), (b)(iv)(B) and (c)(ii) may be waived in extraordinary cases for any associated person of a broker, dealer or municipal securities dealer who demonstrates extensive experience in a field closely related to the municipal securities activities of such broker, dealer or municipal securities dealer or as permitted pursuant to Supplementary Material .04 of this rule. Such waiver may be granted by

(A) a registered securities association with respect to a person associated with a member of such association, or

(B) the appropriate regulatory agency as defined in section 3(a)(34) of the Act with respect to a person associated with any other broker, dealer or municipal securities dealer.

(ii) The requirements of paragraph (d)(ii)(A) and (e)(ii)(A) may be waived by the Board in extraordinary cases for a municipal advisor representative or municipal advisor principal.

(i) Continuing Education Requirements

(i) Continuing Education Requirements for Brokers, Dealers, and Municipal Securities Dealers—This paragraph prescribes requirements regarding the continuing education of certain registered persons subsequent to their initial qualification and registration with a registered securities association with respect to a person associated with a member of such association, or the appropriate regulatory agency as defined in Section 3(a)(34) of the Act with respect to a person associated with any other broker, dealer or municipal securities dealer ("the appropriate enforcement authority"). The requirements shall consist of a Regulatory Element and a Firm Element as set forth below.

(A) Regulatory Element

(1) Requirements—No broker, dealer or municipal securities dealer shall permit any registered person to continue to, and no registered person shall continue to, perform duties as a registered person, unless such person has complied with the requirements of subparagraph (i)(i)(A) hereof. Each registered person shall complete the Regulatory Element on the occurrence of their second registration anniversary date and every three years thereafter or as otherwise prescribed by the

Board. On each occasion, the Regulatory Element must be completed within 120 days after the person's registration anniversary date. A person's initial registration date, also known as the "base date," shall establish the cycle of anniversary dates for purposes of this subparagraph (i)(i)(A). The content of the Regulatory Element shall be determined by the Board for each registration category of persons subject to the rule.

(2) Failure to Complete—Unless otherwise determined by the Board, any registered persons who have not completed the Regulatory Element within the prescribed time frames will have their registrations deemed inactive until such time as the requirements of the program have been satisfied. Any person whose registration has been deemed inactive under this clause (i)(i)(A)(2) shall cease all activities as a registered person and is prohibited from performing any duties and functioning in any capacity requiring registration. Such person may not receive any compensation for transactions in municipal securities, however, such person may receive trails, residual commissions or like compensation resulting from such transactions completed before the person's inactive status, unless the dealer with which the person is associated has a policy prohibiting such trails, residual commissions or like compensation. A registration that is inactive for a period of two years will be administratively terminated. A person whose registration is so terminated may reactivate the registration only by reapplying for registration and meeting the qualification requirements of the applicable provisions of this rule. The appropriate enforcement authority may, upon application and a showing of good cause, allow for additional time for a registered person to satisfy the program requirements.

(3) Disciplinary Actions—Unless otherwise determined by the appropriate enforcement authority, a registered person will be required to retake the Regulatory Element and satisfy all of its requirements in the event such person:

(a) becomes subject to any statutory disqualification as defined in Section 3(a)(39) of the Act;

(b) becomes subject to suspension or to the imposition of a fine of $5,000 or more for violation of any provision of any securities law or regulation, or any agreement with or rule or standard of conduct of any securities governmental agency, securities self-regulatory organization, the appropriate enforcement authority or as imposed by any such regulatory or self-regulatory organization in connection with a disciplinary proceeding; or

(c) is ordered as a sanction in a disciplinary action to retake the Regulatory Element by any securities governmental agency, the appropriate enforcement authority or securities self-regulatory organization.

The retaking of the Regulatory Element shall commence with participation within 120 days of the registered person becoming subject to the statutory disqualification, in the case of clause (a) above, or the completion of the sanction or the disciplinary action becomes final, in the case of clause (b) or clause (c) above. The date that the disciplinary action becomes final will be deemed the person's new base date for purposes of subparagraph (i)(i)(A).

(4) Reassociation—Any registered person who has terminated association with a broker, dealer or municipal securities dealer and who has, within two years of the date of termination, become reassociated in a registered capacity with a broker, dealer or municipal securities dealer shall participate in the Regulatory Element at such intervals that apply (second registration anniversary and every three years thereafter) based on the initial registration anniversary date rather than based on the date of reassociation in a registered capacity.

Any former registered person who becomes reassociated in a registered capacity with a broker, dealer or municipal securities dealer more than two years after termination as such will be required to satisfy the program's requirements in their entirety (second registration anniversary and every three years thereafter), based on the most recent registration date.

(5) Definition of Registered Person—For purposes of this subparagraph, the term "registered person" means any person registered with the appropriate enforcement authority as a municipal

securities representative, municipal securities principal, municipal securities sales principal or financial and operations principal pursuant to this rule.

    (6) Delivery of the Regulatory Element—The continuing education Regulatory Element program will be administered through Web-based delivery or such other technological manner and format as specified by the Board.

(B) Firm Element

    (1) Persons Subject to the Firm Element—The requirements of this subparagraph shall apply to any person registered with a broker, dealer or municipal securities dealer and qualified as a representative or principal in accordance with this rule or as a general securities principal and who regularly engages in or supervises municipal securities activities (collectively, "covered registered persons").

    (2) Standards for the Firm Element

        (a) Each broker, dealer and municipal securities dealer must maintain a continuing and current education program for its covered registered persons to enhance their securities knowledge, skill, and professionalism. At a minimum, each broker, dealer and municipal securities dealer shall at least annually evaluate and prioritize its training needs, develop a written training plan, and conduct training annually on municipal securities for covered registered persons. The plan must take into consideration the broker, dealer and municipal securities dealer's size, organizational structure, and scope of business activities, as well as regulatory developments and the performance of covered registered persons in the Regulatory Element.

        (b) Minimum Standards for Training Programs—Programs used to implement a broker, dealer or municipal securities dealer's training plan must be appropriate for the business of the broker, dealer or municipal securities dealer and, at a minimum must cover training in ethics and professional responsibility and the following matters concerning municipal securities products, services and strategies offered by the broker, dealer or municipal securities dealer:

            (i) General investment features and associated risk factors;

            (ii) Suitability and sales practice considerations;

            (iii) Applicable regulatory requirements.

        (c) Administration of Continuing Education Program—A broker, dealer or municipal securities dealer must administer its continuing education programs in accordance with its annual evaluation and written plan and must maintain records documenting the content of the programs and completion of the programs by covered registered persons.

    (3) Participation in the Firm Element—Covered registered persons included in a broker, dealer or municipal securities dealer's plan must participate in continuing education programs as required by the broker, dealer or municipal securities dealer.

    (4) Specific Training Requirements—The appropriate enforcement authority may require a broker, dealer or municipal securities dealer, individually or as part of a larger group, to provide specific training to its covered registered persons in such areas the appropriate enforcement authority deems appropriate. Such a requirement may stipulate the class of covered registered persons for which it is applicable, the time period in which the requirement must be satisfied and, where appropriate, the actual training content.

(ii) Continuing Education Requirements for Municipal Advisors

  (A) Persons Subject to Continuing Education Requirements—The requirements of this paragraph shall apply to any person qualified as either a municipal advisor representative or a municipal advisor principal with a municipal advisor in accordance with this rule (collectively, "covered persons").

  (B) Standards for a Continuing Education Program

    (1) Each municipal advisor must maintain a continuing and current education program for its covered persons to enhance their municipal advisory knowledge, skill, and professionalism. At a minimum, each municipal advisor shall at least annually evaluate and prioritize its training needs,

develop a written training plan, and conduct training annually on municipal advisory activities for covered persons.

The plan must take into consideration the municipal advisor's size, organizational structure, and scope of municipal advisory activities, as well as regulatory developments.

(2) Minimum Standards for Training Programs — Programs used to implement a municipal advisor's training plan must be appropriate for the business of the municipal advisor and, at a minimum must cover the following matters concerning municipal advisory activities, services and strategies offered by the municipal advisor:

(a) Fiduciary duty obligations owed to municipal entity clients; and

(b) Applicable regulatory requirements.

(3) Administration of Continuing Education Program—A municipal advisor must administer its continuing education program in accordance with its annual evaluation and written training plan and must maintain records documenting the content of the programs and completion of the programs by covered persons.

(C) Participation in the Continuing Education Program—Covered persons included in a municipal advisor's plan must participate in continuing education programs as required by the municipal advisor.

(D) Specific Training Requirements—A registered securities association with respect to a municipal advisor that is a member of such association, or the Commission, or the Commission's designee, with respect to any other municipal advisor ("the appropriate examining authority"), may require a municipal advisor, individually or as part of a larger group, to provide specific training to its covered persons in such areas the appropriate examining authority deems appropriate. Such a requirement may stipulate the class of covered persons for which it is applicable, the time period in which the requirement must be satisfied and, where appropriate, the actual training content.

(E) Each municipal advisor that is also subject to the Standards for the Firm Element as required by Rule G-3(i)(i)(B)(2) is permitted to satisfy the requirements of Rules G-3(i)(i)(B) and G-3(i)(ii), if the municipal advisor:

(1) Develops a single written training plan, if such training plan is consistent with the separate evaluations of the training needs as required under subparagraphs (i)(i)(B)(2)(a) and (i)(ii)(B)(1); and

(2) Conducts annual training for both covered persons and covered registered persons, if such training is consistent with the written training plan(s) and such training meets the minimum standards for training programs required by subparagraphs (i)(i)(B)(2)(b) and (i)(ii)(B)(2).

---

30. MSRB Rules: G-7 – Information Concerning Associated Persons

Summary: Requires dealers to obtain information from their associated personnel concerning their qualifications to engage in municipal securities business and contemplates that this information will be filed with the appropriate regulatory agency.

(a) No associated person (as hereinafter defined) of a broker, dealer or municipal securities dealer shall be qualified for purposes of Rule G-2 of the Board unless such associated person meets the requirements of this rule. The term "associated person" as used in this rule means (i) a municipal securities principal, (ii) a municipal securities sales principal, (iii) a general securities principal engaging in activities listed in Rule G-27(b)(ii)(C)(3), (iv) a municipal securities representative, (v) a municipal securities sales limited representative, (vi) a limited representative – investment company and variable contracts products, and (vii) a municipal fund securities limited principal.

(b) Every broker, dealer and municipal securities dealer shall obtain from each of its associated persons (as defined in section (a) of this rule), and each associated person shall furnish to the broker, dealer or municipal securities dealer with which such person is or seeks to be associated, a completed Form U4 or similar form prescribed by the Commission or a registered securities association for brokers, dealers and municipal securities dealers other than bank dealers or, in the case of a bank dealer, a completed Form MSD-4 or similar form prescribed by the appropriate regulatory agency for such bank dealer.

(c) To the extent any information on the form furnished by an associated person pursuant to section (b) of this rule is or becomes materially inaccurate or incomplete, such associated person shall furnish in writing to the broker, dealer or municipal securities dealer with which such person is or seeks to be associated a corrected form or a statement correcting such information.

(d) For the purpose of verifying the information furnished by an associated person pursuant to section (b) of this rule, every broker, dealer and municipal securities dealer shall make inquiry of all employers of such associated person during the three years immediately preceding such person's association with such broker, dealer or municipal securities dealer concerning the accuracy and completeness of such information as well as such person's record and reputation as related to the person's ability to perform his or her duties and each such prior employer which is a broker, dealer or municipal securities dealer shall make such information available within ten business days following a request made pursuant to the requirements of this section (d).

(e) Every broker, dealer and municipal securities dealer shall maintain and preserve a copy of the form furnished pursuant to section (b) of this rule, and of any corrected forms or additional statements furnished pursuant to section (c) of this rule, until at least three years after the associated person's employment or other association with such broker, dealer or municipal securities dealer has terminated.

(f) Every broker, dealer and municipal securities dealer shall maintain and preserve a record of the name and residence address of each associated person, designated by the category of function performed (whether municipal securities principal, municipal securities sales principal, municipal securities representative or financial and operations principal) and indicating whether such person has taken and passed the qualification examination for municipal securities principals, municipal securities sales principals, municipal securities representatives, municipal securities sales limited representatives, municipal fund securities limited principals or financial and operations principals prescribed by the Board or was exempt from the requirement to take and pass such examination, indicating the basis for such exemption, until at least three years after the associated person's employment or other association with such broker, dealer or municipal securities dealer has terminated.

(g) Every broker, dealer and municipal securities dealer which is a member of a registered securities association shall file with such association, every bank dealer shall file with the appropriate regulatory agency for such bank dealer, and every broker, dealer or municipal securities dealer other than a bank dealer which is not a member of a registered securities association shall file with the Commission, such of the information prescribed by this rule as such association, agency, or the Commission, respectively, shall by rule or regulation require.

(h) Any records required to be maintained and preserved pursuant to this rule shall be preserved in accordance with the requirements of sections (d), (e) and (f) of rule G-9 of the Board.

31. MSRB Rules: G-10 – Delivery of Investment Brochure

Summary: Requires dealers and municipal advisors to provide certain notices to customers and clients within specified timeframes.

(a) Each broker, dealer and municipal securities dealer (collectively, a "dealer") shall, once every calendar year, provide in writing (which may be electronic) to each customer the following items of information:
   (i) a statement that it is registered with the U.S. Securities and Exchange Commission and the Municipal Securities Rulemaking Board;
   (ii) the website address for the Municipal Securities Rulemaking Board; and
   (iii) a statement as to the availability to the customer of an investor brochure that is posted on the website of the Municipal Securities Rulemaking Board that describes the protections that may be provided by the Municipal Securities Rulemaking Board rules and how to file a complaint with an appropriate regulatory authority.

(b) Each municipal advisor shall promptly, after the establishment of a municipal advisory relationship, as defined in MSRB Rule G-42(f)(v), and no less than once each calendar year thereafter during the course of that municipal advisory relationship, or promptly, after entering into an agreement to undertake a solicitation of a municipal entity or obligated person, as defined in Rule 15Ba1-1(n), 17 CFR 240.15Ba1-1(n), under the Act, and no less than once each calendar year thereafter during the course of that agreement, provide in writing (which may be electronic) to the municipal advisory client, the following items of information:
   (i) a statement that it is registered with the U.S. Securities and Exchange Commission and the Municipal Securities Rulemaking Board;
   (ii) the website address for the Municipal Securities Rulemaking Board; and
   (iii) a statement as to the availability to the municipal advisory client of a municipal advisory client brochure that is posted on the website of the Municipal Securities Rulemaking Board that describes the protections that may be provided by the Municipal Securities Rulemaking Board rules and how to file a complaint with an appropriate regulatory authority.

(c) For the purposes of this rule, a municipal advisory client shall include either a municipal entity or obligated person for whom the municipal advisor engages in municipal advisory activities, as defined in Rule G-42(f)(iv), or a broker, dealer, municipal securities dealer, municipal advisor, or investment adviser (as defined in section 202 of the Investment Advisers Act of 1940) on behalf of whom the municipal advisor undertakes a solicitation of a municipal entity or obligated person, as defined in Rule 15Ba1-1(n), 17 CFR 240.15Ba1-1(n), under the Act.

---

32. MSRB Rules: G-20 – Gifts, Gratuities and Non-cash Compensations

Summary: Prohibits dealers and municipal advisors from giving gifts or providing services in excess of $100 to another person in relation to the municipal securities activities of such person's employer and limits the giving and acceptance of non-cash compensation by dealers, subject to exceptions.

(a) Purpose. The purpose of this rule is to maintain the integrity of the municipal securities market and to preserve investor and public confidence in the municipal securities market, including the bond issuance process. The rule protects against improprieties and conflicts of interest that may arise when regulated entities or their associated persons give gifts or gratuities in relation to the municipal securities or municipal advisory activities of the recipients' employers.

(b) Definitions. For purposes of this rule, the following terms have the following meanings:

  (i) "Cash compensation" means any discount, concession, fee, service fee, commission, asset-based sales charge, loan, override or cash employee benefit received in connection with the sale and distribution of municipal securities.

  (ii) "Municipal advisor" shall, for purposes of this rule, have the same meaning as in Section 15B(e)(4) of the Act, 17 CFR 240.15Ba1-1(d)(1)-(4), and other rules and regulations thereunder.

  (iii) "Non-cash compensation" means any form of compensation received in connection with the sale and distribution of municipal securities that is not cash compensation, including, but not limited to, merchandise, gifts and prizes, travel expenses, meals and lodging.

  (iv) "Offeror" means, with respect to a primary offering of municipal securities, the issuer, any adviser to the issuer (including, but not limited to, the issuer's financial advisor, municipal advisor, bond or other legal counsel, or investment or program manager in connection with the primary offering), the underwriter of the primary offering, or any person controlling, controlled by, or under common control with any of the foregoing; provided that, with respect to a primary offering of municipal fund securities, "offeror" shall also include any person considered an "offeror" under FINRA Rules 5110, 2320, or 2341 in connection with any securities held as assets of or underlying such municipal fund securities.

  (v) "Person" means a natural person.

  (vi) "Primary offering" means a primary offering as defined in Securities Exchange Act Rule 15c2-12(f)(7).

  (vii) "Regulated entity" means a broker, dealer, municipal securities dealer or municipal advisor, but does not include the associated persons of such entity.

(c) General Limitation on Value of Gifts and Gratuities. No regulated entity or any of its associated persons shall, directly or indirectly, give or provide or permit to be given or provided any thing or service of value, including gratuities, in excess of $100 per year to a person (other than an employee or partner of such regulated entity), if such payments or services are in relation to the municipal securities or municipal advisory activities of the employer of the recipient of the payment or service. For purposes of this rule the term "employer" shall include a principal for whom the recipient of a payment or service is acting as agent or representative.

(d) Gifts and Gratuities Not Subject to General Limitation. The general limitation of section (c) of this rule shall not apply to the following gifts, provided that they do not give rise to any apparent or actual material conflict of interest:

  (i) Normal Business Dealings. Occasional gifts of meals or tickets to theatrical, sporting, and other entertainments that are hosted by the regulated entity or its associated persons, and the sponsoring by the regulated entity of legitimate business functions that are recognized by the Internal Revenue Service as deductible business expenses; provided that such gifts shall not be so frequent or so extensive as to raise any question of propriety.

  (ii) Transaction-Commemorative Gifts. Gifts that are solely decorative items commemorating a business transaction, such as a customary plaque or desk ornament (e.g., Lucite tombstone).

  (iii) De Minimis Gifts. Gifts of de minimis value (e.g., pens, notepads or modest desk ornaments).

  (iv) Promotional Gifts. Promotional items of nominal value displaying the regulated entity's corporate or other business logo. The value of the item must be substantially below the $100 limit of section (c) to be considered of nominal value.

  (v) Bereavement Gifts. Bereavement gifts that are reasonable and customary for the circumstances.

  (vi) Personal Gifts. Gifts that are personal in nature given upon infrequent life events (e.g., a wedding gift or a congratulatory gift for the birth of a child).

(e) Prohibition of Use of Offering Proceeds. A regulated entity that engages in municipal securities activities or municipal advisory activities for or on behalf of a municipal entity or obligated person in connection with an offering of municipal securities is prohibited from requesting or obtaining reimbursement of its costs and expenses related to the entertainment of any person, including, but not limited to, any official or other personnel of the municipal entity or personnel of the obligated person, from the proceeds of such offering of municipal securities. For purposes of this prohibition, entertainment expenses do not include ordinary and reasonable expenses for meals hosted by the regulated entity and directly related to the offering for which the regulated entity was retained.

(f) Compensation for Services. The general limitation of section (c) of this rule shall not apply to compensation paid as a result of contracts of employment with or compensation for services rendered by another person; provided that there is in existence prior to the time of employment or before the services are rendered a written agreement between the regulated entity and the person who is to perform such services and such agreement includes the nature of the proposed services, the amount of the proposed compensation and the written consent of such person's employer.

(g) Non-Cash Compensation in Connection with Primary Offerings. In connection with the sale and distribution of a primary offering of municipal securities, no broker, dealer or municipal securities dealer, or any associated person thereof, shall directly or indirectly accept or make payments or offers of payments of any non-cash compensation. Notwithstanding the foregoing and the general limitation of section (c) of this rule, the following non-cash compensation arrangements are permitted:

(i) gifts that do not exceed $100 per individual per year and are not preconditioned on achievement of a sales target;

(ii) occasional gifts of meals or tickets to theatrical, sporting, and other entertainments; provided that such gifts are not so frequent or so extensive as to raise any question of propriety and are not preconditioned on achievement of a sales target;

(iii) payment or reimbursement by offerors in connection with meetings held by an offeror or by a broker, dealer or municipal securities dealer for the purpose of training or education of associated persons of a broker, dealer or municipal securities dealer, provided that:

(A) associated persons obtain the prior approval of the broker, dealer or municipal securities dealer to attend the meeting and attendance is not preconditioned by the broker, dealer or municipal securities dealer on achievement of a sales target or any other incentives pursuant to a non-cash compensation arrangement permitted by subsection (g)(iv);

(B) the location is appropriate to the purpose of the meeting, which shall mean an office of the offeror or the broker, dealer or municipal securities dealer, a facility located in the vicinity of such office, a regional location with respect to regional meetings, or a location at which a significant asset, if any, being financed or refinanced in the primary offering is located;

(C) the payment or reimbursement is not applied to the expenses of guests of the associated person; and

(D) the payment or reimbursement is not preconditioned by the offeror on achievement of a sales target or any other non-cash compensation arrangement permitted by subsection (g)(iv).

(iv) non-cash compensation arrangements between a broker, dealer or municipal securities dealer and its associated persons, or a company that controls the broker, dealer or municipal securities dealer and the associated persons of the broker, dealer or municipal securities dealer, provided that:

(A) the non-cash compensation arrangement is based on the total production of associated persons with respect to all municipal securities within respective product types distributed by the broker, dealer or municipal securities dealer;

(B) the non-cash compensation arrangement requires that the credit received for each municipal security within a municipal security product type is equally weighted; and

(C) no entity that is not an associated person of the broker, dealer or municipal securities dealer participates directly or indirectly in the organization of a permissible non-cash compensation arrangement.

(v) contributions by any person other than the broker, dealer or municipal securities dealer to a non-cash compensation arrangement between a broker, dealer or municipal securities dealer and its associated persons, provided that the arrangement meets the criteria in subsection (g)(iv).

33. MSRB Rules: G-37 – Political Contributions and Prohibitions on Municipal Securities Business

Summary: Prohibits dealers from engaging in municipal securities business and municipal advisors from engaging in municipal advisory business with municipal entities if certain contributions have been made to officials of such municipal entities within the preceding two-year period, and requires dealers and municipal advisors to disclose certain political contributions and other information.

(a) Purpose. The purpose and intent of this rule are to ensure that the high standards and integrity of the municipal securities market are maintained, to prevent fraudulent and manipulative acts and practices, to promote just and equitable principles of trade, to perfect a free and open market and to protect investors, municipal entities, obligated persons and the public interest by:

    (i) prohibiting brokers, dealers and municipal securities dealers (collectively, "dealers") from engaging in municipal securities business and municipal advisors from engaging in municipal advisory business with municipal entities if certain political contributions have been made to officials of such municipal entities; and

    (ii) requiring dealers and municipal advisors to disclose certain political contributions, as well as other information, to allow public scrutiny of such political contributions, the municipal securities business of dealers and the municipal advisory business of municipal advisors.

(b) Ban on Municipal Securities Business or Municipal Advisory Business; Excluded Contributions.

    (i) Two-Year Ban.

        (A) Brokers, Dealers and Municipal Securities Dealers. No dealer shall engage in municipal securities business with a municipal entity within two years after a contribution to an official of such municipal entity with dealer selection influence, as defined in paragraph (g)(xvi)(A) of this rule, made by the dealer; a municipal finance professional of the dealer; or a political action committee controlled by either the dealer or a municipal finance professional of the dealer.

        (B) Municipal Advisors. No municipal advisor (excluding a municipal advisor third-party solicitor) shall engage in municipal advisory business with a municipal entity within two years after a contribution to an official of such municipal entity with municipal advisor selection influence, as defined in paragraph (g)(xvi)(B) of this rule, made by the municipal advisor; a municipal advisor professional of the municipal advisor; or a political action committee controlled by either the municipal advisor or a municipal advisor professional of the municipal advisor.

        (C) Municipal Advisor Third-Party Solicitors.

            (1) Municipal Advisor Third-Party Solicitors. No municipal advisor third-party solicitor shall engage in municipal advisory business with a municipal entity within two years after a contribution to an official of such municipal entity with dealer selection influence, municipal advisor selection influence or investment adviser selection influence, as defined in paragraph (g)(xvi)(A), (B) or (C) of this rule, as applicable, made by the municipal advisor third-party solicitor; a municipal advisor professional of the municipal advisor third-party solicitor; or a political action committee controlled by either the municipal advisor third-party solicitor or a municipal advisor professional of the municipal advisor third-party solicitor.

            (2) Regulated Entity Clients of a Municipal Advisor Third-Party Solicitor. If a contribution is made by a municipal advisor third-party solicitor; a municipal advisor professional of the municipal advisor third-party solicitor; or a political action committee controlled by either the municipal advisor third-party solicitor or a municipal advisor professional of the municipal advisor third-party solicitor, the following shall apply.

                (a) In the case of an engagement of the municipal advisor third-party solicitor by a dealer to solicit a municipal entity on behalf of the dealer, if the contribution is made to an official of a municipal entity with dealer selection influence, the prohibition on municipal securities business in paragraph (b)(i)(A) of this rule shall apply to the retaining dealer for two years following the contribution.

   (b) In the case of an engagement of the municipal advisor third-party solicitor by a municipal advisor to solicit a municipal entity on behalf of the municipal advisor, if the contribution is made to an official of a municipal entity with municipal advisor selection influence, the prohibition on municipal advisory business in paragraph (b)(i)(B) of this rule shall apply to the retaining municipal advisor for two years following the contribution.

(D) Cross-Bans for Dealer-Municipal Advisors. In the case of a regulated entity that is both a dealer and a municipal advisor (a "dealer-municipal advisor"), the prohibition on municipal securities business in subsection (b)(i) of this rule shall also apply in the case of a contribution to an official of a municipal entity with dealer selection influence by a municipal advisor professional of the dealer-municipal advisor or a political action committee controlled by a municipal advisor professional of the dealer-municipal advisor; and the prohibition on municipal advisory business in subsection (b)(i) of this rule shall also apply in the case of a contribution to an official of a municipal entity with municipal advisor selection influence by a municipal finance professional of the dealer-municipal advisor or a political action committee controlled by a municipal finance professional of the dealer-municipal advisor.

(E) Orderly Transition Period. A dealer or municipal advisor that is engaging in municipal securities business or municipal advisory business with a municipal entity and during the period of the engagement becomes subject to a prohibition under subsection (b)(i) of this rule may, notwithstanding such prohibition, continue to engage in the municipal securities business or municipal advisory business (except soliciting), as applicable, to allow for an orderly transition to another entity to engage in such business and, where applicable, to allow a municipal advisor to act consistently with its fiduciary duty to the municipal entity; provided, however, that such transition period must be as short a period of time as possible and that the prohibition under subsection (b)(i) of this rule shall be extended by the duration of the orderly transition period.

(ii) Excluded Contributions. A contribution to an official of a municipal entity will not subject a dealer or municipal advisor to a ban on business under subsection (b)(i) of this rule if the contribution meets the specific conditions of an exclusion set forth below.

   (A) Voting Right/De Minimis Contribution. The contribution is made by a municipal finance professional or municipal advisor professional who is entitled to vote for the official of the municipal entity and the contribution and any other contribution made to the official of the municipal entity by such person in total do not exceed $250 per election.

   (B) Contributions Made Before Becoming a Dealer Solicitor or Municipal Advisor Solicitor. The contribution is made by a natural person who: (1) at the time of the contribution was not a municipal finance professional or municipal advisor professional; (2) became and is a municipal finance professional, or municipal advisor professional, or both, solely on the basis of being a dealer solicitor and/or municipal advisor solicitor; and (3) since becoming a municipal finance professional and/or municipal advisor professional has not solicited the municipal entity; provided, however, that this non-solicitation condition is not required for this exclusion after two years have elapsed since the making of the contribution.

   (C) Contributions Made by Certain Persons More Than Six Months Before Becoming a Municipal Finance Professional or Municipal Advisor Professional. The contribution is made by a person who is either or both of the following: (1) a municipal finance professional solely based on activities as a municipal finance principal, dealer supervisory chain person, or dealer executive officer, and the contribution was made more than six months before becoming a municipal finance professional or; (2) a municipal advisor professional solely based on activities as a municipal advisor principal, municipal advisor supervisory chain person, or municipal advisor executive officer, and the contribution was made more than six months before becoming a municipal advisor professional.

(c) Prohibition on Soliciting and Coordinating Contributions and Payments.

    (i) Contributions. No dealer or municipal finance professional of the dealer shall solicit any person (including but not limited to any affiliated entity of the dealer) or political action committee to make any contribution, or coordinate any contributions, to an official of a municipal entity with dealer selection influence with which municipal entity the dealer is engaging, or is seeking to engage in municipal securities business. No municipal advisor or municipal advisor professional of the municipal advisor shall solicit any person (including but not limited to any affiliated entity of the municipal advisor) or political action committee to make any contribution, or coordinate any contributions, to an official of a municipal entity with municipal advisor selection influence with which municipal entity the municipal advisor is engaging, or is seeking to engage in municipal advisory business. In the case of a municipal advisor third-party solicitor, the prohibition on soliciting and coordinating contributions in this subsection (c)(i) shall apply to the solicitation or coordination of contributions to an official of a municipal entity with dealer selection influence, municipal advisor selection influence or investment adviser selection influence, as defined in paragraph (g)(xvi)(A), (B), or (C) of this rule, as applicable, by the municipal advisor third-party solicitor, or any municipal advisor professional of the municipal advisor third-party solicitor. In the case of a dealer-municipal advisor, the prohibition on soliciting and coordinating contributions in this subsection (c)(i) shall apply to the solicitation or coordination of contributions to an official of a municipal entity with dealer selection influence or an official of a municipal entity with municipal advisor selection influence by the dealer-municipal advisor, any municipal finance professional of the dealer-municipal advisor and any municipal advisor professional of the dealer-municipal advisor.

    (ii) Payments. No dealer, municipal advisor, municipal finance representative, municipal advisor representative, dealer solicitor, municipal advisor solicitor, municipal finance principal or municipal advisor principal shall solicit any person (including but not limited to any affiliated entity of the dealer or municipal advisor) or political action committee to make any payment, or coordinate any payments, to a political party of a state or locality where the dealer or municipal advisor is engaging, or is seeking to engage in municipal securities business or municipal advisory business, as applicable.

(d) Prohibition on Circumvention of Rule. No dealer, municipal advisor, municipal finance professional or municipal advisor professional shall, directly or indirectly, through or by any other person or means, do any act which would result in a violation of sections (b) or (c) of this rule.

(e) Required Disclosure to Board.

    (i) Each regulated entity must submit to the Board by the last day of the month following the end of each calendar quarter (these dates correspond to January 31, April 30, July 31 and October 31) Form G-37 containing, in the prescribed format, the following information:

        (A) for any contribution to an official of a municipal entity (other than a contribution made by a municipal finance professional, municipal advisor professional, non-MFP executive officer or non-MAP executive officer of the regulated entity to an official of a municipal entity for whom such person is entitled to vote if all contributions by such person to such official of a municipal entity, in total, do not exceed $250 per election) and payments to political parties of states and political subdivisions (other than a payment made by a municipal finance professional, municipal advisor professional, non-MFP executive officer or non-MAP executive officer of the regulated entity to a political party of a state or political subdivision in which such person is entitled to vote if all payments by such person to such political party, in total, do not exceed $250 per year) made by the persons and entities described in subparagraph (e)(i)(A)(2) below:

            (1) listing by state, the name and title (including any city/county/state or political subdivision) of each official of a municipal entity and political party that received a contribution or payment during such calendar quarter;

            (2) the contribution or payment amount made and the contributor category for such contributions or payments during such calendar quarter, as specified below:

(a) If a regulated entity, the identity of the contributor as a dealer and/or municipal advisor (disclose all applicable categories);

(b) If a natural person, the identity of the contributor as a municipal finance professional, municipal advisor professional, non-MFP executive officer or non-MAP executive officer of the regulated entity (disclose all applicable categories); or

(c) If a political action committee, the identity as a political action committee controlled by the regulated entity or any municipal finance professional or municipal advisor professional of the regulated entity;

(B) for any contribution to a bond ballot campaign (other than a contribution made by a municipal finance professional, municipal advisor professional, non-MFP executive officer or non-MAP executive officer of the regulated entity to a bond ballot campaign for a ballot initiative with respect to which such person is entitled to vote if all contributions by such person to such bond ballot campaign, in total, do not exceed $250 per ballot initiative) made by the persons and entities described in subparagraph (e)(i)(B)(2) below:

(1) listing by state, the official name of each bond ballot campaign receiving a contribution during such calendar quarter, and the jurisdiction (including city/county/state or political subdivision) by or for which municipal securities, if approved, would be issued;

(2) the contribution amount (which, in the case of in-kind contributions, must include both the value and the nature of the goods or services provided, including any ancillary services provided to, on behalf of, or in furtherance of the bond ballot campaign), the specific date on which the contribution was made, and the contributor category for such contributions during such calendar quarter as specified below:

(a) If a regulated entity, the identity of the contributor as a dealer and/or municipal advisor (disclose all applicable categories);

(b) If a natural person, the identity of the contributor as a municipal finance professional, municipal advisor professional, non-MFP executive officer or non-MAP executive officer of the regulated entity (disclose all applicable categories); or

(c) If a political action committee, the identity as a political action committee controlled by the regulated entity or any municipal finance professional or municipal advisor professional of the regulated entity;

(3) the full name of the municipal entity and full issue description of any primary offering resulting from the bond ballot campaign to which a contribution required to be disclosed pursuant to paragraph (e)(i)(B) of this rule has been made, or to which a contribution has been made by a municipal finance professional, municipal advisor professional, non-MFP executive officer or non-MAP executive officer during the period beginning two years prior to such person acquiring such status that would have been required to be disclosed if such person had acquired such status at the time of such contribution and the reportable date of selection on which the regulated entity was selected to engage in the municipal securities business or municipal advisory business, reported in the calendar quarter in which the closing date for the issuance that was authorized by the bond ballot campaign occurred; and

(4) any payment or reimbursement, related to any contribution to any bond ballot campaign received by the regulated entity or any of its municipal finance professionals or municipal advisor professionals from any third party that are required to be disclosed pursuant to paragraph (e)(i)(B) of this rule, including the amount paid and the name of the third party making such payment or reimbursement.

(C) listing by state, the municipal entities with which the regulated entity has engaged in municipal securities business or municipal advisory business during such calendar quarter, along with the type of municipal securities business or municipal advisory business, and, in the case of municipal advisory business engaged in by a municipal advisor third-party solicitor, the listing of the type of municipal advisory business shall be accompanied by the name of the third party on behalf of which business was solicited and the nature of the business solicited (municipal securities business, municipal advisory business and/or investment advisory services—disclose all applicable categories);

(D) any information required to be included on Form G-37 for such calendar quarter pursuant to subsection (e)(iii) of this rule;

(E) such other identifying information required by Form G-37; and

(F) whether any contribution listed in this subsection (e)(i) of this rule is the subject of an automatic exemption pursuant to section (j) of this rule, and the date of such automatic exemption.

The Board shall make public a copy of each Form G-37 received from any regulated entity.

(ii) No regulated entity shall be required to submit Form G-37 to the Board for any calendar quarter in which either:

(A) such regulated entity has no information that is required to be reported pursuant to paragraphs (e)(i)(A) through (D) of this rule for such calendar quarter; or

(B) such regulated entity has not engaged in municipal securities business or municipal advisory business, but only if such regulated entity:

(1) had not engaged in municipal securities business or municipal advisory business during the seven consecutive calendar quarters immediately preceding such calendar quarter; and

(2) has submitted to the Board completed Form G-37x setting forth, in the prescribed format, (a) a certification to the effect that such regulated entity did not engage in municipal securities business or municipal advisory business during the eight consecutive calendar quarters immediately preceding the date of such certification, (b) certain acknowledgments as are set forth in said Form G-37x regarding the obligations of such regulated entity in connection with Forms G-37 and G-37x under subsection (e)(ii) of this rule and Rule G-8(a)(xvi) or Rule G-8(h)(iii), as applicable, and (c) such other identifying information required by Form G-37x; provided, however, that if a regulated entity has engaged in municipal securities business or municipal advisory business subsequent to the submission of Form G-37x to the Board, such regulated entity shall be required to submit a new Form G-37x to the Board in order to again qualify for an exemption under this clause (B). The Board shall make public a copy of each Form G-37x received from any regulated entity.

(iii) If a regulated entity engages in municipal securities business or municipal advisory business during any calendar quarter after not having reported on Form G-37 the information described in paragraph (e)(i)(A) of this rule for one or more contributions or payments made during the two-year period preceding such calendar quarter solely as a result of paragraph (e)(ii)(B) of this rule, such regulated entity shall include on Form G-37 for such calendar quarter all such information (including year and calendar quarter of such contribution(s) or payment(s)) not so reported during such two-year period.

(iv) A regulated entity that submits Form G-37 or Form G-37x to the Board shall submit an electronic version of such form to the Board in such format and manner specified in the current Instructions for Forms G-37, G-37x and G-38t.

(f) Voluntary Disclosure to Board. The Board will accept additional information related to contributions made to officials of municipal entities and bond ballot campaigns and payments made to political parties of states and political subdivisions voluntarily submitted by regulated entities or others, provided that such information is submitted otherwise in accordance with section (e) of this rule.

(g) Definitions.

(i) "Regulated entity" means a dealer or municipal advisor and "regulated entity," "dealer" and "municipal advisor" exclude the entity's associated persons.

(ii) "Municipal finance professional" means:

(A) any "municipal finance representative" - any associated person primarily engaged in municipal securities representative activities, as defined in Rule G-3(a)(i), other than sales activities with natural persons;

    (B) any "dealer solicitor" - any associated person who is a municipal solicitor as defined in paragraph (g)(xiii)(A) of this rule;

    (C) any "municipal finance principal" - any associated person who is both (1) a municipal securities principal or a municipal securities sales principal; and (2) a supervisor of any municipal finance representative (as defined in paragraph (g)(ii)(A) of this rule) or dealer solicitor (as defined in paragraph (g)(ii)(B) of this rule);

    (D) any "dealer supervisory chain person" - any associated person who is a supervisor of any municipal finance principal up through and including, in the case of a dealer other than a bank dealer, the Chief Executive Officer or similarly situated official and in the case of a bank dealer, the officer or officers designated by the board of directors of the bank as responsible for the day-to-day conduct of the bank's municipal securities dealer activities, as required by Rule G-1(a)(1)(A); or

    (E) any "dealer executive officer" - any associated person who is a member of an executive or management committee (or similarly situated official) of a dealer (or, in the case of a bank dealer, the separately identifiable department or division of the bank, as defined in Rule G-1(a)); provided, however, that if the persons described in this paragraph are the only associated persons of the dealer meeting the definition of municipal finance professional, the dealer shall be deemed to have no municipal finance professionals.

    Each person designated by the dealer as a municipal finance professional pursuant to Rule G-8(a)(xvi) is deemed to be a municipal finance professional and shall retain this designation for one year after the last activity or position which gave rise to the designation.

  (iii) "Municipal advisor professional" means:

    (A) any "municipal advisor representative" – any associated person engaged in municipal advisor representative activities, as defined in Rule G-3(d)(i)(A);

    (B) any "municipal advisor solicitor" – any associated person who is a municipal solicitor (as defined in paragraph (g)(xiii)(B) of this rule) (or in the case of an associated person of a municipal advisor third-party solicitor, paragraph (g)(xiii)(C) of this rule);

    (C) any "municipal advisor principal" – any associated person who is both: (1) a municipal advisor principal (as defined in Rule G-3(e)(i)); and (2) a supervisor of any municipal advisor representative (as defined in paragraph (g)(iii)(A) of this rule) or municipal advisor solicitor (as defined in paragraph (g)(iii)(B) of this rule);

    (D) any "municipal advisor supervisory chain person" – any associated person who is a supervisor of any municipal advisor principal up through and including, in the case of a municipal advisor other than a bank municipal advisor, the Chief Executive Officer or similarly situated official, and, in the case of a bank municipal advisor, the officer or officers designated by the board of directors of the bank as responsible for the day-to-day conduct of the bank's municipal advisory activities, as required by 17 CFR 240.15Ba1-1(d)(4)(i); or

    (E) any "municipal advisor executive officer" – any associated person who is a member of the executive or management committee (or similarly situated official) of a municipal advisor (or, in the case of a bank municipal advisor, the separately identifiable department or division of the bank as defined in Section 15B(e)(4) of the Act and 17 CFR 240.15Ba1-1(d)(4)(i) thereunder); provided, however, that if the persons described in this paragraph are the only associated persons of the municipal advisor meeting the definition of municipal advisor professional, the municipal advisor shall be deemed to have no municipal advisor professionals.

    Each person designated by the municipal advisor as a municipal advisor professional pursuant to Rule G-8(h)(iii) is deemed to be a municipal advisor professional and shall retain this designation for one year after the last activity or position which gave rise to the designation.

  (iv) "Bank municipal advisor" means a municipal advisor that is a bank or a separately identifiable department or division of the bank as defined in Section 15B(e)(4) of the Act and 17 CFR 240.15Ba1-1(d)(4)(i) thereunder.

(v) "Bond ballot campaign" means any fund, organization or committee that solicits or receives contributions to be used to support ballot initiatives seeking authorization for the issuance of municipal securities through public approval obtained by popular vote.

(vi) "Contribution" means any gift, subscription, loan, advance, or deposit of money or anything of value made:

    (A) to an official of a municipal entity:

        (1) for the purpose of influencing any election for federal, state or local office;

        (2) for payment of debt incurred in connection with any such election; or

        (3) for transition or inaugural expenses incurred by the successful candidate for state or local office; or

    (B) to a bond ballot campaign:

        (1) for the purpose of influencing (whether in support of or opposition to) any ballot initiative seeking authorization for the issuance of municipal securities through public approval obtained by popular vote;

        (2) for payment of debt incurred in connection with any such ballot initiative; or

        (3) for payment of the costs of conducting any such ballot initiative.

(vii) "Issuer" means the governmental issuer specified in Section 3(a)(29) of the Act.

(viii) "Municipal advisor" means a municipal advisor that is registered or required to be registered under Section 15B of the Act and the rules and regulations thereunder.

(ix) "Municipal advisory business" means those activities that would cause a person to be a municipal advisor as defined in Section 15B(e)(4) of the Act, 17 CFR 240.15Ba1-1(d)(1)-(4) and other rules and regulations thereunder, including: (A) the provision of advice to or on behalf of a municipal entity or an obligated person with respect to municipal financial products or the issuance of municipal securities, including advice with respect to the structure, timing, terms, and other similar matters concerning such financial products or issues and (B) the solicitation of a municipal entity or obligated person, within the meaning of Section 15B(e)(9) of the Act and the rules and regulations thereunder.

(x) "Municipal advisor third-party solicitor" means a municipal advisor that is currently soliciting a municipal entity, is engaged to solicit a municipal entity, or is seeking to be engaged to solicit a municipal entity for direct or indirect compensation, on behalf of a dealer, municipal advisor or investment adviser (as defined in Section 202(a)(11) of the Investment Advisers Act of 1940) that does not control, is not controlled by, or is not under common control with the municipal advisor undertaking such solicitation.

(xi) "Municipal entity" has the meaning specified in Section 15B(e)(8) of the Act and the rules and regulations thereunder.

(xii) "Municipal securities business" means:

    (A) the purchase of a primary offering (as defined in Rule A-13(f)) of municipal securities from a municipal entity on other than a competitive bid basis (e.g., negotiated underwriting);

    (B) the offer or sale of a primary offering of municipal securities on behalf of any municipal entity (e.g., private placement);

    (C) the provision of financial advisory or consultant services to or on behalf of a municipal entity with respect to a primary offering of municipal securities in which the dealer was chosen to provide such services on other than a competitive bid basis; and

    (D) the provision of remarketing agent services to or on behalf of a municipal entity with respect to a primary offering of municipal securities in which the dealer was chosen to provide such services on other than a competitive bid basis.

(xiii) "Municipal solicitor" means:

    (A) an associated person of a dealer who solicits a municipal entity for municipal securities business on behalf of the dealer;

    (B) an associated person of a municipal advisor who solicits a municipal entity for municipal advisory business on behalf of the municipal advisor; or

(C) an associated person of a municipal advisor third-party solicitor who solicits a municipal entity on behalf of a dealer, municipal advisor or investment adviser (as defined in Section 202(a)(11) of the Investment Advisers Act of 1940) that does not control, is not controlled by, or is not under common control with such municipal advisor third-party solicitor.

(xiv) "Non-MAP executive officer" means an associated person in charge of a principal business unit, division or function or any other person who performs similar policy making functions for the municipal advisor (or, in the case of a bank municipal advisor, the separately identifiable department or division of the bank, as defined in Section 15B(e)(4) of the Act and 17 CFR 240.15Ba1-1(d)(4)(i) thereunder), but does not include any municipal advisor professional, as defined in subsection (g)(iii) of this rule; provided, however, that if no associated person of the municipal advisor meets the definition of municipal advisor professional, the municipal advisor shall be deemed to have no non-MAP executive officers. Each person listed by the municipal advisor as a non-MAP executive officer pursuant to Rule G-8(h)(iii) is deemed to be a non-MAP executive officer.

(xv) "Non-MFP executive officer" means an associated person in charge of a principal business unit, division or function or any other person who performs similar policy making functions for the dealer (or, in the case of a bank dealer, the separately identifiable department or division of the bank, as defined in Rule G-1(a)), but does not include any municipal finance professional, as defined in subsection (g)(ii) of this rule; provided, however, that if no associated person of the dealer meets the definition of municipal finance professional, the dealer shall be deemed to have no non-MFP executive officers. Each person listed by the dealer as a non-MFP executive officer pursuant to Rule G-8(a)(xvi) is deemed to be a non-MFP executive officer.

(xvi) "Official of such municipal entity" or "official of a municipal entity," without further specification, means any person who meets the definition of at least one of paragraphs (g)(xvi)(A), (g)(xvi)(B), or (g)(xvi)(C) of this rule.

(A) "Official of a municipal entity with dealer selection influence" or "official of such municipal entity with dealer selection influence" means any person (including any election committee for such person) who was, at the time of the contribution, an incumbent, candidate or successful candidate: (1) for elective office of the municipal entity which office is directly or indirectly responsible for, or can influence the outcome of, the hiring by the municipal entity of a dealer for municipal securities business; or (2) for any elective office of a state or of any political subdivision, which office has authority to appoint any person who is directly or indirectly responsible for, or can influence the outcome of, the hiring by a municipal entity of a dealer for municipal securities business.

(B) "Official of a municipal entity with municipal advisor selection influence" or "official of such municipal entity with municipal advisor selection influence" means any person (including any election committee for such person) who was, at the time of the contribution, an incumbent, candidate or successful candidate: (1) for elective office of the municipal entity which office is directly or indirectly responsible for, or can influence the outcome of, the hiring by the municipal entity of a municipal advisor for municipal advisory business; or (2) for any elective office of a state or of any political subdivision, which office has authority to appoint any person who is directly or indirectly responsible for, or can influence the outcome of, the hiring by a municipal entity of a municipal advisor for municipal advisory business.

(C) "Official of a municipal entity with investment adviser selection influence" or "official of such municipal entity with investment adviser selection influence" means any person (including any election committee for such person) who was, at the time of the contribution, an incumbent, candidate or successful candidate: (1) for elective office of the municipal entity, which office is directly or indirectly responsible for, or can influence the outcome of, the hiring by the municipal entity of an investment adviser (as defined in Section 202(a)(11) of the Investment Advisers Act of 1940) for investment advisory services; or (2) for any elective office of a state or of any political subdivision, which office has authority to appoint any person who is directly or indirectly responsible for, or can influence the outcome of, the hiring by a municipal entity of an investment adviser for investment advisory services.

(xvii) "Payment" means any gift, subscription, loan, advance, or deposit of money or anything of value.

(xviii) "Reportable date of selection" means the date of the earliest to occur of: (A) the execution of an engagement letter; (B) the receipt of formal notification (provided either in writing or orally) from or on behalf of the municipal entity that the dealer or municipal advisor has been selected to engage in municipal securities business or municipal advisory business; or, (C) solely in the case of a dealer, the execution of a bond purchase agreement.

(xix) "Solicit," or "soliciting," except as used in section (c) of this rule, means to make, or making, respectively, a direct or indirect communication with a municipal entity for the purposes of obtaining or retaining an engagement by the municipal entity of a dealer, municipal advisor or investment adviser (as defined in Section 202(a)(11) of the Investment Advisers Act of 1940) for municipal securities business, municipal advisory business or investment advisory services; provided, however, that it does not include advertising by a dealer, municipal advisor or investment adviser.

(h) Operative Terms. The prohibitions under this rule on engaging in municipal securities business and municipal advisory business shall result from a contribution and be of the scope and length of time as provided under Rule G-37 as in effect at the time that such contribution is made.

(i) Application for Exemption. Upon application, a registered securities association with respect to a dealer that is a member of such association, or the appropriate regulatory agency as defined in Section 3(a)(34) of the Act with respect to any other dealer, may, conditionally or unconditionally, exempt such dealer from a prohibition on municipal securities business in subsection (b)(i) of this rule. Upon application, a registered securities association with respect to a municipal advisor that is a member of such association, or the Commission, or the Commission's designee, with respect to any other municipal advisor, may, conditionally or unconditionally, exempt such municipal advisor from a prohibition on municipal advisory business in subsection (b)(i) of this rule. In determining whether to grant such exemption, among other factors, the following shall be considered:

(i) whether such exemption is consistent with the public interest, the protection of investors, municipal entities and obligated persons and the purposes of this rule;

(ii) whether such regulated entity (A) prior to the time the contribution(s) which resulted in such prohibition was made, had developed and instituted procedures reasonably designed to ensure compliance with this rule; (B) prior to or at the time the contribution(s) which resulted in such prohibition was made, had no actual knowledge of the contribution(s); (C) has taken all available steps to cause the contributor involved in making the contribution(s) which resulted in such prohibition to obtain a return of the contribution(s); and (D) has taken such other remedial or preventive measures, as may be appropriate under the circumstances, and the nature of such other remedial or preventive measures directed specifically toward the contributor who made the relevant contribution and all employees of the regulated entity;

(iii) whether, at the time of the contribution, the contributor was a municipal finance professional or a municipal advisor professional or otherwise an employee of the regulated entity, or was seeking such employment, or was a municipal advisor professional or otherwise an employee of a municipal advisor third-party solicitor engaged by the regulated entity or was seeking such employment;

(iv) the timing and amount of the contribution which resulted in the prohibition;

(v) the nature of the election (e.g., federal, state or local); and

(vi) the contributor's apparent intent or motive in making the contribution which resulted in the prohibition, as evidenced by the facts and circumstances surrounding such contribution.

(j) Automatic Exemptions.

(i) A regulated entity that is prohibited from engaging in municipal securities business or municipal advisory business with a municipal entity pursuant to subsection (b)(i) of this rule as a result of a contribution made by a municipal finance professional or a municipal advisor professional, or a municipal advisor professional of a municipal advisor third-party solicitor on behalf of such regulated entity may exempt itself from such prohibition, subject to subsection (j)(ii) and subsection (j)(iii) of this rule, upon satisfaction of the following requirements: (A) the regulated entity must have discovered the contribution which resulted in the prohibition within four months of the date of such contribution; (B) such contribution must not have exceeded $250; and (C) the contributor must obtain a return of the contribution within 60 calendar days of the date of discovery of such contribution by the regulated entity.

(ii) A regulated entity is entitled to no more than two automatic exemptions per 12-month period.

(iii) A regulated entity may not execute more than one automatic exemption relating to contributions by the same person regardless of the time period.

---

34. SEC Rules and Regulations, Securities Exchange Act of 1934: Section 3(a)(39) – Definitions and Application of Title (Statutory Disqualification)

(39) A person is subject to a "statutory disqualification" with respect to membership or participation in, or association with a member of, a self-regulatory organization, if such person—

(A) has been and is expelled or suspended from membership or participation in, or barred or suspended from being associated with a member of, any self-regulatory organization, foreign equivalent of a self-regulatory organization, foreign or international securities exchange, contract market designated pursuant to section 5 of the Commodity Exchange Act (7 U.S.C. 7), or any substantially equivalent foreign statute or regulation, or futures association registered under section 17 of such Act (7 U.S.C. 21), or any substantially equivalent foreign statute or regulation, or has been and is denied trading privileges on any such contract market or foreign equivalent;

(B) is subject to—

(i) an order of the Commission, other appropriate regulatory agency, or foreign financial regulatory authority—

(I) denying, suspending for a period not exceeding 12 months, or revoking his registration as a broker, dealer, municipal securities dealer, government securities broker, government securities dealer, security-based swap dealer, or major security-based swap participant or limiting his activities as a foreign person performing a function substantially equivalent to any of the above; or

(II) barring or suspending for a period not exceeding 12 months his being associated with a broker, dealer, municipal securities dealer, government securities broker, government securities dealer, security-based swap dealer, major security-based swap participant, or foreign person performing a function substantially equivalent to any of the above;

(ii) an order of the Commodity Futures Trading Commission denying, suspending, or revoking his registration under the Commodity Exchange Act (7 U.S.C. 1 et seq.); or

(iii) an order by a foreign financial regulatory authority denying, suspending, or revoking the person's authority to engage in transactions in contracts of sale of a commodity for future delivery or other instruments traded on or subject to the rules of a contract market, board of trade, or foreign equivalent thereof;

(C) by his conduct while associated with a broker, dealer, municipal securities dealer, government securities broker, government securities dealer, security-based swap dealer, or major security-based swap participant, or while associated with an entity or person required to be registered under the Commodity Exchange Act, has been found to be a cause of any effective suspension, expulsion, or order of the character described in subparagraph (A) or (B) of this paragraph, and in entering such a suspension, expulsion, or order, the Commission, an appropriate regulatory agency, or any such self-regulatory organization shall have jurisdiction to find whether or not any person was a cause thereof;

(D) by his conduct while associated with any broker, dealer, municipal securities dealer, government securities broker, government securities dealer, security-based swap dealer, major security-based swap participant, or any other entity engaged in transactions in securities, or while associated with an entity engaged in transactions in contracts of sale of a commodity for future delivery or other instruments traded on or subject to the rules of a contract market, board of trade, or foreign equivalent thereof, has been found to be a cause of any effective suspension, expulsion, or order by a foreign or international securities exchange or foreign financial regulatory authority empowered by a foreign government to administer or enforce its laws relating to financial transactions as described in subparagraph (A) or (B) of this paragraph;

(E) has associated with him any person who is known, or in the exercise of reasonable care should be known, to him to be a person described by subparagraph (A), (B), (C), or (D) of this paragraph; or

(F) has committed or omitted any act, or is subject to an order or finding, enumerated in subparagraph (D), (E), (H), or (G) of paragraph (4) of section 78o(b) of this title, has been convicted of any offense specified in subparagraph (B) of such paragraph (4) or any other felony within ten years of the date of the filing of an application for membership or participation in, or to become associated with a member of, such self-regulatory organization, is enjoined from any action, conduct, or practice specified in subparagraph (C) of such paragraph (4), has willfully made or caused to be made in any application for membership or participation in, or to become associated with a member of, a self-regulatory organization, report required to be filed with a self-regulatory organization, or proceeding before a self-regulatory organization, any statement which was at the time, and in the light of the circumstances under which it was made, false or misleading with respect to any material fact, or has omitted to state in any such application, report, or proceeding any material fact which is required to be stated therein.

---

35. SEC Rules and Regulations, Securities Exchange Act of 1934: 17f-2 – Fingerprinting of Securities Industry Personnel

(a) Exemptions for the fingerprinting requirement. Except as otherwise provided in paragraph (a)(1) or (2) of this section, every member of a national securities exchange, broker, dealer, registered transfer agent and registered clearing agency shall require that each of its partners, directors, officers and employees be fingerprinted and shall submit, or cause to be submitted, the fingerprints of such persons to the Attorney General of the United States or its designee for identification and appropriate processing.

(1) Permissive exemptions. Every member of a national securities exchange, broker, dealer, registered transfer agent and registered clearing agency may claim one or more of the exemptions in paragraph (a)(1) (i), (ii), (iii) or (iv) of this section; Provided, That all the requirements of paragraph (e) of this section are also satisfied.

(i) Member of a national securities exchange, broker, dealer or registered clearing agency. Every person who is a partner, director, officer or employee of a member of a national securities exchange, broker, dealer, or registered clearing agency shall be exempt if that person:

516| Overview of the Regulatory Framework

(A) Is not engaged in the sale of securities;

(B) Does not regularly have access to the keeping, handling or processing of (1) securities, (2) monies, or (3) the original books and records relating to the securities or the monies; and

(C) Does not have direct supervisory responsibility over persons engaged in the activities referred to in paragraphs (a)(1)(i) (A) and (B) of this section.

(ii) Registered transfer agents. Every person who is a partner, director, officer or employee of a registered transfer agent shall be exempt if that person:

(A) Is not engaged in transfer agent functions (as defined in section 3(a)(25) of the Securities Exchange Act of 1934) or activities incidental thereto; or

(B) Meets the conditions in paragraphs (a)(1)(i) (B) and (C) of this section.

(iii) Registered broker-dealers engaged in sales of certain securities. Every partner, director, officer and employee of a registered broker or dealer who satisfies paragraph (a)(1)(i)(B) of this section shall be exempt if that broker or dealer:

(A) Is engaged exclusively in the sale of shares of registered open-end management investment companies, variable contracts, or interests in limited partnerships, unit investment trusts or real estate investment trusts; Provided, those securities ordinarily are not evidenced by certificates;

(B) Is current in its continuing obligation under §§ 240.15b1-1 and 15b3-1(b) to update Item 10 of Form BD to disclose the existence of any statutory disqualification set forth in sections 3(a)(39), 15(b)(4) and 15(b)(6) of the Securities Exchange Act of 1934;

(C) Has insurance or bonding indemnifying it for losses to customers caused by the fraudulent or criminal acts of any of its partners, directors, officers or employees for whom an exemption is being claimed under paragraph (a)(1)(iii) of this section; and

(D) Is subject to the jurisdiction of a state insurance department with respect to its sale of variable contracts.

(iv) Illegible fingerprint cards. Every person who is a partner, director, officer or employee shall be exempt if that member of a national securities exchange, broker, dealer, registered transfer agent or registered clearing agency, on at least three occasions:

(A) Attempts in good faith to obtain from such person a complete set of fingerprints acceptable to the Attorney General or its designee for identification and appropriate processing by requiring that person to be fingerprinted, by having that person's fingerprints rolled by a person competent to do so and by submitting the fingerprint cards for that person to the Attorney General of the United States or its designee in accordance with proper procedures;

(B) Has that person's fingerprint cards returned to it by the Attorney General of the United States or its designee without that person's fingerprints having been identified because the fingerprints were illegible; and

(C) Retains the returned fingerprint cards and any other required records in accordance with paragraph (d) of this section and §§ 240.17a-3(a)(13), 17a-4(e)(2) and 240.17Ad-7(e)(1) under the Securities Exchange Act of 1934.

(2) Other exemptions by application to the Commission. The Commission, upon specified terms, conditions and periods, may grant exemptions to any class of partners, directors, officers or employees of any member of a national securities exchange, broker, dealer, registered transfer agent or registered clearing agency, if the Commission finds that such action is not inconsistent with the public interest or the protection of investors.

(b) Fingerprinting pursuant to other law. Every member of a national securities exchange, broker, dealer, registered transfer agent and registered clearing agency may satisfy the fingerprinting requirement of section 17(f)(2) of the Securities Exchange Act of 1934 as to any partner, director, officer or employee, if:

(1) The person, in connection with his or her present employment with such organization, has been fingerprinted pursuant to any other law, statute, rule or regulation of any state or federal government or agency thereof;

(2) The fingerprint cards for that person are submitted, or are caused to be submitted, to the Attorney General of the United States or its designee for identification and appropriate processing, and the Attorney General or its designee has processed those fingerprint cards; and

(3) The processed fingerprint cards or any substitute records, together with any information received from the Attorney General or its designee, are maintained in accordance with paragraph (d) of this section.

(c) Fingerprinting plans of self-regulatory organizations. The fingerprinting requirement of section 17(f)(2) of the Securities Exchange Act of 1934 may be satisfied by submitting appropriate and complete fingerprint cards to a registered national securities exchange or to a registered national securities association which, pursuant to a plan filed with, and declared effective by, the Commission, forwards such fingerprint cards to the Attorney General of the United States or its designee for identification and appropriate processing. Any plan filed by a registered national securities exchange or a registered national securities association shall not become effective, unless declared effective by the Commission as not inconsistent with the public interest or the protection of investors; and, in declaring any such plan effective, the Commission may impose any terms and conditions relating to the provisions of the plan and the period of its effectiveness as it may deem necessary or appropriate in the public interest, for the protection of investors, or otherwise in furtherance of the purposes of the Securities Exchange Act of 1934.

(d) Record maintenance -

(1) Maintenance of processed fingerprint cards and other related information. Every member of a national securities exchange, broker, dealer, registered transfer agent and registered clearing agency shall maintain the processed fingerprint card or any substitute record when such card is not returned after processing, together with any information received from the Attorney General or its designee, for every person required to be fingerprinted under section 17(f)(2) of the Securities Exchange Act of 1934 and for persons who have complied with this section pursuant to paragraph (b) or (c) of this section. Every substitute record shall state the name of the person whose fingerprint card was submitted to the Attorney General of the United States, the name of the member of a national securities exchange, broker, dealer, registered transfer agent or registered clearing agency that submitted the fingerprint card, the name of the person or organization that rolled the fingerprints, the date on which the fingerprints were rolled, and the date the fingerprint card was submitted to the Attorney General of the United States. The processed fingerprint card and every other substitute record containing the information required by this paragraph, together with any information received from the Attorney General of the United States, shall be kept in an easily accessible place at the organization's principal office and shall be made available upon request to the Commission, the appropriate regulatory agency (if not the Commission) or other designated examining authority. The organization's principal office must provide to the regional, branch or satellite office actually employing the person written evidence that the person's fingerprints have been processed by the FBI, and must provide to that office a copy of any criminal history record information received from the FBI. All fingerprint cards, records and information required to be maintained under this paragraph shall be retained for a period of not less than three years after termination of that person's employment or relationship with the organization.

(2) Record maintenance by designated examining authorities. The records required to be maintained and preserved by a member of a national securities exchange, broker, or dealer pursuant to the requirements of paragraph (d)(1) of this section may be maintained and preserved on behalf of that member, broker, or dealer by a self-regulatory organization that is also the designated examining authority for that member, broker or dealer, Provided That the self-regulatory organization has filed in accordance with § 240.17f-2(c) a fingerprinting plan or amendments to an existing plan concerning the storage and maintenance of records and that plan, as amended, has been declared effective by the Commission, and Provided Further That:

(i) Such records are subject at any time, or from time to time, to reasonable periodic, special or other examinations by representatives of the Commission; and

(ii) The self-regulatory organization furnishes to the Commission, upon demand, at either the principal office or at the regional office complete, correct and current hard copies of any and all such records.

(3) Reproduction of records on microfilm. The records required to be maintained pursuant to paragraph (d)(1) of this section may be produced or reproduced on microfilm and preserved in that form. If such microfilm substitution for hard copy is made by a member of a national securities exchange, broker, dealer, registered transfer agent or registered clearing agency, or by a self-regulatory organization maintaining and storing records pursuant to paragraph (d)(2) of this section, it shall at all times:

(i) Have available for examination by the Commission, the appropriate regulatory agency (if not the Commission) or other designated authority, facilities for the immediate, easily readable projection of the microfilm and for the production of easily readable and legible facsimile enlargements;

(ii) File and index the films in such a manner as to permit the immediate location and retrieval of any particular record;

(iii) Be ready to provide, and immediately provide, any facsimile enlargement which the Commission, the appropriate regulatory agency (if not the Commission) or other designated examining authority by their examiners or other representatives may request; and

(iv) For the period for which the microfilm records are required to be maintained, store separately from the original microfilm records a copy of the microfilm records.

(e) Notice requirement. Every member of a national securities exchange, broker, dealer, registered transfer agent and registered clearing agency that claims one or more of the exemptions in paragraph (a)(1) of this section shall make and keep current a statement entitled "Notice Pursuant to Rule 17f-2" containing the information specified in paragraph (e)(1) of this section.

(1) Contents of statement. The Notice required by paragraph (e) of this section shall:

(i) State the name of the organization and state whether it is a member of a national securities exchange, broker, dealer, registered transfer agent, or registered clearing agency;

(ii) Identify by division, department, class, or name and position within the organization all persons who are claimed to have satisfied the fingerprinting requirement of section 17(f)(2) of the Securities Exchange Act of 1934 pursuant to paragraph (b) of this section;

(iii) Identify by division, department, class, title or position within the organization all persons claimed to be exempt under paragraphs (a)(1)(i) through (iii) of this section, and identify by name all persons claimed to be exempt under paragraph (a)(1)(iv). Persons identified under this paragraph (e)(1)(iii) shall be exempt from the requirement of section 17(f)(2) of the Securities Exchange Act of 1934 unless notified to the contrary by the Commission;

(iv) Describe, in generic terms, the nature of the duties of the person or classes of persons, and the nature of the functions and operations of the divisions and departments, identified as exempt in paragraph (e)(1)(iii) of this section; and

(v) Describe the security measures utilized to ensure that only those persons who have been fingerprinted in accordance with the fingerprinting requirement of section 17(f)(2) of the Securities Exchange Act of 1934 or who are exempt under paragraph (a)(1)(iv) of this section have access to the keeping, handling or processing of securities or monies or the original books and records relating thereto.

(2) Record maintenance. A copy of the Notice required to be made and kept current under paragraph (e) of this section shall be kept in an easily accessible place at the organization's principal office and at the office employing the persons for whom exemptions are claimed and shall be made available upon request for inspection by the Commission, appropriate regulatory agency (if not the Commission) or other designated examining authority.

(3) Exemption from the notice requirement. A registered transfer agent that performs transfer agent functions only on behalf of itself as an issuer and that receives fewer than 500 items for transfer and fewer than 500 items for processing during any six consecutive months shall be exempt from the notice requirement of paragraph (c) of this section.

Made in the USA
Coppell, TX
26 February 2022

74079218R00289